Common Logarithms of Numbers

n	0	1	2	3	4	5	6	7	8	9	Proportional parts				
											1	2	3	4	5
5.5	7404	7412	7419	7427	7435	7443	7451	7459	7466	7474	1	2	2	3	4
5.6	7482	7490	7497	7505	7513	7520	7528	7536	7543	7551	1	2	2	3	4
5.7	7559	7566	7574	7582	7589	7597	7604	7612	7619	7627	1	1	2	3	4
5.8	7634	7642	7649	7657	7664	7672	7679	7686	7694	7701	1	1	2	3	4
5.9	7709	7716	7723	7731	7738	7745	7752	7760	7767	7774	1	1	2	3	4
6.0	7782	7789	7796	7803	7810	7818	7825	7832	7839	7846	1	1	2	3	4
6.1	7853	7860	7868	7875	7882	7889	7896	7903	7910	7917	1	1	2	3	3
6.2	7924	7931	7938	7945	7952	7959	7966	7973	7980	7987	1	1	2	3	3
6.3	7993	8000	8007	8014	8021	8028	8035	8041	8048	8055	1	1	2	3	3
6.4	8062	8069	8075	8082	8089	8096	8102	8109	8116	8122	1	1	2	3	3
6.5	8129	8136	8142	8149	8156	8162	8169	8176	8182	8189	1	1	2	3	3
6.6	8195	8202	8209	8215	8222	8228	8235	8241	8248	8254	1	1	2	3	3
6.7	8261	8267	8274	8280	8287	8293	8299	8306	8312	8319	1	1	2	3	3
6.8	8325	8331	8338	8344	8351	8357	8363	8370	8376	8382	1	1	2	3	3
6.9	8388	8395	8401	8407	8414	8420	8426	8432	8439	8445	1	1	2	3	3
7.0	8451	8457	8463	8470	8476	8482	8488	8494	8500	8506	1	1	2	3	3
7.1	8513	8519	8525	8531	8537	8543	8549	8555	8561	8567	1	1	2	3	3
7.2	8573	8579	8585	8591	8597	8603	8609	8615	8621	8627	1	1	2	3	3
7.3	8633	8639	8645	8651	8657	8663	8669	8675	8681	8686	1	1	2	2	3
7.4	8692	8698	8704	8710	8716	8722	8727	8733	8739	8745	1	1	2	2	3
7.5	8751	8756	8762	8768	8774	8779	8785	8791	8797	8802	1	1	2	2	3
7.6	8808	8814	8820	8825	8831	8837	8842	8848	8854	8859	1	1	2	2	3
7.7	8865	8871	8876	8882	8887	8893	8899	8904	8910	8915	1	1	2	2	3
7.8	8921	8927	8932	8938	8943	8949	8954	8960	8965	8971	1	1	2	2	3
7.9	8976	8982	8987	8993	8998	9004	9009	9015	9020	9025	1	1	2	2	3
8.0	9031	9036	9042	9047	9053	9058	9063	9069	9074	9079	1	1	2	2	3
8.1	9085	9090	9096	9101	9106	9112	9117	9122	9128	9133	1	1	2	2	3
8.2	9138	9143	9149	9154	9159	9165	9170	9175	9180	9186	1	1	2	2	3
8.3	9191	9196	9201	9206	9212	9217	9222	9227	9232	9238	1	1	2	2	3
8.4	9243	9248	9253	9258	9263	9269	9274	9279	9284	9289	1	1	2	2	3
8.5	9294	9299	9304	9309	9315	9320	9325	9330	9335	9340	1	1	2	2	3
8.6	9345	9350	9355	9360	9365	9370	9375	9380	9385	9390	1	1	2	2	3
8.7	9395	9400	9405	9410	9415	9420	9425	9430	9435	9440	1	1	2	2	3
8.8	9445	9450	9455	9460	9465	9469	9474	9479	9484	9489	0	1	1	2	2
8.9	9494	9499	9504	9509	9513	9518	9523	9528	9533	9538	0	1	1	2	2
9.0	9542	9547	9552	9557	9562	9566	9571	9576	9581	9586	0	1	1	2	2
9.1	9590	9595	9600	9605	9609	9614	9619	9624	9628	9633	0	1	1	2	2
9.2	9638	9643	9647	9652	9657	9661	9666	9671	9675	9680	0	1	1	2	2
9.3	9685	9689	9694	9699	9703	9708	9713	9717	9722	9727	0	1	1	2	2
9.4	9731	9736	9741	9745	9750	9754	9759	9763	9768	9773	0	1	1	2	2
9.5	9777	9782	9786	9791	9795	9800	9805	9809	9814	9818	0	1	1	2	2
9.6	9823	9827	9832	9836	9841	9845	9850	9854	9859	9863	0	1	1	2	2
9.7	9868	9872	9877	9881	9886	9890	9894	9899	9903	9908	0	1	1	2	2
9.8	9912	9917	9921	9926	9930	9934	9939	9943	9948	9952	0	1	1	2	2
9.9	9956	9961	9965	9969	9974	9978	9983	9987	9991	9996	0	1	1	2	2
n	0	1	2	3	4	5	6	7	8	9	1	2	3	4	5

The Statistical Method in Business,
applications of probability and inference
to business and other problems

FREDERICK A. EKEBLAD, School of Business, Northwestern University

JOHN WILEY & SONS, INC., NEW YORK · LONDON

The Statistical Method in Business, *applications of probability and inference to business and other problems*

to Dorothy Sebbens Ekeblad

Preface

The Statistical Method in Business is primarily a basic text for an introductory course in business statistics. The material has proved suitable for undergraduates, primarily juniors, and for first-year graduate students. The book is also adaptable for a course in economic statistics.

The point of view is expressed by the subtitle, *Applications of Probability and Inference to Business and Other Problems*. The statistical method is seen as a unified body of thought concerned with the basic human problem of uncertainty and the corollary problems of risk-taking and decision-making. The emphasis throughout the text is on *a* method of thought rather than a collection of methods, or a collection of mechanical tricks of the trade.

The spirit of the book can be best expressed by saying that we continually ask questions that we cannot completely answer. This seems to be a perfectly logical result of any serious investigation of a method of dealing with uncertainty. It would seem contradictory to be certain about how to deal with uncertainty. Such a spirit has a price. The reader will often feel confused and frustrated, and we hope that such feelings are a consequence of the inherent nature of the problem rather than the uncertainty of fuzzy prose.

Partially to compensate for the difficulties inherent in the subject matter, an attempt has been made to minimize the role of those parts of the statistical method which trouble beginning students but which cause no trouble in practical problems. We really *know* how to calculate many things in many ways. It is a chore to learn these calculations, however, and difficulties with this chore can easily distract a person from coming to grips with the more fundamental difficulties of the general philosophy of the statistical method. Therefore, the mathematical demands of the book are quite modest and can easily be satisfied by the entrance requirements of most colleges.

Controversy about how best to handle problems of uncertainty is inherent in the subject. We make no effort to evade the controversies that involve the underlying philosophies guiding people in their use of the statistical method. Some feel that controversy does not belong in an introductory treatment. Our feeling is quite the contrary. Most students get only an introduction, and, if the introduction is sterilized of all the conflicts that plague and vitalize the subject, the student is either being fed "pap" or he is being indoctrinated. In either case he is ill-prepared to handle any of the infectious ideas he is likely to be fed when he leaves the shelter of the textbook.

Although our orientation is primarily toward business problems, we try to take maximum advantage of the versatility of the statistical method by introducing many concepts in a nonbusiness setting. We thus draw on the general experience of the reader to clarify an idea before we attempt to apply it to relatively strange business situations.

The scope of business statistics has grown substantially in recent years. The proliferation of specialized techniques and applications has expanded the materials well beyond the space limits imposed by the typical course and book. The advent of the electronic computer promises to accelerate this proliferation. More than ever, therefore, we must leave out many topics that would be essential in a more extended coverage. For example, we have substantially reduced the space devoted to collection of data, tables, and charts. This reduction intends no discounting of the practical significance of these topics. It merely reflects our judgment that these topics can best be handled elsewhere.

The omission of some traditional topics has made room for other things. The most significant of these topics are:

1. The statistical method is presented as an integral part of the whole process by which human beings acquire and use knowledge. Such a presentation provides a realistic appraisal of the role that can actually be played by the statistical method.
2. A chapter is devoted to the problem of pooling accumulated knowledge with new information. It is here that we make an acquaintance with "Bayesian analysis," as it is currently called.
3. A chapter is also devoted to the problem of making inferences about future samples from information supplied by past samples. This is the general problem of inference that makes special cases of the two traditional problems:
    a. Inferences about a sample from a known universe.
    b Inferences about a universe from a known sample.

4. An introduction is provided to an approach to time series forecasting that develops a rational base for explicitly estimating the degree of uncertainty involved in a forecast. Traditional analysis results in forecasts with undetermined error allowances.

Our approach to statistical inference is sufficiently different to warrant mention here. The approach is basically pragmatic. We start with a known universe. (We choose to use attribute data rather than the customary continuous variables because of convenience of exposition and also because attribute data bring out issues that get lost when we use continuous variables.) We then generate all possible random samples from this universe. Each sample is used to make inferences about the mean of the universe as though we did not already know the mean. All such inferences are then analyzed to see if they make sense in view of the known facts. We are next led step by step to a method of making inferences that seems to work reasonably well. This process confronts us with the philosophical and practical implication of Bayes's theorem and Bayes's postulate that the "equal distribution of ignorance rule" is applicable to the problem of inference. We obtain an inference method that is fundamentally Bayesian, with a slight modification in the mechanics of calculating probabilities.

The problems and questions at the end of each chapter are designed to supplement the text in addition to guiding the student in his evaluation of how well he has grasped the main features of the exposition. Generally there is only one problem or question of a given type. It is relatively easy to make variations to provide any desired degree of duplication for purposes of drill, extra emphasis on certain points, etc. Some of the problems anticipate material of later chapters. Other problems tend to go beyond the text coverage.

Most of the problems are not practical in any real sense. Practical problems become quite complex and involve many issues other than the statistical ones. The problems are generally not trivial, however. Their solution has practical significance to real-life problems. Some of the problems are "for fun." Statistics is not an easy subject, and any opportunity to have fun or make fun helps considerably in the struggle.

The material in the book is more than sufficient for a one-semester or one-quarter course. With minor supplementation and/or with more intensive coverage of problem materials the book is sufficient for two semesters. One very useful way to supplement the text is to assign students special projects to give them personal experience with real data. A very popular project requires each student to forecast the sales of some company, say, by quarters for the next year and then by annual totals 2 years hence, 5 years hence, and 10 years hence. Such a project is much more challenging if the students are required to state their forecasts with a meaningful error band and with some percentage of confidence that the actual will fall within the stated band. The struggle to set meaningful and defensible error bands is very educational, and also quite sobering.

Most of the material of the book has been used in some way with many students. In fact, students have stimulated much of the development because they insisted that they understand what they were doing and why they were doing it. I am happy to acknowledge my indebtedness to the more persistent of the students, which I am sure will surprise some of them.

Students are not the only persons who have helped me. Professor Albert Bennett at Brown University first stimulated my interest in statistics, and Professor Arthur Tebbutt nurtured and sustained this interest, first at Brown and subsequently at Northwestern. Several colleagues have contributed much to my understanding of statistics and of the many problems of practical application. I feel particularly indebted to Arthur Auble, John Dillinger, Loring Farwell, Zenon Malinowski, John O'Neil, and Zenon Szatrowski.

A special debt exists to those who kindly gave their time to read various parts of the manuscript with critical care. Foremost among these have been Boris Parl and Dirk Van Alstyne of Northwestern, William Clarey of Bradley University, Morris Hamburg of the University of Pennsylvania, and Eugene Lerner of City College of New York.

I also wish to thank Deans Donham and Anderson for making it possible for me to have the uninterrupted time needed to put the finishing touches on a labor of many years.

Finally, there are those persons whose help over the years has been so unstinting and personal that it would be unduly sentimental to say more than just thanks. By naming none, I mean to include all.

FREDERICK A. EKEBLAD

Evanston, Illinois
April 21, 1962

Contents

The Statistical Method in Business, applications of probability and inference to business and other problems

chapter 1
The nature of the statistical method

The statistical method has been called many things; we choose to call it a method for making *inferences* about *unknown* events on the basis of a *systematic* analysis of *past experience*. *Inferences* are simply *guesses* dignified by the prior exercise of logical thought; undignified guesses can sometimes be just as effective.

We make inferences about the *unknown* rather than the known simply because it is our ignorance about an event that forces us to guess. Since there is much that we do not know about all the problems that beset us, we find ourselves continually guessing. We even guess about something we could know if we took the time and trouble to learn. We apparently enjoy guessing. Otherwise how do we explain the widespread popularity of games of chance, games that we have created in order to make guessing synonymous with entertainment? We have no shortage of opportunities to apply the statistical method; our shortage is more of effective techniques and in a willingness to apply the techniques we do have.

The statistical method makes inferences from *past* experience, or from knowledge about *past* events, because that is the only kind of experience there is. We have no crystal balls that enable us to see future events before they happen. Hence, the starting place for all inferences is some record of the past. It is understood, of course, that no inference is any better than the quality of the historical data on which it is based.

Although it is more common to think of "inferring the unknown" in the context of the past and the future, we find ourselves dealing with many problems in which the "unknown" is a current fact (to somebody) or in which the unknown is itself some historical event. For example, when we play cards, our hand is known to us but unknown to our opponents (unless they peek). Thus they must make

1

decisions based on *guesses* about our hand, just as we must make decisions based on guesses about theirs. Similarly, businessmen must make guesses about the resources of their competitors, and vice versa. The police detective investigating a crime must make guesses about the various events that have already occurred. A jury may have the same problem at a later date.

Although the statistical method is of widespread applicability and has many features that apply with equal force regardless of the area of application, we put much greater emphasis on applications in the business area. This emphasis becomes more noticeable in the later chapters. The earlier chapters are dominated by our efforts to uncover the fundamentals of the statistical method, fundamentals that apply to all sorts of problems. Thus our illustrations tend to be somewhat varied, with the particular hope that they refer to events that have already come into the experiences of most of the readers.

1.1   A Simple Game

Games can be fun and also informative, particularly when they reveal the problems of guessing in their starkest simplicity. Let us look at a series of games of increasing complexity in order to uncover many of the essential features of the challenge to the statistical method.

The game is played with a conventional deck of playing cards. Suit does not count in the game. The deck is *known* to contain four 1's (aces), four 2's, . . . four 11's (jacks), four 12's (queens), and four 13's (kings). The method of play is as follows:

1. A player selects any number he wishes and places a wager of $1.00.
2. A card is drawn from the deck. If it is the number he selected, he wins $13.00, including the $1 he bet. If it is not his number, he loses his $1.

The problem is very simple, namely, the determination of what number to call. Since we know what cards are in the deck, all we have to be concerned about is what card will be drawn out at any given time. We have several ways of trying to figure out what card will be drawn. The simplest and quickest way is to not try to find out and to act as though we do not know which of the thirteen cards will be drawn. By this line of reasoning, we would decide that because we do not know which card will be drawn, we will assume that each card has the same chance of being drawn. Or, in other words, we would assume that in a long series of drawings, each of the thirteen cards would have been drawn about the same proportion of times as each other card. It, therefore, really makes no difference to us which card we select.

On the other hand, we may decide to "smarten up" by studying the drawing process and its results. Let us first consider the results of some drawings. Let us assume we have observed the results of 45 consecutive drawings. (Each card is replaced after it is drawn, and *thus the deck is the same for each drawing*.) Table 1.1 lists the results.

What can we find out from studying these results? We might first ignore the order of drawing and count the number of times each card was drawn. Table 1.2 shows the results.

The most interesting feature of this experience is the large number of 7's and 8's and the few 10's and 12's. The question is whether this experience just happened as it did and has no practical significance, or whether it suggests that perhaps some of these cards have higher chances of being drawn than others. Unfortunately, there is no way to give a definite answer to this question. We must talk entirely in terms of *probabilities*. For example, even if the expectation were that these cards would come up equally often *in the long run,* we know that they wouldn't come up equally often in only 45 drawings. The question really is whether it is reasonable to tolerate as many, say, as seven 8's in 45 drawings and still believe that the chances of an 8 are no better than any other card, or whether we should decide that this is enough evidence to justify the belief that 8 will come up more often in the future because it has come up more often in the past (or at least during our experience of the past).

Before we can rationalize such questions, we must estimate the probabilities that certain things could happen if certain conditions prevailed. Here, for example, we might start with the *assumption*

TABLE 1.1

Results of 45 Drawings from Playing Card Deck

(Replacement of card after each drawing)

8 →	7	13	5	4	10	13	6	7	5
5	3	1	6	1	3	3	8	4	7
1	6	4	8	8	9	7	8	9	1
7	2	5	9	2	8	5	8	7	12
2	11	1	11	7					

TABLE 1.2

Number of Times Each Card Was Drawn in 45 Drawings

Card	Frequency
one	5
two	3
three	3
four	3
five	5
six	3
seven	7
eight	7
nine	3
ten	1
eleven	2
twelve	1
thirteen	2
	45

that the conditions surrounding the card drawings are such that each card does have the same chance of being drawn as each other card. If this is so, the probability is only about 1 out of 50 of getting as many as seven 8's in 45 drawings. (How to calculate such probabilities is discussed later.) This seems unlikely enough to cause us to suspect that perhaps the assumption is not correct. Perhaps we should assume that the probability of an 8 *is* greater than for the other cards (with the exception of the 7). On the other hand, the probability is about 1 out of 4 that at least one card will come up 7 or more times in 45 drawings. Here, the card "happened" to be an 8 and a 7.

We could calculate the probabilities for other possible assumptions, but it is not important for us to do so now. It is more important for us to look briefly at the problem of deciding what meaning we should attach to the probabilities we have already calculated. To do this most effectively we should formalize our descriptions a little more. First, let us write exactly what we know about these card drawings. We know that:

1. Each card *exists* in the deck the same number of times as each other card;

2. The cards are numbered 1 through 13 (there are no 26's, etc.);
3. Forty-five consecutive drawings resulted in the numbers shown in Table 1.2.

Unfortunately, we do not *know* enough about the cards to be able to tell exactly what card will be drawn next. Hence we must supplement our knowledge with some *belief, assumption,* or *hypothesis.* But, we might assume all manner of things. How do we decide what hypothesis we should really adopt? The most important criterion in judging the quality of an hypothesis is that it *must be consistent with the facts.* This criterion seems obvious, and that it is. It is, however, the kind of obvious thing that we need to be continually reminded of. We all have a tendency to retain hypotheses that have grown dear to us even when the facts no longer support them.

We test the usefulness of a hypothesis by calculating the *probability that the given factual events could have occurred if the hypothesis were true.* For example, let us set up the hypothesis that the cards are equally likely. From this we calculate by standard procedures (discussed in later pages) that there are only two chances out of 100, or .02, of getting seven or more 8's. Suppose we decide that only .02 is very rare in our judgment and that the facts are inconsistent with the hypothesis. Obviously, then, we discard the hypothesis, or belief, because we must retain the facts. But possibly we do not think .02 is very rare, and we are perfectly willing to continue to accept the hypothesis on the grounds that the occurrence of as many as seven 8's was just a "matter of chance." Of course we might decide this either way and either way might be correct. To help us decide we have to determine *how important* the .02 is to *us.* Suppose we conclude that our hypothesis was wrong; namely, we conclude that the chances are greater than 1/13 of getting an 8. Naturally we would now bet on the 8. What would this policy cost us if, in truth, the chances of an 8 were no greater than 1/13? This would obviously depend on the conditions of the game. If the 8 were paid off at the same rate as all other numbers, and if the 8 had the same chance as all the other numbers, and if we always played the 8 because we erroneously believed the 8 were more likely, our erroneous belief costs us nothing.

If, on the other hand, we pay more for an 8 because we believe it is more likely, and if, in fact, it is not, we would be paying a penalty for our erroneous belief.

Let us now summarize the kind of policy we might adopt for playing this game in the light of what we know about it and of what we might choose to guess, or hypothesize. We would definitely choose 8 (or 7) as long as we do not have to pay a premium for this choice over other numbers. We do this because the facts (seven 8's in 45 trials) suggest to us that there is a greater chance for an 8 than for most of the other numbers. Even if we are wrong in this belief, this decision costs us nothing because we are quite sure that the chances of an 8 are, on the evidence, no lower than for any other number. Thus we have nothing to lose by choosing 8, and we might have something to gain. This is obviously a very good position to be in for any situation.

But let us suppose we have to pay a premium to play 8. How high a premium would we be willing to pay? If pressed, of course, we would be willing to pay as much as we *thought* it were worth. We might believe, for example, that since 8 has occurred more than *twice* as often as most of the numbers, we would be willing to pay *twice* as much for the privilege of choosing it. The point is very simple: People decide things according to *what they believe to be true.* Their success will generally be directly related to how closely their beliefs are consistent with the facts. But we are never able to test how well a belief coincides with the facts except on a *probability* basis. Thus we are always beset with *uncertainty.*

We have deliberately asked questions to which there is no definitive answer. We come up, therefore, with no definitive answer. But we are not doing this just to play games. *The essential characteristic of all practical problems is that they do not have definitive answers.* But they must be dealt with as though they do have answers. Hence we must *choose* an answer based upon what we *believe,* and we *hope* that what we believe is *consistent with the facts.* Although we hope never to eliminate all confusion, because to do so would be to throw the problem away too, we do hope to uncover systematic ways of working ourselves through the confusion in such a manner that we will at least be confused about the right things.

More of an effort might have been made to gain additional knowledge about the game and its results, and if these efforts were somewhat successful, there would be less uncertainty. For example, why stop at 45 sample drawings? Why not make 100 or 1000? Why not, indeed? There is no question about the fact that more drawings will provide more information and would enable us to have more confidence in our ultimate selections. But additional drawings take additional time, and time is costly. Somewhere, we have to stop studying a problem and start solving it. Where this point should be is a matter of judgment again, but there are ways of assessing the situation to guide us in exercising this judgment. Such ways are also discussed in later pages.

We should mention that additional things could be done to gain more knowledge other than just adding to the number of sample trials. For one, we could examine the trials we already have to see if there is any evidence of *systematic order* to the numbers. For example, were there more large numbers near the end of the trials? Was a large number generally followed by a small number? And so forth. There is almost no end to this sort of analysis.

Another, and quite different, thing we might do to gain more knowledge about these card drawings is to study very carefully not only the results of the drawings but also those other things that were going on while the drawings were being made. For example, was there any relationship between the number of times the deck was shuffled and the number drawn? Between the distribution of the bets and the number drawn (maybe a certain amount of "cheating" is going on)? And so forth. It is likely we could gain increased knowledge by such *association* of one thing with another. This is something we discuss at considerable length later; however, we have to ignore this method of gaining knowledge in this problem because we are given no information on those things that might have been going on during the drawings.

1.2   A Little More Complex Game

Simple as the last game was, we managed to run into trouble as we tried to figure out a policy to help us choose a card. Even though we knew exactly what was in the deck, and even though we had the experience of 45 drawings, the nature of the problem still left us with some uncertainty about how often we should expect a given card to be drawn. We saw the possibility of several different policies we might adopt in choosing a card; but no policy we could select gave us any assurance that it was the best policy.

Now let us make the game a little more like real-life problems and therefore more complicated. We now consider the same game, but without any knowledge of what is in the deck. All we know about the deck is that there are 100 cards in it; and each card has a number of any size whatsoever on it. Our problem is still the same as before, namely, what number will be drawn? But now we have no way of predicting what will come out of the deck based upon what we know is in it. So let us move immediately to the consideration of how we would interpret any experience we might have with cards that we might have observed being drawn.

Suppose the first card drawn is a 17. It is then returned to the deck. What number would we select for the next drawing and *how much* confidence would we have in our selection?

We would have to select 17 on the simple argument that that is the only number that we know is in the deck. Any other number we select may not even exist.

How much confidence should we have in this selection? This depends on how many 17's we think there are in the deck. Our present knowledge indicates there may be anywhere from 1 to 100 17's. For this reason we would hesitate strongly to bet anything on our choice of 17 unless we were paid off at odds of at least 99 to 1.

Let us quickly summarize the progress we have so far made in gaining knowledge about the cards that might come out of this deck. Before we had seen any card, we would have to admit that our knowledge was nil, or 0; or conversely that our ignorance was infinite. If somebody had asked us what we thought the probability was of drawing, say, a 25, we would have had to admit that as far as we knew it was somewhere between 0 and 1. But now that we have seen a 17, we have reduced our ignorance somewhat. We could now say that the probability of a 17 is somewhere between .01 and 1.00; or that the probability of a 25 is somewhere between 0 and .99. If we wished to express this decrease in ignorance mathematically, we could say that knowledge of the 17 has enabled us to reduce our ignorance from a range of 1 to a range of .99, or a reduction of 1%.

Now let us draw another card. Suppose it is again a 17. What does this tell us? It certainly does not tell us *definitely* that there are at least two 17's in the deck because we might have drawn the same 17 again. On the other hand, is it *reasonable* to assume that we have drawn two 17's in a row if there is only one of them in the deck? The probability of two 17's in a row if there is only one in the deck is only $.01 \times .01$, or .0001, or 1 out of 10,000. This is such a rare event under the hypothesis of only *one* 17 that we may decide to reject this hypothesis in favor of one that would make two 17's in a row appear to be less rare. For example, we might assume that there are ten 17's in the deck. If this were so, the probability of two in a row would be $.1 \times .1$, or .01. This still is not very often, but it certainly is considerably more often than .0001.

Of course we could make many different assumptions about the number of 17's in the deck. Each assumption would make it possible for us to calculate the probability of drawing two 17's in a row. Table 1.3 lists some of such assumptions and their associated probabilities. Which assumption should we adopt? Again we discover that it depends on judgment about what is at stake. To make the situation more concrete, let us assume we are offered the following choice of wagers: If we select 17, we would be paid off at 9 to 1 if it came up on the third draw. On the other hand, if we selected "not 17" and 17 did not come up, we would be paid off at 1 to 9. What bet should we take? Obviously, if we believe that there are at least ten 17's, we take the first bet; if we think there are fewer than ten 17's, we take the second. Or perhaps we are so confused that we do not wish to take either!

TABLE 1.3

Relationship between Hypothesis about the Number of 17's in the Deck and the Probability of Getting Two 17's in a Row

Hypothesis: No. of 17's in Deck	Probability of Two 17's in a Row
1	.0001
2	.0004
3	.0009
4	.0016
5	.0025
6	.0036
7	.0049
8	.0064
9	.0081
10	.0100
11	.0121
12	.0144
13	.0169
14	.0196
15	.0225
.	. . .
20	.0400
25	.0625
30	.0900
.	. . .
40	.1600
50	.2500

The last decision of taking no position is, of course, perfectly proper. We have in effect decided not to play this game. The decision to avoid a "decision" is one that all of us make many times a day in all sorts of problem situations. Sometimes it is the proper thing to do; other times, however, it is indicative of an unwillingness to face up to a problem that is going to be decided one way or another whether we participate in it or not. Also there is the fact that we will never really give ourselves a chance to make a *correct* decision, *of any consequence*, unless we are willing to take the risk of making an *incorrect* decision. There is much truth in the old proverb "nothing ventured, nothing gained." All business decisions are made in a context which suggests the possibility that the decision may be wrong. We just hope that on the average our decisions are based on correct hypotheses often enough to result in a reasonable net profit for the company.

Let us decide that we believe that there are at least ten 17's in the deck. This means that now we think the probability of a 17 on the next drawing is between .10 and 1.0. Note that the range of our uncertainty about the probability of a 17 is less than before the second 17 was drawn. Then it was .01 to 1.0; now it is .10 to 1.0, or 9.09% less. Thus the knowledge gained by the second drawing enabled us to reduce our ignorance another 9.09%. (We should also note that now we would estimate the probability of a 25 as somewhere between 0 and .90 instead of between 0 and .99.)

When could we be sure that we knew the probability of drawing a 17? The answer is that we never could. More drawings would enable us to decrease our ignorance, but we could never really reduce our ignorance to zero, although we might get very close to zero. Table 1.4 gives us some idea of the rate at which additional drawings would decrease our ignorance about the probability of a 17. This table assumes that we keep getting 17's. This assumption makes it considerably easier to make the necessary calculations to illustrate the principle; any other assumptions could be made.

Figure 1.1 shows the material of Table 1.4 in graphic form. Here it is quite easy to see that the rate of reduction of ignorance declines rather substantially after about 20 trials. In other words, a law of diminishing returns sets in; additional investment of time to gain more knowledge results in a smaller rate of return. There would come a time, of course, in any practical situation where further investment to increase knowledge would not be justified by the return.

TABLE 1.4

Rate at Which Ignorance about the Probability of a 17 is Reduced by Additional Drawings

(It is assumed that a 17 is drawn each time)

Number of Drawings	Estimated Probability of a 17 on the Next Draw *	Range of Ignorance
0	0.0000–1.0000	1.0000
1	.0100–1.0000	.9900
2	.1000–1.0000	.9000
3	.2154–1.0000	.7846
4	.3163–1.0000	.6837
5	.3981–1.0000	.6019
6	.4642–1.0000	.5358
7	.5180–1.0000	.4820
8	.5623–1.0000	.4377
9	.5995–1.0000	.4005
10	.6310–1.0000	.3690
11	.6580–1.0000	.3420
12	.6813–1.0000	.3187
13	.7016–1.0000	.2984
14	.7196–1.0000	.2804
15	.7357–1.0000	.2643
16	.7499–1.0000	.2501
17	.7644–1.0000	.2356
18	.7743–1.0000	.2257
19	.7847–1.0000	.2153
20	.7943–1.0000	.2057
.	. . .	. . .
25	.8318–1.0000	.1682
30	.8576–1.0000	.1424
.	. . .	. . .
40	.8913–1.0000	.1087
50	.9120–1.0000	.0880
.	. . .	. . .
100	.9550–1.0000	.0450
500	.9908–1.0000	.0092
1000	.9954–1.0000	.0046

* The probability band is estimated such that the lower limit would lead to a probability of .01 for the given sequence of 17's. For example, the probability of *12* 17's in a row is .01 if there are *68* 17's in the deck.

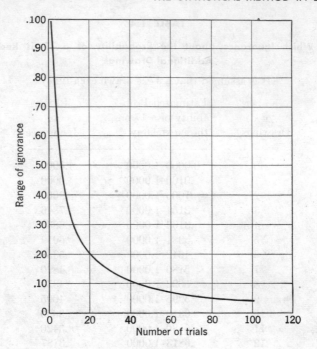

Fig. 1.1 Rate at which ignorance about the probability of a 17 is reduced by additional drawings.

1.3 Comparing the Two Games

Before we introduce a third game, let us briefly summarize and compare the problem situations created by the two games so far discussed.

First, we note that our decision problem was basically the same in both cases, namely, we had to select the number that we thought would occur in the next drawing. In neither case did we know what would occur.

Second, we note that in both cases we became concerned with how often we thought a given number might be drawn. In other words, we became concerned with the *probability* that a given number would occur on a given draw.

Third, we note that the real difference between the two games showed up when we tried to estimate the probabilities of any given number occurring. In the first game we knew what was in the deck. From this knowledge we were able to directly estimate probabilities.

Some people might say that from this information we would know the probabilities. We prefer not to take this position for reasons that are brought out later. In fact, we also looked at 45 trials from the first game. This additional information, although very welcome, caused us to have some doubt that the probabilities inferred from the cards *in* the deck were exactly the same as the probabilities we would infer from what we had observed come *out* of the deck. Therefore, let us not forget that we had some uncertainty about what the probabilities were that a given number would be drawn.

Our problem of estimating the probabilities in the second game were much more serious, however, than they were in the first game because we knew absolutely nothing about what was *in* the deck *except* insofar as we could infer what was in the deck based on our experience with what had been drawn *out* of the deck. The greater uncertainty considerably complicated our problem of deciding on a definitive policy for selecting a number to bet on.

1.4   A Third Game with a Little More Complexity

Disconcerted as we may feel because of our uncertainty about what strategies we should employ in the two previous games, we now have to accept that there is even worse to come.

The third game is exactly the same as the second except that now we are going to play a game in which the deck is changed after each drawing. At no time do we know what is in any deck, and at no time do we know if the succeeding deck is the same as or different from the last deck. For example, if we get a 17 out of the first drawing from the first deck, we have no assurance that the second deck will even have a 17 in it. Similarly, we have no assurance that the second deck does not have all 17's.

Just so we may more clearly appreciate the enormity of the problem now facing us, imagine ourselves sitting down to a friendly(?) game of bridge played with an unknown deck. The only information we could obtain about the deck is what we are able to observe and remember as the hands are being played. *And* to make it worse, the physical deck is changed after each deal and we do not know whether the cards are the same as before, bigger than before, more hearts than before, etc. *Also* keep in mind that, while we were learning by experience, we have been bidding and playing just as though we knew what we were doing!

Considering the challenge that most people believe the game of bridge to be under its present rules of a *known* and *constant* deck, imagine the challenge of the game with an *unknown* and possibly *changing* deck. A first reaction probably is that such a game would be impossible, and no ordinary people could or would play such a game. But let us analyze the situation. First, let us note that *all* the players are presumably equally ignorant. We would not be playing against someone who necessarily knew more than we did. The other person experiences the same twinges of fear as we do. His guesses are just as wild as ours. As soon as we realize his predicament, we are not quite so upset about our predicament. We may even have room in our heart for compassion for that other person!

The third game brings to the forefront one of the most significant features that predominates in many practical situations, and that is that *how much* we know about a situation is often not as important as how much we know *compared* to competitors. In fact, it is a commonplace observation that if a business is easy to learn, in the sense that we feel as though we know what we are doing in such a business, many people enter the business. The resulting competition makes it no easier to make a profit than if we had gone into a more difficult business, where the difficulties served to reduce the number of people who thought they knew something about it.

If we grant that there may be some sense in playing such a game, the next question is to determine how we go about gaining as much knowledge as possible as the game proceeds. The answer is very simple. We analyze the results of the game as they unfold. We relate the figures to each other to try to discover any *system* or *pattern* that may exist. As we think we have discovered such patterns, we begin to incorporate them into our decision-making rules. If we can discover patterns sooner than our competitors, we will gain an advantage. If, on the other hand, we act on patterns that are not really there, we might find ourselves at a disadvantage.

How we proceed to analyze experience in order to abstract most effectively any systems or patterns of behavior is the challenge of the remainder of this book. There are many routine procedures which we can follow that experience suggests will generally be very helpful. Such routines are explained and discussed. On the other hand, there is no routine procedure that can be developed to substitute for all personal judgment. Our basic problem is that of *uncertainty*, the same kind of uncertainty we have experienced as we tried to figure out how to play these games. We can never reduce this uncertainty to zero, and, therefore, the need to exercise faith and courage in our hypotheses will always be present. We might express our purpose as the one of learning how to reduce uncertainty and to cope with uncertainty, rather than the one of eliminating uncertainty.

1.5   A Practical Example

Counterparts of the problems of playing our third game exist in many practical situations.   Let us examine a relatively simple practical illustration for such analogous problems.

Manufacturing operations often result in the occasional production of unsatisfactory units of product. Such units are then rejected and often become classified as scrap. An excessively high production of such scrap is to be avoided if the company is to keep its costs under control. The control of scrap has two parts to it. One task is to be able to identify when the scrap rate has become too high. The other task is to know what to do to reduce the scrap when it is too high. The second task usually involves such things as quality of raw materials, engineering aspects of the production process, training and supervision of workers, etc. These factors are outside the bounds of this book. We are concerned, however, with the first task, that of deciding when the scrap rate is too high.

If we were to interview the typical shop foreman in order to find out how he was able to decide when the scrap rate was too high, we would very likely find that he based his decisions on "experience." His experience would have given him an idea of the *capabilities* of the materials, men, and machines to produce a certain proportion of satisfactory units of product. He would be unreasonable to expect a scrap rate below the minimum dictated by these capabilities. He would have discovered that efforts to reduce scrap below such a minimum level resulted in reductions in the over-all rate of production, excessive anxieties on the part of workers, etc.

He also would have learned that there would be a minimum amount of unavoidable *fluctuation* in the daily scrap rate even though the production process was still operating properly.

In a particular machine shop that had been doing fairly standard work over a period of several months we found that the foreman had decided that a daily scrap rate of 2.5 to 7.5% was satisfactory. If the daily rate went below 2.5%, he checked to see if the workers had become so concerned about producing scrap that they had slowed down their rate of production. If the daily rate went above 7.5%, he checked to find the cause of this excessive rate. He felt that a rate between 2.5% and 7.5% was about right. His attempts to pinpoint the causes of the lower and higher rates within this range were generally unsuccessful. Such attempts also consumed some of his time that he could more profitably apply elsewhere. They also caused some irritations among the workers, who felt that he was getting too fussy and was trying to do the impossible.

Our interest in the foreman's problem is centered on the relationship of his experience to his decision to control daily scrap between 2.5% and 7.5%. We looked at a record of 45 days of experience as reproduced in Table 1.5. The most notable, and possibly discouraging, feature of these scrap percentages is that they vary. For example, during this 9-week period the scrap percentage has been as low as .93 (4th day of the 8th week) and as high as 12.37 (4th day of the 5th week). This is the variation that the foreman would like to control.

Let us now put this scrap control problem in terms analogous to those of our simple card games. Let us imagine that the *production process* that has generated these scrap percentages is like our deck

TABLE 1.5

Percentage of Scrap Produced

Week	Day	% of Scrap	Week	Day	% of Scrap	Week	Day	% of Scrap
1	1	6.86	4	1	5.36	7	1	5.61
	2	4.02		2	6.12		2	7.97
	3	6.53		3	5.72		3	5.07
	4	9.42		4	7.63		4	8.27
	5	4.41		5	8.76		5	1.68
2	1	7.13	5	1	7.38	8	1	3.47
	2	11.69		2	6.11		2	6.28
	3	7.84		3	8.41		3	6.82
	4	4.96		4	12.37		4	.93
	5	6.19		5	4.90		5	8.63
3	1	6.43	6	1	5.83	9	1	7.69
	2	8:05		2	6.74		2	4.83
	3	6.05		3	8.50		3	2.96
	4	3.81		4	5.23		4	7.09
	5	5.94		5	7.07		5	6.92

of cards. This process, just like our deck, has all sorts of scrap percentages in it. Each day one of these percentages occurs, just as though it were drawn out of a deck by a random selection procedure. If we compare the scrap percentages on two successive days, we are uncertain as to whether any observed difference is due to chance or whether it is due to a change in the production process itself, and thus the equivalent of a change in the deck. Naturally, if it represents a change that indicates a worsening in the process, the foreman would like to initiate corrective procedures. Otherwise he would prefer to leave it as it is.

The question is: How can he tell the nature of the given variation? It is obvious that every time the foreman initiates corrective procedures he is taking the risk that he will be searching for a will-o'-the-wisp, or that he will change to an actually poorer process. On the other hand, every time he leaves the process as it is, he takes the risk that the process has actually gone out of control and will continue to produce an unsatisfactory rate of scrap on the average. No matter what he decides, he takes the risk of doing the wrong thing. If this kind of risk bothers him, he perhaps should return to his former job as a machine operator.

1.6 Our Task

The concepts and methods of trying to gain understanding of problems like the scrap problem are going to be the subject of practically all the discussion in the remainder of this book. Such concepts and methods have a much wider application than to just problems like that of the scrap percentage. We find that most of the concepts are quite simple. We have been using most of them through most of our lives. Our attempt to put labels on these concepts and to formalize their relationships causes us no trouble if we form the habit of continually relating our discussion to our own familiar problems. The methods we use and/or refer to vary from things that are common knowledge to the fifth-grader to things that are best handled by professionals.

Actually, the primary virtues needed for successful analysis of historical experience of the scrap percentage sort are patience, persistence, and imagination. These are frequently more important than knowledge of fancy methods or the ability to articulate about concepts. The work routine in the analysis of data has only two basic parts: First, we ask a question about the data; second, we answer the question by rearranging the data. For example, we might ask: "How often has the scrap percentage been over 9.0?" We answer the question by a simple count of the relative frequencies of the various scrap percentages. Or, we might ask: "Are the scrap percentages getting any larger as time passes?" We might try to answer this question by comparing the average daily percentage during the last two weeks with that during the first two weeks. Or, we might ask: "Are the scrap percentages any higher in general on Friday than they are on Tuesday?" We answer this by comparing the average Friday percentage with the average Tuesday percentage. And so forth.

Patience and persistence become necessary because the value of many questions cannot be determined until after they have been answered, and by then all the work of rearrangement has been done, including that part of it that we now wish we had not bothered to do. It is easy to be discouraged if our first questions lead to fruitless results. This is particularly true if we are being judged by the results we produce rather than by the time and effort we put in.

Imagination is needed to help us think of good questions and also of various ways of rearranging the data. Too much imagination, of course, may get us into trouble because we never run out of new questions and new methods, and hence we may spend too much time with the same data, thus leaving ourselves no time to accumulate some additional evidence. Sometimes it is better to get impatient and to quit an analysis after a moderate amount of effort. Unfortunately there is no way to avoid the risks and consequences of quitting too soon or too late because we have no way of predetermining what is too soon or too late.

1.7 The Notions of Universe and Sample

Let us take a minute now to formalize a few terms. From now on we refer to our deck as a *universe*.[1] This term applies whether our deck is real or whether it is a figment of our imagination as in the case of the scrap producing process. More formally, a universe is "a collection of things which contains all the things which we think might occur under some particular circumstances." Rarely, most

---

[1] The word "population" is also commonly used to mean the same thing. We usually use the term universe; however, we occasionally use population. We should be prepared for both in writings on statistical method.

often in games of chance, we might deal with a universe that we *know* contains certain things.

A *sample* is a part of the universe. It might contain only one item; or it might contain all the items and thus be the same as the universe. A sample as large as a universe is generally only a conceptual possibility rather than a reality. The sample may refer to some items that are *in* the universe; or it may refer to items that *are to be generated* by the universe; or it may refer to items that have *already been generated* by the universe. Thus we would refer to our 45 scrap percentages that have occurred over a 9-week period as a *sample* of the scrap percentages that might have been generated by the *universe* of scrap percentages.

We have more to say later about different classes of universes and samples and the relationships between them.

1.8   A Conceptual Scheme

We are now ready to propose a conceptual scheme to help us in our thinking about problems of the sort described above, problems that are characterized by uncertainty and which are, therefore, prime subjects for the statistical method.

We conceive of our problem as one of predicting what sample will occur at some defined period of time. In order to do this, we must somehow develop a picture of what universe this sample will come out of. The only basis we have for developing this picture is our experience with past samples. Each of the past samples came from its own past universe. Possibly such past universes are identical; perhaps they are not. At any rate, we infer what these past universes were like on the basis of the samples that we have observed.

Starting now at the other end of the sequence, we proceed in our analysis as follows:

1. We examine *historical samples* of evidence.
2. We infer from these samples the conditions we think prevailed in the *historical universes* out of which these samples came.
3. We infer from these historical universes the *future universe* out of which we think our sample item will come. This future universe may or may not be the same as the past universes.
4. We predict the sample we think will occur. Since we cannot know exactly what will occur, we express the prediction in *probability* language. Generally this involves *three* numbers. *Two* of the numbers specify the *limits* within which we think the sample will occur. The third number expresses the confidence we have, or the probability, that the sample will be within the limits.

For example, after analysis of our past experience with the scrap percentage, we might come up with the statement that "we are 80% confident that tomorrow's scrap percentage will be between 4.7 and 6.3%." By expressing it this way we make clear the degree of uncertainty we feel about what the scrap percentage really will be. It also serves to remind us that since we really do not know why the scrap percentage will vary between 4.7% and 6.3%, there would be no point in investigating the cause of a scrap percentage, say, of 5.9%. At the same time, since this range of uncertainty about scrap tells us what we *do not know* about scrap, it sets our sights for finding out more if we are of a mind to learn more. In other words, it tells us what there still is to learn.

Contrast this "three-numbered answer system" with the typical system of expressing answers when we do not know the exact answer. For example, let us suppose we were asked right now for the correct time. Without looking at our watch or at a clock, or without asking somebody else, what would we say? Unless we were very unusual, we would probably say something like "8:30" or possibly "about 8:30." But, of course, we really do not know the exact time, even though we have used an exact number in expressing it. We perhaps think we cover ourselves when we say "about," and in a sense we do. But, how big is the "about"? Is it plus or minus one minute, or is it plus or minus twenty minutes? How can one tell how uncertain we are about the time if we don't tell him?

Can we be *sure* that the time is "8:30 plus or minus 20 minutes"? For example, would we bet $1000 to a dime that it is? If we were really sure, we certainly would make such a bet because it would be like finding a dime. The chances are that we wouldn't be *sure*. But if we are not sure, how confident are we? 90%? 99%? How can one tell how confident we are if we don't tell him?

The time example is, of course, generally trivial, unless we are running a railroad. But we all have problems we deal with that are important—important enough, say, so that we really should do some acute thinking about them. If our thinking never gets beyond the "about," or the "usually," or the "fairly often" stage, we are being sloppy. Naturally it is not easy to pin down our thinking about a problem to a point where we can achieve a range and a percentage confidence. But it can be done. As a matter of fact, *every* business decision that involves money now or ultimately (and which one does not?) *implies* a degree of confidence on the part of the man who makes the decision whether or not he realizes what that degree of confidence is.

It is particularly important for professional analysts to develop the habit of expressing the results of their analyses in the form of a range and a percentage confidence. They generally are the only ones who have intimate knowledge of the evidence used in the analysis. They are really the only ones who can give a reasonably accurate idea of what degree of uncertainty is associated with the analysis and the evidence. If they tell the sales vice president that the evidence suggests that "sales next year should be about $56,500,000," how does the vice president know whether he should be really prepared for sales as low as $51,000,000 or as high as $60,000,000? He will not know unless they tell him. Nevertheless he is going to make many decisions based on what *he* thinks would be a reasonable maximum and minimum. But what he thinks may not be consistent with what the evidence suggests. Since people seem to have a rather natural reluctance to pin themselves down unless they have to, vice presidents probably are not going to get specifically stated confidence or tolerance limits unless they insist on them.

Probably another reason why we seem to have a natural reluctance to specify limits to our estimates is that to do so is an explicit confession of ignorance. It is bad enough to pin our own thinking down to a point where we are conscious of our ignorance; it is even worse to confess it to the boss.

PROBLEMS AND QUESTIONS

1.1 You very likely feel that you have some prior knowledge about the probability of drawing a 7 out of an ordinary card deck. You may have had some actual experience with card drawings, or perhaps read a book about them, or perhaps a "more experienced hand" told you about them. Or perhaps you used "logic" to figure out the probability of a 7 on the basis of the content of the deck and your impressions about the drawing process.

(*a*) Considering only your prior knowledge, what is your reaction to the statement that "the probability of a 7 on a single drawing from an ordinary deck is 1/13"?

(*b*) Given the additional knowledge that is shown in Table 1.1, would you make any modifications in your reactions? Explain.

1.2(*a*) What do you understand is meant by the statement "the probability of a head on the toss of a coin is 1/2"?

(*b*) Assume that the statement given in (a) is correct. How many heads should we expect in 10 tosses? 100 tosses? 1,000,000 tosses?

1.3 Analyze the results given in Table 1.1 for any evidence of system or pattern to the results. For example, are the numbers getting bigger? Are they alternately getting bigger and then smaller? And so forth. (Note: The order in which the numbers occurred is from left to right beginning with the first row.)

1.4 Given the information in Table 1.1 and any prior knowledge you think you have, what odds would you give that the next card drawn will be a 2? Explain.

1.5 Consider the problem of our second game, the one in which we did not know the content of the deck but in which we did feel that the deck was constant.

(a) How many 17's in a row would you wish to see before you would be willing to bet 50 cents at even money that the next card was a 17? (Hint: Use the material of Tables 1.3 and 1.4 to help your thinking.) Explain your answer.

(b) Suppose the stake was increased to $5.00. Would this change in stakes have any effect on your answer in (a)? Explain.

1.6 Outline the history of your experience with some event that you have had to deal with over time. This event might be your problem of getting up in the morning at some desired time; or your problem of hitting a golf ball so it lands in some prescribed limits, such as the fairway. Be as specific as you can about any progress you might have made in reducing uncertainty about the event. Also, explain how you can tell whether a departure from the planned event just happened or whether it indicates a need for an adjustment in your planning activities. (For example, if you hit the golf ball into the rough, do you adjust your swing, etc. on the next shot or do you continue as before on the assumption that the bad shot was just luck?)

1.7 Take some problem that you have had, possibly the same one you referred to in Question 6, and express it in terms of the third game. That is, identify the deck or universe; indicate the nature of the event-generating process. Has this universe been shifting over time? How can you tell? Are you sure of this? If you are not sure, how confident are you that the universe is shifting, or has shifted, the way you say it has? Use numbers in expressing this confidence.

1.8 Answer the following questions about the history of scrap percentages as given in Table 1.5.

(a) How often was the scrap percentage

    1. Less than 4.5%?
    2. Less than 6.6%?
    3. More than 5.8%?
    4. More than 8.4%?
    5. Between 2.0% and 3.6%?
    6. Between 2.5% and 7.5%?

(b) Make the best guess you can about the probability that the next day's scrap percentage will be higher than 8.4%. Explain the basis of your estimated probability.

(c) Assume that you are going to bet $1 on the correctness of your probability estimate given in (b). What odds would you be willing to give that you are right?

(d) What was the "average" scrap percentage?

(e) Might you have determined the "average" in some other way? Why did you do it the way you did?

(f) Within what range did the middle 50% of the scrap percentages fall? The middle 2/3's?

(*g*) Were the percentages higher the last two weeks than they were the first two weeks? How much higher? Or lower?

(*h*) Were the Monday percentages higher or lower than the Friday percentages? Would you be willing to plan on a continuation of this difference if you were the foreman?

1.9 What percentage of future scrap percentages would you expect to have the values indicated by the six parts to Question 1.8a? (Hint: Keep in mind that you cannot possibly know these answers. You must do some guessing. So do not come up with a "one-number" answer.)

1.10 Were the differences you discovered between the first two weeks' percentages and those of the last two weeks sufficiently great to cause you to believe that the universe of scrap percentages had shifted between those two periods? Explain and justify your answer.

1.11 Answer the following questions to the best of your ability. *Use only the knowledge you now have.*

(*a*) How heavy is a Woondot?

(*b*) What is the temperature right now in Rangoon?

(*c*) What is today's closing price of General Motors common stock on the New York Stock Exchange?

(*d*) How much do you weigh?

(*e*) How much does a 6-foot-tall adult American male weigh?

(*f*) How much does the first string defensive tackle of the Chicago Bears Professional Football Club weigh?

chapter 2
Some fundamental concepts

2.1 Variation, or Differences

The universal existence of *variation* is one of the most significant aspects of our environment. Many scientists believe that there are no two objects, or two parts of any object, exactly alike. The existence of *apparent* identity of objects is not looked at as evidence of *true* identity, but only as evidence of *inadequate perception*. Advance in any area of man's knowledge has generally proceeded hand-in-hand with the development of more refined measuring instruments, including not only physical measuring instruments such as electronic microscopes, but also the more abstract measuring instruments such as intelligence tests. It is obvious that we cannot take into account differences we cannot even perceive. Our lack of precision of measurement in the social sciences (including business) is one of the prime causes of frustration in that area, a frustration in marked contrast to our apparent success in the physical area. In fact, some people associate science with precision and on this basis ridicule the idea that the social sciences are scientific at all. This is a mistake. It is preferable to associate science with a method of inquiry rather than with the accuracy of the observations made in the inquiry.

The universal existence of variation is at once a problem and an opportunity. The problem arises because universal variation puts us on the horns of a dilemma. If we try to act at all times as though all things are different from each other, we would probably freeze into a state of inaction. This would happen because we would believe that our past experience provided us with no guide to the future. By definition, so to speak, the future is automatically different from the past. On the other hand, if we act as though some things are the same when actually they are different, our action is subject to error. For example, an action that assumes that mushrooms and toadstools are the same is not only subject to error, but also to error of some consequence.

The opportunity arises because universal variation provides man with an unlimited number of objects, both animate and inanimate, which can combine or be combined in an unlimited number of combinations and for the potential creation of new realities. In fact, it is here that we find the basis of progress—and also the basis of retrogression. One of the strongest arguments for a democratically organized society is that it allows for the fullest possible development of individual differences and hence for the greatest potential progress. At the same time, of course, there is the companion risk of retrogression.

2.2 What Differences Make a Difference?

The preceding paragraphs have pointed out that we believe we live in a world of universal variation where everything is different from everything else and where everything today is different from what it was yesterday. Although this notion of universal variation is a very fundamental philosophical truth, it can cause all kinds of trouble if we try to act on it in the solution of all routine problems. We now have to face up to the problem of how we can tell when it is appropriate to act as though things were the same when we believe they are truly different.

The answer is quite simple. We treat things as the same when their differences "don't make any difference." Casual observation of the behavior of anybody, including ourselves, will soon convince us that a difference which makes no difference to a person will be ignored or assumed away. It is absolutely essential that a person ignore some differences in order to have the time and energy to pay attention to others. It is a mixed blessing that people differ widely on what differences they think make a difference. It can be good in that in a relatively free society somebody is paying particular attention to almost any area of differences that we can think of, plus a lot more areas that we cannot think of. Einstein, for example, spent a good part of his lifetime studying differences that even he could not see but only suspect. The average person thought him strange for spending so much of his time on such supposedly meaningless differences, rather than on so-called important differences such as the sharpness of the crease in his trousers. It turned out, of course, that the differences he was concerned with bid fair to make quite a difference to all of us.

Disagreement on what differences make a difference can be bad because such disagreement often leads to disagreeableness and conflict. Many people have real difficulty in permitting others to ignore differences which to them are quite important, and vice versa. Part of the problem of growing up is to gain a sense of values or a recognition of what differences really make a difference, to the adults, that is. The six-year-old child is very concerned about the size difference between two pieces of pie and cares not one whit for how his friend feels about who gets which piece. The adult is very much more concerned about how his friend feels than he is concerned about the size of the pieces of pie. Educators are still faced with the problem (and seem to be as mystified as ever in finding a solution) of how to persuade students that certain differences make a difference other than in the teacher's mind. Should the student be drilled in the detailed differences on the theory that he has to first know what the differences are before he can understand their importance? Or should he be plunged into situations where the differences do make a difference on the theory that he will soon be stimulated to find out what these differences are that are causing all his trouble? Or should there be a mixture of these two theories, with others, in proportions infinitely varied? Or should the teacher not waste time trying to convince the student of the importance of the differences under discussion and concentrate mostly on the "grade nerve." The teacher in effect tells the student that "the difference between a grade of A and a grade of B (a difference the student does appreciate) is equivalent to a recognition of the difference between a logarithm and a quadratic equation (a difference many students would not really appreciate)." This indirect technique for getting people to pay attention to differences they might otherwise ignore is quite common in our society. The worker is taught the importance of noticing the difference between a piston of 3.006 in. in diameter and one of 3.008 in. by associating such a difference with, say, a difference of $8.50 in his paycheck. The thief is taught the difference between earning $100 and stealing $100 by associating such a difference with the difference between freedom and a jail cell.

Most people are not aware of any conscious process whereby they *note* a difference, *evaluate* the importance of the difference, and then *decide* to ignore or consider the difference in their daily affairs. Most of the differences in the objects around us are ignored simply because they are not even perceived. Part of the ability to perceive seems to be inborn. Some people have a better "ear for music" than others regardless of comparative training and of effort applied. The other part of perception ability seems to be related to how much a person practices or studies. To a very large extent we perceive only those differences we have been *told* to look for. It is the rare person who makes it a practice of perceiving differences even where he had not been told to expect them. The average person acquires most of his ideas of what differences exist and which ones are important from other people: his parents, his teachers, his companions, etc. To a very considerable extent these ideas are pressed onto a person before he is ready to consciously and willingly accept them, and certainly before he has had the experiences that enable him to judge for himself whether the differences are really important or are just sham differences. It is necessary that this be the procedure if man is going to make any progress. Each of us has to be brought up to date, so to speak, before we can proceed to make our own contributions to the determination of what differences make a difference. As an anonymous person once expressed it, "this world would never have gotten anyplace if each of us had to reinvent the wheel."

But like most good things, the procedure of rather forcibly passing on man's accumulated wisdom from one generation to another has its bad side too. The elements of wisdom in one age may not be applicable in another, a possibility known to any teenager. But what we have learned at great pain in one age is not lightly tossed aside, especially if it has become part of the stock-in-trade of a professional teacher. Sellers of knowledge, as it were, can be just as tenacious in preserving a market for their brand of knowledge as the seller of buggy whips was in trying to preserve his market. Also there is the problem that some of man's ideas about what differences make a difference have been wrong. Although good and workable ideas probably have a better chance of surviving than bad or wrong ideas, this doesn't mean that bad ideas cannot do a great deal of harm before they do die.

Each person, then, has a substantial personal responsibility as he tries to find out what differences exist, which ones really do make a difference, and which ones can be safely ignored. He must put considerable faith in the knowledge and integrity of others so he can be brought up to date. At the same time he must preserve a sufficient degree of skepticism and of independent judgment so he can do some of his own sorting and some of his own seeking.

We are continually concerned with differences or variation in the pages to follow. Most of our concern, however, is with the observation and analysis of differences as we find them, rather than with the problem of the *importance* of the differences. Where the question of importance is more or less a technical one, that is, subject to objective analysis, we have something to say. If, however, the question of importance revolves around value judgments, we merely call attention to the problem and make no effort to solve it.

2.3   Kinds of Knowledge

Since we are going to devote considerable time to the problem of how to best use the the the knowledge we have and also to the problem of how to acquire additional knowledge, it is useful at this point to take a few minutes to discuss the various kinds of knowledge that we have occasion to deal with. This discussion also makes it possible for us to be more explicit about the kind of approach we are planning to use in later pages.

Knowledge of Why

The most useful kind of knowledge is that which tells us **why** an event occurs. If we know **why,** in the sense that we know the *cause,* or causes, of the event, we have taken the first step in learning how to *physically* control the event. Given this kind of control, we can then make the event happen or not happen as we see fit; or perhaps we can then control the *intensity* of the event.

Knowledge of **why** does not necessarily lead to ability to physically control the event. We may know the causes of an event but be unable to control these causes, thus being unable to control the event. For example, we might know the causes of a tornado without being able to affect such causes and thus prevent a tornado or alter the path of a tornado. But, of course, knowing the causes, we would better be able to *predict* the path of a tornado; then we could take steps to remove things and persons from that path.

As we would expect, knowledge of **why** something occurs is most difficult to find out. We actually know the causes of very few things that happen. We naturally have had greater success with man-made things. Since man has built an automobile, he knows the causal system that makes an automobile behave the way it was *designed* to behave. If the automobile does not behave properly, we can use our knowledge of its causal system to fairly quickly put our finger on the difficulty and then make the proper repair. We have a bit more difficulty when we find that the human body is not working properly, or when the economic or political systems are not working properly. Since we did not build these systems, we are never quite sure of the causal connections among the parts. In fact, we even have disputes about whether such systems are or are not working properly, with some people pointing with alarm and others recommending relaxed patience. With the human body, we have apparently discovered that some parts, like the tonsils and the appendix, are quite superfluous, at least in the sense that the body seems to function the same both with and without such organs. Whether that is because these organs are really superfluous, or whether other organs, as yet unknown to us, take over their functions when they are removed, or whether they really do make a difference that we have not yet been able to perceive are questions still to be answered.

One of the theoretical advantages of a planned, engineered, regulated, or built society, in contrast to a relatively free society that grew without planning, is that we would be able to fix it when it broke down because we would know what it was made of. Such a society would have to be quite simple, however, because we could not understand it otherwise. People would also have to agree on what kind of society we would build, and this is very difficult to accomplish without help from the military. Incidentally, the use of *force* to control events is quite common, whether it is the playpen to restrict the movements of the child or the atomic submarine to modify the behavior of nations.

The paucity of knowledge that man has of why things happen as they do has not deterred him from acting as though he did know why. Although such behavior appears to be arrogant and dangerous, and, in fact, is often just that, there seem to be good psychological reasons for behaving that way. We seem to have an almost pathological need to act "logically" and "sensibly." But how can we act "logically" if we don't know **why?** We cannot, of course. So we invent reasons, preferably good ones, that is, reasons acceptable to our boss, or to our parents, or to our conscience, etc. Most of the time these reasons are at best trivial and superficial; and at worst they are wrong.

Notions of why something happens are essentially theoretical or hypothetical. Generally speaking we do not *know* **why.** We *believe* or *assume* **why.** The tendency of most of us to not state the assumptions under which we act, and often to not even be aware that we have made any assumptions, leads us to believe that we really know when actually we should only assume that we know. This tendency can establish solid blocks to further learning because, if we already "know," there is "nothing further to learn" and we won't make the effort.

Knowledge of When

Most people are singularly uninformed about the *causal system* which makes it possible to turn a small switch and witness, in the comfort of their living room, events which are taking place thousands of miles away. They really have no need to know. It is sufficient for their purposes if they know that, most of the time, **when** they turn the switch the picture appears on the television set. If for some unknown reason or reasons the set does not work properly, a telephone call will bring a serviceman who most of the time will correct the difficulty for less than $10. Although the serviceman is more sophisticated on technical television matters than the typical user, even he is surprisingly ignorant of a good part of the causal system that gets a picture at the flick of a switch. He will likely work from a manual that was written by the engineers of the manufacturer. The manual usually has many phrases like:

When you find flip-flop, the difficulty may be corrected by replacing tube No. 6A4c, or by turning the hold knob to the right. If none of these works, the difficulty is then likely to be with the anterior section of the spherical oscillator. *Do not attempt to adjust this.* Replace the whole section. Return the replaced section to the factory.

Thus even the repairman knows little of the *theory*, or the **why,** of the mechanism he works on. His knowledge consists almost exclusively of the "**when** you see this, you will likely see this" kind. This is obviously a very useful kind of knowledge. It is equally obvious it is not of the same kind or of the same order as that possessed by the electronics engineer, whose, in turn, is not of the same order as that of the theoretical physicist.

Knowledge of **when** is acquired by *associating* things with each other, usually as a result of observation of past events. We associate rain with clouds, basketball players with tall men, Cadillacs with wealthy owners, July (in Chicago) with heat, etc. At least by the time he is born, and maybe sooner, the baby starts associating events with each other. The sounds of footsteps, of clinking pans, of agitated water, etc. soon become associated with being fed, being bathed, being cuddled, etc. Even the most unimaginative baby soon learns to associate the sounds he himself can make and the actions that generally follow. He then makes his first attempts to *control* what happens by consciously making selected vocal sounds, or noises.

It is primarily our knowledge of **when** that enables us to reduce many activities of life to a routine. Such knowledge enables us to predict events and thus plan for them. It is essential that we reduce many decisions to routine in order to release the conscious mind so it can reflect on decision problems in new areas. Most "controls" in business are basically routine decision-makers based on *association* or *knowledge of when* which enable people to make decisions without the pain of conscious mental activity. Thus the executive can delegate many of his *decisions* without also delegating the decision-making *function*.

Knowledge of How Often

When we play any one of the great number of conventional card games, we do have some knowledge about the card that is going to be dealt to us. One thing we know for sure, for example, is that we will not be dealt the "17 of hearts." But we do not know the causal system that results in the particular card selected, or at least we are not supposed to know. Hence we really do not know **why** we get the card we do, although we may have some superstitions about why. Also we do not know **when** we will get a certain card because, if the game is honest, there is no relationship between how the cards are shuffled, cut, and dealt and the particular card drawn at a particular time. The knowledge that we do possess is very real, however, and we may call it knowledge of **how often** a given card will be dealt. We would expect, for example, that the Ace of Spades will be dealt *on the average* 1/52 of the time. This does not mean that exactly one out of every 52 cards dealt to us will be the Ace of Spades. It means only that *in the long run* we would expect that 1/52 of all our thousands of cards would be Aces of Spades.

Knowledge of **how often** is obviously inferior to knowledge of **when** and knowledge of **why**. If we know only **how often** something will happen, we do not know its schedule for happening and our problem of planning is more difficult. Since there is no schedule known to us, the event is never really "due" or "overdue" to happen. We can deal with such events only on a probability basis, and most people find this somewhat disconcerting.

Despite its obvious inferiority to knowledge of **why** and of **when,** knowledge of **how often** is still of considerable value. The most striking illustration of its usefulness is the insurance business, one of the most stable and predictable of all businesses. An insurance company bases its rates not on *who* is going to die and *when* he is going to die, but on **how often** "somebody" is going to die in a given time period. In order to lend stability to their predictions, and thus to have some control over their income and outgo, the insurance company will try to have as many policyholders as practical, thus coming as close as possible to that long run.

This same kind of knowledge also underlies all honestly operated commercial gambling games. The proprietor, or anybody else, does not know who will win nor *when* any given person will win, but he does know quite accurately **how often** "anybody" will win. He quite naturally sets up the game so that this how often is infrequent enough so he, the proprietor, is the only likely winner in the long run. Incidentally, the commercial gambling operation is about as close to a pure illustration of **how often** knowledge that man can imagine. The game is *deliberately* designed to reduce to zero any knowledge of **why** or **when** something will happen. Thus, unless the game breaks down or becomes imperfect, it is literally impossible to devise a system to beat the game. A proper system requires knowledge of when a given event will occur. The only way we can beat a game of chance is to be lucky. To be smart helps not at all.

Blending the Various Kinds of Knowledge

Most situations we encounter in real life find us using knowledge of more than one kind. We find that any decision we make, or any action we take, is based on some of each kind of knowledge. We rarely know exactly why anything happens, although we often act as though we do. Our knowledge of **when** is usually imperfect in the sense that we don't know *exactly* when but only *about* when. As a matter of fact, even when we say or act as though we know that something will happen at about a certain time, in reality we are not sure it will happen at that time or any other time. When a railroad establishes a schedule, it specifies the times we might use as a guide to the true times. It does not guarantee the time and it takes no responsibility whatsoever for any inconvenience, expense, or distress we may be caused by its failure to be on time.

In reality, all knowledge is fundamentally of **how often,** with the counting of **how often** under certain restricted conditions.[1] To il-

---

[1] These are the conditions that define what it is that is to be counted. For example, we might decide to count the relative frequency of noontime temperatures at Midway airport in Chicago for every day during a 3-year period. We might find, say, that a noontime temperature of 46° to 50° occurred 8% of the time. However, if we had counted temperatures only for the month of July, we might find that a noontime temperature of 46° to 50° occurred only 1/2 of 1% of the time. Thus the change in restrictive conditions changes the relative frequency of these temperatures.

TABLE 2.1

Actual Time of Arrival of the "6:05 P.M. Train"

(Recorded only to the nearest minute)

Time of Arrival	Frequency of Occurrence
6:00 or earlier	6
6:01	0
6:02	2
6:03	1
6:04	4
6:05	19
6:06	12
6:07	8
6:08	7
6:09	9
6:10	6
6:11	3
6:12	5
6:13	0
6:14	2
6:15 or later	16
	100

lustrate, let us look at the problem of the railroad schedule. We might ask the question: "Exactly *when* does the 6:05 P.M. train arrive?" The answer would be that it arrives at different times, or at least it has arrived at different times in the past. Let us look at Table 2.1 which gives us the record of the last 100 arrivals measured to the nearest minute.

It is obvious that it would be incorrect to answer the question of when this train arrives by stating a *specific* time. All we really know is **how often** the train has arrived at certain specified times. (Note

Sometimes a change in conditions does not change the relative frequency of some phenomenon. In this case the conditions are irrelevant for the purpose. For example, 1/13th of all the cards in a deck are 6's. Also 1/13th of all the red cards are 6's. Knowledge of card *color* is, therefore, irrelevant if we are interested in the card *number*. Knowledge of the month is not irrelevant if we are interested in Chicago temperatures.

also that we know that it has *not* arrived at some other times.) Some proper answers to the question of when this train has arrived might be:

1. It has arrived between 6:045 and 6:055 19% of the time.
2. " " " " 6:035 " 6:065 35% " " "
3. " " " " 6:015 " 6:125 76% " " "
Etc.

In other words, there are *many* different answers we might properly give to the question. Every one is correct in the sense that every one is consistent with the facts. Which one a person actually gives depends on how much confidence he would like to have in his answer. The more confidence he would like to have, the broader must be his coverage of the various things that might happen. If he wishes to be sure that his answer is correct, he really should answer that the "6:05 arrives sometime, or maybe never." This leads, of course, to a ridiculous answer, which, although it is correct, is no answer at all when it comes to giving somebody some idea of when he should plan to be at the station to meet the train. So, in order to make the answer practically useful, it is necessary to be less than sure that the answer covers all possibilities. Or, to use words we have used before in connection with the scrap control problem, to give a really useful answer to the question of when the train arrives means that we must give an answer that might be wrong. We also must give an answer that interprets **when** as covering some *range* of values rather than some specific value.

Again, we should remind ourselves that people typically do not think, and certainly do not talk, in the terms indicated above. To the typical person, the "6:05" arrives at "about 6:05" and that is all. But if that is all, it is evident that the question of the time is essentially trivial to the people concerned or that somehow "about" has acquired a generally understood meaning so that it requires no further specification. Perhaps "about" is understood to mean no further away than plus or minus 15 minutes. In most everyday affairs certain conventions have grown up which lead to generally accepted tolerances by which the group lives.

2.4 Amount of Knowledge

Table 2.2 presents the record of the last 100 arrivals of the "8:15 P.M." train for the same railroad. The most important thing to note

TABLE 2.2

Actual Time of Arrival of the "8:15 P.M." Train

(Recorded only to the nearest minute)

Time of Arrival	Frequency of Occurrence
8:10 or earlier	12
8:11	3
8:12	1
8:13	5
8:14	3
8:15	11
8:16	7
8:17	4
8:18	6
8:19	8
8:20	7
8:21	6
8:22	5
8:23	3
8:24	4
8:25 or later	15
	100

here is that there has been greater variation in the arrival time of the "8:15" than there has been in that of the "6:05." We can see this if we compare the percentage of time that the two trains have arrived within specified minutes of the schedule time. Table 2.3 summarizes this comparison. In a sense, then, we know more about when the "6:05" will arrive than we do about when the "8:15" will arrive. We know more because we are able to state the arrival time with greater confidence. For example, we are 53% confident that the "6:05" will arrive within 3.5 minutes of its scheduled time, whereas we are only 37% confident that the "8:15" will arrive within those limits. If we wished, we could quantify the amount by which this knowledge is greater and say that it is 43% greater $[(53 - 37)/37]$. Actually we generally do not wish to quantify differences in knowledge this way, but it suffices at the moment to illustrate the fact that

TABLE 2.3

Comparison of Arrival Times of the "6:05" and the "8:15"

Departure from Schedule	% of Arrivals "6:05"	% of Arrivals "8:15"
Plus or minus .5 minutes	19	11
" " " 1.5 "	35	21
" " " 2.5 "	44	30
" " " 3.5 "	53	37
" " " 4.5 "	62	48

there are quantifiable differences in the amount of knowledge we might have. As we shall see in a moment, we find it more convenient to measure *ignorance* than we do to measure *knowledge*.

2.5 A Word about Ignorance

We are all aware of the fact that ignorance is the antithesis of knowledge. Complete ignorance would be the equivalent of zero knowledge, and vice versa. Thus it is possible to talk equally well in terms of ignorance as in terms of knowledge. Let us take a look first at a case of zero knowledge, or of complete ignorance. We may recall that one of the questions at the end of the last chapter asked how heavy a "Woondot" is. We probably had no idea what a "Woondot" is and hence no idea of how heavy one is. It may weigh only .0003 oz. On the other hand, it might weigh 73 million tons, or even more. It may even have a negative weight, and if it were not tied to the earth, would have soared into space. Thus we are forced to admit that the weight of a "Woondot" is somewhere between minus infinity and plus infinity pounds. This is, of course, a large range of uncertainty, or of ignorance.

Now let us look at something we know exactly. Since it is so hard to find illustrations of exact or complete knowledge except for things that we have defined that way, let us take something that we know by definition. A good example is the value of a playing card. We know that the 7 of clubs is exactly the 7 of clubs and not the 6½ of clubs because it is so written on the card. When we play cards, we have no problem that perhaps this particular 6 of clubs is one of the biggest 6's and hence is really bigger than this particular 7 of clubs which happens to be one of the smallest 7's. Anybody who argued this way would be thrown out of the game! We can say, therefore, that we have zero ignorance about the value of the card, or we have complete knowledge.

When we know something, but not everything, we find that we can state answers only within certain limits. We found this to be so in the scrap problem, in the various games, and in the arrival time of the trains. The range of uncertainty we had in any of the above really expressed the *degree of ignorance* we had about the particular phenomenon. We "do not know when the train will arrive between the limits of 6:00 P.M. and 6:10 P.M., although we are reasonably (68%) confident it will arrive some time within those limits." If perchance the railroad were to improve its operations so that we could then say that "the 6:05 will arrive 68% of the time between 6:02 and 6:08," we would now be less ignorant than before about the arrival time. If we wished, we could say that we were 40% less ignorant $[(10 - 6)/10]$.

Whenever we desire to improve our accuracy of estimation in a problem, or what amounts to the same thing, to reduce our range of ignorance, we take steps to try to *learn* something. After taking such steps, we quite naturally are interested to see whether we had any success in our efforts to learn. We find that it is very convenient to then measure the amount by which this learning process *reduced our ignorance*. We find it very difficult to specify what we know and then to measure how much we have added to our knowledge. It is much easier to specify what we do not know and then measure how much we reduce what we do not know.

There is also a psychological advantage in concentrating on our ignorance rather than on our knowledge. When we are aware of how much we do not know, we are psychologically receptive to the need for reducing this ignorance. Also we are aware of how much reduction is possible. By concentrating on what we know, we might easily be satisfied with that and make no effort to learn more.

2.6 Luck, Chance, and Randomness

We are all familiar with luck, that pixy that makes footballs take funny bounces and that largely accounts for the success of the other fellow! Let us analyze what we call luck to see if it has any relationship to what we have been talking about before. Basically, it seems that we use luck as an antonym for skill. We use lucky to characterize a person who has achieved success with no apparent benefit of skill or knowledge. We picture an ignorant person blundering along but somehow becoming the recipient of good fortune. In essence, then, it seems that we use luck as a synonym for *successful behavior based on ignorance.* When a person acts or decides in ignorance, we say that the outcome is in the hands of Lady Luck; or, in other words, the outcome is *not* under the control of the person acting or deciding.

Chance also refers to some sort of pixy that determines events over which we have no control. A game of chance is a game so designed that skill and knowledge are not factors in the outcome. It is sometimes called a fair game because nobody has any advantage over anybody else, regardless of a person's age, sex, education, experience, wealth, etc. If skill and knowledge do become factors in a game of chance, then it is no longer a game of pure chance, although there may still be chance elements in the game. The winner of a game of pure chance is lucky and the loser is unlucky. The fact that such games have results independent of a person's skill and knowledge is such a game's main attraction. Anybody might win; and it is no reflection on a person's intelligence to lose; although it is surprising that so many people, particularly children, take considerable personal satisfaction in winning, even implying that winning somehow or other makes them a kind of superior being.

In essence, luck and chance refer to the same pixy.

Random is a word that we use frequently in subsequent pages. We talk about random samples, random events, random processes, etc. Although we eventually give rather specifically-worded definitions of these things, it is sufficient for our present purposes to simply note that random events are caused by the same pixy that causes chance events. In fact, we use the words chance and random interchangeably.

Now these are all important words and phrases. When we use them we should have some fairly clear idea of what they mean. Our question is: Exactly what, or who, is this pixy that goes around determining these strokes of fortune? The best and most straightforward answer is that this pixy is a whole collection of factors and forces that combine to produce the given result. The forces are many and/or are at the moment indiscernible. The pixy is no magic or cosmic force.

Let us take a look at the problem of determining whether a coin is going to come up heads or tails, or what is the same problem, whether the coin that has rolled under the bed has come up heads or tails. It is clear that whether the coin comes up heads or tails depends on such mundane factors as (1) how a person holds the coin, (2) the amount of friction between the fingers and the coin, (3) the angle of release of the coin, (4) the force of release of the coin, (5) the direction of release, (6) the humidity of the air, (7) the density of the air, (8) the velocity and direction of the wind, (9) the resiliency and uniformity of the surface the coin strikes, etc. If we had precise knowledge of all these factors, and of those not mentioned, it is very likely that we could rather successfully predict the result of the toss. In other words, the result of the toss follows rather directly from these and similar forces. It does not follow from some cosmic force whose nature is forever hidden from man. The forces exist, even though *we* are ignorant of them. We may be ignorant because we are at the moment incapable of measuring these forces. Or, more likely in this case, we are ignorant of these forces because we have decided that the cost of measuring them is too great considering the value of being able to predict the result of a coin toss.

We must admit that the view that luck, chance, and random all refer to a collection of presently unmeasured forces is essentially philosophical in the sense that it represents a faith or a belief. I have never tried to really measure the forces affecting the toss of a coin. Nor do I know anybody who has. But I have faith that the forces exist, and they exist completely irrespective of whether I know what they are or how they behave. I have faith that they are there to be identified and measured whenever we develop our skills and desire to the point that makes us want to measure them. The validity of this view cannot be easily proved or demonstrated. All we can do is argue for the practicality of this way of looking at chance. The most important practical argument is that as long as we have this belief we do not find the *door of knowledge shut to us*. If, on the other hand, we adopt the view that luck, chance, and random are absolute forces whose nature is forever hidden from us, it is only natural for us to stop trying to add to our knowledge. Our progress will stop as soon as we decide that there is no more to know. We are probably all familiar with at least one person who has decided that he has no more to discover or learn.

Another way of expressing this particular view of the nature of chance is to say that chance has nothing whatever to do with the *event* itself. Rather chance refers to man's *knowledge about* the event. In other words, chance is a personal thing; it is a product of the human mind, a pure invention; it does not exist in the sense that a stone exists. The weather in all its aspects has gone on for centuries and will probably go on for many more centuries, quite oblivious of what man has known about the weather and has been saying about the weather. It is highly doubtful that man's increasing knowledge of the weather, an increase that has considerably improved man's ability to forecast the weather, thereby enabling man to label weather phenomena as being due less and less to chance, has in any significant way affected the weather. When we find ourselves labeling an event as a chance event, what we are really doing is confessing our ignorance about the event. But since human beings do not like to confess their ignorance, they project their ignorance to the event and blame their inability to understand the event on the event rather than on their own ignorance. This represents a certain kind of cleverness, but it also results in a certain amount of self-delusion.

Another notable and interesting feature of this way of looking at chance is that it is now possible, and *logical,* for two different people to label the same event as chance or as not chance because they happen to have different amounts of knowledge about the event. Thus the two people might logically act differently with respect to the event. For example, if we and a friend (some friend!) toss a coin to see who pays for the dinner, and if our friend (who is doing the tossing) knows what he is doing, the coin comes up heads because that was what he had decided on. But we think he does not know, so we think the toss is random. He thinks of the event as being entirely predetermined; we think of it as being chance. We both act rationally considering what each of us knows. But he is going to win, not because he is any smarter than we are in the sense that he thinks more logically or more rapidly, but because he knows something we do not. An advantage in knowledge will often offset an advantage in intelligent use of knowledge. The most clever guesser is at the mercy of someone who knows.

2.7   Conscious vs. Subconscious Knowledge

So far we have talked about knowledge in an essentially abstract way. We have made no reference really to the person who has it and to where he has it. Although we treat such matters more elaborately in the next chapter, it is useful to call our attention here to the most obvious of all the distinctions that can be made in the various storage facilities that man has for his knowledge. The distinction is between *conscious* knowledge, which is essentially knowledge we know we have and can transmit to others, and *subconscious* knowledge, which is knowledge that we cannot specifically identify and cannot pass on to others. Some wit once said that conscious knowledge is the kind we talk about but do not use, whereas subconscious knowledge is the kind we use but do not talk about! The same kind of distinction is being made to a certain extent when we say that a person "knows how to do it, but can't do it," whereas another person "can do it, but doesn't know how to do it." This probably sounds somewhat like doubletalk. A good example of what is meant would be a superathlete like Babe Ruth. He could and did hit a baseball quite well; but he did not know how he did it in the sense that he could explain to somebody else how to hit a baseball. There have been many successful businessmen who could run a business; their success proved it. But they were complete failures when it came to knowing how they ran their business in the sense that they could help their successors to run the business.

We are all aware of the fact that we do some things with conscious thought and some things with no apparent thought at all. We also know that we frequently do some things better if we do not think about them. For example, most of us typically walk with far more grace than we exhibit if we walk across a stage before 1000 people.

We would hesitate to try to assess the relative importance to us of our conscious knowledge and of our subconscious knowledge. In later pages our discussions are almost exclusively confined to conscious knowledge. This is not because we consider it more important, but only because this is the only kind we can talk directly about.

2.8 Knowledge, Ignorance, and Decision-making

We become conscious of the problem of making decisions only when we are aware of alternatives or choices, and we are aware of alternatives only when we are aware that we do not know exactly what to do. Hence we have to take action despite a certain amount of ignorance and therefore uncertainty. Fortunately many of our problems are trivial enough or have enough room for error that we do not have to overly concern ourselves with how to best make our choices. In fact, often the problem is so trivial, or we are so indifferent to it, that we deliberately leave the decision to chance even though we know how to do better. For example, most people just go to the bus stop and wait for the bus with no thought of the bus schedule. This is because the bus generally runs often enough so that we feel we can afford to wait the 10 minutes or so that might be the maximum interval. But if the possible waiting time is long enough to be valuable to us, we take the time, trouble, and perhaps money necessary to gather more specific knowledge of the bus schedule and thus plan our arrival at the stop so we save some of the time.

Since so many people wistfully hope that there must be some formula whereby we can make decisions about many matters, it is useful to remind ourselves that this will always be a hope rather than a reality. There can be no complete formula for decision-making for the simple reason that the problem of decision arises only when we are partially ignorant; and if we are partially ignorant, we are bound to be somewhat uncertain about the decision to make. But, although we have no complete formula, we do have ways of analyzing what we do know so we get the most out of it without at the same time getting too much out of it! It may sound surprising, but it is nevertheless true that we often have as much risk of getting too much out of what we know as we have of getting too little.

2.9 Probability

The essential tool in dealing with problems in which we have only partial knowledge is the probability calculus. Since this connotes mathematics to some people, it all seems quite forbidding. But it does not really have to be this way. Actually we all use probability concepts every day with no thought about the mathematics of it. In fact, the cat lying in the bushes waiting for the unwary rabbit is using probability concepts in the selection of the particular bush, the particular time, etc. The cat does not *know* he is going to catch a rabbit, but he figures he has a "pretty good chance" based on his past experience.

Exactly what do we mean when we make such statements as "the probability of a head on the toss of a coin is 1/2 or .5"? We might mean either one of two things. We might be talking strictly in abstractions. Then we would be thinking of a "fair" coin, which by definition is so constructed and so thrown that each side has exactly the same chance of coming up. We might immediately infer from this that the coin would logically always stand on end, thus giving us 1/2 head and 1/2 tail! But we do not want to mean this, so we add the further condition that the coin cannot stand on end! It must come up heads or tails. How often will it come up heads? We answer this by in effect picturing a coin teetering on its edge but unable to really stay on its edge. Sometimes it falls one way; sometimes the other. But, by definition, so to speak, it will fall one way just as often as it will fall the other way *in the long run*. If the coin alternates heads and tails, thus apparently coming as close as possible to the condition of an equal number of heads and tails, we quite logically recognize this *system* in the results and treat the coin toss as a completely solved problem with no uncertainty and no need for probability calculations. It should be clear, then, that the concept of the long run is of the essence in understanding what is meant by probability. But before we tackle the problem a little bit more, let us look at the other way we might interpret the statement that "the probability of a head on the toss of a coin is .5."

The second way to start looking at the problem of probabilities for coin tosses is to start with real coins that are actually going to be tossed, rather than with abstract coins that exist only in our imaginations. If somebody asks whether we would guess heads, tails, or edge, we might take a scientific, or at least an apparently scientific approach, to the problem. *We study the coin and the tossing process.* Let us say we do this with our hands and our eyes and our other unaided senses. Let us suppose further that after about 15 minutes of such study we have come to the following conclusions:

1. It must be almost impossible for this coin to be tossed and end up on its edge because we have found it almost impossible to stand the coin on its edge. So let us for the moment rule out this possibility.
2. We have found no evidence to support the belief that the coin is more likely to come up heads than it is to come up tails, and vice versa. So let us *assume for the moment* that the coin is just as likely to come up heads as it is to come up tails. Or, in other words, let us assume that the probability of a head is .5.

There are two very important aspects to note about this second approach to the problem of what we might mean when we talk about probabilities. First, note that we make very clear that whatever we say about the probability we say only on the basis of *assumptions* we are making, and furthermore, we emphasize the *tentative* character of the assumptions by the qualifying phrase, for the moment. In other words, we are prepared to change our assumptions whenever additional evidence suggests the possible superiority of other assumptions. And, of course, if we change our assumptions, we change the probabilities. The fact that we would do this tells us that we really are not associating the probabilities *with the coin*, but rather with the *assumptions* that we choose to make about the coin. Thus we are really tieing probability statements to our degree of knowledge about something rather than to the something itself.

Second, note that we arrived at the equal chance hypothesis by indirection. In a sense we never really said that heads and tails were equally likely. What we said was that we could see no evidence that suggests that one is more likely than the other. In fact, we are quite convinced that either heads is more likely than tails or that tails is more likely than heads. It is incredible to us that this coin, or any coin, is so perfectly balanced that it is truly just as likely to come up one way as the other. But, unfortunately for us, at the moment we just do not know which is more likely. Therefore we tentatively assume that they are equally likely. But we are going to change that assumption as soon as we have enough additional evidence.

We might raise a question as to why all this fuss about these two possible ways of looking at the probability statement when they both come out at the same place and result in a probability of .5 for a head. The point is that the first way of looking at the statement takes the probability as a *given and unchangeable and true fact;* whereas the second way says the same thing but treats it as a *deduced and tentative assumption.* The second viewpoint is strongly preferred to the first for many reasons that are obvious in view of the discussion in the preceding pages. Later discussion also reveals additional advantages.

This is a good time to pursue a little further the notion that additional evidence might cause us to change our hypothesis about the probability of a head on the toss of a given coin. Knowing only what we could find out about the coin by examining it with our un-aided senses, we decided that the probability of a head (or of a tail) is .5. If we now had to call the result of a toss in advance, it is a matter of indifference to us whether we call heads or tails. We might even toss another coin and use its result to tell us what to call on this one! Let us suppose we decided to call heads. The coin is tossed, and it does come up heads. We now have some additional knowledge about this coin. We have now had some actual experience with the tossing of this coin. Prior to this everything was speculation. What can we make of this experience? It seems appropriate to make two observations:

1. Since we know that the coin has come up heads when tossed, we have more confidence that it can again. We cannot say the same thing about tails because we have not yet seen tails *as the result of a toss.*
2. If in truth there is a greater probability of heads than of tails, we

should see more heads than tails as a result of the tossing. And we
have seen more heads than tails.

This evidence and the observations we made from the evidence
now lead us to state a new tentative hypothesis about the probability
of a head. We now might say that "if the probability of a head is
different from that of a tail, it is more likely to be in favor of heads
than to be in favor of tails." We would now lean, ever so gently,
toward calling heads rather than tails on the next toss. We say,
ever so gently, because the leaning is based on very slim evidence,
namely, only one toss. But let us not forget that *slim as the evidence
of only one toss is, it is evidence and we should not ignore it.* Just
for fun, let us quantify the extent of the leaning that we now feel by
stating that we believe now that the probability of a head is at least
as high as .50001. The difference between .50000 and .50001 may
seem very trivial, and it does seem difficult to see how we can take
much practical advantage of such a small difference, but the point,
however, and this is not trivial, is that every shred of evidence should
tell us something we did not know before, even if only a shred. It
is not proper to let additional evidence accumulate and then ignore
it. When we ignore additional knowledge, we are letting our knowledge become sterile, which is wasteful. But even worse, we are failing to take advantage of opportunities to alter our behavior to increase our rate of success in our acts and decisions.

Let us pursue further the logic behind our leaning toward calling
heads on the next toss because we believe that if there is a difference
in the probabilities, it is in favor of heads. Let us suppose that our
original hypothesis is still correct, namely, that the probability of
a head is the same as that of a tail. Then it is a matter of indifference to us whether we call heads or tails. But, if our second hypothesis of a little higher probability for heads is correct, we should call
heads rather than tails. So now we have two hypotheses to guide
(or confuse) us. One is, call heads or tails; it makes no difference.
The other is, call heads. Anyone can see that if we call heads, we are
being consistent with both hypotheses. Or, in other words, we have
nothing to lose by calling heads if the first hypothesis is true, and we
have something to gain by calling heads if the second hypothesis is
true. And we all know that we are living in the best of all worlds
when we can make decisions that cost us nothing but yet which might
lead to a gain!

How do we feel if the second toss also results in a head? We
should now lean even more to a belief that the probability of a head

is more than .5, say even as high as .5001. And the more heads in a row we get like this, the more we would lean in this direction. For example, I for one would be willing to bet $6 to $4 that the 11th toss would also be a head if the first 10 tosses had been heads! Would you take this bet?

Suppose the second toss had turned out to be tails. Now, of course, we would be back to our original hypothesis before we had seen any tosses, namely, that of equal probability for heads and tails. Our experiences with the two tosses would have tended to confirm what we had believed on the basis of just examining the coin.

We are now ready to state a general policy for problems that involve uncertainty. We can do this best by setting down a series of propositions that seem to make sense.

1. Since we do not *know* what we should do or decide, we must base our action on something that we *believe* is as close to the truth as we can get *at the moment*.
2. We prefer to label such a belief as a *hypothesis*. Technically, a hypothesis is "something assumed for the purpose of argument." We have this preference because this word tends to remind us that we are basing our action on assumption and not on fact. It reduces the possibility that we will develop such a strong attachment to our beliefs that we will continue to hold them in the face of substantial contradictory evidence. Or, even worse, we become so convinced that our beliefs are right that we no longer continue to accumulate additional evidence.
3. Our hypothesis should be as consistent as possible with *all* the knowledge at our command. In this connection we should keep in mind that *fact* and *experience* have an almost sacred quality about them. Whenever we find our hypotheses somewhat inconsistent with our experience, there should be no question about which should give ground, namely, our hypotheses. We cannot deny the fact that "experience is the best teacher," and we should always listen when experience speaks.
4. Since we cannot state or calculate a probability until we have adopted some hypothesis, it is proper to state that all probabilities are *hypothetical* in character. They are not *factual*. They tell us how often we should expect something to happen, or to be true, *provided our assumption is correct*. If our assumption is incorrect, then things are not going to happen the way we expect them to.

Although we may be rather well persuaded that these propositions do make a kind of sense, we may still be bothered by some other notions we hold about probability, notions that we are not sure are consistent with these propositions. For example, we may have in the past had an inclination to believe that if a series of coin tosses had shown more heads than tails, it was logical to call tails now because tails "was due." Our reasoning probably went something like this:

1. The probability of a head is .5. Thus, in the *long run*, there should be as many heads as tails.
2. We have had more heads than tails. If we are going to end up with as many tails as heads, we are going to have to have more tails than heads in the remaining tosses.
3. Therefore "tails is due."

The trouble starts with the first statement. This statement implies that we *know* that there will be an equal number of heads and tails in the long run. But we do not know this at all; nor is there any way we could know this. Moreover, the statement errs in referring to the *number* of heads and tails. Probability statements should and do refer only to the *proportion* expected in the long run, and even then not to any exact proportion for any exact and finite number of events. Suppose somebody tossed a coin 1,000,000 times and got exactly 500,000 heads and 500,000 tails and then claimed that this was evidence of a fair coin fairly tossed. What would be your reaction? My reaction would be that this is evidence of something 'quite the contrary. I would be very suspicious that he was so determined to prove that this was a fair coin fairly tossed that he *controlled* the tosses and made the results conform to what he thought I would expect them to be. In other words, his results are "too good to be true," and I just do not believe them. I might expect the results of 1,000,000 tosses to be such that the *proportion* of heads is in the *neighborhood* of .5, say between .498 and .502. But I certainly don't expect the proportion to be *exactly* .5. Recognition that things can be too good to be true is one of the problems of the card sharp who knows how to manipulate the deal. To allay suspicion, he will deal so the results will appear to look like chance. But he might easily overdo this and make them look too much like chance, and he will, therefore, be suspected by an intelligent opponent.

The second statement tends to collapse now; but it is also based on another notion that frequently causes trouble, the very kind of trouble that is exhibited by the third statement. This notion is that somehow the universe out of which the sample items are being taken has only so many items in it, and that as we draw certain items there must be fewer of them left. Sometimes the conditions of the problem are exactly this way, the most notable case being that of card games. For example, when we deal cards, we find that the longer we do not deal the Ace of Spades the *greater* is the probability that it will be the next card. In fact, if the Ace of Spades is not among the first 51 cards dealt, it is *certain* to be the 52nd card.

But the conditions of the coin tossing are certainly not this way. No matter how many times we toss the coin, and no matter how many heads we get, we have not changed the proportion of heads in the universe unless the tossing process wears a bias into the coin. We cannot deal out all the heads the way we can deal out all the cards. In fact, it is reasonable to assume that the mechanical act of tossing a coin is completely independent of the probability of getting heads and tails on subsequent tosses. It is never appropriate to believe that heads is due because it has not arrived yet.

Most practical problems are more analogous to the coin-tossing situation than they are to the card-drawing situation. It is much more appropriate for us to look for the sort of thing we have *already seen* than to look for what we *have not seen*. If we see a basketball player miss 25 shots in a row, he is not "due" to start making baskets. If anything, he is "due" to be dropped from the first team. Similarly, if a businessman fails in five consecutive businesses which he has tried to run, he will not now make a million because he has already lost so much. He is probably a very bad businessman, and you would be well-advised not to invest any of your money in his next venture. But these judgments are self-evident when expressed this way. Any problems we tend to have in this area probably stem from the fact that most of our conscious experience with probability has been with card games, and we unthinkingly apply what are perfectly good card game principles to other problems in probability which are subject to rather different conditions.

2.10   *Real* Differences vs. *Apparent* or *Statistical* Differences

Suppose we have two decks of ordinary playing cards and we deal five cards out of each deck at random. The two sets of five cards will almost certainly be *different* from each other. For example, the average size of the numbers on one set will be larger than that of the numbers on the other set. This is a difference in fact and, if we were playing a game that depended on the average size of the numbers, one hand would be better than the other; and this difference in the numbers probably would be translated into a difference in the scores of the players. However, if we were to repeat this experiment many times, we have a feeling that the differences between the hands would "tend to average out." In other words, differences like this tend to disappear in the long run. In dealing with differences of this type, we must have two policies, one for the *short-run*, where the differences will exist and will have to be dealt with as such, and one for the *long-run* where the differences will tend not to exist and where we might ignore them.

Now let us consider two other decks of cards. One is an ordinary deck, with the numbers running from 1 to 13. The other deck, however, has numbers running from 3 to 15. We again deal sets of five cards from each deck and compare the numbers. Again we will find them almost always different. Sometimes the cards from the first deck will be larger. Other times the cards from the second deck will be larger. In general, however, knowing what we know about the two decks, we would expect the cards in the second deck to *average* two units higher. Thus *all* the differences between the five card hands will *not* average out.

It should be clear, then, that any *observed* difference between two things or two groups of things might very well be made up of some combination of two distinct and important kinds of differences, one the kind that will tend to average out in the long run, and the other the kind that will persist into the long run. The differences that we believe will average out we call *apparent, statistical, chance,* or *random* differences. The differences that we do not expect to average out we call *real* or *statistically significant* differences. It is essential in practical problems that we try to separate these two differences. For example, if we base a long-run policy on a difference that tends to average out in the long-run, this policy must fail because the difference is bound to disappear. Unfortunately, it is not at all easy to separate these differences. All of us make daily mistakes in classifying differences. We label one difference as chance and go on and ignore it when actually it is real and will persist. We label another difference as real when it is actually chance. We say much in subsequent pages about the problems and techniques in identifying differences.

2.11   Practically-significant Differences vs. Statistically-significant Differences

We spent some time earlier on the question of what difference makes a difference? In that discussion we tacitly assumed that we were dealing with *real* or *statistically-significant* differences. We were quite sure that one piece of cake was really larger than another, but we were not so sure that this difference "made any difference to us." Since we are now in danger of getting ourselves tangled up in words, let us bring these various ideas about differences together and try to clarify their distinctions. At the same time, let us add a fourth type of difference that we have occasion to run across. The fourth type we call a *sham* difference because it is a difference that we do not think exists at all, either in the short-run or in the long-run. This kind of difference arises because human beings are not perfect in their perceptions. We not only fail to note differences that do exist, we note differences that do not exist. For example, if a person were asked to count the number of pennies in a bushel basket, he would come up with a certain answer. But we do not trust him or his counting ability completely, so we have somebody else check his count. He counts 17 pennies fewer than the first person did. What happened to those 17 pennies? Or did nothing happen to them, and all this difference means is that either one or the other, or both, cannot count accurately.

So now let us list in proper order the questions we might ask of an *observed* difference.

1. Does this difference really exist, or is it due only to errors in perception? If it really exists, then we ask
2. Is this a chance difference, the kind that exists only in the short-run, or
3. Is this a real and permanent difference that will persist into the long-run?
   And finally, if we decide that there is a chance and/or a real difference to be concerned with, we ask
4. What difference does this difference make to us? What gains and losses are associated with it? Or is it of such trivial consequence to us that we can ignore it?

To summarize now, we can say that

1. *Sham* differences are those that we do not think really exist at all.
2. *Chance* differences exist, but only in the short-run. They tend to average out in the long-run.
3. *Statistically-significant,* or *real,* differences exist in both the short and long-run.
4. *Practically-significant* differences are non-sham differences that make a difference to us, and we therefore must pay attention to them.

2.12   Short-run vs. Long-run in Decision-making

Let us suppose you and a friend have just finished a fine steak dinner at a good restaurant. Now the check appears amounting to

$10. Each of you had intended to pay half, but your friend has found that this dinner and your congeniality have stimulated his sporting blood. He suggests that you and he toss a coin to see who pays the whole check. You have absolutely no reason to believe that this will not be a fair proposition. You are convinced that your best hypothesis is that you are just as likely to win and pay nothing as you are to lose and pay $10. Of course, you could turn down his offer and pay $5. What decision are you going to make? Because you are intelligent and systematic, you decide to analyze your problem as rationally as possible.

The first thing you do is set down your alternatives.

Decision	Amount I'd Pay	Proba-bility I Would Pay It	Net Expected Cost
1. Refuse offer to toss coin	$ 5	1.00	$5
2. Toss coin {If win:	$ 0	.50	$0} Total: $5
{If lose:	$10	.50	$5}

This analysis reveals that the net expected cost is going to be $5 whether you pay for your own or whether you toss a coin. It looks as though it makes no difference whether you toss or not. You are just about to accept his offer to toss when a horrible thought occurs to you. The thought is that although to toss for $10 dinner checks will cost you $5 on the average and in the *long-run*, this particular toss is certainly going to result in your actually spending *$0* or *$10*. So now you must face up to the question of whether you can afford to spend $10 *right now*, in the *short-run*, for this dinner. You don't bother to ask yourself whether you can afford to spend $0! You know you can do that. Let us suppose you happen to have just $10 in your pocket, plus a nickel that you can use for the tossing. Now you make up another table of your alternatives.

Decision	Money I Would Have Left
1. Refuse offer to toss coin	$ 5.05
2. Toss coin {If win:	$10.05
{If lose:	$ .05

We can be quite sure that when you walk out of this restaurant you will have one of those three amounts of money in your pocket. There is absolutely no question in our mind which amount you would prefer. But, unfortunately, in order to get a chance at the *most* preferred amount, you must take a chance on ending up with the *least* preferred amount. And now we realize something else: the $5 you will gain if you win is not worth as much to you as the $5 you will lose if the toss goes against you.

So now you are just about to turn down his offer, when another thought flashes through your mind. You ask yourself: "I wonder what kind of a sport he will think I am if I refuse to toss for the check?" "He's willing to take exactly the same risk that I'm on the verge of turning down, so he'll probably think I have no sporting blood at all if I turn him down." "Now I don't know what to do. I never should have tried to get rational about this in the first place."

What you will finally do will depend on your *personal* evaluation of the worth to you of his opinion about your sporting blood and the amount by which you discount $5 won compared to $5 lost. The wealthier you are, the less you will tend to discount the $5 and the more likely you are to accept the offer to toss; unless, of course, you are convinced that one of the reasons you are wealthy is because you have made it a practice to never engage in unnecessary gambles, such as this.

Most people are willing to toss a coin to see who pays for the "cokes," probably because the amount involved is trivial (although the principle of discounting still applies), and because they would like to be considered as having at least that amount of sporting blood. Very few people, however, are willing to toss coins for $100 bills. The reason is that, although such a practice will result in a person's breaking even in the *long-run*, he is almost certain to be a winner or a *loser* in the *short-run* and very few of us can afford to take that risk. In fact, what will tend to happen is that most of us would go broke in the short-run and thus never have a chance to break even in the long-run.

But actually the situation can be even worse than this. We may even have an "edge" in the long-run, in the sense that the "game" favors us, say, by 5%. Thus, we are almost certain to win in the long-run, *if we survive*. If, however, we get greedy and try to win too fast in the short-run, we are almost certain to run into a streak of bad luck and get wiped out and thus never get to see the long-run. Many businessmen make this mistake of trying to make money too fast and end up going broke and selling out to somebody who is less greedy and thus better able to survive. The first rule of success in any venture is survival. That is why it is essential to hold back some of our resources, some reserves so to speak, to protect ourselves against an unfortunate outcome to our current short-run commitments. The age-old proverb, "don't put all of your eggs in one basket," expresses this principle.

PROBLEMS AND QUESTIONS

2.1 Describe briefly the differences you are able to find between:

(*a*) Two "identical" dining room chairs.

(*b*) Two "identical" automobiles—same manufacturer, same model, same body style, same color, same trim, or, in short, exactly the same in every technical feature.

(*c*) Two "identical" nails.

(*d*) Two "identical" pencils.

(*e*) Two drawers in the same file cabinet.

(*f*) Two signatures that you have written.

(*g*) Two peas in the same pea pod.

(*h*) Two identical twins of your acquaintance.

2.2 Describe briefly the important characteristics that are exactly the same for any two objects that you are familiar with, *as far as you know.*

Might these identical characteristics be different if you compared them with a microscope or other instrument?

2.3 Give an illustration of a "difference" that "doesn't make any difference" to you. Describe the nature of the difference and how you know that it exists. Explain why it doesn't make any difference to you.

2.4 Describe a difference which *you* think makes a difference but which your mother, or your father, or your brother, etc., thinks makes no difference at all. Try to explain the basis of such a difference in taste or opinion.

2.5 Outline some simple causal system you are familiar with. For example, the causal system that makes it possible for the light to light when you flick the switch; or the causal system that makes it possible for your ball point pen to make a visible line.

State what causes what and also the sequence of action if there is one.

Does this system always work?

How do you tell when it isn't working?

How do you diagnose the difficulty or difficulties if it isn't working?

How do you repair the difficulty?

Are you sure that all your answers to the above are correct?

2.6 In each of the following cases indicate whether knowledge about the first element of the pair would help you in estimating the second element. State the way in which it would help. Be as specific as possible. Note any assumptions you are making.

(*a*) A man's height—the same man's weight.

(*b*) Speed of an automobile—distance required to stop it.

(*c*) July 1, 1960, New York City—noonday temperature, New York City.

(*d*) December 1, 1973, New York City—noonday temperature, New York City.

(e) Color of playing card—number on face of card.

(f) Man's hat size—same man's I.Q.

2.7 Describe something you have *learned* during the last week. Explain how this additional knowledge has enabled you to *better* control your activities and problems. *How much* bette.? Be as specific as possible.

2.8 Describe something you have *unlearned* during the last week, that is, something that you used to think was true, but which you now think is untrue. Do you feel that you are now better off even though in a sense you now know less than you might have thought you did? Explain.

2.9 Using no other knowledge than what you already have, answer the following questions by giving the *lowest* value and the *highest* value you would expect. Select these values as though you were going to bet 4 to 1 that the answer will be within the stated limits and *as though* you really expected somebody to take the bet. In other words, don't state limits so broad that only a fool would bet against you.

(a) How much does this book weigh?

(b) How far is it from Springfield, Massachusetts to Springfield, Illinois?

(c) How far did Arnold Palmer hit his drive off the first tee in the opening round of the 1960 National Open?

(d) How many automobiles were sold in the United States during 1960?

(e) What will the Gross National Product be in the United States during the current calendar year?

(f) How many games will your favorite basketball team win this season?

2.10 What role does chance play in determining the following events? Split your answer into two parts. In one part indicate the role of chance within the limits of *your* knowledge. In the other part indicate what *you think* the role of chance would have been in the mind of an "expert" in the given field. In some cases you may be the "expert."

(a). Your going to college.

(b) The number of Buicks sold by General Motors during the calendar year 1955.

(c) The grade you received in that math course you had in your first year of high school.

(d) The grade you are going to receive in this course.

(e) The time you got out of bed this morning.

2.11 Write a brief essay—no more than 1000 words—on one of the following. Pick out the one that you know best how to do.

(a) How to drive an automobile.

(b) How to set the dinner table.

(c) How to walk.

(d) How to walk across the street.

(e) How to smile.

(f) How to hit a golf ball.

(g) How to fall asleep.

(h) How to cut your fingernails.

(i) How to sell magazines from house to house.

(j) How to supervise Girl (or Boy) Scouts on an overnight hike.

(k) How to make a speech.

2.12 Suppose you had observed the results of a carnival wheel for its last four spins. The results were, in order, 26, 8, 19, 26. If you are going to make a play, what number would you bet on for the next spin of the wheel. The wheel has 48 numbers running from 1 to 48. Explain the logic of your selection.

2.13 (a) A card is to be drawn from an ordinary deck. What is the probability that it *will be* the 4 of diamonds? Explain.

(b) A card *has already* been drawn from an ordinary deck. It is lying face down on the table. What is the probability that it *is* the 4 of diamonds? Explain.

2.14 A combat pilot is definitely exposed to a risk when he flies a mission. Most nations have a policy of limiting the number of missions a pilot will be asked to fly before he is given some sort of relief. What is the rationale behind such a policy?

If you were a flight commander and had a particularly important mission coming up, would you prefer to use pilots who had already survived many missions or would you prefer pilots who had flown relatively few missions? Explain.

2.15 If you were a baseball manager and needed the best batter (the one most likely to get a hit) you could get in a crucial spot, which of the following two batters would you choose? Explain your choice.

One has made eight consecutive hits. This batter has never hit safely nine times in a row to your knowledge. In fact, he had never hit safely more than five times in a row until this last streak. Nine consecutive hits is a club record made 3 years ago by a player now retired.

The other has gone hitless in eight straight turns. He had never gone hitless this long before as far as you know, although he has gone hitless as many as seven times in a row quite frequently.

2.16 Does the saying "The pitcher went to the well once too often" (and got broken) mean that the greater the number of times the pitcher goes to the well, the greater is the probability it will get broken?

Suppose you have two pitchers. One is brand new and has never "been to the well." The other has "been to the well" 1612 times. You are a guest at the house and have been asked to go to the well to get a pitcher of water. The last thing in the world you want to do is break the pitcher. Which pitcher do you take. (As far as you know, the pitchers have equal value to your hostess.)

2.17 Suppose you were offered the privilege of being the proprietor of a game that was so designed that *on the average* in the *long-run* you would retain 10 cents per dollar bet on the game. The rules of the game were such that you paid off a winner at odds of 8 to 1 although the odds against winning were 9 to 1. You would have to supply the capital necessary to operate the game. Winning and losing in the game is a matter of chance. The unit of betting in the game is $1.

It is obvious that a person should be able to earn some money in the long-run by operating this game. Therefore this privilege must have some value.

What is the maximum price you would be willing to pay for the privilege of operating this game? Assume that you have estimated your potential volume of business as averaging 10 plays per hour, 8 hours per day, and 5 days per week.

Hint: This is a deceptively difficult problem to work out in a completely formal manner. But do not be discouraged too quickly. Remember that privileges of this sort have been bought and sold many times by people far less intelligent than you. They arrived at the answer "intuitively."

Some of the questions you will have to answer are

1. How much capital will I need to give me a reasonable(?) chance of surviving one year's play? Two years' play? Etc.

2. If I took this same capital and invested it in United States government bonds, I could earn 4.0% with practically no risk at all. What extra risks do I take when I try to raise the expected return by "buying" this game?

Your thinking about the price you offer for this privilege should help to clarify your understanding of the problem of following a policy that gives you a fair chance of surviving the short-run vicissitudes of chance at the same time as you try to make a fair average return in the long-run. This is, of course, a problem that pervades all of business and with a complexity far greater than the complexity of this simple game situation.

2.18 A given punch press operation in your factory is engineered to turn out 95% acceptable pieces. It has been discovered that to reduce the defective pieces below 5% would cost too much in labor, materials, and tools. Periodic inspections are made to prevent some preventable cause from pushing the percent defectives higher than 5%. Whenever there is strong reason to believe that the percentage of defectives is more than 5%, the process is stopped and the operator looks for the cause. Of course, sometimes the operator is fooled by his inspection results and goes looking for causes and doesn't find any, thus losing valuable production time. Other times he is fooled into letting the process run when he should have stopped it, thus producing too much scrap.

(a) Suppose the last inspection of ten pieces revealed one piece defective. Should the process be stopped for a search for the "trouble"? Explain your decision.

(b) Suppose an inspection of ten pieces revealed two defectives?

(c) Four defectives?

(d) Suppose an inspection of five pieces reveals one defective? Do you note any difference between ten pieces with two defectives and five pieces with one defective? What is the difference?

Hint: One way to approach this problem is to start with the hypothesis that the universe of pieces has 5% defectives. Thus the probability that any piece will be defective would be 1/20 or .05, and the probability that a piece would be satisfactory would be 19/20 or .95. The basic calculation needed to answer part (a) is to calculate the probability of getting ten pieces with one defective out of a universe with 5% defectives. This is done by multiplying the probabilities for the ten separate pieces together, viz. .05 (defective) $\times$ .95 (good) $\times$ .95 $\times$ .95 $\times$ .95 $\times$ .95 $\times$ .95 $\times$ .95 $\times$ .95, or to calculate .05 $\times$ (.95) [9], which equals ? .

2.19 What is the practical significance to business policy of our inability to predict events except within some range of error? Or, in other words, if you did not know exactly what your labor cost was going to be per unit of product during the next fiscal year, what steps would you take to protect yourself against unfavorable labor cost variations? Suppose you had to deal with a union?

chapter **3**

Sources of knowledge

It is self-evident that knowledge does not exist in the abstract. It can be used only insofar as it becomes part of the chemistry of the human body and thus can have some influence over the behavior of the human being. (The same thing can be said of any living object. We are going to confine our attention, however, primarily to the use of knowledge by human beings.) Man's knowledge of the chemistry of the human body is not complete, so it is not possible for us to specify exactly how the human body acquires, stores, and uses knowledge. Our treatment of the subject is further handicapped by our own inexpertness in the general fields of study such as biology, physiology, psychology, neurology, etc., and we approach the subject somewhat apologetically. It is essential that we make some approach, however, if we are to get an idea of the limitations of the methods of solving problems that we are going to talk about in later chapters. We have occasion to state rather often, for example, that formal statistical methods can be used successfully only to solve *part* of most practical problems. It is important that we have some idea of what part we are solving and what part we must necessarily leave to solution devices that cannot easily be formalized and communicated.

3.1 Perception Devices

Human Senses

It is customary to believe that the human body becomes aware of its environment through the medium of the five senses. We sometimes talk of a "sixth" sense as a sense that we cannot identify specifically, or are even sure exists, but which we find convenient to appeal to when we cannot otherwise identify how the apparent perception took place. Specialists in the field have been able to make some very useful subclassifications of the senses that relate the given sense to what it is that is being perceived. For example, the ability to see color is not the same as the ability to see the distance of an oncoming object.

Our interest in the senses is not in the specific characteristics of each, but rather in certain general characteristics of all of them. The first characteristic we note is that each sense has a *limited range.* There are "sounds" that we cannot hear, "odors" we cannot smell, etc. Man's first inkling that this was so probably came from his observation of the behavior of animals. Animals frequently acted as though they could hear things we could not. Thus one of the primary reasons man had for domesticating the dog was to supplement his own limited senses. The reason it is important to recognize this limitation of our senses is that it serves to remind us that there are probably all kinds of things going on around us of which we are not aware. This recognition is both humbling and a challenge, a challenge to try to extend the range of our senses by one device or another. And, of course, we have had some success in meeting that challenge.

A second general characteristic to note is that the range of perception *varies from person to person.* At the same time, we note that, fortunately, this variation usually is not uniform for all senses. If person A has a wider perceptive range than B when it comes to seeing, he might have a narrower range when it comes to hearing. In fact there is some evidence that weakness in one sense is often associated with strength in other senses. The rare and gifted person is the one who has wide range in all his senses.

A third thing we note about our senses is that their range, or acuity, *varies over time* for each of us. Training can sharpen them. On the other hand, fatigue can dull them. The aging process also affects them, usually adversely. Some of the variation appears random to us; in other words we cannot explain it, nor can we predict it.

Fourth is the factor of the degree of *control* we have over our senses. Some of this control is *voluntary.* We are able to deliberately focus our looking, our listening, our sniffing, etc. We are also able to raise and lower our threshold of consciousness. For example, the student studies with the radio on because he doesn't "hear the radio." The city-dweller has almost permanently raised his threshold of consciousness against "city-noises" that would mean sleepless nights for the newly-arrived farm-boy. Our ability to control is limited, however. There is always a sound, or a sight, or an odor, or a touch that will reach our consciousness no matter how high we try to raise our threshold and shut out the stimulus.

When we mention consciousness, we are led to wonder about the degree to which our senses still receive messages even though we are not consciously aware of them. Although we have considerable uncertainty about the process by which subconscious learning goes on, we have substantial evidence that it does. In fact, some psychologists have been so impressed by this evidence that they are inclined to believe that practically all *effective* learning takes place at the subconscious level. In other words, they believe that we *do* what we *are*, not what we *say* or what we *think* we are. And what we really are is buried in our subconscious. They believe that we cannot, and will not, take any voluntary action that is not consistent with the condition of our subconscious.

Another interesting characteristic of our senses is their *power*, both absolute and relative, *to convey knowledge*. Is a picture really worth a thousand words? If we were restricted to the use of only one of our senses to learn all we could about an elephant, would we rather see, hear, touch, smell, or taste one? Fortunately, we do not have to make choices like this. Most of us are able to use our senses all together, and here we find another interesting property of our senses: It is not unusual to find that the senses seem to stimulate each other to greater effort. To hear a noise makes you want to see what produced it. The infant crawling on the rocky beach first sees the stones, then feels them, then bangs them together, then puts them in his mouth, then cries when his mother takes them away and moves him back on the sand! On the other hand, sometimes we find some senses completely dominating others. To feel the crisp cool air, smell the smoke of the campfire, hear the steak sizzling, by now that steak is predestined to taste good, even with dirt.

This is perhaps enough discussion of the human senses to remind us of some important truths. These truths are going to be persistently relevant, even though not always explicitly mentioned, as we pursue the problem of building and using statistical controls in business. Again we use the simple technique of a list of "propositions" that we take as having a reasonable measure of truth.

1. The environment in which we operate has an infinite number of variations.
2. Our knowledge of this environment is useful to us only insofar as it is part of the chemistry of the body.
3. We acquire this knowledge only through the medium of our senses, including both those known to us and possibly others not known to us at this time.
4. Our senses have certain limitations.
    (a) Limited range

    (b) Variable performance
       i From person to person
      ii From time to time
     iii From place to place
    (c) Involuntary in action to some extent
    (d) Subject to actual error

5. Hence our knowledge of our environment is necessarily limited and in some cases incorrect.

6. Thus all our actions are subject to errors caused by what we do not know and by those things that we know but which are not true.

7. Fortunately, we are not as bad off as the above might lead us to believe. We are not really aware of most of the mistakes we are making because our perceptions are too narrow for us to realize they are mistakes. We are not disturbed by what we do not know, because we do not know enough. Ignorance is truly bliss, if we do not have somebody reminding us how ignorant we are.

Augmenting the Human Senses

The more intelligent of men across the centuries have been fully alerted to the limitations of their own unaided senses, and they took steps to do something about them. We have already mentioned man's early use of the dog. Another animal that quickly comes to mind as one we have used in recent decades to supplement our senses is the mouse. The mouse has been used by the coal miner to detect the developing presence of gas in the tunnels. But the most spectacular achievements of man in augmenting his senses have not been through the use of animals. They have been through the creation of physical instruments. Most of these instruments are so commonplace today that we do not fully appreciate their fundamental importance to the development and maintenance of a complex civilization.

3.2   Memory Devices

We not only have the problem of properly exposing our natural and augmented senses to the phenomena around us, we have the further problem of storing what we have thus learned. Also, we not only have to store them until the day we need them, but we have to know where we have stored them, and we have to know how to gain access to this storage place. And none of this happens easily and automatically.

Storage Facilities of the Human Body

The problem of the human memory has been the subject of much research. One theory hypothesizes that we never actually forget anything. Every stimulus is reputed to make some impression, however faint, on the nervous system, and this impression never really disappears even though the conscious mind may never be able to recall it. Even if this is true, we still do not know if it affects behavior by acting through the lower nervous system. We do know, however, that we may never be able to *communicate* this knowledge because we are never able to get it into the conscious nervous centers. The inability to communicate is often disastrous in many practical situations. For all practical purposes it is just as though we did not have the knowledge, assuming we do.

Augmenting the Human Memory

Man has been equally ingenious in augmenting his memory as he has been in augmenting the range of his senses. Record-keeping and picture-making go back through the ages. The twentieth century has witnessed the development of sound-recording to add to the substantial improvements that have taken place in the printing and photographic arts. In fact, we are now running into the problem of providing storage facilities for the ever-mounting volume of paper. Business has developed record-keeping to a fine art. It would be difficult to exaggerate the profound importance of the almost revolutionary developments that have taken place in the 1940's and 1950's in the communication and record-keeping arts. Executives of today know in hours and minutes what executives of yesterday knew in weeks and months, if they ever knew at all. This has substantially increased the span of effective control of the single executive team and has made possible the substantial growth that has taken place in the size of individual businesses. Of course, it has also paved the way for big organizations of all types, including political organizations. If we fear bigness in any institution, we are not so sure that further advances in the communication and recording arts is an unmixed blessing.

3.3 Sampling Problems in the Perception and Recording of Historical Data

Two Distinct Kinds of Sampling Problems

We previously had occasion to define a sample as an item or a group of items that has actually occurred. We now add the qualifying phrase, *as far as we know*. This serves to remind us that it is entirely possible that the phenomenon we are dealing with may actually have occurred many times without our knowing it. Although we necessarily must take action within the limits of what we know, we do not want to be so presumptuous as to believe that we know all that there is to know. One of our sampling problems is that *what we know is only a sample of what was available to be known;* and, furthermore, other people have different samples from ours. This is the sampling problem that predominates when the Gallup Poll asks the opinions of 100 people in a city in order to draw conclusions about the opinions of all the people in the city. This is also the problem when we sample a bowl of soup for saltiness by tasting one spoonful of it. What bothers us, of course, is that *what we know* may be *significantly different,* to us, from what was *available to be known.* If it is significantly different, then we will likely act incorrectly. Gallup says A will win, but actually B will.

The other kind of sampling problem arises because *what actually happens* at any time is not the only thing that *could have happened* at that time. For example, let us suppose we throw a dart at a target. This is not a sample of throws that we have made at this target. This is the whole record because we have actually thrown it just this once. But we still have a sampling problem as soon as we try to use this experience to predict the result of our next throw. This problem arises because we do not fully understand why that particular result of the throwing occurred. Within the limits of our knowledge, we can easily conceive of different possible results that might have occurred as we tossed this dart. In addition, because we can conceive of several possible things that might have occurred, even though they did not, we can now conceive of several possible things that might occur on the next toss.

It is important to note that both kinds of sampling problems have exactly the same basic root: our ignorance. On the one hand, we are ignorant of things that have actually happened or that exist; on the other hand we are ignorant of the generating mechanism that produces the results even when we know all the results. Fortunately, it is usually not necessary to try to separate these two problems in practical situations. We generally lump their manifestations together and treat them as one problem. What is necessary, however, is to recognize that either or both of these sampling problems will exist in every practical situation.

Sample Generating Processes

In order to improve our understanding of the problem of sampling errors, we must think about the various distinguishable processes that might regulate the occurrence of sample items. We start by looking at the various kinds of *universes* out of which the samples might come. Actually we have already done this, but now we are going to formalize and organize the treatment.

The Nature of the Universe, or Population, or Generating Source from Which Samples Might Come. We have previously defined a universe as a "collection of things which contains all the things which we think might occur under the specified conditions of the problem at hand." We retain this definition. Universes can be classified with respect to whether they are *known* or *unknown, real* or *hypothetical,* and *finite* or *infinite.* We make these distinctions not because we believe that practical problems involve all possible combinations of these types; rather we do it to clarify our thinking about the problems of sampling. For example, we have occasion later to make believe we have certain types of universes in order to develop certain principles in a simple and easily understood context. In addition, we discover that some types are simpler to work with than others, and we find it practical to sacrifice a little accuracy to save effort as we work on actual problems.

The difference between a known and an unknown universe should be self-evident. All of the conventional games of chance illustrate known universes. The reason we know them is very simple: we constructed the games. It is quite difficult to think of any other illustrations of known universes. In most practical problems, if not all, we can only guess about what is in the universe. In fact, the reason we frequently take a sample is to help us in making this guess.

A *real* universe is one which *exists,* in the usual meaning of the term. It has a physical existence. It can be seen and touched, etc. The universes of some games of chance exist in this sense, but not of most of them. Whenever the game deals with *single* events, as in roulette, the universe is real. But if the game deals with *combinations* of events, as is true for most card games and some dice games, the universe does not really exist. For example, where is the universe out of which we are going to "draw" a sample of five pennies, which in effect is what we are doing when we toss five pennies? If we *think* about it, we will discover that there are 32 different combinations of the five pennies that might occur. But those combinations do not exist except in our mind. If we wished, we might put each combination on a slip of paper, put the slips in a bowl, and draw one out at random. We have now converted the *hypothetical* universe of coin tosses into a *real* universe of slips of paper. The primary difficulty most people have with hypothetical universes, and unfortunately most problems involve hypothetical universes, is that they can contemplate the universe only if they think about it and work at it.

A *finite* universe is a universe that has a *limited* number of items in it. If we draw items out of this universe and do not replace them, we will eventually exhaust all the items and the universe will have disappeared. An *infinite* universe, on the other hand, is inexhaustible. The real importance of the distinction lies in the fact that *sampling without replacement from a finite universe causes the universe itself to change.* Tomorrow's possibilities, therefore, are different from yesterday's because of yesterday's samples. A simple illustration of a finite universe is a deck of cards as used in most card games. For example, if we play poker and do not recognize that the cards already dealt in a hand have something to do with the cards that might occur on the next deal, we are doing a lot to encourage people to invite us to play with them but little to enhance our chances of winning. But how about tossing coins or throwing dice? How many "throws" are there in a pair of dice? Do we change the universe of possibilities every time we throw the dice? Of course we do not (except for the neglible factor of wear). How big is the universe of pitches "in the arm" of a major league pitcher? To what extent does some sampling (throwing) strengthen the arm and enlarge the universe? To what extent does sampling tire the arm and contract the universe? To what extent does rest "replace" the universe? To what extent does age change the universe? These and similar questions can be asked about all sorts of practical activities, and the answers are important to us because the answers we give tell us what to expect tomorrow.

Surprisingly enough, although the *concept* of the infinite puzzles many people, we find it much easier to work with problems if we believe that the universe is infinite than if we believe it is finite. In fact, many problems just do not exist for us if we believe the universe is infinite. For example, let us look at the problem of farming. If the farmer believes that his farm has soil with an inexhaustible supply of those chemicals that his corn crop "takes out" of it, he worries not at all about the problem of the optimum combination of use, rest, and renewal he should adopt. His philosophy is that "there is always more where that came from." Our society has to continually wrestle with the issues of conservation and replacement of natural resources. What makes these issues "issues" is that we do not know the actual extent of the resources we have, and we do not know the future rate of use. We must guess, and different people guess differently. This problem is further complicated by the question of how far into the future our thinking proceeds.

Fortunately, we have many problems where the universe, though finite, is so big, considering the rate of use or of sampling, that our answers turn out to be essentially the same whether we treat the universe as finite or infinite. For example, let us suppose we participate in a lottery with a total of 1,000,000 contestants. There are 100 prizes, the prizes graded down in value from the 1st to the 100th. The first sample determines the winner of the first prize, etc. No person can win more than one prize. It is obvious that our chances of winning the 100th prize (assuming we have not won a prior prize) are greater than were our chances of winning the first prize, 1 out of "only" 999,901 compared to 1 out of 1,000,000. But what is the practical significance of this "greater chance"? Most people would agree that it has none. A difference this small we often call "of the second order of smalls," that is, too small to bother with. We particularly do not bother with it if it is a bother; and we find that frequently the mathematics of dealing with finite universes are much more bothersome than the mathematics of dealing with infinite universes.

Ways by Which Samples Might Come out of a Universe.

To have some understanding of what is in a universe does not really tell us very much about what is going to come out of that universe unless we have some idea of the "coming out" process. There are in general two ways in which samples may be said to come out of a universe, one is by a *random* process and the other is by a *systematic* or *nonrandom* process. It is quite impossible to tell exactly which process really prevails in a given case. In fact, if we adopt the philosophical view expressed in the preceding chapter, we would say that there is no such thing as a true random process. What exist are processes that look to us like what random processes would look like if there were any. In other words, we have created in our minds a model of what a random process is. Whenever we see a process that looks like this model, we treat the process *as though* it were a random process. Although we have stated it several times in preceding pages, it is worth repeating: *When our present ignorance prevents us from identifying any process as systematic, we temporarily treat the process as though it were nonsystematic or random.* Tomorrow we may be smarter and treat it a little differently. In the meantime we follow the very simple, but profound, rule of action: We do the best we can with *what we know now.* We waste no time trying to do the impossible of considering knowledge that we do not have. The suspicion of systematic variation is a good spur for further study. But the mere suspicion is useless to us if it gives us no concrete idea of the system. To say that something is "biased," but then be unable to state the direction and magnitude of the bias is to say nothing that we can use.

Actually man has been creating "living" random models for many years. The item-generating processes in all so-called games of chance are random processes in the sense that these processes are designed to frustrate man's best efforts to detect any systematic behavior to the process. This is not as hard to do as it may seem. All we do is design out all the systematic variations we know about, thus automatically leaving only those variations that we do not know about, and these are random by definition. Of course, if such a design was attempted by a relatively ignorant man with the use of relatively crude materials and relatively crude tools, it is likely that his process would have some systematic variations detectable by a relatively knowledgeable man with relatively sharp tools. One of the most interesting developments of the last couple of decades, considerably stimulated by the birth and growth of the electronic data processing machine, has been the use of random processes to generate tables of random numbers. Appendix B gives sample pages from such tables. These tables are created by developing a process of generating the digits "0" through "9" one after the other in such a way that the *order* of the digits is such that it defies the world's best minds to discover any way of predicting some numbers in the table by referring to any other numbers in the table. You might try such predictions with the sample pages in Appendix B. If you happen to hit some correctly, and you will, test your "system" in other parts of the table before you decide that you are smart rather than lucky.

It is probably obvious that most samples we deal with are not consciously selected by us. They just happen. However, there are occasions when we do consciously select a sample. Sometimes we select a "good" or biased sample, such as when we select our clothes for a job interview and we do not think it is appropriate "to be ourselves." Reflection will reveal that most of our conscious sample selections are biased in our favor, insofar as we know where our favor is. Part of growing up is to learn how to bias our own samples and discount the bias of the other fellow's! But there are times when we want a "completely unbiased" sample because we want to get as close to the truth as is humanly possible with only part of the record.

It is then that we might be able to profitably use a table of random numbers. The important preliminary, however, is to be able to separately identify each item in the universe and attach a number to it different from the number we attach to every other item. This is what was done, for example, in preparing the selective service draft. The *highest* number so assigned then determines the *number* of digits we include in every number we pick out of the random number table. For example, if the highest number we assigned was 4684, we would then select four-digit sequences from the table. The number 6 would be 0006, the number 48 would be 0048, etc. We can start anywhere we wish in the table and go in any direction we wish. The only rule is to proceed in some manner which is independent of the numbers we find. Do not look for any numbers or pass over any numbers because of any personal likes or dislikes. It is usually a good idea to select a random start by selecting a page number, a column number, and a row number by some random process, such as drawing cards out of a deck. Then proceed *systematically* through the table, by taking the numbers in the same order in which we read the words in a book. Or, to be doubly cautious, we could use one table of random numbers to give the page, column, and row in another table! The possibilities are almost limitless once we start by using one table of random numbers to help make random selections in another table.

Tables of random numbers undoubtedly would be used much more in practice than they are if it were not for the difficulties often encountered as we try to identify and number each item in the universe. Certain characteristics of the universe must be known or we cannot identify an item when we see one. The universe must be finite at least, and preferably not very large, or we will be overwhelmed by the numbering job. Sometimes it may take so long to perform the numbering job that we no longer need to know what it was we were sampling to find out!

There are times when we already know the pertinent characteristics of the universe, or at least we think we do. We nevertheless prefer to work with only a sample of this universe, usually for reasons of economy or time. For example, a company may wish to measure changes over time in the average prices it charges for the many items in its product line. The company certainly knows the items in its line and needs no sample of items to find out what these are. We may decide, however, that we can derive a reasonably accurate index of prices by using only a sample of the items. We would deliberately select this sample so it would be a "cross-section" of the full line. We call such a sample a *purposive* sample to distinguish it from a randomly-selected sample. The principal feature that distinguishes a purposive sample from a random sample is embodied in the role of the person doing the selection. In a purposive selection a particular item is included in the sample because the *selector* decides that it is representative of the universe. In a random selection a particular item is included because of the *chance forces* operating; the wishes of the person involved presumably have nothing to do with it. Whether a purposive sample is truly representative depends on the knowledge and skill of the selector and not particularly on the size of the sample or on the variability of the items in the universe, the two factors that are relevant in judging the probable accuracy of a random sample.

Size and Direction of Errors in Using Samples to Represent a Universe

It would be miraculous indeed if a sample of any kind from a universe of any kind were to lead to exactly the same conclusions we would get if we were to contemplate the whole universe. We must, therefore, have some concern for the errors we are going to make when we use samples. It would, of course, be very easy to determine the size and direction of this error if we knew the universe and could directly compare the conclusion we get from the universe with the conclusion we get from the particular sample we have. But to do this would make no practical sense because who would be using conclusions from samples if he knew the universe? (Before we say "no one" too quickly, we must note that statisticians have been known to do this, but not for the solution to practical problems. Rather they are doing research into the various ways in which samples might differ from a universe. From this research they hope to learn principles that can be used when we do not know the universe.)

Another relatively easy thing to do is to compare the answer that we get from a sample with the answer that would have been perfect, namely, with the result that actually occurred and which the sample was used to predict. This is the "second-guessing" technique. There are occasions, and we use them, when this technique is the only one apparently available to assess the size of sampling errors.

The typical problem that we try to solve is that of estimating the probable range of the sampling error from only the information provided in the sample itself. At first glance this may seem like quite a trick, even like a bit of charlatanism. But we see that it is not that at all. Even if it were, we would probably still do it because in most problems the information in the sample is the only information we have; and if we did not base our estimation of the sample error on that information, we would base it on nothing.

Logical deduction and experiments with actual sampling processes confirm what common sense suggests as the prime determinants of the size of sampling errors. From a very early age we have all felt better about our conclusions when our conclusions were based on more rather than less evidence. Our intuition tells us that sample errors should be smaller the larger the sample, and our intuition is right. What our intuition does not tell us, however, is the rate at which the sample error gets smaller as the size of the sample gets larger. Fortunately, we have been able to use mathematical logic and experimental evidence to help us discover the relationship between size of error and size of sample. We discuss these results later. In the meantime we continue to rely on our intuition.

The other factor that our intuition tells us is important in drawing conclusions from any evidence is the factor of the *consistency* of the evidence. If every item of evidence introduced in a murder trial points directly and unequivocally at the accused as guilty, the jury is going to easily satisfy itself that it knows what to decide. If, on the other hand, the defense attorney has succeeded in introducing evidence that could point in other directions, the jury is going to have problems because of a greater concern that they might make an error in deciding the verdict. Again, we find that our intuition is sound. The *more consistent* the evidence, the *smaller* is the sample error apt to be.

In a general way, we can say that the size of sample error varies *inversely* as does the size of the sample and the consistency of the sample. Since we find it more convenient to measure the *inconsistency* of the evidence, or its *variation*, we are more likely to say that the size of the sample error varies directly with the variation in the evidence. Intuition with respect to the rate at which sample error declines as the degree of variation declines is probably going to give us the correct answer this time. So we feel very safe if we let ourselves rely on intuition for a little longer.

It should go without saying, assuming we have agreed to this point, that we really cannot predict sample error as exactly as some of the preceding paragraphs may imply. When we said, for example, that the size of the sample error varies inversely with the size of the sample, we did not mean it literally. We should have qualified it by adding, *probably*. Although in general, or in the long-run, or on the average we find the sample error declining as the sample size increases, it may actually increase in size as the sample size increases, especially for very small increases in very small samples. Or, we can say that "as the size of a sample increases, increases in sample error become rarer and decreases in sample error become more frequent."

Another thing that should go without saying is that the above discussion of sample error makes sense only when we are talking about *random* errors. The biased impression we give of the usual state of our dress when we "spruce up" for a job interview does not get any less the more job interviews we have. In fact, it may even get greater as each job interview teaches us how to give an even more biased impression the next time. Similar comments apply to what we called a *purposive* sample, a sample deliberately selected by a person to conform to his idea of what the universe looks like. The error in this kind of sample tends to remain the same no matter how big the sample is. When the selector adds items to this kind of a sample, he just adds items like the ones he had before; so, of course, the sample remains essentially the same. Purposive samples have another characteristic that we should mention. Since the selector has essentially the same kind of a problem that the "expert" card dealer has, namely that of creating a sample that "looks good," he tends to make the same kind of error that the card dealer does. He makes the sample look "too good." He tends to deliberately leave out all "extreme" values, concentrating his results around what he thinks is the average. He also tends to try to achieve some semblance of "balance." The distribution of the items in his sample tends to be quite symmetrical even when the items are not symmetrically distributed in the universe.

The problem of the *direction* of the error in a sample, in contrast to its probable *size,* is quite another matter. If we know the direction of the error, we would, of course, adjust our conclusion in the same direction and thus eliminate the error. If we do not know the direction of the error, but have good grounds for suspecting the direction, again we adjust in that direction, albeit somewhat gropingly. If we have no basis whatsoever for determining or suspecting the direction of the sample error, we are able to make no adjustment for direction and must plan our activities for both directions of error, or even more directions if there are more than two directions to our problem, as there would be, for example, in evaluating the effects of artillery fire.

3.4 Some Practical Considerations in Designing Samples

Although practically all the samples we consider are samples that just arise in the normal course of business, there is some occasion for us to refer to *designed* samples that are intended for specific purposes. It is, therefore, worthwhile to consider some of the highlights of the problem of efficiently designing samples; and it can be only the highlights. The field of sample design has expanded tremendously in recent years. If a person is not a specialist in this field, he is likely to be somewhat behind the latest developments. Many new tools have been developed to facilitate the design of experiments in almost all of the physical and social sciences. Market research techniques and methods have experienced similar advances.

The fundamental purpose that guides all practical sample designs is "to buy the most and best information at the lowest possible price." This is, of course, like saying that "the way to make money in the stock market is to buy cheap and sell dear." Most of us know what we are trying to accomplish. The trick is to figure out how to accomplish it. Nevertheless, it is a good idea to occasionally remind ourselves of this fundamental objective of sample design. It is surprising how often we can get in a rut and forget that information costs money.

The Economics of Sample Design

The collection of information does cost money, and generally the cost goes up as we try to collect more. Nobody will consciously pay this cost unless he feels that the information gained is worth it. The problem of balancing this cost against value received is complicated by the fact that usually we can make only relatively poor advance estimates of the value of information. It almost has to be this way. We cannot really assess the value of information until we have it, and even then we have problems, and we cannot get it until we have paid for it. If we insist on guarantees of our money's worth before we spend any money on research, we will never do any research.

The so-called best guess about the probable gains from collecting some information then becomes the budget guide that tells us the limits within which we should try to keep our expenses. This does not mean that we should spend all the money, although often we do spend all of it. Research gets us involved in the kind of steps that lead from one to the other, and before we know it "we have gone too far to stop now."

The uncertainties about the value of our research efforts make us certain about one thing: we should use all the devices we can to make the data collection process more efficient. So let us turn to some of the more prominent ways we can make our sampling more efficient.

Stratifying the Universe

We noted above that sampling errors are less the more consistent the evidence, or the less variation in the evidence. If we could somehow cut down the potential variation in our sample evidence, we would tend to cut down our errors without having to increase the quantity of our sample. For example, if we were dealing with an ordinary deck of playing cards, we would have to contend with cards in our sample that might vary all the way from 1 to 13. Let us suppose that we were interested in estimating the arithmetic mean of the universe from the information in a sample, say, of five cards. Here we know the universe has a mean of 7. But what kind of estimates might we get from this sample of five cards. We might (though it is unlikely) get an estimate as low as 1.2 (sample of four Aces and one deuce) or as high as 12.8 (a sample of four Kings and one Queen). Thus we might have an error in our estimate of as much as 5.8 in either direction.

How can we cut down this potential error and still use only a sample of five cards? (It should be obvious that we could cut it down by increasing the size of the sample.) The answer is that we could cut it down by splitting up the universe of cards into a set of subuniverses, each with only certain cards in it, and then we could select part of the sample from each of the subuniverses. Suppose, for example, we divide the universe of cards into the following five subuniverses, each having only the cards specified.

Sub-universe	Cards
A	1, 2
B	3, 4, 5
C	6, 7, 8
D	9, 10, 11
E	12, 13

Now let us select our sample of five cards by drawing one from subuniverse A, one from subuniverse B, etc. The lowest possible arithmetic mean we could get in our sample is now the mean of 1, 3, 6, 9, 12, or a value of 6.2. The highest possible mean would be 7.8. It is obvious that this is a considerable improvement over the limits of 1.2 and 12.8 that we had before we stratified the universe.

This is very well, but we do not usually know the universe. And how can we neatly divide the universe up into convenient parts if we do not know what is in the universe? For example, if we wanted to accelerate our rate of learning about the deck of 100 unknown cards we struggled with in Chapter 1, how would we go about dividing that deck into subdecks so that the smallest numbers would be in one subdeck, etc.? The answer is that we could not possibly do it, except by luck, as long as we did not have access to the number-side of the card, unless we were able to detect some distinguishable features on the backs of the cards that bore some relationship to what was on the number-side, or unless, as we say, the cards were somehow "marked" and we knew the markings. Let us assume that the backs of the cards do contain all sorts of distinguishable marks. For example, some of the backs are red in color, some blue, etc. Suppose we sample one card of each color and find the following:

Color	Number
Red	36
Blue	8
Green	23
Black	30
White	106

The first thing we note is that the numbers are certainly different for the different colors, and we are tempted to believe that the white cards have the big numbers and the blue cards the little numbers. But a disturbing thought crosses our mind: even if the numbers are the same for all the colors, we are almost certain to find the numbers different on 5 different cards as long as there are different numbers in the deck. For example, if we divide an ordinary deck of cards into the subuniverses of clubs, diamonds, hearts, and spades and then draw one card from each subuniverse, we are almost certain to get four different numbers; and it would be a mistake to assume from this that the numbers are different from suit to suit.

So we seem to be at a dead end as long as we are restricted to this small sample of only one item from each subuniverse. A larger sample would help to decide the issue. For example, if the next white card were to be an 84 and the next blue card a 3, we would now be more inclined toward the hypothesis that white cards have larger numbers than blue cards. Incidentally, as long as our information about the universe was restricted to what we could guess from samples, we could never be sure that the white cards had larger numbers than the blue cards, although, given large enough samples, we might be "as sure as sure can be."

Now we are ready to move into the real world and talk about stratification of universes as it actually does and must take place in real rather than make-believe problems. Suppose we are a manufacturer of a syrup that we sell to franchised bottlers who make it up into a carbonated "soft drink." We would like to find out more than we presently know about the family rate of consumption of soft drinks in the United States. It would, of course, be ridiculous for us to contemplate polling every family in the United States. So we must sample. There are many questions we are going to have to answer about probable benefits to us of the information, costs per interview, etc. But the only question we are concerned with at the moment is the one of the potential value of stratification of the universe of families *for the purpose of finding out their rate of consumption of soft drinks.*

In order to get the most possible value out of our analogy of the card deck, we can imagine our universe of families as a deck of cards with the rate of consumption of soft drinks on the "number side" (the unknown side) and all other characteristics of these families written on the "up side," the one we can see and examine and sort by if we wish to. What are some of these distinguishable characteristics that we might know about? We could make quite a long list, particularly if we had the United States Census volumes handy. Some things that quickly come to mind are: geographical location, age of family head, number of children in family, ages of children. We can undoubtedly think of many more. We now ask questions of this kind: "Suppose we sorted our cards (families) by geographical location. Would we logically expect to find the rate of consumption generally higher in some locations than in others?" We would probably answer this question in the affirmative. So now, instead of thinking of our sampling problem as selecting families from the universe of United States families, we think of it as selecting samples from a subuniverse of Southeast families, etc. If we are correct in our hypothesis that the rate of consumption varies from one location to another, we will find that our final sampling errors will be less than if we had not stratified. If we are wrong, we will not reduce our sampling errors and will have, in one sense, wasted time and money sorting the families. On the other hand, it would not really be wasteful because we would have at least found out, say, that geography is *not* related to the consumption of soft drinks. Although it is almost always more valuable to find out what is true, we should not underrate the value of finding out what is not true.

Another point we should note about the value of stratification is that at the same time that we are stratifying to reduce sampling errors, we are identifying characteristics of the universe that may be helpful in their own right. In other words, it not only makes sense to classify our families by location in order to reduce sampling errors in our estimates of soft drink consumption, but also it makes sense to us as a manufacturer to do the same thing in our efforts to better organize our marketing activities.

Geographical Clustering of Samples

The usual methods of random sampling frequently scatter the sample items rather widely throughout some geographic area. Although this is ideal from the point of view of providing maximum accuracy for a given sample size, it is quite expensive to pay the expenses of the interviewing staff. It is, therefore, often desirable to sacrifice a little accuracy in order to save money. The sample is designed to yield *clusters* of items so an interviewer can concentrate his efforts in a relatively small area. It is surprising how a well-worked out cluster design can save interviewer expense with only relatively moderate loss of accuracy. The Federal Government, for example, has through such means found it financially feasible to collect many statistics that had heretofore been prohibitively expensive.

Sequential Sampling

One of the basic problems in determining the size of a sample we need for a given problem is that we do not have much information to guide us until after we have collected the sample items. Then, of course, it is too late. If the collection problems are such that it is much more economical to collect all the sample items at once, rather than one after another, it is usually wise to err on the high side in predetermining the minimum sample size. It is much more disconcerting to discover that the sample is too small, than it is to discover that it is too large. Most sampling problems in marketing research are of this type.

There are occasions, however, when the sampling and/or the testing process are so expensive that we wish to definitely minimize the size of the sample. Consider the problem of testing the Atlas missile, for example. The test samples are very expensive and time-consuming to build. In addition, they are no good after they are tested.

We want our sample to be big enough to give us the kind of assurances we need before we decide that the Atlas is now "operational," but we do not want the sample to be any larger than we need to decide this. So what we do is test the samples *one at a time*. After each test we select one of three possible decisions: (1) we abandon the Atlas project, (2) we classify the Atlas as operational, or (3) we test another sample.

Many modifications can be made in the sample design to take advantage of the basic idea that prompts sequential sampling. Collection and testing methods may be such that there are certain convenient or economical sample sizes. For example, perhaps sample lots of ten items each are technically convenient. What we can do is test *sequences* of lots of ten items each. We would then be able to come to a final decision in our problem with an excess of items of no more than nine.

The notions and mathematics of sequential sampling were developed early in World War II and were considered an important contribution to the fantastic production record of American industry. The armed forces of the United States have been very aggressive in their efforts to encourage American industry to develop and adopt more efficient methods of designing and testing samples, and the work based on the notions of sequential sampling has played a leading role in these efforts.

Selection in Some Prescribed Order

Sometimes the universe under investigation is known to exist in some geographical, alphabetical, chronological, or other order. For example a universe of telephone subscribers is listed alphabetically in the telephone book. Potato plants are found in a geographical order in a potato field. A universe of random numbers is found in a random order in a table of random numbers. If we would like to select a *random* sample from such ordered situations, the question of how to do it most efficiently and conveniently immediately arises. We would have no problem with a table of random numbers no matter what order we took them in because the numbers are already in a random order by design. But let us suppose we were interested in sampling telephone subscribers in order to find out their ages. Could we get a valid sample by taking, say, every 50th name in the book? Let us select the first name by use of a table of random numbers and then take every 50th name after that. Is this likely to lead to a sample of too many old people? Too many young people? And so forth. We probably would say no because we have no reason to believe that there would be any relationship between the alphabetical character of a subscriber's name and his age. In other words, it may be perfectly logical to argue that an *alphabetical order* of telephone subscribers leads to a *random order* of ages of telephone subscribers, and the use of an alphabetical order might be perfectly valid for sampling ages.

On the other hand, let us suppose that by some quirk of fate completely beyond our comprehension, an alphabetical listing of subscribers automatically listed the subscribers in order of age. What happens to our sample if we select every 50th name with a random start? We should end up with an almost perfect cross section of the age distribution! In other words, our sampling errors would be at a minimum. In effect, what has happened is that the alphabetical listing has neatly *stratified* the universe for us by age, and we recall that effective stratification can be a very useful device to cut down sampling error.

The practice of not noticing the *order* in which data arise or samples are selected can be a very serious shortcoming to any study. Knowledge of relevant *order* or *system* in phenomena is very precious. In fact, it is what we are always searching for if we are searching for anything. Nevertheless we are all guilty of the habit of assuming that no relevant order exists; we do not, therefore, keep track of the order, and it never can exist as far as we are concerned. Most of us, for example, are very careless about dating events as they happen. We assume that chronological order does not count. Unfortunately for us, it often counts more than we had thought. Even statisticians are guilty of this shortcoming. Rarely, if ever, have we seen a statistician treat a series of coin tosses as a *time series*. He treats the sales of a company as a time series, but he automatically assumes that the chronological order of the coin tosses is irrelevant. We cannot deny, however, that the coin tosses actually occurred chronologically in exactly the same sense that the company's sales did.

We must always be alert to order as we observe events. We can decide on their relevance later.

The only time we can really get into trouble when we sample in some prescribed order is when the record being sampled also corresponds to the same order in the following sense. Suppose, again for reasons beyond our comprehension, that every 50th telephone subscriber is a retired farmer, and that farmers do not retire until they are 70 years of age. The resultant sample would contain nothing but ages 70 years and over and would, of course, be most misleading. Fortunately, only rarely do we find that the rhythm of the selection order happens to coincide with the rhythm in the order of what we are studying.

This discussion of order brings up another important consideration in sample design, and that is the absolute necessity of getting clearly in mind exactly what it is we are sampling. For example, sometimes we hear some one say that they are going to take a "sample of people." But what are "people," or what is a "person"? A "person" is all sorts of things. He is a "height," he is a "consumer of canned peas," he is an "admirer of Richard Nixon," he is a "late sleeper on weekends," etc. Thus no one ever really samples "people." What he does sample is "characteristics of people," and generally only very few at a time. If we are to effectively solve our problems of efficient sample design, we must pay specific attention to exactly what it is we are going to measure. For example, an ordered selection of telephone subscribers might be a reasonably acceptable sample for studying the age distribution of family heads in the community. It would be somewhat less acceptable if we were studying the income distribution of family heads on the grounds that the very low income families would tend to be excluded from telephone subscribership and the book. Similarly, we might find that almost any bucket of water from the Atlantic Ocean would be an acceptable sample for detecting the saline content of the Atlantic Ocean. But just any bucket would not be satisfactory if we were sampling the temperature of the Atlantic Ocean.

The Problem of "Nonresponse"

As Robert Burns said, "The best laid plans of mice and men oft gang' aglie." And sampling plans are no exception. It is one thing to plan to find out something about a person who has been scientifically selected in a sample. It is quite another thing to actually do it. Some people are not at home when we call, even with many calls. Some people do not share our enthusiasm about "research" and the importance of their role in it. Some people lack the means of effective communication, such as would be true for recent immigrants. As the result of these and similar frustrations, the final sample of data will not conform to all the specifications of the original design.

The question that now arises is whether there is any reason to believe that the items that did not get included are significantly different from those that did. The answer to this question is considerably complicated by the fact that we do not have any real information about the missing items, for if we did, they would not be missing. Several courses of action would now be open. We might assume that since we knew of no reason to suspect significant differences, there are none. This is, of course, highly presumptuous on our part and generally not advisable. We could check the opinions of others who have had more experience in similar problems. This might bolster our hypothesis of "no significance" and make us less presumptuous if we adopt it. We might assume results for the missing cases that are about as different from the available data as common sense suggests is possible. Then we pool the assumed results and the actual results and compare our final conclusions with those we would get if we ignored the missing cases. If the conclusions are the same, our problem of missing data has disappeared. If the conclusions are different, we have now defined the magnitude of our problem of missing data and should be in an improved position to decide the next step. For example, we may now decide to expend a little more time, effort, and money on further follow-up of the missing cases. By using our early successes here in further comparisons of the kind we have just made, we will be able to more rationally decide when this follow-up program has gone far enough.

If our best efforts still leave us uncertain about the true significance of the missing data, only one appropriate course of action is left: we must admit uncertainty, and come up with a *range* of final conclusions sufficiently broad to cover the range of our uncertainty.

PROBLEMS AND QUESTIONS

3.1 Illustrate the fact that each of *your* five senses has a limited range by reporting the results of an experiment you perform with each of them. Use your own ingenuity to set up an experiment that "proves" the limited range and also uses *quantities* to measure these limits. For example, you might report that you were able to read a given sign with the naked eye at a maximum distance of *37 feet*. However, with the aid of eyeglasses or binoculars you were able to read the sign at a maximum distance of *143 feet*.

3.2 Suppose an attacking airplane is outside the range of your ability to perceive its existence. In other words, in one sense the plane does not exist as far as you are concerned. If you were charged with the responsibility of defending a city against this "nonexistent" plane, how would you go about it?

3.3 Suppose a competitor of yours has allocated $10,000,000 to be used to promote his business at the expense of yours. Unfortunately for you, however, he doesn't tell you this. Thus, in a sense, this $10,000,000 allocation does not exist as far as you are concerned. How do you defend your company against this "attack"?

3.4 Compare the perceptive abilities of your five senses with those of another person. Report on the *measured* differences.

3.5 Consider these two circumstances:

(*a*) Mr. A lets oily rags accumulate in his basement. One night his house catches fire. At great risk to his own personal safety, Mr. A heroically rescues Mrs. A and his three children from the burning house.

(b) Mr. B takes elaborate precautions to prevent the start of a fire in his home. His home never catches on fire. He dies a natural death one day and goes to his grave without ever once having performed an heroic act as far as anybody knows.

In your consideration of these two cases, see if you can note any relationship to your problem of what to do about the "nonexistent" plane and the "nonexistent" promotion fund.

3.6 Perform experiments and/or keep records over a short period of time to discover any variations that you are able to detect in the perceptive abilities of your five senses. Distinguish among variations associated with

(a) Fatigue—deterioration.

(b) Training—improvement.

(c) "Age"—both deterioration and improvement.

Report on your discoveries. *In addition,* what is there about the aging process that is different from fatigue and/or training?

3.7 Contrast your ability to hear every word your mother said when she was explaining to you exactly why you should drive the car as she said you should, and exactly why you should come home when she said you should, with your ability to hear her every word as you listened in the upstairs hall to her sotto voce report to your father on the progress she had made so far on the children's Christmas present list.

What does this tell you about your ability to control your sensory perceptions?

3.8 Yogi Berra was a well-known catcher for the New York Yankees for many years. (Maybe he still is!) This episode has been purported to have occurred early in his major league career. He was such an eager batter that he often swung at, and hit quite well, pitches that were outside the strike zone. Since it is baseball sacrilege to help the pitcher by swinging at "bad" pitches, Yogi was advised by his coaches to curb his eagerness and to swing only at "strikes." In fact, they urged him to go up to the batter's box and *think* about what the pitcher was doing, what Yogi was doing, etc. So Yogi went up to the box and started thinking. While he was thinking, the pitcher put over three called strikes. Yogi came back to the bench muttering: "How can they expect a man to hit and think at the same time?"

Analyze this episode from the point of view of the general human problem that the *conscious mind* can consider only very few things at a time, in some cases only one, whereas many of our activities involve the simultaneous consideration of almost countless things. Consider also the problem that it is difficult to *improve* our performance of complex duties without application of the conscious mind to the details of those duties.

3.9 It should be obvious to you that you are only a *sample of what you might have been,* both for better and for worse. It should be particularly obvious if you have brothers and sisters. Also, as you look back over the road you travelled you can recall many forks in the road and the many choices you made that caused you to forego many other choices. Without writing your autobiography, sketch briefly the "universe" or "universes" out of which you came.

What kind of a sample are you? Random? Purposive? Biased?

What "universe" do you see ahead of you 10 years from now?

3.10 Identify the following universes with respect to whether they are real or hypothetical, known or unknown, and finite or infinite.

(*a*) The universe out of which you are a sample.

(*b*) The universe of grains of sand on the beach at Atlantic City.

(*c*) The universe of sales of 1960 Rambler cars out of which the actual sales came.

(*d*) The universe of possibilities for head and tail combinations if one tosses five coins at once.

(*e*) The universe of words out of which this string of 13 is a sample.

(*f*) The universe of scrap percentages out of which today's percentage came.

(*g*) The universe of *voters* out of which the last Gallup Poll sample was taken.

(*h*) The universe of *voter opinions* out of which the last Gallup Poll sample of opinions was taken.

(*i*) The universe of opinions out of which your present opinion about questions like this came.

3.11 Suppose we select a sample of 100 from a universe that contains 1000 items in each of the following two ways:

1. We draw out the first item at random. Record the result. Replace the item in the universe. Draw out the second item at random. Record. Replace. And so forth until we have recorded the 100 sample items.

2. We draw out all 100 items at once, again at random. (Incidentally, would this be the equivalent of drawing them out one at a time but without replacement?)

Which sample would you expect to have the smaller sampling error? Why?

Would you be willing to bet $1 to a dime that it actually does have a smaller sampling error? Why or why not?

3.12(*a*) The performance of a batter on a given turn at bat is obviously only a sample of what he might have done. Is it a random sample? Explain.

(*b*) Suppose you have the results of ten successive times at bat for a given player. Would you judge that all these samples came from the same universe? Explain.

3.13(*a*) The performance of a housewife in the baking of biscuits is obviously only a sample of what she might have done. Is it a random sample? Explain.

(*b*) Suppose you have the results of ten successive "bakings" for the same housewife. (That is, you have the recorded results, not the biscuits themselves.) Would you judge that these ten samples all came from the same universe? Explain.

3.14(*a*) The performance of a student on an examination is obviously only a sample of what he might have done. Is it a random sample? Explain. Would your answer be any different for a "surprise" exam than for one announced 10 weeks in advance?

(b) If you had the results of ten successive examinations for a given student in a given course, would you judge that they all came from the same universe? Explain.

3.15(a) The number of hours of life for a given electronic tube is obviously only a sample of what it might have been. Is it a random sample? Explain.

(b) Suppose you had the data on the hours of life of ten electronic tubes taken at intervals from the production line. Would you judge that all ten tubes came from the same universe? Explain.

3.16 Let us get ourselves nicely confused about such a simple matter as the length of a room.

(a) An architect designed the house that contains the room. He specified that the room should be 14.5 ft long. However, he might have specified some other length. Hence this specification is only a sample of what it might have been. What kind of a universe? What kind of a sample?

(b) The carpenter builds the house and makes the room 14.5836 ft long. (Do not ask us how we know this.) He might have made it longer or shorter. What kind of a universe? What kind of a sample?

(c) The buyer of the house measures the length of the room and gets an answer of 14.55 inches. What kind of a universe? What kind of a sample?

(d) The buyer's wife measures the length of the room a week later and gets an answer of 14.4 feet. What kind of a universe? What kind of a sample?

(e) How long *is* the room?

3.17 Analyze any 25 consecutive numbers you find any place you would like to look in the table of random numbers in Appendix B. Is there any system to the sequence? List all "tentative" systems you can find.

Select some other section of the table and test your systems. Report on your results.

3.18 Toss an ordinary coin 15 times in a row. Keep track of the chronological order of the resultant heads and tails. Plot the results of the tosses on a graph with "time" on the horizontal axis. Examine the graph for evidence that the results varied some systematic way with "time."

If you think you have found a "system," test it by tossing the coin five more times and recording the results on the graph.

What conclusions do you draw from this experiment?

3.19 Would you guess that the size of random sampling errors would be greater or less for a sample of 100 diameters of "1/2 inch diameter" bolts than for a sample of 250 diameters of "18-inch diameter" wood telephone poles? Explain.

3.20 Suppose you fancied yourself a budding artist with oil colors. You finally get a chance to show your work to a well-respected critic. He asks you to bring him a "sample of your work." What kind of a sample do you select? Out of what universe or universes did you select it? What kinds of answers to these questions do you think the critic would give? Explain.

3.21 The sales manager of your company is taken ill and you, the assistant sales manager, are asked to take over his duties, at least temporarily. What kind of a sample of your work are you going to give?

Are you going to "run the shop" as you think the sales manager would if he were there? Or are you going to run it as you would if you were sales manager? Or are you going to "seize your big chance" and run the shop with an expenditure of energy, sincerity, etc., that you know you could not maintain over any protracted period of time?

How can the president tell which kind of a sample you are giving?

3.22 Why do most purchasers look below the top layer when they buy a basket of fruit?

3.23 At some time or other you must have been told to "be yourself" by some well- or otherwise-meaning person. Almost everybody has. Apparently your recent behavior impressed them as not a "good" sample of what they thought your true nature (universe) was. What was your reaction at the time? Did you agree with their implied evaluation? Did you protest that the sample of behavior certainly was typical of your nature? Etc.

What difference, if any, was there between your outward reaction, the one you wanted the person to get, and your inward reaction?

3.24 Suppose you are throwing darts at a target for the first time. Your first toss lands 12 inches to the right of the bullseye. You would quite naturally like to make your second toss closer. Do you assume that you missed 12 inches *to the right* because you "aimed wrong" and hence you will now adjust your aim 12 inches to the left of the bullseye? Or do you assume that you missed 12 inches, and *it just happened to be to the right,* because you haven't yet mastered the art of throwing darts? So you aim your second toss the same place you thought you aimed the first one. How do you decide a question like this? (This is the same problem the artillery captain faces as he tries to figure out what the reports of the spotter mean from the point of view of any possible adjustments in the aim of the gun.)

3.25 If you were on a jury and if a conviction on the given charge meant the death sentence, would you be less inclined to vote guilty than if conviction resulted in a sentence of 5 years in prison? If yes, how do you justify a position that in effect says that "whether a man is guilty or not depends on the severity of the punishment. The more severe the punishment, the less likely he is to be guilty"?

Would this problem disappear if we could be *sure* that a man was or was not guilty?

3.26 A sample survey is to be made of American housewives to find out about brand preferences for coffee purchases. It is decided to stratify the universe according to geographical location, age of housewife, years of formal schooling of housewife, and number of people living in household. It is decided to use three divisions for each stratifying factor. The divisions are listed below.

Locations	Age of Housewife	Education	Number in Household
Northeast	Under 25	Less than 10 years	Under 3
South	25 to 40	10 to 14 years	3 to 5
West	Over 40	Over 14 years	Over 5

Census data are available to find out how many housewives there are approximately in each of these categories. From these figures it is possible to calculate the *proportion* of housewives in each category. For example, let us say there are 38% of the housewives in the United States under 25 years of age. We will so design our sample that it will end up with *38%* of the housewives under 25 years of age also. Thus, if coffee brand preferences have anything to do with age of housewife, our results won't be thrown off because we will have the right age distribution of housewives in our sample.

Suppose our final sample matched the proper proportions of housewives in all four categories of stratification. Is this a sufficient condition, or should our final proportions be correct down to the proportion, say, of housewives under 25 *and* living in the northeast *and* having over 14 years of formal schooling, *and* in households with three to five members? Or, in other words, instead of filling in our "quotas" in these four categories independently, must we fill them in simultaneously, thus ending up really with *81* separate "quotas"?

What are the issues involved here? (The first thing you had better do is make sure you know where those 81 separate quotas come from. You can do this by drawing a tree of all the possibilities.)

3.27 Suppose you were supervising a survey and had decided to use "clusters" of people in your sample in order to save some money. Do you feel better or worse about your over-all sampling errors if you find practically *no variation within* clusters and quite a bit of variation between clusters? How would you feel if the reverse were true, namely, quite a bit of variation within clusters, but practically no variation between clusters? The illustrations below should clarify your thinking about the meaning of variation within a cluster and variation between clusters.

Results in Cluster A	Results in Cluster B	Results in Cluster C	Results in Cluster D
5	7	1	1
5	7	2	2
5	7	3	3
5	7	4	4
5	7	5	5

Clusters A and B have no variation *within* them; but they do have variation (of 2) *between* them.

Clusters C and D have quite a bit of variation *within* them, but no variation *between* them.

3.28 Suppose you are playing the following simple game. You and a friend are wagering 10 cents on the outcome of the toss of a coin. (You are waiting for a train which will take the two of you on a 17-hour trip.) Since each of you has adopted the hypothesis that heads and tails are equally likely, it is decided that you will call heads every time, and he tails, rather than waste time between tosses deciding the irrelevancy of "which to call." Since it is your coin that is being tossed, it was agreed that he will do all the tossing.

You nevertheless do have a decision problem after each toss. You must decide whether to make another wager on the agreed-upon terms, or to request some change in the terms. (Be careful that your request for a change in the terms does not imply that you think your friend is cheating unless you do not care whether or not you enjoy his company for the next 17 hours.)

What decision do you make after *each* toss if the following represents the sequence of heads and tails? Justify your decision in each case.

T, T, H, T, T, T, H, T, T, T, T, T, H, T, T, T, T, T, T, H.

(Hint: Calculate the probability that the sequence could have happened up to the given point *if* your hypothesis of equal probability for heads and tails is correct.)

3.29 Suppose we had established control procedures for a given job that instructed the operator to let the process run if he found no more than two defectives in a sample of ten. He is instructed to take such a sample every 15 minutes. Suppose he reports to you after about an hour that he has taken four samples so far and has found exactly two defects in each one. This worries him very much because he knows that the process is designed to yield only 5% defectives in the long run. He has stopped the machine to come to talk to you. What is your reaction?

3.30 Suppose you have a problem such that a telephone book provides an excellent source of all the names of the people in the universe you are concerned with. You would like to take a *random* sample of 200 names by the most *efficient* process possible. What are the comparative merits of using a table of random numbers to pick out 200 numbers which you can use to locate names in the book and of taking every 25th name after a random start (there are approximately 5000 names in the book)? Which method would you recommend? Would the characteristic of the people you were studying make any difference in your recommendation? Explain and illustrate.

chapter **4**

The use of numbers

Numbers are the raw materials of most statistical analysis. The fundamental notions underlying the statistical method can also be applied to non-numerical data, but the power of the statistical method is much more evident when we can quantify our data.

Since we have all been trained in the use of numbers since early childhood, it may seem redundant for us to review the fundamental notions underlying the creation of numbers. We find, however, that it is very easy to be so mesmerized by the intricacies of the manipulation of numbers that we often lose sight of the basic meaning of the numbers. A brief review of once familiar ideas will remind us of the inherent characteristics of our raw materials and curb any tendencies we might have to use elaborate analytical techniques on rather inadequate numerical data.

4.1 Counting and the Number System

The idea of *counting* things is one of the most important ideas man ever had. Of course, the earliest man probably had some idea of *amount,* and some ideas about *more* or *less.* There is plenty of evidence to suggest that most animals can handle these ideas of more or less. But very few of the lower animals, if any, can actually count. For example, the mother cat probably knows all her six kittens. And if one is missing she will probably realize he is gone because she cannot find this particular kitten among the ones she sees. But can she tell that one is missing because all she can see is five? Even if she can do this, and thus in a sense knows she has six kittens, there is still considerable doubt that she is able to brag to her neighbor cat that she has *six* kittens while her neighbor has only *five.*

The fundamental origin of all numbers is the process of counting. This counting may be of *existent* and *separate* things, or it may be of *standard* things that we have created, like an "inch." Man undoubtedly learned how to count the natural things in his environment before he learned how to correlate these things and count how many of one thing were contained in one unit of another thing. For example, he probably knew that he had three caves in which to seek shelter before he knew that one cave was three times as deep as another because it had three times as many spear lengths.

Number Systems

Most of us have been trained in the use of the "tens" system of numbering and think of the 10 numbers as running from 1 to 10. Actually, of course, the 10 numbers that form our system are 0, 1, 2 . . . 9. What we call 10 is really a combination of the two numbers, 0 and 1. Originally the system did run from one to ten, with the basic idea coming from the fingers of the two hands. But it was the invention of the concept of nothing or 0 that really opened the door to the comprehensive development of the system that we know today. The child has some difficulty counting very high at the beginning because he does not grasp the system. Thus he has to memorize his counting. Eventually, however, he does grasp the system, and then he has no trouble counting until he is bored or exhausted. At that time he also becomes at least semiconscious of the idea that our number system is such that there is *no limit to how high we can count*. This limitless range of our number system is very important because it means that there cannot be so many of something that we cannot specifically identify "how many" with our system. Similarly, there can never be too few of something for us to specifically identify.

Eventually the concept of *negative* numbers was created. This meant that the range of our number system was truly infinite. The idea of less than nothing, or, say, of −5, is elusive to say the least. But this is not really the idea behind negative numbers. The idea behind negative numbers is the idea of "take aways" or of subtraction. We also use negative numbers to identify *direction* from some specified point. For example, if we move *forward* 5 feet from where we now are, we might say that our movement was *plus* 5 feet. If we move backward, we might say our movement was *minus* 5 feet. But note that we could have called the forward movement minus and the backward movement plus. This brings us to a fundamental point about the use of numbers. The *actual* number and the *sign*, whether plus or minus, almost always depends on the *particular* origin of measurement we have *chosen*. This number has meaning *only* for that origin. Serious confusion results if we try to interpret the number with no knowledge, or with incorrect knowledge, of the origin of measurement. If I tell you that I have moved back 5 feet, you still have no idea of where I now am unless you knew where I was before I moved.

It is important to remember that *negative quantities* do not really exist. A tank just cannot contain "minus 3 gallons of gasoline." The primary value of the concept of the negative number is in the *manipulation* of numbers by the processes of addition, subtraction, multiplication, and division. The result of the manipulation, or the answer, almost always is a *positive* number. The important rule of interpretation of answers, a rule easy to state but sometimes difficult to apply, is that the *sign* of the answer must make sense in the problem at hand. For example, if we are working on all the cost figures relevant to a given product in our plant and we finally come up with a unit cost of *minus* $3.28, we should check over our figuring before we tell the boss that there is money to be made in manufacturing this product even if we have to pay people to take it away. On the other hand, if we tally all the revenues and expenses of the company during a period and discover that the company had a profit of *minus* $8,647, we have a figure which may very well be true, even though somewhat disconcerting.

Man has invented many other number systems than the "tens" system. Some electronic computers, for example, are based on the binary, or "two number," system. This system has nothing but "0" and "1" in it. In fact, the development of the electronic computer as we know it would be impossible without the binary number system. The "tens" system would be just about hopelessly awkward. The logic behind the binary system is quite simple. An electric circuit is either open or it is closed. The problem of controlling a switch so that a circuit is either open or closed is a lot simpler than the problem, say, of controlling and measuring the voltage of a current so that one voltage represents 0, another voltage 1, etc. through all the numbers of the decimal system. Since we actually operate on a decimal system, the problem of using the electronic computer became one of translating a number in the decimal system to one in the binary system. We can illustrate the numbers in the binary system by showing their equivalents in the decimal system for a few numbers in Table 4.1. We might note, incidentally, that each *digit* in the binary number corresponds to a *circuit* in the computer. Note that it takes three circuits to represent the numbers 4 through 7, 16 circuits to represent the number 10,000, etc.

If a person is of an inquisitive turn of mind, he might note the role that is played by the "powers of two." He might even be able to

TABLE 4.1

Decimal System Equivalents of Binary Numbers

Binary Number	Decimal Number
0	0
1	1
10	2
11	3
100	4
101	5
110	6
111	7
1000	8
10000	16
100000	32
1000000	64
10000000	128

develop a formula for easy conversion of any number in the decimal system to its corresponding number in the binary system, or vice versa.

We mention these other number systems and illustrate the binary system not to be confusing, but to remind us that number systems, including the familiar decimal system, are inventions that man has made to help him solve his problems. Because they are inventions, just like automobiles for example, they are subject to improvements or even replacement, if they cannot solve our problems as well as they might. It is unlikely, however, that there will be an early replacement or significant modification of our decimal system. Too many people understand this system, or at least think they do, to tolerate the introduction of a new system. Our civilization will probably have to decline as did ancient China before a new civilization could be built on a new system of counting.

4.2 Units of Counting

It is possible to count, the way a child counts to 100 for his proud parents, without really counting anything at all. All we do is sound out or write the symbolism we have adopted for the various integers in our number system. This kind of counting, however, is of little or no practical value. To be of value our counting must count *something,* maybe stones, or horses, or red corpuscles, or degrees of heat, etc. In practical work all numbers have *units* attached to them. The number is meaningless if we do not know the unit, or if we know the wrong unit. For example, contrast the problem of defining the meaning of 7 with the problem of defining the meaning of seven books.

One of the first things a youngster learns about counting is that he should always count *like* things, not *unlike* things. For example, we should not add apples and oranges, and certainly not apples and horses. There are times when we wonder whether such things should be taught in grade school. It is certainly true that we should be careful of what we count. It is equally true, however, that we should realize that we rarely, if ever, have the opportunity to count things that are *absolutely* alike or identical. We frequently have the opportunity to count things that are *essentially alike,* or whose differences "do not make a difference." But it is often important to realize that to act as though things are the same, say for purposes of counting, does not make them the same. It takes more perception and more imagination to recognize that apples are *different from each other* than it does to recognize that apples are different from oranges, but it certainly should not be said that it is proper to add apples but not apples and oranges. As a matter of fact, from the point of view of certain units of nutrition possessed by both apples and oranges, a given apple can be more like a given orange than like another apple!

It should be obvious that whether we should count things together as though they had the same unit depends on the *purpose* of the count. The issue is whether the differences being ignored make any difference to the purpose. For example, we might properly count all the *articles* in a house as though they were the same, giving equal attention to a thimble and to a divan. Or we might count the *pieces of bedroom* furniture; or the *articles of clothing;* or the *footwear;* or the *shoes;* or the *ladies' shoes;* or the *pairs of black leather shoes;* or the *pairs of black leather shoes that need polishing.*

Probably most of the mistakes that are made in counting are not because people cannot count but because they do not understand the things they are counting well enough to know one when they see one. They include things they should not and they exclude things they should include.

Counting Integral Units

Many of the things we count have an individual existence that makes it relatively easy to identify them as separate and distinct.

We think of such objects as being integral objects, and we expect the final count to be a "whole number" or an "integer." We normally do not think of "1/2 of a person" or "3 1/2 table lamps." There are times, of course, when we do find it sensible to split some units and use only parts of the whole in our counting. "1/2 an apple," for example, might make sense in some contexts. Rarely, however, do we find it apparently proper to think of fractional parts of living organisms, primarily, we suppose, because we suspect that the fractionalization of a living organism generally kills it. This attitude is often a mistake, however, because the *purpose* behind the count sometimes makes the need for *mental fractionalization* quite imperative. A group of boys choosing sides for a baseball game show much more alertness to this need at times than do many adults. The boys' objective is to make up "fair" sides. When they "add up" the boys on one side they want about the same answer as when they "add up" the boys on the other side. But they really do not count "boys," although it may seem so to the naked eye. What they count is "baseball skill." Boy 1 has one unit of such skill. Boy 2 has 1.75 units; boy 3 only .5 units. They then select boys so that the "skill points" add up. Sometimes this leads to more boys on one side than on the other, which may strike an onlooker as "unfair." The same boys will go to school and grow up and get excited because the population of Hokay is greater than that of the United States.

The essential point being made with the above illustration is that we are almost never solely concerned with the *integral units* we are counting. Rarely do we count the number of people because we are interested in the *number of people*. What we are usually interested in is some *characteristic* that people have, and we are counting the people to somehow add up the characteristic. We would be very foolish, however, to assume that one set of 10 people add up to the same amount of this characteristic as another set. We may wonder why it is done this way instead of counting the characteristic directly. The answer is quite simple. We count the obvious integral unit because we know how to and because there is little room for disagreement about the answer. Of course, it may not be the right answer for the underlying question, but it is the right answer for the question we are asking, namely, "how many people are there?" We as human beings have such a strong urge for the sense of security we get when we "know something," that we have a great tendency to ask ourselves questions to which we do know the answer, albeit both the question and the answer do not reflect a realistic appraisal of what is really at issue. For example, the boys would have to *defend* their decision to have an *unequal* number of boys on the two teams. Most people would automatically *assume* that the same number to a side makes a fair game. Almost anyone can count boys; the counting of baseball "skill points" is quite another matter.

Standard Units

We are now led to the problems of counting *standard,* or *abstract,* units. These are units that do not really exist in a natural and obvious state, at least not after they have been subjected to a certain amount of refinement. They are basically creations of man. Usually they manifest themselves in some *physical* form, usually called a *measuring instrument.* Sometimes, however, the physical instrument takes on such complex characteristics that the typical person does not think of it as a *physical* measuring instrument. An example would be the testing procedure for measuring a person's "I.Q." All of the measurable activities in intelligence testing are physical in character, although we think of the testing as measuring *mental* activities. But, if we think about it, we realize that physical activity is probably the only kind that can go on, even if we have decided to call some kinds of physical activities mental activities. It is conceivable, for example, that someone some day will discover the chemical basis of mental activity and thereby lay the groundwork for making all of us geniuses! Or at least geniuses by today's standards.

Man created *standard* units in an attempt to moderate the main disadvantage of the use of *natural* units, namely the *variation* in natural units. We have already commented briefly on some of the problems of counting natural units. The "foot," originally a man's real foot, and thereby varying from man to man, came to be replaced by a "standard" foot, very carefully defined and *approximately* equalled by all the foot rulers, etc., all over the world. With our repetitive machines we have far outdone nature when it comes to creating essentially similar units of an object. The advantages we gain from this are obvious, as are the risks and disadvantages. We also try to standardize people to a considerable extent. We standardize textbooks, teaching methods, etc.

Despite the seeming similarity of our standard units, the fact is that our standard units also vary. All foot rulers are defined alike, but they still are not of the exact length. In fact, it is very unlikely that any two of them are exactly the same length. We cannot prove the validity of this statement, but the validity of the contrary statement cannot be proved either. Recognition of the lack of strict identity, although important from the point of view of reminding us that there is still standardizing to be done if we wish to and are able to, does not gainsay the fact that our foot rulers are considerably more alike than our feet. And this last point illustrates a very important principle in the interpretation of the value of suggested standard units. The principle is that we should not ask if a unit of counting is *perfect*. We should ask if it is *better* than competing units.

Direct Counting vs. Indirect Counting

We have already hinted several times that there are occasions when we seemingly are counting one thing when we are actually interested in counting something else. Our youngsters, for example, were seemingly counting boys, but actually they were counting "ballplayers" which are not exactly the same as boys, although they might look the same to the uninitiated. It is now time to point out that *indirect* counting is not the exception, but rather the rule. It is more subtly true when we count natural units because we find it so easy to delude ourselves. It is obviously true when we count standard units simply because we really do not count standard units for their own sake; we count standard units because we believe that the natural object involved has the given number of the standard units. For example, suppose we decide to measure the number of inches in the length of a room. (Incidentally, how many rooms have we ever seen with inches in them?) We take a steel tape and stretch it from one end of the room to the other. We then read off the answer and announce that we have measured the length of the room. But we did not do that at all. What we did was measure the length of the steel tape! (And actually the manufacturer of the tape did most of the hard work.) We believe that we placed the tape in such a position relative to the length of the room that we also measured the length of the room when we measured the length of the tape. When we announce the "count," there is little doubt that we read the number off the tape correctly. There is considerable doubt that we placed the tape correctly.

Similarly, when we check the thermometer to measure the temperature, we do not really measure the quantity of heat in the air. What we measure is the height of a column of colored liquid in a glass tube. We believe that the degree of heat in the air correlates closely enough with the height of the liquid so that if we know the height of the liquid we have a satisfactory guess about the heat in the air. And most of the time it is.

The more we think about it, the more we realize that practically all the familiar numbers of our experience were not the result of counting something of direct interest. What was counted was something that we are *able to count*. We then assume that the thing we are able to count is the same as the thing in which we are really interested. The classic example is, of course, the way all of us associate "happiness" with "money."

Thus the question: "What do the numbers mean?" is always relevant. We should develop the habit of asking three questions about the numbers we find. First: "Exactly what was counted or measured?" Second: "Exactly what is it that is purported to have been measured at the same time?" Third: "How close is the relationship between the two things?" After answering these questions, we are now in a position to use the given numbers more intelligently.

After we have trained ourselves to ask the three questions given about the *numbers* we find, we should start to develop the habit of asking the following three questions about the *problems* we find. First: "What is there about our problem that we could understand better if we could measure it *quantitatively?*" Second: "What other things have already been measured, or might be measured, that would give us some knowledge of the quantitative variation of the thing we are interested in?" And finally: "How close is this relationship between the two things?"

Until man *quantified* a phenomenon in his environment, he made little or no progress in understanding the phenomenon, controlling the phenomenon, etc. This has obviously been true in dealing with physical phenomena. It has been less obviously true, but nevertheless almost equally true, in our dealings with what are called psychological, sociological, and other related phenomena. In fact, as pointed out earlier, the evidence is mounting that almost every phenomenon has a physical base, or if not a physical base, it has physical manifestations, and the more quickly we quantify these physical manifestations, the better are we going to be able to deal with such problems. We should not use the obvious limitations of quantification to hold back its development and its extension into many areas heretofore held somewhat sacred, as though to use numbers to characterize the variation in something is somehow to defile it. Business affairs have not been immune to man's persistent struggle to improve his understanding by quantifying the relevant phenomena. In many respects, business has pioneered developments in quantification, although not from any motive other than personal profit. The relentless drive of competitive pressure has forced business to continually extend the scope of its "accounting." (Note count in the root of this word.) The number of numbers generated by one day's business in the United States is fantastic. And there seems to be no end as each firm tries to gain a competitive advantage by creating new numbers before its competitors do. The poor fellow who tries to run his business "by the seat of his pants" stands no more chance today than a fighter pilot "flying by the seat of his pants" would against a jet pilot who knows only what he is told by the myriad dials in front of him. Very few pilots, for example, can compete successfully against an altimeter when it comes to figuring out how high the plane is.

4.3 Some Special Problems in Counting and Measuring

Choice of Units

The *unit* that we count is, of course, at the heart of the counting process. We must know the unit well enough so that we can tell one from the other when we see them. One of the most interesting aspects of the counting process, and one of its most valuable, is that we can count anything upon which we set our mind. It is entirely up to us to decide what unit we are going to count. Since this is so, it is absolutely essential that we consciously define the unit we have decided to use in a given case. If two people use different units in the same application, they are bound to get different *numbers* even though they may get identical *answers*, because the answer involves both the number and the unit.

Since the choice of the unit is completely within our command, common sense suggests that we should choose "good" units. What are some of the desirable qualities of a unit, not necessarily in order of importance? One desirable quality is that the unit be *familiar*, or *generally understood*. Of course, it cannot be familiar when it is first adopted; but, once a unit has attained a substantial degree of familiarity, either because of traditional usage or through education, substantial disadvantages develop, at least temporarily, if we change the unit. Such a change considerably weakens one of the greatest values of numbers, namely, added precision in communication between people. We could communicate a strong impression of our independence and individuality by adopting our private set of units of length, weight, etc., but we certainly could not communicate any notions about height, weight, etc. The rule of familiarity puts a handicap on the process of introducing new units that might be better on many other accounts. The calendar currently used on much of the earth is an illustration of a unit of measuring time that is mainly recommended by familiarity.

Relative uniformity of the size of the unit is probably the most important objective quality of a unit of measure. We note two aspects to the problem of uniformity. A unit might vary from element to element at one moment of time, or all units might vary over time. The human foot as a unit of length is an example. This varies from person to person (and also from left foot to right foot) at any moment of time. It also has varied over time; there is substantial evidence that peoples' feet, particularly in the United States, are getting longer. In our choice of standard units, we try to keep both types of variation to a minimum. We are not always too successful, however, particularly when we deal with some of the more complex units. Our most notable recent failure has been the shrinkage in the value of the dollar over the last few decades. Students are particularly alert to the deficiencies in uniformity of test grade units, both from student to student and over time. The most notable simple thing that we continue to measure with obviously nonuniform units is the month. We have inherited a calendar that is not as serviceable as the American Indian's concept of the moon. Users of business data find their tasks considerably complicated because of our present calendar system. The months not only have different numbers of days; they have different numbers of holidays, workdays, Sundays, etc. It would be simpler if each week had the same number of workdays, each month the same number of weeks, etc. It has been seriously suggested, and strongly supported by all working statisticians, that we start improving the situation.

A unit should also be of a size that leads to *numbers that are convenient to work with*. It is impractical to measure the quantity of coal in ounces because it is generally purchased and used in amounts that would result in awkwardly large numbers. Similarly, the astronomer measures distances between stars in light-years rather than in feet and the computer engineer measures time on the computer in milliseconds rather than in hours. The mathematics student, on the other hand, measures the time it takes him to do his homework calculations in hours.

The person who is doing the work is the best judge of the size of number that is the most convenient to work with. Some people like all the numbers to be between 1 and 100, and all the numbers integers at that! If a person abhors fractions, decimal or common, he can always avoid them by choosing a small enough unit. Probably convention and habit are the prime determinants of what is convenient for most people. What we have been used to and what we have been taught in school are generally easy for us. Anything else is strange and hence difficult.

Another useful attribute of a unit is that it be a part of a system of units of different sizes that are easily converted into one another. For example, the money system of the United States has units of cents, nickels, dimes, quarters, half dollars, etc. These are easily converted into each other. Our system of volume measures, on the other hand, has a set of units that are quite awkward in conversion from one to the other. We go from teaspoons, tablespoons, cups, pints, quarts, gallons, etc., up to barrels. Generally speaking, we find that the most convenient units are those that are based on the decimal system, thus making it possible to shift units by shifting the decimal point.

Choice of Origin

The *origin* of measurement, or the value associated with "0," is often a matter of arbitrary choice. Sometimes what is being counted or measured has a natural origin, a point where 0 makes sense. For example, if we are measuring the length of a board, it makes sense to start at one end of the board, call that 0, and count the number of feet to the other end. Some things we measure, however, do not have any natural origin, or, if they do, we do not know where it is. For example, where is the origin of time? Western civilization has chosen to measure time forward and backward from the birth of Christ. We probably date most of the significant events in our lifetime with reference to our age, a number which we find convenient to measure from our birthday as the origin.

Common sense suggests that we choose a convenient origin if we have a choice. Since the choice of origin is what determines where the positive and negative numbers are going to occur, the most important factor in the choice is the interpretation we wish to put on the negative numbers. For example, the theory of profit measurement and the accounting system that results determine the 0 point, or the point of 0 profit. Many people misinterpret the conventional measurement of profit because they do not really understand the meaning of 0 profit. The most common misinterpretation, probably, is to confuse the profit scale with the cash scale and to assume that 0 profit means 0 cash.

We have further occasion to consider the problem of origin when we discuss the concept of the scale below.

Concept of the Scale

We are all familiar with that measuring instrument called the scale. In common usage it is a device to measure weight. We use the term in a more general sense to refer to any measuring device that has the twin features of an *origin* of measurement and a *unit* of measurement. In this sense, an ordinary foot ruler is a scale. It has an origin at one end (usually not marked as *0* however) and is divided up into inches and fractions of inches. The same foot ruler would still be a scale if we decided to place the origin in the middle and mark off the inches plus and minus from that point. The second scale would now have a −4 where the first one had a +2, etc. It should be obvious that the second ruler is as good for measuring the length of a room as would be the first. However, it is also obvious that the numbers in the final answer will be different unless we choose to translate the result on the second ruler into the same result we would get if we used the first ruler. This could be done very simply by adding 6 to every number that had been read from the second ruler to adjust for the fact that the origin of the second ruler was displaced six units from the origin of the first ruler.

If we wished, we could multiply each number on the ordinary ruler by 10, say, resulting in 90 whereas we had 9 before. For convenience we might call the new numbers "dinches." We could now measure the length of the room with this ruler, getting a result in dinches instead of inches. The room is still the same length. However, our numerical answer would be ten times as big as if we had measured it in inches. We could then convert the answer from dinches to inches by dividing the number of dinches by 10.

We could, of course, shift the origin and change the unit at the same time, thus getting a completely new scale. And, knowing the relationship between the original scale and the new scale, we could translate a result from one scale into its equivalent on the other scale. Either scale would be equally good for measuring a given phenomenon. Naturally we should know which scale we are using when we interpret the final result.

We find the ability to shift back and forth from one scale to another a great convenience in performing certain calculations. The usual routine is to take the results of one scale that is very convenient for measuring and interpretation, translate these results into another scale that is very convenient for calculations, and finally translate the results of the calculation back into the original scale. The final results can be quite misleading, and sometimes quite ridiculous, if we err in the translation process.

It is interesting to note that the whole concept of a scale drawing or scale model flows directly from this concept of the scale and of changing the origin and unit of the scale. We construct a scale drawing whenever we measure something in conventional units, such as feet and inches, and then arbitrarily change the unit so that, say, one inch on the original scale becomes equal to 100 ginches on the new scale. The dimensions of the actual object are then measured on the original scale. A set of numbers results. The model is then drawn by using the same numbers (inches) as though they were ginches. The model should then have all the appropriate *proportions*, although it should be only 1/100th the size of the actual.

The 100 Percent Scale. A scale that has found wide application in many practical problems is the percentage scale. This is an arbitrarily created scale that runs from 0 to 100, although we see shortly that it is sometimes more convenient to think of it as running from 0 to 1. It can be used successfully only where the notion of all, or total, and the notion of 0 make sense and also where it makes sense to think of the various parts that make up this total.

We also use such a percentage scale at times when we are trying to approximate the intensity of attitudes or feelings. For example, a person might attempt to communicate the strength of his "liking" for Brand A cigarettes by making a mark on a 100% scale as shown in Fig. 4.1. We can think of the 100% as being the "total amount of affection" the person has for cigarettes. Since this particular person has a 65% liking for Brand A, it is evident that he definitely *prefers* Brand A to any other brand because the maximum "liking" available for whatever brand is in second place is only 35%.

A special case of the 100% scale is often used when we are interested in the *decision* a person will make because of some attitude or feeling he has. Since a person either votes for a candidate or does not vote for him, only two results are possible. The issue now is to determine what value on the 100% scale we should assign a favorable vote and an unfavorable vote. The convention has been adopted of assigning a value of 100% to a favorable vote or a favorable purchase, and a value of 0 to all other possible decisions. For example, if a person likes Brand A cigarettes more than any other brand, and hence buys Brand A, we would assign a decision rating of 100 to Brand A and a decision rating of 0 to all other brands.

Generally speaking, there are significant mathematical advantages to be derived by using a scale from 0 to 1, with decimal fractions occupying the intermediate values, instead of the 0 to 100% scale. This

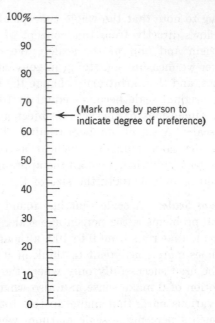

Fig. 4.1 Preference scale for Brand A cigarettes.

would mean that we would be dealing with *proportions* rather than with percentages. The liking for Brand A referred to would be expressed as .65 instead of 65%. We find 65% easier to say than .65, but we find .65 easier to manipulate mathematically. It is no problem to shift back and forth from one scale to another because the numbers on the percentage scale are exactly 100 times the size of the numbers on the proportion scales.

The mathematical advantages of the 0 to 1 scale are particularly important when we are dealing with the decision problem just given. A decision in favor of something would be called 1 instead of 100. If we were dealing with many such decisions, some favorable and some unfavorable (0), we would have a collection of nothing but 1's and 0's. These work very nicely in certain mathematical derivations. This choice is also consistent with many of the practices of our democratic traditions. When citizens vote, they must make definite choices. Person 1 may actually be quite undecided, but leans a shade toward candidate A, say, with a preference rating of .51. He must give his *whole* vote to A, however. Person 2 on the other hand has an unqualified preference of 1.00 for candidate A. He is very happy to give his whole vote to A, and may even wish he had two or more votes to give. The record shows both of these votes exactly the same, namely as unqualified votes for A. The truth would show candidate A with a total preference of 1.51 and candidate B with a total preference of .49. The results of the election show candidate A with 2 votes and candidate B with 0 votes, a result which seems substantially away from the truth, which it is if we consider only those who voted for candidate A. It is quite evident that there is a bias in our measurement in favor of candidate A. However, if we consider the votes for candidate B, we would find a similar bias in favor of B. If we add all the results together, we find these biases somewhat offsetting each other. If A ended up with 53% of the vote, we might say, with caution, that the citizenry apparently had an average preference of .53 for A and an average preference of .47 for B. What this means is impossible to determine, however, from the available information. It might mean that feeling was quite moderate for both candidates, with most people actually not overly concerned about which candidate won. Or feelings might run quite strong, with about 53% of the people 100% for A and unalterably opposed to B, and with about 47% of the people having equally strong but opposite feelings. The latter situation is explosive and might lead to a revolution.

These two extreme possibilities are illustrated in Fig. 4.2. Part A shows a distribution of moderate opinions and Part B a distribution of extreme opinions.

Thus it is obvious that we pay a price in lost information when

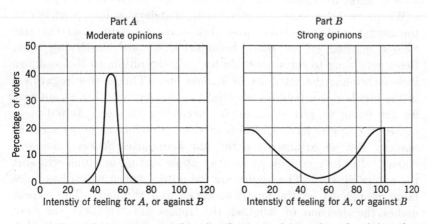

Fig. 4.2 Two of the many possible distributions of intensity of opinion that might prevail on the assumption of an "average" preference of 53%.

we choose the convenience of registering a decision, a preference, or a vote as though it were 1 or 0, with no provision for recording intermediate opinions. It is a good practice in work over which we have some control to ask ourselves whether this convenience of recording only 1's and 0's is worth the sacrifice of information. With the advent of the voting machine, it is conceivable, though not likely, that someday we may cast our vote by registering a degree of preference rather than just giving the whole vote to one candidate and nothing to the others.

The technique of assigning a value of 1 or 0 to something according to whether a given thing is or is not true is used commonly. Its use is not restricted to just those cases in which a decision is being made either for or against something, as in voting, or as in marking True-False questions. We also use it at times when the variable being measured actually takes on a great number, if not an infinite number, of values. For example, we might arbitrarily select a minimum height, say, 6 feet, and label all men that height or more as tall men. We then collect figures on whether a man is tall or not tall. If he is tall, namely, 6 feet tall or taller, we assign a value of 1. If he is not tall, we assign a value of 0. Naturally we do not have as much information about the heights of a group of men if all we know is that 18% of them are tall and 82% of them are not tall as if we knew the heights of the individual men within 1/2 inch. But for some purposes, this restricted information might be enough, in which case there would be no point in collecting any more, and at much greater expense. For example, a basketball coach may very well wish to make his initial sort of the men into tall and not tall players.

When we arbitrarily select certain boundary points, such as in the height problem above, and then sort our items into the size classes marked off by those boundaries, we are classifying these items according to certain *attributes*. By definition, so to speak, an item either has the attribute or it does not. This is true regardless of the number of attributes we might be sorting for. Let us suppose we are going to sort some apples according to size. Actually, of course, the apples have all kinds of sizes, probably as many sizes as apples. But we arbitrarily define the boundaries between five size classes. Let us now look at how an apple sorting machine will sort the apples by size. The apples are fed onto a screen which has holes large enough to let the smallest apples fall through. This screen makes the decision of whether the apples are "smallest" or "not smallest." The "not smallest" apples are then passed along through the machine until they reach another screen. This screen has larger holes than the first one, but still holes not large enough to accept any apples larger than those "medium small or smaller." This screen then decides which apples fall into the medium small class and which do not. The sorting process continues through larger and larger screens until all the apples have been placed in one of the five size classes. Note that the machine never had to make a decision any more complicated than to decide that an apple did or did not fall into a given class. The ability to narrow a decision to only two possibilities is not only highly effective when we use machines to do the deciding, but it is also highly effective when human beings are making the decisions.

Again we remind ourselves that the advantages gained by narrowing our decision problem to a few categories or attributes are not without a price, the price being the assumption that some differences do not make any difference whereas other differences, equally small or even smaller, make a substantial difference. For example, some of the smallest apples differ more in size among themselves than do some of the smallest compared to the medium small. The same thing happens when we grade students A, B, C, etc. There is a greater difference among the B students than there is between some of the A students and some of the B students. But as any student knows, our rating systems attach quite a bit of significance to the difference between an A and a B, but no significance to the difference between two B's. The use of a percentage scale for grading solves some of these problems as it creates others.

The analysis of *attribute classification* data has a theory of its own. For those interested, one of the more comprehensive discussions of attribute analysis is in G. U. Yule and M. G. Kendall, *An Introduction to the Theory of Statistics,* Chapters 1 to 5.

The Problem of "Twice as Much"

As soon as we begin to measure things, we take the next step and start *comparing* the sizes of the numbers that we get. For example, we might compare the distances between towns by saying that "it is *twice as far* from Town A to Town B as it is from Town A to Town C." And just about everybody knows what this means. But what do we mean if we say that "today is twice as cold as yesterday," or "Joe isn't half as smart as Tom." We definitely know how to measure distance in a meaningful way, or, more particularly, with a meaningful *origin*. If one distance measured is 25 miles and the other 50 miles, we have no trouble dividing 50 by 25 and getting 2, which tells us that one is twice as much as the other. But, if yester-

day's temperature was 80°F. and today's is 40°F., is it really twice
as cold today? Suppose it was 2°F. yesterday and 1°F. today? Or
suppose Joe's I.Q. is 105 and Tom's 122. How much smarter than Joe
is Tom?

Thus we see that it makes sense to compare the relative sizes of
some numbers we get, but it makes no sense at all to compare others.
Generally speaking, it is appropriate to compare the relative sizes of
numbers if there is a meaningful origin and if we know where it is.
Otherwise we get rather silly answers, and we get answers which
depend entirely on the arbitrary selection of origin that we made.
For example, it is possible to make any degree of coldness twice as
cold as any other degree of coldness by judicious selection of the
origin of measurement. Whenever we can get any answer we want,
the answer is generally meaningless.

Scales with Apparently Unequal Units

We frequently see scales of measure that seem to have units or
divisions that are unequal in size. The most common illustration
of such a scale is the household measuring cup. Such a cup is used
to measure the *volume*, or cubic content, of the cup or fraction thereof.
The scale, or index, must be shown vertically on the side of the cup
however. If the cup is shaped so that the side makes a 90° angle
with the base, and if both the base and the sides have straight sur-
faces, no problem in making the index exists. If we wished to measure 1/8, we would merely divide the vertical surface into eight *equal*
parts. Rarely, however, do we find measuring cups with these properties. For aesthetic and other reasons, the sides do not make a 90°
angle with the base. Usually the mouth of the cup is larger than the
base, and it takes more vertical distance to make 1/8 of a cup near
the bottom of the cup than it does near the top. Thus the divisions
marked on the side of the cup are not equal. But this is quite proper
because the divisions are not really intended to measure the *vertical
distance*. They are intended to measure the *volume* contained by the
cup if filled to the given point.

The technique of using one scale, such as a vertical scale, to measure something according to another scale (not shown), such as a
volume scale, is quite commonly used. It very often results in a
visible scale that has *unequal* divisions, even though the scale actually represented, but not shown, would have *equal* divisions. If we
use a scale with unequal divisions which cannot be translated into

a meaningful scale with equal divisions, we have a serious problem of interpretation.

The analysis of business problems is often helped by the use of a logarithmic or log scale. It is also sometimes called a ratio scale. The purpose is to compare a set of numbers with respect to their *relative* sizes rather than with respect to their actual numerical difference. For example, 1000 is *twice as large* as 500, as is 2 compared to 1. Interestingly enough, the *logarithm* of 1000 is 3 whereas of 500 it is 2.698970, giving us a *difference in logarithms* of .301030. The logarithm of 2 is .301030 and the logarithm of 1 is 0, also giving us a difference of .301030. Thus if one number is twice the size of another, the difference in their logarithms will be .301030, *regardless* of how big or small the numbers are. If one number is three times as large as another, the difference in their logarithms will be .477121, and so forth. Hence, whenever we are interested in the *relative* sizes of numbers, we find that the logarithms of these numbers show equal differences whenever the relative differences are equal, even though the actual differences between the numbers in the pairs are quite unequal, just as we saw in the example above.

Since it would be very tiresome to actually look up logarithms to compare relative sizes, or actually calculate the relative differences by dividing one number by another, it has seemed appropriate to construct what we call a *logarithmic scale*. This is a scale so constructed that the distances between the numbers listed on the scale is according to the differences between the logarithms of the numbers rather than according to the differences between the numbers themselves. An illustration should make this clear. Table 4.2 shows the logarithms of the first 20 integers.

There are several interesting things to note about this table. First, the difference between successive logarithms declines even though the difference between the successive number equivalents remains constant. This makes sense because the relative differences between successive numbers should be smaller as the numbers get bigger. Eventually, of course, the relative difference between successive numbers gets to be practically 0. Note also that the logarithmic differences between the logs of 1 and 2, 3 and 6, 2 and 4, 4 and 8, 5 and 10, 7 and 14, etc. are all .301030. Those between 1 and 3, 2 and 6, 6 and 18, etc. are all .477121.

If we now make up a scale that is actually laid out so that equal distances represent equal *logarithms*, but, instead of making an index to the scale by writing down the logarithm, we write down the *num-*

TABLE 4.2

Logarithms of First 20 Integers

Number	Differences between Successive Numbers	Logarithm of Number	Differences between Successive Logarithms
1	. . .	0.000000	. . .
2	1	.301030	0.301030
3	1	.477121	.176091
4	1	.602060	.124939
5	1	.698970	.096910
6	1	.778151	.079181
7	1	.845098	.066947
8	1	.903090	.057992
9	1	.954243	.051153
10	1	1.000000	.045757
11	1	1.041393	.041393
12	1	1.079181	.037788
13	1	1.113943	.034762
14	1	1.146128	.032185
15	1	1.176091	.029963
16	1	1.204120	.028029
17	1	1.230449	.026329
18	1	1.255273	.024824
19	1	1.278754	.023481
20	1	1.301030	.022276

ber that has such a logarithm, we would then have a *logarithmic scale*. Figure 4.3 shows the successive stages in the construction of a logarithmic scale. Part *A* shows an ordinary equal division scale with logarithmic values along the vertical axis. Note that equal distances along the scale are matched with equal differences between the logarithms. Part *B* shows exactly the same scale as in *A* except for the change from an index in logarithms to an index of their number equivalents. For example, the logarithm .301030 has been replaced by 2, its number equivalent, the logarithm 1.204120 by 16, its number equivalent, etc. Part *C* shows the same scale and markings as *B* but with additional divisions and markings for the intermediate numbers.

Part *C* is the characteristic form of the logarithmic scale. Ready-

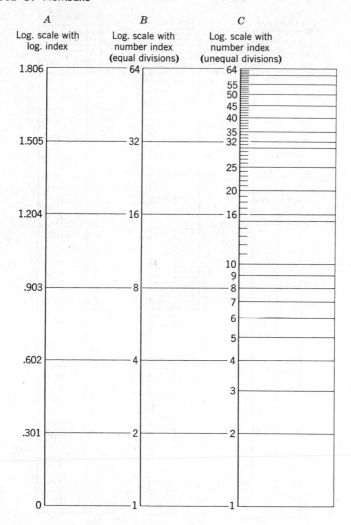

Fig. 4.3 Stages in construction of a logarithmic scale.

made scales of this type can be purchased. Figure 4.4 reproduces some samples of such commercially available paper. We should note some of the most important characteristics of logarithmic scales. First, 0 or any negative number is *never* marked on the index. The technical reason is that there is no logarithm for either 0 or for negative numbers. Another way to see the logic of no 0 and no negative numbers is to measure the relative increase, say, from

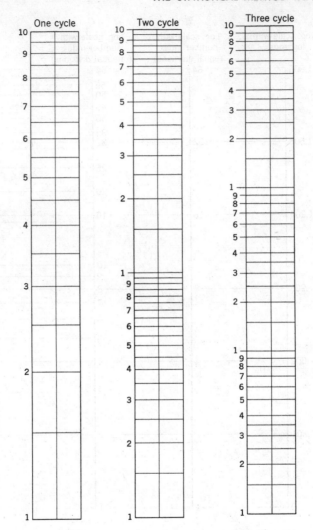

Fig. 4.4   Samples of logarithmic scales.

0 to 25, or from −8 to 124.   It is clear that these measurements cannot logically be made.

Another thing we note is that if we wish to change the scale because our problem is dealing with numbers that start in the neighborhood of 220, we change the markings supplied by the manufacturer by *multiplying* every given index by a *constant*, say, by 200.   Figure 4.5 illustrates such a change.   It is wrong to *add* or *subtract* numbers

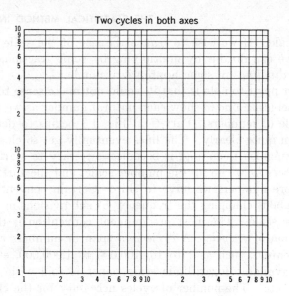

Two cycles in both axes

Fig. 4.4 Continued.

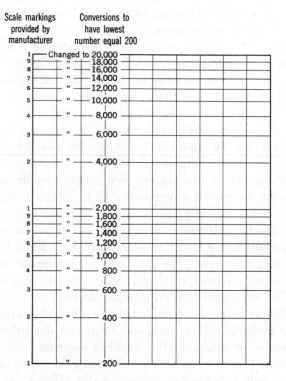

Scale markings provided by manufacturer	Conversions to have lowest number equal 200
1	Changed to 20,000
9	" 18,000
8	" 16,000
7	" 14,000
6	" 12,000
5	" 10,000
4	" 8,000
3	" 6,000
2	" 4,000
1	" 2,000
9	" 1,800
8	" 1,600
7	" 1,400
6	" 1,200
5	" 1,000
4	" 800
3	" 600
2	" 400
1	" 200

Fig. 4.5 Illustration of proper way to change a logarithmic scale.

on a log scale. If we wish to *reduce* the size of the scale markings or index, we can do this by multiplying by some fraction, or, if we prefer, by *dividing* by some appropriate number.

A further point to note is that it would not make sense to continue to have a separate line to show each natural number as we proceeded up the scale of numbers. Part *C* in Fig. 4.3 begins to demonstrate the problem quite clearly. The lines eventually get so close that we cannot distinguish them, and it becomes necessary to start skipping some numbers as we go up the number scale, and the further we go up, the more numbers we have to skip. Certain conventions have grown up about changing the frequency of subdivisions as we go up the number scale. The most predominent convention is that based on the notion of a *cycle*. A cycle is a span of numbers covering a range of tenfold, such as 1 to 10, 100,000 to 1,000,000, etc. Commercially available logarithmic scale paper is sold with one-cycle, two-cycles, etc. The number of cycles necessary for the charting of a given problem depends on the range of the numbers to be plotted. If the largest number is less than 10 times the smallest, one cycle is enough; if the largest is between 10 times the smallest and 100 times the smallest, two cycles are necessary, etc.

Sometimes we would like to compare the relative changes in two or more sets of numbers, such as the comparison of the changes in sales over time of two business firms. If the two series are quite different in magnitude, the two lines would be so far apart on the chart that detailed comparison would be most difficult. Figure 4.6 illustrates the probem. We can improve the situation by using two different scales on the same chart, one for the plotting of one series and one for the other. Figure 4.7 illustrates the improvement over Fig. 4.6 by the use of two scales. We could compare any number of series with the use of any number of logarithmic scales on the same chart.

Incidentally, it is generally not appropriate to use several different scales, or multiple scales, on the same chart if we are using ordinary equal-spaced graph paper, the kind we call *arithmetic* scale paper. We would attempt to compare several series this way only when we are interested in comparing the *relative* or *percentage* variations, and these are properly compared only with the use of logarithmic scales. The use of multiple arithmetic scales results in distortions.

A substitute for commercially-prepared logarithmic paper can be made by using the scales on a slide rule as a guide since the principal scales on a slide rule are logarithmic scales. The C and D scales

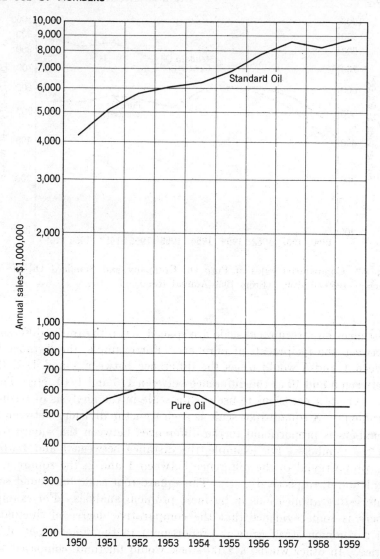

Fig. 4.6 Comparative sales of Pure Oil Company and Standard Oil of New Jersey—1950 to 1959. (From 1959 Annual Reports.)

show one cycle, the A and B scales show two cycles, and the K scale shows three cycles.

There are many other possibilities for special purpose scales in addition to the log scale. The most common of these are the reciprocal scale, the square-root scale, and the probability scale. The

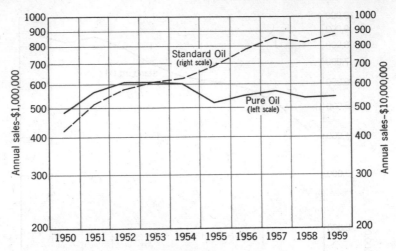

Fig. 4.7 Comparative sales of Pure Oil Company and Standard Oil of New Jersey—1950 to 1959. (From 1959 Annual Reports.)

distances on a reciprocal scale are spaced according to the differences between the reciprocals of numbers. For example, the distance between 1 and 5 would be as the difference between 1 and 1/5; that between 5 and 10 as the difference between 1/5 and 1/10; etc. There are very few occasions to use such a scale in the analysis of business problems. A square-root scale is such that the divisions between the numbers is proportional to the differences between the square roots of the numbers. For example, the distance between 1 and 4 would be proportional to the difference between 1 and 2, the square roots of 1 and 4, respectively, etc. The square-root scale has found some interesting applications in business problem analysis. For example, there is some evidence that the comparative degree of fluctuation of a common stock price is proportional to the *square root* of the price. In other words, a $100 stock would fluctuate compared to a $50 stock in the ratio of about 10 to 7 (the square roots of 100 and 50, respectively) instead of a ratio of about 2 to 1 as the actual prices would indicate. If the rule applied exactly, and if all other factors remained the same, we would expect the $50 stock to rise to $57 while the $100 stock was rising to $110.

The probability scale is really a normal curve scale, the normal curve being a special type of distribution which is widely applied in probability analysis. We touch upon the normal curve and on the probability scale in later pages.

4.4   Accuracy in Counting and Measuring

The numbers which result from the counting process are usually not strictly accurate. If we are counting integral units, such as boxes or chairs, we make mistakes in *identifying* the units, and we make mistakes in the actual counting. When we use standard units, we find that the object being measured almost always has a size that does not correspond to a whole number of units, thus involving us in fractional units; and our perceptive abilities are not sharp enough, even with the aid of instruments, to determine the *exact* size of the object being measured. Furthermore, as pointed out earlier, we do not measure the object directly anyway, thus leaving room for further error as we purport to measure one thing by measuring something else.

It is a good idea to be conscious of the limitations of the accuracy of the numbers with which we deal. Generally speaking we do not know exactly how accurate our numbers are. If we did, we would make the appropriate corrections. Our experience does give us usually some idea, however, of the *probable* magnitude of the errors. Ideally we would like to state our measurements in the form of the confidence we have, or the probability, that the true answer falls within a certain range. For example, if we were to measure the length of the room, we get an answer that we are 90% confident that the room is between 14.45 and 14.65 feet long. We would base such an answer either on repeated independent measurements of the room, treating each measurement as a *sample of all possible measurements*, or we might measure it only once and use our accumulated experience over the years with *many measurements of this type* to estimate the probable error we are subject to here. In any event, we would do our best to indicate to anyone concerned, including ourselves, the limits to accuracy of our basic numbers.

Unfortunately, common practice does not yet approach this ideal. Most numbers originate with no indication of their accuracy. The implication is that they are 100% accurate, although everybody knows that is not true. Physical scientists, of course, have been doing a good job in this connection for many years, and it is to them that we owe most of the conventions that have grown up around the concepts of *significant digits* and *precision* of numbers.

Significant Digits

A digit is defined as *significant* if it is correct within 1/2 of its unit. For example, if we state the length of the room as being 14.5 feet, it is understood that the true length is between 14.45 and 14.55 feet. It is generally assumed that we are *certain* that the true length would be within this range. It would be more appropriate perhaps if we considered it *practically certain* rather than certain. A careful worker never records a digit unless he feels it is significant in the above sense.

The location of the decimal point has nothing to do with the number of significant digits. The decimal point depends only on the size of the unit, and the size of the unit is strictly an arbitrary choice. A convention has grown up which makes it possible to indicate clearly the number of significant digits without complications introduced by the location of the decimal point. This convention is to show all the significant digits, put the decimal point before the last digit, and multiply by the power of ten that will put the decimal point where it belongs for the desired unit of measure. For example, suppose we have a count with four-digit accuracy which results in 4,826,000 if we consider the unit of measure. We make it clear that only four of the seven digits are significant by recording the result as 482.6×10^4. If we had left the number as 4,826,000, it is very possible that someone might assume that the last three zeros are significant. Another way to indicate that only the first four digits are significant is to write 4826 thousands. It is generally a good idea to assume that any zeros at the end of a number are not significant unless we believe that the person who created the number is a very careful worker. Zeros at the beginning of a number should never be counted as significant. For example, the number .00038 has only two significant digits. The number .000380, however, *should have* three significant digits and would have if recorded by a careful worker.

Precision

The *precision* of a number refers to the number of decimal places to which it is recorded. The number .00038 is more *precise* than the number 386, although 386 has more significant digits. Precision is thus associated with the unit of measure and not with accuracy per se. The reason we think of precision as akin to accuracy is that we are normally thinking of two things measured in the same unit. In that case, the more precise number will generally also have more significant digits, such as 369.48 feet vs. 468.5 feet.

4.5   Accuracy of the Results of Calculations from Numbers

The manipulation of partially accurate numbers by the standard methods of arithmetic creates the problem of the accuracy of the final results. The fundamental rule governing the accuracy of calculated results is that *the results cannot be any more accurate than the least accurate number included in the calculation.* Certain arbitrary rules have been adopted to help us abide by this general dictum. Although the rules are not perfect in application, they work well enough for most problems, and they are certainly much better than no rules at all.

Accuracy of Results of Addition and Subtraction

Rule: The *least* accurate number contained in addition and subtraction problems is the *least precise* number.

Thus the answer is no more precise than the least precise number included. The following three examples illustrate the application of the rule. The digits that have been marked out are those that

37.8027	.00378	14,806.29
48603.29	186,000.	26.8
261.832	40.87	.006
.06	9,426.2	973.48
48902.9847	195,467.07378	15,806.576
Rounded: 48902.98	195,000.	15,806.6

must be dropped. Note the rounding operation. If the leftmost digit being dropped is less than 5, no change is made in the last digit retained. If the leftmost digit being dropped is more than 5, the last retained digit is raised by 1. Note that this rule of rounding is consistent with the convention that the last significant digit should be correct within .5. If the leftmost digit being dropped is exactly 5, followed by nothing but zeroes (as far as we know), we then adopt a rule that in the long run will result in rounding up about as often as in rounding down. This rule is to round to the nearest *even* number. The rule might just as well be to round to the nearest *odd* number. The important point is to be consistent. The following examples illustrate the application of the rounding rules. The second number in the column is rounded from the first one in each case.

$$37,802.7 \quad 623.85 \quad 623.95 \quad 438.2 \quad 418.6571$$
$$37,803. \quad 623.8 \quad 624.0 \quad 438. \quad 418.7$$

Generally speaking, the results of addition are a little more accurate than these rules permit us to show. The increased accuracy results because the process of addition provides the opportunity for some of the errors in the original numbers to average out. We would expect to have about as many numbers with *plus* errors as we have with *minus* errors. This apparent gain in accuracy is not enough, however, to justify adding another digit. What it amounts to is: If we had a total, say, of 12,846.84, we would think of it as having a true value between 12,846.835 and 12,846.845. The averaging of errors process may have actually reduced the range to something between 12,846.838 and 12,846.842. We still cannot confidently put a digit in the third decimal place even though we have greater than normal accuracy in the second decimal place.

Accuracy of Results of Multiplication, Division, Squaring, Square Roots, Etc.

Rule: The *least* accurate number contained in multiplication, and similar problems, has the *fewest significant digits*.

The application of this rule is illustrated in the examples below. Note particularly the third example. The number 5 here is an absolute number, not the result of counting or measuring. Hence it really has an unlimited number of significant digits. Thus the num-

	486.97	.07948	63.8406
	$\times 3.18$	$\times 6.1$	$\times 5$
	1548.5646	.484828	319.2030
Rounded:	1550.	.48	319.203
or	15.5×10^2		

ber 5 places no restrictions on the accuracy of the final result. The number of digits in the final answer then depends on the *measured* number with the fewest significant digits. The reason no mention was made of absolute numbers in the discussion of addition and subtraction was that we almost never have occasion to use absolute numbers in these operations. Their use is quite common, however, in multiplication and division.

Since we generally do not multiply more than two numbers together at a time, we cannot rely on the law of averages to help reduce our final errors; it is entirely possible that our final answer is less accurate than these significant digit rules suggest. For example, if we multiply 4.6 by 8.3, the rules suggest an answer of 38. If, however, we are very unlucky, 4.6 may actually be as high as 4.65 and 8.3 as high as 8.35. If this were so, the final answer would be 39 instead of 38. Thus, in a sense, we can actually lose accuracy when we multiply. Fortunately, we have to be very unlucky for this to happen, so we do not worry about the problem very often.

4.6 Size Comparisons Based on Relative Frequency of Occurrence

One of the reasons we measure things is to facilitate comparisons. We have already referred to such comparisons as "twice as long," "twice as heavy," etc. We have also pointed out that there are some scales used that have no meaningful origin and hence no basis of making comparative statements of this type. We are still interested in comparisons however. Another way of comparing things quantitatively is by reference to their *relative frequency of occurrence*. An American male who is 6 feet 4 inches tall is not considered tall because he is 6 feet 4 inches. Rather he is considered tall because relatively few men are taller. It is not his size, but the *rarity* of his size that is important. Actually a man of 6 feet 4 inches is only about 9% taller than a man of average height. There are many dogs that are easily twice as big as many other dogs, but they still would not be considered big dogs because there are so many of them, and also there are many dogs still larger. What makes a grade of 95 on a test worth so much more than a grade of 75 is the rarity of the 95. The students are very quick to recognize the cheapening of the value of a 95 that takes place if 30% of the class achieves 95 or better.

This question of "how big is big?" is not always easy to answer because of the various ways we can answer it, getting apparently quite different results each time. For example, one of the continuing issues in American society has been the matter of "big business." Is a business big because its annual sales volume is $10,000,000 more a year than its average competitor's, or than its average customer's? Or because its volume is 75% more? Or because its volume is the largest of any company in the industry? What should we compare with? All the steel companies are giants compared with department stores, but some steel companies are pygmies compared to United States Steel.

In almost all problems involving the *rating* of people we find what is important is not, say, how much below average a person is, but rather it is the issue of how many people are above him or below him. For example, if the average sales of a salesman in our company are $225,000 per year, we really do not know how bad a salesman is who sells $110,000 until we know how many salesmen sell more or less than $110,000. The $110,000 figure might be at the bottom, or there may be 40% of the salesmen selling less. The distinction would make quite a difference to us if we were the salesman, or the sales manager.

Our ability to measure the relative frequency of things according to some scale of measure can be a very potent tool of analysis and control. We may not know the origin of our scale in a meaningful sense, and we may not really know what is implied by a difference in one unit in our scale, but, if our scale still makes it possible to rank people in the proper order and in the proper frequency, we are still able to make intelligent decisions based on measurements derived from such a scale. For example, we really do not know what a condition of zero intelligence is. Nor do we know what 100 units of intelligence is. Nor do we know how much more intelligence is represented by 125 units than by 120 units. What we think we know is that the average score on a given test for intelligence is 100. We also think that scores on such a test will enable us to properly *rank* people in order of intelligence. We also think we are right when we say a person who scores 150 is very intelligent because very few people have been able to achieve such a high score. But it is fallacious to say that a person who scores 150 is twice as intelligent as a person who scores 75.

The system of percentile ranking, familiar to almost every school child in America, is an illustration of rating or measuring with reference to rank, or relative frequency of occurrence along some scale.

PROBLEMS AND QUESTIONS

4.1 Define briefly but accurately the meaning of the following words and phrases. If possible, make your definition more understandable by using numbers in it.

(*a*) Usually not more than $40
(*b*) Almost always between 60° and 70°
(*c*) Approximately 8%
(*d*) Most of the time over 280 feet

(e) Fairly close to 4 pounds

(f) Good chance of rain tomorrow

4.2   A driving rule often suggested by safety engineers is that "One should leave one car-length between himself and the car just ahead for every 10 miles of speed. Thus at 50 mph one should leave five car lengths."

How many feet are there in a "car length"?

4.3   The professional golfer will often make the following suggestions. Quantify the underlined words. For example, how many pounds of hand pressure should one apply to hold a club *firmly*?

(a) Hold the club *firmly*, but not in a death grip.

(b) Shift *most* of the weight to the left foot as you swing at the ball.

4.4   A new salesman is told by the sales manager to spend *more* time trying to sell those products with a large gross margin than on those products with a small gross margin.

How much more time should he spend?

4.5   You are told by the doctor to soak your injured wrist in *hot* water. How hot?

4.6   *Soft* music has been discovered to be a factor in increasing production in many plants and offices. How soft should it be?

4.7 (a) Measure the length of a room by "pacing it off." Record the result.

(b) Measure the length of the same room by using a *foot rule*. Record result.

(c) Measure the length of the same room by using a device (a piece of string is a possibility) that will stretch from one end to the other. Record the result.

(d) Which result is the most accurate? Explain.

(e) How long is the room? How do you know this?

4.8   What is the value of the pair of shoes you now have on, or last wore? How did you measure this?

4.9   Count the exact number of books you have in your room as of this moment. Have somebody else independently count the number of books.

Compare the results. If they are different, how do you explain the difference?

How many books are there really in the room? How do you know?

4.10   Suppose you worked in a super market and were asked to count the amount of cash in one of the cash registers before you took over the cashier duty. Would you count the checks that some people had presented for payment? Why or why not? Would you count the value of the soap coupons in the drawer? Why or why not? Would you count the register slip that had been signed on the back by the customer because she had inadvertently left her pocket book at home? Why or why not?

How much cash is there in the drawer?

4.11   What is actually being measured when you measure the following things? How accurate is the measurement?

(a) You weigh yourself on a bathroom scale.

(b) You determine the distance between two cities by noting the odometer reading on your automobile both at the beginning and at the end of your trip.

(c) You determine the number of kilocycles in the wavelength of your favorite radio station by reading it off the dial of your radio.

(d) You measure your blood pressure by going to the doctor and asking him to measure it and then to tell you what it is.

(e) You heft two baseball bats to "see" which one is lighter.

(f) You give two applicants for a job a "clerical skill" test. One scored 89 and the other 73.

4.12 The following *units* are in common use. Evaluate each from the point of view of the desirable qualities of a "good" unit.

(a) Ounce

(b) Dollar

(c) Mile

(d) Degrees Fahrenheit

(e) Minute

4.13 If you are asked to estimate the time with no reference to a clock or watch, what is the merit, if any, of stating the estimate in relatively "round" times, such as "3 o'clock," or "3:15," etc. rather than as "3:27 1/2"?

4.14 Interpret the following comparisons

(a) John is 5% taller than Tom.

(b) John is only half as amiable as Tom.

(c) Boiling water is almost seven times as hot as ice at sea level.

(d) Since Tom received a grade of 90 on the exam and John only a grade of 60, it is evident that Tom knew 50% more than John.

(e) John's shirt is only about half as red as Tom's.

(f) Consumers' prices are almost twice as high today as they were twenty years ago.

4.15 Collect figures on the annual dollar sales of the United States Steel Corp. and of the Wheeling Steel Co. for the last 20 years.

(a) Plot both series on the same logarithmic scale.

(b) Plot both series on the same graph but with multiple scales. Design the multiple scales to bring the two series of data as close together as possible.

(c) Comment on the comparative effectiveness of the two graphs in comparing the relative variations in the sales of the two companies.

(d) What did you find out about the history of the sales of the two companies?

(e) Which one do you expect to grow faster over the next 5 years? On what evidence do you base your decision?

4.16 If you ask your hostess to pour you only "half a glass of wine," do you expect the wine to be half-way up the side or do you expect an amount of wine equal to half the cubic content of the glass? How can she tell which you expect?

4.17 One of the arts of designing packages for products is to create the illusion of a greater quantity of product than is actually in the package. One device used is to direct the person's attention to one scale of measure by which the quantity is overstated and away from the true scale.

Study some packages that you are able to find on the shelf of a retail store and identify the two scales involved. Discuss the relationship between the two scales.

4.18 If you were running for political office, at which group would you direct your campaign: "confirmed" Democrats, "confirmed" Republicans, or those near the borderline? Why? How could you tell which were which?

4.19 Assume that your total affection for vegetables can be represented by "1." Make up a scale running from 0 to 1 and mark off on the scale the degree of affection you have for various kinds of vegetables. Do these degrees of affection vary from time to time or from situation to situation? Explain.

4.20 Worker A has been averaging only 20 assemblies an hour in a radio factory compared with an average of 30 assemblies for the whole group. How good a worker is A?

4.21 The company economist forecast the company sales for a given year as $77,500,000. The actual sales turned out to be $83,634,916. How good a forecast was this?

4.22 A student received a grade of 68 in his math class with the class averaging 79. He received a grade of 72 in his English class with the class averaging 77. In what subject did he do the better job? Explain. How much better?

4.23 The ability to make decisions, or "decisiveness," is generally considered to be one of the desirable qualities of a business executive. Explain how you would measure the degree to which a person has this quality or attribute. Indicate the basic unit of measure, the origin (if any), and whether your measure is basically a ranking or rating device rather than one which results in numbers which can be meaningfully compared.

4.24 Perform the indicated calculations and round the result to the appropriate number of significant digits.

(a) Addition

A.	34.8049	B.	478,000	C.	731.0846
	3508.91		36.387		9.0000
	614.357		781.005		86.091
	3.60		1,184.29063		2437.8429

(b) Subtraction

A.	461.82	B.	738.126	C.	1136.284
	−12.07396		−181		−24375.19

(c) Multiplication

A.	1439.563	B.	175,000	C.	4.3894
	×3.41		×37.5		×6

(d) Division

A. $28.3\overline{)94.873}$ B. $6.937\overline{)}.0068$ C. $8\overline{)14.92715}$

(e) Square root

A. $274.183^{1/2}$ B. $497^{1/2}$ C. $.004283^{1/2}$

(f) Logarithm

A. 3.47   B. 124   C. 4,839.260

(g) Antilogarithm

A. .28   B. 2.079367   C. −1.8174

(h) Reciprocal

A. $\dfrac{1}{.347}$ B. $\dfrac{1}{29.006}$ C. $\dfrac{1}{28}$

4.25 It has been somewhat traditional to establish classes of students in the grade schools according to *age*. What is the logic behind this system in contrast to a system that establishes classes according to ability to learn?

4.26 A generation or so ago many public school systems in the United States split the grades into two parts, with a student moving through a grade in two steps rather than one as is more common today. Thus a youngster progressed through 16 steps on his way through grammar school instead of 8 steps. What are the comparative merits of 16 vs. 8 steps? What would you think of a two-step system, with a student spending 4 years in each step?

4.27 If you were designing an ideal grading system, how many categories would you establish? For example, would you be satisfied with a two-category system, with grades of "pass" and "fail," or would you like a system with, say, 100 categories? Explain.

4.28 What are the comparative merits of a wage and salary plan based on only a very limited number of worker categories and one based on as many categories as there are workers? Or, in other words, should all workers on the "same" job get paid the same amount?

4.29 Henry Ford made millions of dollars selling automobiles while offering only a few body styles and no choice of color, horsepower, transmission, etc. Today's manufacturers offer many body styles, many colors and color combinations, many horsepower options, etc. They don't offer everybody a different car, but they certainly come considerably closer than Ford ever did.

What are the business aspects of trying to cover the range of a market with just a few models and trying to cover it with many models?

Why don't toothpaste manufacturers each offer several different models, at least, say, with respect to flavor?

4.30 Why do high-priced restaurants generally offer a more varied fare than low-priced restaurants?

chapter 5

Elements of probability calculations

We defined *probability* as "the relative frequency with which *we expect* an event to occur over the *indefinite long run*." We use the notion of probability to help us deal with events which, as far as we know, occur on no predictable time schedule and because of no known and controllable causes. We emphasize again that probabilities are based on *hypotheses* which we hold. We might base these hypotheses on all kinds of evidence, such as certain physical characteristics of the event in question, our past experience with the event, or even hunch and intuition. Each person is his own boss in selecting hypotheses. The only operating rule is that a person must accept both the rewards and the losses associated with his hypotheses.

5.1 The Fundamental Assumption of Randomness

All mathematical manipulations of probabilities are based on the assumption that the events occur in a *random* manner; a random manner is such that as far as we know there is no relation between the characteristic being sampled and the way in which the sample is selected. After we have established the randomness of the occurrence of the events, and we do this quicker the less knowledge we have, the only other element needed for calculating probabilities is a hypothesis about the relative frequency of the items in the universe. The *relative* quality of the final results will depend on how much knowledge the person has compared to other people. Whenever something is treated as though it were random, it is treated on a base of ignorance. If knowledge were not costly to acquire and if knowledge were always possible to acquire, the ideal practice would be to never assume anything as random.

Our discussion of the concept of randomness in Chapter 2 pointed out that a logical consequence of our definition of randomness is "each event in the universe has the same chance of occurring." The notion of equal chance is what forms the basis of the mathematical models used in probability calculations. There is nothing magical or mysterious about this model. It is something that men have created and which seems to work. It is not a proper question to ask whether this model is right or wrong in a given problem. In a sense, it is always wrong. In another sense, it is always right. The only fair question to ask is whether the model works better than any other solution method currently available. We are quite sure it does not work as well as some methods we hope to have available 10 years from now.

5.2   The Notion of Equal Chance or Equal Probability

A *universe*, regardless of its general character,[1] is conceived of as consisting of a number of *individual* members, each member separate and distinct from each other member and separately identifiable. An ordinary playing card universe, for example, has 52 separate and distinct members. A coin universe has two separate and distinct members. It is events such as these that we are thinking about when we think of equal chance. Thus, fundamentally, the probability of any specific event occuring is $1/N$, with N being the total number of all these individual events in the universe. Any probability that we work with that is greater than $1/N$, such as $15/N$, is a *derived* probability. That is, it is derived from the basic probabilities of $1/N$. We can get probabilities greater than $1/N$ only because we have decided to ignore certain differences between individual events and group some events together as though they were the same. For example, we might ignore the differences in suits between cards in a deck and say that the probability of an 8 is $4/52$. Or, if we are tossing 3 different coins at the same time, we might ignore the individual character of the coins and say that the probability of getting two heads and one tail is $3/8$, thus assuming that we do not care which coins have heads and which coin has the tails. But the probability of any given combination of two heads and one tail would be only $1/8$.

Since in most problems it is absolutely essential that we do com-

---

[1] The various kinds of universes were discussed in Chapter 2.

bine some items and treat them as all of the same kind, for the same reasons that the automobile manufacturer does treat some of his customers as though they all had the same preferences, most practical problems in probability calculations consist of forming the proper *combinations* of items. This is the problem that makes probability calculation so fascinating, and difficult, too. The rest of this chapter is concerned with the main outlines of the available techniques for attacking the problem of calculating the probability of combinations or groups of items.

5.3 Simple Events vs. Complex Events

The King of Hearts is a *simple* event. If we have a set of five cards, such as a set containing the King of Hearts, the Eight of Spades, the Three of Diamonds, the Jack of Spades, and the Nine of Hearts, we have a *complex* event. In general, we can say that a simple event is one that contains only *one* of the individual items in the basic universe. A complex event is one that contains *more than one* of the individual elements in the basic universe. The individual items in a complex event do not have to be *different* in the terms of the problem. For example, if we toss three coins at the same time and get three heads, we have a complex event because we have three heads. The fact that they are all heads is irrelevant to this definition.

Most events we deal with in practice are complex. This is true even in games that we create. Practically all card games involve hands of more than one card. Most dice games consist of tossing more than one die. In more practical affairs we find that a simple event provides so little information on which to base a decision that we automatically find ourselves dealing with complex events as a matter of choice. The baseball manager likes to see the rookie bat more than once before making a decision about him. The teacher likes to ask the student more than one question before determining the grade. The automatic screw machine operator wants to test more than one bolt before he decides to stop the machine for adjustment.

The best way to think about the probabilities of complex events is to first think about the *universe of complex events that is generated by the universe of simple events*. This idea is best communicated by an illustration. Let us use the rather simple case of coin tossing. A simple event is the toss of one coin. The universe of equal probabilities contains one head (H) and one tail (T). If we toss two coins, or one coin twice, we have the complex event of the results of two coin tosses. This universe of equal probabilities contains four events, HH, HT, TH, and TT. The probability, therefore, of any one of these four complex events is $1/4$. Table 5.1 lists the universes of equal probabilities for one coin, two coins, three coins, four coins, and five coins.

The most notable feature of complex events quite evident from the table is that the more complex the event the more events in the universe. In fact, the number of events increases much faster than the number of items in the event. For example, five times as many coins results in 16 times as many events. It is easy to see why a card game with many cards in a hand has many more possibilities than a game with only a few cards in a hand. In this sense, the game of bridge is much more complex than the game of poker. An obvious and important consequence of this phenomenon, namely an increase in the number of possibilities as the complexity of the event increases, is that a *complex event is always less likely to occur than a simple event* from the same basic universe.

Again we remind ourselves that, because of the equal probability assumption, the probability of any event is $1/N$, with N being the number of events in the universe. The only way we can get probabilities greater than $1/N$ is to determine the probability of combinations of events. For example, in the case of tossing four coins, we find the probability of $HHHT$ to be $1/N$, or $1/16$; but the probability of three heads and one tail, with no concern for which coins are heads and which one tails, is $4/16$ because there are four events with three heads and one tail.

Since the probability of a single event is always $1/N$, the determination of such a probability depends only on the determination of N. The first step in determining N is to find its value for simple events. This involves the determination of the number of different distinguishable *values* of the thing being measured. For example, in coin tossing there are only two possible results (we toss the coin again if it lands on end). We might arbitrarily assign a value of 1 to a head and a value of 0 to a tail. In card drawing there are 52 possible results if the suit is considered important. If the suit is not important, there are only 13 possible results.

When we leave game devices and turn to phenomena of the real world, the problem of determining the value of N for simple events becomes considerably more difficult in one sense, and considerably easier in another. For example, suppose we ask ourselves the ques-

TABLE 5.1

Universes of Equally Probable Events for Tosses of Varying Numbers of Coins

1 Coin	2 Coins	3 Coins	4 Coins	5 Coins
H	*HH*	*HHH*	*HHHH*	*HHHHH*
T	*HT*	*HHT*	*HHHT*	*HHHHT*
————	*TH*	*HTH*	*HHTH*	*HHHTH*
2 Events	*TT*	*HTT*	*HTHH*	*HHTHH*
	————	*THH*	*THHH*	*HTHHH*
	4 Events	*THT*	*HHTT*	*THHHH*
		TTH	*HTHT*	*HHHTT*
		TTT	*HTTH*	*HHTHT*
		————	*TTHH*	*HHTTH*
		8 Events	*THHT*	*HTHHT*
			THTH	*HTHTH*
			HTTT	*HTTHH*
			THTT	*THHHT*
			TTHT	*THHTH*
			TTTH	*THTHH*
			TTTT	*TTHHH*
			————	*TTTHH*
			16 Events	*TTHTH*
				TTHHT
				THHTT
				THTHT
				THTTH
				HHTTT
				HTHTT
				HTTHT
				HTTTH
				TTTTH
				TTTHT
				TTHTT
				THTTT
				HTTTT
				TTTTT
				————
				32 Events

tion, "how many different heights might a person be?" We think, of course, that the person might be any one of an *infinite* number of heights *if* we were able to measure the person's *exact* height. In fact, with exact measurement we would find that there are no two people in the world of the same height. If this is startling, keep in mind that a person might conceivably be 5.7380927411748329406 feet tall, a height which is a little different from 5.7380927411748329407 feet. Thus we could consider that N is equal to infinity and that the probability that a person is any given height is $1/\infty$, which is practically 0. If we do not measure these events exactly, but round the measurement to a certain number of significant digits, we discover that some of the events do have the *same values by our measurements*. If we treat these latter values as our basic events, we now discover that the basic events are *not equally probable* because some of them occur more often than others. Thus we are forced to recognize that our inability to measure exactly automatically throws some simple events into the same class and forces us to treat them as though they were identical.

In most practical problems we really do not have any occasion to deal with individual simple events. We deal with combinations or groups of such events, with the various combinations or groups having different probabilities. We could now move to a discussion of how to determine these various group probabilities, but we do not move to such practical problems now, however, because experience suggests that the oversimplifications of games of chance make it possible to understand some basic principles of probability calculation better than if they were discussed in the context of a practical problem. In fact, many of the techniques eventually used in practical problems originated from thinking stimulated by the probability problems of games of chance. In addition, many people find games of chance interesting in their own right.

After we have determined the number of equally probable simple events we have to deal with, we are in a position to derive the number of equally probable complex events that can be generated by these simple events. One way to determine the total number is to *list* all the possible complex events. This can be very time consuming. It can also be very frustrating as we try to avoid leaving out any events or listing any event more than once. The average person does not find it easy to list the events that might happen when we toss only five coins, let alone 10 coins, particularly if we do not know how many events there should be in the list. A simpler way to find out the total number of events is to use a logical procedure. Let us work out a logical procedure for determining the number of complex events for a few coin and card problems.

One logical approach is to draw a *tree* of all the possibilities. Figure 5.1 shows the tree for the possible results for the tossing of four coins. This is rather easy to do correctly because all we do is have any given branch generate two branches, and each of these generates two branches, etc., until we have the desired number of stages. Each event can be determined by tracing all possible paths from the trunk to the tipmost branch. For example, working along the left branches, we have the events *HHHH, HHHT, HHTH, HHTT*. A simple count reveals that there are 16 tips and hence 16 of the four-coin events. If we were interested in five coins, we would split each of the four-coin branches into two branches. And so forth. Of course, drawing trees soon gets tedious, and is, therefore, a rather impractical method. Nevertheless, the technique of drawing trees is very valuable in helping us think through a problem, even if all we do is to draw certain parts of the tree to get some idea of the dimensions of the problem.

Reflection about the problem just given reveals the obvious fact that we can calculate the number of complex events for a given stage by multiplying the number of possibilities at the preceding stage by 2. The possibilities for successive stages would be: one coin—2; two coins—2 × 2, or 4; three coins—4 × 2, or 8; four coins

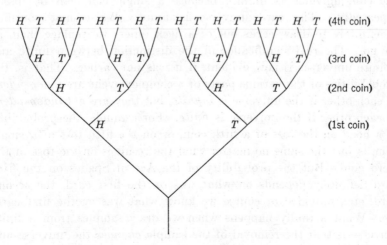

Fig. 5.1 Tree of possibilities for tossing of 4 coins.

—8 × 2, or 16; etc. Another way to conceive of this calculation is to raise the number of basic possibilities (2) to the power equal to the number of coins. For example, the number of possibilities for four coins would be 2^4, or $2 \times 2 \times 2 \times 2$, or 16. The number of possibilities for eight coins would be 2^8, or 256.

Now let us look at the problem of playing cards. We again start with the device of the tree; but we are not going to draw the whole tree because this tree starts out with 52 branches from the main trunk, 51 branches from each of these, etc. We simulate the missing branches by putting a sign on the end of a branch to indicate how many branches are represented by that one. (See Fig. 5.2.)

The most notable difference between the coin problem and the card problem, other than the fact that there are many more possibilities to count with the cards, is that a given card can occur only *once* in the complex event whereas a given value of the coin, such as a head, can occur as many times as items in the complex event. Each branch of the coin tree kept generating two new branches, and this process of generation could go on indefinitely. But each branch of the card tree generates *one fewer* branches than its parent. Eventually the card tree reaches the limit to its growth, namely after 52 generations. The coin tree has no limit. The cause of this difference between coins and cards is the difference in the character of the universes and/or the difference in the way the various parts of the complex event are chosen. In an earlier chapter we made a distinction between finite and infinite universes. In that sense the coin universe is infinite because a single coin can be tossed repeatedly. The card universe is finite. We cannot continue indefinitely to draw cards out of a deck unless we replace them as we go. The real significance of the distinction between finite and infinite universes is now evident, if it was not earlier. That is, the probabilities of the various parts of a complex event are *independent* of each other if the universe is *infinite*, but they are *not independent* of each other if the universe is *finite*. For example, the probability of a head on the toss of a fifth coin, or on the fifth toss of a single coin, is just the same no matter what the result is on the toss of the third coin. But the probability of the Ace of Spades on the fifth card definitely depends on what was on the first card, the second card, etc., provided of course we know what was on the first card, etc. What actually happens when we draw samples from a finite universe is that the removal of the sample *changes* the universe and

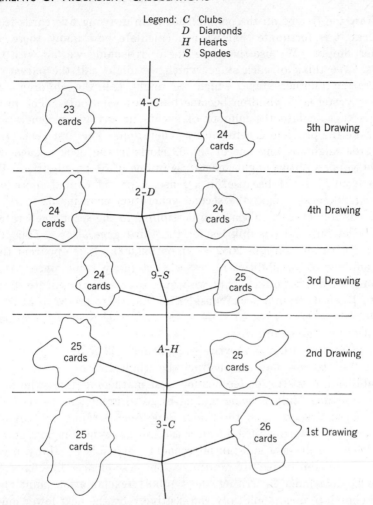

Legend: C Clubs
D Diamonds
H Hearts
S Spades

4-C

23 cards

24 cards

5th Drawing

2-D

24 cards

24 cards

4th Drawing

9-S

24 cards

25 cards

3rd Drawing

A-H

25 cards

25 cards

2nd Drawing

3-C

25 cards

26 cards

1st Drawing

Fig. 5.2 Tree of possibilities for the drawing of 5 cards from an ordinary deck. (Note: The number in the "foliage" refers to the number of "branches" that might have been chosen at that particular drawing in addition to the one that was chosen. The vertical branches represent those chosen.)

all the probabilities of the items still in it, and at the same time, of course, reduces to 0 the probability that a drawn item will be drawn again. This is why a poker hand with two Aces of Spades is considered quite remarkable and suspicious.

Because we realize what a tedious job we would have if we tried to draw the tree of all the possibilities from drawing five cards from a deck, it is fortunate that we can calculate how many there are rather simply. We use the same line of reasoning we did with the coins. We think of each stage, which we might call the parent, as generating another stage, which we might call the children. Of course yesterday's children become tomorrow's parents. The problem is to calculate the number of events in any given generation. We take the problem generation by generation. The first generation of cards might be any one of the 52 cards in the deck. Each one of those possibilities might generate any one of 51 possibilities. We drop from 52 to 51 because, in a sense, a parent cannot reproduce its own likeness. Thus the second generation contains 52×51, or 2652 possible events. Then each possibility in the second generation can beget only 50 possibilities for the third generation. Thus the third generation contains 2652×50, or 132,600. It is apparent that the number of possibilities increases at a fairly rapid pace. It is obvious why it is unlikely that we would ever see a duplicate drawing of 13 cards from a deck, considering that there are $52 \times 51 \times 50 \times 49 \times 48 \times 47 \times 46 \times 45 \times 44 \times 43 \times 42 \times 41 \times 40$ different possibilities for a given drawing.

Incidentally, although to write and calculate $52 \times 51 \times \ldots \times 40$ is far less tedious than to construct the whole tree or to list all the possibilities, it is still too tedious for most mathematicians, who have the interesting fault of being willing to go to great lengths to avoid work. (At first, some of the things done seem strange and complicated and not worthwhile, but after the initial shyness it is apparent that they result in a substantial economy of effort.) Many problems in probability require multiplication of sequences like 52×51, etc. To economize in writing, the symbol ! (exclamation point) has been chosen to mean "multiply consecutively by the next lower number, and then the next lower number until 1 is reached." For example, 5! means to determine the product of 5, 4, 3, 2, 1. 52! means to determine the product of 52, 51, . . . 3, 2, 1. 52!/39! means to determine the product of 52, 51, etc. and then divide the result by the product of 39, 38, . . . 3, 2, 1. Note that this would give exactly the same answer as $52 \times 51 \times \ldots \times 40$. Instead of writing $52 \times 51 \times 50 \times 49 \times 48 \times 47 \times 46 \times 45 \times 44 \times 43 \times 42 \times 41 \times 40$, we write 52!/39!.

To save the actual tedium of calculating, say, 39!, we can use the table given in Appendix C. The name applied to ! is factorial, and we say 39! as 39 factorial.

5.4   Systems for Calculating the Probabilities of Combinations of Items

As already indicated, most problems are more concerned with groups or combinations of events than with single events of equal probability. Now we must not only determine the number of all the equally likely events (N), but we must also determine the number of such events that fall into the given group. We call this number C, and the probability of an event being in such a group we will call C/N.

The Technique of Listing and Counting

The most direct way to determine the probability that one item out of a given group of items will occur is to list all the events, count all of them that fall into a given group, and divide the number in the group (C) by the total number (N). For example, if we look at the list of events for the tossing of five coins as shown in Table 5.1, we are able to count five cases of four heads and one tail. If we form all the groups which would result if we ignore which particular coin is heads or tails, we would get the probabilities as shown in Table 5.2. We find that the 32 equally probable events can be combined into six groups. As we would logically expect, the probability of an item being in a given group is the *sum* of the probabili-

TABLE 5.2

Probabilities of Results of Tosses of 5 Coins—Order of Coins Ignored

Group	Number of Events in Group (C)	Probability of Item Being in Group (C/N)	
$5H, 0T$	1	1/32 or	.03125
$4H, 1T$	5	5/32 "	.15625
$3H, 2T$	10	10/32 "	.31250
$2H, 3T$	10	10/32 "	.31250
$1H, 4T$	5	5/32 "	.15625
$0H, 5T$	1	1/32 "	.03125
Totals:	32 (N)	32/32	1.00000

ties of each of the items in the group. In general, the probability of a group item is equal to or greater than the probability of a single item.

We also note that we now leave the equally probable events behind and are dealing with *different* probabilities for the various groups. But, do not forget that these unequal probabilities are still based on the assumption of equal probabilities for the individual events. All we have done is take 32 equally probable events and combine them into six groups or combinations. It so happens that the probabilities are different for some of the groups because they encompassed different numbers of items. Although this is what almost always happens in practice, it does not have to be that way. For example, if we take the 52 cards in a deck and form the 13 groups which result if we ignore the suit, we find that each of the groups is equally probable, although each group probability (1/13) is greater than the item probabilities (1/52).

The Binomial Theorem System of Counting

The system of listing and counting has obvious limitations. Fortunately, we have other systems of counting and of calculating probabilities of combinations of items. The binomial theorem, probably familiar in at least a limited way, is one such system.

The simplest expression of the binomial theorem is illustrated by $(a + b)^2 = a^2 + 2ab + b^2$. The binomial may be raised to any power, of course. For example, $(a + b)^5 = a^5 + 5a^4b + 10a^3b^2 + 10a^2b^3 + 5ab^4 + b^5$. It is possible to derive each term of the expansion from the preceding term. This system is: To get the coefficient of a term, multiply the coefficient of the preceding term by the exponent of a and divide this product by *1 more* than the exponent of b. Then decrease the exponent of a by 1 and increase the exponent of b by 1.

To get the third term in the above expansion from the second term, we multiply the coefficient 5 by the exponent of a, 4, giving a product of 20. We divide this by 2, which is 1 more than the coefficient of b. The result is 10, the coefficient of the third term. We then reduce the coefficient of a from 4 to 3 and raise the coefficient of b from 1 to 2.

The system just given for expanding the binomial is reasonably efficient if we need all the terms in the expansion. If we wish only certain specific terms, however, we prefer a system that enables us to derive a term without needing a reference to a preceding term or to any other term. We illustrate this system by using the binomial expansion to calculate the probabilities of the various outcomes of the tossing of five coins. The basic binomial is $(.5H + .5T)^5$. The values of the various terms can be calculated as shown in Table 5.3.

Let us first look at column 2 because this shows the relationship to the system we have already used of deriving a term from the preceding term. The first term has a coefficient of 1 with the $.5H$ raised to the 5th power and the $.5T$ to the 0th power. (Any expression raised to the 0th power $= 1$.) The second term has a coefficient of 5/1, which is the exponent of $.5H$ in the first term divided by one more than the exponent of $.5T$ in the first term. The exponent of $.5H$ is then reduced from 5 to 4 and that of the $.5T$ is raised from 0 to 1.

We now derive the third term as shown in column 2. We get the coefficient of the third term by multiplying the coefficient of the second term, which is (5/1), by the exponent of $.5H$ in the second term, which is 4, and then by dividing by one more than the coefficient of $.5T$ in the second term, which is 2. We then lower the exponent of $.5H$ by 1 and raise that of $.5T$ by 1.

All other terms are similarly derived. Note that we have enclosed the two parts of the coefficient in parentheses in each case so that it is clear what part is the coefficient of the preceding term and what part is the new factor.

Columns 3 and 4 are precisely the same as column 2 except for the shorthand introduced for the expression of the coefficients. Column 3 uses the factorial notation referred to on page 132. We should

TABLE 5.3

The Use of the Binomial Expansion to Calculate the Probabilities of the Various Outcomes on the Tossing of 5 Coins

Term No. (1)	Basic Term (2)	Shorthand 1 (3)	Shorthand 2 (4)	Value of Term (5)
1	$(1)(.5H)^5(.5T)^0$	$= \frac{5!}{5!0!}(.5H)^5(.5T)^0$	$= \binom{5}{5}(.5H)^5(.5T)^0$	$= .03125H^5T^0$
2	$(1)\left(\frac{5}{1}\right)(.5H)^4(.5T)^1$	$= \frac{5!}{4!1!}(.5H)^4(.5T)^1$	$= \binom{5}{4}(.5H)^4(.5T)^1$	$= .15625H^4T^1$
3	$\left(\frac{5}{1}\right)\left(\frac{4}{2}\right)(.5H)^3(.5T)^2$	$= \frac{5!}{3!2!}(.5H)^3(.5T)^2$	$= \binom{5}{3}(.5H)^3(.5T)^2$	$= .31250H^3T^2$
4	$\left(\frac{5.4}{1.2}\right)\left(\frac{3}{3}\right)(.5H)^2(.5T)^3$	$= \frac{5!}{2!3!}(.5H)^2(.5T)^3$	$= \binom{5}{2}(.5H)^2(.5T)^3$	$= .31250H^2T^3$
5	$\left(\frac{5.4.3}{1.2.3}\right)\left(\frac{2}{4}\right)(.5H)^1(.5T)^4$	$= \frac{5!}{1!4!}(.5H)^1(.5T)^4$	$= \binom{5}{1}(.5H)^1(.5T)^4$	$= .15625H^1T^4$
6	$\left(\frac{5.4.3.2}{1.2.3.4}\right)\left(\frac{1}{5}\right)(.5H)^0(.5T)^5$	$= \frac{5!}{0!5!}(.5H)^0(.5T)^5$	$= \binom{5}{0}(.5H)^0(.5T)^5$	$= .03125H^0T^5$

be able to make the translation from the coefficients of column 2 to those of column 3 by applying our knowledge about factorial notation.

Now examine the coefficients of the various terms as shown in column 3, and note that they possess a very simple system. The numerator is always 5!. This corresponds to the *number of coins* in our problem. If we were to toss 20 coins, the numerator would be 20!. The denominator always consists of the *two* factorial numbers that correspond to the exponents attached to the parenthetical terms containing the H and the T. If we were to toss 20 coins, and we were interested in the probability of getting 7 heads and 13 tails, we would have to evaluate the term $\dfrac{20!}{7!13!}(.5H)^7(.5T)^{13}$.

The notation shown in column 4 is simply a further economizing on the shorthand of column 3. Since the two numbers in the denominator always add to the number in the numerator, there is no point in writing both of these numbers. Thus $\binom{5}{3}$ is understood to mean $\dfrac{5!}{3!2!}$. Since $\dfrac{5!}{3!2!}$ is the equivalent of $\dfrac{5!}{2!3!}$, $\binom{5}{3}$ is the equivalent of $\binom{5}{2}$. Similarly, $\binom{20}{7}$ is the equivalent of $\binom{20}{13}$. Terms such as $\binom{5}{2}$ are known as *binomial coefficients*.

Column 5 of Table 5.3 shows the results of the indicated arithmetic. The decimal fractions give the probability of getting the particular combination of heads and tails *provided* the basic probability of each is .5.

Binomial Tables. Although the use of the binomial expansion is certainly an improvement over the listing and counting system, it is obvious that the calculations are still quite tedious. For example, if we tossed 50 coins and wished the probability of getting 37 heads and 13 tails, we would have to evaluate the term $\dfrac{50!}{37!13!}(.5H)^{37}(.5T)^{13}$, which is a formidable task. Fortunately, tables are available on binomial probabilities.[1] Sample pages from such tables are shown in

[1] *Tables of the Binomial Probability Distribution,* National Bureau of Standards, Applied Mathematics Series 6, U.S. Government Printing Office, 1950. This volume gives the binomial probabilities for basic probabilities from .01 to .50 in steps of .01 and for sample sizes from 2 to 49.

Romig, Harry G., *50–100 Binomial Tables,* John Wiley and Sons, New York, 1952. This volume gives binomial probabilities for basic probabilities from .01 to .50 in steps of .01 and for sample sizes of 50 to 100 in steps of 5.

Appendix D. For example, the table tells us that there is a probability of about .0071 of getting 39 heads on the toss of 100 coins.

The tables also give the *cumulative* probabilities, that is, the probabilities of getting a result, say, no larger than the one specified. For example, the probability of getting 39 or fewer heads on the toss of 100 coins is about .0176. This is the sum of the probabilities of getting exactly no heads, exactly one head, exactly two heads, etc.

Since binomial probabilities have certain symmetrical properties, the tables provide only the minimum amount of information. This economizes on the size of the book of tables, but it does require a little adaptation on the part of the user. An example of the symmetry is evident if we compare the distribution of $(.4X + .6Y)^5$ with that of $(.6X + .4Y)^5$. These are mirror images of each other as shown in Table 5.4 and Fig. 5.3. The binomial tables show only the

TABLE 5.4

Comparing the $(.4X + .6Y)^5$ Binomial with the $(.6X + .4Y)^5$ Binomial

A. Given: $P(X) = .4$, $n = 5$.

X	Y	$P(X)$, or $P(Y)$	$P(X \geq X)$, or $P(Y \leq Y)$	$P(X \leq X)$, or $P(Y \geq Y)$
0	5	.0778	1.0000	.0778
1	4	.2592	.9222	.3370
2	3	.3456	.6630	.6826
3	2	.2304	.3174	.9130
4	1	.0768	.0870	.9898
5	0	.0102	.0102	1.0000

B. Given: $P(X) = .6$, $n = 5$.

X	Y	$P(X)$, or $P(Y)$	$P(X \geq X)$, or $P(Y \leq Y)$	$P(X \leq X)$, or $P(Y \geq Y)$
0	5	.0102	1.0000	.0102
1	4	.0768	.9898	.0870
2	3	.2304	.9130	.3174
3	2	.3456	.6826	.6630
4	1	.2592	.3370	.9222
5	0	.0778	.0778	1.0000

NOTE: $P(X)$ means probability of X; $P(X \geq X)$ means probability of X equal to or greater than that specified, etc.

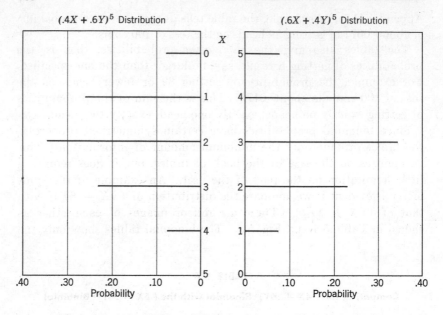

Fig. 5.3 Comparing the $(.4X + .6Y)^5$ binomial with the $(.6X + .4Y)^5$ binomial.

$(.4X + .6Y)^5$ distribution. If our problem requires the $(.6X + .4Y)^5$ distribution, we must interchange X and Y.

Similar symmetry must be used if we use the tables for the cumulative probabilities. For example, the National Bureau of Standards Tables show that the probability of *two or more X's* is .6630 if the basic probability of an X is .4 and if a sample of 5 is taken. Suppose we wished the probability of *one or fewer X's*. The NBS tables do not give this result directly, but it is very easy to derive by subtracting the probability of *two or more X's*, which is .6630, from 1, thus getting a probability of *one or fewer X's* of .3370. If the basic probability had been .6 instead of .4, a little more juggling would be required. *Two or more X's* is the same as *one or fewer Y's*. Hence, if we have a basic X probability of .6 and we wish the probability of two or more X's, we find the probability of one or fewer Y's with a basic probability of .6 and subtract this from 1. But, the probability of one or fewer Y's with a basic probability of .6 is the same as the probability of four or more X's with a basic probability of .4. Thus we arrive at the probability of two or more X's with a basic probability of .6 by subtracting from 1 the probability of four or more X's with a basic probability of .4. This sounds confusing to keep straight, but it becomes easier after working with the tables a bit. (The material in Table 5.4 may be of some help in understanding these steps of adaptation.)

Model Frequency Distributions as Systems of Approximate Counting

Tables of the binomial distribution have been available only in recent years. Before then a person had to do his own calculating or use approximation methods. We find, therefore, that statistical theory and statistical practice has been largely developed in terms of *approximate* methods of calculating probabilities. Such approximate methods would have likely been worked out even if binomial tables had been available over the last half century or so because of certain limitations in the practicality of binomial tables. Since each combination of basic probability (usually called p) and sample size (usually called N) results in a different distribution, binomial tables rather quickly become unwieldy in size if they are to cover a reasonable number of the p,N combinations that are likely to occur in practice. For example, the NBS tables cover 387 oversize pages despite the fact that at least half the combinations are left to be worked out by the user from the material given in the tables. In addition, most practical problems are not perceived clearly enough to justify the calculation of probabilities to several digits of accuracy. Most of the time we need only a rather moderate accuracy of estimation.

For these and other reasons, we find that approximation methods have and will continue to dominate the calculation of probabilities. The most renowned approximation curve is that called the normal. It has also been called the *Gaussian curve* and the *normal law of error*. Its economical use of space can be immediately appreciated by reference to Appendix I, a table of the normal curve that is sufficiently accurate for most practical problems we are likely to encounter.

The Normal Curve as an Approximation to the Binomial. Figure 5.4 shows some pictures of the normal curve. The differences in their apparent shapes are caused by the use of different vertical and horizontal scales. The most commonly used standard shape is shown as B. Here it has the appearance of a bell, and the normal curve is often referred to as a bell-shaped curve. It is important, however, to remember that the normal curve has no actual standard shape. In plotting a distribution to see if it looks normal, care should be taken in choice of scales so that we do not mislead ourselves. The best way to check the normality of a distribution is to

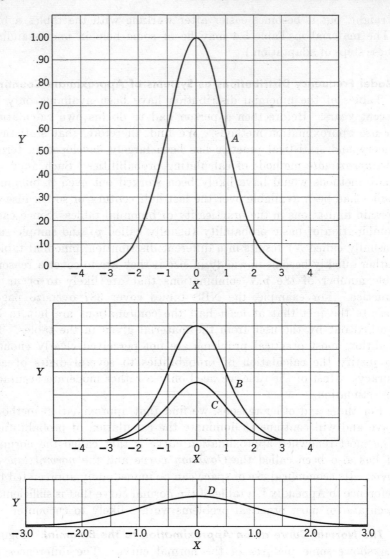

Fig. 5.4 Models of the normal curve.

fit a normal curve to the distribution and evaluate the accuracy of the fit or to plot the distribution on probability paper.

Table 5.5 and Fig. 5.5 compare the binomial and normal curve probabilities for the tossing of 2, 5, 10, 15, and 20 coins. (We discuss the method of estimating the normal curve probabilities shortly.)

TABLE 5.5

Binomial and Normal Curve Probabilities for Tossing of 2, 5, 10, 15, and 20 Coins

2 Coins

Proportion of Heads	Binomial Expecta-tion	Normal Curve Expectation
0	.250	.208
.5	.500	.564
1.0	.250	.208
	1.000	.980

5 Coins

Proportion of Heads	Binomial Expecta-tion	Normal Curve Expectation
0	.031	.029
.2	.156	.145
.4	.312	.323
.6	.312	.323
.8	.156	.145
1.0	.031	.029
	.998	.994

15 Coins

Proportion of Heads	Binomial Expecta-tion	Normal Curve Expectation
0	.000	.000
.0667	.000	.001
.1333	.003	.004
.2000	.014	.014
.2667	.042	.040
.3333	.092	.090
.4000	.153	.153
.4667	.196	.198
.5333	.196	.198
.6000	.153	.153
.6667	.092	.090
.7333	.042	.040
.8000	.014	.014
.8667	.003	.004
.9333	.000	.001
1.0000	.000	.000
	1.000	1.000

10 Coins

Proportion of Heads	Binomial Expecta-tion	Normal Curve Expectation
0	.001	.002
.1	.010	.010
.2	.044	.042
.3	.117	.114
.4	.205	.207
.5	.246	.252
.6	.205	.207
.7	.117	.114
.8	.044	.042
.9	.010	.010
1.0	.001	.002
	1.000	1.002

20 Coins

Proportion of Heads	Binomial Expecta-tion	Normal Curve Expectation
0	.000	.000
.05	.000	.000
.10	.000	.000
.15	.001	.001
.20	.005	.005
.25	.015	.015
.30	.037	.036
.35	.074	.073
.40	.120	.120
.45	.160	.161
.50	.176	.178
.55	.160	.161
.60	.120	.120
.65	.074	.073
.70	.037	.036
.75	.015	.015
.80	.005	.005
.85	.001	.001
.90	.000	.000
.95	.000	.000
1.00	.000	.000
	1.000	1.000

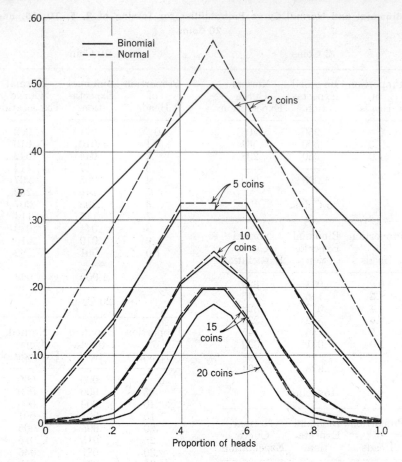

Fig. 5.5 Binomial and normal curve probabilities for tossing of 2, 5, 10, 15, and 20 coins.

It is quite evident that the normal curve probabilities are quite close estimates for as few as five coins. The estimates are so close for 20 coins that the two distributions appear as one in Fig. 5.5. The binomial and normal distributions get closer together as the number of coins, or size of sample, increases. In fact, it can be proved mathematically that the binomial does approach the normal distribution as N increases, with the two coinciding exactly when N reaches infinity.

A very quick way to check the applicability of a normal approximation to a given distribution is to plot the distribution on normal

probability scales. Paper with such scales is available commercially.
Figure 5.6 illustrates the use of such paper for checking the normality
of the distributions of the coins. Table 5.6 shows the *cumulative*
binomial probabilities on which Fig. 5.6 is based. A normal distribution would appear as a *straight* line on a probability scale. Note
that the line is practically straight in the case of the 20-coin distribution.

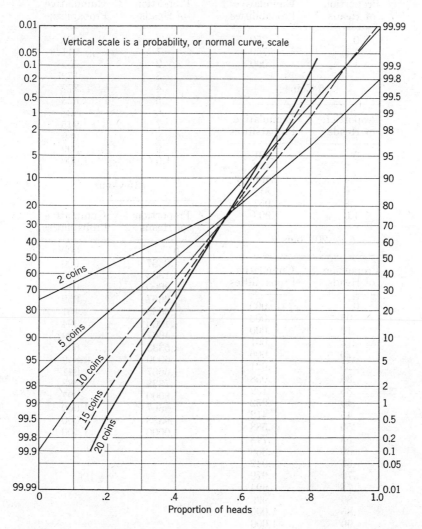

Fig. 5.6 Cumulative binomial distributions of coin tosses for tosses of 2, 5,
10, 15, and 20 coins.

TABLE 5.6

Cumulative Binomial Probabilities for Tossing of 2, 5, 10, 15, and 20 Coins

(The cumulative probabilities are those for the occurrence
of no more than the specified number of heads.)
(Rounding errors prevent some cumulative
probabilities from reaching exactly 1.)

2 Coins

Proportion of Heads	Cumulative Probabilities
0	.250
.5	.750
1.0	1.000

5 Coins

Proportion of Heads	Cumulative Probabilities
0	.031
.2	.187
.4	.499
.6	.811
.8	.967
1.0	.998

10 Coins

Proportion of Heads	Cumulative Probabilities
0	.001
.1	.011
.2	.055
.3	.172
.4	.377
.5	.623
.6	.828
.7	.945
.8	.989
.9	.999
1.0	1.000

15 Coins

Proportion of Heads	Cumulative Probabilities
0	.000
.0667	.000
.1333	.003
.2000	.017
.2667	.059
.3333	.151
.4000	.304
.4667	.500
.5333	.696
.6000	.849
.6667	.941
.7333	.983
.8000	.997
.8667	1.000
.9333	1.000
1.0000	1.000

20 Coins

Proportion of Heads	Cumulative Probabilities
0	.000
.05	.000
.10	.000
.15	.001
.20	.006
.25	.021
.30	.058
.35	.132
.40	.252
.45	.412
.50	.588
.55	.748
.60	.868
.65	.942
.70	.979
.75	.994
.80	.999
.85	1.000
.90	1.000
.95	1.000
1.00	1.000

Before we get too excited, however, about the accuracy of the normal curve as an estimator of the binomial, let us look at some cases in which the basic probability, or p, equals something other than .5. Dice throws offer a common example. Given equal likelihood for each of the six sides on a die, we have a basic probability of 1/6, or .1667, of getting a 6, say. Table 5.7 and Fig. 5.7 compare the binomial and normal curve probabilities for the throwing of 2,

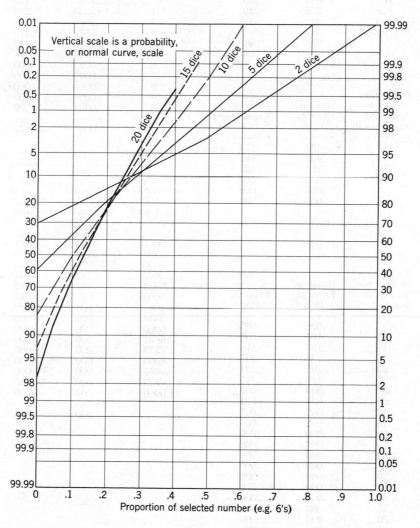

Fig. 5.7 Cumulative binomial distributions of dice throws for tosses of 2, 5, 10, 15, and 20 dice.

TABLE 5.7

Binomial and Normal Curve Probabilities for Throwing of 2, 5, 10, 15, and 20 Dice

2 Dice

Proportion of Any Selected No. from 1 to 6	Binomial Expectation	Normal Curve Expectation
0	.694	.620
.5	.278	.340
1.0	.028	.005
	1.000	.965

5 Dice

Proportion of Any Selected No. from 1 to 6	Binomial Expectation	Normal Curve Expectation
0	.402	.274
.2	.402	.580
.4	.161	.129
.6	.032	.003
.8	.003	.000
1.0	.000	.000
	1.000	.986

20 Dice

Proportion of Any Selected No. from 1 to 6	Binomial Expectation	Normal Curve Expectation
0	.026	.032
.05	.104	.090
.10	.198	.174
.15	.238	.235
.20	.202	.221
.25	.129	.145
.30	.065	.067
.35	.026	.021
.40	.008	.005
.45	.002	.001
.50	.000	.000
.55	.000	.000
.60	.000	.000
.65	.000	.000
.70	.000	.000
.75	.000	.000
.80	.000	.000
.85	.000	.000
.90	.000	.000
.95	.000	.000
1.00	.000	.000
	.998	.991

10 Dice

Proportion of Any Selected No. from 1 to 6	Binomial Expectation	Normal Curve Expectation
0	.162	.125
.1	.323	.288
.2	.291	.325
.3	.155	.179
.4	.054	.048
.5	.013	.006
.6	.002	.000
.7	.000	.000
.8	.000	.000
.9	.000	.000
1.0	.000	.000
	1.000	.971

15 Dice

Proportion of Any Selected No. from 1 to 6	Binomial Expectation	Normal Curve Expectation
0	.065	.062
.0667	.195	.161
.1333	.273	.260
.2000	.236	.260
.2667	.142	.161
.3333	.062	.062
.4000	.021	.015
.4667	.005	.002
.5333	.001	.000
.6000	.000	.000
.6667	.000	.000
.7333	.000	.000
.8000	.000	.000
.8667	.000	.000
.9333	.000	.000
1.0000	.000	.000
	1.000	.983

5, 10, 15, and 20 dice. Although we again note that the accuracy of the normal curve approximation improves with increasing N, just as it did with the coins, we must admit that the errors are still relatively large even when N is 20. It would be even worse if p were smaller than .1667 (or larger than .8333). The convergence of the binomial to the normal as N increases is still true, even when p departs from .5, but the sample size has to be larger for a reasonable approximation the further the departure of p from .5.

Once many people thought the normal distribution described the true state of nature. It even acquired the stature of a law to some (the normal law of error). Many students have been graded according to the normal curve, and are still being so graded. There is nothing inherently wrong with such an application as long as we are aware of what we are doing. Today, we are far less inclined to view the normal curve as anything more than a fairly versatile approximation device, with no presumption that the errors we encounter are due to the failure of the data to conform to the law. We are more inclined to view the errors as simply errors in the use of an approximation device.

Calculating Normal Curve Probabilities. The mathematical equation for a normal curve is the somewhat formidable looking

$$Y = \frac{Ni}{\sigma\sqrt{2\pi}}\, e^{-x^2/2\sigma^2}.$$

The meaning of each of the terms is:

Y = the height of the ordinate for some given value of x.

N = the total frequency in the distribution. This becomes 1 if we use relative frequencies, or probabilities.

i = the size of the class interval used for tallying frequencies. It is much more convenient if we use intervals of constant length.

σ = (sigma) the *standard deviation* of all the items in the distribution. This measures the degree of variation among the x's and is explained below.

π = the familiar constant with a value of 3.14159, which is the ratio of the circumference of a circle to the diameter.

e = another constant with a value of 2.71828. It is the base of the Naperian or *natural* system of logarithms. (Common logarithms use the base 10.)

x = a distance along the X-axis measured from the *arithmetic mean* as an origin, rather than from 0 as an origin.

If we fill in the values for the two constants π and e and assume we are working with relative frequencies, the equation simplifies to

$$Y = \frac{i}{2.5066\sigma} 2.71828^{-x^2/2\sigma^2}.$$

Since the selection of i is arbitrary, the only two unknowns in this equation are the *arithmetic mean* of the universe of possibilities and the *standard deviation* around that mean. The arithmetic mean is very familiar, having been explained probably as early as the fifth grade. It is commonly thought of as "the average." There are other averages, however, and we generally say *mean* when we are referring to the arithmetic average, or arithmetic mean. It is calculated by dividing the *sum* of a set of quantities by the *number* of such quantities in the set. If we use the Greek letter Σ (pronounced sigma), which is the equivalent of the English S (the first letter of the word sum), to signify "take the sum of," and if we use X to represent the values of the various quantities, and N to represent the number of quantities, the calculation of the arithmetic mean can be symbolized in shorthand as follows:

$$\text{Arithmetic mean} = \frac{\Sigma X}{N}.$$

We can simplify even more by using μ_x to represent the mean of X in the *universe*. μ (pronounced mu) is the Greek letter that corresponds to the English m. If we were referring to the mean in a *sample* of X values, we would symbolize it with m_x. Insofar as possible we try to use Greek letters to symbolize values calculated from a universe and English letters to symbolize those calculated from a *sample*. Another common way to symbolize the arithmetic mean is as $\overline{X}$ (pronounced X-bar), or as $\overline{Y}$, or $\overline{Z}$ as the case may be. Although $\overline{X}$ is usually used to symbolize the arithmetic mean of a sample, it is also used when we are talking in general terms, that is, when the distinction between sample and universe is of no importance. The context should make it clear in any given case.

The *standard deviation* is probably a new concept. Its purpose is to measure the *degree of variation* in a set of numbers. Consider the two following groups of numbers. It is quite obvious from direct observation that the numbers in Group A have less variation than those in Group B. The standard deviation of the Group A numbers is 1.4, that of Group B is 4.1, almost three times as great.

Group A	Group B
1	1
2	4
3	6
4	9
5	13

The method of calculating the standard deviation is very interesting. Table 5.8 shows the calculation of the standard deviation of the numbers in Group A. The steps in the calculation are:

1. Calculate the arithmetic mean.
2. Measure the deviation of each item from the arithmetic mean.
3. Square each of these deviations.
4. Determine the sum of these squared deviations.
5. Divide the sum of squared deviations by the number of items.
6. Take the square root of the result.

The logic of the first two steps is probably self-evident. We must measure the deviations from some origin, and the mean seems to be as good as any.

The reason for *squaring* the deviations is probably not so obvious. The deviations are squared in order to solve the problem that the deviations themselves will *always* add to 0 when they are measured from the arithmetic mean, and this will happen regardless of how big the deviations are. The sum of the deviations cannot be used, therefore, to reflect the degree of variation in all the numbers unless

TABLE 5.8

Calculation of the Standard Deviation

X (1)	$X - m_x$ $= (x)$ (2)	$(X - m_x)^2$ $= (x)^2$ (3)	
1	-2	4	$s = \sqrt{\dfrac{\Sigma(X - m_x)^2}{N}} = \sqrt{\dfrac{\Sigma x^2}{N}}$
2	-1	1	
3	0	0	
4	1	1	
5	2	4	$= \sqrt{\dfrac{10}{5}}$
15	0	10	$= 1.414$

we decide to ignore the plus and minus signs. If we ignore the signs, the sum of the deviations will reflect the variations in the numbers, but when we do this we create some serious algebraic problems. We later refer to the *average deviation*, which is what it is called when we ignore signs.

If we are going to use sound mathematical methods to measure the variation, the easiest way is to *square* the deviations, thus solving the problem of signs. This makes the results all positive. We then take steps 4 and 5, which together consist of taking the *arithmetic mean of the squares of the deviations*. Step 6 is forced by step 3. Actually step 3 leads to rather peculiar units of measure. For example, if our original numbers were in units of pounds, the units of the squared deviations are square pounds. At the end of step 5 we would still be in units of square pounds. So logically we take the square root of our result. This returns our computation to units of pounds.

The process of going from pounds to square pounds and back again to pounds is what we were talking about in the preceding chapter when we pointed out that it is sometimes convenient to shift from one unit of measure to another. It also emphasizes the extreme importance of being always conscious of the units of the numbers with which we deal.

Simplifying the Calculation of the Standard Deviation. Although the calculation routine of the standard deviation is not very difficult, particularly if we have a calculator and perhaps also a slide rule and a set of tables of squares and square roots, there are occasions when we can significantly save time and effort by using a simple short-cut device. Before looking at this device, we should be aware that short-cut calculations are exactly like short-cut routes from one part of town to another: There are always more steps in the short-cut than there are in the "long way around." Short-cuts are seemingly complicated until we become familiar with them. Knowing this, we should not let ourselves be overwhelmed at the introduction of a short-cut.

Table 5.9 repeats the calculation of the standard deviation for the same data given in Table 5.8. Note that the answer is exactly the same as in Table 5.8. The short-cut method saves one column of calculation and adds an extra step in the formula. Let us total up to see what the net saving is, if anything. The column saved contained five subtractions. We added a division (division of ΣX^2

TABLE 5.9

Short-cut Calculation of the Standard Deviation

X (1)	X^2 (2)
1	1
2	4
3	9
4	16
5	25
——	——
15	55

$$s = \sqrt{\frac{\Sigma X^2}{N} - \left(\frac{\Sigma X}{N}\right)^2} = \sqrt{\frac{55}{5} - \left(\frac{15}{5}\right)^2}$$

$$= 1.414$$

by N), a squaring (the squaring of $\Sigma X/N$), and a subtraction ($\Sigma X^2/N - [\Sigma X/N]^2$). Thus we traded five subtractions for one division, one squaring, and one subtraction. This certainly does not seem like much, which it is not in this particular case. But let us suppose we had 75 items to handle instead of five. We would now save 75 subtractions and still add only one division, one squaring, and one subtraction, a rather substantial net profit. We may even do better, however. Usually the arithmetic mean has decimal fractions. Our deviations then have decimal fractions, and they are more tedious to square than the original items.

A simple way to remember the short-cut formula is: the square root of the mean of the squares minus the square of the mean. Note that the right-hand term in the formula, $\Sigma X/N$, is the arithmetic mean. Those interested and mathematically inclined should be able to derive this short-cut formula from the basic formula given in Table 5.8.

Using the Normal Curve to Estimate Probabilities. We are now ready for the problem of calculating the probabilities of combinations of events by using the normal curve as an approximation device. We illustrate the procedure by estimating the probabilities for the results of tossing 10 coins. Table 5.10 shows all the necessary calculations. Column 2 shows the basic data, which we have arbitrarily chosen to measure as the proportion of heads showing on a given toss of 10 coins. We could just as well have used the proportion of tails. Columns 3 and 4 show the relative frequencies as they would be determined either by listing all the possibilities or by ex-

TABLE 5.10

Estimating Probabilities of Expected Results From Tossing of Ten Coins—Normal Curve

Combination (1)	Proportion of Heads p (2)	Relative Frequency (3)	f (4)	fp (5)	fp^2 (6)
0H, 10T	0	1/1024 or .000977	.000000	.000000
1H, 9T	.1	10/1024 " .009766	.000977	.000098
2H, 8T	.2	45/1024 " .043945	.008789	.001758
3H, 7T	.3	120/1024 " .117187	.035156	.010547
4H, 6T	.4	210/1024 " .205078	.082031	.032812
5H, 5T	.5	252/1024 " .246094	.123047	.061524
6H, 4T	.6	210/1024 " .205078	.123047	.073828
7H, 3T	.7	120/1024 " .117187	.082031	.057422
8H, 2T	.8	45/1024 " .043945	.035156	.028125
9H, 1T	.9	10/1024 " .009766	.008789	.007910
10H, 0T	1.0	1/1024 " .000977	.000977	.000977
Totals:		1024/1024 " 1.000000	.500000	.275001

$$\mu_p = .5000 \qquad \sigma_p = .1581$$

$p - \mu_p$ (7)	$\dfrac{p - \mu_p}{\sigma_p}$ (8)	Proportionate * Height of Ordinate (9)	Y_p (10)	f (11)
−.5	−3.16	.0068	.0017	.0010
−.4	−2.53	.0407	.0103	.0098
−.3	−1.90	.1645	.0415	.0439
−.2	−1.26	.4521	.1141	.1172
−.1	− .63	.8201	.2069	.2051
0.0	0.0	1.0000	.2523	.2461
.1	.63	.8201	.2069	.2051
.2	1.26	.4521	.1141	.1172
.3	1.90	.1645	.0415	.0439
.4	2.53	.0407	.0103	.0098
.5	3.16	.0068	.0017	.0010
			1.0013	1.0000

$$Y_0 = \frac{1 \times i}{2.5066\sigma} e^0 = \frac{i}{2.5066 \times .1581} = .2523$$

* See table of normal curve ordinates in inside rear cover.

panding the binomial. Column 5 has the calculations necessary for determining the arithmetic mean. Each term is the sum of all the events in a given class and is calculated by multiplying the value of the events in a class by the number of events. For example, there are .043945 of the tosses that will result in .2 heads, or, about 439 tosses out of 10,000 will show two heads and eight tails. Since all the events in a class are the same, we sum them by multiplying their common value by the number of them. We then add all the class sums to determine the total sum, which is .50000. We then divide by the total number of items, which is 1 (see the total of column 4, getting an arithmetic mean of .5. We thus discover the very important result that the arithmetic mean of the distribution of complex events will be exactly the same as the arithmetic mean of the simple events which generated the complex events. In other words, we expect the average proportion of heads to be .5 in the long run regardless of how many coins we toss.

Column 6 shows the *class* sums of the squares of the p values. For example, the third result of .001758 is the square of .2 multiplied by .043945. (Actually the calculation was performed by multiplying .008789 by .2, or fp by p. This is easier since we already have the fp in column 5.) The total of these class sums of squares gives us .275001, which is now used to calculate the standard deviation. The formula is

$$\sqrt{\frac{\Sigma fp^2}{N} - \left(\frac{\Sigma fp}{N}\right)^2}.$$

This is the equivalent formula to the one we used earlier of

$$\sqrt{\frac{\Sigma X^2}{N} - \left(\frac{\Sigma X}{N}\right)^2}.$$

We have replaced X with p because we are now working with *proportions* (based on a scale that runs only from 0 to 1) instead of *variables* (based on a scale that presumably runs indefinitely). We introduced f because our data have already been grouped into classes and f tells us the number of events in the given class. We could have used f in the first formula, but since it would have been 1 in each case because the events were kept separate from each other, we left it out entirely. The standard deviation was calculated to be .1581, as shown at the bottom of the table. It is interesting to note that this result of .1581 could also have been obtained by calculating

$$\sqrt{\frac{\mu_p(1 - \mu_p)}{n}}.$$

which equals

$$\sqrt{\frac{.5 \times .5}{10}}.$$

This is, of course, a much more efficient way to calculate the standard deviation for problems of this sort. We discover in a later chapter that this is the way we normally do it.

Now that we have the arithmetic mean and the standard deviation, we are ready to calculate probabilities from the normal curve. Columns 7 through 10 show the necessary calculations. Column 7 calculates the deviations from the mean. These are the x's in the equation for the normal curve. Fortunately, from now on we can take advantage of a table to considerably simplify our work. The table provides us with the values of

$$e^{\frac{-x^2}{2\sigma^2}}$$

for various values of x/σ. Column 8 shows the calculation of x/σ for each value of x given in column 7. Column 9 shows the values from the table (inside front cover of book) for each value of x/σ.

Our next step is to calculate $i/2.5066\sigma$, which is the value of Y when x equals 0. It is also the value of Y corresponding to the arithmetic mean of X, or of p in this case. Since this value of Y is greater than for any other value of x, it is usually called the *maximum ordinate*. Performing the indicated calculation yields a result of .2523, as shown in the bottom of Table 5.10. When we multiply each value in column 9 by .2523, we get the expected value of Y for each value of p as shown in column 10. These are the normal curve estimates that we are seeking.

Column 11 is a duplicate of column 4 with the figures rounded to four decimal places.

By comparing the normal curve figures of column 10 with the binomial figures of column 11 we can quickly assess the closeness of the approximation. The closeness is even more remarkable if we round both sets of figures to two decimal places. We then find exact agreement in all but two of the 11 classes, and these differ by only .01.

The Poisson Distribution as an Approximation to Probabilities. We have already noted how the normal curve is a poorer approximation to the probabilities of dice throws than of coin tosses. The difficulty is caused by the skewness, or asymmetry, that develops when the basic probability departs from .5. Mathematical statisticians have developed other approximate distributions than the normal to handle such problems. One of the most useful of these, and the only one we discuss, is the *Poisson* distribution, after S. D. Poisson, who first published it in Paris in 1837.

Let us introduce the Poisson distribution by applying it to the simple problem of estimating the probability of getting five 4's on the toss of 12 dice. We assume a basic probability of a 4 of 1/6, which we call p. We then calculate the *arithmetic mean* number of 4's we would expect on the tossing of 12 dice. We call the number of dice N. Thus we have $Np = 12 \times 1/6 = 2$. Np is usually abbreviated to m, a practice we follow. At this point of our analysis, we can see that the getting of *five* 4's on the toss of 12 dice is an above average occurrence, considering we would expect all such outcomes to have a *mean* of 2.

A Poisson estimate of the probability of five 4's is made by solving

$$e^{-2} \cdot \frac{2^5}{5!}, \quad \text{or} \quad \frac{2^5}{e^2 \cdot 5!}.$$

If we substitute 2.71828 for e and solve, we get a probability of .03609.

The binomial probability of getting five 4's on the toss of 12 dice would be $\binom{12}{5} \left(\frac{1}{6} p \right)^5 \left(\frac{5}{6} q \right)^7$, or $.0284 p^5 q^7$. (We use p to identify the probability of the event we are interested in—the occurrence of a 4 in this case—and we use q to refer to "not p," or to all other events that might occur.) Thus we see that the Poisson probability of .03609 is too high by .0077, or by 27%. This is not a small error, and it is probably too large for most practical problems. It is, however, not significantly worse than a normal curve estimate, which is .021.

Table 5.11 and Fig. 5.8 compare the Poisson, binomial, and normal curve probabilities for all possible number of 4's. The most striking feature of the comparison is that the Poisson and normal approximations tend to be on opposite sides of the binomial. (We remind ourselves that the binomial is taken as the truth.) The most important

TABLE 5.11

Binomial, Poisson, and Normal Probabilities for the Occurrence of 4's on the Throwing of 12 Dice

No. of 4's Occurring	Binomial Probability	Poisson Probability	Normal Probability	Error in Poisson	Error in Normal
0	.112	.135	.093	.023	.019
1	.269	.271	.231	.002	.038
2	.296	.271	.309	.025	.013
3	.197	.180	.231	.017	.034
4	.089	.090	.093	.001	.004
5	.028	.036	.021	.008	.007
6	.007	.012	.003	.005	.004
7	.001	.003	.000	.002	.001
8	.000	.001	.000	.001	.000
9	.000	.000	.000	.000	.000
10	.000	.000	.000	.000	.000
11	.000	.000	.000	.000	.000
12	.000	.000	.000	.000	.000
Totals:	.999	.999	.981	.084	.120

feature for us, however, is that the Poisson approximations are closer in general than are the normal. Note that the total error is only .084 for the Poisson compared with .120 for the normal.

Actually, of course, we would probably use neither the Poisson nor the normal as an approximation in a problem as easy as this to handle with the binomial. We have already discovered that we find the normal curve a practical device when the sample gets too large to be handled conveniently with the binomial, a point that is reached rather quickly if we do not have a table of binomial probabilities handy. The same reasoning applies to the Poisson. In fact, we are most likely to use the Poisson when the sample is extremely large, in some cases practically infinite in size. Such a statement should be explained, but first we must return to our formula for the Poisson and examine some of its general properties.

We estimated the Poisson probability of five 4's on the throw of 12 dice by the expression

$$e^{-2} \cdot \frac{2^5}{5!}.$$

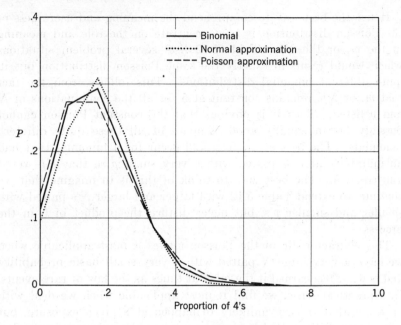

Fig. 5.8 Binomial, Poisson, and normal probabilities for the occurrence of 4's on the toss of 12 dice.

We can put this in general form by replacing the numbers with symbols, giving us

$$e^{-m} \cdot \frac{m^c}{c!}.$$

The constant 2.71828 is e; m is Np, or the size of sample multiplied by the basic probability, and c is the number of times the event in question is taken to occur. The most remarkable property of this formula is not evidenced by what is in it but rather by what is *not* in it, at least not in it explicitly. This property is the independence of the formula from N, *the size of the sample*. Our formula for the normal curve had the same property; but then we were dealing with a distribution that always has the same form except for scales of measure variations. The Poisson distribution takes many different forms very similar to the way the binomial takes many forms. In fact, one form of the Poisson is the normal form, the limit it approaches as m increases. An m of 20, for example, yields a Poisson distribution that is so close to normal that only a very unusual practical problem would not be satisfied by a normal approximation to the Poisson.

Hence the best way to comprehend the meaning and usefulness of the Poisson distribution is to concentrate on the role and meaning of the m, or the Np. Table 5.12 lists several problem situations which would result in exactly the same Poisson distribution but in quite different binomial distributions. This follows from the fact that m, or Np, remains constant at 5 for all the combinations of N and p listed. Thus it is obvious that the constant Poisson cannot possibly be an equally good estimate of all these quite different binomials. The best estimate would occur for a binomial that had an infinitely large N paired with a very small p so that Np would still equal 5. The best way to think of this is to imagine that we continue to extend Table 5.12 with larger and larger N's paired with smaller and smaller p's, but never disturb the product of 5 in the process.

This characteristic of the Poisson makes it most applicable when we have a very large N paired with a very small basic probability and is what has earned it the label at times as the law of rare events. In a practical sense, we find it most applicable when we deal with an event that is very unlikely to happen at a given exposure, but which nevertheless does happen because of the tremendous number of exposures. Insurance companies and safety councils find a great use for the Poisson because they frequently deal with the probability of the occurrence of accidents. For example, chances of getting killed by lightning are very small, so small that we can afford to ignore the possibility, unless, of course, we take steps to substantially increase the probability, say, by holding steel rods in our hands in the

TABLE 5.12

Relationship Between the Binomial and Poisson Distributions for an Np Constant at 5

N	p	Np, or m	Binomial	Poisson
10	.50	5	$(.50p + .50q)^{10}$	$e^{-5}\dfrac{5^c}{c!}$
25	.20	5	$(.20p + .80q)^{25}$	"
100	.05	5	$(.05p + .95q)^{100}$	"
500	.01	5	$(.01p + .99q)^{500}$	"
5,000	.001	5	$(.001p + .999q)^{5,000}$	"
5,000,000	.000001	5	$(.000001p + .999999q)^{5,000,000}$	"

middle of an open field during a thunder storm. However, people get killed by lightning almost every day around the earth, some days more than others. We attribute such deaths, despite the low probability, to the *very high exposure rate*, which is the equivalent of our N. If we were to tally the number of days on which no persons were killed by lightning, the number of days on which one person was killed, etc., we would very likely discover that the distribution of the tallies would conform quite closely to a Poisson distribution.

Practical Methods of Calculating Poisson Probabilities. Although the direct application of the Poisson formula is somewhat easier than the direct application of the binomial, particularly for cases of large N, it still is tedious enough to justify the use of calculation aids. The most prominent of the tables of Poisson probabilities are those prepared by Molina.[1] Appendix F contains selections from the tables published by Hartley. We have reproduced these tables rather than Molina's because of their inclusion of the χ^2 (chi, pronounced "ki") distribution, a distribution we have occasion to refer to in a later chapter.

We illustrate the use of Appendix F by showing how to get the Poisson probabilities for our earlier example of the number of 4's we might get if we tossed 12 dice. Let us first find the probability of getting five 4's. Thus we have an m of 2 and a c of 5. We first search the top rows of Appendix F until we find the column headed by an m of 2.0. The entries in this column tell us the probability of getting a c *less than* that specified in the *extreme right column*. (Pay no attention to the extreme left column headed by v. This is used when we use the table for χ^2 estimates.) For example, the .94735 that is opposite the c of 5 is the probability of getting *4 or fewer* occurrences of the specified event. Since we are interested in the probability of *exactly 5*, we can achieve our objective by subtracting the probability of *4 or fewer* from the probability of *5 or fewer*. (Alternatively, we can think of 4 or fewer as the same as *fewer than 5*, etc.) The latter probability is opposite the c of 6 and is shown as .98344. Thus the probability of *exactly five* 4's is .98344 − .94735, or .03609, the same result we derived by formula.

Perhaps it seems curious that the table lists the *cumulative* probabilities, or the probabilities of all the c's below a specified value, rather than the probabilities for specific c values. The reason is the factor of convenience. Most practical problems require us to esti-

---

[1] Molina, E. C., *Poisson's Exponential Binomial Limit,* D. Van Nostrand Co., Princeton, N.J., 1949.

mate the probabilities for *groups* of *c* values, such as the probability
of a *c less than* a certain value, or *more than* a certain value, or
between two certain values. Rarely do we find it necessary to estimate the probability of a *specific c* value, except for illustrative purposes in a statistics textbook. Even then it is relatively simple to
take the difference between two of the tabled values. We illustrate
some of the typical practical problems below. Also try some on your
own later by doing some of the problems at the end of the chapter.

Miss Thorndike has constructed a chart, or nomagraph, to represent the Poisson tables. A reproduction is shown in Appendix E.
This has been found to be very useful and convenient for many
sampling problems in statistical quality control work. Naturally
it does not permit the accuracy of the tables, but it is accurate
enough for most situations. Note that this chart uses the *pn* instead
of the *m*, or *Np*, we have been using. We can illustrate the use of
the chart by redoing our five 4's on the toss of 12 dice problem. The
horizontal axis shows the value of *pn*, or *Np*, or *m*, which is 2 in our
case. We start at this point and trace the vertical line upward until
we touch the diagonal curved line corresponding to a *c* of 5. We then
read horizontally from this point to find the indicated probability on
the vertical axis. (A ruler of some kind is useful to guide the eye.)
We estimate a probability of about .982. This is the estimated
probability of getting *five or fewer* 4's on the toss of 12 dice. (Note
that the tables referred to earlier associated the probability with
fewer than five, rather than *five or fewer*. This illustrates a common
problem in statistical work, namely, a lack of standardization in the
use of terms, symbols, etc.) If we now go back to the vertical line
above the *np* of 2 and read across from where it strikes the *c* = 4
diagonal, we find an estimate of about .946, which is the probability
of *four or fewer* 4's. The difference between .982 and .946, or .036,
is the estimated probability of exactly five 4's on the toss of 12 dice.
This is, of course, very close to the .03609 we derived from the table.
(We have to admit that our ability to read a chart accurately is
considerably improved by prior knowledge of the correct answer!)

Some Practical Problems Involving the Poisson Distribution

Example A. A bolt manufacturer has a boltmaking machine which,
when producing large lots, turns out an average of .04 defective
bolts. But the machine and the materials are subject to variations
which can lead to an undesirably high proportion of defectives.
When such a situation is suspected strongly enough, the machine
is stopped and any indicated adjustments are made in the process.

There are several issues we would have to discuss before we could handle such a problem with reasonable intelligence, a discussion we get into in later chapters. One factor that we are sure is involved, however, is the probability that a given number of defectives might occur in a sample even though the process is producing only .04 defectives on the average. Suppose, for example, that the quality inspector takes a sample of 50 bolts at random and finds that there are four defectives in the sample. What is the probability of getting *at least* four defectives in a sample of 50 if the basic probability is .04? We quickly calculate our Np of $50 \times .04$ and get 2. In our table in Appendix F we find that there is a Poisson probability of .85712 of getting *fewer than four* defectives. We subtract .85712 from 1 and find an estimated probability of .1429 of getting *at least* four defectives in a sample of 50 even though the process is averaging .04. (Whether or not we should recommend stopping the machine "because the process is producing too many defectives" is a very interesting question we pursue later.)

(It is interesting to note that the binomial probability of this event is .1391 and the normal curve probability is .0743, the latter an obviously poor estimate.)

Example B. An automobile manufacturer periodically inspects the paint surface of a finished car for evidences of surface blemishes. If the number appears excessive, steps are taken in the surface preparation processes, or the paint mixing, or the paint application, and other operations to correct the apparent lack of minimum quality. What makes this a very interesting problem is that we have no way of determining the size of the sample. Most of the blemishes are very small, less than 1/8 inch in diameter. The paint surface contains thousands of square inches. Thus there are almost countless opportunities for a blemish to occur, particularly if we consider that a given 1/8 inch of surface can overlap with many other potential 1/8 inches of surface. It is also evident that the probability that any 1/8 of surface will have a blemish must be very small. If it were not, the whole surface would have quite a few blemishes, and the manufacturer's reputation would be in jeopardy.

Let us suppose that the manufacturer has set a standard of an average of five minor blemishes per automobile. (Large or conspicuous blemishes are caught in the more cursory 100% inspection that is made of every car.) What is the probability that a car might have *at least* nine blemishes even though the process is still averaging only five per car? We enter the Poisson tables at $m = 5$ and find the entry opposite $c = 9$, or .93191. We subtract this from

1 and get an estimate of .068 of getting a car with at least nine blemishes even though the average will be only five.

We are not able to contrast this estimate with the binomial or normal curve estimates because to make the latter we must know the separate values of N and p, and thus it is necessary to use a Poisson estimate whether we wish to or not. Fortunately, this is a very good example of the most appropriate conditions for the use of the Poisson—a very large N with a very small p.

Example C. A manufacturer of sanitary napkins has 10 independent automatic machines to make the product. The loss of production when a machine breaks down is so serious that the company maintains an eleventh machine as a standby. When a given machine breaks down, the operator calls the maintenance department and then resumes production on the spare machine. The original machine then becomes the spare when it has been repaired. Occasionally, however, a second machine will break down while a first machine is still being repaired. In fact, there are sometimes three or more machines all down at the same time. When such bottlenecks develop, the operators are "off production," a considerable cost to the company even though the operators can be diverted to less productive duties in another department.

The company's problem is to find the best possible combination of number of spare machines to have available (it could always add a twelfth machine, for example) and number of maintenance men to have in order to speed up repairs when a breakdown occurs. This is obviously a very complicated problem, and well beyond our modest goals. It is called the queuing problem and is quite common in business, as we can attest from experiences in waiting for service in a bank, a restaurant, or on a telephone call to a business concern with limited switchboard capacity. One feature of the problem that we can work on, however, is the determination of the probability that a given number of breakdowns might occur in a given time interval. We use some simplifying assumptions to facilitate our calculations, assumptions that we do not explicitly specify but which become obvious in seriously solving the problem.

Let us assume that experience of the company has been that it takes 2 hours on the average to repair a machine. Thus, if breakdowns are spaced so that there never is more than one breakdown in a given 2-hour interval, the company is never without a machine for an operator. The company's experience has been that machine breakdowns have averaged one every 5 hours, or .4 per 2-hour period.

What is the probability of having two or more machines down during a given 2-hour period? We have an Np of .4 and a c of 2. Appendix F tells that there is a probability of .93845 of fewer than two breakdowns, or .062 of at least two. Similar calculations could be made for other numbers of breakdowns.

Note that this is also a problem in which we have no way of determining N and p separately. Any given 2-hour period contains countless opportunities for a machine to break down. It might break down during the first minute, or the 274th second, or the 4826th millisecond, etc. In other words, a 2-hour repair period might start *at any moment* during a given 2-hour clock period. The probability of a breakdown at any moment is very small, of course.

5.5 Discrete vs. Continuous Variables

Our calculation of probabilities has so far been restricted to variables that assume only specific sizes, such as five 4's on the toss of 12 dice, or three blemishes in a paint surface, or six defective bolts. We restricted ourselves in order to simplify the introduction to the problem of estimating probabilities.

We now take note that, theoretically, *strictly specific* numerical values exist in only a very small proportion of our practical problems, and even then they exist as strictly specific values only by definition, so to speak. Practically all the measurements we make are subject to error. Hence our numbers are *rounded* to some degree of accuracy. Such a number is not really a *specific* value, but rather is the center of some *range* of values. For example, a person measured as 6.1 feet tall might be anywhere from 6.05 feet to 6.15 feet tall. If we had a distribution of men's heights and were calculating the probability that a man would be 6.1 feet tall, we would calculate the probability that he was between 6.05 and 6.15 feet tall. An *exact* height would have to be carried out to an infinite number of decimal places. There would be an *infinite* number of such exact heights available. The probability of any one of them would be $1/\infty$, or 0.

When we deal with a phenomenon that varies by infinitesimal amounts over its full range, such as is true for human heights, or weights, we call such a phenomenon a *continuous* variable. As we have just seen, the probability of some *specific* value of a continuous variable would be 0. To get a probability of more than 0 we must combine several such specific values into a range or class of values.

A certain amount of such grouping automatically takes place when we use rounded numbers, as we must because of our limited abilities of perception.

We call a phenomenon a *discrete* variable if its nature is such that only certain values of it exist within the range of its coverage. Other values just do not exist at all. For example, the 7 1/2 of hearts just does not exist in a deck. A family just cannot have 4 1/2 children. We are tempted to say that a paint surface just cannot have 4 1/2 blemishes, or that a sample of 50 bolts just cannot have 4 1/2 defective bolts. But second thought reveals that in a sense they *can*, even though our method of measurement does not recognize them. A blemish becomes a blemish only when the observer is able or willing to see it. A defect in the paint surface has to be of a certain intensity to be recorded. It is also obvious that some defects or blemishes are worse than others. Thus a defect is not a specific and unchanging thing, like the 7 of hearts. It is actually a range of things. One set of seven defects would not be the same as some other sets. We treat them as the same for convenience of recording; it would be incorrect to consider them as really the same.

The binomial and Poisson distributions are discrete in the sense

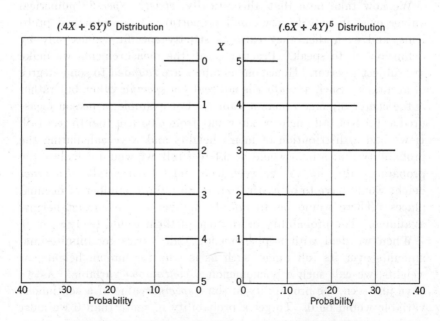

Fig. 5.9a One method of charting a discrete distribution.

.that they provide the probabilities for only specific values of a variable. The in-between values do not exist and have no probability. If we wished to be very technical, we would draw a chart of the binomial or Poisson as shown in Fig. 5.9A rather than as shown in Fig. 5.9B. The thin horizontal lines represent the probabilities for the specific values indicated on the vertical axis. The blank spaces in between the lines do not represent anything. Compare Fig. 5.9 with Fig. 5.10 and note what happens as the power of the binomial increases. The lines get closer together because there are now a greater number of specific values on the horizontal axis. If we raise the power of the binomial high enough, the lines would touch each

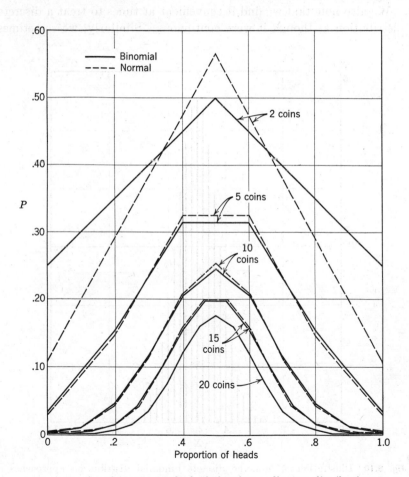

Fig. 5.9b An alternate method of charting a discrete distribution.

other and would make a solid black area as shown in Fig. 5.11. In effect, the binomial distribution has become *continuous*. (The same thing happens to the Poisson as N, and hence m, increases, given a specific p.) It is at this point that the binomial becomes the *normal* distribution, which is a *continuous* distribution.

It should be obvious, now, that the accuracy of the normal curve (a continuous distribution) as an approximation to the binomial (a discrete distribution) depends on how discrete the binomial is. If the gaps between the event values are very large, the binomial is very discrete and the normal is a poor approximation; if the gaps are very small, the binomial is almost continuous and the normal is a good approximation.

We also note that we find it convenient at times to treat a discrete distribution as though it were continuous. Similarly, we sometimes

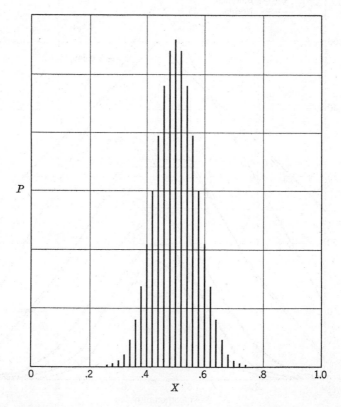

Fig. 5.10 Illustration of how the discrete binomial distribution approaches a continuous distribution as the size of sample increases.

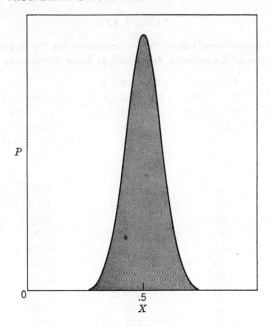

P

0   .5
                           X

Fig. 5.11 Illustration of how the discrete binomial distribution becomes continuous when the sample becomes infinitely large.

consider it convenient to do the reverse. Cultivate the habit of being conscious of whether the variable is discrete or continuous, and then note whether it is treated consistently with what it is or whether some approximation device is being used.

Normal Curve Estimates of Coin-Toss Probabilities Assuming a Continuous Distribution

Let us look at the problem of estimating the probabilities of the various results that might happen when we toss 10 coins. Instead of treating the results of the tosses as a discrete variable as in our normal curve estimates shown in Table 5.10, we now treat them as though they were *continuous*. Table 5.13 shows the necessary calculations.

Column 1 shows the results of the tosses in ranges, or intervals, of values instead of in the specific values as shown earlier. For example, instead of saying that the proportion of heads was .40, we say it was between .35 and up to but not including .45. (The reason we specify the limits to the intervals as having the lower limit in-

TABLE 5.13

Normal Curve Approximations to the Probabilities for the Results of Tossing 10 Coins—Use of Cumulative Probabilities for a Continuous Variable

Proportion of Heads p (1)	Distance from Mean to Further Limit x (2)	Distance in Standard Deviation Units x/s (3)	Proportion of Area from Mean to Further Limit † (4)	Estimated Probability f_c (5)
−.05–.05 *	.55	3.48	.4997	.002
.05–.15	.45	2.85	.4978	.011
.15–.25	.35	2.21	.4864	.044
.25–.35	.25	1.58	.4429	.114
.35–.45	.15	.95	.3289	.203
.45–.55	.05⎱ .05⎰	.32⎱ .32⎰	.1255⎱ .1255⎰	.251
.55–.65	.15	.95	.3289	.203
.65–.75	.25	1.58	.4429	.114
.75–.85	.35	2.21	.4864	.044
.85–.95	.45	2.85	.4978	.011
.95–1.05	.55	3.48	.4997	.002
				.999

* Lower Limit Inclusive, $m_p = .50$, $s_p = .1581$

† See table of normal curve areas on inside rear cover.

clusive, which is the same as saying upper limit exclusive, or of saying, .35 up to but not including .45, is to remove the ambiguity of where to put a value of .45. Of course, that is not really a problem here because there are no such values, but in a really continuous series it would be a problem.) In effect, we are treating each actual value, such as .40, as though it were the middle of a range of values. Also, we make the various ranges just large enough to barely touch each other. Thus, when we finish, our series runs continuously from one end to the other. It is probably surprising that our first interval runs from −.05 to .05 since a minus proportion of heads is a literal impossibility; however, it is necessary to engage in this fiction in order to complete the series, so to speak. If we did not do this, the 0 value would be restricted to only half the interval of all the other values, and this would lead to incorrect estimates of the probabilities.

What we now try to do is estimate the probabilities for each of these intervals. We do not do this directly because the tables of the normal curve are not set up this way. Actually we are going to do the same kind of thing we did when we used the Poisson Tables to estimate the probability of exactly five 4's. We are going to determine two probabilities which straddle the interval, and then we are going to take the difference between them. The process is illustrated in Fig. 5.12. We would like to estimate the probability for the interval from 1 to 2. This involves determining the area of the shaded section of the distribution. (Recall that the total probability, or the total area, is 1.00.) The table gives us the area projected by the distance between 0 and 1, and also the area projected by the distance from 0 to 2. If we take the *difference* between these two values, we have the area (probability) projected by the interval from 1 to 2.

Just as we used the normal curve before, we now take our origin of measure at the arithmetic mean, which is .50 in this case. We measure the distance from the mean to the further limit of the given interval. These distances are shown in column 2. Note that the middle interval contains two such distances because the mean is inside that interval. We divide each of these distances, or deviations, by the standard deviation. (This is the same standard deviation we calculated in Table 5.10.) These results are in column 3. We proceed to the table of normal curve areas on the inside rear cover, which gives us the *area* under the normal curve from the mean to any specified point, and look up the required areas. These are shown in column 4. We take the difference between each of a pair of these to get the final probabilities as shown in column 5. For example, column 4 tells us that the area from the mean to .25 is .4429 and the area from the mean to .35 is .3289. Therefore, the area between .25 and .35 is the difference, or .114.

The estimates shown in column 5 are not quite the same as those shown in column 10 of Table 5.10, but they are reasonably close.

We now refer to some of the important features of the table of normal curve areas as presented on the inside of the rear cover.

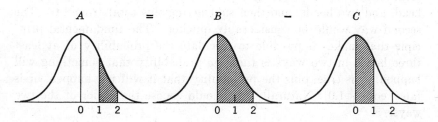

Fig. 5.12 Estimating a probability as a difference between two other probabilities.

Note that the probabilities in the body of the table run from .0000 to .4999997. The latter probability is very close to .5, and would be .5 if we rounded .4999997 a little. The reason the table stops in the neighborhood of .5 instead of 1.0 is that it covers only *half* of the full distribution. But this is really all that is necessary because the other half would be exactly the same since the distribution is perfectly symmetrical.

The probability never really reaches .5 because the normal curve theoretically has an infinite range, there being no upper or lower limit along the horizontal axis. The assumption of an infinite range is not really bothersome in practice, where most of the series we work with do have a finite range, because the probabilities are very close to .5 for values of x/s of 3.5 or more. This is the basis of the statement that "events more than 3.5 standard deviations from the mean almost never happen."

It is a good idea to memorize a few of the values from this table. Some useful things to know are:

1. About 2/3 of the cases are included within one standard deviation of the mean. (Actually it is .6826, which is twice .3413.)
2. About 19 out of 20 cases are within two standard deviations of the mean. (Actually it is .9544, which is twice .4772.)
3. Only about 3 cases out of 1000 will be more than three standard deviations from the mean.

5.6   Some Miscellaneous Aspects of Probability Calculations

Indirect Calculation of Probabilities

If we were interested in the probability of getting at least three heads on the toss of 10 coins, we could determine this by adding together the probabilities of three heads, four heads, etc., up to the probability of 10 heads. On the other hand, we could also get the same answer by adding together the probabilities of no heads, one head, and two heads, and then subtracting this total from 1.0. The second way would be considerably quicker. The fundamental principle that makes it possible to calculate the probability of at least three heads in two ways is that the probability that something will happen, or is true, plus the probability that it will not happen, or is false, equals 1.0. Naturally, we should choose the easier of the two ways.

There are some problems in probability that are quite deceptive if we try to calculate the probability directly. It is much better to calculate that the event will not happen and subtract this from 1.0 than to try to calculate the probability that it will happen. Consider this apparently simple problem. Suppose two dice are going to be tossed. A person offers to bet $1 that at least one 1 or one 2 will appear. Our first inclination is to take this bet because we figure that we have four numbers (3, 4, 5, 6) on our side and he has only two numbers on his, thus giving us 2 chances to his 1. If we had time to list the 36 equally probable things that can happen when we toss two dice, we would find that we would be foolish to take this bet. How can we easily calculate the probability of getting at least one 1 or one 2? We do it by first calculating the probability that we will *not*. The probability that the first die does not have a 1 or a 2 is 2/3. The probability that the second die also does not have a 1 or a 2 is also 2/3. The probability that neither of them has a 1 or a 2 is $2/3 \times 2/3$, or 4/9. Hence, the probability that at least one 1 or one 2 will show is 5 out of 9, and our friend was hoping to take a little advantage of us by offering us only an even bet.

A similar problem that has become a classic is what is called the "birthday problem." Suppose there were 30 people in a room. Somebody offers to bet us that at least two of the people have their birthday on the same day in the same month. Immediately, we think of 365 days in the year and only 30 people, and we are very happy to take the bet. But we will probably lose because actually there are seven chances out of 10 that at least two of the people do have the same birthday. Here again we find it much more desirable to calculate the probability indirectly. It is a very difficult and tedious task to calculate directly the probability that at least two people have the same birthday. It is not so difficult to calculate the probability that it will not be true, and to subtract the result from 1.0. Let us take the 30 people in order. The first person can have any birthday out of the 365 possibilities (we ignore leap day as a very minor modification). The second person has only 364 days left for his birthday if he is not going to duplicate the 1st person's. The third person has only 363 possibilities without duplication, etc. We can now calculate the probability of no duplications as follows

$$\frac{365}{365} \times \frac{364}{365} \times \frac{363}{365} \times \cdots \frac{336}{365} \quad \text{which equals} \quad \frac{365!}{335!365^{30}}.$$

This gives an answer of .294. When we subtract this from 1.0, we get .706. Of course this calculation is not the sort of thing we can do in our head, but it certainly is easier than the direct calculation, or easier than listing the 365^{30} different combinations of 30 birthdays that can exist.[1]

The moral of the examples just given is not to jump too fast in picking out the method of calculating probabilities. The shortest way to the correct answer is often the indirect way.

Conditional Probabilities

We have seen that we cannot calculate any probabilities until we know, or assume, certain *conditions*. The two primary conditions are N, the size of the sample, and p, the basic probability if we are working with the binomial. The normal curve requires knowledge about m, the mean, and s, the standard deviation. The Poisson requires knowledge of Np, or m, the *mean* number of occurrences expected in the long run. Thus it is proper to state that *all probabilities are conditional*. Given the conditions, which are really the *base of knowledge* from which the probabilities are calculated, we usually find rather general agreement on what the probabilities are in a given situation. In other words, the mechanics of calculation are generally not controversial. Disagreement arises because different people tend to assume different conditions, either legitimately because of different knowledge bases, or illegitimately because of failure to assess properly the available information. After asserting the conditional character of *all* probabilities, we now find it necessary to recognize that certain conventions have grown up about the labeling of various types of probabilities. These conventions have appropriated the adjective conditional for a more restrictive type of probability than that which we have been talking about. For example, suppose we are asked to estimate the probability that an adult American male chosen at random will weigh between 170 and 180 pounds. Our offhand guess might be a probability of .11. But, if we are now given the *additional* information that the man in question is 5′11″ tall, we would revise this probability of .11 to, say, .28. It is this latter probability that is typically called a *conditional probability*, in this case the "probability that an adult American male weighs between 170 and 180 pounds *given the condition* that he is 5′11″ tall."

If we adopt this conventional nomenclature, we call the "proba-

---

[1] If you would like to know the probabilities for other than 30 people and you do not wish to do your own calculations, you can find a partial listing in *Introduction to Finite Mathematics* by Kemeny, Snell, and Thompson, Prentice Hall, 1957, p. 125.

bility that an adult American male weighs 170 to 180 pounds" the *unconditional probability*. But, we might ask what we should call the "probability that an adult American weighs 170 to 180 pounds," or the "probability that an American weighs 170 to 180 pounds," or the "probability that a human being weighs 170 to 180 pounds," etc. It is immediately apparent that all probabilities have restrictive conditions of some sort.

Hence we prefer to think of all probabilities as conditional probabilities. This helps to prevent one of the most common errors made in the application of probability concepts, namely, the failure to be alert to the *particular conditions* which must necessarily surround any probability. For example, it is not uncommon for cardplayers to appeal to the laws of probability in selecting a particular strategy. Such a policy presumably makes their action scientific. However, it is scarcely scientific if the particular probability calculation is based on conditions which do not prevail. The probability of a 5-card deal from a deck having all five cards of the same suit is only 1 out of 500. But, if we are playing against an opponent who obviously has at least four spades because the four are facing upward, and if this opponent has been betting as though the fifth card is also a spade, we would be well advised to substantially revise our notion of the probability that *that particular hand* has five spades in it. The 1 out of 500 is rather completely irrelevant under the *given conditions*. (Of course, if we happen to have been lucky enough to have visually spotted what our opponent's fifth card is, the information conditions are now such that we *know* whether he has five spades or not, thus pushing the probability to either 1 or 0. The motive for cheating in games of chance is to acquire additional information in order to improve probability estimates.)

Since many practical problems provide us with alternative sets of conditions which we may analyze and use, it is useful to have some terminology to distinguish between two separate conditional probabilities. We prefer to use the terms of *conditional* and *subconditional*. For example, the group of all 5′11″ adult American males is a *subgroup*, or subset, of the group of adult American males. Hence it seems appropriate to call probabilities dealing with this subgroup subconditional and those associated with the larger group conditional. Of course, if our problem shifts so we also become concerned with the even larger group of American males, the probabilities associated with the now subgroup of adult American males become subconditional.

Subconditional Probabilities and Subuniverses. It is probably apparent that the notion of group and subgroup is precisely the same as universe and subuniverse and of set and subset that we encountered earlier. Thus a subconditional probability is simply a probability for a universe that is subsidiary to a larger universe that has already been referred to in the given context.

Some Useful Shorthand

Discussions of probability are generally more satisfactory if the appropriate conditions are specified for any given calculation or indicated calculation. For example, we might make frequent use of a statement such as, the probability of five heads on the toss of 12 coins is .19336, given that the probability of a head on the toss of one coin is .5. This is somewhat tedious to write out. Hence we have adopted some simple shorthand. In shorthand the above statement becomes

$$P(H^5 \mid N = 12, p = .5) = .19336.$$

We use capital P to stand for probability. We then enclose in parentheses what it is we are getting the probability of. The first element within the parentheses always refers to the specific event in question, such as five heads, or H^5, in this case. We then erect a vertical line. This line is really the symbol for the word given. Everything to the right of this line refers to the *conditions* that are presumed to define the universe out of which the specific event is to come, or has come. The necessary and sufficient conditions in this case are the number of coins, or, more generally, the *size of the sample,* and the *basic probability* of getting a head on the toss of one coin. We can take these two conditions and proceed to expand the appropriate binomial from which we can get the probability.

The fundamental challenge of most practical problems is to specify the appropriate conditions; they are those that satisfy the practical conditions of the problem and also are manageable from a calculation point of view. Sometimes we really do not know how to calculate the probabilities for some sets of conditions. Then we must modify the conditions so we can make an estimate. These modifications naturally distort our concept of an ideal solution. In other cases we know how to calculate the probability for the conditions, but we find it too tedious. Again we modify and accept a less than ideal solution.

Some Useful Theorems in Probability Calculations

Suppose we are going to draw cards from an ordinary deck with the fundamental assumption that each card is equally likely. Let us call these conditions X. What is the probability that the drawn card will be a spade? In symbols, we can answer by saying

$$P(S|X) = \tfrac{1}{4} = \tfrac{13}{52}. \qquad (S \text{ stands for spade.})$$

A useful way to picture this problem is shown in Fig. 5.13. The large enclosure represents all the cards in the deck. Each of the smaller subensclosures represents the number of spades, hearts, etc. Note that the subenclosures do not overlap at any points. This is because it is impossible for a card to be both a spade and a heart, for example, at the same time. Such events are *mutually exclusive events*. If we know that a given event has occurred, such as a spade, we know that all other mutually exclusive events have not occurred.

Now consider the problem of the probability of the drawn card being a 4. Figure 5.14 shows the distribution of the 13 mutually

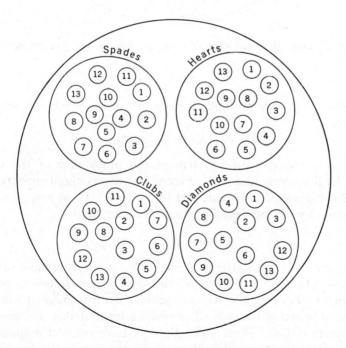

Fig. 5.13 Diagram of distribution of cards in a deck by suit, and then by number within suit.

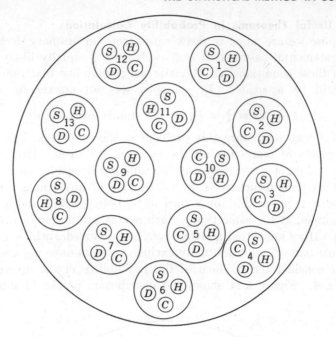

Fig. 5.14 Diagram of distribution of cards by number, and then by suit within number.

exclusive events which divide a deck by card number.   In symbols we have

$$P(4|X) = \tfrac{1}{13} = \tfrac{4}{52}.$$

We next consider the problem of the probability of the card's being both a spade and a 4.   Figure 5.15 shows the distribution of the 52 cards classified by suit and by number.   These are, of course, also mutually exclusive events.   In symbols we have

$$P(S \text{ and } 4|X) = \tfrac{1}{52}.$$

We could also calculate this probability by referring back to Figs. 5.13 and 5.14.   We now consider the sampling operation as having *two stages*.   For example, we can consider the first stage in Fig. 5.13 as that of selecting the *suit*.   The probability that this selection will be a *spade* is 1/4.   Then, *given* that we have selected a spade, we can calculate the probability that we would select a 4 in the second stage.   This would be 1/13.   If we now multiply these two probabilities together, we have $1/4 \times 1/13 = 1/52$, the same answer we obtained above. Similarly, we could have first selected the number (see Fig. 5.14) and secondly selected the suit. We would then have the probability of getting the 4 of spades as $1/13 \times 1/4 = 1/52$, again the same answer as above.

When we combine several stages this way, we call the final probability a *joint*, or *compound*, probability. We can symbolize the above operations as

$$P(S \text{ and } 4 \,|\, X) = P(S \,|\, X) \cdot P(4 \,|\, S, X) = \tfrac{1}{4} \cdot \tfrac{1}{13} = \tfrac{1}{52}$$

$$\text{or } P(4 \,|\, X) \cdot P(S \,|\, 4, X) = \tfrac{1}{13} \cdot \tfrac{1}{4} = \tfrac{1}{52}.$$

Since, in the case of a card deck, the probability of a 4 is *independent* of the suit, we could have calculated the same answer by just multiplying the probability of a spade by the probability of a 4, namely

$$P(S \text{ and } 4 \,|\, X) = P(S \,|\, X) \cdot P(4 \,|\, X) = \tfrac{1}{4} \cdot \tfrac{1}{13} = \tfrac{1}{52}.$$

Suppose, however, that all the 4's in the deck were also spades, but with there still being 13 spades and four 4's in the deck. We would

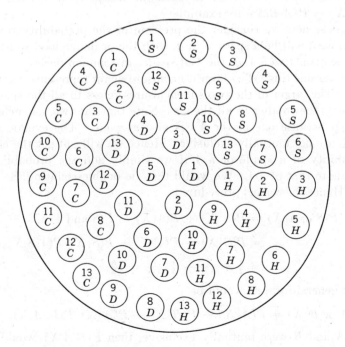

Fig. 5.15 Diagram of distribution of cards by suit and number.

still obtain the same answer as before if we assumed independence of suit and number. This is obviously wrong. The first formula will give the correct answer because it will allow for the fact that, *knowing* that we have a spade, the probability of a 4 is now 4/4.

In symbols we would have

$$P(S \text{ and } 4 \,|\, Y) = P(4 \,|\, Y) \cdot P(S \,|\, 4, \, Y) = \tfrac{1}{13} \cdot \tfrac{4}{4} = \tfrac{1}{13},$$

$$\text{or } P(S \,|\, Y) \cdot P(4 \,|\, S, \, Y) = \tfrac{1}{4} \cdot \tfrac{4}{13} = \tfrac{1}{13}.$$

(Note that we have substituted Y for X to recognize the change in the conditions of the deck.)

If we let A represent the suit and B the number and X the general conditions in the universe, we can write the more general formula for the probability of two joint events

$$P(A \text{ and } B \,|\, X) = P(A \,|\, X) \cdot P(B \,|\, A, X)$$

$$\text{or } P(B \,|\, X) \cdot P(A \,|\, B, X). \tag{5.1}$$

Since this formula involves the *multiplication* of probabilities, it is often called the *multiplication theorem*. We have used it many times in the preceding pages without realizing it as such. Our use has so far been restricted to cases of *independent* events where $P(A \,|\, X) = P(A \,|\, B, X)$, for example.

Suppose now we consider the problem of the probability that the drawn card will be a spade *or* a 4, with the or understood to also include a spade *and* a 4, or the 4 of spades in common parlance. Figure 5.16 diagrams this. The largest enclosure again represents the whole deck. The larger of the two subenclosures refers to all the spades in the deck, the smaller to all the 4's. Note that the two subenclosures overlap because one of the 4's is also a spade. The events, spade and 4, are not mutually exclusive. Hence we will not get the correct probability of a spade or a 4 if we simply add the probability of a spade to that of a 4. We would then be double-counting the overlap. Hence the correct procedure is

$$P(S \text{ or } 4 \,|\, X) = P(S \,|\, X) + P(4 \,|\, X) - P(S \text{ and } 4 \,|\, X)$$

$$= P(S \,|\, X) + P(4 \,|\, X) - P(S \,|\, X) \cdot P(4 \,|\, S, X)$$

$$= \tfrac{1}{4} + \tfrac{1}{13} - \tfrac{1}{4} \cdot \tfrac{1}{13} = \tfrac{16}{52}.$$

The general formula would be

$$P(A \text{ or } B \,|\, X) = P(A \,|\, X) + P(B \,|\, X) - P(A \,|\, X) \cdot P(B \,|\, A, X). \tag{5.2}$$

If A and B were mutually exclusive, then $P(B \,|\, A, X)$ would be 0 and the subtraction term would drop out. This is so when we deal

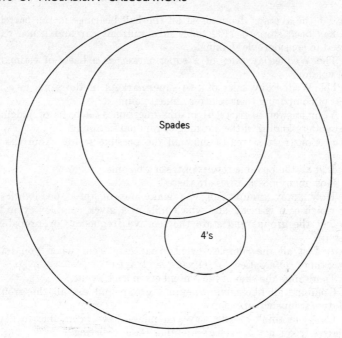

Fig. 5.16 Diagram of the overlap between the set of all spades and the set of all 4's in a playing card deck.

with classified events within the same universe, such as the weights of people. If we have a person who weighs 145 pounds (A), the probability that he also weighs 185 pounds (B) is 0. Hence the probability that a person weighs either 145 pounds or 185 pounds is the simple sum of the probabilities of each of these occurrences.

The formula shown as Eq. 5.2 is known as the *addition theorem,* or the theorem for *adding* the probabilities of alternative events. The formula applies whether or not the events are mutually exclusive. Since we are generally dealing with mutually exclusive events, we often use the formula without the subtraction term.

PROBLEMS AND QUESTIONS

5.1 Would you classify the following samples as random? Explain.

(a) A teaspoon of coffee from a cup to test the coffee's sweetness.

(b) A thermometer reading of the air temperature in your back yard to determine the air temperature in your city.

(c) A 3-hour date with a member of the opposite sex to test her (him) for long-run compatibility.

(d) A handful of ball bearings from the top of a barrel of ball bearings to test for the average diameter of all the ball bearings in the barrel. The barrel has been shipped 1100 miles in a railroad car and hence has been subjected to considerable shaking.

(e) The Wednesday sales of a supermarket as a basis of estimating its annual volume.

(f) The Wednesday sales of two supermarkets in the same city for the purpose of comparing their relative annual volumes.

(g) Your answer to part (b) of this question as a basis of judging your general understanding of the meaning of random sampling.

5.2(a) Construct a tree to show all the possible results from the tossing of 6 coins.

(b) List all the possible results of tossing 6 coins.

(c) How many possibilities are there?

(d) How many groups can you make out of these possibilities if we ignore which coin is heads and which tails in a given complex event?

(e) List the groups and state the relative frequency, or probability, of each group.

5.3(a) List all the complex events that can occur when you roll three dice at a time. (Be patient!) (Example: 1, 4, 6)

(b) Determine the sum of the 3 numbers in each event.

(c) Combine all like numbers into a group and list all the groups and the relative frequency of each.

(d) Can you think of any way you might have been able to determine the relative frequency of each group other than by listing?

5.4 What is the total number of possibilities for a sample drawn from each of the following universes? Show your method of calculation.

(a) Sample of one toss of 7 coins from a universe of 7 coins.

(b) Sample of one throw of 6 dice from a universe of 6 dice.

(c) Sample of one toss of 4 coins and 3 dice from a universe of 4 coins and 3 dice.

(d) Sample of 13 cards from a deck of 52 cards.

(e) Sample of 10 names drawn from a telephone book with 5000 names if:

1. A name is replaced after being drawn.

2. A name is not replaced after being drawn.

(f) Sample of five ants from an anthill to determine the average length of all the ants in the anthill. (How many ants in an anthill?)

(g) Sample of one trip through a maze that has the following sequence of *number* of choices at the successive turning points: 3, 2, 4, 5, 3.

5.5 Evaluate the following. You may use tables if you wish.

(a) $7!$ (b) $52!$ (c) $\dfrac{12!}{5!}$ (d) $\dfrac{365!}{21!344!}$ (e) 6^{28} (f) $2.718^{-4} = \dfrac{1}{2.718^4}$

5.6 Use the binomial theorem to calculate the probabilities of the various combinations that result from the tossing of six coins.

5.7 Evaluate the following:

(a) $\dbinom{5}{2}$ (b) $\dbinom{12}{4}$ (c) $\dbinom{12}{8}$ (d) $\dbinom{7}{2,5}$ (e) $\dbinom{12}{4,3,5} = \dfrac{12!}{4!3!5!}$ (f) $\dbinom{52}{13}$

5.8 Use binomial terms to calculate the probabilities of the following:

(a) Six heads on the toss of 9 coins.

(*b*) 50 heads on the toss of 100 coins. (Note how small this is even though it is the most probable result.)

(*c*) Eight 5's on the roll of 12 dice.

(*d*) 26 5's on the roll of 130 dice.

(*e*) Four defectives in a sample of 10 bolts if the probability of a defective is .2.

(*f*) Would five defectives in a sample of 10 bolts be quite convincing evidence that the process was generating more than 20% defectives? Show calculations and explain basis of decision.

5.9 Use the normal curve to approximate the probabilities of getting the various results from the tossing of 6 coins. Let 0 heads be 0, one head .167, two heads .333, etc. You can check your result for the calculation of the standard deviation by seeing if it agrees with

$$\sqrt{(.167 \times .833)/6}.$$

5.10 Calculate the standard deviation of the following sets of numbers without the use of any short cuts.

(*a*)	2	(*b*)	27	(*c*)	.324	(*d*)	2	(You may find it more con-
	4		34		.571		6	venient to group the like items.)
	7		41		.068		3	
	9		46		.249		5	
	13		58				3	
(*e*)	1286						4	
	2572						3	
	3858						5	
	5144						4	
	6430						4	

5.11 Calculate the standard deviation of the same series as in Problem 10 with the use of any short cuts you find handy.

5.12 Calculate the standard deviation of the series in Problem 10*e* by taking the following steps:

(*a*) *Divide* each number by 1286.

(*b*) Calculate the standard deviation of the resultant series by the short-cut method.

(*c*) *Multiply* the result by 1286.

(*d*) Compare your answer and the amount of work with what you did in Problems 10*e* and 11*e*.

5.13 Use the Poisson formula

$$Y_c = 2.71828^{-m} \cdot \frac{m^c}{c!}$$

or the Poisson Table to estimate the following probabilities. (Remember that a number raised to a negative power is the same as 1 divided by that number to the same positive power.)

(*a*) The probability of seven 5's on the roll of 100 dice.

(*b*) The probability of two defects in a sample of 10 welds if the welding operation is supposed to be generating only 2% defects.

(*c*) The probability of two or fewer defects under same conditions as in (*b*).

(d) The probability of three or more defects under same conditions as in (b).

(e) The probability that there will be no more than 3 defects in the surface of a piece of plate glass if $m = .5$.

(f) The probability that exactly two people out of 1000 policyholders will be killed by an accident that has a probability of .000006 of happening to a person. If your company had to pay claims on two such accidents, would you feel that you had any evidence that the accidents have been "rigged," and that the company would be justified in spending a little money on an investigation? Explain.

5.14 Use the Thorndike Chart for the following problems:

(a) All the parts of Problem 13.

(b) The probability of 26 or more 6's on the roll of 130 dice? (What is the difference between rolling 10 dice 13 times and rolling 130 dice at once?)

(c) The probability of two or more 6's on the roll of 10 dice? Why are your answers different in (b) and (c)?

(d) The probability of between two and four machine breakdowns in an hour out of a total of 20 machines if the probability of a breakdown is .05.

5.15 Use the normal curve to estimate the probabilities of the various results from the tossing of six coins. Let 0 heads be $-.083$ to $.083$, one head $.083 - .250$, etc.

Compare your results with those you got in Problems 2, 6, and 9.

5.16 Use the normal curve to estimate the following probabilities:

(a) Probability of a sample value of 6 or more if the universe has a mean of 4 and a standard deviation of 1.5.

(b) Probability of sample value of less than 8 if $m = 10$ and $s = .8$.

(c) Probability of sample value of between 5 and 9 if $m = 15$ and $s = 4.7$.

(d) Probability of sample value of 6 or more if $m = 8$ and $s = 1.5$.

5.17 Identify the following variables as being either discrete or continuous.

(a) The number of rooms in a house.

(b) The number of rooms in a house for purpose of getting an idea of the amount of living space in the house.

(c) The annual sales of a company from year to year.

(d) The rate of time-lost accidents per 1000 man-hours of exposure.

(e) The proportion of people who indicate a preference for a given brand of tooth paste.

(f) Manual dexterity of a group of workers.

5.18 In grading some examination papers an instructor discovers that two students who sat next to each other had identical wording in one of the answers. The answer was wrong. It contained 12 words. What kind of evidence is this that the two students cooperated with each other in some way during the examination?

5.19 What is the probability that at least one 5 will show up on the roll of 2 dice? Show your calculations.

5.20 What is the probability that at least three cards out of five playing cards will be hearts? Show calculations.

5.21 What is the probability that at least three cards out of five playing cards will be the same suit? Show calculations.

5.22 The probability that any one component in a rocket will fail is .001. The rocket has 500 component parts.

(a) What is the probability that the rocket will function properly?

(b) If it were desired to have a rocket that gave a .9 probability of a successful firing, how many parts would it be necessary to eliminate? (The parts would be eliminated through design improvements.)

(c) The probability of successful firing could also be improved by reducing the probability of failure of a component part. To what level must the probability of a component failure be reduced in order to give a .9 probability of a successful firing?

5.23 The probability that a trailer truck will fail to negotiate a given curve on a highway is .000001 if the truck does not exceed a speed of 30 mph coming into the curve. The probability of failure increases to .001 at 40 mph, .01 at 50 mph and to .1 at 60 mph. A given truck failed to negotiate the curve, crashed through the guard rail and struck and seriously injured two people. In the investigation the driver claimed that he was not traveling over 30 mph and that something went wrong with the steering. What is the probability that the driver was lying, or at least inaccurate in his perception of his true speed? (There is no way to check the steering.)

How fast would you estimate that the driver was really traveling? How much confidence do you have in the correctness of your estimate? (Make sure that your estimate covers some range.)

5.24 Your firm manufactures a product that must be protected from temperature variations. It is relatively expensive to provide this protection. There are times when very little protection is needed because of the actual temperature prevailing. The decision on how much artificial protection to use is based on the weather forecast for the critical time period. Two sources of such forecasts are used, the local office of the United States Weather Bureau and a local private forecasting service. A check of the past record of these two sources reveals that they both have had a record of success of .9 in forecasting the temperature within a tolerable range.

(a) If both forecasters agree on a given forecast, what is the probability of a correct decision if you follow their advice? What critical assumption did you make in calculating this probability?

(b) Suppose the two forecasters disagree. How good a decision technique would it be to flip a coin to see which forecaster you will follow? Can you think of a better way to make the decision?

(c) A careful check of the historical records reveals that the two forecasters agree on their forecasts 98% of the time. Are their forecasts independent of each other? Explain. (Note: Independent does not necessarily refer only to the issue of whether there is or is not any actual communication or collaboration between the two forecasters. It is conceivable, for example, that both use essentially the same evidence and essentially the same techniques for analyzing that evidence. Their answers would thus tend to agree even though the people involved operated independently of each other. We are concerned with whether their answers are independent.)

5.25 Your company has a warehouse right on the waterfront at an eastern United States port. A hurricane has been moving up the coast with a currently estimated probability of .03 of causing rains and tidal floods that will result in 4 feet of water on the first floor of the warehouse. You are responsible for deciding whether to spend the money to have the warehouse emptied on the first floor. The company has no hurricane insurance.

What factors would you weigh in making your decision? What probabilities would be important? Explain.

chapter 6

Some useful analytical tools

Our discussion of the normal curve introduced the arithmetic mean and the standard deviation, the two most commonly used analytical tools in statistical work. These are only two members of a family of analytical tools. It is now important for us to introduce other members and show how each of the various tools can play a special role in a particular problem. Thus fortified, we will be able to pursue further study of the statistical method without being distracted by the necessity to stop and explain a tool that the current problem makes useful.

The various tools we discuss are all aimed at our basic problem of dealing with an event that might have all kinds of values, the typical situation in all decision problems. The *distribution* of such possible values is our main concern. We have already discovered that we can deal with such distributions in many ways. We discovered we could *list* all the possible values. Although this list is easy to understand, it is very tedious, and sometimes impossible, to complete. Hence we searched for shorthand ways of summarizing such a list. One shorthand way was the *binomial theorem* system of counting. Although the binomial theorem system was more efficient than the listing system, it also gets very tedious, although tables are now available that can help considerably to expedite the routine work. We then discovered that we could often make *useful approximations* to a distribution by such model distributions as the Poisson and the normal. In the case of the normal, we discovered that all we needed were the arithmetic mean and standard deviation of the desired distribution and a table of the normal curve, a table that can be conveniently summarized on one page of a book. We could then estimate the relative frequencies, or probabilities, for any desired values within the distribution.

If our practical problems were all such that normal curve approximations were adequate, we could stop our discussion with the arithmetic mean and the standard deviation. Unfortunately this is not so. Many events in business and economic problems have distributions that do not fall into convenient patterns. It is then that we must improvise and use other analytical devices, such as the median in place of the arithmetic mean, and quartiles and deciles in place of the standard deviation. Such other analytical devices are our concern in this chapter.

Since the crucial issue in many practical problems is that of deciding when we can use the mean and standard deviation with reasonable impunity rather than being forced by the shape of the relevant distributions to resort to less convenient devices, we also find it necessary to pay particular attention to those devices that help us to gain a quick impression of the *shape* of the relevant frequency distributions. We have already used some *charts* of frequency distributions as such a device. In this chapter we elaborate a bit on the use of charts to represent a picture of a distribution. We also refer to some *mathematical* tools for measuring the degree to which a distribution lacks symmetry. If a distribution is not symmetrical, we say that it is *skewed,* and we call measures of lack of symmetry measures of *skewness.*

Since we cannot analyze a frequency distribution until we have one, we also discuss the process of constructing frequency distributions from *real data,* rather than from artificial data such as the hypothetical results of coin tosses.

6.1　Averages

It has been customary to introduce children to "the average" in the fifth grade in the American school system. The average is defined as the *sum* of the set of numbers divided by the *number* of numbers in the set. This early indoctrination has rather thoroughly implanted in our culture the notion that there is such a thing as *the* average. Actually, of course, the problem is not quite so simple. At the same time that the child *calculates* the average in the approved way, he *thinks* of an average as something that connotes ordinary, or usual, or middle. The *mathematical* properties of his calculation are generally of no concern. In fact, the typical youngster is not at all aware of what those mathematical properties imply.

We become concerned with the subject of averages because we often *represent* a set of numbers by a single number, or average. It is important that we know what it is about the set that we are representing, and also that what we are representing makes practical sense in our problem. We should mention, too, that the subject of averages is very important in its own right, quite apart from any particular use we make of averages in this book. We have been dealing with averages in one form or another almost continuously since we became aware of our environment. We should now find it useful to try to organize our notions about averages as they affect our day-to-day conduct.

Three General Purposes Dictate the Choice of an Average

Although there are many more than three different averages, there really are only three general purposes for which averages are used. Any particular average will be found to fall under one of these three purposes:

1. The purpose requires the average to be *as close as possible* to all the items of the group. Such an average is often called a *least-error* value.
2. The purpose requires the average to *coincide exactly* with the event being predicted. In other words, being close does not count. Common sense suggests that the best value to choose from the group is the one that *occurs most often*. Such an average is often called the *most probable* value.
3. The purpose expresses no interest in *individual* items. (The above two purposes are very much interested in individual items.) Rather it expresses an interest in *combinations* of items. The combination of items that is most meaningful, and hence most commonly used, is the *total* of the items.

The Least-Error Value.   Although we deplore the practice, it is very common to make a *single-valued* estimate of something, such as the company sales for the coming year. (We much prefer that the sales forecast be expressed as a *range of expectation* with an *associated probability* in order to reflect explicitly the degree of uncertainty involved.) It is obviously important for the forecast to be *close* to the true value. The size of the error does make a difference. Hence we wish the forecast to be *as close as possible* to what is likely to happen.

We can make the problem more concrete by taking a much oversimplified example. Let us assume that our analysis of all pertinent (as far as we know) factors affecting our company's sales led us to believe that any one of the following sales volumes might occur with equal probability:

$$12, 14, 17, 18, 24 \text{ (millions of dollars)}$$

What forecast would we make, keeping in mind that we want our forecast to be as close as possible to the right answer? A useful approach to the problem is to put these 5 possibilities in perspective by placing them along a scale as follows:

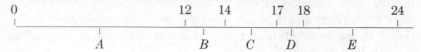

It is obviously foolish to select a value such as *A* because we can get closer to all five of the possible results by moving to the right until we reach 12. If we then move from 12 to *B*, we get further away from 12, but we get closer to the other four possibilities. If we quantify the value of such a movement from 12 to *B*, we can say that for each *increase* in error of $1000 with respect to 12, we *decrease* our error a total of $4000 with respect to 14, 17, 18, and 24, thus giving us a net decrease of $3000. It pays, therefore, to move to 14. If we continue past 14 to the point *C*, we would now be moving away from two of the possibilities and closer to three of them. This gives us a net reduction in error of $1000. It is, therefore, worthwhile to move to 17. If we proceed from 17 to *D*, we would move away from three of the possibilities and toward only two, thus *increasing* error by $1000, and the value that gives us the *least deviation* from all the possible values, therefore, is 17.

We can now say that the least-error value is the one that has as many values above it in size as it has below it in size. Such a value is called the *median*. If there are an *even* number of possibilities, there is no single median. Any value either equal to or between the two middle values would satisfy the least-error criterion. We can see that this is so if we eliminate 18 from our set of possibilities. Note that any movement between 14 and 17 results in moving closer to *two* of the items and further away from *two* of the items, resulting in a net change of total error of zero. Sometimes we are indifferent to which of the set of least-error values we choose. So we would be in this particular example [1] which assumes that only the specified items could occur. However, in most practical prob-

---

[1] If in truth only these four items could occur, we might still argue for either 14 or 17, rather than for any value in between, on the grounds that the extremes are equally good as the in-between values as far as minimizing error is concerned. But they have an additional advantage. Choice of either of these, or both, permits us to enjoy the thrill of being exactly right, an impossibility if we choose a value that cannot occur. Such a thrill has some value to most people, even if only psychological.

lems no such limitations exist. Gaps in the sample information are due to limitations in the size of the sample, not to the fact that certain values cannot occur. Thus we can imagine values in this indifference range. We must make an assumption about the way these values are distributed. In the absence of specific information to the contrary, we usually apply the equal distribution of ignorance rule and assume that the missing items are equally spaced throughout the indifference range. The next step is to apply the least-error concept to these equally spaced items. This concept suggests that the *middle* value among all these imagined possibilities is the best one to use. We usually calculate the middle value by taking half the sum, or the arithmetic mean, of the two middle values in the sample. Here we would get 15.5.

The Most Probable Value. If our problem is such that our answer must be *exactly* right, prudence suggests that we should be right *as often as possible,* with no concern for the amount of error when we are wrong. The proper value to select for such a problem is the one that is expected to have the *highest probability* of occurring. We call such a value the *mode.* Since the value that has occurred most often is the most likely value to occur most often in the future (we assume no shifts in the universe), the mode is simply the most frequent value that has occurred.

Although the mode has often been called the most logical of all the averages, connoting what is usually thought as average, there are really very few practical situations in which it is proper to use the mode. Since its use should be limited to those cases where we must be *exactly* right, it can logically be used only when we can tell whether we are exactly right. Our limited abilities of perception make it impossible to know when we are exactly right except where we have set up certain defined rules or standards. For example, we know we are exactly right when we guess the 4 of spades and it occurs. We know this because the 4 of spades is what it is by definition. There is no 4.00078 of spades, for example. But, if we guess a man's height as 6 feet, how can we ever be sure that he is 6 feet tall?

We say, therefore, that we should use the mode only when we are dealing with things that are so defined that we have no trouble distinguishing one thing from another. Even then we would not use the mode unless it was clear that the size of an error is of no significance. One of the best ways to test whether we wish a *least-error value* or a *most probable value* in a given problem is to imagine that we have already made an estimate and are now comparing it with the actual result. Or better still, compare two hypothetical estimates with a presumed actual value. For example, suppose we have two sales estimates of $5 million and $15 million dollars. The actual happens to be $14.7 million. If we feel better with an estimate of $15 million than we do with an estimate of $5 million, it is clear that it is important to us to be close. If $15 million is no better than $5 million, it is not important to be close, and "a miss is as good as a mile." It is, of course, very important to be close with a sales forecast.

Combinations of Items—Totals. If we were trying to estimate the *total* cost of a group of items which we had produced, we could make such an estimate by multiplying the number of items in the group by the *arithmetic mean* cost of an item. We defined the arithmetic mean as

$$\overline{X} = \frac{\Sigma X}{N}.$$

It is clear from this definition that $N \cdot \overline{X} = \Sigma X$. It is equally clear that $\Sigma X / \overline{X} = N$.

Thus we see that the most important characteristic of the arithmetic mean is its algebraic relationship to the *total* and to the *number* of items. Although most of us first learned to calculate the arithmetic mean as "the average," there is really nothing inherent in its calculation that results in a value that could properly be called an average in the sense of a typical or usual item. The arithmetic mean becomes an average in the typical sense only by coincidence, certainly not by definition. The coincidence occurs when the distribution of items happens to be *symmetrical*. Figure 6.1 gives illustrations of symmetrical distributions. A single-humped symmetrical distribution such as in *A* would have its mean, median, and mode all equal to each other. Thus we might *calculate* the *mean* even though we want the *median*, and no harm is done. A rectangular distribution as in *B* would have the mean equal to the median also, but the distribution has as many modes as it has items because each item occurs equally often. A bimodal distribution as in *C* again has the median equal to the mean. The two modes suggest the possibility that two overlapping distributions, each with its own mode, have been combined and perhaps had better be separated if at all possible. An example of such a bimodal distribution

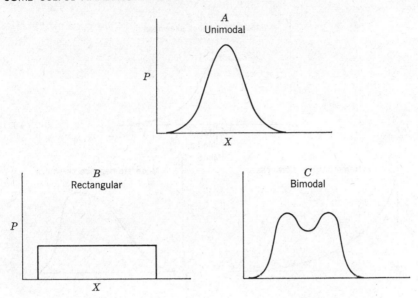

Fig. 6.1 Three examples of symmetrical distributions.

would be a distribution of the heights of adult humans with no distinction as to sex.

Figure 6.2 shows some examples of asymmetrical, or skewed, distributions. Part *A*, with *positive* skewness, is a type of distribution that occurs quite often in business and economic data. Note that the mean is larger than the median, which in turn is larger than the mode. If the skewness is only moderate, we find that the distance between the mode and median is about twice that between the median and the mean, a relationship that makes it possible to estimate any one of these from the other two. Part *B* illustrates what is called a reverse-*J* distribution, a distribution with substantial positive skewness. The above relationship among the median, mean, and mode would not hold in this case. A *negatively*-skewed distribution as in *C* is more a curiosity than a fact in business data. It is so rare that, if we see one, we should suspect the method of collecting the data, or we should suspect that artificial restraints have been put on the phenomenon being measured.

The fact that the mean *might* be equal to the median has been the cause of considerable chaos in the use of averages. For reasons we examine shortly, the mean rather completely dominates the choice of average to use. What causes chaos is that usually no explicit

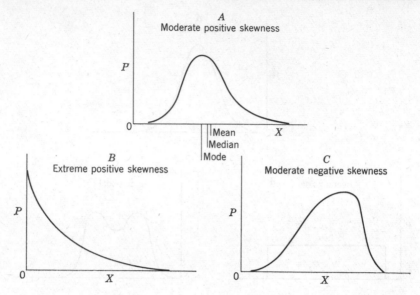

Fig. 6.2 Three examples of skewed distributions.

statement is made as to whether the mean is selected because it *is* the mean and is the correct value to use when we are interested in the *total*, or whether the mean is selected because we believe the distribution is sufficiently symmetrical to make the mean a reasonable approximation to the *median*, the value that we really want.

The Harmonic Mean to Represent a Total. Although the arithmetic mean fortunately satisfies most problems that require knowledge of the total, there are circumstances under which it is not appropriate. We can best understand the circumstances by recognizing that almost all measurements are really *rates*, and that all rates can be expressed in two ways, with one way being the reciprocal of the other. For example, a production rate for a man can be expressed as X pieces per hour or as Y hours per piece. Thus 20 pieces per hour would be the exact equivalent of .05 hours per piece. In our automobile 30 miles per hour is the equivalent of .03333 hours per mile.

Table 6.1 contrasts the two ways of presenting the production rates of three workers. Note that the first way, pieces per hour, shows the *output varying* from worker to worker and the *time constant*. The second way shows the *time varying* and the *output constant*. Suppose we had the problem of estimating how long it would take

TABLE 6.1

Contrasting Ways of Showing Production Rates of Workers

Man	Pieces per Hour	Hours per Piece
A	3	.33333
B	4	.25000
C	6	.16667

these three men, or any given number of similar men, to fill a production order of 200 pieces. We would suppose that we could solve
such a problem by using the average output per man per hour or
the average hours per man per piece. The proper average in each
case would seem to be the arithmetic mean because we are interested in the *total* output or the *total* time. The mean pieces per
hour is 4.3333. The mean hours per piece is .2500. Dividing 200
pieces by 4.3333 pieces per hour, we find that it will take 46.154 man-
hours to turn out 200 pieces. Multiplying 200 pieces by .2500 hours
per piece, we find that it will take 50 man-hours to turn out 200
pieces. Something is wrong with at least one of these calculations.
The 50 hours calculated from the arithmetic mean of .2500 hours per
piece is wrong here. This calculation assumes that each man will
produce the *same number of pieces* during the production period.
Such an assumption would be correct if work rules were such that
each man is assigned the same quota and would quit for the day
when he had filled his quota. Most work rules are not of this sort,
but rather such that each man works the *same amount of time,* with
the fast workers producing more than the slow workers during that
time.

Note the assumption of equal number of pieces results in more
man-hours than the assumption of equal amounts of time. This is
as we would expect. If we restrict the output of fast workers to the
same amount as for slow workers, we would obviously reduce the
over-all average rate of output, or conversely, increase the average
time required.

Having concluded that the arithmetic mean of pieces per hour
gives us the right answer and the arithmetic mean of hours per piece
the wrong answer in this case, we next must decide what we should
do if our data are expressed as hours per piece. Probably the easiest
thing to do, and the most logical, would be to convert the data to

pieces per hour and use the arithmetic mean. If we had some
cogent reason for the final answer to be expressed in hours per piece,
we could convert back by taking the reciprocal of the arithmetic
mean of pieces per hour. The reciprocal of 4.3333 pieces per hour
is .23077 hours per piece. Note that 200 pieces multiplied by .23077
hours per piece will give us a total man-hours of 46.154, the same
result as dividing 200 by 4.3333.

The process of taking reciprocals of a set of numbers because the
wrong factor is constant in the original set, taking the arithmetic
mean of the reciprocals, and then converting back to the original
form by taking the reciprocal of the arithmetic mean, results in
calculating the *harmonic mean* of the original set of numbers. Thus
we would call .23077 the harmonic mean of the three numbers, .3333,
.25000, and .16667. Using familiar symbols, we can express the
formula for the harmonic mean as

$$H = \frac{1}{\dfrac{\sum \dfrac{1}{x}}{N}} = \frac{N}{\sum \dfrac{1}{x}}.$$

Because the harmonic mean is rather strange to most people, we
should not use it if we can avoid it. We should simply convert our
data and use the more familiar arithmetic mean. The following
routine may help to decide when such conversion is needed.

1. First, find out what factor is varying in the *real situation*. In our
   problem it would be output per worker, not hours of work.
2. Second, find out what factor is varying in the series of data. In our
   problem it would be output per worker if we had the pieces per hour
   data; it would be hours of work if we had the hours per piece data.
3. Third, if the answers to the above two questions are the same, as they
   would be if we had the pieces per hour data, the arithmetic mean of
   the given data is correct. If the answers are different, the given data
   must be converted by taking reciprocals of the numbers. The arithmetic mean of these reciprocals would then give a correct answer.

Other Combinations of Items. Although to add a set of numbers
is certainly the most common and most meaningful way to combine
numbers, it is not the only way. Another thing we could do is
multiply a set of numbers. For example, our pieces per hour data
could be added to get a total of 13 pieces per hour; they could be
multiplied together to get the product 72 ?. We use the question
mark because we have a definite problem of units here. The unit
implied by our mathematics would be cubic pieces, or, if you prefer,

pieces cubed. Just to state such units is to reveal their ridiculous character.

Thus we can say that the product of a set of numbers usually makes no sense if the various numbers have some unit attached to them unless our ultimate interest results in the disappearance of this unit. The unit disappears only when we are basically concerned with *rates of change* from one number to another or with *ratios* of elements in one set to corresponding elements in another set. For example, let us suppose we had an investment fund that had the values as shown in column 2 of Table 6.2. Then let us suppose we made the vague request that we would like to know the average value of the fund during this period. We say vague because we have failed to state our purpose, and without the purpose we can calculate several answers.

Before we discuss the eight different answers shown in the lower section of Table 6.2, let us explain the logic of the use of the logarithms. We use the logs as a calculation tool to simplify the multiplying of the numbers together, and, even more important, to simplify the taking of the proper root of the resultant product. Turn to column 4 for clarification of the procedure. Here we determine the *total* of the logarithms of each of the fund values. The total of logarithms is really the mathematical equivalent of the *product of the fund values*. We then *divided* the total of the logarithms by 5, thus getting the arithmetic mean of the logarithms. To divide the total of logarithms by 5 is the mathematical equivalent of taking the 5th root of the product of the fund values. We then took the antilogarithm of 2.067432 and got a value of $116,800. The result of this routine of calculation is the *geometric mean*. In familiar symbols the routine can be summarized as

$$\text{Geometric Mean} = \sqrt[n]{X_1 \cdot X_2 \cdots X_n}$$

or

$$G = \text{antilog} \frac{\Sigma \log X}{N}$$

It is clear that the geometric mean is strictly a function of the *product* of the items. If this product has no meaning, it is extremely difficult to attach any significance to the nth root of that product. As pointed out above, this product usually has no meaning if the numbers multiplied together have some unit attached to them, such as dollars, bushels, pounds, feet, quarts, etc.

Now let us turn to the discussion of the eight answers. The arithmetic mean of the five fund values is $117,600. This has no

TABLE 6.2

Alternative Ways of Determining the Average Value of an Investment Fund

Year (1)	Value of Fund—End of Year $1000 (2)	Ratio of Fund Value to that in Preceding Year (3)	Logarithms of Fund Values (4)	Logarithms of Ratios (5)
1955	100	—	2.000000	—
1956	108	1.0800	2.033424	.033424
1957	115	1.0648	2.060698	.027268
1958	125	1.0870	2.096910	.036230
1959	140	1.1200	2.146128	.049218
Totals:	588	4.3518	10.337160	.146140
Arith. Mean:	117.6	1.08795	2.067432	.036535
Median:	115	1.08350	2.060698	.034827

Antilogarithms

Mean:	116.80	1.0878
Median:	115	1.0835

Value of Fund at End of 1957 if
  (1) Arithmetic mean *value* had prevailed:

                                       117.6

  (2) Median *value* had prevailed:

                                         115

  (3) Geometric mean *value* had prevailed:

                                       116.80

  (4) Geometric *median value* had prevailed:

                                       115

  (5) Arithmetic mean *rate of change* had prevailed:
      $100 \times (1.08795)^2$ 118.364

  (6) Median *rate of change* had prevailed:
      $100 \times (1.08350)^2$ 117.397

  (7) Geometric mean *rate of change* had prevailed:
      $100 \times (1.0878)^2$ 118.331

  (8) Geometric *median rate of change* had prevailed:

                                         115

significance as such because the total from which it came has no significance. The lack of meaning in the total is quite clear when we realize that we might as well have evaluated the fund every 6 months, or even every week, giving us a total about twice as big, or 52 times as big.

The *median* of $115,000 would have significance if we thought that our experience with this fund would be of value in predicting our experience with a new fund also starting out at $100,000. If we had no way of predicting how long we would be able to let such a fund accumulate, other than that we would definitely liquidate it at the end of 4 complete years, if not sooner, we might argue that the best single estimate of the value of the fund at this relatively unknown liquidation date would be $115,000. We might add that this solution assumes that the *time order* of the varying rates of accumulation is of significance. The *median rate of change* of the fund, ignoring the time order, is +8.35%. (See column 3.) If we let this compound for 2 years, we get an expected value of the fund at the end of 2 years of $117,400. (See solution 6.)

The *geometric mean* value of the fund of $116,800 has no practical significance because the product on which it is based has no significance.

The *geometric median* value of the fund of $115,000 has the same significance as the median because it is, of course, exactly the same answer. Examine the way these two measures were calculated and see that they will always yield the same answer.

The *arithmetic mean rate of change* of 8.795% has no significance because the total on which it is based has none. (It should go without saying that a ratio of 1.08795 is the equivalent of a rate of change of 8.795%.) The fund value of $118,400, therefore, which is based on this rate of change also has no practical significance. (See solution 5.)

The *geometric mean rate of change* of 8.78% has at least mathematical significance, even though its practical significance is illusory. If this rate had prevailed in *each* of the 4 years of accumulation, instead of the actual rate, the fund would have still had a value of $140,000 at the end of 1959. That this is so makes it clear that we went to considerable extra work in calculating this rate. We could have obtained the same answer more economically by taking the 4th root of the ratio of the 1959 fund to the 1955 fund, or

$$\sqrt[4]{\frac{140}{100}}.$$

This calculation is further simplified by using logarithms, the answer being

$$\text{antilog } \frac{\log 140 - \log 100}{4}.$$

It is very easy to prove that these two methods give the same answer by proving that the *product* of the ratios in column 3 is exactly the same as the ratio of 140 to 100. Let us write out all the terms of the ratios and take their product:

$$\frac{108}{100} \times \frac{115}{108} \times \frac{125}{115} \times \frac{140}{125} = \frac{140}{100}$$

Note that all the terms between 100 and 140 cancel.

Where have we ended up, then, in our attempt to answer the question of "What was the average value of the fund?". It seems it is fair to say we have ended in a state of confusion. We apparently set out to illustrate the use of the *product* of a set of numbers and of its derivative concept, the *geometric mean*. We seem to have demonstrated that neither the product nor the geometric mean of these fund values has any meaning. We did go a step further, however, in calculating the product of the *ratios* of successive fund values. This product does have at least mathematical meaning. Note that when we took the ratios, we *canceled out the unit*. For example, 1.0800 in column 3 has no unit. Hence the product of such ratios does not cause us to end up with such absurd answers as in quintic dollars, which is what we get when we take the product of the five fund values. We also discovered that the product of these ratios is the mathematical equivalent of the single ratio of 140 to 100. Thus, if we know what this ratio means, we know what the product of all the individual ratios means.

Part of our confusion was caused by our not knowing why we wanted to know the average value of the fund. Not knowing, we let our imagination run and hence developed eight different averages. We eliminated three because they were based on meaningless totals or products. They are numbered (1), (3), and (5) in the table. Since three of the remaining five turned out to be the same, we are now reduced to only three open to consideration. To choose among these, we must ask and answer why anybody would wish to know the average value of such a fund. We discussed one possible purpose when we were considering the median value and the median rate of change. There we discovered that $115,000 was an appropriate answer if we assumed that the time order of the rates of change was indicative of the kind of time order that might prevail in the future. If not, an answer of $117,400 was appropriate.

The only remaining possibility is the use of the geometric mean rate of change. This would be meaningful *only if* the investment conditions were such that the fund must be committed for 4 years with no possibility of liquidation at a prior date. This is, of course, a very rare situation. The closest thing to it occurs with the Series E bonds of the Federal Government. The advertised rate of interest on such bonds is the average rate of return only if the bonds are held to maturity. Redemption at any prior date results in a rate of return less than the advertised rate. Thus the advertised rate is really the *maximum* rate we might earn if we bought such bonds. We would really be quite foolish if we purchased such bonds as though the maximum rate were the average rate. The reader is left to figure out an appropriate average rate for Series E bonds to compare with the expected rate of return on an alternative investment.

Clear-cut examples of the proper use of the geometric mean are not easy to find. We try again in the chapter on index numbers. In the meantime, we should not accept unthinkingly any presumably correct use of the geometric mean.

Other Factors in the Choice of an Appropriate Average. Although the three purposes mentioned dominate the choice of an average and *should prevail over any other consideration,* there are times when the distribution is sufficiently symmetrical for the three primary averages, mean, median, and mode, to be practically the same size. It is then that other criteria enter the arena of choice.

Relative Stability in Sampling. Figure 6.3 compares a distribution of means of random samples with one of medians. The samples each contained three items. The universe was symmetrical. Note the greater spread of the medians. This illustrates a very important weakness of the median compared to the mean: the median in general is more subject to sampling errors than the mean. Thus it is entirely possible for the *mean* of a random sample to be a better estimate of the *median* of the universe than the *median* of the sample would be.

Therefore, whenever it is reasonable to assume that the universe is symmetrical, we definitely prefer to use the mean of the sample as our average, even though our purpose requires the least-error value or the median.

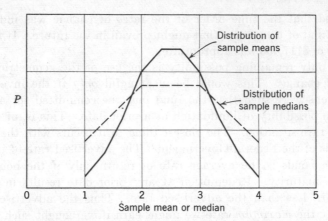

Fig. 6.3 Comparison of distributions of means of random samples and medians of random samples. (Universe consists of the numbers 1, 2, 3, 4. All possible samples of 3 items each are included in the distributions.)

Susceptible to Algebraic Manipulation. Another weakness of the median is that it bears no precise algebraic relationship to the distribution from which it is calculated. Hence it becomes very difficult to manipulate the median mathematically. The mean, on the other hand, has a precise relationship to the *total* and the *number* of items in the distribution. It is not surprising, therefore, that the basic structure of mathematical statistics is built around the arithmetic mean. It cannot be overemphasized, however, that the fundamental assumption underlying this mathematical structure is that the universe is at least *symmetrical*. We say at least because sometimes the even more restrictive assumption of *normality* has to be made.

Again we conclude stating that we prefer the mean to the median as a *least-error* value *if* the appropriate assumptions are reasonable.

Transforming Data to Make Them Symmetrical. Our preference for the mean over the median can at times be so strong that we make an effort to convert a skewed distribution into one that is reasonably symmetrical. This conversion should not be carried out by any arbitrary throwing away of some of the items of evidence, a technique sometimes used in time study. Rather it should be done by the application of a standard mathematical procedure. Table 6.3 illustrates such a mathematical transformation of data. The original series, *X*, is definitely skewed. Note that the arith-

TABLE 6.3

Transforming a Skewed Series to a Symmetrical Series by the Use of Logarithms

X	Log X
1	.000000
2	.301030
4	.602060
8	.903090
16	1.204120
32	1.505150
64	1.806180
127	6.321630

$$\overline{X} = 18.14 \qquad .903090$$
$$\text{Median(Md)} = 8 \qquad .903090$$
$$\text{Gm} = 8 \text{ (antilog of .903090)}$$

metic mean of 18.14 is substantially larger than the median of 8. The distribution of the logarithms of X is symmetrical, however. Note that the median and mean of the logs are both equal to .903090. Also note that in this case the *geometric* mean of the original data will equal the median.

We can do other things than use logarithms. We find many physical phenomena that seem to follow a square-root law in the sense that one variable varies as the square root of another variable. Then we might find it convenient to work with the square roots of the original items rather than with the items themselves. Another possible transformation device is the reciprocal, which we used in the calculation of the harmonic mean. We can also combine logarithms with reciprocals, etc.

The work involved in doing this sort of thing can be quite substantial and very frustrating if our efforts turn out to be fruitless. The use of special graph paper, constructed on the same principles as logarithmic paper and probability paper, can facilitate our efforts to make a skewed series reasonably symmetrical. We must confess, however, that relatively little success has been had in transforming skewed business data into symmetrical data by some simple device. We should hesitate to devote much time to a search for a proper transformation unless we have very strong reasons to prefer the arithmetic mean to the median.

Mathematical Properties of Mean and Median. We already have noted that the median is a least-error value (p. 188) and that the sum of the deviations around the mean equals 0 (p. 149). We now note that the mean is a *least-squared-error* value. These three mathematical properties are illustrated in Table 6.4.

Column 2 illustrates that the sum of the deviations from the mean equals 0. This is the property that makes it possible to use short-cut methods of calculating the mean. It also considerably simplifies much of the mathematics of manipulating the arithmetic mean. It also tells us that the mean divides a series into two parts so that the sum of all the items above the mean equals the sum of all the items below the mean. It is thus analogous to the center of gravity. It should be clear that this would mean nothing in a practical problem unless it were meaningful to add the items in a series.

Column 3 illustrates the process of getting the sum of the *squares* of the deviations from the mean. This is fundamental to the calculation of the standard deviation, and the squaring is done to systematically convert all the minus signs to plus signs. The sum of these squared deviations, 338, is the smallest sum of squared deviations it is possible to get with this series of five numbers. If we measure these squared deviations from any other value than 10, the *arithmetic mean,* we find their sum to be larger than 338. For example, column 6 measures them from the median, or 7 in this case, resulting in a sum of 383. It is easily proved by the use of calculus that the sum of the squared deviations is a minimum when

TABLE 6.4

Illustration of Mathematical Properties of the Arithmetic Mean and the Median

X (1)	$X - \overline{X}$ (2)	$(X - \overline{X})^2$ (3)	$\lvert X - \overline{X} \rvert$ (4)	$\lvert X - \text{Md} \rvert$ (5)	$(X - \text{Md})^2$ (6)
2	-8	64	8	5	25
4	-6	36	6	3	9
7	-3	9	3	0	0
12	2	4	2	5	25
25	15	225	15	18	324
50	0	338	34	31	383

$\overline{X} = 10; \text{Md} = 7$

they are measured from the arithmetic mean. This explains why the mean is often called the least-squares value.

Although the least-squares property is very useful in calculations, it should not be interpreted as having any other practical significance. If least-squares estimates have any practical use, it is because they are the same as arithmetic-mean estimates, not because they are least squares. As a matter of fact, rarely does a squared error make any sense at all. For example, we would hesitate to tell our boss that the given sales estimate was expected to be accurate with 80% confidence within a range of 300,000,000 square dollars. If a squared error makes no sense, then, of course, it makes no sense as such to minimize them.

Column 5 illustrates the calculation of the sum of the deviations around the median, with the *direction of the deviation being ignored*, thus making all the signs plus. We proved by the use of a graph (p. 188) that this sum is a minimum when it is measured from the median. Note that the sum is 34 if we measure from the mean in this case.

The fact that we generally are interested in a *least-error* value even though we usually calculate a *least-squares* value is a persistent complication in the application of statistical methods. It forces us to be continually alert to the *shape* of the distribution with which we work, the fundamental requirement being that the distribution be essentially symmetrical.

6.2 Frequency Series

We have already had substantial contact with frequency series in our study of coin and dice throws. The frequency series arose because we had decided to treat some individual events as though they were the same even though they were conceptually or actually different. For example, if we toss five coins and get a result of *HHTTH*, this is obviously different from a result of *THHTH*. This difference makes a difference to us, however, only if the *order* of the heads and tails counts. If the order does not make a difference to us, we find it desirable to treat these two events as the same, thus giving us a *frequency* of 2 for the event of three heads and two tails.

Another interesting thing we discovered in our analysis of the frequency distributions of coins and dice was the tendency of such distributions to conform quite well to the normal, or Gaussian, distribution. We achieved considerable economy of time and effort by using the normal distribution as an approximation device.

Frequency Distributions of Coin Tossing Data

We now direct our attention to the construction of frequency series from actual sample data. We can illustrate one of the problems that arises by examining some actual results of a coin tossing experiment. Table 6.5 compares the universe of long-run expectations with two separate experiments in tossing five coins 100 times. First note that the two experiments yielded different results, the most notable difference being the skewness in the first distribution. If we assume that both of these experimental distributions were generated by the same universe, and this seems reasonable since the same set of five coins was used for both, we can explain these different results only by labeling them due to fluctuations of random sampling. (This is really another way of saying that the differences were due to reasons unknown.) Hence we might assume that the differences are strictly short-run and would disappear if we made the sample large enough in each case. In fact, we might go even further and assume that both of these distributions would then be the same as the hypothesized universe.

TABLE 6.5

Universe of Long-run Expectations Compared with Results of Two Experiments in the Tossing of 5 Coins 100 Times

Number of Heads	Universe of Long-run Expectancy *	Actual Frequency for 100 Tosses	
		Experiment #1	Experiment #2
0	3	6	2
1	16	17	19
2	31	33	29
3	31	33	30
4	16	8	17
5	3	3	3
	100	100	100

* Based upon the hypothesis that the probability of a head is .5 for each of the 5 coins.

We are thus brought to what is the real problem for us. The typical practical situation finds us in possession of only one set of results of the kind shown in Experiment 1 or 2. We are quite sure that if we obtained another set, the results would be different from the first, and that both would be different from the unknown universe of long-run expectations. Our typical problem, then, is making the best guess we can about the universe distribution from the information provided by *one* sample distribution. In doing this we must answer questions like this: Is the universe really *symmetrical* even though the sample shows some skewness? (Cf. Experiment 1.) Does the universe have a basically *smooth* distribution as we proceed from one frequency class to another? Does the universe have about the same degree of variation in it as the sample, or might the sample have left out a proper share of extreme items? And so forth.

It should be obvious that our answers to these and similar questions are subject to *uncertainty*. Therefore we concentrate on coming up with not a *single* answer to such questions, but really a *set* or *class* of answers, with the set big enough to properly reflect the degree of ignorance we have about the location of the true answer.

An Important Qualification. In order to simplify our discussion over the next several pages, we are going to assume away the problem that the universe may be changing over the period under study. We are going to treat our sample items as though they all came from the same universe. This would be a very dangerous assumption in most practical problems, and we do not make it later. But for the moment it will enable us to concentrate on other issues.

Some Actual Data

Table 6.6 lists the first 200 charge sales on a given day in a neighborhood hardware store in the order in which they actually occurred. Since we are assuming that no shifts were taking place in the universe during the day, that is, there were no tendencies for the sales to get larger or smaller in any systematic way as the day progressed, we ignore the chronological order henceforth. The important thing is *how often* sales of various sizes occurred.

The Facts as We Find Them. Figure 6.4 portrays graphically the 200 unit sales in order of size. The tiers are used in order to concentrate the data in a reasonably small area for more effective comprehension of their pattern of variation.

The most important point to note about the unit sales is the *variation in their frequency* as we progress along the scale from 0. The density appears to increase until we reach $2.00 to $2.50, and then

TABLE 6.6

Unit Charge Sales of Neighborhood Hardware Store: In Order of Occurrence

1.04	2.00	11.80	1.24
.75	1.25	3.00	1.28
4.28	1.23	2.27	1.39
.82	5.39	5.22	1.85
.91	34.16	4.92	8.59
2.98	2.03	5.09	1.74
3.30	4.50	12.35	5.12
1.98	2.58	4.28	5.90
4.04	17.79	1.05	.72
9.27	4.70	1.96	3.09
4.50	2.00	.88	26.84
1.91	5.54	32.83	6.95
2.64	8.00	2.14	42.18
4.15	10.30	6.16	.60
3.50	11.48	3.91	.31
10.47	2.17	2.55	7.11
4.37	5.04	1.79	1.80
10.97	2.16	2.07	1.46
.61	4.92	19.95	1.88
4.60	2.58	6.38	10.08
.67	11.00	2.75	1.04
.40	4.85	.41	2.34
2.15	25.80	2.99	12.63
5.23	3.25	2.47	2.12
2.07	2.17	3.14	5.40
2.00	1.90	2.25	9.75
1.67	17.28	5.69	71.25
2.45	3.74	3.06	4.09
6.54	3.67	.84	5.64
2.02	12.06	2.15	1.40
13.94	34.16	6.26	1.02
1.00	4.00	2.50	3.08
6.94	6.50	.55	4.74
1.96	4.75	3.25	1.09
2.49	17.90	.81	14.55
4.94	36.95	5.54	2.54
3.30	14.49	15.16	5.28
2.02	3.93	1.91	2.26
2.46	1.79	4.07	2.19
1.15	1.02	4.33	2.54
3.20	7.77	4.15	1.10
12.00	6.10	15.99	1.02
2.50	6.10	1.24	13.83
4.19	8.28	1.44	5.64
2.64	.70	2.10	3.16
2.08	7.38	5.98	2.37
5.48	2.37	2.50	2.52
1.68	4.02	1.96	3.25
3.48	6.70	5.63	3.08
.85	.80	5.43	3.79

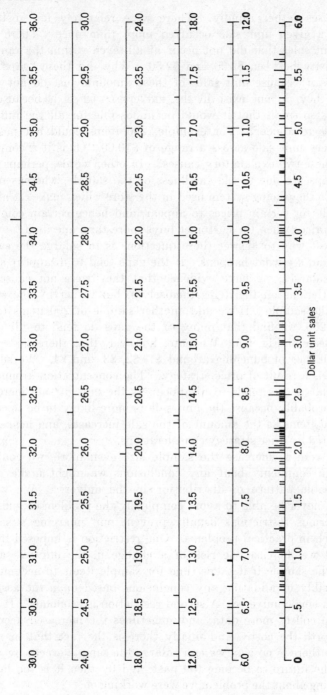

Fig. 6.4 Graphic presentation of 200 unit sales of a neighborhood hardware store.

it decreases rather rapidly. There were relatively few instances wherein a given unit sale occurred more than once. There were many unit sales that did not occur at all, even within the range of high density between $2.00 and $2.50. Why did these "gaps" appear? Is it because unit sales of these amounts just do not occur because they do not exist in the universe? Or is it because our sample is so small that it would be impossible for all the different unit sales to appear? For example, 200 items could not possibly cover every unit sale across a range of $10.00. Or is it a combination of these two explanatory causes? In other words, perhaps some of the gaps are due to the smallness of the sample, whereas others are due to the pricing system used in the store which makes it almost impossible for certain prices to appear, and hence certain combinations of prices when the customer buys more than one item.

The best way to answer these questions is to enlarge the sample of data and see what happens. If the gaps tend to disappear as the sample enlarges, we have evidence that they were not caused by any restrictions on the items themselves, but rather by the smallness of the sample. If we add another sample of 200 items to our original 200, we find that many of the gaps do tend to fill up as can be seen in Fig. 6.5. We note, however, that there does seem to be evidence of bunching around $1, $2, $3, and $4. We suspect that this is a result of price strategy. The concentration around the even dollar marks tends to disappear as the unit of sale increases. This is probably because the unit sale is more likely to be made up of *several* items as the amount of the sale increases, and hence it is less affected by price strategy considerations.

If we were to increase the sample size even more, we could be still more confident about any conclusions we might make about the probable pattern of distribution in the universe. We would, however, never be able to avoid completely the problem of guessing. Three serious restrictions usually prevent our enlarging a sample very much in practical problems. One restriction is imposed by the fact that we increase the risk of a change in the universe as we enlarge the sample if it takes time for sample items to accumulate, thus possibly invalidating any conclusions based upon the assumptions of a single universe. A second restriction is economic. It costs money to collect more data, and sometimes the increased accuracy is not worth the cost. And finally there is the fact that in many problems there is no way we can enlarge the sample except by waiting for the future to become the past, and by then it is too late to do anything about the problem we were working on.

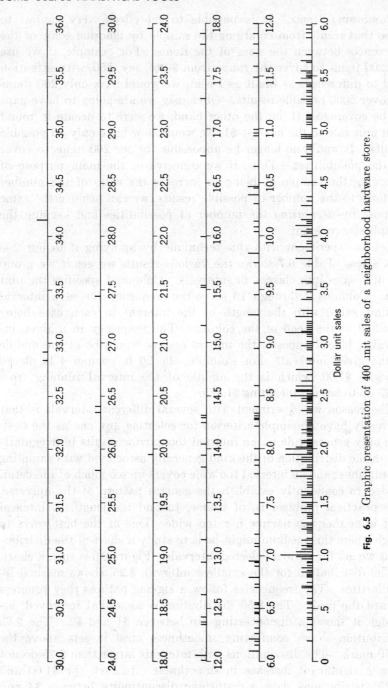

Fig. 6.5 Graphic presentation of 400 unit sales of a neighborhood hardware store.

Dollar unit sales

Combining Items. It is possible to get effects very similar to those that result from enlarging the sample by ignoring some of the differences between the sizes of the items. For example, if we use our 200 items to cover the range from $0 to, say, $50, with attention paid to differences as small as 1 cent, we would have only 200 items to cover 5000 possible results. Obviously we are going to have gaps in the coverage. If, on the other hand, we were to decide to round each unit sale to the nearest $1, we would now have only 50 possible results. It would no longer be impossible for our 200 items to cover all the possibilities. Thus, if we conceive of the main purpose of enlarging the sample as being to increase the *ratio* of the number of items to the number of possible results, we can achieve the same purpose by *decreasing* the number of possibilities and keeping the sample size constant.

Let us experiment with this technique by applying it to our 200 unit sales. Table 6.7 shows the various results we get if we group the unit sales into classes, or intervals. Column 1 specifies the unit sale. Columns 2 through 10 show the frequency for each interval of unit sales, with the length of the interval in each case being specified at the head of the column. The frequency in a given interval is placed opposite the unit sales that would be at the middle of the given interval. For example, the 26 in column 4 is placed opposite $1.00, which is the middle of the interval running from $.625 up to but not including $1.375.

The reason we experiment with several different intervals is that we really have no simple criterion for selecting any one as the best. The only general rule is: an interval too narrow results in irregularities in the distribution of the kind generally associated with sampling fluctuations; and an interval too wide covers up too much of the detail needed to confidently establish the general pattern of the universe. The practical problem is, of course, to find the length of interval that is neither too narrow nor too wide. One of the best ways to judge where this medium might be is to study a chart of the distributions we get for various selected intervals. Figure 6.6 is such a chart.

The distribution for the smallest interval, $.25, shows marked irregularities. The frequencies follow a zig-zag path as they progress toward the peak. The $.50 distribution is somewhat improved, although it shows a disconcerting dip between $1 and $2. The $.75 distribution shows comforting smoothness until it gets above the $7.50 mark. The distributions with intervals larger than $.75 do not show a significant increase in smoothness. In fact, the $1.00 and $1.25 distributions show a disturbing discontinuity between $4 and

TABLE 6.7

Frequency of Unit Charge Sales of a Neighborhood Hardware Store. Selected Intervals.

Dollar Unit Sales	Length of Interval								
	$.25	.50	.75	1.00	1.25	1.50	2.00	2.50	3.00
.00	0	0		3	----				
.125	----								
.25	1	----	6			----			
.375	----								
.50	5	9		----					
.625	----		----						
.75	9	----			32				
.875	----								
1.00	11	21	26	33		39	51		
1.125	----								
1.25	6	----						79	
1.375	----		----		----				
1.50	4	9		----					93
1.625	----								
1.75	7	----	30			----			
1.875	----								
2.00	19	30		43	56	----			
2.125	----		----						
2.25	13	----							
2.375	----								
2.50	13	21	29	----		42		----	
2.625	----				----				
2.75	3	----							
2.875	----		----						
3.00	7	11		28			62		
3.125	----								----
3.25	8	----	17		23	----			
3.375	----								
3.50	2	9		----					
3.625	----		----						
3.75	3	----						56	
3.875	----				----				
4.00	7	11	17	18		50	----		
4.125	----								
4.25	7	----							
4.375	----		----						
4.50	3	9		----	27				60

TABLE 6.7 (Continued)

Dollar Unit Sales	Length of Interval								
	$.25	.50	.75	1.00	1.25	1.50	2.00	2.50	3.00
4.625	----								
4.75	4	----	13			----			
4.875	----								
5.00	6	10		20			40	----	
5.125	----		----		----				
5.25	3	----							
5.375	----								
5.50	6	11	13	----		26			
5.625	----								
5.75	4	----			19				
5.875	----		----						
6.00	4	5		13			----		----
6.125	----								
6.25	2	----	9			----		30	
6.375	----				----				
6.50	3	5		----					
6.625	----		----						
6.75	1	----							
6.875	----								
7.00	3	3	4	7	8	9	13		
7.125	----								
7.25	0	----							
7.375	----		----						
7.50	1	1		----				----	16
7.625	----				----				
7.75	1	----	3			----			
7.875	----								
8.00	1	2		3			----		
8.125	----		----						
8.25	1	----			4				
8.375	----								
8.50	1	2	2	----		4			
8.625	----								
8.75	0	----						6	
8.875	----		----		----				
9.00	0	0		2			5		----
9.125	----								
9.25	1	----	1			----			

TABLE 6.7 (Continued)

Dollar Unit Sales	\$.25	.50	.75	1.00	1.25	1.50	2.00	2.50	3.00
9.375	----								
9.50	0	1		----	3				
9.625	----		----						
9.75	1	----							
9.875	----								
10.00	1	2	3	4		5	----	----	
10.125	----				----				
10.25	1	----							
10.375	----		----						
10.50	1	2		----					9
10.625	----								
10.75	0	----	3		4	----			
10.875	----								
11.00	2	2		3			7		
11.125	----		----						
11.25	0	----						10	
11.375	----				----				
11.50	1	1	2	----		6			
11.625	----								
11.75	1	----							
11.875	----		----						
12.00	2	3		4	5		----		----
12.125	----								
12.25	1	----	3			----			
12.375	----								
12.50	0	2		----				----	
12.625	----		----		----				
12.75	1	----							
12.875	----								
13.00	0	0	1	1		2	6		
13.125	----								
13.25	0	----			2				
13.375	----		----						
13.50	0	0		----					8
13.625	----								
13.75	1	----	2			----		5	
13.875	----				----				
14.00	1	2		3			----		

TABLE 6.7 (Continued)

Dollar Unit Sales	$.25	.50	.75	1.00	1.25	1.50	2.00	2.50	3.00
14.125	----		----						
14.25	0	----							
14.375	----								
14.50	2	2	2	----	3	5			
14.625	----								
14.75	0	----							
14.875	----		----						
15.00	0	1		2			4	----	----
15.125	----				----				
15.25	1	----	1			----			
15.375	----								
15.50	0	0		----					
15.625	----		----						
15.75	0	----			2				
15.875	----								
16.00	1	1	1	1		1	----		
16.125	----								
16.25	0	----						3	
16.375	----		----		----				
16.50	0	0		----					5
16.625	----								
16.75	0	----	0			----			
16.875	----								
17.00	0	0		1	1		3		
17.125	----		----						
17.250	1	----							
17.375	----								
17.50	0	1	2	----		3		----	
17.625	----				----				
17.75	1	----							
17.875	----		----						
18.00	1	2		2			----		----
18.125	----								
18.25	0	----	1		2	----			
18.375	----								
18.50	0	0		----					
18.625	----		----						
18.75	0	----						3	

TABLE 6.7 (Continued)

Dollar Unit Sales	Length of Interval								
	$.25	.50	.75	1.00	1.25	1.50	2.00	2.50	3.00
18.875	----				----				
19.00	0	0	0	0		0	1		
19.125	----								
19.25	0								
19.375	----		----						
19.50	0	0		----	1				1
19.625	----								
19.75	0	----	1			----			
19.875	----								
20.00	1	1		1			----	----	
20.125	----		----		----				
20.25	0	----							
20.375	----								
20.50	0	0	0	----		1			
20.625	----								
20.75	0	----			0				
20.875	----		----						
21.00	0	0		0			0		----
21.125	----								
21.25	0	----	0			----		0	
21.375	----				----				
21.50	0	0		----					
21.625	----		----						
21.75	0	----							
21.875	----								
22.00	0	0	0	0	0	0	----		
22.125	----								
22.25	0	----							
22.375	----		----						
22.50	0	0		----				----	0
22.625	----				----				
22.75	0	----	0			----			
22.875	----								
23.00	0	0		0			0		
23.125	----		----						
23.25	0	----			0				
23.375	----								
23.50	0	0	0	----		0			

TABLE 6.7 (Continued)

Dollar Unit Sales	$.25	.50	.75	1.00	1.25	1.50	2.00	2.50	3.00
					Length of Interval				
23.625	----								
23.75	0	----						0	
23.875	----		----		----				
24.00	0	0		0			----		----
24.125	----								
24.25	0	----	0			----			
24.375	----								
24.50	0	0		----	0				
24.625	----		----						
24.75	0	----							
24.875	----								
25.00	0	0	0	0		0	1	----	
25.125	----				----				
25.25	0	----							
25.375	----		----						
25.50	0	0		----					2
25.625	----								
25.75	1	----	1		1	----			
25.875	----								
26.00	0	1		1			----		
26.125	----		----						
26.25	0	----						2	
26.375	----								
26.50	0	0	1	----	----	1			
26.625	----								
26.75	1	----							
26.875	----		----						
27.00	0	1		1	1		1		----
27.125	----								
27.25	0	----	0			----			
27.375	----								
27.50	0	0		----				----	
27.625	----		----		----				
27.75	0	----							
27.875	----								
28.00	0	0	0	0		0	----		
28.125	----								
28.25	0	----			0				

TABLE 6.7 (Continued)

Dollar Unit Sales	$.25	.50	.75	1.00	1.25	1.50	2.00	2.50	3.00
				Length of Interval					
28.375	----		----						
28.50	0	0		----					0
28.625	----								
28.75	0	----	0			----		0	
28.875	----				----				
29.00	0	0		0			0		
29.125	----		----						
29.25	0	----							
29.375	----								
29.50	0	0	0	----	0	0			
29.625	----								
29.75	0	----							
29.875	----		----						
30.00	0	0		0			----	----	----
30.125	----				----				
30.25	0	----	0			----			
30.375	----								
30.50	0	0		----					
30.625	----		----						
30.75	0	----			0				
30.875	----								
31.00	0	0	0	0		0	0		
31.125	----								
31.25	0	----						0	
31.375	----		----		----				
31.50	0	0		----					1
31.625	----								
31.75	0	----	0			----			
31.875	----								
32.00	0	0		0	0		----		
32.125	----		----						
32.25	0	----							
32.375	----								
32.50	0	0	1	----		1		----	
32.625	----				----				
32.75	1	----							
32.875	----		----						
33.00	0	1		1			1		----

TABLE 6.7 (Continued)

Dollar Unit Sales	\$.25	.50	.75	1.00	1.25	1.50	2.00	2.50	3.00
				Length of Interval					
33.125	----								
33.25	0	----	0		1	----			
33.375	----								
33.50	0	0		----					
33.625	----		----						
33.75	0	----						3	
33.875	----				----				
34.00	0	2	2	2		2	----		
34.125	----								
34.25	2	----							
34.375	----		----						
34.50	0	0		----	2				2
34.625	----								
34.75	0	----	0			----			
34.875	----								
35.00	0	0		0			2	----	
35.125	----		----		----				
35.25	0	----							
35.375	----								
35.50	0	0	0	----		0			
35.625	----								
35.75	0	----			0				
35.875	----		----						
36.00	0	0		0			----		----
36.125	----								
36.25	0	----	0			----		1	
36.375	----				----				
36.50	0	0		----					
36.625	----		----						
36.75	0	----							
36.875	----								
37.00	1	1	1	1	1	1	1		
37.125	----								
37.25	0	----							
37.375	----		----						
37.50	0	0		----				----	1
37.625	----				----				
37.75	0	----	0			----			

TABLE 6.7 (Continued)

Dollar Unit Sales	Length of Interval								
	$.25	.50	.75	1.00	1.25	1.50	2.00	2.50	3.00
37.875	----								
38.00	0	0		0			----		
38.125	----		----						
38.25	0	----			0				
38.375	----								
38.50	0	0	0	----					
38.625	----								
38.75	0	----						0	
38.875	----		----		----				
39.00	0	0		0			0		----
39.125	----								
39.25	0	----	0			----			
39.375	----								
39.50	0	0		----	0				
39.625			----						
39.75	0	----							
39.875	----								
40.00	0	0	0	0		0	----	----	
40.125	----				----				
40.25	0	----							
40.375	----		----						
40.50	0	0		----					0
40.625	----								
40.75	0	----	0		0	----			
40.875	----								
41.00	0	0		0			1		
41.125	----		----						
41.25	0	----						1	
41.375	----				----				
41.50	0	0	0	----		1			
41.625	----								
41.75	0	----							
41.875	----		----						
42.00	0	1		1	1		----		----
42.125	----								
42.25	1	----	1			----			
42.375	----								
42.50	0	0		----				----	

TABLE 6.7 (Continued)

Dollar Unit Sales	$.25	.50	.75	1.00	1.25	1.50	2.00	2.50	3.00
42.625	----		----		----				
42.75	0	----							
42.875	----								
43.00	0	0	0	0		0	0		
43.125	----								
43.25	0	----			0				
43.375	----		----						
43.50	0			----					1
70.50	0			----					1
70.625	----								
70.75	0	----	0		0	----			
70.875	----								
71.00	0	0		1			1		
71.125	----		----						
71.25	1	----						1	
71.375	----				----				
71.50	0	1	1	----		1			
71.625	----								
Totals:	200	200	200	200	200	200	200	200	200

Note: Horizontal lines mark limits of intervals. Frequencies are shown opposite the midpoint of the interval.

$6. All the distributions make the positive skewness quite clear. Practically all of them show a peak at, or very close to, a unit sale of $2.00.

Let us select the distribution with an interval of $.75 as the best of those so far considered, and then ask ourselves why we think it is the best. Our basic argument would be that it provides the *optimum combination of smoothness and detail*. A smaller interval gives us more detail, which would be good, but only at the sacrifice of smoothness. A larger interval gives us less detail, which is bad, and with no significant increase in smoothness. We now ask ourselves why we put so much emphasis on smoothness. First, and more importantly, we believe that most *universes* are *smooth* in their

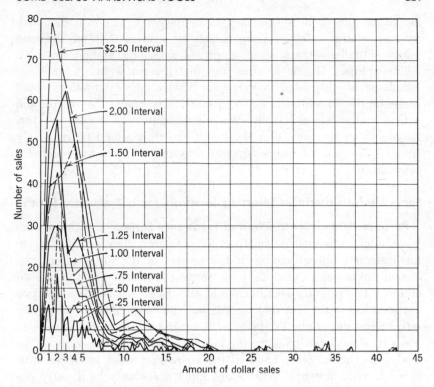

Fig. 6.6 Graphic presentation of unit charge sales of neighborhood hardware store—frequencies for selected intervals.

distributions. This is not usually supported by direct evidence because we are always dealing with samples, and samples are always irregular to some extent. We have found, however, just as we did when we enlarged our sample of unit sales to 400, that larger samples generally are more regular in distribution form than are smaller samples. We reason, therefore, that still larger samples would be even smoother, and that the universe itself would be definitely devoid of irregularities.

Second, we put so much emphasis on smoothness of the distribution because it is *convenient*. A universe is much easier to deal with if it has a regular shape. Such regularity is necessary, in fact, if we are going to represent the distribution by some mathematical model, as we did in an earlier chapter when we used the model of the normal curve to represent the various specific forms of the binomial. In fact, the pull of convenience is so strong that we are frequently willing to sacrifice a little accuracy to achieve it. For example, with the unit charge sales we have reason to suspect that the universe might actually contain some untoward bunching around the even dollar points. If this is true, the distribution would show some lumpiness as illustrated in Fig. 6.7. This kind of lumpiness would present quite a problem if we were to try to represent the distribution with a mathematical model. We might arbitrarily smooth out this lumpiness on the basis that the resulting errors would be relatively trivial. We can, of course, overdo this and sacrifice too much for convenience.

Some Useful Criteria in Selecting Intervals for a Frequency Series

Purpose Behind Construction of Frequency Series. Two basic purposes might prompt the construction of a frequency series: first to facilitate our understanding of the nature of the distribution, and second to present the data in a form convenient for the use of others. The primary significance of the difference between the two purposes lies in the fact that the person who constructs the frequency series from the original data *has the original data in his possession* and can always fall back on the original data for some parts of his analysis. On the other hand, if the frequency series is all we have to work with, any final conclusions must necessarily be directly determined by the frequency series rather than by the original data. Insofar as the frequency series does not adequately describe the original data, such final conclusions are subject to error.

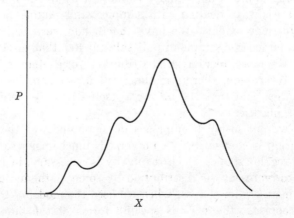

Fig. 6.7 Illustration of a lumpy frequency distribution.

When we construct a frequency series from the original data, we are usually concerned with trying to discover the general shape of the universe. In addition, we are usually hopeful that the general shape conforms reasonably well to some standard distribution like the normal. Our procedure is very similar to what we have done with the unit sales data to this point. In addition we often chart the original data in a *cumulative frequency* form to facilitate smoothing and to compare the result with a standard distribution. We found it very convenient to chart our binomial distributions in a cumulative form to see better what was happening as we increased the size of our samples.

Presentation of data in the form of a frequency series provides two advantages. It enables the presentation of masses of data in a very small space and it preanalyzes the data. It is most appropriate only when the sample of data is fairly large, say, at least 150 items. If the sample is much less than 150, the economy of space provided by the frequency series is less spectacular and the risks of error in the preanalysis increase. With small amounts of data it is usually better to make our own mistakes by constructing a series ourselves than to restrict our analysis to only what can be done with the pre-constructed frequency series. Occasionally it is necessary to present even small samples in the form of frequency series in order to conceal the identity of the specific items. Such concealment is often required in order to get cooperation from the suppliers of the original information. For example, a woman might be willing to admit her age is between 30 and 40 years although she would not admit the exact year.

Sometimes the sample of data is so large that we feel that for all practical purposes the resultant distribution will look very much like the universe. Then, if we have no reason to believe that the universe has gaps in it or has some points of unusually heavy concentration, we often will preset the intervals and collect the data by just tallying the proper interval locations. Thus we never actually record a specific item.

Intervals Should Be of Constant Length If at All Reasonable. One of the points of interest in studying a frequency series is what happens to the frequency from interval to interval. If the intervals themselves have varying lengths, it is very difficult to separate that part of the change in frequency due to the change in interval length from that part due to a real change in frequency. It is obvious, for example, that large intervals will tend to have greater frequencies than small intervals. Equal-sized intervals will also considerably facilitate the analysis of the series, whether by mathematics or by charts, as we see later.

Unfortunately, there are many series in business and economic data which are so skewed in their distributions that adherence to the equal interval rule creates more problems than it solves. Our unit sales series illustrates the dilemma. An interval small enough in size to present a reasonable amount of detail in the areas where the bulk of the data falls results in a great number of empty intervals in the higher ranges of the data. The compromise solution is to lengthen the intervals as the data thin out and even possibly to provide what is called an open end to cover all the items that fall above a certain value (or below a certain value if the data are skewed negatively, which is very rare in business data). These compromises will force some modification of analytical procedures, but the problems are certainly not insurmountable. For example, it should be pointed out that the length of the intervals usually has no effect whatsoever on the cumulative frequency chart.

Intervals Should be Mutually Exclusive. The intervals should be so defined that a particular item can fall in only *one* interval, and there must be an interval for every possible item. Unfortunately, it is much more difficult to unequivocally define an interval than we might imagine. It is important here to keep clearly in mind the distinction between a *discrete* variable, one that varies in steps, and a *continuous* variable, one that theoretically and actually varies by infinitesimal amounts. If a series is discrete, there would be *gaps* in the data themselves, and we solve our problem of unequivocally defined intervals by matching the gaps between items of data with gaps between the intervals. For example, if we were classifying families by number of children in them, we might use intervals as follows:

> 0–1 children
> 2–3   "
> 4–5   "
> etc.

If the series is continuous, such as in a distribution of heights of human beings, the limits of adjacent intervals theoretically butt against each other, with nothing at all in between. We know, however, that limitations of perception result in rounded measurements, thus presenting the appearance of gaps. For example, if our measurements are rounded to one decimal place, there is no measurement recorded between 5.8′ and 5.9′. We know, nevertheless, that the 5.8 might actually be as large as 5.85 and 5.9 as small as 5.85, thus theoretically eliminating the gap.

A theoretically perfect solution to the problem of intervals for a continuous series cannot be achieved without using footnotes because there is no other way to state the intervals so that no one will be misled. To make our discussion concrete, let us assume we have measurements rounded to one decimal place. If we write our intervals, say, as 1.00–1.95, 2.00–2.95, etc., there would be no problem where to put a given item. All the numbers from 1.0 to 1.9 go into the 1.00–1.95 interval, all those from 2.0 to 2.9 into the 2.00–2.95 interval, etc. The true intervals, however, would be .95–1.95, 1.95–2.95, etc., and the midpoints of the intervals would be 1.45, 2.45, etc. This follows from the fact that the number, 1.0, might actually be as small as .95. If we state the interval as 1.00–1.95, a person using the series might make two incorrect assumptions. He may assume the data are accurate to two decimal places, and he may assume the midpoint is 1.475. If we state the interval as .95–1.95, he again may assume 2-decimal-place accuracy. In addition, he may be confused by the fact that the upper limit of one interval is also the lower limit of the next interval. We can eliminate both problems by using footnotes. For example, the footnotes may read:

1. Lower limit of interval is included, upper limit excluded.
2. Data actually accurate to only one decimal place.

Some people prefer to eliminate the first footnote by stating the intervals as ".95 up to but not including 1.95," etc. This method takes quite a bit of space in the body of the table, however.

Location of the Arithmetic Mean and Median in a Frequency Distribution. It is an advantage to know the arithmetic mean and the median of a series before we select the class boundaries. If the median and the mean are almost equal in size, this indicates that the over-all distribution will be fairly symmetrical. We should then select boundaries for the interval containing the median and the mean so that they will be as close as possible to the midpoint of that interval. If the mean and the median are significantly different in size, the distribution is skewed in the direction of the mean. For example, the arithmetic mean income per family in the United States, and in every other country, is significantly larger than the median, particularly before taxes are deducted. This difference is caused by the skewness in the direction of the high incomes.   Figure 6.8 illustrates the situation.   Note that the peak frequency is to the left of the median, which is to the left of the mean.   Also note that the distance from the median to the mean is about half as large as the distance from the median to the mode, the value associated with the peak frequency.   This approximate 2 to 1 ratio of these distances is fairly typical of moderately skewed series.   This ratio does not hold too well, however, if the skewness is as large, say, as in our unit sales series.   Our first sample of 200 has an arithmetic mean of \$5.72 and a median of only \$3.14.   If the 2 to 1 ratio prevailed, the mode would be only \$1.85.   Figure 6.2 shows that a better estimate of the mode would place it somewhere between \$2.00 and \$2.50.   Our second sample of 200 has an arithmetic mean of \$4.90 and a median of \$3.42. The 2 to 1 ratio would place the mode at \$2.68, a figure which seems to be too high.

Logic suggests that the mode of the distribution should be near the center of the interval in which it falls and that the interval which contains the mode should also have the highest frequency.   Unfortunately, there is no simple way to estimate the mode until we have already selected our intervals and tallied the items.   Since such a prior selection influences the location of the mode, we run some

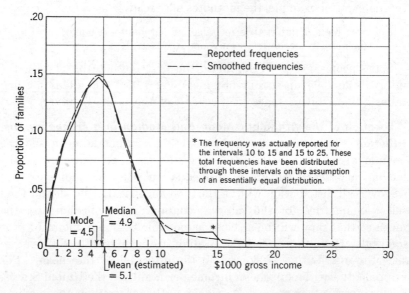

Fig. 6.8 Distribution of family income in Vermont, 1959.   (Source: United States Census of Population, 1960—Vermont; p. 69.)

risk of reasoning in a circle. The ideal solution would be to select many intervals which differ both in size and boundaries for the same size, and select the final distribution which resulted in the best compromise between smoothness and detail, with no explicit concern for the mode. The mode of the resultant distribution would then be about as good an estimate of the true mode as we might make. But an approach like this involves considerable labor; hence it is seldom used. Rather we trust to luck and postconstruction analysis to locate the mode.

Actually we are not overly concerned with the location of the mode except as a criterion for the selection of interval boundaries. As we have seen, the mode has practically no use in business problems and almost never has to be calculated for its own sake.

Interval Boundaries and Midpoints Should Be Relatively Round Numbers. This condition has a very appealing ring, and there are occasions when it has merit. However, we cannot achieve this objective without introducing some bias to the results we get from calculations of the distribution. For example, let us suppose we decided to round our intervals from .95–1.95 to 1.0–2.0. This would have the obvious merit of stating our intervals with the same number of decimal places as the data, thus eliminating the need for a footnote on accuracy. It also results in round numbers. It will, however, put numbers into the interval that would be *measured* as running from 1.0 to 1.9 but which actually would run from .95 to 1.95. (In this and subsequent discussion we are assuming that the upper limit is excluded from the interval.) The typical person probably would assume that the midpoint of an interval running from 1.0 to 2.0 would be 1.5 instead of the true midpoint of 1.45. He would also assume that the interval ran from 1.0 to 2.0. If he uses the 1.5 instead of the 1.45 in his calculations, his results would have an upward bias in some cases. Of course, this bias is only .05, and many people may be willing to have it in a given problem for the convenience of the round numbers. Nevertheless a careful worker should know that the bias is there and know what he is ignoring if he so decides. If we are constructing the frequency distribution for others to use, we definitely should provide information about any bias.

The primary argument for relatively round numbers is convenience of calculation. This is not so important as a few years ago. With modern calculators and modern methods of short-cut calculation we are better advised to be more concerned with the accuracy of our data than with the "roundness" of our numbers. An example of how easy it is to solve the problem of round numbers when we are at the calculation stage would be the rounding of 1.45 to 1.50, 2.45 to 2.50, etc., by *adding* .05 to all the numbers *before* performing a calculation. Then when we have finished, we merely *subtract* .05 from our answer if appropriate. We say "if appropriate" because there are some calculations, such as the standard deviation, that would be unaffected by the addition of .05 to all the numbers.

The Problem of Lumpiness or Discontinuities in the Data. We have already noted the possibility that our unit sales data had an apparent tendency to concentrate around the even dollar points, particularly at the lower values of the series. We used Fig. 6.7 to illustrate the problem. We decided to ignore the problem in our treatment of the unit sales data. It is important, nevertheless, that we now note what we would have done if we had not decided to ignore the problem.

We would have done two things. First, we would have selected intervals in such a way that the dollar points would have been reasonably close to interval midpoints. Second, we would have made the intervals small enough so that intervals adjacent to those that had the dollar points would have appropriately low frequencies, thus highlighting the fact that the dollar-point concentrations did exist. The resultant lumpiness would then be quite obvious, and appropriately so. It would be inappropriate to worry about midpoints corresponding to concentration points and then choose intervals so broad that the lumpiness gets smoothed over, thus encouraging people to assume that the series has no concentration points other than the single one around the mode.

6.3   Charts of Frequency Series or of Probability Distributions

We have already used charts extensively in our discussions. We have found them a very useful tool to help us acquire a mental picture of the way in which a variable may be varying and to compare the particular distribution with some pattern we might have in mind, thus helping us to decide whether any conformity to a pattern is close enough to justify the hypothesis that the pattern is a fair representation of the series of data involved. It is possible sometimes to make probability calculations to test the conformity of fact with hypothesis. Even these calculations, however, involve some assumptions about the shape of the distribution we are dealing with, a shape best suggested by looking at a chart. Thus we find charts helpful even if only preliminary to using mathematical calculations.

One of the most important functions of a chart is to provide guidance for *interpolating* between given items in order to infer the values of items which we do not yet have but which we suspect can occur nevertheless. In fact, the whole process of inference is essentially a process of interpolating, and practically all statistical methods are interpolation methods. In a sense there is no need to be persuaded to practice the art of interpolation, or the related art of extrapolation. We all seem to have an intuitive urge to read between the lines, so to speak. Where we may need a little persuasion is to consider the possibility that apparently new and strange interpolation methods may be useful additions to our present stock of tried and true methods!

Figure 6.9 illustrates five alternative ways of picturing a frequency distribution. Each has its counterpart in the presentation of a *cumulative* frequency distribution as shown in Fig. 6.10. Part *A* presents only the coordinate dots. The location of the dot with respect to the variable is no problem for the cumulative distribution. It is for the noncumulative form, however. The problem exists because the dot must represent an *interval*, such as from .95 up to but not including 1.95. Where should we place the dot in the interval? The convention is to place the dot at the *midpoint* of the interval. If the items were symmetrically distributed through the interval, the midpoint would correspond to both the median and the mean of the items in the interval. But, of course, the items are rarely symmetrically distributed, either actually or theoretically, with the possible exception of the middle interval in an over-all symmetrical distribution. What the midpoint represents, then, is really a concession to convenience. The determination of the median or mean of the interval requires some assumptions about the over-all distribution. Unless the assumption of normality is reasonable, we find ourselves getting into a veritable maze of difficulties in trying to locate the median or mean, and we choose to struggle along with the midpoint and its obvious bias. In general the midpoints are too far away from the center of the distribution. Note also that the bias in the lower half tends to balance that of the upper half. Thus, we can see that a standard deviation calculated from the midpoints would be too large; but an arithmetic mean would be about right.

Part *B* of Fig. 6.9 uses a vertical bar to represent the frequency

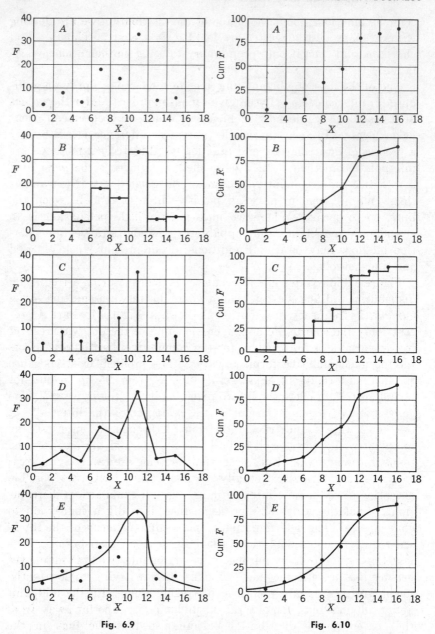

Fig. 6.9

Fig. 6.10

Fig. 6.9 Alternative forms of frequency distribution charts.

Fig. 6.10 Alternative forms of cumulative frequency distribution charts (no. of cases with value *less than* specified X).

in an interval. The assumption of an even distribution within an interval, implied by the use of the midpoint in Part A, is now made explicit. The result is the appearance of a set of steps as we go from interval to interval. This type of chart is called a *histogram*. Its apparent counterpart in Fig. 6.10 requires connecting the dots with *straight* lines. Such a *linear change* in the total, or cumulative, frequency is the equivalent of assuming that the frequency in an interval is equally spaced.

The use of vertical lines as in Part C of Fig. 6.9 is particularly appropriate when we are dealing with a *discrete* series. We used this form when charting some of our binomial distributions. This mode of presentation emphasizes that there are gaps in the data and that there is no need to solve the problem of how best to interpolate between recorded items.

The cumulative distribution counterpart of Part C of Fig. 6.9 consists of *steps* as we proceed from one value to the next. This mode of presentation is consistent with the idea that the frequencies change in *jumps* when we are dealing with a discrete series. This follows from the fact that there would be no X values falling between those for which the frequencies are given.

Part D of Fig. 6.9 is the result of connecting the midpoints given in Part A. This form is usually called a *frequency polygon*. The use of such connecting straight lines represents a relatively crude attempt at providing a basis for *interpolating* between the recorded frequencies. This method of interpolation assumes that the intermediate frequencies change at rates that are related to the frequencies that *straddle* the point of interest. This assumption is generally more valid than the assumption of equal frequencies that is implied by the use of a histogram as in Part B of Fig. 6.9.

The cumulative distribution counterpart of the frequency polygon requires that the points be connected with *curved* lines as shown in Part D of Fig. 6.10. There is no simple way to draw the exact curve that would correspond to the polygon line. The curves in Part D of Fig. 6.10 have just been drawn by eye.

Part E represents an attempt to draw a picture of the distribution of the *universe* from the sample dots shown in Part A. Note that no attempt is made to draw the curve through the sample dots. Rather, the curve generally goes between the dots. It may seem curious that no obvious attempt was made to draw the curve so it was a little less dispersed than the dots, thus tending to offset some of the bias caused by placing the dots at midpoints. The reason is that samples tend to *understate* the dispersion of a universe. We have occasion to explain this understatement later. By drawing our curve in between the dots, we are letting the overstatement of dispersion caused by the use of midpoints balance somewhat the understatement caused by the use of a sample.

The curve shown in Part E of Fig. 6.10 is probably the best basis for interpolating the frequencies of subintervals. The estimated frequency would be calculated by taking the difference between the cumulative frequencies indicated for the two boundaries of the subinterval. For example, let us estimate the frequency for the subinterval between \$4.50 and \$5.00 for our distribution of unit charge sales. Figure 6.11 shows the cumulative distribution of such sales and also a smooth curve fitted by eye to that distribution. The smooth curve indicates 68.75% of the sales falling below \$5.00 and 64% falling below \$4.50. Thus we estimate that 4.75% of the sales would fall between \$4.50 and \$5.00.

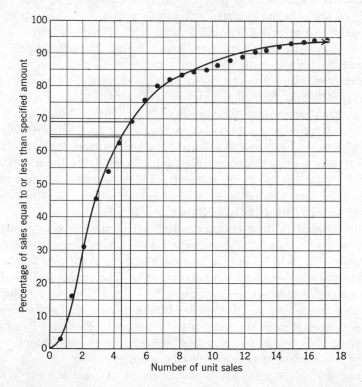

Fig. 6.11 Cumulative frequency distribution of 200 unit charge sales of a neighborhood hardware store with smooth curve fitted by eye to represent the universe of such sales.

Charting Frequency Series with Unequal Intervals or with Open Ends

If a frequency distribution has unequal intervals, adjustments must be made in the recorded frequencies before we can draw a proper chart. In effect we must recreate the frequencies that would have existed if equal intervals had been used. We can now see one of the advantages of equal intervals in the first place. Table 6.8 shows the distribution of the 200 charge sales of our hardware store as it might typically be presented for the use of others. Note that an interval of $.75 is used until we get to a value of $7.375. The interval then increases to a width of $1.50. It stays at $1.50 until we reach $14.875, where it increases to a width of $3.00. The series

TABLE 6.8

Relative Frequency of Unit Charge Sales of a Neighborhood Hardware Store (200 Unit Sales in Sample)

Dollar Unit Sales	Proportion of Unit Sales
Under .625 *	.030
.625–1.375	.130
1.375–2.125	.150
2.125–2.875	.145
2.875–3.625	.085
3.625–4.375	.085
4.375 5.125	.065
5.125–5.875	.065
5.875–6.625	.045
6.625–7.375	.020
7.375–8.875	.025
8.875–10.375	.020
10.375–11.875	.025
11.875–13.375	.020
13.375–14.875	.020
14.875–17.875	.020
17.875–20.875	.010
20.875 and over †	.040
	1.000

* Lower Limit Inclusive: Sales actually occurred only to nearest cent.
† Arithmetic mean of items in this class is $38.02.

TABLE 6.9

Revision of Table 6.8 Distribution to Equalize Length of Intervals

Dollar Unit Sales	Proportion of Unit Sales
−.125–.625 *	.0300
.625–1.375	.1300
1.375–2.125	.1500
2.125–2.875	.1450
2.875–3.625	.0850
3.625–4.375	.0850
4.375–5.125	.0650
5.125–5.875	.0650
5.875–6.625	.0450
6.625–7.375	.0200
7.375–8.125	.0125
8.125–8.875	.0125
8.875–9.625	.0100
9.625–10.375	.0100
10.375–11.125	.0125
11.125–11.875	.0125
11.875–12.625	.0100
12.625–13.375	.0100
13.375–14.125	.0100
14.125–14.875	.0100
14.875–15.625	.0050
15.625–16.375	.0050
16.375–17.125	.0050
17.125–17.875	.0050
17.875–18.625	.0025
18.625–19.375	.0025
19.375–20.125	.0025
20.125–20.875	.0025
20.875 and over †	.0400
	1.0000

* Lower Limit Inclusive: Original data accurate to nearest cent.

† The highest sample item was $71.25. Arithmetic Mean of items in this class is $38.02.

then becomes open after $21.875. The simplest assumption we can make about the frequencies in the extra-wide intervals is that they are equally spaced. We might assume that the $8.875 to $9.625 interval has a frequency of 1.0%, just half the frequency in the full interval. Common sense suggests that there probably would be slightly more than 1.0% of the frequency in the lower half and slightly less than 1.0% in the upper half of the interval. We are, however, well out on the tail of this distribution, thus making the curve fairly close to horizontal. Hence the assumption of equal frequency is not so bad. In fact, considering the errors in plotting a graph and the limited perceptive ability of the eye, it is entirely possible that the difference between the assumed equal distribution and the so-called truth is within the limits of these crudities. We would not say this if we were interpolating in the interior ranges of the data, however. Fortunately we rarely find the extra-large intervals in the interior ranges.

If we follow this policy of equally distributing the frequencies in the larger intervals, we get frequencies as shown in Table 6.9 and in Fig. 6.12. Note what we did on the chart with the open ends. We closed the lower end by assuming that there would be no sales of less than 0. This seems reasonable, although there might be some logic to including "sales returns" in the unit sales distribution as though they were negative sales. We attached an arrow at the upper end to indicate that the distribution continues. Thus we have spread the 4.0% of the sales that were $21.875 or more over an in-

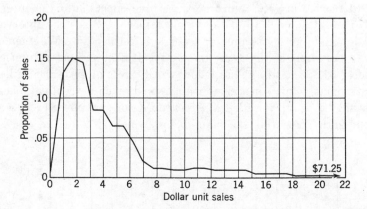

Fig. 6.12 Graphic presentation of frequency distribution of unit charge sales of a neighborhood hardware store. (It has been assumed that the frequencies in the extra large intervals are equally distributed. See Tables 6.8 and 6.9.)

definite range. This indefiniteness bothers some people because they think that the upper limit of the series should be explicitly stated. We handled the problem by appending a footnote to the table which specifies the highest unit sale in our sample of 200 and also the arithmetic mean of all the sales in the open class. This appended information can be very useful to a person who would like to make some calculations from the given distribution. It can be a very challenging task to estimate the arithmetic mean of a distribution with open ends if there is no specific information about the total of the items in the open class.

6.4   Interpolating in a Frequency Series

When we interpolate in a frequency series, we assume that each item within an interval occupies its own individual space and that all the spaces are equal. For example, the interval $1.375 to 2.125 of our unit sales series contains 15% of the 200 items. Hence we divide the interval into 15 equal spaces, with each of the given items assumed to be located at the middle of its space. (If we were working with the 200 items instead of the percentage of items, we would have divided the interval into 30 spaces. The principles and final answers would remain the same.) See Fig. 6.13. If we wished to estimate the value below which 25% of the sales occurred, we would proceed as follows. Since the two intervals below $1.375 contain a total of 16% of the items (see Table 6.8), we must proceed another 9% to reach the 25% point. We go nine spaces into the interval, $1.375 to 2.125, or 9/15 of the whole interval. Since the interval is $.75 long, we go a distance of 9/15 × $.75, or $.45. We then add this to the value of the lower boundary, $1.375, and get a final estimate of $1.825 as the value below which 25% of the sales fell.

Any point below (or above) which some given percentage of cases is estimated to fall is called a *percentile*. For example, $1.825 would be the 25th percentile, the point below which 25% of the cases are

$1.375 $2.125

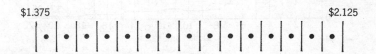

Fig. 6.13 Illustration of spacing assumption for interpolating in a frequency series.

estimated to fall and above which 75% are estimated to fall. It
has become somewhat of a convention to count the percentiles from
the bottom of a series. Thus a student scoring at the 95th percentile
on a test would be scoring higher than one who scored at the 5th
percentile. We have already noted that the 50th percentile is spe-
cially named as the median. The 25th and 75th percentiles are
called the first and third *quartiles*, respectively. The 10th, 20th, etc.
percentiles are often called the first, second, etc. *deciles*.

All of these percentile measures are generally calculated by the
method just described for the 25th percentile. Note that the fundamental assumption is that the interval that contains the indicated
percentile has as many equal spaces as there are items in that interval.
This assumption is not strictly correct, but the errors in using it are
considered to be small, particularly in view of the difficulties caused
by a more realistic assumption.

6.5 Short-cut Calculation Methods

We found a short-cut method of calculating the standard deviation quite advantageous (p. 150), and now we generalize this short-
cut procedure to better appreciate its versatility.

Suppose we wish to calculate the arithmetic mean of the following
five numbers: 50, 75, 100, 150, 225. Following the definition of the
mean, we would add these five numbers and divide by 5, getting a
total of 600 and a mean of 120. If we *divide* each of the numbers
by 25, we would get the series 2, 3, 4, 6, 9. The mean of the latter
series is 4.8, which when *multiplied* by 25 would give us 120. If we
let k represent a number such as 25, what we have done can be expressed as

$$\overline{X} = k \frac{\sum \dfrac{X}{k}}{N}.$$

Of course, k can be any value we wish it to be, including a decimal
fraction. Thus it is proper to divide (or multiply) all the numbers
in a series by any arbitrary number, take the mean of the result,
and then multiply (or divide) by the arbitrary number to return to
the original units of the series. We should be no more bothered by
this process with arbitrary numbers than by the same process that
we use when we convert dollars to cents and back again, or feet to
inches and back again, etc.

Let us now subtract 100 from each of our five numbers, resulting in the series -50, -25, 0, 50, 125, and then take the arithmetic mean of the resultant five numbers, getting a result of 20. If we now add the 100 back in, we get a final result of 120. If we let C represent a number such as 100, what we have done can be expressed as

$$\overline{X} = C + \frac{\Sigma(X - C)}{N}.$$

C can be any arbitrary number, either positive or negative.

If we wish, we can subtract 100 from all our numbers and divide the resultant series by 25, getting a final series of -2, -1, 0, 2, 5 and a mean of .8. If we multiply .8 by 25 and add 100, we again end up with 120. Note that the order in which we make these adjustments is important. If we had added 100 and multiplied by 25, we would have obtained a ridiculous answer.

These processes of shifting the *origin* of measure (subtracting C) and changing the *unit* of measure (dividing by k) can be combined into a single formula as

$$\overline{X} = C + k\frac{\Sigma\left(\dfrac{X - C}{k}\right)}{N}.$$

The trick in practice is to choose values for C and k so that the calculation of the mean is expedited. We illustrate how this can be done in the next section.

The same transformations can be used to expedite the calculation of the standard deviation. Interestingly enough, however, the value of the standard deviation is not affected by adding or subtracting C; and we do not have to reverse the process at the end of the calculation.

Table 6.10 illustrates the application of these transformations to the calculation of the standard deviation. These seem confusing at first but study this table column by column and any confusion should clear up. Columns 1 through 3 show the calculation of the mean and standard deviation by straightforward application of their definitions. Column 4 shifts the origin of measure from 0 to 100. The result is called d for convenience of reference. Column 5 calculates $d - \overline{d}$. Note that it turns out to be exactly the same as x in column 2. It can be seen that the standard deviation of d is exactly the same as the standard deviation of X, thus verifying that the standard deviation is independent of the origin of measure of the series. In

TABLE 6.10

Short-cut Methods of Calculating the Standard Deviation

X	$X - \bar{X}$, or x	x^2	$X - C$, or $X - 100$ $= d$	$d - \bar{d}$	$\dfrac{X}{25}$	$\left(\dfrac{X}{25} - \dfrac{\bar{X}}{25}\right)$	$\left(\dfrac{X}{25} - \dfrac{\bar{X}}{25}\right)^2$	$\dfrac{d}{25}$	$\left(\dfrac{d}{25}\right)^2$
(1)	(2)	(3)	(4)	(5)	(6)	(7)	(8)	(9)	(10)
50	-70	4,900	-50	-70	2	-2.8	7.84	-2	4
75	-45	2,025	-25	-45	3	-1.8	3.24	-1	1
100	-20	400	0	-20	4	$-.8$	.64	0	.0
150	30	900	50	30	6	1.2	1.44	2	4
225	105	11,025	125	105	9	4.2	17.64	5	25
600	0	19,250	100	0	24	0	30.80	4	34

A. Arith. Mean $= \dfrac{\Sigma X}{N} = \dfrac{600}{5} = 120 = \bar{X}$.

B. $\bar{X} = C + \dfrac{\Sigma(X - C)}{N} = 100 + \tfrac{100}{5} = 120$.

C. $\bar{X} = C + \dfrac{\sum \dfrac{X - C}{k}}{N} \cdot k = 100 + \tfrac{4}{5} \cdot 25 = 120$.

D. Standard Deviation $s = \sqrt{\dfrac{\Sigma(X - \bar{X})^2}{N}} = \sqrt{\dfrac{\Sigma x^2}{N}} = \sqrt{\dfrac{19250}{5}} = 62.05$.

E. $s = k \sqrt{\dfrac{\sum\left(\dfrac{X}{k} - \dfrac{\bar{X}}{k}\right)^2}{N}} = 25\sqrt{\dfrac{30.80}{5}} = 25 \times 2.482 = 62.05$.

F. $s = k \sqrt{\dfrac{\sum\left(\dfrac{X - C}{k}\right)^2}{N} - \left(\dfrac{\sum\left(\dfrac{X - C}{k}\right)}{N}\right)^2} = 25 \times \sqrt{\dfrac{34}{5} - \left(\dfrac{4}{5}\right)^2}$

$= 25 \times 2.482 = 62.05$.

column 6 we show the results of dividing X by 25. If we divide the sum of this column by 5, we get 4.8, which is 1/25 of the mean of X. Columns 7 and 8 carry out the necessary calculations to determine the standard deviation of $X/25$. We find this standard deviation to be 2.482, which is 1/25 of the standard deviation of X.

We are now ready for columns 9 and 10. Column 9 is the result of dividing d (see column 4) by 25. Note that column 9 does not add to 0, which it would if d had been measured from the mean of 120 instead of 100. Column 10 squares the column 9 values. The sum of column 10 is not the proper sum for the determination of the standard deviation because the deviations were not measured from the mean. A correction must be made to allow for the error. The size of the error is equal to the difference between the mean and the origin actually used. The mean is 4.8. (Remember that all our numbers have been divided by 25, thus explaining how we get from 120 to 4.8.) We measured our deviations from 4.0, or from 100/25, and each value in column 9 is too large by .8. Since we squared each of these values, we also squared the error. We correct this error by *subtracting* $.8^2$, or .64, from the mean of the values in column 10. The square root of this yields 2.482, which when multiplied by 25 gives us the correct standard deviation of 62.05.

The whole process can be summarized by the formula

$$s = k \sqrt{\frac{\sum \left(\frac{X - C}{k}\right)^2}{N} - \left(\sum \frac{X - C}{k}\right)^2}.$$

Note that we must finally multiply by k to reverse the original division by k. No such reversal is necessary to adjust for the subtraction of C, because the standard deviation is independent of the origin of measure. The second term under the radical is always *subtracted* from the first term. The first term can never be too small because of the least-squares property of the mean. There are two values that might be chosen for C that are worth commenting on. When C equals 0, the formula reduces to the equivalent of the formula we used in the preceding chapter (p. 150), the only difference being the change in the unit by use of k. We expressed that formula as "the square root of the mean of the squares minus the square of the mean."

When C equals the mean, the formula reduces to the calculation of the deviations from the mean itself. Note that the second term under the radical becomes equal to 0 then because the operation within the parentheses would be the summation of the deviations from the mean, which we have learned always equals zero.

6.6   Calculating the Mean and Standard Deviation From a Frequency Series

The calculation of the mean and standard deviation from a frequency series involves only minor modifications of the procedures hitherto discussed. Table 6.11 illustrates the procedures by applying them to our hardware store unit sales series. Column 3 is the midpoint of each interval with the exception of the last interval, which is represented by the arithmetic mean of the items in that interval. The fundamental assumption is that the midpoints are reasonable approximations to the *means* of items within intervals. We know that the midpoints tend to be too small in the lower intervals and too large in the upper intervals, but we expect that these errors will come close to canceling. Column 4 gives the estimates for the total of the items within an interval and is calculated by multiplying the frequency by the midpoint. The total of this column gives us the estimated total of all the items. Division by N, the total frequency, gives us the estimate of the arithmetic mean, a value of $5.72.

Column 5 shows the deviation of each midpoint from the mean. Hence we are now assuming that the midpoint is an adequate representation for each item within an interval to measure its deviation from the mean. However, we know that the true mean or median of an interval is actually closer to the general mean than the midpoint. Thus the deviations from the midpoint are too large, and the standard deviation based on them is in general too large. Attempts have been made to develop a correction for this error, the most notable that of Sheppard. Sheppard's correction formula should be applied only when N is fairly large, say, 1000 or more, and also when the distribution is not very skew. Neither condition is satisfied by our distribution, so we make no attempt to correct our standard deviation.

Column 6 multiplies each deviation by its frequency. This column should add to zero. It does not because of rounding errors. Column 7 is the product of columns 5 and 6 and gives us the sum of the squares of the deviations from the mean. This sum is then divided by N, or 1, giving a result of 57.9339 square dollars. We call this result, namely the mean of the squares of the deviations from the mean, the *variance*, a concept we run across frequently in later pages. The square root of the variance gives us the standard deviation, or $7.61.

The calculations to this point are the result of following the straightforward definitions of the mean and standard deviation. The remainder of the columns illustrate the application of various short-cut devices, some of which seem not to be really short-cuts.

Column 8 can be used in place of columns 5, 6, and 7 in getting the standard deviation. Column 8 is the product of columns 3 and 4. If we divide the sum of this column by 1 and subtract the

Calculation of the Arithmetic Mean and the Standard Deviation from the

Dollar Unit Sales (1)	Proportion of Sales f (2)	Midpoint of Interval † X (3)	fX (4)	$X - \bar{X}$, or x (5)	fx (6)	fx^2 (7)
Under .625 *	.030	.3125	.009375	−5.4064	−.162192	.876875
.625–1.375	.130	1.0000	.130000	−4.7189	−.613457	2.894842
1.375–2.125	.150	1.7500	.262500	−3.9689	−.595335	2.362825
2.125–2.875	.145	2.5000	.362500	−3.2189	−.466740	1.502389
2.875–3.625	.085	3.2500	.276250	−2.4689	−.209856	.518113
3.625–4.375	.085	4.0000	.340000	−1.7189	−.146106	.251142
4.375–5.125	.065	4.7500	.308750	−.9689	−.062978	.061019
5.125–5.875	.065	5.5000	.357500	−.2189	−.014228	.003115
5.875–6.625	.045	6.2500	.281250	.5311	.023900	.012693
6.625–7.375	.020	7.0000	.140000	1.2811	.025622	.032824
7.375–8.875	.025	8.1250	.203125	2.4061	.060152	.144732
8.875–10.375	.020	9.6250	.192500	3.9061	.078122	.305152
10.375–11.875	.025	11.1250	.278125	5.4061	.135152	.730645
11.875–13.375	.020	12.6250	.252500	6.9061	.138122	.953884
13.375–14.875	.020	14.1250	.282500	8.4061	.168122	1.413250
14.875–17.875	.020	16.3750	.327500	10.6561	.213122	2.271049
17.875–20.875	.010	19.3750	.193750	13.6561	.136561	1.864891
20.875 and over ‡	.040	38.0200	1.520800	32.3011	1.292044	41.734442
	1.000		5.718925		.000027	57.933882

$$\bar{X} = \frac{\Sigma fX}{N} = \frac{5.718925}{1} = \$5.72. \qquad \bar{X} = C + \frac{\Sigma fX'}{N} = 4.75 + .9689 = \$5.72.$$

$$s = \sqrt{\frac{\Sigma f(X - \bar{X})^2}{N}} = \sqrt{\frac{\Sigma fx^2}{N}} \qquad \bar{X} = C + k\,\frac{\Sigma f\left(\dfrac{X - C}{k}\right)}{N} = 4.75 + .375 \times 2.583801$$

$$= \sqrt{\frac{57.933882}{1}} = \$7.61. \qquad\qquad = 4.75 + .9689 = \$5.72.$$

* Lower Limit Inclusive.
† Except for last interval.
‡ 38.020 is arithmetic mean of items in interval.

square of the arithmetic mean, we get the variance. The square root of this then gives us the standard deviation of $7.61, the same answer as before. This calculation saves 18 subtractions and 18 multiplications over the first method and adds only one multiplication and one subtraction, a net saving of 34 operations.

The remaining columns do not enable us to save on the *number* of operations. They merely result in transforming the given numbers into other numbers which we hope are easier to work with, either because the new numbers are smaller or because they are "rounder," or both.

6.11

Frequency Distribution of the Unit Sales of a Neighborhood Hardware Store

fX^2 (8)	$X - C = X'$ ($C = 4.75$) (9)	fX' (10)	$(X' - \overline{X}')$ $= x'$ (11)	$\dfrac{X - C}{k} = d$ ($k = .375$) (12)	d' ($k = .75$) (12a)	fd (13)	fd^2 (14)
.002930	−4.4375	−.133125	−5.4064	−11.8333	−5.9167	−.354999	4.200810
.130000	−3.7500	−.487500	−4.7189	−10	−5.0	−1.300000	13.000000
.459375	−3.0000	−.450000	−3.9689	−8	−4.0	−1.200000	9.600000
.906250	−2.2500	−.326250	−3.2189	−6	−3.0	−.870000	5.220000
.897812	−1.5000	−.127500	−2.4689	−4	−2.0	−.340000	1.360000
1.360000	−.7500	−.063750	−1.7189	−2	−1.0	−.170000	.340000
1.466562	0	0	−.9689	0	0	0	0
1.966250	.7500	.048750	−.2189	2	1.0	.130000	.260000
1.757812	1.5000	.067500	.5311	4	2.0	.180000	.720000
.980000	2.2500	.045000	1.2811	6	3.0	.120000	.720000
1.650391	3.3750	.084375	2.4061	9	4.5	.225000	2.025000
1.852812	4.8750	.097500	3.9061	13	6.5	.260000	3.380000
3.094141	6.3750	.159375	5.4061	17	8.5	.425000	7.225000
3.187812	7.8750	.157500	6.9061	21	10.5	.420000	8.820000
3.990312	9.3750	.187500	8.4061	25	12.5	.500000	12.500000
5.362812	11.6250	.232500	10.6561	31	15.5	.620000	19.220000
3.753906	14.6250	.146250	13.6561	39	19.5	.390000	15.210000
57.820816	33.2700	1.330800	32.3011	88.72	44.36	3.548800	314.849536
90.639993		.968925				2.583801	418.650346

$$s = \sqrt{\frac{\Sigma fX^2}{N} - \left(\frac{\Sigma fX}{N}\right)^2}$$

$$= \sqrt{90.639993 - 5.7189^2}$$

$$= \$7.61.$$

$$s = k\sqrt{\frac{\Sigma fd^2}{N} - \left(\frac{\Sigma fd}{N}\right)^2}$$

$$= .375\sqrt{418.6503 - 6.6760}$$

$$= .375 \times 20.297 = \$7.61.$$

In column 9 we subtract \$4.75 from each of the X values. The reason is to try to get the sum of column 10 as close to 0 as we can. We try to select the number we subtract so it is as close to the mean as possible but still keep it reasonably round and also equal to the midpoint of one of the intervals. Note that \$4.75 is the midpoint of an interval and that it is in the neighborhood of the mean. We might as well have chosen to subtract \$5.50. This maneuver does not seem to help us much here because all we have accomplished is to replace columns 3, 4, and 5 with columns 9, 10, and 11 to reduce the sum of column 4, \$5.718925, to the sum of column 10, \$.968925.

This seems scarcely worthwhile; in fact, here it was a bad bargain. (We merely note that columns 5 and 11 turn out to be identical, a result we should expect.)

Actually we knew that columns 9, 10, and 11 would turn out to be a poor bargain; rarely does it turn out otherwise. The main purpose of doing these calculations was to demonstrate their uselessness and to prepare the groundwork for column 12. Column 12 divides each value in column 9 by $.375. If we ignore the first and last figures, we note that we have finally achieved some nice numbers to work with. It was no accident that we chose to divide by $.375. This is half the size of the primary interval of $.75. If all the intervals had been the same width, we would have divided by $.75. But the existence of the variable width intervals causes the kind of problem shown in column 12a. Note that column 12 eliminates most of the decimal fractions shown in 12a. We now carry out the calculation of the mean and standard deviation as though we were working with the variable d instead of the variable X. We find that d has a mean of 2.5838 and a standard deviation of 20.297. Note that we have attached no unit to either of these numbers. Actually they are in "units of $.375," which is the equivalent of "half a class interval" for most of the intervals.

Since $d = (X - C)/k$, we can convert d to X by solving that equality for X. This gives us $X = C + kd$, or $4.75 + $.375 \times 2.5838$, or $5.72, the same answer as by the direct calculation.

Since the standard deviation is independent of the origin of measure, we convert 20.297 merely by multiplying by $.375, again getting $7.61.

In actual practice, if we were to use the short-cuts as indicated in columns 12, 13, and 14, columns 4 through 11 would be eliminated entirely. Since column 3 is needed only to help measure the deviations in units of $.375, we can also eliminate this if we are able to do this mentally. Column 3 would definitely be eliminated if we were working with equal intervals. In fact, the advantages of equal intervals are so substantial in performing the above type of calculations that it is worth seeing how easy the job would have been if we had used equal intervals in our unit sales series. Table 6.12 shows a series with $5.00 intervals used throughout. Note that all the calculations in the table are easily done in our head. Note particularly how simple the d column is if we use the class interval of $5.00 as a unit. On the other hand, also note that the series is not very descriptive of the bulk of the detail in the series, burying 68% of

TABLE 6.12

Illustration of Effect of Equal Intervals on Ease of Calculations from a Frequency Series (Data are unit sales of a hardware store.   200 items in sample.)

Dollar Unit Sales	Proportion of Sales f	d	fd	fd^2
0–5 *	.680	−2	−1.360	2.720
5–10	.175	−1	−.175	.175
10–15	.075	0	0	0
15–20	.030	1	.030	.030
20–25	.000	2	0	0
25–30	.010	3	.030	.090
30–35	.015	4	.060	.240
35–40	.005	5	.025	.125
40–45	.005	6	.030	.180
45–50	.000	7	0	0
50–55	.000	8	0	0
55–60	.000	9	0	0
60–65	.000	10	0	0
65–70	.000	11	0	0
70–75	.005	12	.060	.720
	1.000		−1.300	4.280

$$C = \$12.50 \qquad \overline{X} = C + k\,\frac{\Sigma f\left(\dfrac{X - C}{k}\right)}{N} = 12.50 + 5.00\,\frac{-1.30}{1} = \$6.00.$$

$$k = 5.00$$

$$d = \frac{X - C}{k} \qquad s = k\sqrt{\frac{\Sigma fd^2}{N} - \left(\frac{\Sigma fd}{N}\right)^2} = 5\sqrt{4.28 - (-1.3)^2}$$

$$= 5 \times 1.6093 = \$8.05.$$

* Lower Limit Inclusive.

the items in the 0 to $5.00 interval.   In addition, the mean and standard deviation are both somewhat larger than appropriate.

The Problem of Open Ends

Although our series of unit sales had an open end, we were provided with the arithmetic mean of the items in the open class.   Usually such information is not available.   If it is not, we must make some estimate of this value or give up the idea of calculating the mean or standard deviation from such an open-end series. Theories that might be useful in making such estimates are outside the range of this book. Fortunately, open ends become necessary only when a distribution has extreme skewness. Then the arithmetic mean would be a relatively poor approximation to a least-error value, and, unless our purpose dictated the mean because we were interested in the *total* of the series, it would be inappropriate to use the mean anyway. We would then prefer the median, which fortunately would not be bothered by the open end unless the median happened to fall in the open class, a very unlikely circumstance.

6.7   Other Measures of Variation

The only measure of variation we have considered so far is the standard deviation. The standard deviation is a very useful measure provided the distribution is normal, or nearly so. We can then use tables of the normal curve to estimate probabilities based on the standard deviation. If the distribution is not approximately normal, or cannot be transformed into a nearly normal form, the standard deviation has limited practical meaning. It then becomes necessary to use other devices to estimate the proportions of cases that fall between given values of the series.

The Quartile Deviation

The quartile deviation, or semi-interquartile range, is commonly used when skewness makes the standard deviation inappropriate. It is usually stated as half the distance between the 1st and 3rd quartiles. For example, the 1st quartile of our unit sales distribution is $1.825 and the 3rd quartile is $5.817. Half the difference between these is $1.996. If we compare this with the standard deviation of $7.612, we can see how inappropriate the standard deviation is for estimating relative frequencies in this unit sales distribution. The normal curve indicates .676 of a standard deviation would include 50% of the cases if laid off on either side of the mean. Here it would mean 50% of the cases would fall between $.58 and $10.86. Actually this band would contain about 86% of the cases.

The quartile deviation is often used in conjunction with the median, the argument being that the median plus and minus one quartile deviation should cover 50% of the cases. The median of our unit sales series is \$3.27. Thus we would expect 50% of our unit sales to fall between \$1.28 and \$5.27. Actually 56% of the cases are within this band. Again the problem is caused by the substantial skewness in this series. In a case such as this it would be preferable to state merely that it is estimated 50% of the cases fell between the two quartiles of \$1.825 and \$5.817 without trying to relate the quartile deviation to the mean or the median, relationships which are meaningful only when the distribution is at least reasonably symmetrical, if not reasonably normal.

The Range

The *range* is the difference between the smallest and largest value in the series; it covers 100% of the *sample* cases. It has very little applicability for its own sake and is very erratic from sample to sample. Rarely does it make practical sense to try to encompass all the possibilities within the scope of our expectation. To do so would be to try to protect ourselves against all eventualities, a policy that usually leads to inaction and frustration.

The range has been found very useful in recent years in statistical quality control applications. The range is a rather good basis for estimating the standard deviation if the sample is small, say less than 15, and if the universe is thought to be approximately normal. The advantages of the range are its relative ease of calculation and relatively simple concept, two great advantages when we are dealing with routine calculations which must be performed hastily by ordinary shop workers.

Other Measures of Relative Frequency

Although tradition has concentrated primarily on the standard deviation (in conjunction with the normal curve), the quartile deviation, and the range as devices for stating the relative frequency of cases within specified limits, the percentiles can also be used as a basis for a so-called measure of dispersion. We could, for example, directly determine the range within which the middle 80% of the cases fell by using the 10th and 90th percentiles.

The Average or Mean Deviation

The average, or mean, deviation is the arithmetic mean of the deviations from the median, with the signs of the deviations being ignored. It is sometimes calculated from the mean rather than the median, although the median is preferred because the median minimizes such deviations. Table 6.13 shows the calculation of the

TABLE 6.13

Calculation of the Average Deviation of Unit Charge Sales of Hardware Store

Dollar Unit Sales	Proportion of Sales f	Midpoint of Interval † X	$|X - \text{Md}|$	$f|X - \text{Md}|$	Cum-f
0–.625 *	.030	.3125	2.9575	.088725	.030
.625–1.375	.130	1.0000	2.2700	.295100	.160
1.375–2.125	.150	1.7500	1.5200	.228000	.310
2.125–2.875	.145	2.5000	.7700	.111650	.455
2.875–3.625	.085	3.2500	.0200	.001700	.540
3.625–4.375	.085	4.0000	.7300	.062050	.625
4.375–5.125	.065	4.7500	1.4800	.096200	.690
5.125–5.875	.065	5.5000	2.2300	.144950	.755
5.875–6.625	.045	6.2500	2.9800	.134100	.800
6.625–7.375	.020	7.0000	3.7300	.074600	.820
7.375–8.875	.025	8.1250	4.8550	.121375	.845
8.875–10.375	.020	9.6250	6.3550	.127100	.865
10.375–11.875	.025	11.1250	7.8550	.196375	.890
11.875–13.375	.020	12.6250	9.3550	.187100	.910
13.375–14.875	.020	14.1250	10.8550	.217100	.930
14.875–17.875	.020	16.3750	13.1050	.262100	.950
17.875–20.875	.010	19.3750	16.1050	.161050	.960
20.875 and over	.040	38.0200 ‡	34.7500	1.390000	1.000
	1.000			3.899275	

$$\text{Median} = \text{Md} = 2.875 + \frac{.500 - .455}{.085} \times .75 \qquad \text{Average Deviation} = \text{A.D.}$$

$$= 2.875 + .397 \qquad\qquad \text{A.D.} = \frac{\Sigma f|X - \text{Md}|}{N}$$

$$= \$3.27. \qquad\qquad\qquad = \frac{3.899275}{1}$$

$$= \$3.90.$$

* L.L.I.

† Except last interval.

‡ Arithmetic mean of interval.

average deviation for the unit sales series. The average deviation from the median is $3.90. If it had been measured from the mean, it would have been $4.54.

We should never really use the average deviation as a basis of estimating the frequency of cases between specified limits. It can be used when the distribution is essentially normal, but then the standard deviation would be much preferred. Its preferred use is as a basis for estimating the *total* error in a series of estimates. Since it is an arithmetic mean of the deviations, it has all the properties and uses of the arithmetic mean, including an algebraic relation to the total. In this use it is a logical companion to the median. The median minimizes the error of estimate and the average deviation tells the size of this minimum error.

The Median Deviation

As we might expect, we could calculate the median of the deviations from the median. A little reflection convinces us that this gives the same answer as the quartile deviation if the distribution is symmetrical. In the unit sales the median deviation is $1.80, compared with a quartile deviation of $2.00, the difference caused by the skewness in the series. The median deviation would be preferred to the quartile deviation in a skewed series because it does accurately indicate the range around the median within which 50% of the items fell.

Measures of Relative Variation

All the measures of variation so far referred to are measured in the units of the given series. As such they are affected by this unit. There are times when it is useful to be able to compare the variations in different series independent of their units of measure. We did something like this when we compared the sales of two companies on a logarithmic scale (p. 112). The simplest way to eliminate the effects of the unit is to divide the measure of variation by some average, preferably the average most logically connected with the given measure of variation. For example, if we divide the standard deviation of the unit sales by the arithmetic mean of the sales, we get 1.33. This measure is given the special name of the *coefficient of variation*, and is usually symbolized by V.

We might also divide the quartile deviation by the median, getting $2.00/$3.27, or .61; or the average deviation by the median, getting $3.90/$3.27, or 1.19; or the median deviation by the median, getting $1.80/$3.27, or .55.

Measures of relative variation are also useful when we are comparing the variations of two series which have quite different *magnitudes* even when measured in the same units. For example, a neighborhood drugstore has an arithmetic mean unit charge sale of $2.64 and a standard deviation of $2.12. This results in a coefficient of variation of .80. If we compare this with the V for the hardware store unit charge sales of 1.33, we get the impression that there is about 65% greater variation in the hardware store sales than in the drugstore sales. If we compare the two standard deviations of $2.64 and $7.61, we get the impression that there is about 188% greater variation in the hardware store sales.

6.8   Measuring Skewness

The importance of the skewness of a distribution should be clear because we have been forced to refer to it so many times in preceding pages. We would naturally expect, therefore, that the measurement of the degree of skewness would play a key role in almost any statistical analysis. Surprisingly enough, we rarely find the degree of skewness being calculated. Most people seem to be willing to rely on some visual impression of the degree of skewness, and others seem quite satisfied with intuitive notions they have without even a visual examination of a chart.

There are probably two major reasons for the rather general disregard of the quantitative determination of skewness. One reason is that we have had little success in developing a measure of skewness that is completely satisfactory from the theoretical point of view and from the point of view of being easy to calculate and understand. An associated factor is that we have had even greater difficulty in developing a simple way of measuring the sampling errors in any given measure of skewness.

The second reason is psychological. The existence of skewness is a substantial inconvenience in most statistical analysis. Most of the generally known statistical measures and most of the easily available tables, such as the normal curve, assume a reasonable conformity to at least a symmetrical distribution, and in some cases a normal distribution. As soon as we explicitly realize that our distribution is significantly skewed, we also have to recognize that almost all of the techniques we know are inapplicable except with a degree of error. Thus there is a great tendency to look the other way, as it were, when the issue of skewness comes up and make believe that it is not really an issue at all. In other words, we find it more comfortable to assume that a universe is essentially symmetrical if we do not know how much skewness there is in the sample than if we do!

A good measure of skewness should have three properties. It should:

1. Be a pure number in the sense that its value is independent of the units of the series and also of the degree of variation in the series;
2. Have a value of zero when the distribution is symmetrical; and
3. Have some meaningful scale of measure so that we could easily interpret the measured value.

Thus an ideal measure of skewness might be one which varied in size from 0 to 1 and in which fractional values, such as .35, could be meaningfully interpreted as representing, say, 35% skewness on a known linear scale of skewness, or as representing an amount of skewness that could be placed in some ranking of the amount of skewness we find from experience in various series. An example of the experience type of scale would be the way we measure the significance of a batting average of .325. Most every American boy knows that this is a high batting average in the sense that very few ballplayers are able to achieve it. Similarly, we might be able to say that a skewness of .35 is very high because there are relatively few times in which a value of that or more has occurred. However, if we measure skewness on a linear scale from 0 to 1, with no knowledge of how often we might find certain values, it would be perfectly appropriate to assume that a skewness of .35 is moderately small.

Of the several methods of measuring skewness that have been developed we discuss three formulas, the first is

$$Sk = \frac{\text{Mean} - \text{Median}}{s}.$$

This formula obviously satisfies the requirement of being a pure number because the unit of the series cancels out in the division. It also has a value of zero in a symmetrical distribution. Although it is not obvious, it can be proved that this ratio has a maximum value of 1.

If we apply this formula to our unit sales data, we get

$$Sk = \frac{\$5.72 - \$3.27}{\$7.61} = +.32.$$

The question now is to determine how much skewness is represented by .32. It is moderately low on the 0 to 1 scale. Unfortunately, we

find that skewness is rarely measured, and we have no ready standard to judge whether .32 is high or low on an experience scale. We
might say somewhat authoritatively that we suspect that .32 is actually quite high, a value that is rarely exceeded. The knowledge
that a sample of weights of adult American females yields a skewness
of .17 and the distribution of family incomes in the United States,
before taxes, for the year 1947 was estimated to be .19 may be helpful.

The second measure of skewness we refer to is based on an extension of the ideas underlying the calculation of the mean and the
standard deviation. The sum of the deviations from the mean
always equals zero. If, however, we *cube* these deviations, the
sum of the cubes definitely equals zero if the distribution is *symmetrical* but probably does not equal zero if the distribution is
skewed. Furthermore, we can say that in general the likelihood
of the sum's being zero is less the greater the departure from symmetry, and we are able to say that the sum of the cubes of the
deviations from the mean is a function of the degree of skewness.
More particularly, we say that

$$\gamma_1 \text{ (gamma)} = \frac{\mu_3}{s^3},$$

where

$$\mu_3 = \frac{\Sigma f(X - \overline{X})^3}{N}.$$

Table 6.14 illustrates the calculation for our unit sales series.
Note that the short-cut method was used and that both μ_3 and s
were left in units of $.375. The answer of 3.15 is somewhat difficult
to interpret. There is no limit to the value of γ_1 so we cannot be
helped by relating 3.15 to its potential limiting value. Again we
have rather limited experience to tell us how often a γ_1 of 3.15 occurs.
A guide might be the fact that the weights of a sample of adult
American females has a γ_1 of .95 and the distribution of United
States family income in 1947 had a γ_1 of 8.76.

The third measure of skewness we refer to is based on the notions
of the mean and the median as is the first one. However, instead
of considering the *values* of these in the units of the given series,
we now refer to their *percentile equivalents*. The median is equivalent to the 50th percentile by definition. The mean would also
be equivalent to the 50th percentile if the distribution were sym-

TABLE 6.14

Calculation of Coefficient of Skewness of Unit Charge Sales of Hardware Store

(*Note:* This table is a continuation of Table 6.11. The additional information required is fd^3, which is calculated here as though it were Column 15 of Table 6.11.)

fd^3
(15)

− 49.709445
−130.000000
− 76.800000
− 31.320000
−   5.440000
−   .680000
0
.520000
2.880000
4.320000
18.225000
43.940000
122.825000
185.220000
312.500000
595.820000
593.190000
27933.450834
29518.941389

Coefficient of skewness $= \gamma_1 = \dfrac{\mu_3}{s^3}$

$$\mu_3 = \frac{\Sigma f(X - \overline{X})^3}{N}$$

$$= \frac{\Sigma fd^3}{N} - 3\frac{\Sigma fd^2}{N}\cdot\frac{\Sigma fd}{N} + 2\left(\frac{\Sigma fd}{N}\right)^3$$

$$= 29{,}518.9414 - 3 \times 418.6503 \times 2.5838 + 2 \times 2.5838^3$$

$$= 26{,}308.3144$$

$$\gamma_1 = \frac{26{,}308.3144}{20.297^3}$$

$$= 3.15$$

metrical. Departure of the mean from the 50th percentile can thus be taken as evidence of skewness. The specific formula we use is

$$Sk = \frac{P_m - .50}{.50},$$

where P_m is the percentile equivalent of the mean. This measure has a maximum value of 1 and a minimum value of 0, if we ignore signs. The sign indicates the direction of the skewness just as for the first two measures.

If we apply this formula to our unit sales series, we first calculate P_m. We do this by matching the mean of $5.72 with its percentile equivalent. We can see from Table 6.11 that $5.72 falls in the interval $5.125 to $5.875. Since 69% of the cases have a value less than \$5.125 and 75.5% have a value less than \$5.875, we know immediately that the value of P_m falls between 69% and 75.5%. A linear interpolation gives us an estimated value for P_m of

$$69\% + \frac{\$5.72 - \$5.125}{\$.75} \times 6.5\% = 69\% + 5.2\% = 74.2\%.$$

Substituting 74.2% in our formula, we get a skewness coefficient of

$$\frac{.742 - .50}{.50} = .484, \text{ or } 48.4\%.$$

The simplest way to interpret the magnitude of the skewness based on this percentile concept is to refer back to P_m. We can say, for example, that the skewness of unit sales is such that there are about three chances out of four that a given sale will be less than the arithmetic mean (ignoring sampling errors in our information). Or, if we prefer, we can say that the odds are 3 to 1 in favor of an item being less than the mean. Contrast this with the 1 to 1 odds for a symmetrical distribution.

The income distribution had a P_m of .64, and the female weight distribution had a P_m of .56.

6.9 Kurtosis

If we further extend the idea of raising deviations from the mean to some power, we might raise these deviations to the *fourth* power and then take the arithmetic mean of the results. We could then take the *fourth* root in order to get back to the original units of the series. The term *moment* has been applied to such measures based on various powers of the deviations. A general formula often used is

$$\mu_k = \frac{\Sigma f x^k}{N},$$

where k refers to the particular power used. If we wish, we can take the kth root of μ_k. Note that the square root of the second moment about the mean is the familiar standard deviation; we referred to the third moment in our discussion of measures of skewness. The fourth moment, or $(\Sigma f x^4)/N$, is the basis of measuring a characteristic of a frequency series called *kurtosis*. The most commonly used formula for kurtosis is

$$\gamma_2 = \frac{\mu_4}{\mu_2{}^2} - 3.$$

This is a pure number also. Note that the numerator would have the same unit as the denominator. The 3 is subtracted because a normal curve yields a value of 3 for the ratio of μ_4 to $\mu_2{}^2$. Thus γ_2 has a value of zero for a normal curve. If a curve has a relatively high proportion of cases in the tails compared with the normal curve, then γ_2 will be positive because of the greater effect of extremes on the value of μ_4 than on the value of μ_2. Figure 6.14 illustrates a curve with a positive kurtosis and compares it with a normal curve. Figure 6.15 shows the same distribution on probability paper.

We have little occasion to calculate the kurtosis of a distribu-

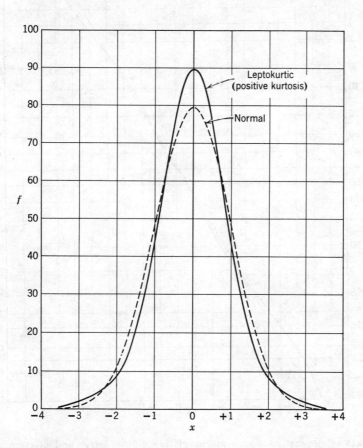

Fig. 6.14 Comparative shapes of normal curve and of curve with positive kurtosis (leptokurtic curve). (Note: Both curves have the same standard deviations.)

tion. Although it has considerable importance in theoretical statistics, it is very tedious to calculate and very difficult to interpret in most applied problems. It will have its greatest significance to us when we consider the t distribution later. In fact the distribution illustrated in Figs. 6.14 and 6.15 is a t distribution.

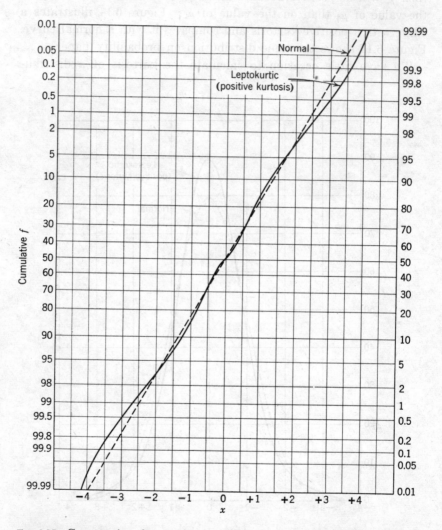

Fig. 6.15 Comparative shapes of cumulative normal curve and of cumulative leptokurtic curve—probability scale. (Note: Both curves have the same standard deviations.)

6.10   The Predominance of the Arithmetic Mean

Review the various calculations referred to in this and earlier
chapters and note that the process of adding a series of numbers and
then dividing by the number of numbers appears over and over
again.   We can illustrate this point by gathering together several
of the measures that involve this process:

$$\text{Arithmetic mean} = \left(\frac{\Sigma X}{N} \right)$$

$$\text{Geometric mean} = \text{antilog} \left(\frac{\Sigma \log X}{N} \right)$$

$$\text{Harmonic mean} = \frac{1}{\dfrac{\Sigma \dfrac{1}{X}}{N}}$$

$$s = \sqrt{\frac{\Sigma x^2}{N}}$$

$$\mu_k = \frac{\Sigma f x^k}{N}$$

The circled areas call attention to this process of taking the arithmetic mean of some variable.   The essential process is one of doing
something, as it were, to an original set of numbers and then taking
the arithmetic mean of the result.   Often, we undo what we did and
return to the original units of the series.   In fact, if we do not undo
it or if we do not convert to a pure number, we end up with
reasonably absurd units that defy practical interpretation.

It is very helpful in trying to understand statistical formulas to
remember that practically all the formulas consist of two parts.   One
part involves transforming the units of the series, by taking logarithms, or by squaring, for example, and then possibly transforming
back *after* the other part of the formula takes the arithmetic mean.
Some formulas are working formulas and, for example, might omit
the process of dividing by N because it happens to conveniently cancel out in the total operation.   But the mean is certainly buried somewhere in the formula, and it is usually worthwhile to dig it out be-

cause it is a fact that the essentially *statistical* part of the analysis takes place where the mean is taken; and if we do not know where the mean is taken and of what it is taken, we are in a position to rather completely misunderstand the import of what we are doing.

We have occasion to introduce additional tools in later chapters. We try to call attention to where the averaging process takes place and its significance in the given analysis. The fact that the fundamental statistical operation consists of taking the arithmetic mean should greatly simplify the seemingly complex formulas.

PROBLEMS AND QUESTIONS

6.1 State the average you would use in each of the following situations. Give specific reasons for your selection. In some of the cases you will feel that an average is only a partial answer to the problem. Do not let such a feeling deter you from selecting the best possible average.

(a) The average height of grammar school children for determining the best height for a drinking fountain.

(b) The average temperature during a winter day for estimating the heating needs to maintain an indoor temperature of 72°F.

(c) The average muzzle velocity of a 16″ artillery shell for purposes of estimating the best range setting to strike a given target.

(d) The average daily sales of newspapers in a given drugstore to make the best possible estimate of the appropriate number of papers to order. (Note: Assume that the sales figures to be averaged have not been affected by any "out of stock" limitations.)

(e) The average caloric content of one pound of round steak for inclusion in a table of caloric contents of various foods.

(f) The average speed in miles per hour of three ferry boats for estimating the number of trips that the boats can make between two river points during a 24-hour period.

(g) The average daily attendance at a movie theater for purposes of estimating:

1. The total monthly revenue;
2. The number of ushers needed on any given day.

(h) The average of your examination grades in a course for purpose of determining your course grade.

6.2 In your high school algebra course there were probably such problems as "If John takes 6 days to dig a ditch, Tom takes 4 days to dig the same ditch, and Harry 3 days to dig this ditch, how many days will it take for all three men together to dig the ditch?" The answer came from solving for X in the equation

$$\frac{1}{6} + \frac{1}{4} + \frac{1}{3} = \frac{1}{X}.$$

Show the analogy between this kind of a problem and the need for the harmonic mean in some cases when we are interested in the total of some items.

6.3 Given the variable X, find a value M so that $\Sigma(X - M)^2$ is a minimum. (You will need ability with calculus to solve this problem.)

6.4 Given the variable X and that $M = (\Sigma X)/N$, prove that $\Sigma(X - M) = 0$. (You can do this with elementary algebra.)

6.5 Below are presented the 200 additional unit charge sales referred to in the text.

Sample of 200 Unit Charge Sales of a Neighborhood Hardware
Store (This sample of 200 occurred immediately after—
in time—the 200 sales referred to in the text.)

(Data listed in order of size. The chronological order is
assumed to be irrelevant.)

$ .20	1.14	1.74	2.44	3.43	4.75	6.32	10.04
.35	1.14	1.79	2.47	3.46	4.76	6.45	10.38
.41	1.22	1.79	2.50	3.49	4.81	6.47	10.38
.47	1.30	1.80	2.54	3.49	4.83	6.56	10.45
.51	1.30	1.83	2.55	3.50	4.94	6.74	10.46
.56	1.35	1.85	2.55	3.57	4.95	6.79	10.65
.70	1.37	1.88	2.59	3.58	4.95	6.80	10.91
.71	1.40	1.91	2.70	3.59	5.07	6.90	10.95
.72	1.44	1.92	2.75	3.79	5.10	6.95	11.59
.85	1.48	1.95	2.75	3.79	5.13	7.08	11.71
.87	1.50	1.95	2.80	3.87	5.26	7.09	11.90
.88	1.50	1.96	2.85	3.90	5.28	7.20	12.06
.93	1.54	2.00	2.93	3.90	5.31	7.85	12.37
.94	1.54	2.00	2.96	3.95	5.34	7.89	12.42
.98	1.54	2.02	2.98	4.00	5.35	8.22	12.94
.98	1.55	2.05	3.08	4.03	5.43	8.27	13.15
1.00	1.57	2.07	3.08	4.04	5.43	8.32	14.04
1.00	1.57	2.07	3.08	4.09	5.49	8.33	14.29
1.02	1.58	2.22	3.08	4.10	5.50	8.39	15.52
1.02	1.59	2.23	3.10	4.12	5.53	8.95	15.53
1.02	1.60	2.28	3.13	4.13	5.87	9.27	16.75
1.03	1.60	2.31	3.17	4.50	5.94	9.45	23.96
1.05	1.64	2.37	3.28	4.65	6.19	9.56	26.40
1.06	1.73	2.40	3.41	4.70	6.21	9.83	27.44
1.09	1.74	2.40	3.42	4.72	6.21	9.83	32.91

(*a*) Construct the best frequency series you can of such data using *equal* intervals. Defend your choice of intervals by the use of appropriate charts.

(*b*) Construct the best frequency series you can of such data using variable-sized intervals if you wish. Defend your choice of intervals.

(*c*) Use charts to compare your two frequency series with the ones given in the text for the first 200 unit charge sales. Assume that the proprietor had only the information provided by *one* of these two sets of 200. Use what you have found out about the other 200 to estimate the errors he would make if he assumed that his sample of 200 represented the pattern of the universe.

6.6 It was pointed out in the text that the process of "rounding" numbers by combining them into intervals produced effects similar to those resulting from enlarging the sample. Common sense suggests that we couldn't make such apparent gains without some price. Discuss what we lost when we combined items into intervals. How would you try to balance the value of what you lost against the cost of adding more items to your sample? Do you suspect that there might be a sort of "law of diminishing returns" operating on either the cost or gain function? Explain.

6.7 Was there any evidence of "lumpiness" in your distribution of 200 items? What significance would this evidence have to you as the proprietor of a small hardware store? Would it make any difference to you if your wife (rather than a hired clerk) was the bookkeeper?

6.8 The construction of a frequency series obviously results in some steps being taken to use the *sample* of data as a basis for estimating the distribution of items in the *universe*. It is equally obvious that only *some* steps are taken unless one carries his analysis to the point of drawing a smooth curve and then reconstructs his frequencies to conform to this smooth curve. How would you explain what your frequency series does represent if you find that it is somewhere between an exact replica of the original sample and an estimate of the universe?

6.9 The assumption that items are equally spaced through some interval is an application of the "equal distribution of ignorance" rule, or the "rule of insufficient reason" to use unequal spaces. Analyze the logic behind the equal distribution of ignorance rule as a device to choose among alternatives when you have insufficient knowledge to rationally weight the alternatives. What other rule or rules might you apply?

6.10 Suppose you were using some sample evidence to make an estimate of some characteristic of a universe, such as the mean of the universe. If one method of estimation gave you the same chance of your estimate being too high as it did of its being too low while another estimate was such that the arithmetic mean of such estimates (if you were to make many of them) would equal the desired universe value, which method would you choose? Give reasons. (Assume that the distribution of estimates is skewed so that the two methods would give different answers.)

6.11 Calculate the following measures from your frequency series of the second group of 200 unit sales.

(*a*) Arithmetic mean.
(*b*) Median.
(*c*) Semi-interquartile range.
(*d*) Median deviation.
(*e*) Mean deviation.
(*f*) Standard deviation.
(*g*) Range within which the middle 60% of the cases fall.
(*h*) Percentile equivalent of the mean.
(*i*) Coefficient of skewness by each of three methods given in text.
(*j*) Coefficient of variation.

6.12 Give a practical interpretation of each of your answers in 11.

6.13 What differences exist between the sample of 200 analyzed in the text and the sample you analyzed? Do you judge that they are real differences which should be considered by the proprietor in his planning? Or are they of a sort that would cause you to be willing to combine the two samples as though they both came from the same universe? Defend your conclusions.

6.14 Suppose the coefficient of skewness for a sample of 200 unit sales of a different hardware store turned out to be .36 when measured by the formula

$$Sk = \frac{P_m - .50}{.50}.$$

How much less skewness does this distribution have compared with the one used in the text? Compared with the one you analyzed?

chapter 7

Making inferences about the unknown, or the problem of intelligent guessing

We now have most of the tools and ideas we need to tackle the central issue of any practical problem that involves uncertainty, namely, how to make the most intelligent guesses we can about the things we do not know. Since we try to work out methods of guessing that conform to some simple rules of logic, we dignify such guesses by calling them *inferences*. We warn, however, that we are, in fact, guessing, and our methods should be judged by whether or not they work as well as by whether or not they appear logical.

7.1   A Simple Example of Our Basic Problem

It is helpful now to review some of the material from the introductory chapter. Again we use the device of a simplified example to dramatize the main issues.

Suppose there are 10 fish bowls on a table. The bowls have been painted so we cannot see the contents. Each bowl contains a large number of small balls about the size of marbles. Some of the balls are purportedly white. The rest of them are nonwhite. We are to select any one of the bowls we wish and set it aside. We are then offered a bet of $5 to $2 that a random sample of five balls from this bowl will have one, two, or three white balls. Or, if we wished, we could accept the bet the other way around, namely, $2 to $5 that a random sample of five balls will contain four or five white balls. To help us decide which bet we would like to take, we are permitted to draw a random sample of five balls from any one of the remaining nine bowls; or, if we wished, we could select our total of five balls from the nine bowls in any combination we wished, such as one ball each from five of the bowls.

This is quite obviously a guessing game. Unless we peek, or cheat, or have inside information, there is no way that we can make a completely rational choice in this situation. But let us head into the problem to see if we can be rational about some parts of it.

The first decision we have to make is our choice of one of the 10 bowls. Since we presumably know nothing about the contents of any of the bowls, we have no rational basis of choice. Hence we choose one by any method we wish, including a hocus-pocus method if that gives us any psychological satisfaction. The important thing is to not kid ourselves that our method is rational.

The second decision is to choose our informational sample of five balls from the remaining nine bowls. Again we are handicapped by complete lack of knowledge of the contents of the bowls. We must therefore proceed by assumption, hypothesis, or guess. We do not know that, perhaps, the 10 bowls all have the same proportion of white balls; or that the proportions are all different. We would prefer that the bowls were all the same because we would then find that our five informational balls would definitely be relevant to the first bowl that we had selected. If the bowls are different, we might be up against an extreme situation in which the first bowl has all white balls whereas the bowl from which we select the informational balls has no white balls. We can avoid being misled by such a situation by selecting our five informational balls from five different bowls, one ball from each.

Suppose we select one ball from each of five bowls and find that four of the five are white.

We must now decide whether to bet $2 against $5 that a sample of five balls from the first bowl will contain four or five white balls, or to bet $5 against $2 that the sample will contain one, two, or three white balls. If we knew the proportion of white balls in the first bowl, our problem would be much simpler. For example, if we knew that the bowl contained 50% white balls, we could expand the binomial $(.5W + .5C)^5$ and easily estimate the probability of getting four or more white balls in a sample of five. (It is .1875.) Since odds of 2 to 5 are fair if the probability of four or more is .2857, we would prefer to bet against four or more at these odds. Hence we would bet $5 against $2 that there will be three or fewer white balls. (.2857 is calculated by dividing 2 by 7, 7 being the total chances associated with 2 to 5 odds.)

Since we do not know the proportion of white balls in the bowl, we must *guess*, or *infer*. The only basis we have for such an inference is the informational sample of five balls, four of them being white. Common sense indicates that we should be more inclined to believe that the bowl contains a *relatively large proportion* of white balls, given this sample with four white balls, than we would be if our sample had contained only one white ball. The issue, however, is whether this inclination is strong enough to push the probability of four or more white balls from the first bowl beyond .2857, the dividing line between the two bets. The answer is not at all easy to determine in a rational manner. Its determination involves those logical procedures that fall under statistical inference, the topic that concerns us in this and succeeding chapters. Before outlining our plan of attack, we find it profitable to review the conceptual scheme we introduced in the first chapter.

7.2   Another Look at Our Conceptual Scheme

Figure 7.1 presents a diagram that illustrates the flow of ideas as we move from historical data to inferences about future samples. The broad arrows indicate the direction of flow. The whole process of inference starts with the so-called historical facts. They might be the number of white balls in a sample of five. Or they might be the output of a worker during his first month on the job. Or they

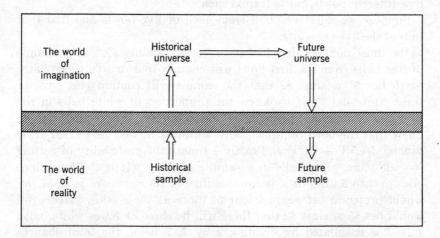

Fig. 7.1   Flow diagram for inferring unknown and/or future events from known and/or historical events.

might be the various prices of a company's common stock during the last two weeks, etc. These facts are then treated as though they were only a *sample of what could have happened*. We might have had a sample with four white balls instead of two white balls. Or the worker might have produced 847 units instead of 769, etc. We find it easy to recognize that the universe, or generating mechanism, which produced the particular sample facts might have all sorts of characteristics. The universe might contain 70% white balls, or 40%, or 26%, etc. The worker might be capable of averaging 826 pieces per month, or 806, or 904, etc. *There is no way that we will ever be able to know such a characteristic of the universe* unless we are dealing with games or the like. Hence we can deal with such a characteristic only by using our imagination.

Note that we separate the world of reality, where we find our sample facts, from the world of imagination, where we find our *inferences* about the kinds of universes which we believe have generated the past samples and/or will generate the future samples.

One of our very real practical problems is to judge whether the universe that will generate the future sample facts is the same as that which generated the past sample facts. We do not know, for example, whether our 10 bowls have different proportions of white balls. We do not know whether our worker is improving with practice or worsening with age. But we must make decisions about such events that are based on some sort of assumption about the prevailing conditions.

After delving into the world of imagination, we must return to the world of reality and make a decision about the kind of future sample facts we expect to encounter. Our success in anticipating these sample facts is the real test of whether our imaginings have been worthwhile. The most elegant logic will be useless if the forecasts are not reasonably accurate.

The process of going from historical facts to inferences about future facts can be very haphazard unless we discipline our thinking by insisting that we assign *probabilities* to the truth of the various inferences we make. In fact, the attempt to assign probabilities in some rational manner distinguishes the statistical method from other methods we might use to arrive at decisions. Any decision in practical affairs necessarily implies some probabilities, quite irrespective of whether the decision-maker has consciously assigned them or not. Sometimes we feel a sense of frustration as we try to explicitly assign probabilities in any practical situation. When we do, we should remind ourselves that everybody else does too.

Another way of picturing our conceptual scheme is in the form of a tree diagram like that shown in Fig. 7.2. We start at the extreme left with the facts, the historical sample, or S_h. From these facts we make inferences about the various historical universes that

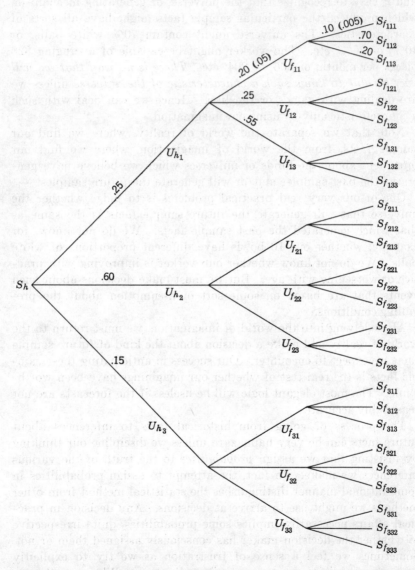

Fig. 7.2 Tree diagram illustrating the inference steps as we proceed from knowledge of a historical sample to inferences about a future sample.

might have generated these facts, or U_h. We have restricted these inferences to only three in order to make the tree manageable within the bounds of the page. Note that we have assigned probabilities to each of these inferences. Also note that these probabilities add to 1, as they must because our inferences should cover all the possibilities and one of them must be true.

The next set of branches shows the various inferences we might make about the *future* universe, or U_f. We show the associated probabilities only for the topmost set. Note that again the three branch probabilities add to 1. (Ignore the number in the parentheses for the moment.)

Finally we come to the last set of branches. These show the various *future samples* that we infer from the particular future universe that we had previously inferred. These branches are labeled S_f. Again note that the assigned probabilities add to 1.

Now let us consider the probabilities that are shown in parentheses. These are the probabilities that our particular inferences to that point are correct. Let us trace out the inferences along the topmost branches. We start with a probability of .25 that U_{h_1} is true. Then, *given* that U_{h_1} is true, we infer that there is a probability of .20 that $U_{f_{11}}$ is true. The probability that both U_{h_1} and $U_{f_{11}}$ are true would be .25 × .20, or .05, as shown in parentheses. This is a *joint*, or *compound*, probability. Finally, given that U_{h_1} and $U_{f_{11}}$ are true, there is a probability of .10 that $S_{f_{111}}$ is true. The joint probability that U_{h_1}, $U_{f_{11}}$, and $S_{f_{111}}$ are all true would be .25 × .20 × .10, or .005.

If we were to assign probabilities to all the branches in this tree and calculate all the joint probabilities, we would find that the final joint probabilities at the extreme right of the tree would add to 1. This would mean the actual future sample must have some one of the various possible values shown in the list of S_f's. Similarly, we would find that the joint probabilities associated with the occurrence of the various future universes would also add to 1 because this future universe must take on one of the listed values.

Since we are basically interested in *future samples* in our practical problems, it would be nice if we could avoid all the intervening steps, and associated arithmetic, between the historical facts and our inferences about future samples. Our tree would then look like Fig. 7.3. We find that there are occasions under which we are able to make such direct inferences. However, we could not understand and appreciate such occasions until we have learned to "climb the tree" by taking advantage of the "footholds" provided by the intervening branches.

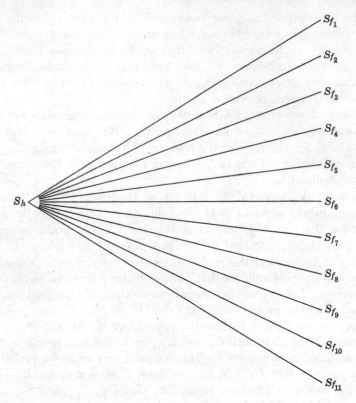

Fig. 7.3 Tree diagram illustrating the paths of inference when we go from past samples directly to inferences about future samples.

7.3 How We Are Going to Study Our Problems of Inference

Although the conceptual scheme just given is quite simple, our attempts to formalize the procedure, and particularly to *quantify* the relevant probabilities, will very likely be troublesome if we try to do too much at once. We are, therefore, going to take the stages one at a time insofar as practicable. This chapter is basically concerned with the *exposure* of the fundamental problems that develop as we try to infer the characteristics of a universe from information supplied by a sample; the next chapter develops a method of handling these problems. In both chapters we ignore the possibility that the universe may be shifting, or that the various samples may have come from different universes.

In Chapter 9 we discuss the relationship of probabilities to the practical problem of decision-making, confining our attention to problems that involve actions based on certain beliefs we might hold about a *universe*.

In Chapter 10 we consider the problem of *pooling* all the information we might have about a problem in making inferences about a universe. For example, past experience may lead to the belief that the universe of coin tosses is so constituted that 50% of the tosses will be heads in the long run. Suppose we then observe a sample of 10 tosses which shows 80% heads. How do we relate our original experience and belief with this result? Do we now believe that these coins will produce more than 50% heads when they are tossed? Or do we basically ignore the new sample evidence and continue to believe what we believed before we saw it? This is the issue of relating old information to new, or the issue of pooling information.

In Chapter 11 we give explicit consideration to the problem of making inferences about future *samples*. We consider both the method that works through inferences about universes and the direct method which goes directly from the past sample to the future sample.

In Chapter 12 we apply all the ideas and techniques we have developed in Chapters 7 through 11 to the problem of making inferences about a *continuous variable*, such as the unit sales of a hardware store, or the size of the Federal Debt, or the height of an adult American male. Prior to this we confine ourselves to the problem of inferences about *attribute data*. These are data that are measured in such a way that they can take on only values of 1 or 0. We approach our problems of inferences with attribute data because we then gain the advantages of simplicity of understanding. At the same time, we can also uncover quite vividly some problems in inference that get obscured, or are assumed away, if we work with continuous variables.

7.4 The Behavior of Random Samples From a Known Universe

The best way to begin our speculations about the kind of universes from which a given sample came is to study the reverse process, namely, the kinds of samples that can come from a *known* universe. We have already discussed this problem (Chapter 5) of the probabilities of getting various sample results from a given universe. We now supplement the earlier analysis.

The Basic Model We Use

We are going to try to develop most of the basic ideas involved in making inferences about a universe by referring to a simple model of a universe. We use this model universe to generate sample information, and we then take the sample information and generate inferences about the universe from which these samples came and check these inferences against the known characteristics of the universe. We should thus be able to see quite clearly whether our methods of making inferences work and in exactly what way they work. At the same time we can check other possible systems of making inferences.

The model universe we use consists of an infinite number of objects, each subject to a simple test of being satisfactory for some purpose. These objects could be some specified part for an automobile, for example. We happen to know that 30%, or .30, of all the parts are satisfactory. We call a satisfactory part A. Thus .70 of the parts are not satisfactory; we call these $\bar{A}$ (not A). Since we would like to treat our problem mathematically, we must assign numbers to the factor of a part's being satisfactory or not satisfactory. We arbitrarily assign a value of 1 to a satisfactory part and a value of 0 to an unsatisfactory one. (The assignment of these particular numbers considerably simplifies our subsequent calculations without significantly prejudicing our results. Thus we can learn quite a bit at a relatively small cost in arithmetical labor.)

Let us now examine this universe quantitatively. The objects are identifiable by the number 1 or the number 0. Of all the objects .30 are 1's and .70 0's. Let us call this variable (from 1 to 0) X. We can now carry out the familiar calculations as shown in Table 7.1.

Although all these calculations are pretty familiar by now, we review certain features because of their pertinence to what follows. Note that P is the *relative* frequency and thus adds to 1. We also use P to mean probability, a usage consistent with our interpretation of a probability as a relative frequency of occurrence in the indefinite long run. One of the conveniences of using *relative* frequencies is illustrated in the calculation of the arithmetic mean, etc. Note that we divide the sums of the PX's, etc. by 1 to get the arithmetic means.

Although the calculations for the mean, the variance, the crude skewness, and the coefficient of skewness are all carried out in a straightforward way in the table, we indicate the alternative ways

TABLE 7.1

Analysis and Summary Description of Universe of Automobile Part 3496

Condition of Part	Value of Part X	Relative Frequency P	PX	$X - \overline{X}$ or x	Px	Px^2	Px^3
$\overline{A}$	0	.70	0	$-.30$	$-.21$	.063	$-.0189$
A	1	.30	.30	.70	.21	.147	.1029
		1.00	.30		0	.210	.084

$$\overline{X} = \frac{.30}{1} = \pi \qquad\qquad L_x = .084 = \pi\tau(\tau - \pi)$$

$$\sigma_x^2 = .21 = \pi\tau = \pi - \pi^2 \qquad K_x = \frac{.084}{(.21)^{3/2}} = \frac{\tau - \pi}{\sqrt{\pi\tau}} = .873$$

$$\sigma_x = .46$$

of calculating these results with sole reference to π and τ. It is customary to label the arithmetic mean of the numbers 1 and 0 in a universe as π. (This assumes, of course, that only the numbers 1 and 0 can occur.) The value of π also is always equal to the *proportion* of the given element in the universe. τ is then taken to equal $1 - \pi$, or in this case .70.

Verify each of the calculations in Table 7.1 by substituting the values of .30 and .70 for π and τ, respectively, in the appropriate formulas. The ease of doing this should make clear one of the advantages we pick up by restricting our model to values of 1 and 0.

Figure 7.4 shows where we now stand. The top part of the figure indicates our universe of 30% satisfactory parts, or the domain of knowledge. We have also listed the results of the analysis made in Table 7.1. The lower part of the picture is the domain of ignorance. This is where all the samples from this universe are. We hope to illuminate this area by making *inferences* about the kinds of samples we might get from this known universe.

The Results of Drawing Random Samples

We are going to imagine taking samples of five items from our universe and assume that these samples are selected in such a way that we are unable to detect any relationship between the process of selection and the results we get. We treat these samples, therefore, as though they were generated by a random process. We have pre-

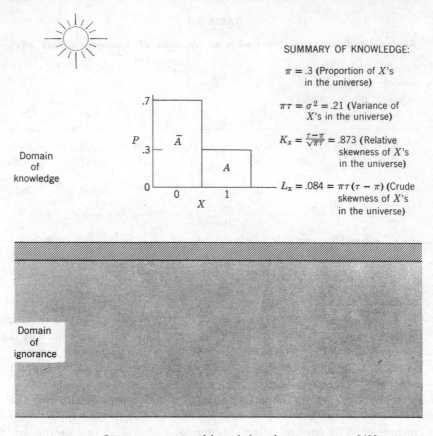

SUMMARY OF KNOWLEDGE:

$\pi = .3$ (Proportion of X's in the universe)

$\pi\tau = \sigma^2 = .21$ (Variance of X's in the universe)

$K_x = \frac{\tau - \pi}{\sqrt{\pi\tau}} = .873$ (Relative skewness of X's in the universe)

$L_x = .084 = \pi\tau(\tau - \pi)$ (Crude skewness of X's in the universe)

Domain of knowledge

Domain of ignorance

Fig. 7.4 Our present state of knowledge about auto part 3496.

viously defined a random process as one in which *we are ignorant* of any relationship between the process and the results, and our notion of randomness is simply a model we have constructed to treat something we do not know anything about. We do not argue that there *is* no relationship between the process of selection and the results that occur. We merely note that *we* know of no such relationships, and we must treat the process as though there were none. It is not surprising, then, that since randomness is a result of ignorance, we find ourselves making random errors.

We could, of course, actually construct a model universe of the type we have defined. We could then actually draw samples of five items out of this universe and study the sample results and make conclusions about the kinds of samples we can get from this universe.

Such conclusions would be based on experience. The more such samples we had, and hence the more experience we had, the more specific could be our conclusions. Such an experiment would be quite tedious for us to perform. Some probably would not be satisfied even if we took 1000 such samples. We could considerably speed up such an experiment by *simulating* the drawing process on an electronic computer. We would program (give it instructions) the computer so it would search a table of random numbers for sets of five items. The computer could conduct the search, and find results, at a prodigious rate, thus spewing out random samples of 5 far faster than we could draw them, say, out of a big bowl. We could then program the computer to analyze the samples and indicate in a summary way what resulted.

We are neither going to actually draw the samples nor are we going to program the computer in this way. We are going to assume that we know enough about what the results would be so that we do not wish to waste our time or computer time on such an experiment. Our problem is so simple that it was experimentally analyzed years ago. We are reasonably well satisfied that the binomial theorem, for example, predicts quite well the kinds of results the experiment gives. In fact, it gives us better results than the experiment. The experiment must somehow end before all possible samples have been selected and the results of the experiment will always be a fraction of what could be. The binomial theorem enables us to proceed immediately to an estimate of what would happen if we actually did carry out all possible experiments.

It is worth noting that there are many problems in probability and inference that we do not understand very well, in the sense that we do not have any ready formulas to predict the outcomes of infinite experiments. These are the problems for which we should use the computer to help us search out likely formulas. As pointed out earlier, most of the logical inventions in probability and statistics were initially a response to observable phenomena, and the clues to what a good formula should look like came from experience. If we can learn how to simulate experience on the computer, the potential rate of progress is amazing. It is now possible to have the computer generate more experience in a few hours than heretofore we have been able to generate in years or decades; however, we can remind ourselves that the computer can do only what we tell it, although certainly very quickly. It even makes mistakes in a hurry!

Our procedure is to exploit the binomial theorem to indicate what kinds of samples of 5 will come out of this universe in the *long run*.

Figure 7.5 continues the analogy begun in Fig. 7.4. We find that only six different kinds of samples can occur, the distinguishing feature being the *number* of satisfactory parts in the sample, a number which can run from 0 to 5. Each of these results is pictured in the lower part of the diagram. We have calculated the mean, the variance, the crude skewness, and the coefficient of skewness for each possible sample.

We have also noted the *relative frequency* with which we would expect each of these samples in the *long run*. These are shown along the light ray leading to a given sample. For example, the extreme left ray shows $P(p = 0|\pi = .3, N = 5) = .16807$. This is shorthand for: the probability of getting 0 satisfactory parts, *given* that there are .3 satisfactory parts in the universe and that we are taking samples of 5, is equal to .16807. If we change 0 to something else, say to .2 as we do for the next ray to the right, there is a change in the probability even though π and N remain the same. Similarly, if we change π, we change the probability, or if we change N. Since each of these factors does make a difference in the probability, it is a good idea to cultivate the habit of explicitly specifying them. It is very easy to make rather serious blunders in the use of probabilities if we misinterpret the *conditions* which necessarily must accompany any statement of probability. [It is conventional to use capital P to signify probability. The event we are getting P for is enclosed in parentheses. The first item in parentheses is the event itself, here, $p = 0$. (This is small p and refers to the *proportion* of 1's in the given sample if only 1's and 0's can occur.) We then draw a vertical line to separate the event from the *conditions* under which the event is presumably being generated. These conditions are essential. There is no way that a probability can be calculated except for some given conditions.]

The diagrams at the very bottom of Fig. 7.5 summarize the results from these six possible samples. Section A summarizes the various values for the sample *means*, here called the sample p's. This is the distribution we pay most attention to. Part B summarizes the sample *variances*. Part C summarizes the sample *skewnesses*. All of these distributions take into account the relative frequency with which each sample is expected to occur.

Since we are going to make only passing references to the distributions of the variance and of the skewness, let us make such references first. The most important thing to note about the sample variances is that their arithmetic mean is *less* than the variance in the universe. Note that the universe variance is .21 and the *mean* of

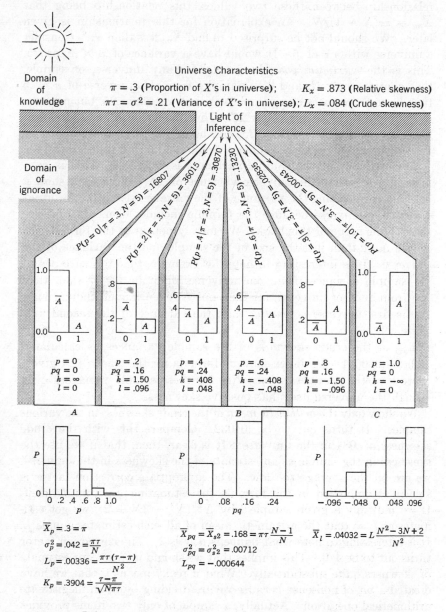

Fig. 7.5 Inferences about samples of five items from a known universe.

the sample variances is .168. Note also that there is a known exact relationship between these two values, this relationship being that $\overline{X}_{pq} = \pi \tau (N - 1)/N$. An explanation for this relationship is given later. We should not be surprised to find $\overline{X}_{pq}$ less than $\pi \tau$. Consider a universe with a π of .5. It would have a variance of .5 $\times$ .5, or .25. This is the *maximum possible variance* for any universe, or sample, that contains only 1's and 0's. Samples from this universe of $\pi = .5$ thus have some cases of a sample variance *less than* .25, but no cases of a sample variance *more than* .25. Thus the mean of such variances must necessarily be *less than* .25, and hence less than the variance of the universe. A parallel argument would hold for all other universes.

The variance of the sample variances is .0071232. This is considerably less than the universe variance of .21. We do not show a formula for deriving the variance of the variances from the information in the universe because the formula includes elements that are outside the scope of this book. We merely note that the formula involves more than just the size of the sample and the variance of the universe. It is interesting to note, for example, that the variance of the sample variances from one universe might be *larger* than they are from another universe, for the same N, even though the variance in the first universe is *smaller* than the variance of the second universe.

L_{pq}, or the crude skewness of the sample variances, is calculated to be $-.000644$. Again we show no formula for the reason just given. Note that the skewness is *negative* for these sample variances even though the universe itself has positive skewness.

We show only the *arithmetic mean* of the crude skewness in the various samples. It turns out to be .04032. Compare this with the crude skewness of .084 in the universe. It is clear, then, that if we use the skewness in the sample as an estimate of the skewness in the universe, we are on the average too low. The appropriate correction factor is shown as embodied in the formula for estimating $\overline{X}_l$ from L itself. If we multiply a given sample l by $N^2/(N^2 - 3N + 2)$, we get estimates of L so that the arithmetic mean of all such estimates equals L. It is interesting to note what happens if N is 2. The correction factor turns out to be 4/0. This implies that we should increase our estimate of skewness quite substantially. What it really means is that we have created a bit of nonsense because we are dividing by 0, an illegitimate arithmetical operation. Actually, a sample of only two items provides us with no information at all about the skewness in the universe. All samples of two items are *automatically symmetrical* regardless of how much skewness there is in the universe. It should be obvious, then, that it is a bit of nonsense to base any estimate of skewness on only two items.

Now let us return to the distribution of sample means, here called p's. Since we are going to be spending quite a bit of time with such distributions, it is a good idea to make very clear exactly how we have calculated the summary results shown at the base of Part A. Table 7.2 shows the detail of the calculations. The important features of each column are as follows:

> Column 1 These are the *only possible* proportions of satisfactory units that can occur in samples of 5. These proportions are the equivalent of samples having 0 satisfactory units, 1 satisfactory unit, etc., up to a maximum of 5 satisfactory units.
>
> Column 2 These are the *probabilities* of getting samples with the given p's. Thus we are saying that we expect to get samples with 0 satisfactory units .16807 of the time *in the long run*. The

TABLE 7.2

Analysis of Distribution of Sample Arithmetic Means (p's) for Simple Random Samples of 5 Items Each from a Universe with an Arithmetic Mean (π) of .3

Sample p (1)	P (2)	Pp (3)	$(p - \bar{p})$ (4)	$P(p - \bar{p})$ (5)	$P(p - \bar{p})^2$ (6)	$P(p - \bar{p})^3$ (7)
0	.16807	0	$-.3$	$-.050421$	.0151263	$-.00453789$
.2	.36015	.072030	$-.1$	$-.036015$	.0036015	$-.00036015$
.4	.30870	.123480	.1	.030870	.0030870	.00030870
.6	.13230	.079380	.3	.039690	.0119070	.00357210
.8	.02835	.022680	.5	.014175	.0070875	.00354375
1.0	.00243	.002430	.7	.001701	.0011907	.00083349
	1.00000	.300000		0	.0420000	.00336000

$$\overline{X}_p = \bar{p} = .30 = \pi; \ \sigma_p{}^2 = .042 = \boxed{\frac{\pi\tau}{N}} = \frac{.3 \times .7}{5}$$

$$L_p = .00336 = \boxed{\frac{L}{N^2}} = \frac{\pi\tau(\tau - \pi)}{N^2} = \frac{.3 \times .7(.7 - .3)}{25} = \frac{.084}{25}$$

$$K_p = \frac{.00336}{.042^{3/2}} = \frac{.00336}{\sqrt{.042^3}} = \frac{.00336}{.008607} = .3904 = \boxed{\frac{K}{\sqrt{N}}} = \frac{\tau - \pi}{\sqrt{N} \times \sqrt{\pi\tau}}$$

$$= \frac{.7 - .3}{\sqrt{5 \times .7 \times .3}} = \frac{.4}{\sqrt{1.05}} = \frac{.4}{1.0247}$$

probabilities given here were taken from a table of the binomial. At least check them against the table, or possibly check them by calculating the binomial itself!

Column 3 This is the multiplication of each p by its corresponding P, or multiplying each sample mean by the relative frequency of its expected occurrence. The sum of this column is the arithmetic mean of *all the sample means*.

N.B. A very important characteristic of the means of random samples is now apparent, namely, that *the arithmetic mean of all sample means is equal to the mean of the universe*.

Column 4 Here we show the deviations of each sample mean from the universe mean. Since they are not yet weighted by their probabilities, the sum of column 4 is meaningless.

Column 5 Here we multiply each deviation in column 4 by its probability in column 2. We sum these weighted deviations and get 0. This is as we expect because we know that the *sum of the deviations from the arithmetic mean always equals 0*.

Column 6 Here we have the weighted *squared* deviations. They were calculated by multiplying column 4 by column 5. The sum is the sum of all the squared deviations. Since N equals 1, this is also the *mean* of the squared deviations and hence what we call the *variance*. If we were to take the square root of this, we would have the *standard deviation* of the sample p's.

Note that we could have calculated the same result of .042 by dividing the *variance of the universe* ($\pi\tau$, or .21) by the *number of items in the sample* (here 5). This is a very important result and is *always true*. Its truth is quite independent of the shape of the universe. We almost always calculate the variance of sample means by this formula rather than by the tedious process of a direct calculation from a distribution of all possible sample means as we did here.

Column 7 Here we make the next logical step after squaring the deviations. Now we *cube* them. (Although we do not do it here, or elsewhere, we should note that the next logical step is to raise these deviations to the 4th power. The omission of this step, and of the steps up to even higher powers of deviations, is what prevented us from saying very much about the distributions of sample variances and sample skewnesses. We would need these higher powers to say more.)

We are interested in the cubes of deviations because they indicate something about *skewness*. The sum of the cubes is 0 if there is no skewness. Here we find a result of .00336. This indicates a *positive skewness* in the distribution of sample means.

The calculations below the columns show that we could have obtained this same result by dividing the crude skewness in the universe (L) by the *square* of the sample size. This is also a very important result. Again we emphasize that it is *always true* and is *completely independent* of the distribution form of the universe. We can now see why we asserted in an earlier chapter that the normal curve is a rather good approximation to the distribution of sample means even though the universe is quite skewed *provided* the sample is reasonably large. The crude skewness of sample means varies inversely as the *square* of the sample size.

The *coefficient* of skewness of sample means is also calculated; it is .3904. Again we find that we could have calculated this directly from the universe information, using the universe K and dividing it by the *square root* of N. Note that the relative skewness does not disappear as fast as does the crude skewness. The reason is quite simple. The relative skewness is calculated by dividing the crude skewness by the *cube of the standard deviation*. As N increases, we find the crude skewness decreasing quite rapidly in the *numerator* of the ratio. But, also as N increases, we find the standard deviation decreasing in the *denominator* of the ratio. The net result is that the *ratio* does not decrease with N as rapidly as does the *numerator*.

Now that we, to an extent, understand the behavior of samples as they are generated by a random process from a *known universe*, we are in a better position to infer what is an unknown universe on the basis of a *known sample*.

7.5 Inferring the Mean of a Universe from Information Provided by a Random Sample

The typical practical situation is illustrated in Fig. 7.6. All of our knowledge is in the sample domain. Our problem is to make inferences about the universe domain from this sample information.

We first must face a philosophical issue. The characteristics of the universe are in fact *fixed* in the same sense that the characteristics of a deck of playing cards are fixed. *Several* different samples could have been drawn from this single universe. We might argue, therefore, that the universe is a *constant* and the sample is a *variable*. This argument is relevant only if we *know* the universe and are *guessing* about the sample. If we do not know the universe, the situation is quite different. We now have a case in which we know the sample and are guessing about the universe. Therefore, *as far as we know*, the universe might have *several* characteristics and the sample has only the *specific* characteristics given. Hence we must treat the universe as though it were a variable and the sample as though it were a constant.

Some analysts object to treating a constant universe as though it

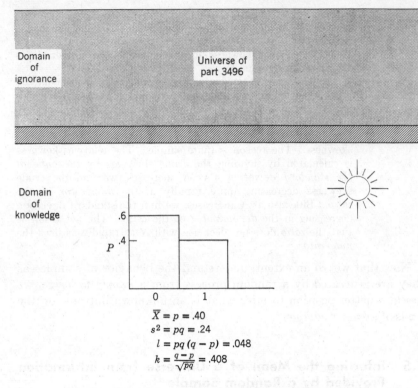

$$\overline{X} = p = .40$$
$$s^2 = pq = .24$$
$$l = pq\,(q - p) = .048$$
$$k = \frac{q - p}{\sqrt{pq}} = .408$$

Fig. 7.6 Our present state of knowledge about part 3496.

were a variable. We answer this objection by pointing out that we must always treat a problem in terms of what *we* know about the situation, not in terms of what the situation really is. If our knowledge is scanty, prudence requires that we allow for all the possible values some unknown constant might have. We should understand, then, that when we treat a universe as though it were a variable, we do not do this because we think the universe really is a variable but because we do not know the precise value of the relevant constant.

Summary Characteristics of Our Sample

Note that we have calculated the same summary figures for our sample of five auto parts as we did for our universe. We find that the sample has a mean of .4, or 40% satisfactory parts. It has a variance of .24, a crude skewness of .048, and a coefficient of skewness of .408. What might we now say about the universe from which this sample came?

If we say that "the universe has a mean of .4," we are making a statement about the mean which will be right on the average, in the sense that the arithmetic mean of all such statements would give us the true universe mean. We are able to say this because we have already learned that the *arithmetic mean of all possible sample means is equal to the mean of the universe.* (See the previous section.)

Similarly, we could say that "the universe has a variance of .30" (the sample variance of .24 times $N/(N-1)$, or times 1.25). We make this adjustment in the sample variance because we have discovered that the arithmetic mean of sample variances is too small. (See Section 7.4.) After making this adjustment, we can now say that *the arithmetic mean of all such estimates of the universe variance will equal the true universe variance.*

It may seem absurd to make an estimate of the universe variance of .30 when we know that the *maximum possible* variance of the universe is .25. (The variance of a distribution of 1's and 0's is equal to $\pi\tau$, and $\pi\tau$ can never be larger than .25.) And it *is* absurd in a way. We are led into such an absurd statement if we insist that our estimates have their *arithmetic mean* correspond to the truth, or the universe value that is being estimated. It is thus apparent that we should attach no magical properties to any method of making estimates that satisfies the arithmetic mean criterion. It is quite clear here that we should abandon the arithmetic mean criterion for another general criterion that comes to better terms with common sense. Since further discussion of this issue is beyond the scope of this book, we merely advise an adjustment of the sample variance for its downward bias *up to the logical maximum of .25*, but no further. Thus, in this case, we would adjust the sample variance of .24 up to the maximum value of .25.

A parallel line of reasoning leads us first to estimate that the universe has a crude skewness of .100. [This is the sample crude skewness multiplied by $N^2/(N^2 - 3N + 2)$.] Again we find our estimate larger than a known maximum, in this case a maximum of .0967. Hence we would reduce the estimate to .0967. We make no attempt to make the best single estimate of the coefficient of skewness in the universe.

If we now combine these so-called best single estimates of the mean, variance, and skewness and come up with a universe that has a mean of .40, a variance of .25, and a crude skewness of .0967, we would have a "best single estimate" of the universe. We find the task of constructing such a universe quite formidable, almost like constructing a Frankenstein monster, with a leg from here, a head from there, a torso from somewhere else, etc. We are sure, however, that the resultant universe does not conform to any customary binomial distributions because this combination of mean, variance, and skewness is a logical impossibility for a binomial distribution. We feel confident that we could eventually find a distribution form that would have these characteristics, at least approximately. But we are not going to bother to look for it because we are quite sure we would have no practical use for it after we found it because it would be only a *single* estimate of the unknown universe. Such a single estimate is almost certainly wrong (we are certain it is in this case). To have an estimate that is almost certainly wrong, and to not know its margin of error, is to have no reliable base for rational action. What we could try to do, of course, is first make this best estimate, then make a next best, and a second next best, etc. until we have a whole collection of estimates of this universe. Such an approach is conceptually possible, and it probably would be somewhat rewarding. However, it would involve some very formidable challenges, and we must confess that we are not quite up to them here, and not just because this is an introductory book.

We are actually going to lower our sights somewhat and not even try to describe the universe fully. We are going to confine ourselves to the relatively modest task of estimating the *mean* of the universe. We take up the parallel task of estimating the *variance* of a universe in a later chapter (Chapter 12). Nowhere do we try to estimate both of these things at the same time.

One Approach to Inferences About the Universe Mean

We start reasoning about the mean of the universe with the *best single estimate we have at the moment* and that is a mean of .40. But we are quite sure that the true mean might be larger than .40 or smaller than .40. The problem, then, is to determine how much larger or how much smaller, and then to determine how often it might be a given amount larger or a given amount smaller. In other words, we would like the equivalent of a probability distribution of the possible values of the unknown universe mean. How do we go about generating such a distribution?

The simplest and most straightforward approach to the problem of generating a probability distribution of the unknown universe mean based on information supplied by a random sample is to *let the sample act as though it were the universe* and let the unknown, and hence variable, *universe act as though it were the sample*. What we are going to do, then, is follow a consistent procedure of *letting knowledge beget inferences.* We have previously used the procedure to let our knowledge about a universe beget inferences about a sample. We are now going to let our knowledge about a sample beget inferences about a universe. We have no trouble doing this consistently as long as we concentrate on *knowledge* and *inference* as the keys, rather than on *universe* and *sample,* which are not the keys, although the distinction between universe and sample is certainly relevant to many things we are going to do.

We call an inferred probability distribution of the unknown universe mean the *inference distribution of the unknown universe mean,* and we call the probabilities in such a distribution the *inference ratios.* We use inference here rather than probability in order to reduce the possibility of misunderstanding. Thus we plan to use *inference* when our knowledge is in the *sample* domain and we are making statements about the universe. We use *probability* when our knowledge is in the *universe* domain and we are making statements about the sample.

Figure 7.7 pictures a possible set of inferences about π (we call such an inference π_I). Note that we have done exactly what we did in Fig. 7.5. We have used information in the domain of knowledge to generate inferences in the domain of ignorance. The *inference ratios* referred to in the rays leading to the various possible values of π_I are taken directly from a table of the binomial distribution, in this case for a mean (p) of .4 and N of 5; it would be good to verify them. We comment only on the leftmost one. It is written $I(\pi_I = 0 | p = .4, N = 5) = .0778$. This is shorthand for "the *inference ratio* of a value of π_I of 0, *given* a sample of five items with a mean of .4, is equal to .0778."

Again we have the problem of some absurd answers. If π really had a value of 0, of course, all samples would have p's of 0. Similarly, if π really had a value of 1, all samples would have a p of 1. Our inference ratios of .0778 and .0102 are thus apparently nothing but nonsense because common sense suggests they should have values of 0. Nonsense or not, we now are going to work with the inference ratios of .0778 and .0102 because we find it very convenient and also because we can discover some properties of inferences that would be obscured otherwise. Actually, our problem is caused by working with very small samples and because we have arbitrarily restricted the values of our basic data to 1's and 0's. If we worked with larger samples and/or continuous variables, the problem of absurd answers would disappear. Perhaps we would be more tolerant of these absurdities if we imagined that a case of π_I of 0 is really a case of π_I of 0 to .1. Similarly, a π_I of .2 represents the range from .1 to .3, etc., up to a π_I of 1 representing the range from .9 to 1. We have merely decided to arbitrarily represent these ranges by certain specific values.

Figure 7.8 shows the inferences of Fig. 7.7 in the form of a single distribution. Here we show π_I along the horizontal axis. It runs from a minimum of 0 to a maximum of 1. We indicate the location of the sample p of .4 by the arrow. The vertical axis shows the inference ratios. (Keep in mind that these are the equivalent of probabilities.)

We would like to think that the distribution of Fig. 7.8 is a fair representation of the likely values of the unknown π, but we must admit that at this stage it has only one property that gives us any comfort, namely, it is that this distribution has a mean of .4, thus equal to the sample mean; and we know that the universe mean does

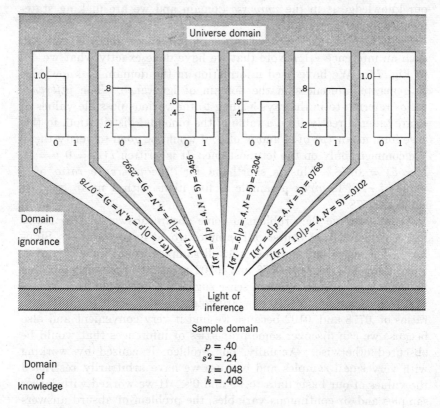

Fig. 7.7 Tentative inferences about π_I based on a random sample.

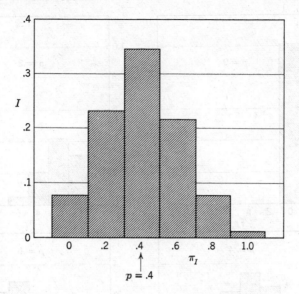

Fig 7.8 Inference distribution of π_I based on a sample of 5 with a p of .4.

equal the arithmetic mean of all the sample means. If, say, our inference distribution had a mean different from .4, we would be concerned because we would fear that the arithmetic mean of all such inferences would not be the universe mean. It is proper, then, for us to do a little more testing before we accept Fig. 7.8 as a fair and proper picture of the likely values of π_I.

Summary of All Possible Inferences that Could be Made from All Possible Samples

We make this test by considering all the other possible sample results and making inferences about π from each of them, and then we *average* all these inferences.

Figure 7.9 shows all such possible inference distributions, including that from a p of .4. Table 7.3 shows the same information in tabular form. Let us turn our attention to the table. The columns are headed by the various selected values of π_I. The rows are identified by the various possible sample p's. Since our samples contain only five items each, we know that there are no other possible values of p than the ones listed. No such restriction applies to the π_I's. We know that π in truth might have a value of .36947, or any other value of an infinite set of values running from 0 to 1. We show only the

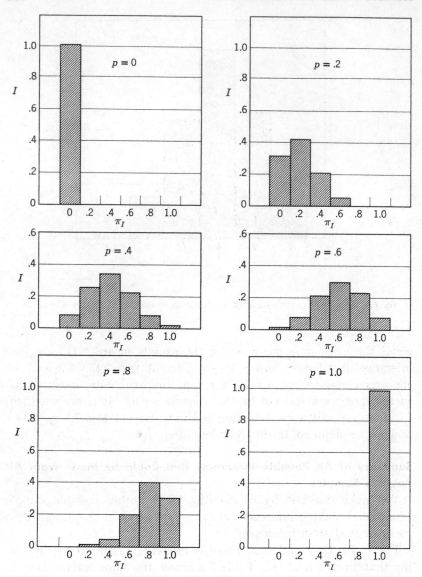

Fig. 7.9 Inference distributions of π_I based on all possible values of p in samples of five items.

values of 0, .2, .4, .6, .8, and 1. It is obvious, then, that we are letting each of these six selected values represent a set of values. In essence, we are letting 0 represent 0 to .1, .2 represent .1 to .3, etc. These are quite crude intervals. We justify their use at the moment because

TABLE 7.3

Matrix of Inference Ratios for All Possible Values of π_I Based on All Possible Values of p for Samples of 5 Items

[The body of the matrix shows $I(\pi_I|p, N = 5)$]

π_I

p	0	.2	.4	.6	.8	1.0	Σ
0	1.0000	.0000	.0000	.0000	.0000	.0000	1.0000
.2	.3277	.4096	.2048	.0512	.0064	.0003	1.0000
.4	.0778	.2592	.3456	.2304	.0768	.0102	1.0000
.6	.0102	.0768	.2304	.3456	.2592	.0778	1.0000
.8	.0003	.0064	.0512	.2048	.4096	.3277	1.0000
1.0	.0000	.0000	.0000	.0000	.0000	1.0000	1.0000

they keep our model as simple as possible; we use more refined intervals later. The crudities cause us no real trouble now with respect to the main purposes of our present investigations.

Examine the row identified by p equal to .4 and you will see the same set of inference ratios for the various values of π_I that we showed in Figs. 7.7 and 7.8. The other rows give the appropriate ratios for the other values of p. All of these ratios are obtainable from a table of the binomial. We should spot check these against such a table in order to satisfy ourselves that we understand exactly how they are determined. Note that each *row* has a sum of 1.0000. This should be so because π *must have some value*, and we claim that we have included that value somewhere in the row. We show no sums for the columns. Such sums would imply *equal weights* for each value of p, and we know that such equal weights would not be true under any circumstances.

Averaging the Inference Ratios. We are now ready to average these inferences as soon as we determine the *appropriate weights* to use. The appropriate weights would depend on the *relative frequency* with which we would expect the various values of p to occur. These relative frequencies depend on the *true value of π* in the universe. Since we started out with a universe with a π of .3, let us

TABLE 7.4

Probability Vector of All Possible Values of p for Samples of 5 from a Universe with a π of .3

p	$P(p \mid \pi = .3, N = 5)$
0	.1681
.2	.3602
.4	.3087
.6	.1323
.8	.0284
1.0	.0023
	1.0000

assume that our "unknown" universe does have a π of .3. Table 7.4 shows the expected relative frequency, or probability, of the various values of p for samples of five from a universe with π equal to .3.

We can now see where our inferences lead us. Table 7.4 indicates that we get a sample p of 0 in .1681 of all samples from a universe with a π of .3. This means that we make the inference about π shown in the first row of Table 7.3 .1681 of the time. Similarly, we make the inference shown in the second row $(p = .2)$ .3602 of the time, etc. If we now multiply each row of inferences shown in Table 7.3 by its relative frequency of occurrence shown in Table 7.4, we have weighted each inference about π according to the relative frequency with which we would be making such an inference. Table 7.5 shows the results of such a multiplication. (Note that we have called Table 7.3 a *matrix* of inference ratios, and Table 7.4 a probability *vector*. These are terms used in matrix algebra, a subject which may be unfamiliar. If so, it is sufficient to know that a *matrix* is essentially a *table with rows and columns*. A *vector* is simply a special case of a matrix that has only *one* row; or, it could also have only *one* column. Thus we talk about a *row vector*, which is a matrix with only one row, and a *column vector*, which is a matrix with only one column. Thus we might call Table 7.3 a *matrix* and Table 7.4 a *column vector*. Those exposed to matrix algebra will note that Tables 7.3 through 7.7 are parts of a system of *matrix multiplication*.)

All of the inference ratios in Table 7.5 are the result of multiplying the *corresponding* unit in Table 7.3 by the appropriate row probability given in Table 7.4. For example, .1681 in the upper left-hand

TABLE 7.5

Matrix of Weighted Inference Ratios for All Possible Values of π, Given that $\pi = .3, N = 5$

[The body of the matrix shows $I(\pi_I | p, N = 5, \pi = .3)$]

π_I

p	0	.2	.4	.6	.8	1.0	
0	.1681	.0000	.0000	.0000	.0000	.0000	.1681
.2	.1180	.1475	.0738	.0184	.0023	.0001	.3601
.4	.0240	.0800	.1067	.0711	.0237	.0031	.3086
.6	.0013	.0102	.0305	.0457	.0343	.0103	.1323
.8	.0000	.0002	.0015	.0058	.0116	.0093	.0284
1.0	.0000	.0000	.0000	.0000	.0000	.0023	.0023
	.3114	.2379	.2125	.1410	.0719	.0251	.9998

corner of Table 7.5 is the result of multiplying 1.0000 from Table 7.3 by .1681 from Table 7.4; .1475 just southeast of the .1681 is the result of multiplying .4096 from Table 7.3 by .3602 from Table 7.4; .0738 in column 3, row 2 of Table 7.5 is the result of multiplying .2048 in column 3, row 2 of Table 7.3 by .3602 in the second row of Table 7.4; etc. Note that the rows add to the same probabilities as we had in Table 7.4 (except for slight rounding errors). This is as we would expect because we started with rows that each added to 1.0, and 1 multiplied by any number should give us the number.

Another way to visualize the material of Table 7.5 is in the form of a tree. Figure 7.10 shows the series of branches. We start with a universe with a π of .3. This universe is then used to generate samples of five items each. These samples could have the p values indicated by the six branches emanating from the trunk. They would occur with the long run frequency indicated at each branch. These correspond to the probabilities given in Table 7.4. Then, given a particular sample p, we could generate inferences about π. These inferences are shown by the six branches that emanate from each of the sample p's. Two probabilities are designated for each of these 36 branches. The first one is the probability (or inference ratio) of the particular π_I, *given* the value of p. Note that these probabilities add to 1

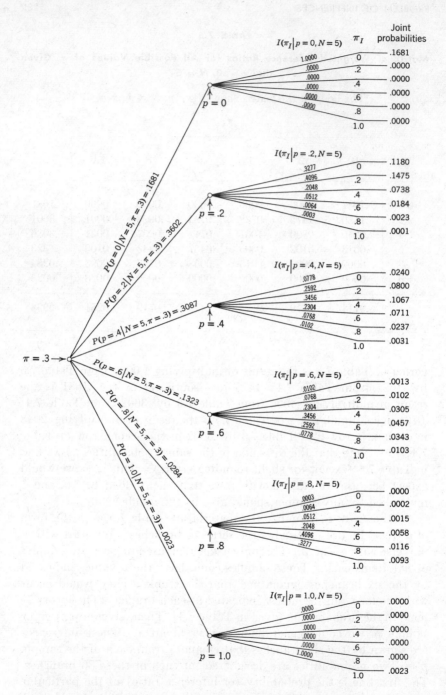

Fig. 7.10 Tree of inference ratios for all possible values of π_I given that $\pi = .3$, $N = 5$.

within each set of six branches. These probabilities correspond to those in Table 7.3. The probabilities shown at the tips of the branches, and labeled the *joint* probabilities, are the result of multiplying the probability of the π_I by the probability of the p that generated the inference. These are the probabilities that correspond to those shown in Table 7.5. Note that *all 36 of these together* add to 1.

Our primary interest in Table 7.5 is in the *column totals.* Here we have the *average* (arithmetic mean) of *all* the different inferences we might make about π based on *all* the possible samples of five items we could get from the universe. Let us call this collection of column totals the *average inference ratio vector* for estimates of π, in this case the inferences based on samples of five items each. In Table 7.6 we rewrite this *average inference ratio vector* as a column vector. We then analyze this vector by calculating the mean, variance, and skewness.

The first and most important thing to note is that the arithmetic mean of all the inferences about π is equal to .300, the value of π in the universe. In other words, if we use the binomial based on the sample p's to generate estimates of π, we find that the arithmetic mean of all such estimates will equal the π in the universe. Thus any errors we make in estimating π will average out in the arithmetic

TABLE 7.6

Analysis of Average Inference Ratio Vector of Estimates of π_I Based on Samples of 5, Given that $\pi = .3$

π_I	I	$I \times \pi_I$	$(\pi_I - \overline{\pi}_I)$	$I(\pi_I - \overline{\pi}_I)$	$I(\pi_I - \overline{\pi}_I)^2$	$I(\pi_I - \overline{\pi}_I)^3$
0	.3114	0	$-.3$	$-.09342$	.028026	$-.0084078$
.2	.2379	.04758	$-.1$	$-.02379$	.002379	$-.0002379$
.4	.2125	.08500	.1	.02125	.002125	.0002125
.6	.1410	.08460	.3	.04230	.012690	.0038070
.8	.0719	.05752	.5	.03595	.017975	.0089875
1.0	.0251	.02510	.7	.01757	.012299	.0086093
	.9998 *	.29980		$-.00014$ †	.075494	.0129706

* Departure from 1.0000 due to rounding errors.
†   "   "   0   "   "   "   "

$\overline{\pi}_I = .2998 = .300$

$\sigma_{\pi_I} = .0755 = \pi\tau \times \dfrac{2N - 1}{2N} \times \dfrac{2}{N} = .21 \times .9 \times .4$

$L_{\pi_I} = .0130$

mean sense. This seems to be a reasonably desirable feature of any estimating procedure.[1] Although we should be quite pleased to find the arithmetic mean of our inferences equaling the true value of π, we should not then automatically assume that the inference ratios that accompany these estimates are meaningful in any probability or relative frequency sense. In fact, it is easily demonstrated that there are many different distributions of π_I that will average out at the true value. However, these different distributions would give quite different inference ratios and hence would give quite different impressions of the chances that the true π falls within any specified limits within the distribution. We examine this problem as soon as we finish commenting on the variance and skewness of this average inference ratio vector.

The variance of this average inference ratio vector is .0755. Note that this same result could have been obtained by multiplying the universe variance of π_T by the expression

$$\frac{2N-1}{2N} \times \frac{2}{N}.$$

This expression looks more formidable than it actually is. Note that the first half $(2N-1)/2N$ is practically equal to 1 if N is any size at all. For example, if $N = 10$, then $(2N-1)/2N = .95$. Thus if N is large, we can treat this part as equal to 1, thus leaving us with $2/N$. As a matter of fact, if we had used the $(N-1)$ binomial instead of the (N) binomial in generating our inferences, we would have found that the variance of the average inference ratio vector would have been exactly $\pi_T(2/N)$.[2] The variance of sample means (p's)

---

[1] We might also argue that it would be a desirable feature to make estimates that have a minimum error in the sense that the sum of all possible errors, signs ignored, is as small as possible. It is the *median* of a set of numbers that minimizes the sum of the deviations if the signs are ignored. If the distribution is symmetrical, the mean will equal the median and we can simultaneously have estimates that have minimum error and errors that will average out. If the distribution is skewed, it is impossible to satisfy both these desirable conditions at the same time. We must then make a choice. Since the distribution we are working with is skewed, we face such a choice here. We have chosen to satisfy the condition of averaging out our errors rather than of minimizing them. We make this choice mostly for convenience.

[2] We may ask why anybody would consider using $N-1$ instead of N in making inferences about π. For example, although we had samples of 5 items, we might have used 4 to generate the binomial. The logic for using 4 would be this:

is equal to $\pi\tau/N$. Hence we can say that the variance of the average inference ratio vector *tends* to equal *twice* the variance of sample p's. Another way to look at it is this: Each sample is the basis of a distribution of sample p's, or of π_I's. Each of these distributions has a variance of pq/N. When we add all these distributions together to get the total, or average, inference ratio vector, we find that this total distribution tends to have *twice* the variance of its members.

We merely note that the average inference ratio vector has a crude skewness of .0130. Since the crude skewness of the universe is .084, this makes the average inference ratio vector skewness about 1/6 of the universe skewness. The formula that expresses the exact relationship is quite forbidding. We note only that the skewness tends to disappear quite rapidly as N increases.

7.6 Checking the Accuracy of the Probabilities Implied by the Inference Ratio Distributions

The second test we must apply to our inference ratio distributions is that of determining their accuracy in estimating the probability that π does in fact fall within specified values of π_I. (The first test, discussed above, established that the inferences did in fact *average out* to the correct value of π.) In applying this test of the accuracy of the *specific inference ratios* we use a much larger sample than before. This larger sample makes it possible to see things that are somewhat obscured if we use a sample of only five items. Table 7.7 shows the *inference matrix* for all possible samples of 50 items from a universe that contains an unknown number of 1's and 0's. The numbers in the body of the matrix (*reading horizontally*) are taken from tables of the binomial distribution. The probabilities are

---

The variance of a binomial distribution varies *inversely* with N. That is, the larger the N, the smaller the variance. The variances of random samples are in general *too small*. In fact, the average sample variance is equal to the universe variance $\times$ $(N-1)/N$. Since we base each of our inference ratio distributions on the sample information, these distributions in general have variances which are smaller than they would be if they were based on the variance in the universe. If we wish to correct for this deficiency, we should use $N-1$ for our binomial inference ratio distributions. Incidentally, if we do use $N-1$ instead of N, we find that the mean of all our inferences will be the true π, just as in using N. However, our average inference ratio vector will have a larger variance than if we had used N.

TABLE 7.7

Inference Matrix * for Binomially Distributed Samples of 50

	p	0	.02	.04	.06	.08	.10	.12	.14	.16	.18	.20 Vector	.22	.24	.26	.28	.30	.32	.34	.36	.38	.40
Π_r																						
.00	1000	0	0	0	0	0	0	0	0													
.02	364	372	386	184	90	35	13	3	1			0										
.04	130	271	276	231	204	139	86	45	20	7	3	0	0									
.06	45	145	226	173	163	181	141	129	86	53	20	11	2	0	0							
.08	15	67	143	102	106	185	147	141	108	87	58	27	7	3	1	0						
.10	5	29	78	203	106	154	171	147	154	135	108	68	33	11	3	1	0					
.12	2	11	38	83	133	167	171	147	161	141	135	107	64	28	11	3	1	0				
.14	1	4	17	45	86	129	157	161	141	152	142	135	108	68	35	13	5	1	0			
.16	1	2	7	22	50	87	124	149	152	142	145	120	141	107	68	36	15	6	2	0	0	
.18	0	0	2	10	26	53	81	120	142	145		142	135	107	71	42	19	8	3	1	0	
.20	1	0	1									106	73	45	22	11	5	2	1	0	0	
→ .20 Vector		0	1	4	13	30	55	87	117	136	140		127	103	75	50	30	16	8	4	2	1	0

	.42	.44	.46	.48	.50 Vector	.52	.54	.56	.58	.60	.62	.64	.66	.68	.70
.22	2	1	0												
.24	5	2	1	0											
.26	12	6	3	1	1	0									
.28	22	13	7	3	1	1	0								
.30	37	24	14	8	4	2	1	0							
.32	56	38	25	15	8	4	2	1	0						
.34	77	57	40	25	15	8	4	2	1	0					
.36	97	78	58	40	26	15	8	4	2	1	0				
.38	112	97	78	59	41	26	16	8	4	2	1	0			
.40	117	110	96	78	59	41	27	16	9	4	2	1	0		
.42	115	116	109	96	78	59	42	27	16	9	4	2	1	0	
.44	100	112	114	109	96	78	59	42	27	16	9	4	2	1	0
.46	82	101	113	113	108	96	78	60	42	27	16	9	4	2	1
.48	61	82	97	109	112	108	96	79	60	42	27	16	9	4	2
→ .50 Vector	42	60	79	96		96	79	60	42	27	16	9	4	2	1
↑ .20 Vector	60	74	96	108		112	108	96	78	60	42	27	16	9	0

(p scale across top: 0 .02 .04 .06 .08 .10 .12 .14 .16 .18 .20 .22 .24 .26 .28 .30 .32 .34 .36 .38 .40 .42 .44 .46 .48 .50 .52 .54 .56 .58 .60 .62 .64 .66 .68 .70 .72 .74 .76 .78 .80 .82 .84 .86 .88 .90 .92 .94 .96 .98 1.00)

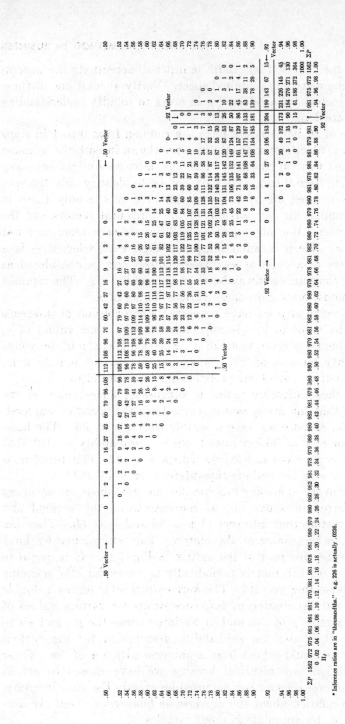

* Inference ratios are in "thousandths." e.g. 226 is actually .0226.

rounded to the nearest thousandth in order to accentuate the general pattern of the matrix in a limited space. Verify at least one of these horizontal vectors for a selected p in order to solidify understanding of what we are doing.

A sample of 50 items *might* have a p running from 0 to 1 in steps of .02. These 51 different possibilities are shown in both the leftmost and rightmost vertical columns. The true universe π *might* have *any* value running from 0 to 1. We have chosen to identify only the specific values marked off by steps of .02. We choose only these in order to simplify our comparisons of the horizontal vectors and the vertical vectors. We might just as well have chosen more or fewer values for π_I. Keep in mind that, in reality, each selected π_I is a *representative* of a class of π_I. These classes can be considered as bounded by the points midway between the specific π_I's. The topmost and bottommost rows show these various values of π_I.

For each value of p we have generated a distribution of inference ratios for the value of π_I. It appears as though some values of π_I are *impossible* for a given value of p. For example, a p of .06 yields no probability for a π_I of .28. This is, of course, not strictly true; but *it is true* if we round our probabilities to thousandths.

Each of these inference ratios is *supposedly* an estimate of the probability that the given sample came from the specified universe. For example, suppose we have a sample with a p of .36. The horizontal vector at $p = .36$ indicates there is a probability of .101 that this sample came from a universe with a π of .32. Our problem is this: *How close to the truth is this inference ratio of .101?*

Rather than try to answer this specific question about the accuracy of .101 referred to above, let us concentrate on the vertical and horizontal vectors that intersect at $p = .50$ and $\pi_I = .50$. They are marked off in the center of the matrix. For convenience we have reproduced just this part of the matrix in Fig. 7.11. It is useful to refer back to the full matrix periodically as we explain the meaning of these intersecting vectors. The *horizontal vector* serves a double duty; it is the distribution of *inference ratios* for various values of π_I, *given* a sample p of .50, and, if we interchange the p's and π's in our matrix, it is also the *probability distribution* for the various values of p we would expect from a universe with a π of .50. These two distributions are identical because we have chosen to act as though *knowledge about a sample* provides exactly the same inference base for speculation about the universe as *knowledge about the universe* provides for speculation about samples.

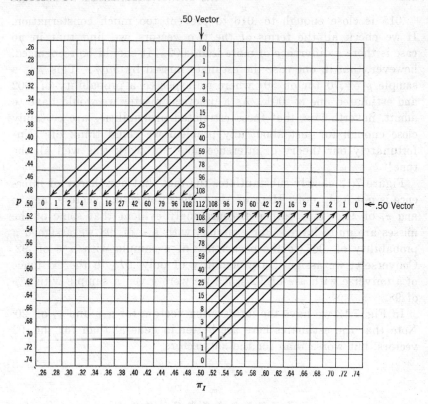

Fig. 7.11 Comparison of inference and probability vectors—$\pi = .5$, $N = 50$. (See Table 7.7.)

The *vertical vector* at $\pi_I = .50$ is nothing more than a cross section of the horizontal vectors. More particularly, here it represents the various probabilities that *would have been assigned* to the truth of a π of .5 given the various specified sample p's. The arrows connect terms of the vectors which should have the same values *if our theory of inference were perfect*. For example, if we are given a π of .36, we would assign a probability of .016 (the sixth term in from the left on the horizontal vector) to the occurrence of a random sample of 50 items with a p of .50. Conversely, given a sample of 50 with a p of .36, we would expect to assign a probability of .016 to the existence of a universe with a π of .50. We note, however, that our inference method has actually assigned a probability of .015 to a π_I of .50, given a p of .36.

.015 is close enough to .016 to prevent too much consternation. If we check all the terms of the two vectors, we find that in no case is there a difference of more than .002. It should be recognized, however, that in one case the estimate missed by 50%. This was a sample p of .70 (or of .30) where we expected a probability of .002 and estimated one of .001. As a practical matter we would have to admit, nevertheless, that these estimated probabilities are certainly close enough for just about any problem we could think of. Unfortunately our theory of inference does not work this well all the time!

Figure 7.12 clearly substantiates the fact that our theory of inference is not foolproof. Here we show the intersecting vectors for a p and π_I of .92. It is rather discouragingly evident that some of the misses are quite large. For example, with a π of .98 we assigned a probability of .067 to the occurrence of a sample with a p of .92. Conversely, we assigned a probability of only *.015* to the existence of a universe with a π of .92 when we were given a sample with a p of .98.

In Fig. 7.13 we have the intersecting vectors for a p and π_I of .20. Note that the estimates here are better in general than for the .92 vectors, but worse than for the .50 vectors.

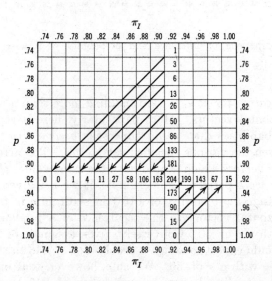

Fig. 7.12. Comparison of inference and probability vectors: $\pi = .92$, $N = 50$. (See Table 7.7.)

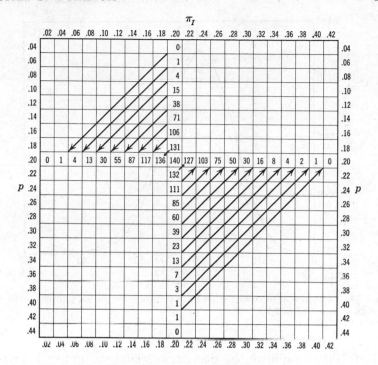

Fig. 7.13 Comparison of inference and probability vectors: $\pi = .20$, $N = 50$.

The Cause of the Errors in the Inference Ratios

Figure 7.14 clearly demonstrates that the errors in the inference ratios are definitely systematic. Note that the inference ratios are always *below* or equal to the direct probabilities for values of p below .20 and always *above* or equal to the direct probabilities for values of p above .20. (We are confining our attention to the intersecting vectors at π and p of .20.) It looks as though a simple corrective action would be to rotate the distribution of inference ratios clockwise. This would bring the two distributions into almost perfect agreement. To accomplish this, however, we would have to alter all our *horizontal vectors* because the vertical vectors are simply cross sections of the horizontal vectors. If we alter these horizontal vectors, we do two things that we do not like to do. First, we would have abandoned the *binomial distribution* as our inference distribution, and we are reluctant to do this because we do not have at hand any other simple class of distributions to substitute for the binomial

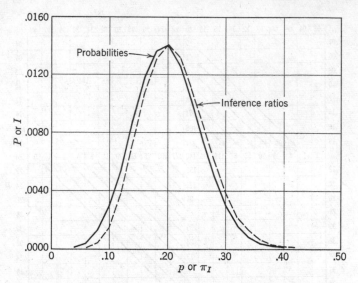

Fig. 7.14 Comparison of converse and direct probabilities for samples of 50 with $\pi = .20$. (See Table 7.7.)

and still do the required job. Second, we would end up with inferences that *would not average out at the true value of* π. We must admit that there is no inherent magic in averaging out at π but to do so does give us a sense of security that we hesitate to abandon until we have something else.

Let us examine the *condition that would definitely make the intersecting vectors identical.* Table 7.8 illustrates an ideal inference matrix wherein all the inference ratios are exactly equal to their companion direct probabilities. The fundamental condition to accomplish this is that *all the horizontal vectors must have the same probabilities.* Thus the vectors differ only with respect to their *means.* All the vectors have the same *variance* and the same *skewness.* Our problems would be solved if we could eliminate the correlation that exists among the mean, variance, and skewness in our samples. A mean of .50 is accompanied by the *maximum variance* of .25 and by *0 skewness.* It is impossible to have a sample with a mean of .50 and, say, with a variance of .20 or with a skewness of .068. As the mean departs from .50, the variance *decreases* and the skewness *increases.* If it were possible for any given mean to be paired with any given variance and with any given skewness, we would find that our horizontal vectors would *average out* to have the

TABLE 7.8

Ideal Inference Matrixes

Symmetrical Probability and Inference Vectors

```
0  1  5 11 18 30 18 11  5  1 │  0
   0  1  5 11 18 30 18 11  5 │  1 │  0
      0  1  5 11 18 30 18 11 │  5 │  1  0
         0  1  5 11 18 30 18 │ 11 │  5  1  0
            0  1  5 11 18 30 │ 18 │ 11  5  1  0
   ─────────────────────────────────────────────
               0  1  5 11 18 │ 30 │ 18 11  5  1  0
   ─────────────────────────────────────────────
                  0  1  5 11 │ 18 │ 30 18 11  5  1  0
                     0  1  5 │ 11 │ 18 30 18 11  5  1  0
                        0  1 │  5 │ 11 18 30 18 11  5  1  0
                           0 │  1 │  5 11 18 30 18 11  5  1  0
                             │  0 │  1  5 11 18 30 18 11  5  1  0
```

Skewed Inference and Probability Vectors

```
0 1 2 4 6 9 15 25 20 12  5  1 │  0
  0 1 2 4 6  9 15 25 20 12  5 │  1 │  0
    0 1 2 4  6  9 15 25 20 12 │  5 │  1  0
      0 1 2  4  6  9 15 25 20 │ 12 │  5  1  0
        0 1  2  4  6  9 15 25 │ 20 │ 12  5  1  0
  ───────────────────────────────────────────────
           0  1  2  4  6  9 15 │ 25 │ 20 12  5  1  0
  ───────────────────────────────────────────────
              0  1  2  4  6  9 │ 15 │ 25 20 12  5  1  0
                 0  1  2  4  6 │  9 │ 15 25 20 12  5  1  0
                    0  1  2  4 │  6 │  9 15 25 20 12  5  1  0
                       0  1  2 │  4 │  6  9 15 25 20 12  5  1  0
                          0  1 │  2 │  4  6  9 15 25 20 12  5  1  0
                             0 │  1 │  2  4  6  9 15 25 20 12  5  1  0
                               │  0 │  1  2  4  6  9 15 25 20 12 5 1 0
```

same variance and same skewness, thus satisfying our desired condition. We say average out because *individual* horizontal vectors would sometimes have *small* variance and sometimes *large* variance due to fluctuations of sampling. The same would be true of skewness.

In Table 7.7 we note that the *variances of the horizontal vectors are essentially the same* near the *center* of the matrix. This explains why our inference ratios are good estimates of the direct probabilities if π equals .50. The estimates would be almost as good if π equaled .48, or .46, etc. We begin to get significantly poorer estimates only when the variance begins to decline significantly.

It is also important to note that the inference ratios do not become poor estimates until we get near the *tails* of the distributions. The *maximum probability* for a given vector is always exactly correct, the next adjacent probabilities are nearly correct, the next a little less correct, etc. Thus we do not begin to make large errors until we get to the small probabilities, the very ones that are not so likely to occur. For example, if π equals .30, we find a probability of .122 that a sample p of .30 will occur. When a p of .30 does occur, we assign a probability of .122 to a π_I of .30, and we have assigned the exactly correct probability. If our sample happens to have a p of .28, we assign a probability of .117 to the existence of a π_I of .30. This compares with the direct probability of .119; if we get a p of .26, we assign an inference ratio of .100 instead of the correct .105; if our sample has a p of .22, we assign an inference ratio of .052 to the existence of a π_I of .30 instead of the correct .060. But note that, although we make a relatively large error in our estimate of the probability of π_I of .30 when we have a sample p as low as .22, *we do not make this error very often because a p of .22 does not occur very often.* It is appropriate to state that this method of stating inference ratios is such that *the cases of small errors occur more frequently than the cases of large errors.* Therefore our total errors are moderately small.

The Importance of the Size of the Sample to the Accuracy of Inference Ratios

The errors in the inference ratios decline as the sample size increases. The decline is not because the variances in the horizontal vectors become more uniform, because they in fact do not become more uniform. The relative differences between the variances remain precisely the same regardless of the size of the sample. For example, the variance associated with a p of .5 is always about twice as large as the variance associated with a p of .146 regardless of the size of N. (See Table 7.9 and note that the relative sizes of the numbers are the same in columns 2, 3, 4, and 5.) What does happen as N increases is that the *relevant* horizontal vectors are so close together with respect to a given p that we become concerned only with a very small

TABLE 7.9

Variances of Binomial for Various Values of p and Various Sizes of Samples

p	pq	$\dfrac{pq}{.25}$ *	$\dfrac{pq}{5}$	$\dfrac{pq}{100}$
(1)	(2)	(3)	(4)	(5)
0	0	0	0	0
.05	.0475	.19	.0095	.000475
.10	.0900	.36	.0180	.000900
.15	.1275	.51	.0255	.001275
.20	.1600	.64	.0320	.001600
.25	.1875	.75	.0375	.001875
.30	.2100	.84	.0420	.002100
.35	.2275	.91	.0455	.002275
.40	.2400	.96	.0480	.002400
.45	.2475	.99	.0495	.002475
.50	.2500	1.00	.0500	.002500

* This column expresses each value of pq as a ratio to the pq of .25 that is associated with a p of .5.

segment of the total matrix, and the variances of the horizontal vectors are then practically the same. For example, note the case of a p of .3. If N equals 1, we get a variance of .21 and a standard deviation of .458. If we use the normal curve probabilities as a crude basis of estimating the range of the bulk of the probabilities around a p of .30, we find that plus and minus 1 standard deviation of .458 would be necessary to cover about 2/3 of the cases. Thus we would be running across the vectors from a p of 0 (we rule out p values of less than 0) to the neighborhood of a p of .75. Such a range of p vectors certainly gives us plenty of opportunity to be distressed by the changes in the variances. But now consider the case if N equals 10,000. Here we have a standard deviation of only .00458. If we go to plus and minus 3 of these, we should include about .9975 of all the frequencies. (The normal curve estimate would be quite good with such a large sample.) Thus we would find our relevant p vectors all within the span of a p of .285 and a p of .315. It should be obvious that the variances of these vectors would be practically identical and that our inference ratios would be almost exactly the same as the direct probabilities.

7.7   A Summary of the Properties of the Binomial Distribution as an Estimator of the Probability Distribution of the Value of the Unknown π

We uncovered several concepts and ideas in our exploration of what happens if we use the binomial distribution as an estimator of the value of the unknown π. Since we encounter these concepts and ideas again and again, it is useful to summarize them in order to fix them in our minds.

1. Does the probability distribution of an *unknown* universe value exist? We have found that there is a distribution of the unknown π that has many of the properties of a probability distribution. We have not learned as yet how to estimate the probabilities *precisely*, but we have demonstrated that we can estimate them close enough for many practical problems. We would argue that such estimated probabilities are subject to exactly the same kinds of interpretations as are the probabilities generated from a *known* universe about an unknown sample or samples.

2. The binomial distributions have the property that the arithmetic mean of all the inferred distributions results in the exact true value of the unknown π. This means that repeated estimates produce errors which average out in the arithmetic mean sense. This seems to be a useful property of an estimating procedure and one we would always try to have if it is possible without sacrificing some other useful properties. We see other useful properties shortly.

3. Our use of the binomial inferences required that we make *no assumptions whatsoever* about the mean, variance, or skewness of the universe other than what was implied by the sample itself. In other words, we did not impose any restrictions on our inferences owing to any notions we might have about the universe, either by assumption or from prior knowledge. The importance of our *not* making any assumptions becomes clearer in later discussion when we *do* make some assumptions.

4. The binomial distributions are very handy to work with; they have known properties and can be generated by a relatively simple formula. The tedium of calculating binomial probabilities can be relieved by tables.

5. The binomial distribution is *discrete*. It provides probabilities for only certain specific values of π_I; however, other values of π_I are possible. If we wish to use the binomial distribution to estimate probabilities for the other values of π_I, we must *interpolate* between the specific discrete values. We would thus be treating the binomial distribution as though it were a *continuous* distribution. There is nothing inherently wrong in treating the binomial distribution as a continuous distribution. To do so, however, involves some rather tedious calculations to find the interpolated probabilities for the sub-

intervals. No one has yet performed such calculations and published them in a table, primarily because there seems to be no pressing demand for such interpolated values.

6. Errors in the use of binomial probabilities as estimates of the probability that a given π_I is in fact the truth are caused by the *variation in the variance* of the distribution for different sample values of p. If we could allow p to vary without accompanying *systematic* variation in the variance of the distribution of π_I, we would solve our problem of errors in our probability estimates. We emphasize the word *systematic* because we would not be concerned with *random* variations in the variance. Random variations would tend to average out, thus leaving us with *constant* variance *on the average*.

7. Errors in the use of binomial probabilities to estimate the probability distribution of π_I tend to decline as the size of the sample increases. This decline is caused by the reduced variance in p as N increases.

8. The errors in the probabilities are more serious on the tails of the distribution than they are in the middle of the distribution. Thus the error in the probability varies inversely with the size of the probability. The net result is that small errors occur more often than large errors.

9. The binomial distribution gives probabilities for π_I equal to 0 or 1 that are obviously wrong. If we have a sample with, say, .25 defective pieces, common sense suggests that this sample could not possibly come from a universe with 0 defectives, or from one with 100% defectives. The binomial distribution based on a p of .25 suggests *positive* probabilities for a π_I of 0 or of 1, however. This sort of nonsense could be considerably reduced if finer interpolations were made for the values of π_I. This also would not appear to be quite so much nonsense if we interpreted a π_I of 0 to actually refer to a range of π_I from 0 to, say, .10. Thus, apparently discrete estimates of probabilities of π_I for values of 0, .2, .4, .6, .8, and 1.0 could be interpreted as estimates of the probabilities for π_I values in the intervals: 0–.1, .1–.3, .3–.5, .5–.7, .7–.9, .9–1.0. The existence of positive probabilities in the two extreme *intervals* would not appear so shocking.

The problem with the boundaries of 0 and 1 exists in some form with any estimating method. Fortunately, the restrictive impact of these boundaries declines as the sample size increases. Later we show how we can solve the problem of boundaries by using an inference model that has no boundaries, for example, the normal distribution.

7.8 The Underlying Logic of a Theory of Inference

Since we have already discussed the problem of developing some procedure for making inferences about the unknown mean of a universe, it may seem strange that we postpone to now any explicit discussion of the logical requirements of an inference method. We feel that we will be in a better position to appreciate the logic after we have seen some of the problems a theory of inference faces.

We now make an assertion that would have seemed to be quite bold a few pages back. Let us first make the assertion in the form of a special case: We would like our theory of inference to be so constructed that if the probability of a sample p of .20 is .158, *given* a universe π of .40, the probability of a π of .40, *given* a sample p of .20, should also be .158, both statements, of course, for a given sample size. In symbols we would like to be able to assert the validity of the following equality:

$$P(p = .20 \,|\, \pi = .40, N) = P(\pi = .40 \,|\, p = .20, N).$$

Or, more generally, we would like to assert the validity of

$$P(p \,|\, \pi, N) = P(\pi \,|\, p, N).$$

If we call the probability on the left side of this equation the *direct* probability and the probability on the right side the *inverse* probability, we can now say that we would like our direct probabilities to equal our inverse probabilities. The direct probabilities are those calculated about samples from a known universe. The inverse probabilities are those calculated about universe inferences from a known sample.

The fundamental condition for this equality to be true is that *each sample mean (p) should be able to occur with each possible sample variance, and with each possible sample skewness.* Table 7.8 illustrated such a condition for a case of zero skewness and for a case of significant positive skewness.

7.9 The Next Step

We now have a fairly clear idea of the essential conditions for an ideal theory for making inferences about the mean of a universe from information supplied by a random sample. We also have a theory for making such inferences which works quite well if the sample is reasonably large and/or if the universe π is in fact in the neighborhood of .50. Our next step is to develop modifications of this initial theory that will improve our estimates for small samples and for π values some distance from .50. This is the task of the next chapter.

PROBLEMS AND QUESTIONS

7.1 Stay within the bounds of your present knowledge and analyze each of the following prediction problems. Describe the historical sample information which you have. Infer the universe and any expected shifts in the universe. Make a probability inference about the event.

(a) What time (to the minute) will you go to bed tonight?

(b) How much (to the pound) will you weigh tomorrow morning?

(c) How far is it (to the yard) from where you now are to the nearest source of a drink of water?

(d) What will the United States Gross National Product be (to the billion $) during the current calendar year?

(e) How many people (to the hundred thousand) will be unemployed in the United States next July 1?

7.2 Given each of the universes referred to, and given the drawing of an infinite number of *random* samples of the specified size, make inferences about the relative frequency of all the possible sample means. Use tables of the binomial. π refers to the universe proportion, N to the size of the sample.

(a) $\pi = .2; \ N = 5.$

(b) $\pi = .8; \ N = 5.$

(c) $\pi = .2; \ N = 8.$

(d) $\pi = .4; \ N = 20.$

7.3 Suppose that the information given in Question 2 represented *hypotheses* that you were making about the true conditions of a universe. Would you make wagers consistent with the probabilities you calculated with respect to specific samples that could be drawn? For example, if the events in question were the number of defective radio tubes in a sample of five, and if your inference was that there was a probability of .1 of getting two defective tubes out of five, would you be willing to bet $.10 to $1 that the next sample of five would have two defectives? Why or why not? Would you bet $10 to $100? Why or why not?

If you decide not to bet $10 to $100, would you be willing to bet $100 to $10 that there *will not* be two defectives in the next sample of five? Why or why not?

If you decide to bet on *neither* side of the issue, what *do* you plan to do?

7.4 For each of the sets of inferences you derived in Question 2 calculate and interpret the following. Use the direct calculation and then check by use of the formulas based on π and τ as given in Table 7.2.

(a) The arithmetic mean of the set. $(\bar{X}_p)$

(b) The variance of the set. (σ_p^2)

(c) The standard deviation of the set. (σ_p)

(d) The crude skewness of the set. (L_p) (Remember: the L is for (L)opsidedness.)

(e) The coefficient of skewness of the set. (K_p) (Remember: the K is for (K)ockeyedness.)

7.5 The problem of "bias" in sample results can be very perplexing. Consider the case of the sample variance, or standard deviation, as an estimate of the universe variance, or standard deviation. The table below shows the expected sample results with samples of five from a universe with a π of .5 and thus a variance of $\pi\tau$, or .25.

Sample p (1)	Sample pq (2)	Probability P (3)	Ppq (4)	Adjusted Variance $p'q'$ (5)	$Pp'q'$ (6)	"Corrected" Adjusted Variance $p''q''$ (7)	$Pp''q''$ (8)
0	0	.03125	0	0	0	0	0
.2	.16	.15625	.025000	.20	.031250	.20	.031250
.4	.24	.31250	.075000	.30	.093750	.25	.078125
.6	.24	.31250	.075000	.30	.093750	.25	.078125
.8	.16	.15625	.025000	.20	.031250	.20	.031250
1.0	0	.03125	0	0	0	0	0
		1.00000	.200000		.250000		.21875

If we take the sample variances as we find them, we end up with an arithmetic mean of estimates of .2 as shown in column 4. If we adjust each sample variance for the mean error and pay no attention to the fact that some of the adjusted variances will be impossibly high, we would have estimates with an arithmetic mean of .25, which is the actual universe value. (See column 6.) If we arbitrarily reduce all impossibly high estimates to the maximum of .25 (see column 7), we get an arithmetic mean estimate of .21875 (column 8).

(a) What policy would you follow in making estimates in a practical problem?

(b) What is the logic of requiring estimates to have an arithmetic mean equal to the true value?

(c) What other criteria might we use for defining whether or not an estimate tends to have bias? (Hint: Could any other average be used than the mean?)

(d) Suppose you had adopted the criterion that an estimate of the variance should be as close as possible to the universe value. Analyze the estimates shown in column 2 to see how close they are to the true value of .25. Compare the closeness of the column 2 estimates with that of the column 5 estimates. With the column 7 estimates.

What conclusions do you draw now?

7.6 Make up an inference matrix like that in Table 7.3 for samples of four instead of five.

(a) Suppose the universe π were actually .5. There would then be a probability of .3750 of getting a sample of four with a p of .5. According to your matrix, what is the probability (or inference ratio) of a sample of four with a p of .5 having come from a universe with a π of .5? Does this strike you as a logical result considering that there is a .3750 probability of getting such a sample from such a universe? Explain.

(b) Again suppose a π of .5. The probability of a p of .25 in a sample of four is .2500. According to your matrix, what is the probability of a sample of four with a p of .25 having come from a universe with a π of .5? Is this a logical result? Explain. What seems to be the cause of the apparent inconsistency?

7.7 Suppose a universe π of .25 and samples of four.

(a) Determine the probabilities of getting all the various possible sample results from this universe. (In other words, determine the *probability vector* for expected sample results.)

(b) Multiply your matrix of Problem 6 by this probability vector in the manner shown in the text to develop Table 7.5 from Tables 7.3 and 7.4.

(c) Why should the horizontal sums (the sums of the row vectors) give exactly (except for rounding) the same probabilities you have in your *probabilty vector* that you multiplied by?

(d) Determine the sums of the column vectors in the matrix you calculated in (b). These make up the average inference ratio vector. Why should these sums add to 1 (except for rounding errors)?

(e) What meaning do you attach to the "average inference ratio vector" developed in (d).

7.8 Calculate the mean and variance of your average inference ratio vector developed in Problem 7(d). Are your answers what you would expect based on the formulas given in Table 7.6?

7.9 Make up a chart in the manner of Figures 7.11, 7.12, and 7.13 from your matrix of Problem 6 by reproducing the intersecting vectors at $p = .75$ and $\pi = .75$. Test these vectors for correspondence.

7.10 Test the intersecting vectors at $p = .50$ and $\pi = .50$ in the same manner as done in Problem 9. Are the vectors closer when $\pi = .5$ than when $\pi = .75$? If so, why?

7.11 (a) Set up the inference matrix for samples of 20.

(b) Test the correspondence of the intersecting vectors at π and p of .35. Are these vectors closer than you found with your samples of only four?

chapter 8

A theory and method for making inferences about the mean of a universe from information supplied by a random sample

The essence of any modification of the theory of inference outlined in the preceding chapter is to reduce the *differences* between inference ratio vectors. In other words, we would like to develop a set of inference ratio vectors that would be identical except for the displacement caused by variations in the mean. We illustrated this condition in Table 7.8 on page 301.

One approach to this problem is *transforming p* into another variable. The technique of transforming the scale and/or the origin of a variable can sometimes be very effective in simplifying a problem. The transformation that has been performed on p with some success involves the use of *arc sines* of p. In high school geometry it was explained that the sine of an angle in a right triangle is calculated by dividing the length of the side opposite the angle by the length of the hypotenuse. For example, if the side opposite the given angle was 6 inches long and the hypotenuse was 9 inches long, the sine of the angle would be .667. The angle would be about 42°. Thus we can say that the sine of an angle of 42° equals approximately .667. Since the opposite side cannot be any larger than the hypotenuse, the sines of angles between 0° and 90° vary from 0 to 1; p also varies from 0 to 1. If we take p and treat it as though it were the sine of an angle *and then replace p with the corresponding number of degrees in the associated angle,* we have made an arc sine transformation. For example, if we have a p of .40, we would replace it with an arc sine (the angle equivalent) of 23.6°. After making such arc sine transformations, we would carry out all further analysis in terms of the arc sines. Although this method is moderately successful in equalizing adjacent inference ratio vectors, it is not perfect. In addition, it does not open the door to some lines of reasoning that an alternative approach does, lines of reasoning that are of great significance in dealing with the many practical issues we face as we apply any theory of inference, and we, therefore, say no more about the arc since transformation.[1]

The approach we use involves a line of reasoning that has had a somewhat checkered career over the last 2 centuries. The line of reasoning is really based on the application of the equal distribution of ignorance rule, also called the rule of insufficient reason. Although the rule has actually been applied for many centuries, its first *formal* application to the problem of statistical inference is attributed to Thomas Bayes, a Presbyterian minister in England who also had a great interest in probability. A posthumous article called "Essay Towards Solving a Problem in the Doctrine of Chances" was published in 1763, 2 years after the death of Reverend Bayes.[2] Bayes took his problem as

Given the number of times in which an unknown event has happened and failed: *Required* the chance that the probability of its happening in a single trial lies somewhere between any two degrees of probability that can be named.

If we restate Bayes's language to conform to more modern usage, his problem was

Given a sample of size n with proportion of successes equal to p: *Required* the probability that the universe proportion lies between any two specified values.

Or, in symbols, the problem becomes that of determining the value of

$$P(\pi_L \leq \pi \leq \pi_U \,|\, p, n).$$

(L and U refer to lower and upper limits to the value of π.)

Thus, Bayes's problem is precisely the same one that we have been trying to solve.

---

[1] The interested reader will find a very lucid discussion of the arc sine transformation in W. E. Deming, *Some Theory of Sampling,* John Wiley and Sons, New York, 1950, and in Eisenhart, Hastay, and Wallis, *Techniques of Statistical Analysis,* McGraw-Hill, New York, 1947.

[2] Originally published in *The Philosophical Transactions.* The essay has since been republished in *Biometrika,* **45** (1958), pp. 293–315.

Considerable controversy has grown up around the question of the validity of Bayes's work. Substantial creaence was placed in his methods throughout most of the 19th century, and significant extensions of his methods were developed, mostly by LaPlace. However, another school of thought emerged in the 20th century. This school prevailed, with the result that Bayes's methods fell into disrepute, so much so that reputable books did not even discuss his work. We are now in the midst of a revival in interest in the ideas expounded by Bayes, a revival that started at about midcentury.

We cannot provide a thorough exposure to all the elements that have precipitated the controversy. We do hope, however, to cover enough ground to give the more important ideas, ideas that are absolutely crucial for an intelligent application of any method of making inferences.

8.1 Bayes's Theorem

A useful place to start is with a simple example that illustrates the basic idea at the root of all our subsequent analysis. This idea is embodied in what is called Bayes's theorem. (There is some question that Bayes would lay claim to this, or to many other things that have become associated with his name.)

Suppose we have three boxes, marked A, B, and C for convenience of reference. Each box contains 100 small balls. Box A has 20% red balls; Box B has 40% red balls; and Box C has 80% red balls. One of these boxes is to be selected *at random,* with each box having the same chance of being selected as far as we know. We have no way of knowing which box has been selected. We then are to select at random five balls from this box and record the proportion of red balls in the sample. We select the balls one at a time, replacing after each selection in order to maintain a constant universe for each drawing. Suppose that our sample shows .4 red balls. What odds would we require before we would be willing to bet that Box C had been selected? Or, in general, what is the probability that Box A had been selected? Box B? Box C?

Figure 8.1 shows our problem in the form of a tree diagram. The first set of branches show the three possible boxes, with each having a probability of .33 of being selected. The second sets of branches show the probabilities of getting various numbers of red balls *given* a particular box. Note that the probabilities add to 1 within each set of branches. At the tips of the second sets of branches are shown

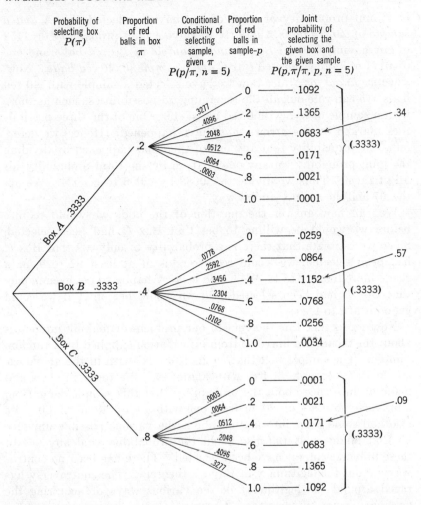

| Probability of selecting box $P(\pi)$ | Proportion of red balls in box π | Conditional probability of selecting sample, given π $P(p/\pi, n = 5)$ | Proportion of red balls in sample-p | Joint probability of selecting the given box and the given sample $P(p,\pi/\pi, p, n = 5)$ |

Fig. 8.1 Tree diagram of problem of selecting first a box and then a random sample of five balls from the box.

the *joint* probabilities of having selected a particular box *and* a particular sample from that box. Note that these joint probabilities add to .33 within each set, the *same* probability as that for selecting the branch from which the set is derived. Also note that *all the joint probabilities together* add to 1 (except for rounding errors). This is a way of saying that our sample of five balls *must* have come from one of these 18 possibilities.

Finally we come to the solution to our problem. Note that there is a joint probability of .0683 of our having selected *Box A and a sample of .40 red balls;* similarly we have a joint probability of .1152 of our having selected *Box B and a sample of .40 red balls* and one of .0171 of having selected *Box C and a sample of .40 red balls.* Now, since *we know for a fact* that we have selected a sample with .40 red balls, we can rule out all the remaining 15 possibilities, such as those with a sample of five with 0 red balls, etc. One of the three possibilities marked by the arrows *must* have happened. Hence, we determine the probability that any one of them has happened by dividing the joint probability of any one of them by the total probability for all of them. Thus we divide the .0683 by .2006 to get .34. We get the .57 and the .09 in a similar way.

We can now answer the question of the odds we would require before we would be willing to bet that Box *C* had been selected. Since we estimate that there is a probability of only .09 that Box *C* had been selected, we would require odds of at least 91 to 9, or a shade more than 10 to 1. We would be very happy to bet even money that Box *B* had been selected, and we would bet on *A* if we could get odds of 2 to 1.

Now let us link this theorem to our problem of making inferences about the mean of a universe from information supplied by a random sample. The sample fact that we had to deal with in the above example was a sample of five with a p of .4. We took this fact and made an inference about the probability that this sample came from a universe with a π of .20, or from one with a π of .40, or of .80. We also had some *prior* information about the various possible universe π's that might exist *and also* about the probability that any one of these universes might have been selected. There has been no controversy about the legitimacy of Bayes's theorem. The controversy has raged around the legitimacy of the various ways of acquiring the necessary *prior information.* Given this prior information, everything thereafter is essentially a matter of routine mechanics.

8.2   Some Useful Language

We will make more rapid progress later if we now agree on a few terms and thus reduce the possibility of misunderstanding. Table 8.1 shows the relevant parts of the tree diagram of Fig. 8.1 in a more convenient form. Columns 1 and 2 identify the three boxes and their *given* characteristics. Column 3 gives the list of probabilities for the selection of the various boxes. This distribution of probabilities

TABLE 8.1

The Use of Bayes's Theorem to Estimate the Probability that a Given Sample Came from Any One of Three Possible Universes

(1) Box	(2) π	(3) $P(\pi)$	(4) $P(p = .4 \mid \pi, n)$	(5) $P(p = .4, \pi \mid p, n)$	(6) $P(\pi \mid p, \pi, n)$
A	.20	.3333	.2048	.0683	.34
B	.40	.3333	.3456	.1152	.57
C	.80	.3333	.0512	.0171	.09
		1.00	.6016	.2006	1.00
		↑ Prior Distribution		↑ Marginal Probability	↑ Posterior Distribution

is referred to as a *prior probability distribution*. It is called prior because it comes *before* the second one which we refer to shortly. Note that this distribution adds to 1 (except for rounding errors).

Column 4 gives the *conditional* probability of getting a sample of five with a p of .4, the conditions in each case being the given π and the size of the sample.

Column 5 gives the *joint conditional* probability of getting *both* a sample with a p of .4 *and* the particular universe. Note that the calculation of this probability requires knowledge of p, π, and n. The *sum* of column 5, or the sum of the joint conditional probabilities is called the *marginal* probability. It is called marginal because it occurs in the *margin* of the table. The important thing to remember about marginal probabilities is that they are always the result of *adding* some specific probabilities together, and they always refer to the probability that some *one* of some *collection* of events has or will occur. In this case, the collection of events is the occurrence of a sample with a p of .4. We could get such an event from Box A, *or* from Box B, *or* from Box C. The probability that a sample with a p of .4 will occur at all is the sum of the probabilities that it will occur in any one of the given specific ways.

Column 6 is simply a redistribution of the probabilities of column 5 so that they add to 1. We justify this redistribution because we *know for a fact* that a sample p of .4 has occurred. The only remaining uncertainty is that of the box from which such a sample came. We call the probabilities in column 6 *posterior* probabilities. They are called posterior because they come *after* the prior probabilities. Note that their calculation requires knowledge about p, π, and n. These posterior probabilities are also sometimes called *revised* probabilities. The logic of this is: *Before*, or prior to, our having any *sample information*, we would assign a probability of .33 to our having selected Box B. *After*, or posterior to, our having the sample information, we assign a probability of .57 to our having originally selected Box B. The posterior probability of .57 is thus a *revision* of the prior probability of .33. The basis of the revision is the information supplied by the sample.

8.3   The Problem of the Source of Prior Information

In the preceding section we were *told* that there were three possible universe values of π, namely, .2, .4, and .8. We were also *told* that each of these possibilities had a probability of being selected of .33 in each case. It is conceivable, of course, that the probabilities of selecting these universes might have been any of an infinite number of possible combinations. For example, the probabilities might have been .10, .38, and .52, respectively. The only condition is that the probabilities add to 1 because, of course, one of the universes must be selected.

Now let us take a slightly different problem. Let us suppose that we are told that a card has a number written on its concealed side. Let us suppose further that we are assured that this number is somewhere between 0 and 1. A complete stranger walks into the room and is apprised of the situation. He then offers to bet us $10 to $2 that the number on the card is somewhere between .2 and .3. He bases this action on his claim that he possesses occult powers. Do we take this bet? If we do not take this bet, is there any set of odds that we would accept? For example, suppose he offered to bet $100 against $1 that the value is between .2 and .3. Keep in mind that there is absolutely no way he can tell what is on the other side of the card, unless, of course, he does have occult powers.

Perhaps we feel quite uncertain about whether or not we should take this $10 to $2 bet. If so, perhaps it would be helpful to give permission to take the *other side* of the bet if we wish to. After all, if we reject the offer of $10 to $2, we must feel that it is not a fair offer. In such a case, we certainly must be willing to take the other side of the bet because we would now be on the advantageous side. Or, perhaps we think the bet is very fair, so fair that it does not make any difference what side of the bet we go on. The essential point is that we *must* make up our mind and take one side or the other! (Note: We are assuming in all this that the money involved is small enough in any case so that we feel that it is more the reputation of our decision-making powers that is at stake rather than any significant amount of money.)

Is there any rational way to decide an issue like the above? It is often argued that this is just the place for an application of the equal distribution of ignorance rule. This rule states that there is a probability of .1 that the card has a number between .2 and .3, because .2 to .3 covers .1 of the range from 0 to 1. The rule suggests that we take the offer of $10 to $2 because the offered odds are *45 times* as great as they should be for a fair bet. (He is offering 5 to 1 when he should be offering 1 to 9.)

It is also sometimes argued that the equal distribution of ignorance rule is the rankest form of nonsense. How, it is asked, can we base so-called rational behavior on a base of complete ignorance? Frankly, we are not too sure whether we consider the rule rational or not, although we lean toward considering it so. What attracts us to the rule is that we do not know *any other rule of behavior* to use in a situation like that described above. We do not believe that anybody else does either, including those who inveigh against the equal distribution of ignorance rule at the same time they are implicitly using it. We all have undoubtedly used the rule many times, perhaps under the name of splitting the difference.

Bayes's Postulate

As the Reverend Bayes contemplated the problem of making inferences about a universe mean on the basis of solely the evidence of a sample, he first imagined that the true mean might have *any value whatsoever between 0 and 1*. He then postulated that each of these possible values was *equally likely* within the bounds of his present knowledge, with his present knowledge being zero. Hence he set up what we now call a *prior distribution* of equally-likely values of π. Some examples of some possibilities for such a distribution are shown in Table 8.2. The values called π_H must be interpreted as the values that *represent* a *range* of values. Generally we use the *midpoint* of the range to represent the values. (This is really another example of the application of the equal distribution of ignorance rule, an application indulged in by all statisticians, including those who object to the rule.) Thus the probability of .2 paired with the π_H of .1 in

TABLE 8.2

Examples of Prior Distributions of Equally Likely Values of π_H

A		B		C	
π_H	$P(\pi_H)$	π_H	$P(\pi_H)$	π_H	$P(\pi_H)$
		0	.1		
				.05	.1
.1	.2				
				.15	.1
		.2	.2		
				.25	.1
.3	.2				
				.35	.1
		.4	.2		
				.45	.1
.5	.2				
				.55	.1
		.6	.2		
				.65	.1
.7	.2				
				.75	.1
		.8	.2		
				.85	.1
.9	.2				
				.95	.1
		1.0	.1		
	1.0		1.0		1.0

the A distribution should be interpreted as the probability of a π_H falling between 0 and .2; similarly, there is a probability of .2 of a π_H between .2 and .4, with this range represented by a π_H of .3. We attach the subscript H to signify that we are referring to hypothetical values of π. The true π has some specific, but unknown, value.

Distribution B seems at first glance to show *unequal* probabilities. Actually, however, the distribution of probabilities is still equal. What is unequal is the size of the intervals used for π_H. The first interval, represented by a π_H of 0 runs from $-.1$ to .1, thus centering on 0. However, the lower half of this interval is meaningless because negative values for π_H are impossible. Hence the probability of a value falling within the $-.1$ to .1 interval is only the probability of a value falling between 0 and .1, a range that is only half the length of the interval from, say, .1 to .3 and represented by a π_H of .2. The same explanation exists for the probability of .1 that is paired with the π_H of 1.0

It is possible, of course, to divide the full range from 0 to 1 into as many intervals as we wish. Distribution C shows what happens when we divide the full range into 10 equal parts. The greater the number of divisions we use, the smaller will become the probability that the true π will fall within any such interval. For example, if we divide the range into 1,000,000 intervals, the probability that π falls in any one will be only .000001.

8.4 A Direct Application of Bayes's Theorem to the Problem of Inferences About π Based on Information from a Random Sample

We are now in a position to apply Bayes's theorem to our problem of making inferences about π. Table 8.3 shows the routine. Column 1 shows the various hypothetical values of π we have arbitrarily selected. We chose these because they are consistent with the values we used in the preceding chapter when we were making inferences based on the direct application of the binomial theorem.

TABLE 8.3

Inferences about π Based on a Prior Distribution of Equal Probabilities and on a Subsequent Sample of 5 Items with a p of .4

(1)	(2)	(3)	(4)	(5)
		$P(p = .4 \mid \pi_H,$	$P(p = .4,$	$P(\pi_H \mid p = .4,$
π_H	$P(\pi_H)$	$N = 5)$	$\pi_H \mid \pi_H, N = 5)$	$\pi_H, N = 5)$
0	.1	0	0	0
.2	.2	.2048	.04096	.2462
.4	.2	.3456	.06912	.4154
.6	.2	.2304	.04608	.2769
.8	.2	.0512	.01024	.0615
1.0	.1	0	0	0
	1.0	.8320	.16640	.9999

Column 2 shows the *prior* probabilities we associate with each of these π_H's. It is important to note that these are based on the assumption of equal likelihood. It is also important to note that these add to 1.

Column 3 shows the conditional probability of getting a random sample of 5 with a p of .4 *given* the truth of the particular value of π_H. The sum of these conditional probabilities is meaningless because it is a function of the arbitrary number of hypotheses. The more hypotheses, the larger the sum.

Column 4 shows the joint conditional probabilities of getting *both* the sample p of .4 *and* the particular value of π_H. The total of these, .16640, is the marginal probability, and it is the probability of getting a sample of 5 with a p of .4 *provided* each of the hypothetical π's is equally likely. We have more to say about the interpretation of such marginal probabilities in a subsequent chapter.

Column 5 is the posterior probability distribution of π_H and represents the probabilities we assign to the truth of the various π_H's *now that we have this sample information*. This is also the object of our search for an inference distribution of π given a sample of 5 with a p of .4.

8.5   Comparing Bayesian Inferences with Binomial Inferences

We can now compare inferences based on Bayes's theorem and equally likely prior hypotheses with those we made in the last chapter based on the direct application of the binomial theorem. Table 8.4 shows all the inference distributions we would get if we applied Bayes's theorem to all the possible results we could get from samples of 5. Note that the probabilities shown in the vector (or column) headed by a p of .4 are exactly the same as our posterior probabilities shown in column 5 of Table 8.3. The other columns have been calculated in exactly the same way as shown in Table 8.3, with the only difference being the different values of p. (We might note parenthetically that column 4 can be omitted in a calculation of Bayesian probabilities *provided* that the relevant probabilities in column 2 are all *equal*. Under such a circumstance, column 4 is just a *proportionate* adjustment of column 3, just as is column 5. Hence one can make a single proportionate adjustment and go directly to column 5 from column 3. It is very important to remember, however, that

TABLE 8.4

**Estimates of Inference Ratios for Various Values of π_I Based on
Posterior Probabilities Calculated From a Prior Distribution
of Equal Probabilities. N = 5**

[Body of matrix contains $P(\pi_I \mid p, \pi_I, N = 5)$]

p

π_I	0	.2	.4	.6	.8	1.0	
0	.7062	0	0	0	0	0	.7062
.2	.2314	.5447	.2462	.0615	.0085	.0002	1.0925
.4	.0549	.3447	.4154	.2769	.1021	.0072	1.2012
.6	.0072	.1021	.2769	.4154	.3447	.0549	1.2012
.8	.0002	.0085	.0615	.2462	.5447	.2314	1.0925
1.0	0	0	0	0	0	.7062	.7062
	.9999	1.0000	1.0000	1.0000	1.0000	.9999	5.9998

column 4 is *implied* even if we skip across it if the relevant probabilities are all equal.)

Let us look at the horizontal vector at $\pi_I = .4$. This vector tells us the probability we would assign to π_I's being .4 if we had a sample of 5 with a p of 0, or of .2, etc. For example, this vector tells us that if we have a sample with a p of .2, we believe that there is a probability of .3447 that this sample came from a universe with a π_I of .4.

How much truth is there in this probability? We can answer this question by first looking at Fig. 8.2 and then at Table 8.5. Figure 8.2 pictures the line of reasoning we are following. We assume that we start with a universe that has a π of .4. This is the trunk shown at the extreme left. We then generate all possible samples from this universe. They are signified by the six branches fanning out from the trunk. Attached to each branch we show the sample p and the probability it could occur. We then use each sample p to generate inferences about π. The binomial inferences are those we worked out in the preceding chapter. They can be found in Table 7.3. The Bayesian inferences are those we have just shown in Table 8.4.

The key inferences at the moment are those for a π_I of .4. They are marked by the arrows at the tips of the branches. We have re-

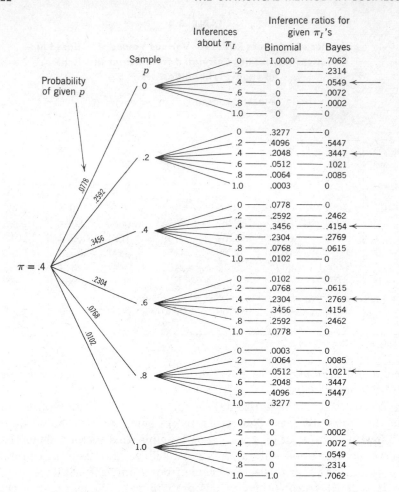

Fig. 8.2 Tree diagram illustrating paths of reasoning as we go from a known universe to inferences about samples from that universe and finally to inferences about the universe from the samples.

produced these particular inference ratios in columns 3 and 4 of Table 8.5. We have also reproduced in column 2 the probabilities of getting given sample p's from a universe with a π of .4. Note that these are exactly the same as shown for the six branches emanating from the trunk of Fig. 8.2. Ideally, we should find the probabilities in columns 2, 3, and 4 all alike. For example, if the probability of getting a sample p of .2 from a universe with a π of .4 is .2592, the

TABLE 8.5

Comparison of Binomial and Bayesian Inference Ratios of π_I With Ideal Probabilities (Given $N = 5$ and $\pi = .4$)

(1) p or π_I	(2) $P(p\mid\pi=.4)$	(3) $I(\pi_I\mid p=.4)$	(4) $I(\pi_I\mid p=.4,\ \pi_H)$	(5) $\mid(3)-(2)\mid$	(6) $\mid(4)-(2)\mid$
0	.0778	0	.0549	.0778	.0229
.2	.2592	.2048	.3447	.0544	.0855
.4	.3456	.3456	.4154	0	.0698
.6	.2304	.2304	.2769	0	.0465
.8	.0768	.0512	.1021	.0256	.0253
1.0	.0102	0	.0072	.0102	.0030
	1.0000	.8320	1.2012	.1680	.2530

probability that a sample p of .2 came from a universe with a π of .4 should also be .2592. Note, however, that the binomial inferences give us a probability (or inference ratio) of .2048 that a sample p of .2 came from a universe with a π of .4. The Bayesian inferences yield a value of .3447, thus being in error on the opposite side.

Columns 5 and 6 of Table 8.5 calculate the absolute differences between the true probability (column 2) and those estimated by the binomial and Bayesian formulas. We find that the binomial estimates are quite good in the middle of the distribution, perfect, in fact; but they make relatively large errors on the tails. This is consistent with what we found when we worked with a sample of 50 in the preceding chapter. The Bayesian estimates are a little closer on the tails, but significantly worse in the central area. The total error (signs ignored) is definitely in favor of the binomial estimates.

These results come as a disappointment because we were hoping to improve on the binomial estimates by the use of Bayes's theorem. We did improve the estimates at the tails, but only at the expense of much poorer estimates in the central region. In the next section we make some additional modifications in our procedures that correct this situation. Before doing so, however, we should call attention to a few other features of Table 8.5 that have some significance.

The binomial estimates (column 3) are in general *too low*. The inference ratios (or probabilities) add to only .8320 instead of the appropriate 1.

The Bayesian estimates are in general *too high*, adding to 1.2012.

The *average* of the binomial and Bayesian estimates would be better in general than either one alone because the two methods tend to make opposite errors.

8.6 Modifying the Method of Calculating Conditional Probabilities in Order to Improve the Bayesian Estimates of Inference Ratios of π_I

Figure 8.3 pictures the method we used in the preceding section to calculate the conditional probabilities of a sample p given some hypothetical π. The shaded section of Part A shows the probability of a p of .4 given a π_H of .4. Part B shows the probability of a p of .4 given a π_H of .2. Similar charts could be drawn for any other values of π_H that we might choose.

Figure 8.4 pictures another way of calculating a conditional probability. Part A shows the whole probability distribution of the various values of p that could occur given that π_H equals .5. The shaded area marks off the probability of getting a p of *.4 or less.* (We are here treating p as a *continuous* variable.)

Part B shows the whole distribution of p given that π_H equals .7. Again we shade in the area for a p of *.4 or less.*

In Part C we superimpose the histograms of Parts A and B. Note the cross-hatched area. This is where $P(p \leq .4 | \pi_H = .7)$ appears now. Note that it is entirely within the *total* shaded area that shows $P(p \leq .4 | \pi_H = .5)$. The numerical values associated with these two

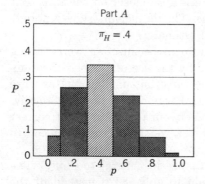
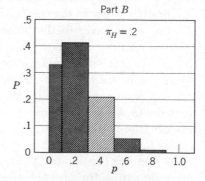

Fig. 8.3 Illustration of the probability of a sample p of .4 in a sample of five items from universes with different π's—p taken as a discrete variable.

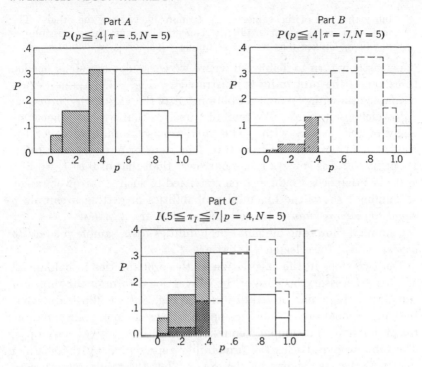

Fig. 8.4 Illustration of method of estimating the probability that π_I lies between .5 and .7 on the basis of cumulative probabilities and the treatment of p as a continuous variable.

areas are .0969 and .3438. (These are taken from the binomial tables in a manner that is explained shortly.)

We now ask ourselves the interpretation we should put on the *difference* between these two areas, or between these two probabilities.

The first thing we note is that the difference is *caused by our change from an hypothesis of a π_H of .5 to one of a π_H of .7 and by nothing else.* Hence we now assert that this difference is an estimate of the probability that π lies between .5 and .7 *given* a sample of 5 with a p of .4. This statement makes sense only if two underlying assumptions are correct:

1. Direct and inverse probabilities tend to equality in the sense that $P(p|\pi) = P(\pi|p)$. We adopted this criterion for a useful theory of inference.

2. The *prior* probability of a π_H of .5 is equal to the *prior* probability of a π_H of .7. This permits us to calculate the difference between $P(p \leq .4|\pi_H = .7)$ and $P(p \leq .4|\pi_H = .5)$ without any concern for the possi-

bility that one of the values of π_H is more likely than the other. The fact that we are not explicitly concerned about these possibilities *definitely implies* that we are assuming *equal prior probabilities*.

Let us now turn to Table 8.6 where we carry out the steps needed to calculate the probabilities illustrated by Fig. 8.4. Again we use a sample of 5 with a p of .4. Column 1 lists the various hypothetical π_H's we choose to pick. We remind ourselves that we may choose as many of these as we wish. The only proviso is that we cover the *full range* of possibilities from 0 to 1 in steps of any size we prefer. If our hypotheses cover a range narrower than that of 0 to 1, we find that our inferences would also be restricted to such a narrower range.

Column 2 shows the binomial probabilities of getting a sample p *equal to or more than .4* for selected π_H that are *.4 or less*.

Column 3 shows the binomial probabilities for a sample p *equal to or less than .4* for selected π_H that are *.4 or more*.

The two steps in the calculation of the probabilities in columns 2 and 3 are necessary because of the conventional form of the tables of cumulative binomial probabilities. In Fig. 8.5 we illustrate what the conventional tables show. Suppose we were to look up in the table the probability of a sample p equal to or less than .4 given a π_H of .5. The table would give us the probability represented by the shading lines *plus* the area shown by the dots. Thus the table treats p as a strictly *discrete* variable and includes *all* of .4 in its calculation. We prefer to treat p as though it were really a *continuous* variable. Thus

TABLE 8.6

Inference Ratios for Values of π_I Based on Differences between Probabilities of p Equal to or Less than .4 for Various Hypothetical Values of π. $N = 5$

π_H (1)	$P(p \geqq .4 \mid \pi_H)$ (2)	$P(p \leqq .4 \mid \pi_H)$ (3)	π_I (4)	$I(\pi_I \mid p = .4,\ \pi_H)$ (5)	$I \times \pi_I$ (6)
0	$0 - 0 \quad = 0$		0	.0451	0
.1	$.0815 - .0364 = .0451$		.2	.2723	.05446
.3	$.4718 - .1544 = .3174$		.4	.3388	.13552
.4	$.6630 - .1728 = .4902$	$.6826 - .1728 = .5098$	.6	.2469	.14814
.5		$.5000 - .1562 = .3438$	.8	.0923	.07384
.7		$.1631 - .0662 = .0969$	1.0	.0046	.00460
.9		$.0086 - .0040 = .0046$	———		———
1.0		$.0000 - .0000 = .0000$		1.0000	.41656

$P(p \mid \pi = .5, N = 5)$

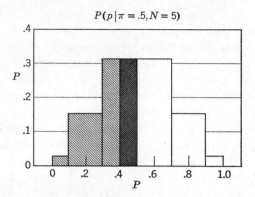

Fig. 8.5 Illustration of effects of treating p as a discrete variable or as a continuous variable.

we think of .4 as really the *middle* point of a range of values running from .3 to .5. Therefore we are interested in only the *lower half* of this .3 to .5 interval.

While we have Fig. 8.5 before us, we should note that if we treat p as a strictly discrete variable and include the dotted area in our calculations, we will find a *larger difference* than before between the $P(p \leq .4 \mid \pi_H = .5)$ and the $P(p \leq .4 \mid \pi_H = .7)$. Thus we will have a *larger probability than before* of a π_I being between .5 and .7. Such larger probabilities would exist for all ranges of π_I. When we add such probabilities, we would get a total *greater than 1*. This is, of course, somewhat illogical. Some people do follow this procedure, however, so they are apparently willing to accept this bit of nonsense in exchange for some other advantages which they think they gain. What these possible advantages are we consider later.

Let us now return to Table 8.6 and trace through the calculations performed there. If we have a hypothetical π_H of .1, we find from the table of the *cumulative* binomial that there is a probability of .0815 of getting a sample p of *.4 or larger;* .0815 is the sum of the probability of a p of .4 (.0729), the probability of a p of .6 (.0081), the probability of a p of .8 (.0004), and the probability of a p of 1.0 (.0000). (Actually these four probabilities add to .0814. The difference from .0815 is due to rounding.) We then subtract .0364 from .0815 to eliminate *half* of the probability shown for .4. The net result is .0451, which we take to be the probability of getting a p *equal to or larger* than .4 *given* a π_H of .1.

Exactly the same procedure is followed to get the estimates for a

π_H of .3 and .4. Check at least one of these to make sure our procedure is clear.

We then reverse our perspective, so to speak, and seek the probability of a p equal to or *less* than .4 for various values of π_H of .4 and *larger*. To help us picture perspective, we might think of ourselves as standing on the horizontal axis of a chart like Fig. 8.5 *at the point corresponding to our hypothetical π_H value*. Then we *face the direction of the particular sample result*, .4 in our example. If our hypothesis happens to be exactly the same as the sample result, then, of course, we find the sample p "at our feet." Most of the time, however, we find the sample p some distance *in front*. The probability we are interested in, or the area under the distribution, is that area on the *other side of p* from where we are standing. We are not at all interested in the area under that part of the curve that is *in back of us* or in the area *between* our π_H and p. What we are doing in column 2 is to first stand at a π_H of 0. We then look beyond the p of .4 and calculate the probability on the far side of .4. We then step up to a π_H of .1 and repeat the procedure, and then to a π_H of .3, and finally to a π_H of .4. If we kept facing and moving in the same direction, we would now find the p of .4 in back of us. So we simply turn about and are looking down at .4. We calculate these "looking-down" probabilities successively from a π_H of .4, .5, .7, .9, and finally 1.0. Column 3 shows the calculations from this perspective.

Again, check at least one of these calculations. It is particularly useful to check one for a π_H of more than .5 because it helps gain some familiarity with the way the tables are set up. Note that the tables show π values (the actual table may call these p) only up to .5. It is then assumed that a person can figure out how to find the appropriate values for higher π values by finding their complements among the π's less than .5. It takes a little practice to do this with reasonable confidence that the answer is right. See p. 137 for some guidance in using the binomial tables.

We had to make two calculations for a π_H of .4. This follows from the fact that it is legitimate to look in both directions from this point.

The corrections are all equal to *half* the probability of a sample p of .4. It is instructive to examine the effects of the corrections for π_H at .4. If we look up from .4, we find the uncorrected probability of a .4 or more to be .6630, whereas the corrected probability is .4902. If we look down from .4, we find an uncorrected probability of .6826 and a corrected one of .5098. The two uncorrected probabilities add to 1.3456, a sum that is obviously too large. Such a finding is the equivalent of standing at some point in a room 20 feet long and discovering that 12 feet of the 20 feet are in front of us and 13 feet of the 20 are in back of us!

The two corrected probabilities add to 1.0 as they should.

In column 4 we list the particular π_I's for which we would like to estimate probabilities. As before, we are using 0 to represent the interval from 0 to .1, .2 to represent .1 to .3, etc. (There is a bit of awkwardness caused by the existence of the boundaries at 0 and 1. The π_I's seem to be at the middle of their intervals except at these boundaries. They are also at the middle at the boundaries if we are willing to imagine the little fiction of the distribution extending down to $-.1$ and up to 1.1. We find it convenient at the moment to engage in this little fiction. It causes us no real trouble and saves us other troubles.)

In column 5 we show the inferred probabilities for the existence of these various π_I values. These are calculated by taking the *differences* between the successive cumulative probabilities we calculated in columns 2 and 3. The .0451 is the difference between 0 and .0451; the .2723 is the difference between the .0451 and the .3174, etc. The exception to this process occurs at the π_I of .4. Since part of the .3 to .5 interval comes from looking *down* from .4 and the other part from looking *up* from .4, we must *add* these two parts together. Thus .3388 is the *sum* of the difference between .3174 and .4902 and the difference between .5098 and .3438.

We find some comfort in the fact that the probabilities in column 5 add up to 1.0, thus conforming to the general rule of all probabilities that the whole set of them must add to 1.0.

In column 6 we have multiplied each π_I by its inference ratio. The total of these turns out to be .41656. Since the sample p is exactly .4, we would prefer that the arithmetic mean of our inferences about π were also .4. In such a case we would then be satisfying the desirable criterion that the arithmetic mean of all our inferences would equal the true value. This criterion is satisfied if the inferences based on any given sample p average out to that sample p.

We are not exactly surprised that our Bayesian inferences are not going to satisfy the criterion of averaging out at the true value. This criterion was one of the things we might have to sacrifice if we were going to improve the accuracy of our inference ratios as estimators of the true probabilities. We also are not exactly surprised that the sum of column 6 turned out to be *larger* than .4 rather than smaller. It is larger because our use of the *prior distribution* of π_H with *equal* probabilities for the various π_H imparts a *bias toward .5* in any inferences that are tied to this prior distribution. What actually happens is that our final inference distribution is really a *weighted average* of the information contained in the prior distribution of π_H and that contained in the sample. The average of our prior distribution is .5. (The assumption of *equal* probabilities for all π_H's results in such an average.) Our final distribution is thus an average of a prior distribution with a mean of .5 and a sample with a mean of .4. It is hence not surprising to find a result larger than .4. If we had worked with a sample with a p of .6, we would have ended up with a mean of .58344, also biased toward .5. In general the bias is greater the closer p is to 0 or 1. There would be no bias if p were .5. The bias declines as the size of the sample increases because the *sample* information would then carry greater and greater relative weight in the average. Theoretically the bias never completely vanishes until the sample is infinitely large.

We have more to say about the relationships of prior distributions and posterior distributions later when we discuss the pooling of information in more general terms than here. Some people would seriously question whether it is legitimate to develop this prior distribution with which we have just been working. They claim that it is based on sheer ignorance and should not carry weight in any conclusions supposedly based on factual evidence. If there was any initial doubt that the assumption of equal probabilities based on the equal distribution of ignorance rule did in fact impart "information" to the final conclusions, such doubt should now be dispelled. Our example above clearly demonstrates that this assumption does impart information in the sense that it does carry weight in the final conclusion, a weight that leads to a bias toward .5. But, at the same time the existence of this bias is realized, keep in mind that we may have to pay the price of a little bias (as defined) in order to get better estimates of the probabilities of π_I.

8.7 Testing the Accuracy of Inference Ratios Based on Modified Estimates of Bayesian Probabilities

(*Note:* From now on we use the term Bayesian probabilities to refer to probabilities that are calculated by reference to *both* a prior distribution and to a sample.)

Let us apply our latest inference method to all possible samples of 10 items. Table 8.7 shows the matrix of all such possible results. The leftmost column lists the 11 possible sample results that can occur from a random sample of 10 items. Each of these results has

TABLE 8.7

Matrix of All Possible Inferences About π_I Based on All Possible Samples of 10 Items Each. Probabilities (Inference Ratios) Are Calculated From a Prior Distribution of Equal Probabilities and From Cumulative Binomial Probabilities Based on a Sample of 10 Items. (See Table 8.6 for illustration of calculation routine)

(Body of table shows: $I(\pi_I | p, \pi_H, N = 10)$)

π_I

p	0	.1	.2	.3	.4	.5	.6	.7	.8	.9	1.0	
0	.401	.402	.141	.043	.010	.003	.000	.000	.000	.000	.000	1.000
.1	.243	.386	.220	.100	.037	.010	.003	.000	.000	.000	.000	.999
.2	.049	.269	.297	.211	.113	.045	.013	.003	.000	.000	.000	1.000
.3	.007	.108	.234	.264	.205	.118	.050	.013	.002	.000	.000	1.001
.4	.001	.029	.121	.216	.249	.203	.121	.049	.011	.001	.000	1.001
.5	.000	.006	.048	.118	.207	.242	.207	.118	.048	.006	.000	1.000
.6	.000	.001	.011	.049	.121	.203	.249	.216	.121	.029	.001	1.001
.7	.000	.000	.002	.013	.050	.118	.205	.264	.234	.108	.007	1.001
.8	.000	.000	.000	.003	.013	.045	.113	.211	.297	.269	.049	1.000
.9	.000	.000	.000	.000	.003	.010	.037	.100	.220	.386	.243	.999
1.0	.000	.000	.000	.000	.000	.003	.010	.043	.141	.402	.401	1.000
	.701	1.201	1.074	1.017	1.008	1.000	1.008	1.017	1.074	1.201	.701	11.002

been used to generate a set of inference ratios for values of π_I. These inference ratios appear as the horizontal vectors. The π_I's are shown as the headings for the vertical vectors.

Let us first examine these vertical vectors. Consider the one headed by π_I of .5. This vector indicates that if our sample of 10 has a p of 0, we assign a probability of .003 to this sample's having come from a universe with a π of .5. What is the probability that a universe with a π of .5 will generate a sample of 10 with a p of 0? The binomial theorem indicates that the probability is .001. The .003 is quite close on a *numerical* basis, being off by only .002. We must admit that it is quite wrong on a *percentage* basis, however.

Table 8.8 compares the entire vertical vector at $\pi_I = .5$ with the desired result as shown by the binomial probabilities. In general the correspondence is quite close, as can be seen by comparing columns 2 and 3. Our problem would have to be very critical to be dissatisfied with estimates as accurate as these.

Column 4 of Table 8.8 shows the results we would get by using the simple binomial as a generator, the first inference method we used.

TABLE 8.8

Comparison of Modified Bayesian Estimates of Probabilities of a π_I of .50
for Various Values of *p* with Probabilities of these Various Values of *p*
Given that π Really Does Equal .5.   *N* = 10

(1) p	(2) $P(p\|\pi = .5)$	(3) $I(\pi_I = .50\|p, \pi_H)$	(4) $I(\pi_I = .50\|p)$
0	.001	.003	.000
.1	.010	.010	.002
.2	.044	.045	.026
.3	.117	.118	.103
.4	.205	.203	.201
.5	.246	.242	.246
.6	.205	.203	.201
.7	.117	.118	.103
.8	.044	.045	.026
.9	.010	.010	.002
1.0	.001	.003	.000
	1.000	1.000	.910

It is obvious that our modification has resulted in significant improvements.

Figure 8.6 makes it possible to make these comparisons visually. The chart also shows the comparisons for π values of .4, .3, .2, .1, and 0. It is quite evident that the modified Bayesian estimates are closer to the true probabilities for all values of π than are those estimates based on the simple binomial. (The results for π values of .6, .7, .8, .9, and 1 are not shown because they would be mirror images of the results shown for π equal to .4, .3, .2, .1, and 0, respectively.) It is also evident that the estimates are poorer the further away we are from a π of .5. However, the Bayesian estimates are not seriously in error until we have a π of 0 or 1.

8.8   Bias in Modified Bayesian Estimates of Inference Ratios for π_I

We started our quest for a theory of making inferences about π by developing inferences so that the *arithmetic mean of all such inferences would be the true universe value.* This seemed like a good idea

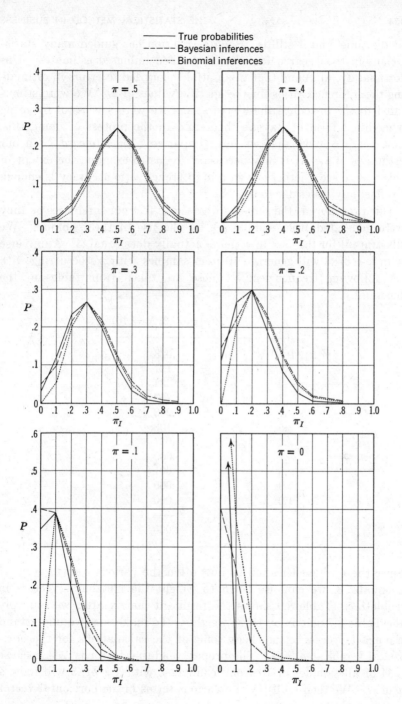

Fig. 8.6 Comparison of inference ratio vectors based on binomial and Bayesian inferences with the true probabilities.

at the time, and it still is. Such a criterion has guided many statisticians in their search for what are called unbiased estimates. Unfortunately, we found that this initial theory led to errors in estimating the inference ratios for the specific values of π_I. We were stimulated to try to reduce these errors, and we were successful by using a modified form of Bayes's theorem. In the process of doing this, however, we know that we have imparted a *bias toward .5* in our estimates of π_I. It is now necessary for us to examine the extent of this bias to see whether our gain in inference ratio accuracy is enough to offset any losses due to this bias.

Our procedure is the same as we used to test our inferences as they were generated from sample p's by the use of the binomial. We illustrate it for the case in which π actually does equal .3. A universe with a π of .3 will generate 10 item samples with p's occurring with the following frequencies: (These are taken from tables of the binomial.)

p	$P(p \mid \pi = .3, N = 10)$
0	.028
.1	.121
.2	.234
.3	.267
.4	.200
.5	.103
.6	.037
.7	.009
.8	.001
.9	.000
1.0	.000
	1.000

Since these frequencies tell us how often the various p's will occur if π equals .3, we can use them to weight the horizontal vectors in Table 8.7. Table 8.9 shows the resultant matrix after we multiply the Table 8.7 matrix by these weights. To make sure we understand the exact process let us check some of the calculations for the horizontal vector at $p = .2$. The proper weighting factor is .234 because .234 of all samples of 10 from a universe with a π of .3 will have a p of .2. We then multiply the various terms in the horizontal vector

TABLE 8.9

Matrix of Inferences About π Generated by Sample p's that Previously Had Been Generated by a Universe With a π of .3; N = 10

[Body of Matrix shows: $I(\pi_I | p, \pi_H) \times P(p | \pi = .3)$]

π_I

p	0	.1	.2	.3	.4	.5	.6	.7	.8	.9	1.0	
0	.011	.011	.004	.001								.027
.1	.029	.047	.027	.012	.004	.001						.120
.2	.011	.063	.069	.049	.026	.011	.003	.001				.233
.3	.002	.029	.062	.070	.055	.032	.013	.003	.001			.267
.4		.006	.024	.043	.050	.041	.024	.010	.002			.200
.5		.001	.005	.012	.021	.025	.021	.012	.005	.001		.103
.6				.002	.004	.008	.009	.008	.004	.001		.036
.7						.001	.002	.002	.002	.001		.008
.8												
.9												
1.0												
	.053	.157	.191	.189	.160	.119	.072	.036	.014	.003		.994

at $p = .2$ as given in Table 8.7 by this .234. The first term is .049 (see Table 8.7). The resultant product is .011 (see Table 8.9). The second term is .269. The resultant product is .063, etc. Note that the sum of these products for this vector in Table 8.9 is .233. This would be .234 except for rounding errors and is what we would expect because we have multiplied a vector that originally added to 1 (Table 8.7) by the number .234. The rest of the matrix is calculated in the same way.

The sums of the vertical vectors give us the total relative frequency with which various inferences about π are made. Since all of these inferences were made solely on the basis of samples that came from a universe with a π of .3, it is instructive to examine this series of sums. For convenience of reference we call this series of sums the *average inference ratio vector* for samples of 10 from a universe with a π of .3.

Table 8.10 compares this vector with the vector we get if we use the simple binomial as an inference generator (our first version for an inference theory).

Column 2 shows the vector based solely on information about p. Column 3 is the product of this vector times the various π_I values. It adds to .3003. Rounding errors prevent it from equalling exactly 3. Thus we confirm our earlier finding, namely that the arithmetic mean of all inferences based on binomials generated from sample p's will equal the true universe π.

Column 4 shows the vector generated by our modified Bayesian technique, or by information about p and "information" about equally-likely hypotheses about π. Its failure to add to 1 is caused by rounding errors. Column 5 is the result of multiplying the column 4 vector by the various π_I values. Here we get a total of .3164. The departure of this from the true value of .3 is *not* caused by rounding errors. Rather it is caused by the bias toward .5 that is imparted by the assumption of equally-likely π_H's. This bias is part of the price we must pay in order to improve our estimates of the specific probabilities for the various π_I's.

Column 6 shows the difference between each π_I value and the true π of .3. Note that the direction of the difference is ignored because we are here concerned only with the size of the difference. Thus column 6 is the amount by which each π_I misses as an estimate of the π of .3. Column 7 multiplies each miss given in column 6 by the

TABLE 8.10

Comparative Analysis of Average Inference Ratio Vectors, One Vector Based on Binomial Inferences from p, the Other Based on Bayesian Inferences from π_H and p. Given: $\pi = .3$; $N = 10$

(1) π_I	(2) $I(\pi_I\|p)$	(3) $I(\pi_I\|p) \times \pi_I$	(4) $I(\pi_I\|p, \pi_H)$	(5) $I(\pi_I\|p, \pi_H) \times \pi_I$	(6) $\|\pi_I - .3\|$	(7) (6) × (2)	(8) (6) × (4)
0	.104	0	.053	0	.3	.0312	.0159
.1	.151	.0151	.157	.0157	.2	.0302	.0314
.2	.185	.0370	.191	.0382	.1	.0185	.0191
.3	.182	.0546	.189	.0567	0	0	0
.4	.151	.0604	.160	.0640	.1	.0151	.0160
.5	.108	.0540	.119	.0595	.2	.0216	.0238
.6	.066	.0396	.072	.0432	.3	.0198	.0216
.7	.034	.0238	.036	.0252	.4	.0136	.0144
.8	.014	.0112	.014	.0112	.5	.0070	.0070
.9	.004	.0036	.003	.0027	.6	.0024	.0018
1.0	.001	.0010	.000	.0000	.7	.0007	.0000
	1.000	.3003	.994	.3164		.1601	.1510

number of times it occurs as indicated by the vector in column 2. The sum of column 7 gives us the total of all our errors if we use p-binomials as estimators of π_I. Ideally, of course, we would like such a total to be as small as possible, even as small as 0 if that were possible.

Column 8 repeats the same process performed for column 7 except that we now use the vector in column 4, the Bayesian estimators, as our relative frequencies of the column 6 errors. Here we find a sum of .1510. (This has a *very slight* downward bias because the total of column 4 is only .994 instead of 1. This bias will not affect our conclusion given below.) Note that this sum of errors is smaller than that for the p-binomial estimators. Thus we can now argue that the bias in the Bayesian estimators is offset by the improvements in the specific probabilities, giving us an over-all better estimation than did our first inference method.

8.9 Summary of Our Theory of Making Inferences About π from Information Supplied by a Sample p

1. The *objective* was to estimate the probability that π had any given range of values. We were to make this estimate on the basis of the information supplied by a random sample. Thus, given p and n, we wished to estimate the value of $P(\pi_L \leqq \pi_I \leqq \pi_U)$, with the L and U referring to the lower and upper limits to the inferred value of π.
2. The criterion that we eventually adopted for a good estimate was: the probability of π_I, given p, should be the same as the probability of p, given π. Or, in symbols, we wished the truth of the equality:

$$P(\pi_I | p) = P(p | \pi).$$

   We assume, of course, that n is the same in both cases.
3. We found that this was impossible to accomplish exactly because of significant variation in inference vectors from one p to the next due to our inability to keep pq constant as p varied. This problem moderated as the size of the sample increased. It also tended to be less a problem near the center of the vector, where the probabilities were high, than on the tails, where the probabilities were low.
4. We were also bothered by nonsense answers near the boundaries of 0 and 1.
5. Our initial inference method did have the desirable feature that it generated inferences that averaged out (in the arithmetic mean sense) at the correct answer.
6. We then set out to try to improve on our first inference method. We did this knowing that we might have to sacrifice some desirable features in order to gain more of others.
7. We tried, and quickly rejected, a straightforward application of

Bayes's theorem to the calculation of *discrete* probabilities. This method led us further astray.

8. We then modified this Bayesian approach by working with *cumulative* probabilities and by treating the binomial distribution as though it were *continuous*. We immediately noted marked improvements in our estimates of the specific probabilities for various π_I values.

9. We then noted that these modified Bayesian estimates would not average out at the true value of π. They imparted a bias toward .5. (Incidentally, it is worth noting that the *un*modified Bayesian estimates would give an even greater bias toward .5.)

10. Finally we tested the modified Bayesian estimates against the *p*-binomial estimates and found that the total errors in estimating the value of the true π were less. We were thus satisfied that the modified Bayesian estimates represented a real improvement over the *p*-binomials.

11. All three methods of making inferences (the *p*-binomial, the discrete Bayesian, and the continuous Bayesian) get better as the sample size increases. In fact, they all converge on the same, and the correct, value of π.

12. The methods vary with respect to the tedium of calculation and with respect to the degree of simplicity of their underlying logic. The generation of the binomial from *p* is probably the simplest to perform and the simplest to comprehend. However, this could become somewhat tedious if we wished to interpolate for π_I values not given directly in the table of the binomial. It should also be noted that some people would find such an interpolation offensive to their sense of logic, despite the fact that it would result in practically useful answers. There is some evidence that more and more people are willing to accept the idea of using the binomial distribution as though it were a continuous series.

13. Unless we find that our problem attaches critical significance to the tail probabilities, where the differences between the methods are most pronounced, we might choose a method almost on the basis of taste and on the availability of convenient binomial tables.

14. Many of the above problems tend to disappear as the size of the sample increases. As a matter of fact, we might switch over to the use of *normal curve* estimates as N achieves some minimum size. All binomial distributions approach the normal as N increases; they also become more obviously *continuous* in their form. We postpone our discussion of such normal curve estimates until a later chapter when we discuss inferences about the mean of a continuous variable.

8.10   The Use of Poisson Probabilities in Making Inferences

We sometimes run into problems in which it is practically impossible to determine the *relative frequency* with which some event can or has occurred in the usual sense in which we use the term relative frequency. The difficulty is caused by the fact that the *opportunities* for the event to occur are almost limitless, and hence uncountable. We gave illustrations of this problem by reference to the probability of a defect in a paint surface and the probability that a machine will break down in some time interval. About all we were able to do is determine *how many* defects occurred in some specified area of the painted surface, or *how many* machines broke down in some specified time interval.

If we specify the *average number of such defects in the universe* as *m* and the number of such defects in a sample as *c*, we find that we can estimate the probability of a given sample *c* from *knowledge* about a given universe *m* by the following formula:

$$Yc = e^{-m} \cdot \frac{m^c}{c!}, \qquad \text{or} \qquad P(c\,|\,m) = e^{-m} \cdot \frac{m^c}{c!}$$

This is, of course, the formula we called the Poisson formula in an earlier chapter. We use this formula with a given *m* and then calculate the probability of each of the possible *c* values. The resultant distribution is what we called the Poisson distribution.

Now let us consider the problem in which we do not know the value of *m*, but we do know the value of *c* in a given sample. What inferences might we then make about the value of *m*? This problem is exactly analogous to our problem of making inferences about π from information about *p*, and we could approach it in exactly the same ways.

We might simply reverse the *c* and *m* and let the information about the sample act as a generator of inferences about the universe. Such inferences would have the same properties we discovered when we let the sample *p* act as a generator of inferences about π. As they apply to *m*, these properties would be:

1. The arithmetic mean of all inferences about *m* would equal *m*.
2. The specific probability of the correct *m* would be estimated exactly.
3. The specific probabilities of *m*'s in the neighborhood of the correct *m* would be more accurately estimated than those on the tails of the distribution.
4. The probabilities of *m*'s *below* the true *m* would be *underestimated;* those for *m*'s *above* the true *m* would be *overestimated*.

If we used a prior distribution of *m* with equal probabilities as a basis of estimation of the probability distribution of m_I (modified Bayesian estimates), we would find:

1. The arithmetic mean of all inferences about *m* would be *greater* than the correct *m*.

2. The specific probability for the correct m would be very slightly *under-estimated*.
3. The specific probabilities for all other m's would in general be more closely estimated than if we had simply reversed m and c as above.

In either case we would find our estimates improving *as c increased*. This follows from the fact that we are really assuming that the p is a statistical constant in the equality $c = Np$. If p is in truth very small, as it should be to make the Poisson approximation work, and if it is constant, N increases proportionately with c. Hence an increase in c is indicative of an *increase in N*. We have learned that our estimates improve with an increase in N. As a matter of fact, the Poisson distribution approaches the normal as m (or c) increases. We might also add that these methods give identical, and perfect, answers if the relevant sampling distributions are truly normal.

PROBLEMS AND QUESTIONS

8.1(*a*) You are given a presumably random sample of four items with a p of .25. You have no other information about the universe from which this sample came. Assume the validity of the equal distribution of ignorance rule and estimate the inference distribution of π_I by assuming equally likely values of π_H in the manner of Table 8.3.

(*b*) Explain the logic, if any, of the equal distribution of ignorance rule. Give an illustration from your own experience in which you have used the rule or its equivalent. (You may not have been aware of such an assumption at the time.)

(*c*) Interpret the sum of the joint-conditional probabilities you calculated in (*a*). (The joint-conditional probabilities are those shown in column 4 of Table 8.3.) Suppose that your answer had been as low as .0000147; what would be your reaction?

8.2(*a*) Complete the inference matrix for a sample of 4 in the manner of Table 8.4. This involves the assumption of equally likely prior values of π_H. Use the short-cut method that omits the calculation of the joint probabilities.

(*b*) Under what circumstances is it appropriate to omit the calculation of the joint probabilities on our way to the calculation of the posterior probabilities?

(*c*) Assume that $\pi = .25$ and $N = 4$ and compare your binomial inferences $[I(\pi_I|p = .4)]$ and your Bayesian inferences $[I(\pi_I|p = .4, \pi_H)]$ with the ideal probabilities $[P(p|\pi = .4)]$ in the manner of Table 8.5.

Do you find results consistent with those we found in Table 8.5?

8.3(*a*) Given that $p = .25$ and $N = 4$, estimate the modified Bayesian inferences about π_I in the manner of Table 8.6.

(*b*) This method assumes that the binomial distribution may be treated as a *continuous* variable. Do you approve? Why or why not?

(*c*) How do you explain the fact that your average inference is larger than .25, the value in the sample?

(*d*) Without doing any further calculation other than a simple subtraction, estimate the average modified Bayesian inference you would make if $p = .75$ and $N = 4$. (Hint: This should be *less* than .75.)

8.4(*a*) Calculate all other modified Bayesian inferences for samples of 4 in addition to the one you calculated in Problem 8.3(*a*).

(*b*) Form a matrix with these inferences in the manner of Table 8.7.

(*c*) Interpret the vertical vector headed by $\pi_I = .25$.

(*d*) Compare this vertical vector headed by $\pi_I = .25$ with the direct probabilities of getting these various sample p's. (In the manner of the first three columns of Table 8.8.)

8.5(*a*) Assume that $\pi = .25$ and that $N = 4$. Calculate the probability vector for various expected values of p.

(*b*) Multiply this probability vector by the modified Bayesian inference matrix you calculated in Problem 8.4(*b*). (In the manner of Table 8.9.)

(*c*) Compare the *average* inference ratio vector made from the column sums of this matrix with the corresponding vector based on simple binomial inferences. (The latter vector comes from the column sums in the matrix calculated in Problem 7.7.)

Follow Table 8.10 as a model.

(*d*) What conclusions do you draw about the relative advantages of modified Bayesian estimates compared with the simple binomial estimates?

8.6 A sample of 20 radio tubes of a given type is tested. All 20 tubes are found satisfactory.

(*a*) What is the probability that all the tubes of this type, and manufactured by this process, are satisfactory?

(*b*) What is the probability that no more than 80% of such tubes are satisfactory?

(*c*) Are you *sure* that your answers in (*a*) and/or (*b*) are correct? (Errors in arithmetic aside.)

8.7 A rookie in the American League fails to hit safely in his first 10 times at bat. What is the probability that he will never get a hit?

8.8 The surface of a bathtub shows three small blemishes. What is the probability that the universe of bathtubs averages four or more defects?

chapter 9

Inference ratios as ingredients in planning and decision-making

In Chapters 7 and 8 we examined the problem of estimating, from sample information, the probabilities (inference ratios) that a universe might have certain π_I values. We paid no real attention to why we would make such inferences nor to what we would do with them after we had them. We now consider the role that such inference ratios might play in facilitating planning and decision-making.

9.1 A Simple Decision-making Model

The president of a cereal manufacturing company with a national market for a consumer cereal called Smoothies felt that his company has been losing market share and decided to fire his sales vice president if the company's market share has fallen below 30%. A survey based on a presumably random sample of 100 consumers reveals that 28% of them express a preference for Smoothies. Should he fire the vice president?

It takes very little imagination (and the vice president would be sure to point this out) to recognize that the true proportion in the universe might still be larger than .30 even though a sample of 100 showed only .28. Maybe this was just an unlucky sample. Another sample might show a p of more than .30.

A rational procedure at this stage would be to generate the inference ratio distribution for the various possible values of π_I. We would then be in a position to make estimates of the probability that the true proportion was above .30 or below .30. Table 9.1 shows three sets of estimates of this inference ratio distribution. In column 2 are shown the ratios we get from the binomial expansion with p

TABLE 9.1

Estimates of Inference Ratios for Various Proportions of *All* Consumers
Who Might Actually Prefer Smoothies. Inferences Based on
Presumably Random Sample of 100 Consumers, 28% of
Whom Expressing a Preference for Smoothies

(1) π_I	(2) $I(\pi_I \mid p)$	(3) $I(\pi_I \mid p, \pi_H)$	(4) $I(\pi_I \mid p)$ †
.12–.14 *	0	0	.001
.14–.16	.002	.002	.003
.16–.18	.008	.005	.009
.18–.20	.024	.020	.025
.20–.22	.055	.052	.054
.22–.24	.099	.096	.095
.24–.26	.145	.145	.143
.26–.28	.173	.174	.170
.28–.30	.169	.170	.170
.30–.32	.137	.139	.143
.32–.34	.093	.095	.095
.34–.36	.053	.056	.054
.36–.38	.026	.029	.025
.38–.40	.010	.012	.009
.40–.42	.004	.004	.003
.42–.44	.002	.001	.001
.44–.46	0	.001	0
	1.000	1.001	1.000

* Lower Limit Inclusive.
† Normal curve approximations.

equal to .28 and N equal to 100. Note that we have gathered the
various point probabilities into intervals. For example, .145 shown
for the .24–.26 interval is made up of *half* the frequency associated
with a π_I of .24 (1/2 of .062), the whole frequency associated with
a π_I of .25 (.073), and *half* of the frequency associated with a π_I of
.26 (1/2 of .082). A more refined method of interpolation would
not split these boundary frequencies exactly in half. However, the
errors of the crude interpolation are quite small and are generally
not worth the trouble of refinement. It might be interesting to check
one of the other recorded ratios in column 2.

Column 3 shows the set of ratios that result if we take a prior distribution of equally probable π_H's and modify it by adding the information supplied by a sample p of .28. The procedure is the one we outlined in Chapter 8. Table 9.2 shows the detail of the calculations for column 3. An examination of this table should help you to refresh your memory of this procedure.

Note that the column 3 ratios tend to be *below* the column 2 ratios for values of π_I *less than* .28 and *above* the column 2 ratios for values of π_I *more* than .28. This is consistent with our previous experience with these two methods. The binomial estimates based only on the sample information have an arithmetic mean equal to the sample p, or .28 in this case. The modified Bayesian estimates (column 3) have a bias toward .5 ($\bar{\pi}_I = .2824$), though certainly not a serious bias in this case. We also found that the modified Bayesian estimates

TABLE 9.2

**Details of Calculation of Modified Bayesian Estimates
Shown in Column 3 of Table 9.1**

(1) π_H	(2) $P(p \geq .28 \vert \pi_H)$	$P(p \leq .28 \vert \pi_H)$	(3) π_I	(4) $I(\pi_I \vert p, \pi_H)$
.14	.000		.14–.16 *	.002
.16	.002 − .000 = .002		.16–.18	.005
.18	.009 − .002 = .007		.18–.20	.020
.20	.034 − .007 = .027		.20–.22	.052
.22	.095 − .016 = .079		.22–.24	.096
.24	.204 − .029 = .175		.24–.26	.145
.26	.360 − .040 = .320		.26–.28	.174
.28	.538 − .044 = .494	.551 − .044 = .507	.28–.30	.170
.30		.377 − .040 = .337	.30–.32	.139
.32		.228 − .030 = .198	.32–.34	.095
.34		.122 − .019 = .103	.34–.36	.056
.36		.057 − .010 = .047	.36–.38	.029
.38		.023 − .005 = .018	.38–.40	.012
.40		.008 − .002 = .006	.40–.42	.004
.42		.003 − .001 = .002	.42–.44	.001
.44		.001 − .000 = .001	.44–.46	.001
.46		.000 − .000 = .000	.46–.48	.000
				1.001

* Lower Limit Inclusive.

of the individual ratios were somewhat better than the p-binomial estimates. But here again we find the differences quite small.

In column 4 we show by way of contrast the estimates we would get if we assumed that the π_I's were *normally* distributed. This distribution is, of course, *symmetrical*, whereas the other two are skewed positively, or to the right. The mean of the normal distribution is also .28. It is evident that these normal curve approximations are reasonably close to the other two distributions. We might be forgiven if we chose among these three methods on the basis of taste and convenience rather than on the basis of theoretical accuracy. Unless we forget, we might remind ourselves that the modified Bayesian estimates would be the closest to the truth. (Table 9.3

TABLE 9.3

**Details of Calculation of Normal Curve Estimates
Shown in Column 4 of Table 9.1**

(1)	(2)	(3)	(4)	(5)	(6)	(7)
π_I	$\pi_I - p$	$\dfrac{\pi_I - p}{\sigma_p} = Z$	$I(\pi \leq \pi_I)$	$I(\pi \geq \pi_I)$	π_I	$I(\pi_I \mid p)$
.12	−.16	−3.55	.000		.12–.14 *	.001
.14	−.14	−3.10	.001		.14–.16	.003
.16	−.12	−2.66	.004		.16–.18	.009
.18	−.10	−2.22	.013		.18–.20	.025
.20	−.08	−1.77	.038		.20–.22	.054
.22	−.06	−1.33	.092		.22–.24	.095
.24	−.04	−0.89	.187		.24–.26	.143
.26	−.02	−0.44	.330		.26–.28	.170
.28	0	0	.500	.500	.28–.30	.170
.30	.02	.44		.330	.30–.32	.143
.32	.04	.89		.187	.32–.34	.095
.34	.06	1.33		.092	.34–.36	.054
.36	.08	1.77		.038	.36–.38	.025
.38	.10	2.22		.013	.38–.40	.009
.40	.12	2.66		.004	.40–.42	.003
.42	.14	3.10		.001	.42–.44	.001
.44	.16	3.55		.000	.44–.46	.000
						1.000

* Lower Limit Inclusive.

shows the detail of calculating the normal curve approximations. Note that it is necessary to make an estimate of σ_p in order to carry out the calculations. This estimate is made with $N - 1$, or 99, as a divisor rather than with 100 in order to adjust for the downward bias in sample variances.)

Since the company president has simplified his problem to the point where he is concerned only with whether Smoothies' share of market is above or below .30, we do the same with our probabilities. Table 9.4 shows the results of cumulating our inference ratios above and below .30 for the three methods of estimation. The differences in the estimates are certainly not of any great practical significance.

TABLE 9.4

Probability That Smoothies' Share of Market is Above or Below .30

	Binomial	Modified Bayesian	Normal
$I(\pi_I \leq .30)$	.675	.664	.670
$I(\pi_I \geq .30)$	.325	.336	.330
	1.000	1.000	1.000

The Probability Matrix

The sample survey results obviously provide *inconclusive* evidence on the question of whether the true market share is above or below .30. The president cannot fire the vice president without taking the chance (approx. .33) that the action is wrong because the market share had not really fallen below .30. Similarly, the president cannot retain the vice president without taking the chance (approx. .67) that the retention is wrong because the market share had fallen below .30. Table 9.5 summarizes these options and the probabilities of their being chosen correctly or incorrectly. We call such a table a *probability matrix*.

If the president fires the vice president, there is a .67 probability that his decision is *correct*. Note that we record this option as a *gain*. There is a probability of .33 that such a firing is an *incorrect* decision. We record this option in the *loss* column. Similarly we record the probabilities for correctly or incorrectly keeping the vice president. Note that the row and column sums are all equal to 1.

TABLE 9.5

**Probability Matrix for Problem of Whether to Fire the Sales Vice President
(Based on sample of 100 with p = .28 and on derived
probability that $\pi_I \lesseqgtr .30$)**

	Gain	Loss	
Fire Vice President	.67	.33	1.00
Keep Vice President	.33	.67	1.00
	1.00	1.00	

This follows from the fact that we must either gain or lose when we make a decision, and that we must either fire the vice president or keep him.

The Consequence Matrix

The president undoubtedly expects to gain some advantage for the company if he correctly fires the sales vice president. For example, the new vice president would facilitate the recovery of lost market share, or he might retard the rate of loss of market share. Let us suppose that the president assesses the value of such a correct action as $150,000.

On the other hand, if the sales vice president is incorrectly fired, the company would be expected to suffer some loss, or expense, or loss of revenue, etc. For example, there would be the cost associated with hiring a new vice president who may not be as good as the one we fired. There are also the possible effects flowing from a feeling among the remaining staff that the vice president had been unfairly dealt with, etc. Let us suppose the president assesses the cost of such an incorrect action as $500,000.

There are corresponding gains and losses associated with correctly or incorrectly keeping the vice president. Let us suppose the president estimates that it is worth $200,000 to correctly keep the vice president, and that it will cost $100,000 to incorrectly keep him.

Table 9.6 shows these possible *consequences* in a matrix very similar to that for the probability matrix. A correct firing shows $150,000 in the gain column. An incorrect firing shows $500,000 in the loss column. A correct keeping shows a gain of $200,000. An incorrect keeping shows a loss of $100,000.

TABLE 9.6

Consequence Matrix for Problem of Whether to Fire the Sales Vice President

	Gain	Loss
Fire Vice President	$150,000	$500,000
Keep Vice President	$200,000	$100,000

The Pay-off Matrix

Common sense suggests that the president would like to make a decision about the sales vice president that will maximize the company's gain or minimize its loss. If we multiply the gains and losses of the *consequence matrix* by the probabilities of their occurring as shown by the *probability matrix*, we will be able to assess the probable losses or gains associated with a decision about the sales vice president. Table 9.7 shows the results of such a multiplication. We call the resultant matrix the *pay-off matrix*. Each cell value in the pay-off matrix is the product of the values in the corresponding cells of the probability and consequence matrixes. For example, the $100,050 is .67 × $150,000.

By adding the rows of the pay-off matrix we are now able to determine the *expected economic consequences* of firing or retaining the sales vice president. We find that we expect to lose $64,500 if we fire the vice president and to lose $1000 if we keep him. There is thus an apparent advantage of $63,500 in keeping the vice president.

It is interesting to note that this is a situation in which either decision results in an apparent *loss*. We, in effect, then choose the lesser of the two evils, as it were. Sometimes we face decisions where all options are apparently going to lead to expected *gains*. We then choose the one with the maximum expected gain. Finally, there

TABLE 9.7

Pay-off Matrix for Problem of Whether to Fire the Sales Vice President

	Gain	Loss	Net Gain (Loss)
Fire Vice President	$100,500	$165,000	($64,500)
Keep Vice President	$ 66,000	$ 67,000	($ 1,000)

would be cases in which some options give expected gains and others expected losses. Again we choose that with the maximum expected gain.

9.2 Another Example with a Different Consequence Matrix

Let us see what happens to our sales vice president with *no change in the facts about the market* but with a change in the way *the president assesses the consequences of his decision.* Table 9.8 shows a revised consequence matrix and hence a revised pay-off matrix for the same problem as before. The probability matrix remains the same.

It is now evident that the sales vice president should be fired!

TABLE 9.8

Revised Decision-making Model on Problem of Firing the Sales Vice President

A. Consequence Matrix:

	Gain	Loss
Fire Vice President	$250,000	$400,000
Keep Vice President	$150,000	$250,000

B. Pay-off Matrix:

	Gain	Loss	Net Gain (Loss)
Fire Vice President	$167,500	$132,000	$ 35,500
Keep Vice President	$ 49,500	$167,500	($118,000)

9.3 Is the Company's Share of Market More Than .30?

We started out on this problem of what to do about the sales vice president with the idea that he would be fired if the company's share of market had fallen below .30. We discovered, of course, that we cannot make a judgment about the company's share of market without considering the consequences of those actions that flow from such a judgment. We saw that in one case the vice president was retained,

thus on the assumption that the share of market had not fallen below
.30. In the other case he was fired, thus on the assumption that
share of market had fallen below .30. And this despite no change
in the facts about share of market!

Thus we see that what the president is willing to believe about
share of market depends on what he is planning to do because of
that belief and on how he assesses the consequences of his contemplated actions. The only possible *abstract* answer to the question
of share of market is one which shows the *whole probability distribution* of possible answers. Any attempt to use only part of this
distribution as though this part contained the truth automatically
involves us in risk of error and hence in the need for evaluation of
the consequences of that risk.

9.4   Truth as an Abstraction vs. Truth as a Personal Belief That Regulates Our Behavior

The notion that what we should believe about share of market
depends only partly on the *facts* about share of market is as profound
as it is disconcerting. Such a notion makes it perfectly rational for
a person to now act as though something is true and then act as
though it is false, with no change in the available information in
the interim. People do this quite regularly. Who among us has
never been told to "put your money where your mouth is," and,
when so told, then proceeded to modify his beliefs. We all are aware
of the different consequences that flow from talking as though something were so and acting as though something were so. That is why
political commentators have much less difficulty making decisions
than senators, and senators less trouble than presidents. Similarly
a jury finds it much less difficult to convict a man if the penalty is
mild than if it is severe, all quite independent of the weight of the
evidence. That is why, for example, a defense lawyer might very
rationally try to maneuver the prosecution into asking for the death
penalty on the theory that the jury would not vote guilty on that
penalty, although it would on, say, a 20-year jail term.

Some people have a strong philosophical objection to the notion
that it is rational for people to believe what they wish to believe
in the light of their own evaluation of consequences. Such objectors
argue that truth is a property of the *events* in question (an event
such as share of market) and not a property of the *person* acting
with respect to the events. They fear that such a notion grants

everybody such wide latitude in what he can do rationally that the notion of rationality becomes a useless guide because there would be no such thing as irrational behavior. But, of course, there probably is no such thing as irrational behavior in the sense that any person ever knowingly behaves contrarily to what his reason tells him to *at the moment he has to make the decision.* Tomorrow he may decide that he should have behaved differently, but that does not mean that yesterday he was irrational. It is very easy to confuse rational behavior with behavior that turns out to have been correct, however we determine what is correct.

The philosophical arguments pro and con the desirability of some objective standards of truth are certainly worth considerable discussion. Such a discussion, however, would carry us well outside the proper bounds of this book. We are more concerned here with certain practical issues that arise daily in a society as dominated by division of labor as ours is. From a philosophical point of view, we find it very easy to argue that each person should take personal responsibility for interpreting his own facts. If a person had a job in which he was merely supposed to *report* the facts, he would report them in the form of probability distributions. For example, the United States Weather Bureau office in Chicago would make no commitment on the next day's temperature. It would report the best estimate it could make of the full probability distribution of the expected temperatures. The newspapers would publish this distribution, and all the readers who had any real concern with the next day's temperature would multiply this distribution by their own personal consequence matrix! They would then decide what to wear, where to go, etc., on the basis of the resultant pay-off matrix. Since the probability distribution would usually cover quite a range of possible temperatures, the weather bureau would never really be wrong, nor, of course, would it ever really be right. The only people who could then do any meaningful griping about the quality of job being done by the weather bureau would be those who felt that the bureau was stating incorrect probabilities (how could we determine this?) or that the bureau was perhaps showing more uncertainty about the outlook than more assiduous research would reveal. Most of the people probably would stop complaining about, or even commenting on, the job being done by the weather bureau. They would look for some other agency as a scapegoat for their need to feel that they could do some other fellow's job better than he is doing it!

The fact is that most of us have neither the time, the energy, nor the inclination to spend our days making up probability, consequence, and pay-off matrixes for the myriad of events that press down on us. We necessarily, and in a sense willingly, have adopted a master pay-off matrix that tells us what subsidiary pay-off matrixes we ourselves will work on and which ones we will leave to the *judgment of others*. In effect, we tell the weather bureau: "Pick out that part of the probability distribution of the expected temperature that *you think* makes sense for the citizenry at large. I'll learn to adapt to whatever you decide, or gripe to my Congressman." The weather bureau now finds itself on the spot. So it does what we all do when we find ourselves on the spot. It takes immediate steps to get off the spot. It does this by taking refuge in some notion of objective truth! Thus the bureau absolves itself of any personal responsibility for what it says about the next day's temperature.

Since all of us find ourselves in a position similar to that of the weather bureau, where we are asked to make decisions for which we do not wish to take personal responsibility, we are very happy to collaborate in a more or less general conspiracy to develop objective procedures for making these decisions. We are thus able to blame something else rather than ourselves when things go wrong, and we at the same time can pontificate on our objective and scientific procedures.

We have, of course, overdrawn the case somewhat. Actually there are some very practical arguments for assigning some of our responsibilities to others. The trick is to assign those that can be handled best by others and to devise a way of assessing how well they are handling the responsibilities. In effect, we delegate the job of determining the probability matrix and the consequence matrix. The delegate then merely tells us what to do. We then assess the outcome. If the outcome strikes us as typically unfavorable, we are led to make up a probability matrix, a consequence matrix, and a pay-off matrix on the question of *whether we will continue to delegate this job to this person*. We would make a mistake as a general rule to meddle with the matrixes he is using to do the job he has been assigned.

9.5　Some Commonly Accepted Standards of Objective Truth

Although no person who thinks about it finds it easy to develop notions about objective truth, the same person can appreciate the practical value of having people more or less agree on some general standards of what constitutes an objective truth. In other words, we are not sure we know what objective truth is, or even that there is such a thing. Nevertheless we are willing to adopt some standards about it in order to facilitate communication. Most work and social groups not only develop their own jargon, they also develop implicit notions of how true something has to be to be considered true. This is another way of saying that the group learns how to adopt a generally agreed upon criterion of *acceptable risk*. A member of such a group is expected to adhere to these accepted standards as one of the conditions of remaining in good standing within the group. This is true whether we are trying to remain in good standing within a drag-racing club or a university of scholars. The primary argument for the currently accepted standards is the same in either group, namely that they are good standards because the group thinks they are good standards. If we find the standards unpalatable, we leave the group.

The Notion of 50–50

If we leave consequences entirely aside, we are bound to be attracted to the notion that something is true if there is at least a .5 probability of its being true. Correspondingly, something is false if there is a less than .5 chance of its being true. There seems to be no offhand reason why we should adopt a more stringent standard for truth than for falsity, or vice versa.

The notion of 50–50 used to play a rather dominant role in statistical work. The probable error, the middle 50% range, used to be much calculated and much quoted. If a person acted as though the truth were within the probable error range, he had an even chance of being right. If he were told that something was true by a person who believed in the 50–50 rule, he knew that he had at least an even chance of success if he acted on that information. More than that he did not know.

The Notion of 2 to 1

The 50–50 rule (consequences aside) seems to be a good rule if we must act as though something is either true or false. But sometimes a third act is available. This is the act associated with "I don't know." Thus a person can conceive of *three* conclusions he might make about an event: True, False, Do not Know. What is more natural, then (consequences aside), than to divide the probability scale into three equal parts? If the probability is less than .33, the event is called false, if it is more than .67, it is called true, and if the probability is between .33 and .67, the evidence is inconclusive. Thus when we call something true by this rule, we believe that there is at least a 2 to 1 chance that it is true, and similarly when we call something false. The rest of the time we say we do not know.

This rule is being used far more than we realize. It so happens that "the mean plus and minus one standard deviation" covers about 2/3 of the cases if a distribution is normal or nearly so. Many people make conclusions from evidence by stating the one standard deviation limits, thus suggesting that an action based on such a conclusion has a 2 to 1 chance of being right. We hesitate to decide whether the popularity of the 2 to 1 rule is because of the logic of the 2 to 1 or because of the aura of respectability that has come to surround the standard deviation.

The Rule of Modesty or of Conservatism

As soon as we admit the possibility that we find the evidence inconclusive, we open the door to the possibility of attaining a reputation by demonstrating that humbleness and modesty are also useful traits. We worry so much about drawing hasty, premature, and ill-founded conclusions that we end up drawing practically no conclusions unless the evidence is overwhelming, or at least we think we are drawing no conclusions. As a matter of fact, life's problems press in on us in such a way that the decision of "no conclusion" is nothing more than a decision to continue the old policies in effect. There is nothing inherently wrong in this, but it is important to know that that is what we are doing when we "postpone" a decision until more evidence comes in. Most of us derive considerable comfort in the continuance of the familiar routines. We require rather substantial contrary evidence before we abandon old ways. We are very likely to become quite "scientific" and demand "proof" before we make any "hasty and ill-founded" conclusions. For example, the evidence that has linked cancer to cigarette smoking has done more to stimulate a scientific attitude among smokers than anything they ever learned in a science course in school. The subtleties of argument that people have been able to deduce to cast doubt on the cancer-causing hypothesis would do justice to some of the world's most profound philosophers who have tried to discover the real meaning of truth. Some have let their scientific enthusiasm run so high that they have finally decided that they have proved that nothing is true!

The application of the rule of modesty generally leads to the requirement of odds in the neighborhood of 9 to 1, or 19 to 1, or 99 to 1, etc., before we label something as true, or false. There is no particular magic in these numbers, although we might think so if we are superstitious about 9's. Actually, they developed out of a round number philosophy. Equivalent statements would be 1 out of 10, 1 out of 20, and 1 out of 100. Why 1 out of 50, or 49 to 1, never attained currency is a useful subject of research for a psychologist.

Unless we leave this section with the idea that we have been making sport with this modesty rule, we remind ourselves that it is not obstinacy that causes most of us to adopt the slogan that "a bird in the hand is worth two in the bush." It is just that we have learned that it is a good idea to get odds before we risk something *we already have* for something we *"might get."* This is just another way of saying that we really find it impossible to leave consequences aside. The people who already have something are generally less inclined to experiment to get more than are those who do not have anything to lose. Nonsmokers find it much easier to accept the notion of a link between cigarettes and cancer than do smokers and tobacco companies. What is surprising is not that this is so but that people seem to be surprised that it is so.

The "It Is So Because It Cannot Be Proved It Is Not" Rule, or Vice Versa

Some people have rather badly misinterpreted what we have called the modesty rule. They have accepted the stringent requirement that the apparent odds be quite high before they can be persuaded to change a belief or an hypothesis. Unfortunately, however, they have not always been too careful in their initial selection of hypotheses. (Or, perhaps they have been very careful, but very subtle!)

The misinterpretation stems from the notion of the *null hypothesis*, a notion that has had considerable prominence in statistical work. Originally this notion referred to an hypothesis that stated that "there is *no* difference between these two phenomena." For example, let us suppose that we are testing the effectiveness of two different types of advertising copy. We initially adopt the hypothesis that *there is no real difference between the effectiveness of the two types of copy.* We then collect evidence which shows any *observed* differences in effectiveness. But, of course, we well know that there would be some observed differences in sample evidence even though there was no *real* difference. We liken the situation to that of drawing playing cards out of a deck. In this case we happen to know that two decks of cards are identical, hence we are not misled into believing that the cards have higher numbers in one deck than in the other because we happened to *observe two samples* of five cards each which showed higher numbers from one deck than from the other. We brush off such an observed difference as due to chance and continue to believe that *there is no difference between the two decks.* An analogous line of reasoning tells us to brush off an observed difference between advertising copies as due to chance unless the chance is so low that it would be imprudent to count on it. For example, if the observed difference could have occurred by chance only .01 times on the hypothesis of "no difference," we might be pardoned for abandoning the hypothesis of "no difference." Of course, as soon as we abandon an hypothesis of "no difference," we automatically have adopted one of "some difference." (The determination of the size of the "some" was a neglected problem for many years.)

Thus the adjective null was appropriate (null means "nothing"). The attendant notion that we should not abandon a null hypothesis unless the odds were at least 9 to 1 is obviously a very conservative rule. Such a rule provides us with a very strong presumption to treat things as though they were the same unless we have rather strong evidence that they are different. This rule is practiced quite widely in American life. Our concept of democracy has strong leanings towards treating people as though they were the same unless there are definite reasons to the contrary.

A person might grant the practical logic in the notion of the null hypothesis with a conservative rejection rule without, however, granting the logic of its extension to cover all kinds of hypotheses. As so often happens with such things, the original meaning of the null hypothesis has been lost over the years. Some people now treat all hypotheses as though they were null hypotheses. They use the conservative rejection rule and naturally have trouble refuting their hypotheses. They take what to them is the next logical step and argue that we should act as though the hypothesis is true because we have not been able to clearly demonstrate its falsity. This is a dangerous practice. What very often happens is that the evidence is so scanty that we should hesitate strongly to say any more than "we do not know." It really is not at all difficult to dream up all sorts of hypotheses that cannot be proved false. To then call these true must be some sort of nonsense. Similarly, it is not at all difficult to dream up all sorts of hypotheses that cannot be proved true. Lack of overwhelming proof certainly does not make them false, however.

9.6 The Policy We Follow in Drawing Conclusions from Evidence

We leave the hiring and firing of vice presidents to presidents. Our task is the more modest one of estimating the probabilities that are appropriate to the given facts. We lack the knowledge that is essential to the setting up of appropriate consequence matrixes. We have shown the mechanics of deriving a pay-off matrix, or a decision matrix, from the underlying probability and consequence matrixes in order to clarify the role that is played by the probability estimates. Although we are convinced that probability calculations should play a very important role in decision-making, whether in business, politics, military strategy, personal life, etc., and probably an expanding role, we are equally convinced that the probabilities are not the whole story. We must always accept personal responsibility for our decisions. To take refuge in statistical formulas to justify decisions is to abdicate our responsibilities. Such abdication would also mean that we would have failed to utilize in our decisions that great welter of accumulated experience, both conscious and unconscious, that as yet has not yielded to reasonably precise quantification. In fact, most of the great historical decisions that have been made that have affected the future of nations and companies probably never would have been supported by a rational consideration of the probabilities.

Our discussion in subsequent pages concentrates almost exclusively on the problems of estimating probabilities. Our frequent references to practical affairs should be interpreted as attempts to link our calculations to such affairs, not to provide a complete decision-making mechanism for dealing with such affairs.

9.7 Confidence Intervals—Abbreviated Probability Distributions

Up to this time we have emphasized the importance of estimating the *entire* probability distribution of the value of some unknown event, such as the proportion of the people who prefer Smoothies. To report only *part* of this distribution tends to prejudice the final decisions to some extent because any user must then confine his analysis to only those parts that are presented. For example, if we state that the evidence supports the statement that we are 90%

confident that Smoothies' share of market lies between .21 and .36 (see Table 9.1 for data that support this statement), the president is automatically restricted in the kinds of decisions he can make. When a statistician has made such a report, he has implicitly usurped some of the president's decision-making function. The president is probably in no position to supplement such probability statements. He will tend to accept the word of the statistician for what it is worth. Sometimes such statements are not worth very much, and some presidents are smart enough to know it.

The practice of summarizing a probability distribution by some simple *confidence interval* like the above is much more common than is the practice of reporting the whole distribution. Both statisticians and decision-makers have been at fault for the fostering of this practice. Statisticians have been handicapped by the apparently great difficulties that have stood in the way of the development of rational procedures for estimating all the required probabilities. The flavor of some of these difficulties is apparent in the preceding chapters. Hence there developed a willingness to accept the notion that rational confidence statements were legitimate at the same time that the notion of a complete probability distribution was rejected. It is easy to look back and wonder about a logic that permitted us to take any part of a probability distribution but which forbade our putting all the parts together.

Decision-makers also contributed to the fostering of this practice of reporting abbreviated probability distributions in the form of confidence intervals, mostly because they were human beings, as were the statisticians too. As we know, a good deal of administration theory is designed to pinpoint the responsibility for decision-making. Human beings in general, however, seem to have a distaste for making unpleasant decisions, particularly decisions that involve firing people, dismissing students, and the like. Hence decision-makers are often very happy to point the finger of responsibility away from themselves. Since other people will resist if the finger is pointed at them, the best place to point is at some inanimate object, like a confidence interval. This is particularly useful if the object is surrounded with an aura of scientific respectability. A pre-set confidence interval is very handy to make a decision that is "forced on us by the facts." Of course, confidence intervals that do not support the desired decision frequently get disqualified on the grounds of "biased sample," "errors in measurement," "not the whole picture," etc. Statisticians were often human enough to be somewhat thrilled that their results were being used to make important decisions. Their feelings when their results were ignored or ridiculed were often not expressible.

The preceding remarks may lead to the belief that confidence intervals, or abbreviated probability distributions, have no proper place in high-level practical statistical work. This is not true, however. They definitely do have a place; but their place should not dominate the scene. The practical necessity to estimate the range within which some value probably falls has been recognized for centuries. Engineers have been concerned with this problem under the name of tolerance limits. Although it is true that engineers have sometimes implicitly assumed that all or practically all of their products should fall within their tolerance limits, practical experience usually revealed some failures. In fact, this predilection of engineers for 100% or practically 100% confidence intervals has probably had a considerable effect on the general popularity of relatively high confidence coefficients (the 90%, or 99%, etc., is known as a *confidence coefficient*). Engineering and production problems have played a significant role in the development of rules of thumb in practical statistical work. Many of these rules have been borrowed for other applications with little regard for their origins and their practical meaning.

The important thing for us to keep in mind is that the selection of a proper abbreviation from a probability distribution should be made with explicit consideration given to the appropriate consequence matrix. There is no particular trick to the *calculation* of a 60% interval vs. a 90% interval. The practical problem is the decision of which to calculate. So now let us get to the task of calculating confidence intervals on the assumption that we have been told which coefficients we should use.

Calculating a Confidence Interval: Use of Tables of The Cumulative Binomial Probabilities

Suppose we have a random sample of 40 items with a p of .25. What limits should we set on π_I so that we can be 90% confident that the true π falls within the limits?

We assume that we are satisfied if there is no more than a .05 chance that the true π is above our upper limit and no more than a .05 chance that it is below our lower limit. Since the distribution is skewed, this is not the same as requiring the 90% to cover the smallest possible range, although the difference between the two possible intervals is negligible.

Our approach to this problem is illustrated in Fig. 9.1. Part A shows how we locate the value of the *lower limit* to the interval, called π_{I_L}. The sample p of .25 is taken as a *fixed point* along the horizontal axis. We then search for a π_I that will generate a distribution of p's so that there is a .05 probability of getting a p of .25 or larger. Suppose that π_H is such a π and the pictured curve is the generated distribution. The shaded area to the right of $p = .25$ would then contain .05 of the area under the curve. An examination of the table of the cumulative binomial for $r = 10$ (equivalent of $p = .25$) and $n = 40$ reveals that the appropriate hypothetical π lies between .14 and .15. If we make a linear interpolation, we find that an appropriate π_{I_L} is

$$.14 + \frac{.05 - .0453}{.0672 - .0453} \times .01 = .142.$$

We can now state that $P(p \geq .25 \mid \pi_H = .142, n = 40) = .05$. Then, following the rule of inverse probabilities used in Chapters 7 and 8, we turn this statement around to read $P(\pi_I \leq .142 \mid p = .25, n = 40, \pi_H) = .05$.

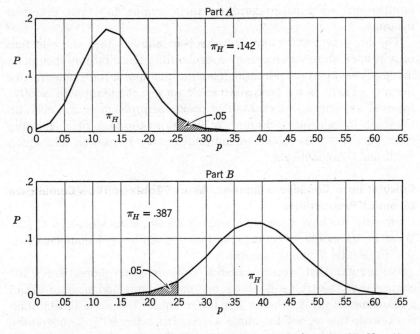

Fig. 9.1 Estimating a 90% confidence interval: given that $p = .25$, $N = 40$.

Part B of Fig. 9.1 illustrates the same argument for determining the *upper limit* to the interval. We are now concerned with the probability of getting a sample p of *.25 or less* given some value of π_H, and we wish this probability to be .05. The use of the binomial table is not straight-forward this time. The table shows the probabilities for a given *r-value or more*. We wish the probabilities for a given *r-value or less*. First we note that the probability of r of *11 or more* is the same as *1 minus the probability of 10 or less*. For example, the table tells us that the probability of an r of 11 or more is .4161 if $\pi_H = .25$. Hence it follows by subtraction that the probability of 10 or less must be $1 - .4161$, or .5839.

If this characteristic of the table is fixed in our minds, we can now see that we look in the column for $r = 11$, $n = 40$ until we find the nearest figure to .95. We find that .95 would fall between a π_H of .38 and .39. Using a linear interpolation as before, we estimate π_H as

$$.38 + \frac{.95 - .9400}{.9537 - .9400} \times .01 = .387.$$

From this we state that $P(\pi_I \geq .387 \,|\, p = .25,\ n = 40,\ \pi_H) = .05$. We put these two statements together and say that there is a .90 probability that π_I falls between .142 and .387 given the evidence of a sample of 40 with a p of .25. Note that the lower limit is closer to .25 than is the upper limit. This is caused by the fact that the upper limit was based on a variance of $.387 \times .613$, which is larger than the variance used for the lower limit, which was $.142 \times .858$.

The limits of .142 and .387 are known as conservative limits. They actually cover more than 90% of the inference distribution and are made conservative because we treat p as though it were a *discrete* variable. When we calculated the probability of an r of 10 or more, we included the full range of the 10, which really runs from 9.5 to 10.5. This is the same problem we noted in Chapter 8, and which we illustrated in Fig. 8.5. To adjust for this conservatism we would have to subtract half of the probability associated with $r = 10$ from our cumulative probabilities. Table 9.9 shows the procedure.

This adjustment contracts the intervals from .142—.387 to .151—.376. Most people would probably rather accept the conservatism than the tedium of the adjustment. It is important to remember, however, that this adjustment can be quite important if N is moderately small. We discovered as much in Chapter 8 when we were working on the entire inference distribution instead of just selected parts of it as we are doing here.

TABLE 9.9

Adjusting Confidence Intervals for Conservatism
Given: $p = .25$, $n = 40$. Wanted: 90% Confidence Interval of π

(1) π_H	(2) $P(p \geq .25\,|\pi_H)$	(3) $P(p \leqq .25\,|\pi_H)$	(4) $P(p = .25\,|\pi_H)$	(5) $\frac{1}{2} \times$ (4)	(6) $P(p > .25\,|\pi_H)$	Interpolations
.15	.0672		.0373	.0186	.0486	$.15 + \dfrac{.05 - .0486}{.0702 - .0486} \times .01$
.16	.0952		.0499	.0250	.0702	$= .151$
					$P(p < .25\,|\pi_H)$	
.37		.0768	.0389	.0194	.0574	$.38 - \dfrac{.05 - .0442}{.0574 - .0442} \times .01$
·38		.0600	.0315	.0158	.0442	$= .376$

Calculating a Confidence Interval: Use of a Normal Curve With Symmetrical Limits

With a sample as large as 40 and with p in the neighborhood of .25, we might find that the normal curve will make a reasonable approximation to the 90% confidence interval of π. Our first task is to estimate the standard deviation of the universe, and from that the standard deviation of the sample p's. Since the only information we have about the standard deviation of the universe is that supplied by the sample, we use the sample standard deviation as the basis of our best estimate. We say "basis" because we must adjust the sample standard deviation for the fact that sample standard deviations are in general too small in the sense that the arithmetic mean of all sample standard deviations is less than the standard deviation of the universe. The adjustment can be made as follows:

$$\sigma^2 = s^2 \, \frac{N}{N-1}.$$

Thus in our problem we get an estimate of σ^2, called $\hat{\sigma}^2$, of

$$.25 \times .75 \, \frac{40}{40-1} = .1923.$$

We estimate the standard deviation of sample p's by the formula

$$\hat{\sigma}_p = \sqrt{\frac{\hat{\sigma}^2}{N}} = .069.$$

Note that the above two operations involved first a multiplication by N and then a division by N. If we combine these two formulas, we can eliminate this multiplication and division. Thus we would get

$$\hat{\sigma}_p = \sqrt{\frac{s^2}{N-1}} = \sqrt{\frac{.25 \times .75}{40-1}} = .069.$$

Figure 9.2 illustrates the line of reasoning we will now follow. In fact, it illustrates two lines of reasoning. Since we get the same answer in either case, we can exercise our preference. Part A illustrates the case in which we are really using the sample information as the basis of generating a probability or inference distribution of the unknown universe π. This is the process some people object to because they do not like to think about an unknown universe value as though it were a random variable. If we agree with this objection, we would prefer the line of reasoning as exhibited in Part B.

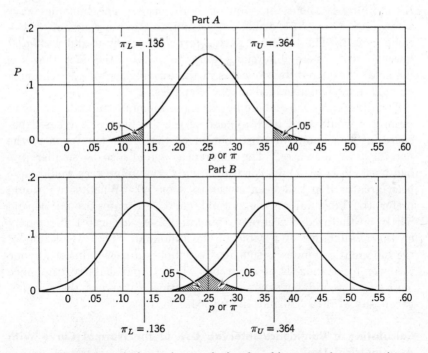

Fig. 9.2 Illustration of alternative methods of making normal curve estimates of the 90% confidence interval. (Note: These curves are not drawn to strict scales.)

The vertical lines are drawn through Parts A and B to make it clear that both methods give precisely the same values for π_L and π_U.

Just as when we were using the binomial, we wish to find values for π_L and π_U so that the excluded areas (shaded in the charts) contain .05 of the cases, respectively. We now search the normal curve table for the value of Z that will cut off .05 of the tail of the normal curve. $[Z = (\pi - p)/\sigma_p]$ We find that the appropriate Z is 1.645. If we substitute this value in the equation $Z = (\pi - p)/\sigma_p$, we get $1.645 = (\pi - .25)/.069$. This gives a value for π_U of .364.

A simple rearrangement of terms makes it possible to express this formula as

$$\pi_U = p + Z\sigma_p.$$

The value for π_L is similarly calculated from the formula $\pi_L = p - Z\sigma_p$, resulting in an answer of .136.

If we compare the normal curve approximations to those we derived earlier from the binomial, we find the differences to be just about what we would expect. The range between the upper and lower limits is about the same in both cases. The binomial gave a range of $.376 - .151$, or .225. The normal gave a range of $.364 - .136$, or .228. The binomial gave a *larger* upper limit and a *smaller* lower limit. These differences were caused by the fact that the binomial considered the *skewness* in the distribution of π_I. The normal curve method averaged out the skewness.

The differences shown here between the binomial and normal curve estimates would tend to disappear as the sample size increased because, as you know, the distribution of the mean (p) tends to the normal as N increases. The differences would also be smaller if p had been closer to .5 and, correspondingly, the differences would have been greater if p had been closer to 0 or 1.0. Whether we would prefer the binomial or the normal curve estimates would depend partly on the needed accuracy (binomial more accurate) and partly on the availability of a table of the binomial. The calculation of the binomial estimates is sufficiently tedious to cause almost anyone to lower his standards of accuracy. This is particularly true since most of us would not know what practical difference there is between, say, .151 to .376 and .136 to .364.

Calculating a Confidence Interval: Use of the Normal Curve With Asymmetrical Limits

In the above application of the normal curve we made a *single estimate* of the standard deviation of p based on the value of p itself. We know, however, that the standard deviation of p is really a function of the unknown π. Since the unknown π might have all sorts of values, the standard deviation of p also might have all sorts of values, in fact, one value for each of the possible π values. For example, we obtained an upper limit of .364 for π in the preceding section. Using this in the formula

$$\sigma_p = \sqrt{\frac{\pi - \pi^2}{N}},$$

we get a σ_p of .076. [Note that we use N instead of $N - 1$ because here we are working with the *universe* proportion (albeit assumed).] Similarly we would get a σ_p of .054 with our lower limit of π of .136. Our single estimate had a value of .069.

If we wish, we might use a value of σ_p to get the *upper* limit of π that is appropriate for this π. We would do likewise for the lower limit of π. Since we cannot calculate σ_p until we know π_L and π_U, we must estimate σ_p, π_L, and π_U simultaneously. The procedure is to replace the σ_p in the formula $\pi = p + Z\sigma_p$ with the value of σ_p as expressed in terms of π. Doing this, we get

$$\pi = p + Z\sqrt{\frac{\pi - \pi^2}{N}}.$$

(Note that $\pi\tau$ is the same as $\pi - \pi^2$.) A little rearrangement of this expression and the application of the formula for the solution of a quadratic equation results in the somewhat formidable-looking

$$\pi_I = \frac{Z^2 + 2Np \pm \sqrt{(Z^2 + 2Np)^2 - 4Np^2(Z^2 + N)}}{2(Z^2 + N)}.$$

If we substitute in this expression the values given in our problem, we get

$$\left[\frac{1.645^2 + 2 \times 40 \times .25 \pm \sqrt{(1.645^2 + 2 \times 40 \times .25)^2 - 4 \times 40 \times .25^2(1.645^2 + 40)}}{2(1.645^2 + 40)} \right],$$

and subsequently values for π_I of .376 and .156.

Calculating a Confidence Interval: Comparison of Results from Alternative Methods

To facilitate comparison of the various results we have derived in our efforts to estimate the 90% confidence limits of π, we have

Method	Interval	
	π_L	π_U
A. Discrete binomial	.142	.387
B. Continuous binomial	.151	.376
C. Symmetrical normal	.136	.364
D. Asymmetrical normal	.156	.376

gathered all our results together in Table 9.10. We assume that Method B gives the most correct result. It is interesting to note that Method D gives the same upper limit as Method B but too high a lower limit. This is as we would expect. The upper limit is determined from a distribution centered on .376 and with a variance of $.376 \times .624$. With $N = 40$, we would expect the normal approximation to the binomial to be quite good, and it is. The lower limit is determined from a distribution centered on .151 or .156 and with a variance of $.151 \times .849$ or $.156 \times .844$. The normal curve tends to be a relatively poor approximation to the binomial when π varies this much from .50, even with N as large as 40. The error in the approximation is always on the side of making the interval too short.

Differences like those shown in Table 9.10 would tend to get greater the smaller the sample size and the more p varied from .5. Conversely, all of these methods tend to give the same answers as N increases and as p gets closer to .5. The choice we make among the methods depends on the degree of accuracy apparently required by our problem and on the availability of calculation aids such as tables and desk calculators. Method C is clearly the least accurate, but it is also clearly the easiest to do if tables of the binomial are unavailable.

9.8 Hypothesis Testing, or Tests of Significance

It is a well-known fact that all of us, including the lower animals, make decisions and regulate our behavior according to what we believe to be true. The hungry squirrel will dig in the ground in the early spring looking for the nuts he believes are there, either because he believes he buried some in the fall or because he believes other squirrels buried some; or maybe he digs because his mother taught him to dig when he was hungry. At any rate, the squirrel has a problem if he does not find a reasonable number of nuts as a result of his first efforts. He might assume that he is not finding many nuts because he is just unlucky. If he reacts this way, he retains his hypothesis that there really are some nuts and continues his digging, maybe even with redoubled effort.

On the other hand, he might decide that he is not finding many nuts because there are not many nuts to be found. In this case he rejects the original hypothesis that started him to digging. What he does thereafter will depend on what kind of a squirrel he is: he may dig in another area, he may try to steal from other squirrels, he may just lie down and die, etc. As a matter of fact, his quickness to abandon his hypothesis that there are some nuts will also depend on what kind of a squirrel he is and on what other options he has for finding food other than by digging. A lazy squirrel, for example, would have a strong tendency to quickly abandon any hypothesis that involved the work of digging. A squirrel who got pleasure out of digging might continue with the "dig for food" hypothesis long after any reasonable squirrel would have abandoned it for other hypotheses.

To a statistician, testing a hypothesis means merely to *calculate the probability* that some observed sample events could have occurred *if the hypothesis is true*. It does not mean to determine whether the hypothesis is right or wrong, or whether we should act as though it is right or wrong. Whether we should believe that an hypothesis is right or wrong depends on more than the simple probability that a given set of events could have occurred if the hypothesis is true. Just as in the case of the squirrel, what we should believe also depends on the other options available and on what kind of people we are.

The Routine of Hypothesis Testing

The procedure for testing an hypothesis has five clearly distinguishable steps. They are:

1. State the *hypothesis* or belief that is to be tested. This is really a statement of the *universe conditions*. For example, the president of the Smoothies Company might state the hypothesis:
    35% of all the people prefer Smoothies.

2. Consult and clearly specify the available *evidence*. For example, the president notes that:

> 28 people out of a sample of 100 people express a preference for Smoothies.

3. Specify any *assumptions* needed to make it possible to estimate the probability that the given *sample* evidence could have been generated by the *hypothetical universe*. For example, the president might assume:

    a. The sample of 100 was essentially *random*. This would be random in the sense that nobody involved with the problem is able to discern any correlation between the selection procedure and the likelihood of a preference for Smoothies.

    b. The distribution of sample means is reasonably well approximated by a normal curve. (The president might just as well assume that it is not and hence require the greater accuracy of a binomial estimate.)

4. *Calculate the probability* that the given sample evidence could have occurred if the hypothesis is true. For example, in the market share problem we would calculate the probability of a *sample p of .28 or lower* from a universe with a π of .35. The normal curve approximation to this probability is .07. (We discuss the calculation of this below.)

5. Make a *decision* about the hypothesis. This decision would depend on such things as:

    a. The probability just calculated. The smaller the calculated probability, the less attractive does the hypothesis become.

    b. The *practical availability* of alternative hypotheses that would be associated with higher probabilities. For example, if the president feels that he must believe that the true market share is either as high as 35% or it is as low as 25%, he would be much more likely to hang on to the 35% notion than he would if it were practical to believe that the market share was in the neighborhood of 30%. (We may wonder why the president would ever box himself in so that his only options were 35% and 25%. This is a good question and well worth further thought. Review the number of times we have done something or said something in the past that had the effect of severely restricting our available options and thus forced us to choose between options that would seem quite silly to someone without our background. People, business firms, and nations all have "hostages to fortune" that tie their hands, as it were, as they face the developing future.)

    c. The consequence matrix for the available options. This is not usually as easy to specify quantitatively as we implied when we used one in our simple decision-making model. Actually the *consequence* of any event is also subject to uncertainty just as the *event itself* is. For example, we are uncertain as to *whether we will* have lung cancer before our 60th birthday. But let us suppose we were *certain* that we would. We would still be *uncertain about the consequences* to us of getting lung cancer. We may believe, for example, that medical progress may be such that lung cancer will be no worse than tuberculosis by the time we have it. It is obvious that *our hypotheses about the consequences* will have something to do with our willingness to hold certain *hypotheses about events* that are associated with such consequences.

The Mechanics of Calculating the Probability Associated with a Given Hypothesis and with Given Sample Events

We have already calculated probabilities so many times that it is fair to state that what follows is a simple review of things we have done before. Let us take the problem of the president of the Smoothies Company. He believes that Smoothies' market share is 35%. What are the chances of getting only 28 people out of a random sample of 100 who express a preference for Smoothies *if* the market share really is 35%?

We first calculate the standard deviation of the sample p's for samples of 100 *from a universe with a π of .35*. This is

$$\sigma_p = \sqrt{\frac{\pi\tau}{N}},$$

or

$$\sqrt{\frac{.35 \times .65}{100}},$$

and hence .0477. We then find out how many of these σ_p's it takes to reach from .35 down to .28. It takes $(.35 - .28)/.0477$, or 1.468 of them. This is the value of Z for use in finding normal curve probabilities. The normal curve table shows that there is a .07 probability of getting a sample p this far below the universe mean.

Figure 9.3 pictures what we have done. We have erected a normal curve based on a π of .35 and with a standard deviation of .0477. The shaded area is that part of the lower tail of this curve that falls below .28. Hence we can now say that there is a probability of .07 (within the limits of a normal curve approximation) of getting a sample of 100 with 28 or fewer Smoothies adherents even though 35% of all the people prefer Smoothies. (The binomial distribution would show a probability of .08 instead of .07.)

9.9 Routine Hypothesis Testers

The burden of decision-making is so great on all of us, whether in personal, business, social, political, etc. affairs, that we are often

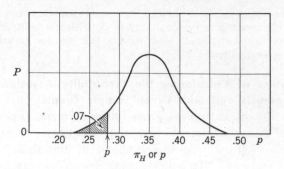

Fig. 9.3 Probability of getting a random sample p of .28 or less if π_H equals .35 and N equals 100 (normal curve approximation).

willing to pay a small price to lighten this burden. The rewards that flow from the development of routine decision-makers can be quite substantial both from the point of view of getting the job done and from the easing of anxiety. Consider, for example, the problem of deciding whether it is safe to drive our car through an intersection. In the absence of traffic lights, stop signs, yield right of way signs, etc. we would have to approach the intersection with considerable caution. We would have to be alert to the capabilities of our car to stop, to turn, to accelerate, etc., and to the possible appearance of a car on our right, our left, in back of us (the fellow in back may be assuming we are not going to slow down). It does not take much imagination to realize that modern automobile traffic would be an impossibility without the lights to tell us when "it is safe" to cross. The benefits from our lighting system are so great that most of us do not fret about the times when we can clearly see that it is safe but the light is red and says "no." (Pedestrians seem to have much less respect for the decisions of the lights than do drivers.)

The primary *mechanical requirement* of a routine decision-maker, or hypothesis tester, is an unambiguous system of signaling. The signal may be a particular color, a particular number, a bell, etc. Frequently it is sufficient to have a signal solely to *reject* the operating hypothesis. The absence of any signal means "leave well enough alone." For example, many automobiles no longer have an oil pressure gauge. It has been replaced with a red light that lights only when the oil pressure has fallen below a predetermined safe level.

The primary *philosophical requirement* is a willingness to tolerate a certain amount of error or variation in the phenomenon we are dealing with. The best way to handle this philosophical problem is to *ignore* the tolerable variation after we have made up our mind that it is economic to not try to control it. If we continue to worry about it after we had presumably decided that it was tolerable, we have not as yet achieved the primary benefit from a routine decision-maker, namely, the need to no longer *think* about that decision problem. This is what businessmen mean when they say that they make a decision and then *forget* about *that* problem. What we do, in effect, is to make a decision about a *system* for decision-making, and we have to have enough sense to then let the system do the deciding.

It is surprisingly difficult to devise a decision-making system and trust the system to make the decisions. Most people seem to have an almost uncontrollable urge to *try to beat their own system*. This means that the system never really has a chance to be fairly tested. The system is allowed to make the decision only when it agrees with what the person would decide if he did not have a system. All other times the system is overruled. This very often happens when a system is first installed. The person who formerly made the decisions quite naturally has serious doubts that a so-called mechanical monster can do at least as well as he did, or even well enough to justify releasing his mental energies for other more important tasks. So the mechanical decisions are checked very carefully. Naturally the machine makes mistakes that would be obvious to any reasonably intelligent person, just as the intersection light is sometimes red when any one can see that the intersection is likely to be clear for the next 30 seconds. These mistakes are recounted with great glee. What is even worse, the machine is sometimes prevented from making such obvious mistakes, and, in fact, the same decision-making process as before is in effect.

9.10 Predicting the Performance of a Routine Decision-maker—The Operating Characteristic Curve

Let us suppose that a simple routine decision-maker of the following kind has been installed to control the operation of an automatic machine:

a. Every 1000 cycles of the machine a sample of 10 pieces is taken off in the order in which the machine produces them.
b. These pieces are immediately measured for length on a "go, no-go" gauge which tells whether or not the piece is shorter than some specified maximum length.

c. If *two or fewer* of the 10 pieces fail to pass the test, the process is allowed to continue operating; if *three or more* pieces are too long, the process is stopped and an adjustment is made on the machine.

(We can easily see the stimulation such a system would provide to devise a machine to take the sample, test it, and make the needed adjustment in the basic production machine.)

The engineers assure us that a sample of 10 so selected would be reasonably random.

The quality of the output of this machine depends on the universe proportion of defectives and the luck we have with the samples. It is useful to ask the question of the probability that this process will be stopped for adjustment under various hypotheses about the universe proportion of defectives. Figure 9.4 shows the *operating characteristic curve* of this decision system. Along the horizontal axis we show the various hypotheses we might make about the universe being generated by this machine. The vertical axis shows the probability of getting a sample of 10 with three or more defectives. The curve describes this probability for the various π_H's.

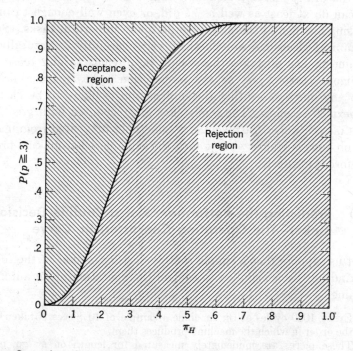

Fig. 9.4 Operating characteristic curve showing the performance of a decision rule that stops a machine whenever a sample of 10 shows three or more defects.

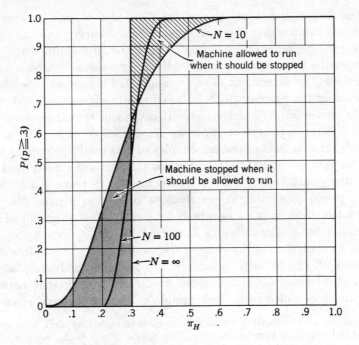

Fig. 9.5 Operating characteristic curves for decision rule based alternatively on samples of 10 items, 100 items, and on the whole universe.

This curve shows that there is a .50 chance that the machine will be stopped if the process is producing 26% defectives and, correspondingly, a .50 chance that it will be allowed to run. It is clear that the higher the proportion of defectives the more likely the machine is to be stopped. For example, there is a probability of .9 of stopping the machine if the universe proportion is .42.

The region to the left of the curve is called the *acceptance region* because it represents the probabilities of getting two or fewer defectives in a sample of 10. The region to the right is called the *rejection region* because it represents the probabilities of getting three or more defectives.

The fact that this decision system is relatively loose is made apparent if we consult Fig. 9.5. Here we also show the operating characteristic curve for a decision system based on a sample of *100*. Suppose that if we knew what quality the machine was producing, we would stop the machine whenever it was producing at more than a 30% rate of defectives. Such knowledge would be indicated by a vertical line on the chart at $\pi_H = .30$. The *dotted* area between the "complete information operating characteristic curve" and the "$N = 10$ operating characteristic curve" shows the probabilities the machine would be stopped even though the process was producing no more than 30% defectives. The *cross-hatched* area shows the probabilities that the process will be allowed to run even though it is producing more than 30% defectives. It is evident that these areas are much less for a sample of 100 than for a sample of 10. It is also obvious that the cost of testing samples of 100 would be greater than that for samples of 10.[1] (It is worth noting parenthetically that the operating characteristic curves shown in Figs. 9.4 and 9.5 indicate that a process operating at exactly 30% defectives is more likely to be stopped than it is to be allowed to run. This may offend our common sense. The difficulty is caused by the *discrete* series. If we try to control at 30%, we have the problem of what to do with a sample with exactly 30% defectives. In a sample of 10, and with a continuous series, 30% defectives would really represent between 25% and 35% defectives. In a sample of 100, 30% would represent

---

[1] Mathematical methods of balancing the costs of collecting more information against the estimated benefits are beyond the scope of this book. Such methods are a part of a rapidly developing attempt to quantify more and more of the decision-making process in business. The most recently published large-scale effort in this area is Robert Schlaifer's book on *Probability and Statistics for Business Decisions,* McGraw-Hill Book Company, New York, 1959. Schlaifer is actually quite critical of much of the earlier work that had been done on such things as operating characteristic curves, hypothesis testing, Type I and Type II errors (discussed below), etc. Nevertheless it appears likely that many of Schlaifer's recommendations will develop to be supplementary to rather than in replacement of many of these things he criticized.

If interested in these and related developments, look at some of the following essentially nonmathematical treatments. (The mathematical demands of Schlaifer's book are also quite modest.)

Bross, Irwin D. J., *Design for Decision,* The Macmillan Company, New York, 1953.

Chernoff, Herman and Moses, Lincoln E., *Elementary Decision Theory,* John Wiley and Sons, New York, 1959.

Luce, R. Duncan, and Raiffa, Howard, *Games and Decisions,* John Wiley and Sons, New York, 1957.

Williams, J. D., *The Compleat Strategyst,* McGraw-Hill Book Company, New York, 1954. (Williams writes in a sufficiently light vein to make a trip through his book somewhat fun—of the sort possible within the limits of a reasonably rigorous treatment.)

Raiffa and Schlaifer have also collaborated on a book that provides much of the mathematical argument that lies behind Schlaifer's book. It is not recommended for someone who is not mathematically sophisticated. Its title: *Applied Statistical Decision Theory,* Harvard Business School, Boston, 1961.

between 29.5% and 30.5%. We have arbitrarily decided to follow the conservative rule and classify the *whole range* represented by 30% as a *rejection area*. We might just as well have classified it as an *acceptance area*. Or, if we wished, we might adopt a decision system such that the occurrence of exactly 30% defectives in a sample tells us to "toss a coin." If it comes up heads, we stop the machine; if tails, we let it run. Thus, in the long run we should find it about equally probable that we will stop the machine or let it run if $p = 30\%$.)

9.11 Type I vs. Type II Errors

It is clear from the operating characteristic curves shown in Figs. 9.4 and 9.5 that there are times when our routine decision-maker will stop the machine when it should let it run, and let it run when it should stop it. We might add that the same thing will happen if the decision is being made by the operator. In fact, this problem is a characteristic of all *two-choice* problems when *we do not know for certain* what choice we should make. This is, of course, why innocent men sometimes go to jail and why guilty men sometimes go free.

The convention is to call it a Type I error when we *reject the truth*. More exactly, we are really talking about some *hypothesis* we have made. For example, if we had set up the hypothesis that the machine is producing satisfactorily (no more than 30% defectives, say), but we then *stopped* the machine on the basis of sample information, we would have exposed ourselves to a Type I error. We might just as well have set up the hypothesis that the machine is *not* producing satisfactorily. We would then expose ourselves to a Type I error if we let the machine *run* on the basis of some sample information.

We make a Type II error whenever we *accept a falsehood*, or whenever we retain a false hypothesis.

An additional convention has been established of always selecting the hypothesis to be tested that is *strongly preferred*. This preference may be a result of accumulated experience with the phenomenon which leads us to believe that it really is true; or it may be a preference growing out of some general moral, political, social, etc., philosophy. For example, the American judicial system requires that an accused person be *presumed innocent*. The *hypothesis of innocence* is thus the one that is being tested by the evidence of the trial.

Thus we see that a Type I error generally consists of rejecting something that we have a strong prior reason to believe is true, or of rejecting something that we *prefer* to believe is true. It is not surprising that it takes substantial evidence to persuade a mother to abandon her hypothesis that her son is innocent of a murder. Thus it happens that many decision processes require probability of the Type I error to be quite small. It is not unusual for people to require this probability to be as low as .10, or .05, or .01, or even .0001. Thus our Smoothies Company president might have such a strong preference for keeping his son-in-law on the payroll that his preferred hypothesis is for a market share of 35%. Since the sample evidence created a risk of as much of .07 of rejecting this hypothesis when it was really true (a Type I error), he naturally refuses such a "large risk" and retains his hypothesis, and his son-in-law's job. The situation might be quite the reverse if his son-in-law were waiting in line for the vice president to stumble!

It should be obvious that an effort to reduce the risk of Type I error automatically increases the risk of Type II error *within the limits of a given set of evidence*. Figure 9.6 illustrates this. Here we show the various optional operating characteristics curves for controlling our machine's output on the basis of testing samples of 10. We set up the hypothesis that the machine is operating satisfactorily. (We prefer this hypothesis to the reverse one because the machine is very expensive and is also subject to rapid obsolescence. The top executives get very unhappy when they see this machine idle. Also scrap is cheap and can be reworked through the machine at moderate cost.) If we decide to stop the machine only when there are at least seven defectives, we will *almost never* stop the machine when the process is producing less than 30% defectives. (Note the negligible part of the No. 7 operating characteristic curve that is to the left of the 30% vertical line.) We would thus have reduced the Type I error to practically zero. However, in doing this, we have substantially increased the probability of letting the machine run when it is in fact producing more than 30% defectives. (Note the large amount of area between the No. 7 line and the vertical line at 30%.) Thus this decision rule (stop at seven or more defectives) will make frequent Type II errors.

The rule to stop on three or more defectives will make far fewer Type II errors than the seven or more rule. However, to achieve this reduction it is necessary to substantially increase Type I errors. The balance we choose between Type I and Type II errors depends on how we assess the consequences of each. It is a relatively simple matter to do the arithmetic of balancing if we are able to quantify the consequences satisfactorily. The important thing is the *ratio*

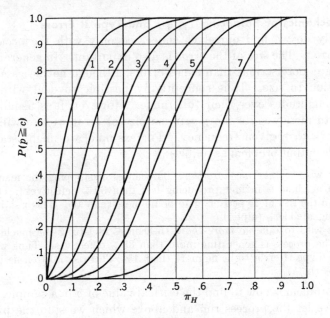

Fig. 9.6 Illustration of relationship between type I and type II errors for various decision boundaries. We assume that we wish to stop the machine if it is producing more than .30 defectives. A type I error is made when we stop the machine even though it is in fact producing *fewer than* .30 defectives. A type II error occurs when we fail to stop the machine even though it is in fact producing *more than* .30 defectives. The number attached to a given operating characteristic curve is the minimum number of defects that we will find in a sample of 10 that will cause us to stop the machine. For example, the curve labeled "3" is for the rule that tells us to stop the machine whenever we find 3 or more defects in a sample of 10.

between the consequences. If they are considered of *equal* value, we balance at odds of .5 to .5. If Type I errors are considered *three times as serious* as Type II errors, we balance at .25 to .75.

As shown in Fig. 9.5, it is possible to reduce the risk of *both* Type I and Type II errors by *increasing the sample size*. The expense of doing this must be justified by the seriousness of these errors. Again we can use our judicial system to illustrate this principle at work. It is common knowledge that a murder trial is always more protracted and considerably more expensive than a simple civil suit for the simple reason that both Type I and Type II errors are considered much more serious in a murder case than they are in a case, say, of trespass.

The Mechanics of Balancing Type I and Type II Errors

Rarely do we find ourselves concerned only with the *occurrence* of an error. The *size* of the error is also important. In general, large errors are more serious than small errors, although not necessarily in proportion to size. It is conceptually possible to deal with these error magnitudes over their full range. However, it is usually sufficient to merely state the *maximum* size of error we are willing to tolerate with a given frequency. For example, we might state our machine output problem as follows:

1. We wish to take *no more than* .05 chances of stopping the machine if the machine is in fact producing less than 30% defectives. Thus we wish the risk of Type I error to be no more than .05. This risk is often designated as α (alpha).
2. We wish to take *no more than* .15 chances of letting the machine run if the process is generating more than 35% defectives. Thus we wish the Type II error to be no more than .15. This risk is often designated as β (beta).

Our problem is now to find the critical value of p in a sample, below which we let the process run and above which we stop the process, *and also* to find the appropriate sample size. To simplify the problem somewhat, we will assume that normal curve approximations are sufficiently accurate. Otherwise trial-and-error procedures would have to be used. If more accuracy is desired, we can make a first approximation with the normal curve and then use this solution to give us a good start on a trial-and-error procedure, say, with binomial tables. Figure 9.7 illustrates our problem. We wish a value, p, so that it cuts off the *upper .05* of the normal curve centered on .30 and

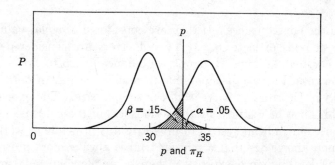

Fig. 9.7 Illustration of nature of problem of finding the unique p and N that will give us a type I error of no more than .05 and a type II error of no more than .15. (Note: Curves are not drawn to scale. They merely illustrate the line of reasoning.)

the *lower .15* of the normal curve centered on .35. We must find a sample size that will give us the unique standard deviations of sample means to accomplish this cut-off point. We can see that if our sample is *too small,* our two normal curves will overlap too much, thus giving us larger risks than we are willing to take. If our sample is too large, we will be wasting money on larger samples than we really need.

We use our now familiar formula for Z. This is $Z = (p - \pi)/\sigma_p$. Our risk of .05 corresponds to a Z of 1.645 and thus an equation of

$$1.645 = \frac{p - .30}{\sqrt{\dfrac{.30 - .30^2}{N}}}.$$

Our β risk of .15 corresponds to a Z of 1.033 and thus an equation of

$$1.033 = \frac{.35 - p}{\sqrt{\dfrac{.35 - .35^2}{N}}}.$$

We now have two equations with two unknowns. A little rearrangement of these will give us

$$(1) \qquad \frac{1}{\sqrt{N}} = \frac{p - .30}{1.645\sqrt{.30 - .30^2}}$$

and (2) $$\qquad \frac{1}{\sqrt{N}} = \frac{.35 - p}{1.033\sqrt{.35 - .35^2}}.$$

Thus the right sides of these equations are equal to each other. If we equate these and solve for p, we get a p of .330. We then find that $N = 270$.

We would have to loosen our standards of control to reduce N below 270. We could express this loosening either as increases in our α and β errors, or as an increase in the spread between our lower limit of .30 and our upper limit of .35.

9.12 The Future Development of Statistical Decision-making Models

We have merely scratched the surface of the potential of statistical models as aids in decision-making. The development of the electronic computer has now made practical a wide variety of applications that were formerly prohibitively expensive of money and time, or that were even impossible because of the tremendous volume of arithmetic involved. Our ability to deal with massive probability, consequence, and pay-off matrixes is no longer limited by the mechanics of calculation. The primary limitations are imposed by the problems of filling in the appropriate values in these matrixes. But the computer helps us even there. We often find it very practical to make up several sets of matrixes. Thus we can see the outcomes under various *assumed* probability and consequence conditions, with the computer running through the calculations fast enough to make such experimental analysis practicable. This type of analysis is particularly valuable when we can predetermine certain critical values for our matrixes. A *critical* value is one which acts as a *dividing line* between one decision and another. For example, our president of Smoothies may have adopted a π of .25 as a critical value, with the decision to fire the vice president of sales following automatically if the sample indicated a π less than .25. Given such a critical value, we no longer bother about the *whole* probability distribution. We concentrate on the simple issue of the probability that π is less than .25.

9.13 Our Next Step

Now that we have fortified ourselves with some ideas about how the estimation of probabilities can be useful in aiding us in making decisions, we are better prepared in learning how to use probability calculations most effectively. This involves the problem of systematically relating the implications of the most recent information available to the ideas and hypotheses we might have accumulated prior to the appearance of this recent information. We have anticipated this problem to some extent in our discussion of hypothesis testing ideas and techniques; but in the next chapter we try to view the issues from a broader point of view.

PROBLEMS AND QUESTIONS

9.1 Assume that the survey of a random sample of 100 consumers had resulted in 25 consumers expressing a preference for Smoothies.

(a) Generate inferences about the true proportion of preference in the universe by the use of:

    1. Direct application of the binomial theorem (cf. column 2 of Table 9.1)

    2. Modified Bayesian estimates (cf. column 3 of Table 9.1)

    3. Normal curve estimates (cf. column 4 of Table 9.1)

(b) Cumulate the probabilities you calculated in (a) and determine the estimated probability (inference ratio) that the universe proportion is *less* than .30; *more* than .30.

(*c*) Make up a probability matrix for the problem of whether or not to fire the sales vice president.

(*d*) Assume the validity of the consequence matrix shown in Table 9.6 and combine this matrix with the probability matrix you constructed in (*c*) in order to derive the estimated pay-off matrix.

(*e*) What is the apparent net expected gain (or loss) if the vice president is fired? If he is retained?

9.2 Logic suggests that there must be some point of indifference where the evidence as summarized by the pay-off matrix shows an equal gain (or loss) regardless of whether the sales vice president is fired or retained.

(*a*) Take the consequence matrix as given and determine the probability matrix that would lead to a no decision pay-off matrix, that is, a pay-off matrix that suggests an indifference to whether the sales vice president was fired or retained.

(*b*) What result in a sample of 100 would correspond to this point of indifference? (For example, a sample *p* of .28 was associated with a probability matrix with a .67 − .33 split in the probabilities. (See Table 9.5.) Your calculation in Question 9.1(*c*) was based on a sample *p* of .25 and resulted in a probability matrix with a ? − ? split in the probabilities. Thus each sample result is paired with its own probability split. Find the *p* that pairs with the split that corresponds to the point of indifference.)

(*c*) Suppose that you were the president and were confronted with a pay-off matrix that expressed indifference to the direction of the decision. What action would you then take?

9.3 Suppose that you were the sales vice president whose fate was to be decided by the results of an analysis of the sort illustrated in Questions 1 and 2 and in the text. Suppose further that the director of market research was to conduct the survey and supervise the necessary calculations to derive the probability matrix. The ultimate result was that the pay-off matrix indicated a pay-off just barely in favor of your dismissal. Thus it was clear that a slight change in the basic probabilities might reverse the recommendation. Inquiry revealed that the normal curve had been used in inferring the probabilities. What would be your reaction?

9.4 The pay-off matrix in Table 9.7 of the text points in the direction of retaining the vice president. Suppose you were the president. You are actually almost completely convinced that you should fire the vice president. You had expected that the results of the analysis would have supported such a decision and are now quite chagrined to find that the results did not. However, you have been so committed to a policy of being fair and objective that you are almost forced to abide by the decision of the matrix. In fact, you are so committed to a policy of being fair and objective that you decide that the fairest thing of all is to collect a larger sample of evidence before making such an important decision. Actually, you suspect that a larger sample will yield the same results as the original sample of 100, namely, a .28 preference rate. Suppose your suspicion is correct about the results of a larger sample.

(*a*) Estimate the minimum size of the *total* sample (including the original

100) that would result in an indifference point if the sample p again came out to be .28.

(b) Again assume that p will be .28. What total sample should be planned in order to result in a pay-off matrix with a net pay-off of $100,000 in favor of firing the vice president?

(c) Suppose that this additional survey is estimated to cost a base amount of $5,000 plus $1.50 for each completed interview. How would you incorporate these costs in your analysis of how much evidence you should try to get in order to decide what to do with the vice president. (There must be some point in any decision problem where the cost of collecting and analyzing additional evidence overbalances the contribution such evidence makes to the decision-making process. In other words, it becomes cheaper to make more mistakes than to increase the research needed to reduce the number of mistakes.)

9.5 The consequence matrix was taken as a fact in the text and in the above problems. Common sense suggests, however, that the figures shown in the consequence matrix are really estimates. Thus they are subject to the same kinds of uncertainties as those we had about the true state of the market preference for Smoothies. Suppose that further analysis on our part resulted in the estimation of the following probability distributions for each of the four categories shown in Table 9.6:

Gain from *Correctly* Firing V.P.—G_f	$P(G_f)$	Loss from *Incorrectly* Firing V.P.—L_f	$P(L_f)$
$ 25,000	.20	$ 0	.25
100,000	.64	500,000	.50
500,000	.16	1,000,000	.25
	1.00		1.00

Gain from *Correctly* Keeping V.P.—G_k	$P(G_k)$	Loss from *Incorrectly* Keeping V.P.—L_k	$P(G_k)$
$ 0	.40	$ 50,000	.60
50,000	.22	100,000	.10
500,000	.38	200,000	.30
	1.00		1.00

(a) Suppose you decided to ignore your uncertainty about the exact consequences of each of these four possible outcomes. What procedure would you follow to reduce each of the above probability distributions to a single figure? Defend your selection.

(b) Suppose you decided to try to allow for your uncertainty about the consequences. What suggestions do you have for making this uncertainty a part of your formal development of a pay-off matrix?

(c) What effect do *varying degrees* of uncertainty about consequences have on the usefulness of a pay-off matrix in decision-making? For example, is it possible that uncertainty about consequences can become so great that the pay-off matrix will approach a point of indifference, and thus will give no guide to the correct decision? Explain.

(d) What is the effect (on the efficacy of a pay-off matrix) of an increased uncertainty about the *facts?* (Hint: a *smaller* sample of evidence increases the uncertainty about the facts.)

9.6 How would you establish the truth of the following statements? Do you find it necessary to use a standard for truth that falls somewhat short of 100% confidence?

(a) If I toss this coin, the probability that it will come up heads is .5.

(b) We should lower the price of our product from $2.79 to $2.39 because we will then be able to increase volume of unit sales by at least 25%.

(c) Since we have 200 antimissile missiles, each with a probability of .70 of operating satisfactorily and destroying its target, an enemy must have at least 300 missiles, each with at least .50 probability of firing properly, in order to have a reasonable chance of striking our major cities and other targets with at least 100 missiles.

(d) We cannot possibly afford to increase the wage rate $.17 per hour without reducing our profit to practically zero. Our accounting records show that the net profit last year was only $.19 per hour of labor input.

(e) I must have a new set of spark plugs installed in my car in order to prevent the motor from stalling at intersections when I slow down or stop.

(f) I must vote for the conviction of this accused burglar because he has been positively identified by the shopkeeper.

9.7 Most people agree that a proper standard of justice is one which treats people impartially. What quantitative criteria would you set up in order to help you achieve justice in each of the following problems?

(a) You wish to pay your workers in such a way that they get "equal pay for equal work," and hence presumably "twice as much pay for twice as much work."

(b) As a judge you wish to assess fines for exceeding the posted speed limit in such a way that the fine is proportional to the increased risk of accident caused by the excessive speed.

1. If the posted limit were 40 mph, would you fine a man twice as much if he had been accused of going 80 mph as you would if he had been going 60 mph? Explain.

2. Would you fine a man less, or even waive the fine, if he had a good excuse, such as rushing to the hospital with an expectant mother?

3. What kind of proof would you require from the arresting officer before deciding how fast the car really was going?

(c) Two youngsters are caught fighting. Interrogation reveals that each claims the other "started it." Might both boys be telling the truth? Explain.

What action would you suggest that would be fair to both boys but which would still reduce the likelihood of either boy's fighting in the future?

9.8 Estimate the 90% confidence interval for the location of the universe proportion of defective radio tubes if a random sample of 50 tubes revealed four defective tubes. Use the following methods:

(a) Cumulative binomial with discrete probabilities.

(b) Adjustment of (a) for conservatism by eliminating the extra probability in the manner of Table 9.9.

(c) Normal curve approximation with a single estimate of the standard deviation of sample means.

(d) Normal curve approximation with a recognition of the fact that the standard deviation of sample means varies as the hypothesis about π varies.

(e) Analyze the differences in the results obtained by the above methods and make any generalizations that you think will be useful in helping you to decide on a method in a practical problem.

9.9 An opinion poll based on a random sample of 100 people revealed that 55 of the respondents expressed a preference for Candidate A in an upcoming election and the remaining 45 expressed a preference for Candidate B.

(a) Estimate the 80% confidence limits for the proportion of all people who prefer Candidate A. Use any method you wish.

(b) Suppose you were the campaign manager of Candidate A. Would your responsibilities in this position have any influence on your choice of method for the estimation of the 80% confidence limits? Explain.

(c) Would normal curve estimates be closer to the true limits in this case with a p of .55 and an N of 100 than they would be in the preceding problem with a p of .08 and an N of 50? Explain.

(d) How would you decide on 80% limits rather than, say, 95% limits, or 60%, etc.?

9.10(a) What is an hypothesis?

(b) List five hypotheses that have governed some of your behavior during the last 24 hours.

(c) Indicate the percentage of confidence you have that each of the above hypotheses is true. Explain the basis of your belief that some of these hypotheses are more reliable than others.

9.11 State some hypothesis that you used to believe true but which you have since replaced with some alternative hypothesis. What was the evidence that first suggested its truth? What evidence caused you to change your mind? Did this new evidence suggest that there had been a change in the underlying conditions, or did it suggest that *your knowledge* of the underlying conditions had changed?

What percentage of confidence do you now have in the truth of the hypothesis that you *now* act on?

9.12 The World-Wide Casualty Company makes frequent use of mail solicitations in trying to get new policyholders. It hires a mailing service to provide the mailing lists and also to handle the mechanical tasks of actually mailing out the particular solicitation pieces. The Casualty Company keeps a record of the responses it has had from various mailings. It analyzes these in order to make more intelligent decisions about the kinds of lists it should continue to use and about the particular mailing services that seem to have the most reliable lists and mailing services. Most mailing services also keep such records so they can make reasonable estimates of the expected responses from various kinds of appeals to various types of listings. Such estimates are frequently used by customers in deciding whether to make a mailing, and if so, to what list.

The World-Wide Casualty Company has recently placed a mailing order with a mailing service on the hypothesis that the mailing of 2800 pieces would result in a 12% response. The actual response turned out to be only 10.5%. How would this result affect your evaluation of the reliability of the original claim of a 12% response? For example, would you be inclined to give this mailing service another chance on the theory that the reduced rate of returns may have been due to chance? What chance would you be willing to take that it was due to chance? Explain.

9.13 You will recall that we discovered that the arithmetic mean of sample variances is less than the variance of the universe. However, if we adjust each sample variance by multiplying it by $N/(N-1)$, we find that the arithmetic mean of such results would now be equal to the true universe variance. However, we also discovered that such a routine adjustment of sample variances sometimes led to nonsense answers that were larger than could logically be possible. What is the difference, if any, between a policy of making such an adjustment except when it is clearly foolish, e.g., except when it would give an answer larger than the known maximum of .25, and a policy of requiring people to stop at an intersection when the light is red except when no car is coming from the other side?

9.14 The operator of a bolt-making machine is required to stop the machine for adjustment whenever the periodic sample of 10 bolts shows two or more defective bolts.

(a) Construct the operating characteristic curve for this routine decision-maker and plot it on a graph.

(b) How did you treat the probability of exactly two defects? That is, did you treat p as a discrete or as a continuous variable?

(c) What difference in your operating characteristic curve is caused by whether you treated p as discrete or continuous? Illustrate your answer by drawing a free-hand sketch of the different OC curves that would result.

(d) Suppose that inquiry revealed that this routine decision-maker was supposed to control quality such that there was a maximum of 12 percent defects in the universe of bolts. What does your OC curve say about the risk that the process would be allowed to run even though the process is unsatisfactory because it is producing more than 12% defectives?

(e) What is the risk that the process will be stopped even though the process is producing fewer than 10% defectives?

(f) What steps would have to be taken in order to have a routine decision-maker with smaller risks than those you estimated in (d) and (e)?

9.15 You are asked to devise a routine decision-maker that will give us the following controls on Type I and Type II errors:

1. We wish to take no more than a .10 chance of stopping the machine if the process is producing 10% or fewer defectives.

2. We wish to take no more than a .05 chance of letting the machine run if the process is producing more than 12% defectives.

(a) Estimate the critical value of p and the size of sample necessary to achieve control within these specified limits.

(b) Suppose the testing process destroyed the bolt. Hence it would be very desirable to minimize the size of the sample to be tested. What changes would have to be made in the process or in the specifications in order to reduce the necessary size of sample?

9.16 Analyze the comparative sizes of the two types of errors involved in the following decisions.

(a) You are on the jury in a treason trial. Conviction carries a death sentence.

(b) You are on the jury in a treason trial. Conviction carries a sentence of life imprisonment with parole possible after 20 years.

(c) You are on the admissions committee of a "preferred" college. If you turn down an applicant, he is very likely to apply elsewhere with a reasonable probability of acceptance.

(d) Suppose you represented a "college of last resort." Your rejects almost never get to college.

(e) Would you rather marry somebody you should not have, or not marry somebody you should have?

(f) You are a military commander who must make decisions about when to commit men and materials to battle. Would you rather lose opportunities for successful attack than waste men in fruitless endeavors; or would you rather waste men than lose opportunities?

(g) You are a businessman who must make the decision about the design of the product. Your designers offer you several options. Would you rather go broke trying to make a major breakthrough in design, or would you rather miss a breakthrough opportunity in the interests of a solvency of longer term?

chapter 10

Pooling information

Most of the problems we run across from day to day are not completely new; and we have contended with them before in one form or another. The new sample evidence that we experience today is not the only evidence that we have experienced on similar problems. In fact, there is psychological evidence to show that the learning process consists of *adding to* and *modifying* what we *already know*. In a sense, new evidence must come to terms with what we already know before it is really discernible.

An attempt to treat sample evidence as though it were completely independent of all prior evidence is an interesting exercise in logic and in objective scientific analysis. Such an attempt, however, does run into the problem that it assumes that yesterday never existed. On the other hand, of course, such an attempt relieves us of the risks associated with the prejudices and misinterpretations of past experiences. Even if it were desirable, however, there is a serious question of whether it is *really possible* for us to ignore our yesterdays as we contemplate today's problems and today's evidence. Most business organizations do not really think so. That is why they make strong efforts to periodically inject new blood into the organization in order to provide a steady pressure for adaptation to change. The older people tend to know what they know too well to be easily swayed by new evidence. In fact, they have trouble even seeing the evidence! The youngsters have little trouble grasping the new evidence because it bulks so large in their accumulated pile! In a real practical sense, yesterday may not have existed for the youngster.

We have already spent some time on this problem of what to do with prior information as we are looking at a new sample of evidence. We tried very hard to act as though there were no prior information as we made inferences about a universe π from a given sample. We discovered that there were certain advantages to such an approach, not the least of which being that we really felt that we had no prior information. However, somewhat surprisingly, we discovered that we could make *better estimates* of π if we assumed a prior distribution of equally-probable π's. We know that this prior distribution carried some weight in our inferences because the average of our inferences had a bias toward .5, which was the average of our prior distribution.

But, just to show how our thinking is strongly influenced by our point of view, let us suppose that we take the view that the most appropriate hypothesis about the π's is that they are *equally probable*. We will hold this view until new evidence causes us to modify it. Suppose the new evidence comes and suggests the possibility that the true π is closer, say, to .3 than it is to .5. Open-minded that we are, we now modify our original hypothesis of equal probability with a mean expectation of .5 to one of unequal probabilities with a mean expectation of, say, .34. We have thus allowed our conclusion to show a *strong bias toward .3*. We are unwilling to throw our original hypothesis completely away, but we are willing to give it a relatively small weight as we *pool* our prior hypothesis with the new information. Should more than that be asked of any man?

Whether or not we find the above point of view at all attractive, we must admit that there is some basis for arguing that the *bias* runs toward the sample p of .30 rather than toward the hypothetical π of .50. Or perhaps it would be better if we dropped the word, bias. It has an invidious connotation and almost automatically causes people to label it bad and deserving of eradication.

We should also mention that analysis of such things as operating characteristics curves, Type I and Type II errors, and tests of significance inadvertently involved the problem of reconciling prior beliefs or hypotheses with new sample evidence. People tend to keep the risks of Type I errors low as a way of balancing the conclusions of accumulated experience against the indications of additional evidence.

In this chapter we propose to extend some of the notions on pooling previously touched on and to make explicit those things previously treated implicitly.

10.1   Kinds of Prior Information

Quantitative vs. Nonquantitative Information

A good deal of the fruits of our past experiences are embodied in the vague raiment of those things we call feelings, attitudes, etc. We find it very difficult to express their nature quantitatively so that we and others can mathematically combine them with new evidence to arrive at quantitatively expressed new conclusions. The closest approach we can make to quantifying these important regulators of behavior is to *quantify the behavior*. If we do this under various kinds of stimuli (sample evidence), we can *deduce* the kinds and intensities of the beliefs that are apparently regulating that behavior. Research like this is very useful in studying *how people actually do pool* their past experiences with new evidence. However, since our interest is in developing apparently rational ways of pooling the old with the new, we leave to others the problems of research into how people actually do it.

We are going to confine our attention solely to those problems of pooling *quantitatively expressed* information. In doing this, we are going to be willing to take moderate risks that the quantification process does not accurately measure the things it presumes to measure. For example, if someone tells us that he likes cake twice as much as ice cream, we will take the risks associated with calling it twice as much when actually it may be only 1.7 as much or three times as much.

Undigested vs. Digested Information: Raw Data vs. an Inference Distribution

The human nervous system is essentially a data-processing system. It tends to digest information the same way the stomach digests food. The output of this data-processing system is a set of conclusions or hypotheses. The original information is essentially lost in the process, or, if it is stored, it is particularly inaccessible. The result is that we can now call forth only the *conclusions* we have made from our past experiences and not the experiences themselves, except, of course, an occasional anecdote that we find fits our conclusions quite well, and which probably never happened that way anyway. We cannot easily determine how much experience or evidence supported the conclusion, or how variable was the experience, the two things about evidence we have discovered it is most important to know.

We would not be overly concerned about this lack of direct evidence on how much and how variable the past experience has been if we could be assured that the conclusions that have been drawn were couched in terms that showed the modesty befitting the paucity and inconsistency of the evidence. Unfortunately, we find it unrealistic to be assured on this matter. Some people, by their very nature, always strongly believe whatever it is that they are currently believing. They leave little doubt that their "conclusions follow inevitably and unquestionably from the evidence," whereas other people tend to be somewhat tentative in all their views. The first type of person tends to swamp any new evidence in his prior convictions; the second type of person gets his prior convictions swamped by the new evidence.

Despite these difficulties in trying to assess the weight of past evidence in supporting a given hypothesis, we do the best we can to deduce its apparent weight from the strength of the convictions expressed in the conclusions. This might result in our letting "men of conviction" overly dominate a situation; however, we hope to reduce the risks of this by giving proper regard to the probabilities in a situation.

10.2 Weights in Pooling Information

As soon as we contemplate combining two sets of information in order to extract a joint conclusion, we run into the problem of the relative weights we should assign to the two sets of information. The problem would be relatively simple if we could be assured that the two sets of information definitely belonged to the same universe. For example, if we were presented with a sample of 10 cards from a deck (not playing cards) and another sample of 5 cards from the *same* deck, we would not hesitate to give the first sample a weight of 2 and the second sample a weight of 1 in any pooling operation. But suppose the first sample occurred last Friday and the second sample occurred today. What assurrance do we have that they both came from the same universe? Perhaps shifts have occurred which would make it appropriate to completely ignore the first sample, thus, in effect, giving it a weight of 0.

To Pool or Not to Pool?

Many people have a predilection toward strong measures in choosing weighting systems for pooling two sets of information. We might add, as a matter of fact, that the literature of statistics implicitly supports such strong measures. This approach to the problem reduces the basic issue to either pooling or not pooling.

Given the decision that the two sets did come from the same universe, weights are then assigned *proportional to the sizes of the two samples*. If one set of information is in a predigested form, we must try to deduce an appropriate N, a challenging task at times.

Modified Weighting Systems

If we find that it is not clear whether the two sets of evidence came from the same universe, and it almost never is, we might try to develop a modified weighting system that allows for the uncertainty about whether to pool and also for the amount of evidence in each set. This is a pretty tricky business and not easily, or even preferably, left to routine procedures. We probably should not use these difficulties, however, as an excuse to fall back on the pool or not pool solution, a solution for which we do have simple routines.

After posting this warning, we now turn to some of the simple routines associated with a "pool or not pool" analysis. We trust that we can work out our own modifications of these routines in order to allow for any indicated modified weight patterns.

10.3   Procedure If Given Two Bits of Sample Information

Suppose we are given two samples of evidence. One sample of five items from a machine process contains one defective item. The other sample, also five items, contains two defective items from the same *apparent* process. The first sample occurred first in time. What can we now infer about the process universe that has been generating these samples? Do we conclude that the process is deteriorating, namely, that the second sample came from a different, and poorer, universe than the first sample? If so, what inference do we now make? Do we decide that a "trend" is at work and that the process has by now deteriorated to an even worse condition than when the second sample was taken?

Or do we infer that the two samples came from the same universe and that the difference between the two samples was strictly a matter of chance? If we believe this, we would pool the two samples with equal weights because they have equal N's. What inference would we then make about the universe π?

The Behavior of Paired Samples from the Same Universe

As an aid to deciding what to do with two samples that may or may not have come from the same universe, it is interesting to examine what happens when we pair samples that have come from the same universe. Let us suppose that we are drawing random samples of two items from a universe that has 10% defectives in it. We then pick out pairs of the samples of two and take the difference be-

TABLE 10.1

**Differences between Means of Paired Samples of 2
from a Universe with $\pi = .1$**

Part A.   Differences between   Part B.   Probabilities of Differences
                Means

p_1	p_2 0	.5	1.0		p_1	p_2 0	.5	1.0	Σ
0	0	$-.5$	-1.0		0	.6561	.1458	.0081	.81
.5	.5	0	$-.5$		.5	.1458	.0324	.0018	.18
1.0	1.0	.5	0		1.0	.0081	.0018	.0001	.01
					Σ	.81	.18	.01	1.00

tween their means.   Table 10.1 summarizes the sort of results we would get if we considered all possible differences between the means in such pairs.   The matrix in Part A shows the differences that would occur for all possible combinations of p_1 and p_2.   Part B shows the probability that a given difference would occur.   These probabilities are the *joint* probabilities for the simultaneous occurrence of the given p_1 and p_2.   For example, the probability of 0 defectives in a sample of two is $.9 \times .9$, or .81.   The probability that p_1 will be 0 at the same time that p_2 will be 0 is $.81 \times .81$, or .6561.   This is the probability shown in the upper left-hand corner of the probability matrix.   The other probabilities are similarly calculated.   Note the symmetry in the table and also in the marginal probabilities.   The total of all the probabilities must be 1.0, thus accounting for all the possible differences.

Table 10.2 analyzes the summary characteristics of these differences.   Here we find that the arithmetic mean of all the differences equals 0.   This is as we would expect.   This is another way of expressing the notion that chance will (in the long run) average out differences between samples taken from the same universe.   The standard deviation of these differences is .30.   An interesting thing about this standard deviation is that it can also be calculated from the formula shown.   This formula is always true and

TABLE 10.2

Summary Characteristics of Differences between Means of Paired Samples of 2 with $\pi = .1$

(1) $p_1 - p_2,$ or d	(2) P	(3) Pd	(4) Pd^2	(5) P *
-1.0	.0081	$-.0081$	.0081	.0027
$-.5$	.1476	$-.0738$	.0369	.1649
0	.6886	0	0	.6649
.5	.1476	.0738	.0369	.1649
1.0	.0081	.0081	.0081	.0027
	1.0000	0	.0900	1.0001

$$\bar{X}_d = 0 \quad \sigma_d = \sqrt{.09}, \text{ or } .3$$

$$\sigma_d = \sqrt{\frac{\sigma^2}{N_1} + \frac{\sigma^2}{N_2}}$$

$$= \sqrt{\frac{.9 \times .1}{N_1} + \frac{.9 \times .1}{N_2}}$$

* Normal curve.

makes it possible for us to calculate σ_d from knowledge of σ and of N_1 and N_2. If the N's are equal, we derive the interesting special case that $\sigma_d = \sqrt{2\sigma_p^2}$, or that the *variance* (square of the standard deviation) of the differences between sample means is equal to *twice* the variance of the means. If we think about this, we realize that this is not so far removed from what intuitive common sense would tell us.

Another very interesting feature of this distribution of differences is that it is *symmetrical* even though the universe is quite *skewed.* This symmetry is always a characteristic of the differences between means of random samples provided that the samples came from the same universe. Thus normal curve estimates of this distribution tend to be quite good even for relatively small samples. For example, in this case the normal curve probabilities are as shown in column 5 of Table 10.2. The closeness to the exact probabilities shown in column 2 is quite remarkable considering how small our samples are.

Estimating the Distribution of Differences between Sample Means from the Same Universe

Let us now return to our two samples of five, one with one defective and the other with two defectives. Let us assume that we have no other information about this process. A possible first step in analysis is to set up the *hypothesis* that both samples came from the same universe. If this is true, we can estimate the standard deviation of this universe by combining the information in the two samples. The two samples together give us a sample of 10 with three defects. Thus our "best" estimate of σ would be

$$\sqrt{pq \cdot \frac{N}{N-1}}, \text{ or } \sqrt{.7 \times .3 \frac{10}{9}}.$$

(The $N/(N-1)$ adjustment is made because sample standard deviations tend to average out smaller than the universe standard deviation.) This works out to be .483. (Failure to make the bias adjustment would give us a $\acute\sigma$ of .458.)

We have discovered that

$$\sigma_d = \sqrt{\frac{\sigma^2}{N_1} + \frac{\sigma^2}{N_2}}.$$

This reduces to

$$\sigma_d = \sigma \sqrt{\frac{1}{N_1} + \frac{1}{N_2}},$$

a form that many people find more convenient to work with. If we substitute our *estimate* of .483 for σ, we get

$$\acute\sigma_d = .483 \sqrt{\tfrac{1}{5} + \tfrac{1}{5}}.$$

This works out to give us a $\acute\sigma_d$ of .305.

We are now ready to estimate the probability that two samples could have differed by at least as much as ours even though they both came from the same universe. We assume that the normal curve will make satisfactory estimates of this probability, an assumption that seems quite reasonable in view of what we found out in the last section about the distribution of differences. Let us measure the observed difference by subtracting p_1 from p_2, thus getting a d of $+.2$. Figure 10.1 illustrates our progress to this point. The curve shown is a normal distribution with a standard deviation of .305 and a mean of 0. Our observed difference of $+.2$ is spotted on the horizontal axis. The probability we are interested in is indicated by the shaded area to the right of .2. We calculate this area by looking up the appropriate Z in the normal curve table. Here $Z = (p_2 - p_1)/\acute\sigma_{p_1 - p_2}$, or $.2/.305$, or .656. (We show $\acute\sigma_d$ as $\acute\sigma_{p_1 - p_2}$ in this formula to emphasize the general character of all formulas for Z, namely that Z is the ratio of some particular difference to the standard deviation of all such differences. In this case the difference in mind is $p_1 - p_2$. We have also had experience with $p - \pi$, and we run into other differences in later work.)

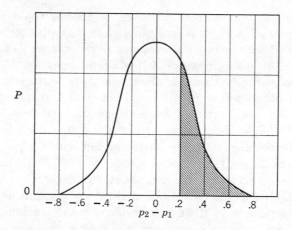

Fig. 10.1 Estimated normal distribution of differences between sample p's from universe, with $\pi_I = .3$ ($N_1 = N_2 = 5$). (Note: Not drawn to exact scale.)

A Z of .656 cuts off a tail area of .256. Thus we estimate that a difference of $+.2$ or more would occur .256 of the time even if these two samples came from the same universe.

Deciding Whether to Pool, and, if so, How to Pool Two Bits of Sample Information

Now that we have a probability to work with, we can turn to the most difficult part of our task, that is, what do we decide to do about the pooling issue. For the first time we have now explicitly come to grips with the question of whether the universe we are dealing with *has remained constant* over the period of our samples. The corollary question, and really the most important question, is to determine what we would now like to say about the universe from which the *next* sample will be taken. We really cannot do anything about the pieces the machine has *already turned out*, but we could prevent the machine from turning out an excessive number of defective pieces *in the future* if we knew when to shut the machine off for adjustment.

As soon as we begin to think about the practical setting that caused us to take the samples in the first place, we begin to project our thinking beyond the apparently simple issue of pooling. What is important is not whether we pool, but what happens to us if we pool and what happens to us if we do not pool. For example, suppose that the results of both samples are sufficiently "good" so that we would let the machine run on the basis of *either sample alone*. Suppose further that the two samples *combined,* or pooled, would also tell us to let the process run. It is now quite clear that whether we pool or not makes absolutely no difference in our decision. The issue of pooling would then be merely an intellectual exercise.

But suppose the first sample alone tells us to let the machine run. (It obviously must have or we would not have had the opportunity to get another sample under the same apparent conditions.) Suppose the second sample alone tells us to stop the machine. Suppose the two samples together tell us to let it run, but with the precautionary note to immediately take another sample of five. Now our decision about pooling affects our decision about the machine!

It is also obvious that our decision about the machine also depends on what happens to us if we incorrectly stop the machine and what happens if we incorrectly let it run, and both of these incorrect decisions must be balanced against corresponding correct decisions. In other words, we need the details of a consequence matrix. And, as before, we would need the details of a probability matrix in order to combine these two matrixes into a pay-off matrix. The decision to pool or not to pool would then automatically pop out. As a matter of fact, we could work up a model that would also permit a moderate amount of variable weighting in the pooling process.

Unfortunately, or fortunately, depending upon our point of view, we cannot take the space needed to develop further any of the routines of building pay-off matrixes.[1] Our task is to uncover some of the problems involved in estimating the probabilities that would be involved. We find it necessary nevertheless to periodically raise the issue of consequence matrixes lest we imply that it is possible to make real decisions about real problems on the basis of probabilities alone. We also must contend with our natural tendencies to either dismiss probabilities as irrelevant or to treat them as the sole determiners of truth, with the middle ground left unattended. We trust that we could all fill in the appropriate consequences if we were dealing with a real problem. In the meantime we try to explore some of the mysteries of probabilities.

Before leaving this section, we should point out that the test of the hypothesis of no difference between the two universes from which the samples came would traditionally have led to a decision to retain the hypothesis. This decision would follow from the widely practiced conservative rule of not rejecting an hypothesis unless the risk

[1] See references on p. 374 for further information on the process of combining probabilities and consequences.

of Type I error is less than some figure in the neighborhood of .10, or .05. Since such a rejection would involve a risk of .26 in this case, the hypothesis of no difference would survive the test. We again remind ourselves that this conservative rule makes little practical sense *unless* we have accumulated previous experiences that provide some presumption for the hypothesis of no difference, a *presumption quite apart from the evidence of the two samples.* Thus, in effect, the conservative rule is testing *old evidence*, although vaguely defined, against *new evidence*, usually quite specifically defined in the form of random samples. Personal judgment is thus a very strong, though implicit, factor in the use of the conservative rule.

Estimating the Inference Distribution of the Differences between the Means (π's) of Two Universes

In the preceding sections we approached the problem of what to do with the two samples by adopting a *prior hypothesis that the two samples came from the same universe.* Another approach to the problem is to make *no prior assumption* about the differences between the two universes, but to let the sample information generate a set of inferences about the kind of differences that might exist. This is exactly what we tried to do in Chapter 7 when we had information from only one sample, namely, let the sample tell us what to infer, with as little prior assumption as possible.

The *best single estimate* we can make of the differences between the means of two universes is the difference observed between the two sample means. The arithmetic mean of all such estimates would equal the actual difference between the universe means. We have already discovered, for example, that the arithmetic mean of differences between means of samples from the *same* universe would be 0. In our case, the observed difference was $+.2$. Thus we can say that the best single estimate we can make is that the two universes have means that *differ by $+.2$.* But, of course, we are well aware of the fact that the true difference might be more or less than $+.2$. The question, then, is to estimate the probability, or inference, distribution of this difference.

This is precisely the same problem we tackled when we estimated the inference distribution for π_I. Unfortunately, our task is made more difficult by the fact that the distribution of differences between means of samples from *different* universes conforms to no simple pattern. The distributions are *skewed*, although this skewness tends to decline as the combined sample size increases. The binomial

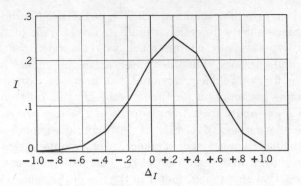

Fig. 10.2 Binomial estimates of inference ratios of Δ_I given: $p_1 = .2$, $p_2 = .4$, $N_1 = N_2 = 5$. (Note: Inference ratios are based on binomial with $p = .6$ and $N = 10$.)

distribution with N equal to the combined sizes of the two samples and with p_d equal to .5 plus *one-half* the difference between the two sample p's tends to approximate this distribution of differences. (We use the subscript d merely to identify this synthetic p as a p that is concerned with differences.) Figure 10.2 and Table 10.3 show such

TABLE 10.3

Binomial Estimates of Inference Ratios of Δ_I. Given: $p_1 = .2$, $p_2 = .4$, $N_1 = N_2 = 5$. (Based on binomial with $p_d = .6$ and $N = 10$)

(1) p_d	(2) $I(p_d)$	(3) Δ_I	(4) $I \times \Delta_I$
0	.000	−1.0	.0000
.1	.002	−.8	−.0016
.2	.011	−.6	−.0066
.3	.042	−.4	−.0168
.4	.111	−.2	−.0222
.5	.201	0	0
.6	.251	.2	.0502
.7	.215	.4	.0860
.8	.121	.6	.0726
.9	.040	.8	.0320
1.0	.006	1.0	.0060
			.1996

an estimated inference ratio distribution based on our two samples of five with p's of .2 and .4. Note that the Δ_I (delta) values run from -1.0 to $+1.0$ and that the maximum probability occurs at a Δ_I of .2, the observed difference between the sample means. Also note that the arithmetic mean of the Δ_I's is .2 (except for rounding errors), again the observed difference. Because we have actually *doubled* the spread of the distribution from the binomial limits of 0 and 1.0, the variance of this distribution of Δ_I is *twice* the variance of the binomial distribution on which it is based.

Table 10.4 shows the inference ratios for Δ_I based on samples with p's of .8 and .5 with N's of 5 and 4, respectively. Study columns 1 and 3, and you can see how we transform p_d into Δ_I. Note that the mean of Δ_I is .300, the observed difference between the samples.

We could modify these inference ratios in Tables 10.3 and 10.4 the same way we modified our binomial estimates of π_I. That is, we could set up equally likely hypotheses for all possible values of Δ and then use the Bayesian technique to get the posterior distribution. This is quite a tedious procedure, and it is rarely done. Actually normal curve approximations are usually used because of their relative simplicity and also because we can easily interpolate for the inference ratios for any selected intervals of Δ_I. Interpolations from

TABLE 10.4

Binomial Estimates of Inference Ratios of Δ_I. Given: $p_1 = 8$, $p_2 = .5$, $N_1 = 5$, $N_2 = 4$. (Based on binomial with $p_d = .65$ and $N = 9$)

(1) p_d	(2) $I(p_d)$	(3) Δ_I	(4) $I \times \Delta_I$
0	.000	-1.000	.0000
.111	.001	$-.778$	$-.0008$
.222	.010	$-.556$	$-.0056$
.333	.042	$-.333$	$-.0140$
.444	.118	$-.111$	$-.0131$
.556	.219	.111	.0243
.667	.272	.333	.0906
.778	.216	.556	.1201
.889	.100	.778	.0778
1.000	.021	1.000	.0210
	.999		.3003

TABLE 10.5

Normal Curve Estimates of Inference Ratios of Δ_I.
Given: $p_1 = .2$, $p_2 = .4$, $N_1 = N_2 = 5$.

(1)	(2)	(3)	(4)	(5)
			Proportionate	
		$\dfrac{\Delta_I - .2}{\hat{\sigma}_d}$	Height of	
Δ_I	$\Delta_I - .2$		Ordinate	I_{Δ_I}
−1.000	−1.2	−3.79	.001	.000
−.8	−1.0	−3.16	.007	.002
−.6	−.8	−2.53	.041	.010
−.4	−.6	−1.90	.164	.041
−.2	−.4	−1.26	.452	.114
0	−.2	−.63	.820	.207
.2	0	0	1.000	.252
.4	.2	.63	.820	.207
.6	.4	1.26	.452	.114
.8	.6	1.90	.164	.041
1.0	.8	2.53	.041	.010
				.998

$$\sigma_d = \sqrt{\frac{.2 \times .8}{4} + \frac{.4 \times .6}{4}}$$
$$= .316$$

Maximum ordinate $= Y_0$

$$Y_0 = \frac{.2}{2.5066 \times .316}$$
$$= .252$$

the crude binomial are somewhat tedious. Table 10.5 shows the calculation of such normal curve estimates when p equals .2 and .4 and both N's are 5. A notable difference exists between our procedure here and that when we made the normal curve estimates assuming the two samples came from the *same* universe. Before, we *pooled* the two samples and made a *single* estimate of σ. Now we do not pool because we do not assume the two samples came from the same universe. Hence we make two separate estimates of σ, one for each universe. The average of these two is *greater* than the estimate we would get if we pooled because we now make a *double* adjustment for bias in sample standard deviations.

The other difference, of course, is that we now center around a mean of .2 rather than a mean of 0.

A comparison of these normal curve estimates with the binomial estimates shows tolerably good agreement. In most practical problems we would find ourselves unable to know what to do with the differences between the two.

What Odds Would We Give that the Process is Now Generating More Defectives Than When the First Sample Was Drawn?

Although we do not have the necessary consequence matrix to really decide whether and, if so, how, to pool the information from these two samples drawn from this machine process, we can try to answer the interesting question of the odds we would be willing to give that the process is now generating more defectives because the second sample shows more defectives than the first. Our inference distribution shown in column 5 of Table 10.5 indicates a total probability of .271 that Δ_I lies between 0 and $-.9$ $(.002 + .010 + .041 + .114 + .207/2)$. (The binomial distribution in column 2 of Table 10.3 shows a probability of .266 for the same thing.) Thus there seems to be about one chance out of four that the true difference is *0 or less*, or three chances out of four that the true difference is *0 or more*. Does this mean that we should now be willing to bet almost 3 to 1 that the process is producing more defectives than formerly?

The answer is that we would, provided we had absolutely no other information about this process. If, however, we have had some undefined past experience with the process that told us that variation of the observed sort has been occurring *in a random manner* for quite some time, we would be very foolish to abandon the lessons of this past experience and be completely persuaded by the siren song of the latest information. In fact, our past experience may be so persuasive that we would be willing to bet nearly even-money that the next sample of five will show fewer than .2 defectives.

10.4 Procedure if Given a Prior Inference Distribution and One Bit of New Sample Information

Let us suppose that the prior information has been predigested. We have no way of recovering the actual information, but we are able to get the conclusions that had been drawn from that information. Let us suppose further that these conclusions are expressed in the form of an inference distribution. Our informant cannot recall where he got his notions, but he is willing to state the confidence he has that the universe proportion has certain values. Table 10.6 shows this inference distribution. Thus he feels that there is a .26 probability that the universe π is .20. (Actually he is using .20 as the center of a range from .15 to .25. Similarly for the other π_I's.) Note that the inference ratios add to 1. In other words, his list of π_I's covers all possible values of π_I.

The universe in question is assumed to have some single *specific* value, that value being unknown of course. We mention this point here because, as we see later, there are problems in which we actually are dealing with *several* universes and in which the sampling process goes through *two* stages. In the first stage, one of the universes is

TABLE 10.6

Prior Information in the Form of an Inference Distribution

π_I	I
0	.08
.2	.26
.4	.34
.6	.23
.8	.08
1.0	.01
	1.00

selected by a process we do not fully understand. Hence we do not know which universe was selected. In the second stage, a sample is selected from the chosen universe. The problem is to infer from the sample information the probability that any one of the universes had been selected. The problem we are working on at the moment is not that of determining which universe had been selected but rather that of determining the unknown value of that universe that *exists*. We can see that there are analogies between these two problems; but they are certainly different problems.

We now suppose that additional evidence arises in the form of a presumably random sample of five items with four successes among the five. If we add this information to what our informant has already told us about this unknown π, what should we now say about the inference distribution of π? As before, our first problem is that of deciding whether his prior experience and the new sample both refer to the *same universe*. It is entirely possible that his inferences are very proper for the situation that *historically existed*, but that they are essentially irrelevant for the present and the future. If we decide that they refer to the same universe, we may pool the two sets of information and come out with an inference set based on both. And, again as before, there is the possibility that we may be so uncertain as to whether we should or should not pool the two sets that we decide to pool with some weight modifications.

We start by assuming that his prior inferences are *correct* and that the new information came from the same universe that his old information came from. We calculate the probability that we could get a sample of five with four successes if his inferences are correct.

Table 10.7 carries out the necessary calculations. Columns 1 and 2 show the prior inference distribution. Column 3 shows the probability we could get a sample of five with a p of .8 given the particular π_I value. For example, given a π_I of .2, we find we have .0064 chances of getting a p of .8 in a sample of five. Column 4 is the *joint* probability of getting both the given π_I and a p of .8. It is simply a multiplication of column 3 by column 2. The *sum* of column 4, the *marginal* probability, tells us the probability of getting a sample of five with a p of .8 *if the prior inference distribution is true*. In other words, the probability that this sample came from one or the other of these universes is the sum of the probabilities that it came from each one of them.

Column 5 is simply column 4 adjusted proportionately so the total probability adds to 1 rather than to .1202. The logic behind this is as follows:

1. We assume that this sample came from one of the specified universes.
2. We also assume that the probabilities in column 2 are *correct*.
3. Hence the probabilities in column 4 give us the correct probabilities that we could get this sample from each of these universes.
4. Since this sample must have (assumptions 1 and 2) come from these and no other universes, the probability that it came from these universes is *1.0*.
5. Therefore we enlarge .1202 to 1.0. This, of course, requires the raising of each of the probabilities proportionately.
6. Finally, we interpret column 5 as telling us the probabilities that *this particular sample* came from each of these universes, *provided* each of these universes had the probability of being true as indicated in column 2.

TABLE 10.7

Testing a New Sample against Prior Information

(1) π_I	(2) $I(\pi_I)$	(3) $P(p\,|\,\pi_I)$	(4) $I(\pi_I)P(p)$	(5) $I(\pi_I'\,|\,p, \pi_I)$
0	.08	0	.0000	0
.2	.26	.0064	.0017	.014
.4	.34	.0768	.0261	.217
.6	.23	.2592	.0596	.496
.8	.08	.4096	.0328	.273
1.0	.01	0	0	0
	1.00		.1202	1.000

If all of our assumptions are correct, we could now argue that the column 5 probabilities, or the *posterior* probabilities, provide us with a *revised* inference distribution of π. It would then represent the result of *pooling* the prior information with the new sample information. That this is so is illustrated in Table 10.8. Part A shows the inference distribution that results from a sample of five with a p of .4. The method of generation is that of the *crude version* of the application of Bayes's theorem. We know how to do better than this, but this version is quick and easy, and sufficient to illustrate our point. It is also a parallel method to that shown in Table 10.7. Part B of Table 10.8 then takes the inference distribution generated in Part A and adds the information in a new sample of five with a p of .8. In other words, we use the *posterior* distribution in Part A as the *prior* distribution in Part B. We then generate a new posterior distribution as shown in column 5 of Part B. In Part C we show what happens if we first *pool the two samples* and then generate an in-

TABLE 10.8

Illustrating the Pooling Characteristics of the Application of Bayes's Theorem. $p_1 = .4, N_1 = 5; p_2 = .8, N_2 = 5$

		Part A				Part B	
(1)	(2)	(3)	(4)	(5) and (2′)	(3)	(4)	(5)
π_H	$P(\pi_H)$	$P(p_1\|\pi_H)$	$P(\pi_H)P(p_1\|\pi_H)$	$I(\pi_I\|p_1,\pi_H)$	$P(p_2\|\pi_I)$	$P(p_2\|\pi_I)I(\pi_I)$	$I'(\pi_I'\|p_2,\pi_I)$
0	.167	0	0	0	0	0	0
.2	.167	.2048	.0341	.246	.0064	.0016	.012
.4	.167	.3456	.0576	.416	.0768	.0319	.245
.6	.167	.2304	.0384	.277	.2592	.0718	.551
.8	.167	.0512	.0085	.061	.4096	.0250	.192
1.0	.167	0	0	0	0	0	0
	1.000		.1386	1.000		.1303	1.000

Part C: $\dfrac{p_1 + p_2}{2} = p = .6; N = N_1 + N_2 = 10$

(1)	(2)	(3)	(4)	(5)
π_H	$P(\pi_H)$	$P(p\|\pi_H)$	$P(\pi_H)P(p\|\pi_H)$	$I(\pi_I\|p,\pi_H)$
0	.167	0	0	0
.2	.167	.0055	.0009	.012
.4	.167	.1115	.0186	.245
.6	.167	.2508	.0418	.550
.8	.167	.0881	.0147	.193
1.0	.167	0	0	0
	1.000		.0760	1.000

ference distribution. The pooled sample would have 10 items with a p of .6. If we now compare column 5 in Parts B and C, we find a very satisfactory agreement.

We may thus conclude that the application of Bayes's theorem to information provided by two samples gives us essentially the same final inference distribution, whether we process the two samples in sequence, or whether we combine the samples and then process the combination.

We still must face the question of whether it was *appropriate* to pool the inference distribution with the new sample. If it is appropriate, we would now have a posterior distribution that gives us a clearer picture of the state of this unknown universe π than before the additional information provided by the new sample. We say clearer because this posterior distribution has less variation than the prior, as it should considering that it is based on more information. As a matter of fact, *if this universe does not change,* and if we keep adding new sample information this way, we will ultimately end up with a final posterior distribution that will converge on the true π. At that point our posterior distribution will show a probability of 1 for this π_I value and probabilities of 0 for all others.

The issue of the appropriateness of the pooling revolves around the *marginal probability* and, of course, the *consequences* of the decision to pool or not pool. Let us concentrate our attention on the marginal probability. We found it to be .1202 (see Table 10.7). How do we evaluate this? The first thing we must do is place this in its proper perspective. We do this by showing the whole distribution of which it is a part. Table 10.9 shows the matrix of all possible joint probabilities we could get if we combined all possible samples of five with our prior distribution.

The column of probabilities listed under the p of .8 is exactly the equivalent of column 4 in Table 10.7. The only differences are rounding errors. The other columns of the matrix were similarly calculated for each of the other possible p's in a sample of five.

First we note that the horizontal sums are equal to the original prior probabilities. (Rounding errors excepted.) This is as we would expect. This is the equivalent of saying that the *total* of the probabilities that a given sample came from a particular universe is equal to the probability that the particular universe prevails, or exists.

The vertical sums are the marginal probabilities. These measure the probability that any given sample could have come from this *whole set* of universes. If, for example, this really were a two-stage

TABLE 10.9

**Matrix of All Possible Joint Conditional Probabilities from a Given
Prior Distribution and All Possible Results of a Sample of 5**

[Body of matrix shows $P(p|\pi_I, N = 5) \times I(\pi_I)$]

p

π_I	I	0	.2	.4	.6	.8	1.0	
0	.08	.078	0	0	0	0	0	.078
.2	.26	.085	.106	.053	.013	.002	.000	.259
.4	.34	.027	.090	.119	.080	.026	.004	.346
.6	.23	.002	.018	.053	.080	.060	.018	.231
.8	.08	.000	.001	.004	.016	.033	.025	.079
1.0	.01	0	0	0	0	0	.010	.010
	1.00	.192	.215	.229	.189	.121	.057	1.003

sampling process, and if in the first stage one of the universes is
selected with the indicated prior probability, and then in the second
stage a sample of five is selected, we would expect a sample p of .2
to occur .215 of the time in the long run. Our sample happened to
have a p of .8. This would occur .121 of the time in the long run,
given the assumptions. We also note that a p of 1.0 would occur
.057 times in the long run. Thus we can say that we would expect a
p of *.8 or more* to occur .178 of the time.

What do these marginal probabilities have to do with the issue
of whether to pool? Let us answer this by assuming an extreme
condition. Let us suppose that our prior distribution had been such
that the marginal probability of a sample p of *.8 or more* had turned
out to be .00002. We would now be in possession of a *very unusual*
sample from this set of prior universes, *or* we would have a sample
that really did not come from this set. In other words, we would
have a strong suspicion that the prior information referred to a
universe different from the one from which this sample came. Again
we find it impossible to rationally state how strong this suspicion
would have to be before we would act on it. It, as before, depends
on our evaluation of the consequences of the pooling decision. If a
person has a very strong attachment to his prior distribution, say,

because it represents the accumulated experience of 20 years' work, he would require the marginal probabilities to be very low before he would dismiss his prior experience as irrelevant to today's problems. Human nature being what it is, it seems likely that more people are pooling information when they should not than people not pooling when they should. (We should mention that we are not considering at all the problem of people who have strongly held prior distributions and then proceed to *ignore* all new information. These people are not pooling, but, of course, for quite different reasons, the main reason being that they do not even see that there is anything that might be pooled.)

Some Relationships among Prior Probabilities, Posterior Probabilities, and Marginal Probabilities

It is evident that the posterior distribution is directly related to the prior distribution and the sample. A change in either the prior distribution or in the sample will change the posterior distribution. The relative importance of the prior distribution and the sample in this pooling operation will depend on the *quantity* of information contained in each and on the *variance* of this information. A *strong* prior distribution is one which has *very small variance,* the strongest possible being one with 0 variance, a type we look at in the next section. Such a strong prior distribution tends to dominate the posterior distribution unless the sample is tremendously large. A man of very strong convictions can be said to have very strong prior distributions. His hypotheses are very little altered by additional information. In fact, some people have such strong prior distributions that the issue of pooling becomes irrelevant. Their prior distributions completely overwhelm the sample evidence. If a person with very strong prior distributions continues to run into very low marginal probabilities, we have evidence that his prior distributions, although very strong, are probably inappropriate to the current problems. In effect we find him labeling almost everything that happens as "unusual."

A *weak* prior distribution is one with *relatively large* variance. The weakest prior distribution is that based on no previous information. We ran into this when we first struggled with the problem of inference. We used Bayes's theorem with *equal probabilities* assigned to all possible π_H's across the full range from 0 to 1.0. We discovered, however, that although this was certainly about as weak a prior distribution as we could imagine, it was not completely defenseless against the sample information. In fact, we did not want it to be completely defenseless because we were hoping to use these equal probabilities to modify the inferences from the sample alone. We did discover that this prior distribution modified the inference ratios and also biased the average toward .5, the average of the prior distribution. But the fact that this was a weak prior distribution was evidenced by the speed with which it tended to become swamped as the size of the sample increased. (The modified Bayesian method and the binomial method converged fairly rapidly as the size of sample increased.)

If we could be assured that our prior distributions were *proper* characterizations of our past experience, we would be less inclined to worry about strong prior distributions dominating a situation over a period of many years of accumulation of additional evidence. The additional evidence would in fact be only a small proportion of the total accumulation. But, unfortunately, we have abundant evidence that many people are temperamentally inclined toward strong prior distributions, just as other people are temperamentally inclined toward weak prior distributions. These evidences often show up at a very early age, say, in the hospital nursery. To apply the pooling operation to these people is essentially a waste of time. Attention to marginal probabilities is absolutely essential if we hope to significantly alter the prior distributions.

In conclusion, we emphasize very strongly that the calculation of posterior probabilities *assumes* that the prior distribution is a *proper* representation of past experience and not a mere outlet for the expression of pipe dreams, prejudices, hopes, etc. It also assumes that the universe that is generating the experiences, old and new, has not changed. If these assumptions stand up well under investigation, the posterior distribution is a reasonable approximation to our current state of effective knowledge. The best index we have to the reliability of these assumptions is the size of the marginal probabilities.

(We might parenthetically note that there are mathematical relationships that exist between the variance of the universe and the variance of the prior distribution, assuming we have used standard inference methods to derive our prior distribution. There are also relationships among the variance of the universe, the variance of the prior distribution and the variance of the marginal distribution. There are similar relationships among the variance of the universe, of the prior and of the posterior distribution. These relationships become very useful if we are trying to estimate the marginal and posterior distributions with, say, normal curve approximations. Limitations of space prevent discussing these relations and their applications.)

10.5   Procedure of Pooling If Given an Unqualified Hypothesis and Sample Information

Most people are not in the habit of consciously maintaining in their minds hypothetical inference distributions derived from their accumulated past experiences. It would not be surprising to find a random sample of 100 businessmen yielding no one who would admit to such a practice. This does not mean that these men do not daily *act as though they had such distributions*. It is also true that moderately skillful questioning could help these men to bring such distributions out of their subconscious minds into their conscious minds, and onto a piece of paper, and from there into a pooling analysis of the sort referred to in the preceding section. Actually, most successful people periodically do review their current operating hypotheses in a conscious way. But they do this in terms other than those we have been using. Also, we find that many people consider this reviewing as part of their private life, so private that even spouses are not allowed in on it. Thus an attempt to pry into this area often results in a rebuff, or a rationalization of the real operating hypotheses so that they look good to the public eye. Mathematical manipulations based on such rationalizations can lead to some amusing posterior distributions at best, or some very serious misconceptions at worst.

Most people have a strong predilection toward consciously expressing their prior distributions in the form of a *single number*. The president of the Smoothies Company will admit that he believes that the market share is *35%*, or even that it is *about 35%*, or sometimes even that it is *at least 35%*. If we try to get more from him, he may even call us strange for thinking that there is any more. Let us suppose that all we can get him to say is 35%. We know and he knows that he does not mean *exactly* 35%, but a vague "about" 35%. How do we pool this information with that appearing in a new sample?

Actually we can proceed exactly as we did when we were given a *distribution* of prior information. Table 10.10 shows the calculations. We put the prior probability of 1 in quotes to signify that it is the best we can say when we have only a single hypothesis. The mar-

TABLE 10.10

**Pooling a Vaguely Specific Prior Distribution with a
New Sample of 100 with a p of .28**

(1) π_I	(2) $I(\pi_I)$	(3) $P(p \leqq .28 \mid \pi_I)$	(4) $I(\pi_I)P(p \mid \pi_I)$	(5) $I(\pi_I' \mid p, \pi_I)$
.35	"1"	.07	.07	"1"
	1.00		.07	1.00

ginal probability of .07 is exactly the same answer we got in Chapter 9 when we tested the hypothesis that $\pi = .35$. If our president retains this hypothesis in the face of a marginal probability of only .07, we would be justified in saying that apparently he has a strong prior preference for the hypothesis of .35. This is exactly the same as saying that he is willing to take only a very small risk of Type I error. If we were to interview this president and probe until we found out how low a marginal probability he would tolerate before he would revise his hypothesis, we would be able to deduce the value system or the consequence matrix (at least the ratios between values) that is apparently guiding his thinking.

We can thus see that the methods of hypothesis testing bear a definite relationship to the problem of pooling prior and new information. In a sense, the testing of a single hypothesis as though it were the only one is simply a special case of the more general case where we have a more explicit statement of the apparent strength of conviction reflected in the prior distribution. It is also worth noting at this time that there is a strong likelihood that a person's prior distribution reflects not only his outlook on the probabilities, but also some of his feelings about the consequences. For example, a person expresses at least part of his fear of consequences in a generally weak prior distribution, probably weaker than that warranted by just the experience of the actual frequency of events. A person who is very much afraid of death from an airplane accident will tend to express this fear by remembering an accident rate that is higher than the truth. Each subsequent accident tends to confirm this prior distribution. The reverse is true for a person who strongly believes that accidents do not happen to him. If we treat these prior distributions as though they were pure probability distributions and subsequently combine the probabilities with a consequence matrix, we may be inadvertently doing a bit of double counting of consequences.

PROBLEMS AND QUESTIONS

10.1 You probably have some prior conviction that the probability of a head on the toss of a coin is .5. Suppose a particular coin is tossed and comes up heads several times in succession. How many such successive heads would you tolerate and still retain your original conviction of a $P(H) = .5$?

10.2 What is the past evidence or past authority that supports your prior conviction that the probability of a head is .5?

10.3 Give an example of some conviction that you hold so strongly that you would continue to believe its truth even in the face of almost overwhelming evidence. Distinguish carefully between something you *say* you believe and something that you really believe in the sense that the belief controls your actions. For example, almost everybody believes in The Golden Rule as an abstraction. Very few people rely on it as a guide to behavior.

10.4 A universe of machine parts is known to have 20% of the parts defective. (Do not ask how it is possible to know something like this. We are just trying to keep things simple—for the moment.) Paired samples of four items each are to be selected at random from this universe.

(*a*) Construct a matrix that shows all the possible combinations of sample p's that can occur. (In the manner of Part A of Table 10.1)

(*b*) Construct the matrix of probabilities that would be associated with each combination. (In the manner of Part B of Table 10.1)

(*c*) Combine all similar differences between paired p's in the form of a frequency distribution. (See Table 10.2, columns 1 and 2.)

(*d*) Calculate the arithmetic mean and standard deviation of this distribution.

(*e*) Check your calculation of the standard deviation by using the formula

$$\sigma_d = \sqrt{\frac{\sigma^2}{N_1} + \frac{\sigma^2}{N_2}}.$$

(*f*) Make normal curve estimates of the expected frequencies and compare them with the ones you calculated by direct application of the binomial.

(*g*) Are the normal curve estimates you made in (*f*) closer than those shown in the text for the case of a universe with $\pi = .1$ and $N = 2$? Measure the degree of closeness in some consistent manner. Is there a logical explanation for this?

(*h*) Repeat parts (*a*) to (*g*) assuming a universe with a $\pi = .2$ and with samples of two. What differences, if any, do you find in the accuracy of the normal curve estimates in this case compared with that in the text for the case of $\pi = .1$? Is there a logical explanation for your results?

10.5 Assume that you have no prior information of any kind about a given machine process. A sample of 10 items is selected at random from the first hour's output. It yields three defective items. A sample of 10 items is then selected from the second hour's output. It has one defective item. What, if anything, happened to the efficiency of the operation between the first and second hour? (Hint: You should answer this question in terms of the *probabilities* involved. A definitive answer is, of course, impossible.)

10.6(*a*) What is the probability that the process referred to in Question 10.5 was generating more defectives during the first hour than during the second hour?

(*b*) What is the probability that the process was generating the *same* proportion of defectives during each of the hours?

10.7 A given machine process is *supposed* to be producing 10% defectives. However, information that has accumulated to date about the process during a period in which the process has been purportedly stable has resulted in the following inference distribution about the universe proportion of defectives:

π_I	I
.10 *	.90
.30	.08
.50	.02
	1.00

* These values refer to the center of an interval of values.

A sample of 20 items has just been tested. It had only one defective.

(*a*) What inferences do you now make about the universe proportion of defectives?

(*b*) What is the probability that the process is now producing fewer than 10% defectives? Would you bet $1 of your own money at these odds? Would you be willing to claim fewer than 10% defectives in your promotional literature? Why or why not?

(*c*) What is the probability that the process has shifted in some way from what was formerly believed as expressed by the prior inference distribution?

(*d*) What is the probability that the new sample evidence is consistent with what was believed prior to its drawing and testing? Explain the basis of your answer.

10.8 You have a "vaguely specific" prior belief that a given setting on a machine will result in 5% defectives. A sample of 10 pieces reveals three defectives. What, if anything, does this additional information do to your belief about the long-run outcome of this particular machine setting? Buttress your argument with appropriate calculations.

10.9 Practical affairs continually confront us with the need to rationalize today's events with yesterday's beliefs. Critically analyze the problem of developing a practical policy for handling this issue of rationalization. For example, what are the merits of a philosophy that

(*a*) Always believes strongly whatever is currently believed, thus leading to so-called forthright and decisive action.

(*b*) Revises these beliefs in steps rather than in infinitesimal gradations.

(*c*) Never admits doubt until we are ready to modify the belief. Consider this question both from the point of view of your personal psychological needs and from the point of view of a business manager who has to be aware of the impact of his beliefs on the people he is managing. (For example, a good college quarterback is permitted to *feel* uncertain that he has chosen the right play, but he apparently should never let the team suspect this uncertainty.)

Also consider the problem of saving face when we discover the need to reject what has previously been sold as an unquestioned truth.

chapter 11

Inferences about later samples from information about prior samples

11.1 We Win (or Lose) with Samples, Not Universes

Up to this point we have concentrated on making inferences about *universes*. We have at times acted as though the universe
was the key element in a decision problem. It is now time to recognize that the universe as such really has no direct practical relevance.
Practical affairs involve *sample events*, not the whole universe. This
is also true of games of chance. We do not play bridge with the
universe of cards, but only with *sample hands* from that universe.
When we buy an automobile, we buy a *sample* of that manufacturer's
universe of cars, and we have to learn to live with that sample. If
we hire a man to do a job, he gives a *sample* of his work, and never
more than that. If a worker stops a machine on the basis of *one*
sample of information, he is not really trying to control the universe
of this machine's output. He is simply trying to assure as best he
can that later *samples* [1] of output will be satisfactory.

The universe is relevant information only insofar as it helps us to
make inferences about these future samples. If we make plans
based solely on the universe characteristics, we are likely to be very
disappointed in the results of our planning. The problem is created
by *variation*, particularly unpredictable or random variation. As
we mentioned in an earlier chapter, it is small solace to know that we
would have won in the long run if we had not gone broke in the short

---

[1] Sometimes the later *samples* are so large that we can safely assume that they
are the *equivalent* of the universe. In this case, inferences about future sample
p's would be essentially the same as inferences about π_I.

run. The ideal set-up is one in which we have a profit-potential universe working for us and also have sufficient reserves to withstand those unlucky samples that are bound to happen sooner or later. If our reserves are thin, then we not only need a profit-potential universe but also to be lucky.

In this chapter we direct our attention to making inferences about *future samples* on the basis of information supplied by some *past sample or samples*. Since we have previously done all the work necessary for this, we are essentially only reorienting some of the past work.

11.2 From Sample 1→to Universe Inferences→to Sample 2 •

To go from sample-to universe-to sample involves the same kinds of mechanics we used when we considered the problem of pooling a past inference distribution with a new sample. The only difference is that we are now going to *predict* what a second sample will be rather than wait to see what it is before we analyze the situation.

Let us suppose we have a presumably random sample of 10 items with three of the items defectives. We would now like to predict the number of defectives in a second sample of 10 items *provided* the universe has not shifted in the meantime. Figure 11.1 shows the tree that outlines the paths of reasoning from our first sample to expectations about a second sample. Our first task is to infer the probability distribution for the various *universe proportions* of defectives that might exist. Table 11.1 shows such an inference distribution. This inference distribution was copied from the fourth row of Table 8.7 on p. 331. It thus has been calculated by what we called the modified Bayesian method. With this inference distribution as a base we now calculate the *marginal* probability of getting any particular sample p, say, for a second sample of 10. (The same procedure would be used for any size sample.) The method of calculating the marginal probability is the same as we have used several times previously, Table 10.7 on p. 403 being a typical example.

In Table 11.2 we summarize the marginal probabilities for all possible values of p that could result from the inference distribution of Table 11.1. This table tells the probability of our getting a second sample of 10 with the given $p_{2,1}$ [1] if we had a first sample of 10 with a p_1 of .3. For example, if a first sample of 10 has this p_1 of .3, there

---

[1] We use $p_{2,1}$ to refer to a p_2 that is conditional on a prior p_1.

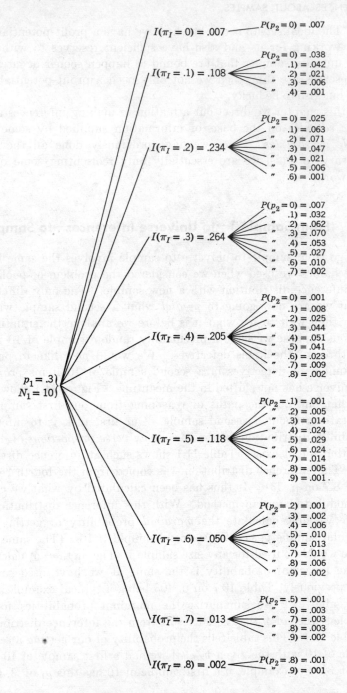

Fig. 11.1 Tree of probabilities for a second sample of 10 based on information from a first sample of 10 with $p = .3$.

TABLE 11.1

Inference Distribution of π Based on a Sample of 10 with $p = .3$

(1) π_I	(2) $I(\pi_I \mid p_1 = .3, N = 10)$
0	.007
.1	.108
.2	.234
.3	.264
.4	.205
.5	.118
.6	.050
.7	.013
.8	.002
.9	.000
1.0	.000
	1.001

TABLE 11.2

Probability of Getting a Succeeding Sample of 10 with the Given p If We Have a First Sample with a p of .3 ($N_1 = 10$)

p_2	$P(p_2 \mid p_1)$
0	.078
.1	.146
.2	.185
.3	.183
.4	.156
.5	.114
.6	.074
.7	.039
.8	.017
.9	.006
1.0	.000
	.998

are only .017 chances that a second sample of 10 would have a $p_{2,1}$ of .8.

It is instructive to compare this inference distribution shown in Table 11.1 with the distribution of marginal probabilities shown in Table 11.2. In Table 11.3 we compare their means and variances. The two means of .318 and .317 differ only because of rounding errors. It is logical to expect that the arithmetic mean of all possible sample means will equal the arithmetic mean of the generating universe, or, in this case, the arithmetic mean of the universe of inferred universe π_I's. We also expected the mean to be higher than .3 because we remember that the modified Bayesian method of inference does result in a bias toward .5.

TABLE 11.3

Comparison of Inference Distribution from a First Sample of 10 with the Distribution of All Possible Second Samples of 10

(1) π_I or $p_{2,1}$	(2) $I(\pi_I)$	(3) $I \times \pi_I$	(4) $I \times \pi_I^2$	(5) $P(p_2\|p_1)$	(6) $P \times p_{2,1}$	(7) $p \times p_{2,1}^2$
0	.007	0	0	.078	0	0
.1	.108	.0108	.00108	.146	.0146	.00146
.2	.234	.0468	.00936	.185	.0370	.00740
.3	.264	.0792	.02376	.183	.0549	.01647
.4	.205	.0820	.03280	.156	.0624	.02496
.5	.118	.0590	.02950	.114	.0570	.02850
.6	.050	.0300	.01800	.074	.0444	.02664
.7	.013	.0091	.00637	.039	.0273	.01911
.8	.002	.0016	.00128	.017	.0136	.01088
.9	.000	.0000	.00000	.006	.0054	.00486
1.0	.000	.0000	.00000	.000	.0000	.00000
	1.001	.3185	.12215	.998	.3166	.14028

$$\bar{\pi}_I = \frac{.3185}{1.001} = .318 \qquad \bar{p}_{2,1} = \frac{.3166}{.988} = .317$$

$$s_{\pi_I}^2 = \frac{.12215}{1.001} - \left(\frac{.3185}{1.001}\right)^2 \qquad s_{p_{2,1}}^2 = \frac{.14028}{.998} - \left(\frac{.3166}{.998}\right)^2$$

$$= .0209 \qquad\qquad\qquad = .0401$$

$$\approx \frac{p_1 q_1}{N_1} = \frac{.3 \times .7}{10} = .0210 \qquad \approx p_1 q_1 \frac{N_1 + N_2}{N_1 N_2} = .21 \times .20 = .042$$

$$\approx \frac{p_1 q_1}{N_1} \cdot \frac{N_1 + N_2}{N_2} = s_{\pi_I}^2 \frac{N_1 + N_2}{N_2}$$

The variance of the sample $p_{2,1}$'s (means) is *larger* than the variance of the inference distribution. This is also a logical expectation. If our *second* samples were *infinitely large*, we would then expect each sample $p_{2,1}$ to have the same value as the π_I of the universe from which it purportedly came, with no sampling variation at all. The distribution of such sample $p_{2,1}$'s would then have the same variance as the distribution of the π_I's. However, if the second samples are not that large, each purported universe will generate several possible $p_{2,1}$'s. This would be an additional source of variation in the $p_{2,1}$'s, that is, additional to the variation caused by the variation in the π_I's. Hence the $p_{2,1}$'s will have a greater variation than the π_I's. At the bottom of Table 11.3 we have shown a formula that gives an *approximate* relationship between the variance of π_I and the variance of $p_{2,1}$. It is clear from this formula that $s^2_{p_{2,1}}$ approaches $s^2_{\pi_I}$ as N_2 increases because $(N_2 + N_1)/N_2$ would then approach 1. For example, if N_2 were 1000, this ratio would be 1010/1000.

11.3 From Sample 1 Directly to Inferences about Sample 2

If we are not really interested in the *inference distribution* from the first sample, but only in the kinds of *second samples* that might be generated, we might short circuit this step of getting the inference distribution. To do this, however, we must make some assumptions about the *form* of the distribution of the marginal probabilities. Unfortunately, they do not conform to any simple binomial or its equivalent. But, again we find that the distribution tends toward the normal as N_1 and N_2 increase. For example, if N_1 increases, the distribution of π_I approaches the normal. The convergence of the distribution of $p_{2,1}$ to the normal with increases in N_1 and N_2 would be more rapid the closer the universe proportion is to .5. A normal approximation to the distribution of $p_{2,1}$ shown in Table 11.3 is relatively poor. We expect such a result with samples as small as 10 and with our basic information suggesting a π of .3. Let us, therefore, illustrate the direct approach to inferences about $p_{2,1}$ by using larger samples.

Our first problem is that of devising a formula for estimating the standard deviation of this distribution of $p_{2,1}$. We saw at the bottom of Table 11.3 that the variance of $p_{2,1}$ as there calculated can be approximated by the formula

$$\hat{\sigma}^2_{p_{2,1}} = p_1 q_1 \cdot \frac{N_1 + N_2}{N_1 N_2}.$$

This is a familiar formula to us. We used this when we were discussing the distribution of the differences between sample p's when the two samples came from the same universe. The similarity is no coincidence. The problem of the distribution of second sample p's as inferred from a first sample p can be restated as the problem of the *differences* that might exist between two sample p's, given that the two samples came from the same universe.

We recall that the variance of the differences between sample p's is a function of the variance of the universe and the sizes of the two samples. If we do not know this universe variance, we make the best estimate we can from the available information, in this case p_1 and N_1. Our best unbiased estimate is

$$\hat{\sigma}^2 = p_1 q_1 \frac{N_1}{N_1 - 1}, \text{ or } .3 \times .7 \frac{10}{9} = .233$$

for our preceding problem. If we have 50 items in the first sample, the estimated universe variance would be

$$.3 \times .7 \times \frac{50}{49} = .214.$$

We next allow for the effects of sizes of samples by multiplying the estimated universe variance by

$$\frac{N_1 + N_2}{N_1 N_2}.$$

Note that it is irrelevant whether sample 1 is relatively large or whether sample 2 is relatively large. The important consideration is the *combined* sizes of the two samples. (The advantage of having sample 1 relatively large is that this is the sample we must use to estimate the universe variance. The size of sample 2 is irrelevant for this purpose.)

Suppose our second sample is to have 20 items. Our estimate of the variance of the distribution of p_2 is

$$\hat{\sigma}^2_{p_1 - p_2} = \hat{\sigma}^2_{p_{2,1}}$$

$$= p_1 q_1 \frac{N_1}{N_1 - 1} \times \frac{N_1 + N_2}{N_1 N_2}$$

$$= .3 \times .7 \times \frac{50}{49} \times \frac{50 + 20}{50 \times 20}$$

$$= .214 \times .070$$

$$= .015.$$

(If we simplify the above formula, we get

$$\hat{\sigma}^2_{p_{2,1}} = p_1 q_1 \frac{N_1 + N_2}{N_2(N_1 - 1)}.\Bigg)$$

We are now ready to carry out the routine for making normal curve estimates of the distribution of $p_{2,1}$. Table 11.4 does this by estimating the height of the ordinates. We might just as well have used the differences between the cumulative probabilities. Column 1 lists the particular $p_{2,1}$ that we choose to represent the full range of $p_{2,1}$. Column 2 converts these $p_{2,1}$ values into values of $p_2 - p_1$,

TABLE 11.4

Expectations about the p of a Second Sample Based on Inferences about Differences between this Second p and the p of a First Sample

(1)	(2)	(3)	(4)	(5)	(6)
			Propor-	Normal Curve Estimates	Binomial
			tionate	Estimates	Estimates
		$\frac{p_{2,1} - p_1}{.122} = Z$	Height of	$P(p_2 \mid p_1,$	$P(p_2 \mid p_1,$
$p_{2,1}$	$p_{2,1} - p_1$		Ordinate	$N_1, N_2)$	of $P(p_{2,1})$ *
0	−.30	−2.46	.049	.008	.003
.05	−.25	−2.05	.122	.020	.015
.10	−.20	−1.64	.261	.043	.045
.15	−.15	−1.23	.469	.077	.088
.20	−.10	−.82	.714	.117	.119
.25	−.05	−.41	.919	.150	.146
.30	0	0	1.000	.164	.161
.35	.05	.41	.919	.150	.141
.40	.10	.82	.714	.117	.109
.45	.15	1.23	.469	.077	.071
.50	.20	1.64	.261	.043	.043
.55	.25	2.05	.122	.020	.021
.60	.30	2.46	.049	.008	.010
.65	.35	2.87	.016	.003	.004
.70	.40	3.28	.004	.001	.001
				.998	.977

$$Y_0 = \text{Maximum ordinate} = \frac{.05}{2.5066 \times .122} = .1635$$

* These are straightforward binomial estimates, and hence they differ slightly from modified Bayesian estimates.

given that $p_1 = .3$.* Column 3 converts these differences into Z units, our standard unit for measuring the normal curve. Column 4 shows the corresponding values from the Table of the Proportionate Height of Normal Curve Ordinates. Column 5 is the result of multiplying the column 4 figures by the maximum ordinate of .1635. Column 6 shows the estimates we get working through inferences about the universe proportion. The correspondence is reasonably close, particularly if we were to round to two decimal places.

11.4   Summary of the Problem and Methods of Making Inferences

Practical problems in inference usually break down into two parts as far as the *probabilities* are concerned. The first part is the problem of guessing, or inferring, the nature of the *universe* that will apparently be generating the samples that will occur. If we are playing a game of cards, we do not have to guess what this universe is because we know what it is. Thus the first part of our problem does not generally exist in games of chance.

The second part of the problem of inference is to guess what kinds of *samples* will *actually* occur. These will be the actual events on which we will be paid off, with the pay-off sometimes being negative. These are the events that we must necessarily provide for in the short-run in order to survive over the long-run and at least partly realize our long-run expectations.

These two problems are further complicated by the fact that the actual universe may shift before it ever generates enough samples to give us a semblance of our long-run expectations. Thus we may find that our earlier samples, possibly classified as unlucky, may never have a chance to be averaged out in the sense that future samples from the *same* universe will eventually overwhelm the first samples. If we have failed to recognize a shift in the universe, we may find ourselves waiting for something that is never going to come.

The greater is our uncertainty about the true state of the universe, the greater is our problem of planning a long-run strategy. We may have to *act* as though a given strategy has a profit potential even though it in fact has a loss potential. Similarly, of course, we may

---

* The effect of this procedure is to assume that $\bar{p}_{2,1}$ will equal .3, the value of p_1. Our estimates, therefore, are unbiased in the sense that our estimates tend to average out at the true value. Contrast this with the Bayesian estimates which have a bias toward .5.

reject a strategy that has a profit potential because we cannot clearly see this potential through the fog of our ignorance.

Uncertainty about the true state of the universe gets compounded as we contemplate the kinds of samples that will actually occur. We would be uncertain about the samples even if we *knew* the universe. We have seen what common sense already indicated, namely that the uncertainty about the samples is a function of three factors: (1) uncertainty about the universe, (2) variation within the universe, whatever its true state is, and (3) the size of the sample. It is these uncertainties that cause us to provide *reserves* against the short-run vicissitudes. In general, the greater the uncertainty, the larger must the reserves be relative to the commitments that have been made.

Practicality requires us to supplement all our notions about the *probabilities* of events with notions about the *consequences* of the occurrence or nonoccurrence of these events. Limitations of space have forced us to concentrate on the probabilities, with only passing consideration of any formal ways of combining probabilities with consequences.

Up to this point we have restricted our attention to information about the phenomenon we were trying to predict. This restriction imposed a greater degree of uncertainty on our solutions than is generally true in practice. In subsequent chapters we consider ways to *associate* information about other phenomena with the phenomenon of interest. We can thus reduce our uncertainties in exactly the same way we reduce our uncertainty about the degree of heat in the air by consulting the reading on a thermometer, although unfortunately we have much less success. We also give more attention than heretofore to whether and how a universe might be shifting through time.

PROBLEMS AND QUESTIONS

11.1 Most people would be willing to toss a coin to determine who will pay for the cokes. However, most of these same people will refuse to toss the same coin for $100 bills. Since the long-run universe probabilities are the same in both cases, there must be something else that causes the different policy. We have previously discussed this difference as being rooted in the different *consequences* that people attach to losing 5 or 10 cents and losing $100. Discuss this same issue in terms of the problem of *having to live with sample results,* not with any long-run expectations.

11.2 We are frequently admonished to avoid short-sighted policies in favor of policies that work over the long pull. We are also advised to take care of today, and tomorrow will take care of itself.

(*a*) Is there any necessary fundamental conflict between the short-run and the long-run? Give illustrations from your own practical experiences.

(b) Can you think of any situations in which you see an opportunity for a long-run gain without any risk of short-run loss?

11.3 Rework problem 17 in Chapter 2 in the light of your present knowledge.

11.4 A sample of five items yields one defective.

(a) What inferences would you make about the universe proportion of defectives?

(b) What inferences would you make about the probability distribution of the number of defectives in a second sample of five on the assumption that the universe remains constant?

1. Estimate this distribution by working through the inference distribution derived in (a).

2. Draw a tree of your line of inferences from the first sample to the second sample via the universe.

3. Estimate this distribution by going directly from the first sample to inferences about the second sample.

4. Critically compare your answers in (a) and (c).

chapter 12

Inferences from information expressed as a continuous variable

We have so far confined our attention to the problem of inferences about *attribute* data, data which can take on only the values of 1 and 0. This gave us certain advantages of exposition. It also enabled us to point up some issues that tend to get buried when we consider variable data. At the same time we labored under some difficulties which now disappear, more particularly the difficulties associated with having our data bounded by limits such as 1 and 0. We now turn to the problem of inferences for *continuous variables*. A continuous variable can take on *any size whatsoever* within the range of the data; our treatment parallels that which we used with attributes.

12.1 Analogy between Methods of Treating Attributes and Methods of Treating Continuous Variables

Brief Summary of Some Important Things We Learned From Our Treatment of Attributes

1. The arithmetic mean of sample means equals the mean of the universe. We found this true for attributes, where $\overline{X}_p = \pi$. It is also true for variables, where $\overline{X}_{\bar{x}} = \mu$ (*mu*, the Greek *m*).
2. The arithmetic mean of sample variances is *less than* the variance of the universe. We found that a simple adjustment could be made to correct for this bias. The formula was $\overline{X}_{s^2} \cdot N/(N-1) = \sigma^2$. If we had only a single sample, the best unbiased estimate of σ^2 would be $s^2 \cdot N/(N-1)$. (If we use attributes $s^2 = pq$.)

    Precisely the same relationship holds for variables.
3. The arithmetic mean of the crude skewness of samples is *less than* the crude skewness of the universe. We have no occasion to use this rela-

tionship so we do not reproduce it here. It is useful to remember, however, that samples in general have less skewness *on the average* than does the universe from which the samples came.

Another important thing to remember about skewness is that a sample can be skewed even though the universe is symmetrical. In fact, a symmetrical sample is a great rarity.

4. The variance of sample means is a direct function of the variance of the universe and an inverse function of the sample size. In formula: $\sigma_p{}^2 = \sigma^2/N$, or if σ^2 is unknown, which is the usual case, $\hat{\sigma}_p{}^2 = \hat{\sigma}^2/N$. Precisely the same relationship holds for variables. The expression is $\sigma_{\bar{x}}{}^2 = \sigma^2/N$, with σ replaced by $\hat{\sigma}$ if the universe variance is unknown.

5. Inferences about π should allow for the *variance and skewness* indicated by the sample. We discovered that such inferences would average out so that the appropriate estimates of π would be made. Thus we set up inference distributions that had the same direction of skewness in them as that in the sample. We ignored the skewness in the sample only when the sample was quite large.

6. If the sample is large, say 50 or more, and if the sample p is near .50, a normal curve approximation is fairly good. (A sample p near .50 would indicate a relatively small skewness.) Our analysis of the binomial distribution revealed that it approached the normal curve as N increased, with the approximation being better the nearer p is to .5. This phenomenon for the binomial is a special case of a general theorem that applies to *all* sampling distributions of the arithmetic mean. This is the central limit theorem, which argues that the means of random samples will tend to a normal distribution as N increases *regardless* of the distribution form of the universe. Figure 12.1 illustrates this convergence tendency for a few different types of universe. It is important to note that skewness is a much more troublesome factor than other departures from normality. A symmetrical universe, regardless of its specialized character, will generate *symmetrically* distributed sample means, with the characteristic shape of the normal curve with its center hump appearing fairly quickly as N increases. A skewed universe never does generate symmetrically distributed sample means, although the skewness does decline as N increases. The crude skewness varies inversely with N^2 and the coefficient of skewness inversely with N. Hence we must use caution in assuming that the normal curve applies if we find evidence of substantial skewness. For example, our data on unit charge sales for the hardware store showed substantial skewness. Normal curve inferences in this case would tend to be poor for samples less than 50, or even much less than 100.

7. Differences between means of independent samples from the *same* universe are always symmetrically distributed and quite close to the normal, even for quite small samples. This relationship applies regardless of the shape of the universe. It also holds for variables.

8. Differences between means of independent samples from *different* universes are symmetrically distributed only if the universes are symmetrically distributed. In such a case normal curve approximations would hold quite well even if N is small. If the universes are not symmetrical, the distribution of differences will be skewed. This skewness will tend to decline as the sample sizes increase, just as we found for the distribution of means from a single universe.

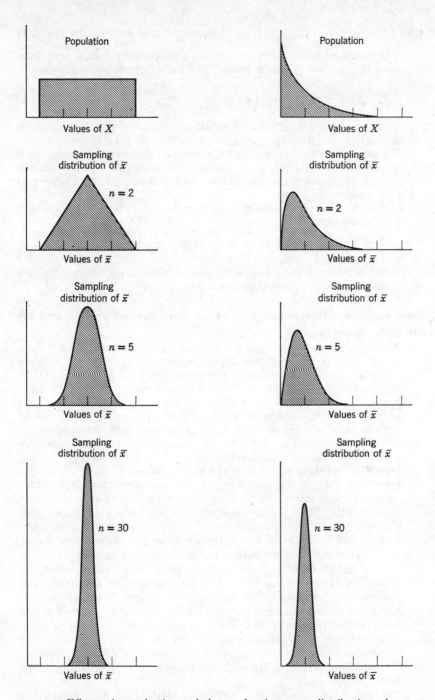

Fig. 12.1 Effects of sample size and shape of universe on distribution of means of random samples. (Reproduced with permission from E. Kurnow, G. J. Glasser, and F. Ottman, *Statistics for Business Decisions,* Richard D. Irwin, Inc., Homewood, Illinois, pp. 182–3.)

9. The variance of the *difference* between two sample means is essentially *twice* the variance of sample means. The basic formula for attributes is:

$$\hat{\sigma}^2_{p_1-p_2} = \frac{\hat{\sigma}^2}{N_1} + \frac{\hat{\sigma}^2}{N_2} = \hat{\sigma}^2 \left(\frac{1}{N_1} + \frac{1}{N_2} \right) = 2\frac{\hat{\sigma}^2}{N_1} \quad \text{if} \quad N_1 = N_2.$$

Note that information from the two samples is pooled to derive a single estimate of the universe variance. This formula holds strictly only on the assumption that both samples came from universes with equal variances. The situation is more complicated otherwise. The formula is approximately correct even with unequal variances and is often used as such an approximation.

Precisely the same formulas apply when we are working with variables. The basic formula is:

$$\hat{\sigma}^2_{\bar{x}_1-\bar{x}_2} = \frac{\hat{\sigma}^2}{N_1} + \frac{\hat{\sigma}^2}{N_2} = \hat{\sigma}^2 \left(\frac{1}{N_1} + \frac{1}{N_2} \right)$$

Again we assume universes with equal variances, and we pool the two samples to arrive at this single estimate.

Some Important Differences between a Continuous Variable and an Attribute Measure

1. Most continuous variables do not have any arbitrary boundaries. Thus we do not run into the sort of problem we did with attributes when we were making estimates near the boundaries. In fact, we generally assume that our continuous variables have no boundaries, in the same sense that the normal curve has no boundaries. Theoretically the normal curve has no boundaries; however, the probabilities decline quite rapidly as we move beyond, say, a distance three standard deviations from the mean. Thus we can fix *practical* boundaries beyond which the probabilities are negligible at the same time we reap the benefits of working with an unbounded distribution.

2. Since a continuous variable can take on any size whatsoever within its natural boundaries, we have an *infinite* number of possible values to work with. This results in certain mathematical advantages. Not the least of these advantages is that it makes it possible for us to make *independent* estimates of the arithmetic mean and the standard deviation. With attributes we were not able to get samples so that a given mean could occur with all possible standard deviations. In fact, we found that each mean was paired with its own standard deviation. The net result of this was that the inference vectors had *different* variances. If a given sample mean can be paired with all possible standard deviations, we find that the inference vectors will all average out to have the *same variance*. This means that we will not have to use any prior hypotheses as we did with attributes. We will thus get good estimates of the inference ratios without necessitating any bias-inducing prior probabilities.

3. The universe distribution of a continuous variable can take on all kinds of shapes. Hence the distribution of sample means can take on all kinds of shapes. Unfortunately, these various distributions do not

belong to any well-regulated family of distributions in the way that the attribute distributions belonged to the family of binomial distributions. Our approach to inferences about the means of variables is thus strictly in terms of *approximations*. We adopt certain model distributions, such as the normal, as the basis of our probability estimates. This tactic gives the appearance of making our procedures easier than when working with the binomial distributions. We should not forget, however, that they are easier only because we are forced to be satisfied with approximations. As indicated a few paragraphs before, distributions of sample means tend to converge on the normal as the sample size increases. Thus most of our big mistakes occur when we work with small samples.

12.2   Inferences About the Mean of a Continuous Variable by the Use of Percentile Equivalents

Let us suppose we are making inferences about the universe mean of the unit sales of our neighborhood hardware store. We combined the 200 raw figures into a frequency distribution. This distribution showed substantial positive skewness. The magnitude of this skewness is indicated by the fact that the mean of $5.72 was located at about the 74th percentile. The mean would be at the 50th percentile if the distribution were symmetrical. A possible approach to inferences about the universe mean is to work through the *percentile equivalent* of the mean. In effect we would be converting our variable data into attribute data for purposes of calculations. If we let a represent sample values below the mean and b represent values above the mean, we could use the binomial, $(.74a + .26b)^{200}$, to generate percentile equivalents of the universe mean. We could then transform these back to unit sales figures. The expansion of this binomial would be quite tedious. We cannot use tables because tables are not conveniently available for an N as large as 200. Most people would find it practical, therefore, to be satisfied with a normal curve approximation to this distribution. This approximation would fail to recognize the skewness involved, but the errors involved would be small. In order to illustrate the use of the percentile equivalent approach we arbitrarily assume that our sample had been only 100. Thus we can use the Romig binomial tables.

Table 12.1 illustrates the calculations for the percentile equivalent approach. Column 1 lists arbitrarily chosen hypothetical π_H's. Column 2 lists the modified Bayesian cumulative probabilities. These are taken from Romig's binomial tables for $N = 100$. The

TABLE 12.1

Inferences About μ Based on Percentile Equivalents—Hardware Store Unit Sales Data.   Given: $\overline{X}$ = \$5.72; Percentile Equivalent equals .74; N = 100

(1) π_H	(2) $P(p \geq .74 \mid \pi_H)$	$P(p \leq .74 \mid \pi_H)$	(3) π_I	(4) I	(5) μ_I
.56	$.0002 - .0000 = .0002$		.54–.58 *	.00	3.6–3.9 *
.58	$.0006 - .0002 = .0004$		.58–.62	.01	3.9–4.3
.60	$.0024 - .0006 = .0018$		.62–.66	.04	4.3–4.7
.62	$.0078 - .0018 = .0060$		.66–.70	.15	4.7–5.2
.64	$.0220 - .0046 = .0174$		.70–.74	.31	5.2–5.7
.66	$.0544 - .0102 = .0442$		.74–.78	.32	5.7–6.3
.68	$.1180 - .0192 = .1088$		.78–.82	.15	6.3–7.4
.70	$.2244 - .0306 = .1938$		.82–.86	.02	7.4–10.1
.72	$.3748 - .0410 = .3338$			———	
.74	$.5525 - .0453 = .5072$	$.5381 - .0453 = .4928$		1.00	
.76		$.3562 - .0407 = .3155$			
.78		$.1972 - .0290 = .1682$			
.80		$.0875 - .0158 = .0717$			
.82		$.0295 - .0064 = .0231$			
.84		$.0071 - .0018 = .0053$			
.86		$.0011 - .0003 = .0008$			
.88		$.0001 - .0000 = .0001$			

* Lower Limit Inclusive.

method of calculation is the same as that shown in Table 8.6. Column 3 shows arbitrarily chosen intervals for π_I. Column 4 shows the inference ratios for these intervals based on the cumulative probabilities given in column 2.   Column 5 shows the unit sales equivalents of the column 3 intervals. The best way to transform from percentile equivalents (the π_I's in column 3) into unit sales is by means of a graph. Figure 12.2 illustrates the procedure.   Here we show the cumulative frequency chart of the frequency series of unit sales given in Table 6.8. A smooth line has been drawn by eye through the observed cumulative frequencies to provide the basis of the interpolations. The procedure is to locate the given percentile on the vertical axis, for example, the .62 percentile. A horizontal line is drawn to intercept the cumulative frequency curve; a vertical is dropped from this point of intersection to the horizontal,

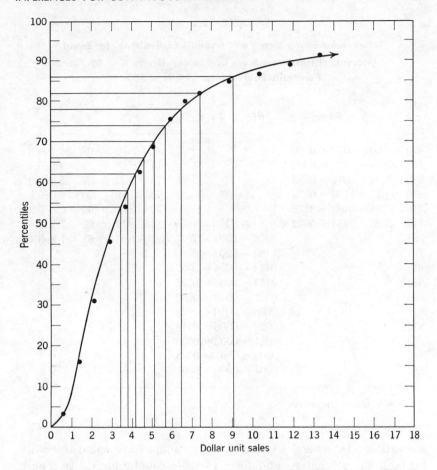

Fig. 12.2 Cumulative frequency curve of unit sales of hardware store. Illustration of transformation of percentile equivalents into dollar unit sales.

or unit sales, axis. The intercepted value is then the unit sales equivalent of the percentile. Such transformations are shown for all the values given in columns 3 and 5 of Table 12.1. We could, of course, use the same technique in reverse to transform unit sales values into percentile equivalents.

Columns 4 and 5 give us the estimated inference ratios for the unknown universe μ. Note an awkwardness caused by the *unequal* intervals for μ_I. We would have been better advised if we had worked out *equal* intervals. We chose the convenient route of using equal intervals for the percentiles and also round numbers for the

TABLE 12.2

**Inferences About μ Based on Percentile Equivalents—for Equal
Intervals of Hardware Store Unit Sales.   Given: $\overline{X} = \$5.72$;
Percentile Equivalent $= .74; N = 100$**

(1) π_H	(2) $P(p \geqq .74 \vert \pi_H)$	$P(p \leqq .74 \vert \pi_H)$	(3) π_I	(4) I	(5) μ_I
.470	$.0000 - .0000 = .0000$		.610–.670 *	.07	\$4.2–4.8 *
.545	$.0001 - .0000 = .0000$		.670–.718	.25	4.8–5.4
.610	$.0044 - .0011 = .0033$		.718–.763	.39	5.4–6.0
.670	$.0815 - .0143 = .0672$		.763–.794	.20	6.0–6.6
.718	$.3588 - .0409 = .3179$		.794–.815	.06	6.6–7.2
.740	$.5525 - .0453 = .5072$	$.5381 - .0453 = .4928$	.815–.830	.02	7.2–7.8
.763		$.3308 - .0391 = .2917$	.830–.840	.01	7.8–8.4
.794		$.1163 - .0203 = .0960$			
.815		$.0411 - .0084 = .0327$			
.830		$.0151 - .0035 = .0116$			
.840		$.0071 - .0018 = .0053$			
.848		$.0038 - .0010 = .0028$			
.853		$.0024 - .0006 = .0018$			
.860		$.0011 - .0003 = .0008$			
.870		$.0004 - .0001 = .0003$			
.880		$.0001 - .0000 = .0001$			

* Lower Limit Inclusive.

percentiles.   In general we find that we cannot have equal intervals
for both the percentiles and their variable counterparts.   In Table
12.2 we show the results of this percentile equivalent method if we
equalize the unit sales intervals.   Figure 12.3 shows the starting
point of an attempt to equalize these unit sales intervals.   We start
with equal intervals on the horizontal axis and estimate the percentile equivalents.   These percentile equivalents become the key
figures for estimating probabilities from the binomial tables.   Table
12.2 summarizes the calculations.   A little free-lance interpolating
is needed to get the probabilities given in column 2.   Otherwise everything proceeds as shown in Table 12.1.

Figure 12.4 pictures our second inference distribution of μ_I.   The
skewness is quite evident, and is in the same direction as the skewness in the sample.   This is as we found it for attributes.   This is
the ideal solution to our problem of making inferences about the uni-

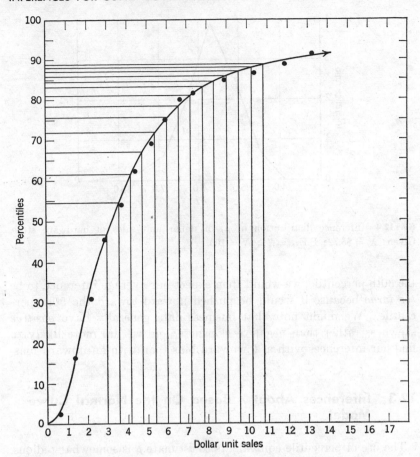

Fig. 12.3 Cumulative frequency curve of unit sales of hardware store. Illustration of transformation of dollar unit sales into percentile equivalents.

verse mean of the hardware sales. If this procedure were repeated for all possible samples of 100, we would find that the indicated inference ratios would be almost exactly correct as indicators of the probability that the universe mean falls within the specified values. The grand mean of all such inferences, however, would likely be a *little less* than the true mean. This bias is the result of using a prior distribution of equally probable π_H's. Since this bias runs toward .5, and our sample mean is at the 74th percentile, we would expect our inferences to average out at something less than .74 and hence something less than the true mean. If our sample mean had been, say, at

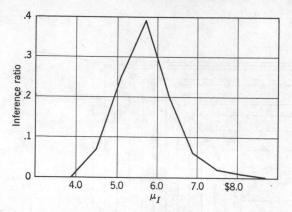

Fig. 12.4 Inference distribution of μ_I of dollar unit sales of hardware store. Given: $\overline{X} = \$5.72$; P.E.$_{\bar{x}} = .74$; $N = 100$.

the 30th percentile, we would then expect our average inference to be *too large* because it would be pushed upward toward the 50th percentile. We might note that business data generally have *positive* skewness rather than negative skewness, and we are more likely to find our inferences with a downward bias than with an upward bias.

12.3 Inferences About μ Based On the Normal Curve Model

The use of percentile equivalents to estimate μ is somewhat tedious. It also presumes the availability of tables of the binomial. Hence it is much more customary to use the normal curve model as the basis of estimates. Table 12.3 shows the now familiar procedure for making normal curve estimates. Here we use cumulative frequencies rather than ordinates of the normal curve. The results are essentially the same in either case. We use the cumulative frequencies because of the close analogy to the use of cumulative frequencies in Table 12.2. Note the calculation of $\hat{\sigma}_{\bar{x}}$ at the base of the table. We use $N - 1$ instead of N because we use s instead of σ. We could have converted s into σ by the relation $\hat{\sigma}^2 = s^2 N/(N - 1)$ and then used N in the formula for the standard deviation of the sample means. The answers would have been the same. This short-cut formula is obviously more convenient. Note that in column 3 we call $(\mu_I - \overline{X})/\hat{\sigma}_{\bar{x}}$ t instead of Z as we have done previously. The significance of this is made clear when we consider the problem of samples somewhat smaller than 100.

TABLE 12.3

Normal Curve Estimates of the Inference Distribution of the Mean of Unit Sales of a Hardware Store. $\overline{X} = \$5.72; s = \$7.61; N = 100$

(1) μ_I	(2) $\mu_I - \overline{X}$	(3) $\dfrac{\mu_I - \overline{X}}{\hat{\sigma}_{\bar{x}}} = t$	(4) $P(\mu_I \leq \overline{X} \mid \overline{X}, \hat{\sigma})$	$P(\mu_I \geq \overline{X} \mid \overline{X}, \hat{\sigma})$	(5) μ_I	(6) $I(\mu_I)$
$3.0	$-2.7	-3.53	.0002		$3.6-4.2 *	.02
3.6	-2.1	-2.75	.0030		4.2-4.8	.09
4.2	-1.5	-1.96	.0250		4.8-5.4	.23
4.8	- .9	-1.18	.1190		5.4-6.0	.31
5.4	- .3	- .39	.3483		6.0-6.6	.23
5.7	0	0	.5000	.5000	6.6-7.2	.09
6.0	.3	.39		.3483	7.2-7.8	.02
6.6	.9	1.18		.1190	7.8-8.4	.00
7.2	1.5	1.96		.0250		—
7.8	2.1	2.75		.0030		.99
8.4	2.7	3.53		.0002		

* Lower Limit Inclusive. $\hat{\sigma}_{\bar{x}} = \dfrac{s}{\sqrt{N-1}} = \dfrac{\$7.61}{\sqrt{99}} = \$7.65$

In Table 12.4 and Fig. 12.5 we compare the percentile equivalent estimates with the normal curve estimates. The difference between the means of the two distributions was caused mainly by our rounding activities. If it were not for these, we would expect the mean based on the percentiles to be slightly smaller because of bias toward .50. The standard deviations are clearly different, and this difference is not caused by rounding errors. (The difference between the normal curve standard deviation of $.75 and the expected standard deviation of $.76 is caused by rounding errors.) The modified Bayesian estimates tend to have a smaller variance because of "information" supplied by the prior distribution of equal probabilities. In effect, there is a pooling of two distributions, one the prior distribution of equal probabilities and the other the binomial distribution based only on the sample information. The variance of the pooled distribution must be less than the smaller of the two variances of the separate distributions. The binomial distribution would have a variance that would be the equivalent of $.76. Hence the Bayesian estimates must have a variance less than $.76.

TABLE 12.4

Comparison of Percentile Equivalent and Normal Curve Estimates of the Mean of Unit Sales of a Hardware Store

	Percentile Equivalent				Normal Curve		
(1) μ_I *	(2) I_p	(3) $I_p\mu_I$	(4) $I_p\mu_I{}^2$	(5) I_z	(6) $I_z\mu_I$	(7) $I_z\mu_I{}^2$
$3.9	.00	.000	.0000	.02	.078	.3042
4.5	.07	.315	1.4175	.09	.405	1.8225
5.1	.25	1.275	6.5025	.23	1.173	5.9823
5.7	.39	2.223	12.6711	.31	1.767	10.0719
6.3	.20	1.260	7.9380	.23	1.449	9.1287
6.9	.06	.414	2.8566	.09	.621	4.2849
7.5	.02	.150	1.1250	.02	.150	1.1250
8.1	.01	.081	.6561	.00	.000	.0000
	1.00	5.718	33.1668	.99	5.643	32.7195

Percentile Equivalent	Normal

$\bar{\mu}_I = \$5.72$ $\qquad\qquad$ $\bar{\mu}_I = \$5.70$

$s_{\mu_I} = \sqrt{33.1668 - 5.718^2}$ $\qquad$ $s_{\mu_I} = \sqrt{\dfrac{32.7195}{.99} - 5.7^2}$

$\qquad = \$.69$ $\qquad\qquad\qquad\qquad = \$.75$

Percentile Equivalent of Mean = .52 (Approximate)

* Midpoint of interval.

The percentile equivalent of the mean of μ_I is estimated to be approximately .52 for the percentile based estimates. It would be .50, of course, for the normal curve estimates because the normal curve is symmetrical. Thus there is only *very moderate skewness* in the inference distribution. *This is a vivid illustration of the effect of increasing sample size on the skewness of the distribution of sample means.*

Whether we prefer the percentile equivalent estimates or the normal curve estimates in a given problem depends on the significance we attach to the differences like those shown in Table 12.4. In many

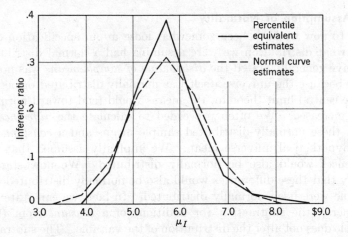

Fig. 12.5 Comparison of the percentile equivalent and normal curve estimates of the universe mean of hardware store unit sales.

problems we find that our notions of consequences are so vague that moderate differences in the probabilities will not make any differences in our decisions anyway. Or at least they should not. Many people would prefer the normal curve approximations because of their relative ease of calculation. If this seems like a lazy man's rule, we might emphasize the *conservative* features of the normal curve estimates. Note that the normal curve estimates show greater uncertainty (greater dispersion) than the percentile equivalent estimates. Many analysts consider this a positive virtue. In other words, it is apparently better to *underestimate* than it is to *overestimate* what we know. This rule is obviously subject to dispute. Perhaps a more defensible rule would be to always try to estimate *as accurately as we can* what we know, with no conscious bias toward under- or over-estimation.

12.4 The *t* Distribution

In the preceding section we called the ratio $(\mu_I - \overline{X})/\hat{\sigma}_{\overline{x}}$ the equivalent of *t* rather than of the more familiar *Z*. We then proceeded to use *t* in the normal curve table just as though it were *Z*. It is now time to make the appropriate distinction between *t* and *Z*.

The Assumption of Normality

Up to now we have been somewhat loose in our specification of exactly what distribution we were assuming had a normal distribution. We have generally stated the *distribution of sample means* was normal, either because the universe itself was normally distributed or because, by the central limit theorem, the means would tend toward normality as N increased. We often proceeded to calculate the *differences* between these normally-distributed sample means and a *constant*, such as a hypothetical universe mean. We implicitly assumed that these differences would also be normally distributed. We now state explicitly that these differences would also be normally distributed if the variable were itself normally distributed. In fact, we can state that, in general, the subtraction (or addition) of a *constant* from (to) a variable does not alter the distribution of the variable. The subtraction merely alters the origin of measure. For example, the distribution of ordinary playing cards is *rectangular*. If we subtract 5 from the value of each card, the resultant distribution is also rectangular.

A second step we often took was to divide these differences by the *standard deviation of such differences*. If the standard deviation is known, it is obviously a *constant*. The division of a variable by a constant does not alter the form of the distribution of that variable. It merely changes its *unit* of measure. Thus, if the variable is normally distributed, the ratios of this variable to some constant is also normally distributed.

We can now be very specific about what Z really is. Suppose we have a set of sample means, or $\overline{X}$'s, that are normally distributed. If we subtract μ from each $\overline{X}$, the resultant differences, or $\overline{X} - \mu$, will also be normally distributed. If we divide these differences by the standard deviation of such differences, or by $\sigma_{\bar{x}}$, the resultant ratios will also be normally distributed. We call such ratios Z. Hence Z is a *normally-distributed ratio*. Its value to us is that it is *independent of the unit* of the series being analyzed and can thus be related to a *standard* normal curve that can be used for all problems involving the normal curve. Thus one table of the normal curve is sufficient for us. We merely take our given normally-distributed variable and transform it into Z. In this way all normal distributions can be transformed into Z. We then look up Z in the normal curve table.

The Case When $\hat{\sigma}$ is a Variable

Let us suppose that the standard deviation we divide by to get Z is *not known*. We then have to estimate it. This estimate might take on many different values. Hence our ratios of *normal* deviates will be to a *variable* rather than to a constant. The resultant ratios will not be normally-distributed. Hence they are not proper Z's. The exact form of their distribution depends on the degree to which $\hat{\sigma}$ varies. Since $\hat{\sigma}$ varies less as the size of sample increases, the exact form of the distribution of these ratios depends on the size of the sample, or more specifically on the number of *degrees of freedom* in the data used to estimate σ. We call these ratios t.

The Notion of Degrees of Freedom

It goes without saying that a conclusion that purports to be based on a certain set of evidence should in fact be related to that evidence. If we find that we can arrive at a given conclusion with no reference to a set of evidence, we are justified in arguing that the conclusion has nothing to do with the evidence. Many of the rules of evidence and the rules of procedure used in our court system are designed to assure reasonably well that the final decision will be based on the evidence *freely given* by the witnesses. It is also true that certain procedural rules must be followed in statistical analysis to prevent us from inadvertently acting as though our conclusions are based on the evidence when in fact they are quite independent of the evidence. It took statisticians quite a few years to learn only a few of the simpler rules to be followed to prevent our promulgating sophisticated nonsense in the guise of "scientific conclusions from unbiased evidence." Sophistication came from the use of analytical methods not easily comprehended by the layman, and nonsense came from the fact that the methods were so complicated that they more or less overwhelmed the evidence and developed conclusions that were foreordained rather than based on the evidence. We have occasion to see how the worst offenses were committed when we study correlation analysis in a later chapter.

We can illustrate the basic notion of degrees of freedom by referring to the problem of attempting to estimate the arithmetic mean and standard deviation of a universe. Suppose we are asked to estimate the arithmetic mean from a *single* number, i.e., from a sample with only *one* item in it. We cannot possibly give an answer unless we know the value of the item in question. The arithmetic mean of such a number is the number itself, and any conclusion we draw about the mean is necessarily based on the value of this item of evidence. But suppose we are asked to estimate the *standard deviation* from a sample of *one* item. We can easily see that the answer is 0, and we can state this *without knowing the value of the item at all*. Obviously this must be nonsense. The fact is that *one item alone* provides us with absolutely no information about the value of the standard deviation. It takes *at least two* items to give us any information about the standard deviation. However, if either of these items alone tells us nothing, it must be only the second one that tells us something. Hence we conclude that the standard deviation is based on $N - 1$ items, or $N - 1$ *degrees of freedom.*

Another way to look at the problem is to consider what must be done in order to calculate something such as the standard deviation. The standard deviation is measured from the *arithmetic mean.* We must therefore know the mean before we can calculate the standard deviation. (This is true even when we use a method of calculation which short-cuts the mean. We may not then actually know the mean, but rest assured that our formula does.) The prior calculation of the mean "uses up" one of the items of evidence in a sense, thus leaving one fewer item to provide evidence about the standard deviation. If we then calculate the standard deviation, we use up another item, leaving only $N - 2$ items to tell us something about, say, the skewness of the data. If we have only two items to begin with, we thus would have no evidence at all about skewness. (We can demonstrate that this is so by calculating the skewness of a 2-item series. We find that all such series have a *0* skewness regardless of the values of the items.)

Thus, if we have ever talked of "drawing conclusions from evidence," we were being more literal than we perhaps thought. In a sense we drew these conclusions from the evidence the same way we would draw a cup of sugar out of a canister. Each time we drew a conclusion we left less evidence, just as each cup of sugar reduced the contents of the canister. Eventually the evidence gets exhausted, just as the canister does. Unfortunately, it is not as easy to see the evidence dwindle as it is to see the sugar disappear. We must understand the notion of degrees of freedom to see the evidence disappear. Otherwise we might go on indefinitely drawing conclusions from the evidence. We would be kidding ourselves, of course, and we would find this out when we discovered that our conclusions were not standing up to the future facts. This is what a person does who draws all sorts of conclusions about human behavior based on his experience with *one* individual, who may even be himself.

A more technical explanation of the use of the degrees of freedom notion by statisticians is as follows. Suppose we have a sample of N items, the items identified as $X_1, X_2, X_3 \cdots X_N$. We calculate the arithmetic mean of these items, and we can now logically argue that this arithmetic mean was based on a sample of N items. Since we did nothing in our calculation to fix, or constrain, the value of any of these N items, we say that the arithmetic mean was based on N *degrees of freedom*. Each item was *free* to take on any value whatsoever *as far as we are concerned*. Suppose we now calculate the *standard deviation* of our N items. To do this, we must take the mean as a *given*, or *fixed*, or *specified*, value (various terms can be applied to connote a lack of freedom). The specification of the mean is the equivalent of the specification of the *total* of the N items. So we can now write the equation

$$X_1 + X_2 + X_3 + \cdots + X_N = N\overline{X} = \Sigma X, \text{ with } \Sigma X \text{ } given.$$

We now conceive of the X's being free to have any values whatsoever as far as we are concerned. It is immediately apparent that *one* of these X's is not really free as long as we insist that the N items must add to the specified total. As soon as $N - 1$ of the items have "chosen" their values, *the Nth item must take on that value that will make the correct total*. The Nth item is thus really determined by the values of the other $N - 1$ items *and by the total*. It is not *free* at all.

For example, suppose a series of 20 items has a mean of $5.00, and thus a total of $100.00. Nineteen of the items are allowed to take on any values that are determined by the evidence-generating process. Suppose these 19 items add to $93.00. The 20th *must* now have a value of $7.00 in order to make the total $100.00.

This is why we say that the evidence available to tell us something about the standard deviation consists of only $N - 1$ *degrees of freedom*. It is useful to recall that the sample standard deviation tends to be *too small on the average* unless we use $N - 1$ instead of N in its calculation. We can now relate this phenomenon to the notion of degrees of freedom.

The notion extends beyond the calculation of the standard deviation. Consider the problem of skewness. The coefficient of skewness depends on the prior calculation of *both* the mean *and* the standard deviation. The specification of the standard deviation really specifies the sum of the *squares* of the items. Thus we would now have a second equation to go with the first one. This second would be

$$X_1{}^2 + X_2{}^2 + X_3{}^2 + \cdots + X_N{}^2 = \Sigma X^2.$$

We now find that $N - 2$ of the items are free to vary. As soon as we know these *and* the specified sum and sum of squares, the remaining two items are easily calculated from the two equations. This is why we say that the coefficient of skewness is based on only $N - 2$ degrees of freedom.

We generally use the symbol k to represent the *number of constraints* or the number of values that are *specified by prior calculations*. The number of degrees of freedom is represented by n and the size of the sample by N. Thus we can define the number of degrees of freedom, n, as equal to $N - k$.

The general notion of degrees of freedom extends beyond the simple mathematical case in which we can count them with little difficulty. The notion applies also to the problem of psychological constraints on the data themselves. For example, if subtle psychological influences cause a respondent or a witness to unknowingly restrict his answers to only certain limited categories, it would be incorrect to treat the responses as though they were freely given. Unfortunately, we do not have any routine procedures to measure the degree of constraint that has been put on the data. Thus it is not unusual to find ourselves using data as though they were "free," except for the calculation restrictions we later impose, when, in fact, the original data were already severely restricted. *Bias* is the term we usually apply to any psychological restrictions we think exist. We should not let the inherent difficulties in measuring the magnitude of this bias deter us from making the attempt. If we are deterred, we might find ourselves in the essentially ridiculous position of using sophisticated technique on naive data.

It might be instructive to speculate on the different interpretations we should put on human behavior that is the result of free choice and that which is the result of coercion. For example, if we could plan the menus at the Waldorf-Astoria so that there was only an average of 5% waste, we could properly qualify as a genius in the art of satisfying peoples' food desires. To have as little waste in serving meals to a military group would take somewhat less than genius. To offer people *real* freedom of choice and to gamble on our ability to anticipate those choices is the fundamental challenge of business. It is so much a challenge that most businesses find it desirable to expend some effort in the arts of persuasion in order to help people make their choices. It is not at all easy to separate that part of a consumer's preference that was the result of persuasion from that part that was based on a real choice for the product. The more we speculate on such matters the more we realize that the notion of degrees of freedom is closely related to our notions on freedom in general.

The Shape of the *t* Distribution

Figure 12.6 illustrates the characteristic shape of a *t* distribution in comparison with the normal. The essential difference is that the *t* is flatter than the normal. Thus more of the frequency is at the tails of the distribution. The degree of flatness is a function of the number of degrees of freedom, with the relative flatness decreasing as *n* increases. The *t* becomes normal when *n* equals infinity. Actually it becomes quite close to normal for as little as 30 degrees of freedom, especially if our concern is mostly with the *interior* sections of the distribution.

Since there is a different *t* distribution for each *n*, we find it too expensive to provide *t* tables with as much detail as we have in a normal table. This lack of detail has probably contributed somewhat to the tendency for statisticians to develop some standard criteria

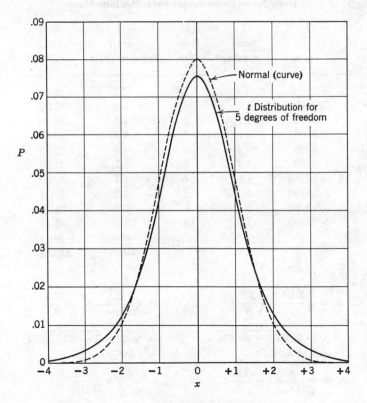

Fig. 12.6 Comparative shapes of normal and *t* distributions.

of risk. We mentioned earlier the historical prominence of the .05 and .01 levels of risk. People just naturally used the criteria that were available in the most popular publications of the t table.

12.5 Inferences About μ Based on the t Distribution

Let us return to the problem of controlling the percentage of scrap in a machine shop, a problem we looked at briefly in Chapter 1. Table 12.5 shows a sample of 10 actual scrap percentages. Column 2 lists the percentages in the order in which they occurred, with the dates given in column 1. Column 4 lists the scrap percentages *in*

TABLE 12.5

Daily Scrap Percentages for a Machine Shop

(1) Date	(2) Scrap Percentage	(3) Item No.	(4) Scrap Percentage-X	(5) X^2
5/2/60	5.2	1	2.2	4.84
5/3/60	4.1	2	3.6	12.96
5/4/60	4.7	3	4.1	16.81
5/5/60	3.6	4	4.3	18.49
5/6/60	2.2	5	4.4	19.36
5/9/60	4.4	6	4.7	22.09
5/10/60	7.1	7	4.7	22.09
5/11/60	4.3	8	5.2	27.04
5/12/60	5.3	9	5.3	28.09
5/13/60	4.7	10	7.1	50.41
			45.6	222.18

$\bar{X} = 4.56\%$

$$s = \sqrt{\frac{\Sigma X^2}{N} - \left(\frac{\Sigma X}{N}\right)^2} \qquad \hat{\sigma} = \sqrt{\frac{\Sigma X^2}{N-1} - \frac{(\Sigma X)^2}{N(N-1)}}$$

$$= \sqrt{22.218 - 20.794} \qquad = \sqrt{24.687 - 23.104}$$

$$= 1.19\% \qquad = 1.26\%$$

$$\hat{\sigma}_{\bar{x}} = \frac{s}{\sqrt{N-1}} = \frac{1.19}{3} \qquad \hat{\sigma}_{\bar{x}} = \frac{\hat{\sigma}}{\sqrt{N}} = \frac{1.26}{3.162}$$

$$= .40\% \qquad = .40\%$$

order of size. We will assume that the time order is irrelevant. In other words, we will assume that the complex mechanism that is generating scrap from day to day is not undergoing any systematic changes. (Complex mechanism refers to all aspects of the *production process*, that is, the raw materials, the machines, the workers, the supervision, etc.) We make this assumption only for purposes of exposition. It is very likely an incorrect assumption, and, in practice, we do not make it until we have exhausted our efforts to detect systematic movements. This assumption enables us to combine these 10 scrap percentages into a *single* sample as though all 10 items came from the same universe, or generating mechanism.

At the base of the table are shown the calculations for the sample mean, the sample standard deviation, the estimated universe standard deviation, and the estimated standard deviation of sample means. The first issue we must face is that of the legitimacy of the assumption that the distribution of sample means of these percentages would be nearly normal. Since the sample is only 10 items, we would be somewhat optimistic to rely on the central limit theorem to justify this assumption. This theorem states that the distribution of sample means *tends toward normality* as the sample size increases. However, the distribution of sample means *starts out*, for samples of size one, by conforming to the *same shape* as the universe. If the universe itself is normally distributed, then, of course, the sample means would be normally distributed regardless of the sample size. The greater the departure of the universe from normality, the poorer the normal curve is as an estimate of the distribution of sample means. Unless our sample has at least 50 items, prudence requires us to check on this universe before making the assumption of normality. If we find evidence of substantial departure from normality, we are far less confident of our ability to make reasonably accurate estimates of the desired inference ratios. Normal curve estimates would be obviously crude. If we used percentile equivalents to make some allowance for skewness, we might be better off than with the normal. On the other hand, the errors in interpolating for percentile equivalents can be quite large when we have small samples. Unfortunately, we do not have any other easy way to handle the problem.

An examination of the distribution of our 10 scrap percentages as shown in column 4 gives us reasonable confidence that the universe of scrap percentages is closely approximated by a normal curve. Our sample appears quite *symmetrical*. It also shows evidence of a bunching in the neighborhood of the sample mean. So let us assume that the distribution of sample means would be quite closely approximated by a normal curve. We remind you that this is the distribution that appears in the *numerator* of the Z or t ratio, whichever is applicable in a given problem. If this numerator does not conform closely to the normal, neither the Z nor the t ratio is very meaningful.

Our next step is to *estimate* the standard deviation of sample means. Two avenues of approach to this are shown at the base of Table 12.5. On the left is shown the sequence which first calculates the standard deviation of the *sample*, with no consideration being given to degrees of freedom. The second step is to estimate the standard deviation of sample means with reference to this sample standard deviation and the number of degrees of freedom.

The second avenue of approach is to first *estimate* the standard deviation of the universe by considering the number of degrees of freedom. This gives us a value of 1.26% rather than the 1.19% which we got for the sample standard deviation itself. The second step is then to use this estimated *universe* standard deviation *and the sample size* to derive an estimate of the standard deviation of sample means. The two avenues lead, of course, to the same result of .40%.

Which avenue of approach we use is essentially a matter of personal choice. There are strong logical arguments for almost never calculating the standard deviation of a sample. In fact, the argument extends to saying that any measure which refers solely to a given sample is really irrelevant for practical problems. We are basically interested in the universe and in future samples. On the other hand, there is a long tradition behind the calculation of sample measures. These measures have been *defined* with reference to a sample. Thus it is probably more practical to conform to traditional definitions and make subsequent modifications than it is to create new definitions that would confuse most people.

Now that we have cleared away these preliminaries, we may proceed to the estimation of inference ratios for various possible values of the universe mean of these scrap percentages. Table 12.6 shows the necessary calculations. The routine is precisely the same as that we have followed for our normal curve estimates. The only difference is that the probabilities in column 4 are taken from a t table rather than a normal table. The t table is in Appendix G. This table has been set up somewhat differently from the normal curve table. The body of the t table shows the probability of getting the given t value *or less*. Since t has a mean of zero, the probability of a t of zero or less is .5. There is a different probability for each number of degrees of freedom. Note that the probabilities in column 4 are calculated

TABLE 12.6

Estimation of Inference Ratios for Selected Values of the Universe Mean of Scrap Percentages

(1) μ_I %	(2) $\mu_I - \overline{X}$ %	(3) $\dfrac{\mu_I - \overline{X}}{\hat{\sigma}_{\bar{x}}} = t$	(4) $P(\mu \leqq \mu_I \mid \overline{X})$	$P(\mu \geqq \mu_I \mid \overline{X})$	(5) μ_I %	(6) I_t	(7) I_z
2.88	−1.68	−4.2	.00115		—2.88 *	.001	.000
3.04	−1.52	−3.8	.00211		2.88–3.04	.001	.000
3.20	−1.36	−3.4	.00394		3.04–3.20	.002	.000
3.36	−1.20	−3.0	.00748		3.20–3.36	.004	.001
3.52	−1.04	−2.6	.01437		3.36–3.52	.007	.003
3.68	− .88	−2.2	.02767		3.52–3.68	.013	.009
3.84	− .72	−1.8	.05269		3.68–3.84	.025	.022
4.00	− .56	−1.4	.09751		3.84–4.00	.045	.045
4.16	− .40	−1.0	.17172		4.00–4.16	.074	.078
4.32	− .24	− .6	.28165		4.16–4.32	.110	.116
4.48	− .08	− .2	.42296		4.32–4.48	.141	.146
4.56	.00	0	.50000	.50000	4.48–4.64	.154	.158
4.64	.08	.2		.42296	4.64–4.80	.141	.146
4.80	.24	.6		.28165	4.80–4.96	.110	.116
4.96	.40	1.0		.17172	4.96–5.12	.074	.078
5.12	.56	1.4		.09751	5.12–5.28	.045	.045
5.28	.72	1.8		.05269	5.28–5.44	.025	.022
5.44	.88	2.2		.02767	5.44–5.60	.013	.009
5.60	1.04	2.6		.01437	5.60–5.76	.007	.003
5.76	1.20	3.0		.00748	5.76–5.92	.004	.001
5.92	1.36	3.4		.00394	5.92–6.08	.002	.000
6.08	1.52	3.8		.00211	6.08–6.24	.001	.000
6.24	1.68	4.2		.00115	6.24—	.001	.000
						1.000	.998

* Lower Limit Inclusive.

by subtracting the table probability from 1. For example, we find $P(\mu \geqq 5.76)$ is equal to $P(t \geqq 3.0)$ or to $1 - .99252$, or $.00748$.

The considerable detail in Table 12.6 aids in comparing the t estimates in column 6 with the normal estimates in column 7. The relative flatness of the t distribution is quite evident, with the tail probabilities somewhat higher than for the normal. If we are working with a problem that is concerned with the extreme tail values, the relative differences between the t estimates and the normal estimates can be quite critical. Note, for example, that the inference ratio in the 3.20–3.36 interval is *4 times* as large for the t than for

TABLE 12.7

Comparison of t Estimates with Normal Estimates of
Inference Ratios of μ.   Given: $\overline{X} = 4.56\%$, $\hat{\sigma} = 1.26\%$, $N = 10$

(1) %	(2) I_t	(3) I_z
2.88–3.36 *	.01	.00
3.36–3.84	.04	.03
3.84–4.32	.23	.24
4.32–4.80	.44	.45
4.80–5.28	.23	.24
5.28–5.76	.04	.03
5.76–6.24	.01	.00
	1.00	.99

* Lower Limit Inclusive.

the normal. On the other hand, if our problem is not concerned with these extreme values, and/or if apparently precise estimates of probabilities are meaningless because of uncertainties about consequences, the differences between the t and normal estimates are trivial. Note the comparisons when we broaden the intervals and round the probabilities as shown in Table 12.7. Very few of us would know what to do with differences of this magnitude. Thus we might as well use the more convenient normal curve estimates if we find them more convenient.

12.6   Confidence Intervals for an Estimated Universe Mean

If we have a problem in which we are interested in only certain parts of the distribution of μ_I, we simply calculate the estimates for those parts. For example, if we wish to develop a confidence range for μ_I so that we would like to feel 90% confident that the true mean falls within the interval, we find the value of μ_I *below* which 5% of the probability lies and also the point *above* which 5% of the probability lies. It is obvious, then, that there must be 90% of the probability between the two points. Let us make such an estimate for our scrap problem. We were given a sample mean of 4.56% and an estimated standard deviation of sample means of .40%. A check of the t table for $n = 9$ reveals that a t of about 1.84 will cut off the outer 5% of the probability. Thus our 90% confidence limits would be estimated as 4.56% $\pm$ 1.84 $\times$ .40%. This works out as 3.82% to 5.30%.

If we had decided to use the normal curve instead of the t, we would get a Z of about 1.65. This would give us 90% limits of 3.90% and 5.22%. Note that this is a narrower range than for t, just as we would expect.

The calculations would proceed exactly the same way for any other confidence coefficient than 90%.

12.7 Testing Hypotheses about the Universe Mean of a Continuous Variable

Suppose the production superintendent of our machine shop has been insisting that the daily average percentage of scrap should not run more than 4.00%. His argument for this belief is based on what he has learned about what some competitive machine shops have purportedly been doing and also on what he believes can be achieved on the basis of his own past experience as a worker and foreman. He notes that the daily average for this two-week period was 4.56%. What action should he take?

We cannot determine a definitive answer to this question unless we have a reliable consequence matrix to combine with our probability estimates, and/or unless we are prepared to take over the superintendent's job, a task that we are probably not too well qualified for. What we can do, however, is help the superintendent to develop an answer by estimating for him some of the probabilities that are involved.

If we have no prior information about the standard deviation of sample means other than that we can derive from the sample, we would have to use the estimate of .40% that we calculated in a preceding section. We can picture our problem as shown in Fig. 12.7. Both curves are of the t distribution for 9 degrees of freedom and for a standard deviation of .40%. Part A centers the distribution on 4.00%, the *hypothetical* universe mean. The shaded area in the right tail represents the probability that we could get a sample of 10 with a mean of 4.56% *or more* if this hypothesis is true. Part B centers the distribution on the *sample mean* of 4.56%. The shaded area in the left tail represents the probability that the universe mean

Part *A*: Probability distribution of $\overline{X}$
around a given hypothetical μ_H

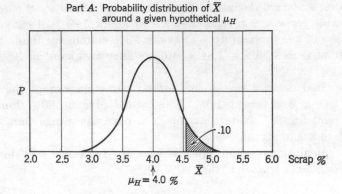

Part *B*: Inference distribution of μ_I
around the given sample $\overline{X}$

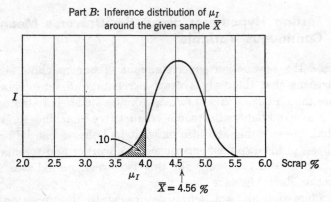

Fig. 12.7 Alternative models for testing hypothesis that the universe mean of scrap percentage is still as low as 4.0% despite a sample of 10 with a mean of 4.56%. (Note: Not drawn to scale.)

is *4.00% or lower* given this sample of 10 with a mean of 4.56% and a standard deviation of 1.19%. Since these curves are both symmetrical and identical in shape, the indicated probabilities are exactly equal. Some people would argue that only Part *A* is a legitimate representation of our problem because it is here that we treat the universe mean as a *constant* (although obviously only hypothetical) and the sample mean as a *variable,* or as a member of a whole hypothetical *family* of sample means. Part *B*, on the other hand, treats the sample mean as a *given constant* and the universe mean as a *variable,* that is, a variable in the sense that it could conceivably have all kinds of values as far as we know. Since both views result in the same answer, we can select either as our model. We prefer the *B* model generally because it appears to us to be more consistent with the practical character of the problem we face, that is, it treats what we *know* (the sample) as a given constant, and it treats what we do not know (the universe) as though it might have several different values (which, of course, it might).

In either case we calculate t and find it to be $(4.00\% - 4.56\%)/.40\%$, or -1.4 if we use the B model and $+1.4$ if we use the A model. The t table tells us that this cuts off a tail probability of .098, or .10. Thus we might say that there is about 1 chance in 10 that the universe mean is 4.00% or lower, given this sample result for a two-week period. If the superintendent has had any other reasons to be concerned about rising scrap percentages, he is very likely to conclude at this time that some steps are necessary to try to reduce scrap. On the other hand, if this recent sample is the first indication in quite awhile that scrap costs may be getting too high, he might very well attribute this sample to a chance occurrence and continue to act as though the universe mean is no higher than 4.00%. At the least, however, he certainly should be alerted to keep a closer watch on the scrap percentages even though he plans no immediate change in policy.

12.8   Pooling Information About the Mean of a Continuous Variable

Pooling Two Samples

It is not unusual to find that we have more than one set of evidence about some phenomenon. We all well know that the generation of sample evidence is a continuous process in real life. If we are alert, we accumulate this evidence and continuously modify our hypotheses about the phenomenon. (Modification may mean no change in some cases.) We faced this problem in our discussion of attributes. There we discovered that the first issue to be settled is that of deciding whether the several sets of evidence should be considered as coming from the same universe, or whether some of the evidence supersedes others. For example, if the daily average scrap percentage for the two weeks succeeding those referred to above turned out to be 4.04%, how do we combine this information with the average of 4.56% we had earlier? Do we decide that the scrap percentage has gone down or do we decide that the difference in the averages was due to chance, in the same sense that we would attribute a poor bridge hand following a good hand as due to chance rather than to a general reduction of the values of the cards in the deck?

Let us take a look at the probabilities involved in such an issue.

As a first approach we might set up the *hypothesis* that these two average scrap percentages did come from the same universe. Given this hypothesis, we then proceed to estimate the probability that a difference of the magnitude observed could have happened by chance. We use the familiar formula for the standard deviation of the differences between two sample means from the same universe, namely

$$\hat{\sigma}_{\bar{x}_1 - \bar{x}_2} = \hat{\sigma} \sqrt{\frac{1}{N_1} + \frac{1}{N_2}} = \hat{\sigma} \sqrt{\frac{N_1 + N_2}{N_1 N_2}}. \tag{12.1}$$

The first sample of 10 resulted in an estimated universe standard deviation of 1.26%. The second sample of 10 yielded an estimated universe standard deviation of .94%. A weighted average of these would be

$$\sqrt{\frac{N_1 \hat{\sigma}_1{}^2 + N_2 \hat{\sigma}_2{}^2}{N_1 + N_2}}.$$

Since the N's are equal in our problem, this reduces to a simple mean of the two standard deviations, or $(1.26 + .94)/2$, or 1.10%. Substituting in Eq. 12.1, we get

$$\hat{\sigma}_{\bar{x}_1 - \bar{x}_2} = 1.10 \sqrt{.1 + .1} = 1.10 \times .447 = .49\%.$$

The appropriate t is $(\bar{X}_1 - \bar{X}_2)/(\hat{\sigma}_{\bar{x}_1 - \bar{x}_2})$, or $(4.56 - 4.04)/.49 = 1.06$. Figure 12.8 illustrates the situation at this point. The curve is

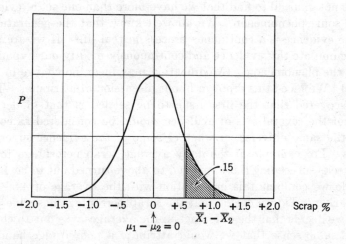

Fig. 12.8 Model for testing hypothesis that two samples came from universes with the same mean. (Note: Not drawn to scale.)

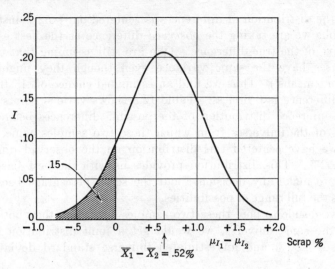

Fig. 12.9 Model for inference distribution of differences between means of two universes from which two given samples have been drawn (see Table 12.8).

a t distribution for 18 degrees of freedom (9 degrees from the first sample and 9 from the second). The horizontal axis shows differences between sample means. The curve is centered on 0 to conform to the hypothesis of "no difference." The observed difference of $+.52\%$ cuts off the shaded area in the right tail. The probability enclosed by this shaded area is the probability of getting a sample difference of $+.52\%$ *or more* if it is true that these two samples came from the same universe. The t table for 18 degrees of freedom shows this probability to be about .15.

Whether .15 is sufficiently rare to cause us to conclude that it is unlikely that both samples came from the same universe depends as usual on the consequences of the available decisions. If we decide that the samples came from *different* universes, this is the same as deciding that the scrap percentage has *declined* over this time interval. This decision would likely mean that there is no real need for an action designed to *lower* the scrap percentage. If, on the other hand, we decide that the two samples came from the *same* universe, we are very likely to then decide that the scrap percentage is running too much above the desired 4.00% level. This would call for some overt action to lower the percentage. This would be a needless action, and possibly a fruitless and costly action, if the percentage already is practically below 4.00%.

An alternative model for the same problem is shown in Fig. 12.9.

Here the distribution of differences is centered on $+.52\%$ instead of 0. Thus we are taking the *observed* difference as the best estimate we have of the true difference. (We are still assuming that the two universes have the same variance even though they might have different means.) Thus we find an estimated chance of .15 that the true difference is 0 or less. Table 12.8 shows various points of the whole inference distribution of the possible differences between the means of the universes from which these two samples came. Note that we have centered this distribution on the observed difference of $+.52\%$. This distribution provides us with the best base from which to make any decision about the scrap percentage because it covers the full range of possibilities.

If we decide to pool these two samples as though they both came from the same universe, we would get a joint distribution with a mean of 4.30% and an estimated universe standard deviation of

TABLE 12.8

**Inferences About Differences between Two Universe Means
of Scrap Percentage**

Given: $\bar{X}_1 = 4.56\%$; $\hat{\sigma}_1 = 1.26\%$; $N_1 = 10$

$\bar{X}_2 = 4.04\%$; $\hat{\sigma}_2 = .94\%$; $N_2 = 10$

Derived: $\hat{\sigma}_d = \hat{\sigma}_{\bar{x}_1 - \bar{x}_2} = .49\%$ Let: $\mu_1 - \mu_2 = D_I$; $\bar{X}_1 - \bar{X}_2 = d$

(1)	(2)	(3)	(4)		(5)	(6)
$\mu_1 - \mu_2 = D_I$	$D_I - d$	$\dfrac{D_I - d}{\hat{\sigma}_d} = t_d$	$P(t \leqq t_d)$	$P(t \geqq t_d)$	D_I	I_{D_I}
-1.04%	-1.56%	-3.18	.00		$-1.04- -.78$	.01
$-\ .78$	-1.30	-2.65	.01		$-\ .78- -.52$	.01
$-\ .52$	-1.04	-2.12	.02		$-\ .52- -.26$	.04
$-\ .26$	$-\ .78$	-1.59	.06		$-\ .26-\ \ 0$	.09
0	$-\ .52$	-1.06	.15		$0-\ .26$	.15
$.26$	$-\ .26$	$-\ .53$	.30		$.26-\ .52$	.20
$.52$	0	0	.50	.50	$.52-\ .78$	.20
$.78$	$.26$	$.53$		.30	$.78-\ 1.04$	.15
1.04	$.52$	1.06		.15	$1.04-\ 1.30$	.09
1.30	$.78$	1.59		.06	$1.30-\ 1.56$	.04
1.56	1.04	2.12		.02	$1.56-\ 1.82$	.01
1.82	1.30	2.65		.01	$1.82-\ 2.08$	.01
2.08	1.56	3.18		.00		——
						1.00

1.10% and a sample size of 20. Table 12.9 shows the inference distribution if we pool these two samples. Note the degree to which the increase in information has narrowed the uncertainty about the value of μ. We would use narrower intervals in practical work in order to provide more detailed probabilities.

TABLE 12.9

Inference Distribution of Universe Mean of Scrap Percentage Based on Pooling of Two Samples. Pooled Mean = 4.30%; Standard Deviation = 1.10%; N = 20

$$\hat{\sigma}_{\bar{x}} = \frac{1.10\%}{\sqrt{20}} = .25\%$$

(1)	(2)	(3)	(4)		(5)	(6)
μ_I	$\mu_I - \overline{X}$	$\dfrac{\mu_I - \overline{X}}{\hat{\sigma}_{\bar{x}}} = t_x$	$P(t \leq t_x)$	$P(t \geq t_x)$	μ_I	I_{μ_I}
2.88%	−1.42%	−5.68	.000			
3.36	− .94	−3.76	.001		3.36–3.84	.04
3.84	− .46	−1.84	.041		3.84–4.32	.49
4.30	0	0	.500	.500	4.32–4.80	.44
4.32	.02	.08		.469	4.80–5.28	.03
4.80	.50	2.00		.030		—
5.28	.98	3.92		.001		1.00

Pooling a Prior Inference Distribution with A New Sample

If we find that part of the information to be pooled is already in the form of an *inference distribution*, and the other part a *sample*, we can use Bayes's theorem to pool two sets of information. We recall that Bayes's theorem involves calculating the joint probabilities of getting the prior distribution and the second sample. This is a tedious operation when applied to variables, particularly here where the small samples require some intricate handling of the degrees of freedom problem. Fortunately, the pooling of a prior distribution with a sample is the equivalent of pooling the prior distribution with the inference distribution derived from the sample. Table 12.10 illustrates the routine.

Column 2 shows the inference ratios based on the first sample of 10 with a mean of 4.56% and a standard deviation of 1.26%. Column 3 shows the inference ratios based on the second sample of 10 with a mean of 4.04% and a standard deviation of .94%. Column 4 is

TABLE 12.10

**Pooling a Prior Inference Distribution with a New Sample
by the Pooling of the Inference Distributions**

(1) μ_I	(2) I_1	(3) I_2	(4) $I_1 \times I_2$	(5) I_j	(6) μ_I	(7) $I_j \times \mu_I$
2.40–2.88%	.001	.002	.000			
2.88–3.36	.007	.023	.000			
3.36–3.84	.045	.235	.011	.05	3.60%	.180%
3.84–4.32	.229	.551	.126	.58	4.08	2.366
4.32–4.80	.436	.173	.075	.35	4.56	1.596
4.80–5.28	.229	.015	.003	.02	5.04	.101
5.28–5.76	.045	.001	.000			
5.76–6.24	.007	.000	.000			
6.24–6.72	.001	.000	.000			
	1.000	1.000	.215	1.00		4.243%

the result of multiplying column 2 by column 3, thus giving us the joint probabilities of the given μ_I values. Column 5 is our desired set of *pooled* inference ratios and is simply the result of proportionately adjusting the column 4 ratios so they add to 1.

Since these pooled estimates are based on exactly the same information we used when we pooled the samples, we should get the same answer in both cases. If we compare column 6 in Table 12.9 with column 5 in Table 12.10, however, we see that the answers are not the same. The most notable difference is in the means of the two distributions.

When we pooled the two samples, we derived an inference distribution with a mean of 4.30%. As shown in column 7 of Table 12.10, the mean when we combine the inference distributions is 4.24%. Thus it is obvious that the second sample, with a mean of 4.04%, apparently carried more weight than the first sample, with a mean of 4.56%, even though each sample had 10 items.

The cause of this unequal weighting is the *unequal standard deviations* of the two samples. We pooled the two sample standard deviations when we pooled the *two samples*. We did this because we believed that the best single estimate of the standard deviation of the universe is that based on the information from the two samples. When we pooled the two inference distributions, however, we pooled two distributions *which had unequal standard deviations*. The second sample generated the *inference* distribution with the *smaller* standard deviation because this second sample itself had a smaller standard deviation. This smaller standard deviation has the same effect as a *larger N* when two distributions are combined. This follows from the formula for the standard deviation of sample means, which is

$$\hat{\sigma}_{\bar{x}} = \frac{\hat{\sigma}}{\sqrt{N}}.$$

It is obvious that $\hat{\sigma}_{\bar{x}}$ can get smaller *either* because of a *smaller $\hat{\sigma}$* or a *larger N*. When we are given only an inference distribution, *we have no way of knowing what part of the $\hat{\sigma}_{\bar{x}}$ is due to $\hat{\sigma}$ and what part is due to N*.

Which of the two pooling procedures would we prefer? We would prefer to pool samples and then make inferences, rather than make inferences and then pool inferences. Thus we would prefer the inference distribution that gives us a joint mean of 4.30% in this problem of scrap percentages. The basis of choice is quite simple. If we pool samples, we can take full advantage of the available information about *both* the sample sizes *and* the sample standard deviations. We need to make assumptions about neither. If, on the other hand, we pool inference distributions, we can use only the *combined effects* of the sample sizes and the sample standard deviations. The pooling operation must then make either implicit or explicit *assumptions about the separate effects of sample sizes and sample standard deviations*. Since the fundamental assumption underlying the pooling operation is that the two sets of information came from the *same universe,* it is automatically assumed that the two sets have the *same standard deviations*. Thus any difference between the standard deviations of the two *inference distributions* is automatically attributed to *differences in sample size*.

The Decision to Pool New Information with Old. So far we have glossed over the issue of *whether* we should pool a prior inference distribution with a new sample. The issue is resolved by an analysis of the probabilities shown in column 4, particularly by the *total* of such probabilities. We referred to this total as the *marginal probability* when we were discussing attributes. In this previous work we discovered that these marginal probabilities enabled us to estimate the probability that the given sample could have come from the possible universes indicated by the prior inference distribution. If this probability turned out to be very low, we would be disinclined to assume that the new sample really referred to the same universe as did the inference distribution, and hence we would hesitate to pool the two sets of information.

The problem we now face is that of making some general statements about the properties of this distribution of marginal probabilities. The *mean* of this distribution would be the same as the mean of the prior distribution. This follows from the well-known fact that the arithmetic mean of all possible sample means will be the same as the mean of the generating distribution. The variance of this distribution is the same as the variance of the distribution of *differences between means of paired samples from the same universe.* The logic of this is clear if we look behind the inference distribution to the sample information that generated it. We would now be considering the différence between the mean of a first sample, or a prior sample, and that of a second sample. If we were to know the variance of this distribution of differences, we could deduce all possible means of a second sample by simply adding the mean of the given prior sample to each of these possible differences. The resultant distribution would have a mean equal to the mean of the prior sample and hence also equal to the mean of the inference distribution. It would also have a variance equal to the variance of the distribution of differences.

The fundamental formula for the variance of the distribution of differences between means is

$$\sigma_{\bar{x}_1 - \bar{x}_2}^2 = \sigma^2 \left(\frac{1}{N_1} + \frac{1}{N_2} \right) = \sigma^2 \frac{(N_1 + N_2)}{N_1 N_2} = \frac{\sigma^2}{N_1} \left(\frac{N_1 + N_2}{N_2} \right).$$

The σ^2 is the variance of the universe, N_1 is the size of the prior sample, or the sample that underlies the inference distribution, and N_2 is the size of the second sample. In the case of our current problem, we have assumed that the only available information is the prior inference distribution and the mean, the variance, and the size of the second sample. The inference distribution is that shown in columns 1 and 2 of Table 12.10. A direct calculation from this distribution reveals that it has a mean of 4.56% and a standard deviation of .47%, or a variance of .225. The second sample has a mean of 4.04%, a variance of .88, and an N_2 of 10.

It is clear that the only thing we know directly that could be substituted in the above formula is the value of N_2. We could make an estimate of σ^2 by using the variance of the second sample; *or* we could make an estimate of σ^2/N_1 by reference to the variance of the inference distribution, which we might call $\sigma_{\mu_I}^2$. We can estimate the variance of sample means, or of inferences about the universe mean, by the formula

$$\hat{\sigma}_{\bar{x}}^2 = \sigma_{\mu_I}^2 = \hat{\sigma}^2/N_1.$$

Since we used the t distribution with $N_1 - 1$ degrees of freedom to estimate the desired probabilities in the manner shown in Table 12.6, the resultant inference distribution will actually end up with a *larger* variance than $\hat{\sigma}^2/N_1$ because the t distribution is *more dispersed* than the normal. Thus the realized $\sigma_{\mu_I}^2$ will be larger than the one used as a base for calculations. For example, the variance used to estimate the inference distribution shown in Table 12.6 was .16. The realized variance of the Table 12.6 distribution was approximately .21. Rounding errors and grouping errors pushed this up to .225 when we combined intervals as shown in columns 1 and 2 of Table 12.10. The greater spread of the t distribution is an inverse function of the degrees of freedom. In fact, if we take the variance of the unit normal curve as equal to 1, the corresponding variance of the t distribution is $n/(n-2)$, with n being the number of degrees of freedom. With a sample of 10, we would have 9 degrees of freedom, and $n/(n-2) = 9/7$. If we multiply .16, our original variance, by $9/7$, we get .206, a result that compares reasonably well with the realized variance of .210. Actually we would expect the calculated realized variance to be a little larger than expected because of grouping error in the calculation of the variance from a frequency distribution.

Thus we can use $\dfrac{N_1 - 3}{N_1 - 1}\sigma_{\mu_I}^2\left(\text{same as }\dfrac{n_1 - 2}{n_1}\sigma_{\mu_I}^2\right)$ as an estimate

of $\dfrac{\hat{\sigma}^2}{N_1}$.

We are still left with the problem of estimating N_1. The only possible approach to this problem is to assume that the unbiased variance of the prior unknown sample was the same as the unbiased variance of the second sample. We thus replace $\hat{\sigma}^2$ with $\hat{\sigma}_2^2$ in the equation $(N_1 - 3)/(N_1 - 1)\sigma_{\mu_I}^2 = \hat{\sigma}^2/N_1$ and solve for N_1. A little simple algebra results in an N_1 of $\hat{\sigma}_2^2/\sigma_{\mu_I}^2 \cdot (N_2 - 1)/N_2 + 3$. If we then substitute this estimate for N_1 in our basic formula for the variance of differences, we get the somewhat formidable-looking

$$\hat{\sigma}_{\bar{x}_1 - \bar{x}_2}^2 = \sigma_{\mu_I}^2\frac{N_2 + 3}{N_2} + \frac{\hat{\sigma}_2^2}{N_2}\frac{N_2 - 1}{N_2}.$$

This formula is not quite as bad as it looks. The left-hand term is simply the variance of the inference distribution with an adjustment; this adjustment ratio approaches 1 as N_2 increases. The right-hand term is the variance of sample means based on the variance of the second sample, also with an adjustment. Also note that this adjustment ratio approaches 1 as N_2 increases.

We are now in a position to substitute the appropriate values in the formula and thus make an estimate of $\hat{\sigma}^2_{\bar{x}_1 - \bar{x}_2}$. If we do this, we obtain

$$\hat{\sigma}^2_{\bar{x}_1 - \bar{x}_2} = .225 \, \frac{10 + 3}{10} + \frac{.884}{10} \cdot \frac{9}{10} = .372, \quad \text{and} \quad \hat{\sigma}_{\bar{x}_1 - \bar{x}_2} = .61\%.$$

Now we can estimate the probability of obtaining a second sample of 10 with a mean of *4.04% or less*, given our inference distribution based on a first sample with a mean of 4.56%. Our *t* ratio is $(\bar{X}_1 - \bar{X}_2)/\hat{\sigma}_{\bar{x}_1 - \bar{x}_2}$, or $(4.56\% - 4.04\%)/.61\%$, or .85. The *t* table for 9 degrees of freedom reveals that this point cuts off about .21 of the tail of the *t* curve.* Thus we estimate that there are about .21 chances of getting a second sample mean of 4.04% or lower, given this particular prior inference distribution. Hence the hypothesis that this sample came from the same universe as this inference distribution seems fairly reasonable, unless the consequence matrix is rather unusual or unless there are other reasons to doubt the hypothesis. Given the acceptability of this hypothesis, we are now willing to pool the two sets of information.

12.9   Estimating the Probability Distribution of Means of Subsequent Samples on the Basis of Information Supplied by a First Sample

Inferences about the means of *future samples* often must be made from prior *sample* information rather than from *universe* information. The problem of going from past samples to future samples is a little easier with variables than it is with attributes. We used two approaches in our attribute analysis. The first approach involved making inferences about the *universe proportion* from the sample information. Then we used these universe inferences to make inferences about future sample proportions. The second approach was based on *differences* between the proportion in the given sample and the possible proportions in the future sample. The first approach used binomial estimates of the probabilities; the second approach used normal curve estimates. Ideally, both approaches should have given the same answers; however, they did not because of the differences between the binomial and the normal for small samples. When we work with variables, we find that the normal

---

* There is some logic to allowing for the degrees of freedom embodied in the inference distribution. Estimation of N_1 from the formula results in 6.5, or 6, and thus in 5 d.f. If we add this to our 9, we get a total of 14. Our probability now reduces to .20 from the .21, a negligible difference.

curve is the only practical basis for estimates unless we wish to get involved with percentile equivalents.

We derive an additional advantage if we work directly from past samples to future samples by means of differences between sample means. By so doing we effectively short cut completely the need to show any concern for the inference distribution of the unknown universe mean. In addition to being a saving in labor, this short cut avoids any philosophical difficulties a person might have about treating an unknown constant (the universe mean) as though it were a random variable. Whenever we have a choice of methods, it is an obvious advantage if we can use a method that provokes the least disagreement.

Our basic formula is the now familiar

$$\hat{\sigma}^2_{\bar{x}_1 - \bar{x}_2} = \hat{\sigma}^2 \frac{N_1 + N_2}{N_1 N_2}.$$

The only thing we do not know is $\hat{\sigma}^2$. As usual we make the best possible estimate of $\hat{\sigma}^2$. In this case the only information we have about $\hat{\sigma}^2$ is that supplied by the variance of the *given* sample. Thus we can rewrite the formula to read

$$\hat{\sigma}^2_{\bar{x}_1 - \bar{x}_2} = \hat{\sigma}_1^2 \frac{N_1 + N_2}{N_1 N_2}.$$

Let us now apply these procedures to our example of the scrap percentages. Our first sample had a mean of 4.56%, a $\hat{\sigma}$ of 1.26%, and an N of 10. What kinds of inferences might we now make about the mean of a subsequent sample of eight items, assuming, of course, that the second sample came from the same universe as did the first? We first specify that the mean of this inference distribution will have the same mean as does the first sample. We estimate its variance by substituting the appropriate values in our formula. Thus we get $\hat{\sigma}^2_{\bar{x}_1 - \bar{x}_2} = 1.59 (10 + 8)/10 \times 8 = .35$. Hence $\hat{\sigma}_{\bar{x}_1 - \bar{x}_2} = .59\%$. We assume that a normal approximation is reasonable, and thus we use the t distribution to estimate probabilities because we do not know the standard deviation of the universe. We have 9 degrees of freedom to work with. (At first glance it may appear that we have 17 degrees of freedom. However, the key fact is the *number of degrees of freedom on which we base our estimate of the standard deviation*. Note that we have information about the standard deviation *only* from the 10 items in the first sample. We have no information at all from the second sample. Everything we say about the second sample is based solely on information supplied by this first sample.)

TABLE 12.11

Inferences About Mean of a Future Sample of 8 Items
Based on a Past Sample of 10 Items

Given: $\overline{X}_1 = 4.56\%$; $\hat{\sigma}_1 = 1.26\%$
Derived: $\hat{\sigma}_{\bar{x}_1 - \bar{x}_2} = .59\%$ (see text)

(1) $\overline{X}_I$	(2) $\overline{X}_I - \overline{X}_1$	(3) $\dfrac{\overline{X}_I - \overline{X}_1}{\hat{\sigma}_{\bar{x}_1-\bar{x}_2}}=t$	(4) $P(\overline{X}_2 \leqq \overline{X}_I)$	$P(\overline{X}_2 \geqq \overline{X}_I)$	(5) $\overline{X}_I$	(6) $P(\overline{X}_I)$
1.44%	−3.12	−5.29	.000		1.44–1.92	.001
1.92	−2.64	−4.47	.001		1.92–2.40	.002
2.40	−2.16	−3.66	.003		2.40–2.88	.007
2.88	−1.68	−2.85	.010		2.88–3.36	.027
3.36	−1.20	−2.03	.037		3.36–3.84	.090
3.84	− .72	−1.22	.127		3.84–4.32	.219
4.32	− .24	− .41	.346		4.32–4.80	.308
4.56	0	0	.500	.500	4.80–5.28	.219
4.80	.24	.41		.346	5.28–5.76	.090
5.28	.72	1.22		.127	5.76–6.24	.027
5.76	1.20	2.03		.037	6.24–6.72	.007
6.24	1.68	2.85		.010	6.72–7.20	.002
6.72	2.16	3.66		.003	7.20–7.68	.001
7.20	2.64	4.47		.001	———	
7.68	3.12	5.29		.000		1.000

Table 12.11 shows the now familiar calculations necessary to develop an inference distribution, in this case for the means of a subsequent sample based on information supplied by a prior sample.

12.10   Inferences About the Standard Deviation of a Continuous Variable

So far we have concerned ourselves only with the *mean* of a distribution. There are occasions when it is desirable to make some estimates of the degree to which *individual items* vary from each other. For example, an automobile battery manufacturer is not only interested in the *average* life of his batteries, he is also interested in the *uniformity* of the life of individual batteries. If the manufacturer guarantees his batteries for 24 months, and if the average life of the batteries is 28 months, there might still be a large proportion of claims for "short-life" if there is wide variation in the lives of individual batteries. In fact, there are many problems in which uniformity, or dependability, or stability of performance is of sufficient importance to cause us to tolerate some deficiency in the average in order to achieve greater uniformity. This is particularly true with respect to individuals who are working as part of a team effort. A person who is very good when he is good, and very bad when he is bad, is frequently not as valuable as another person who is almost never very good or very bad.

In Fig. 12.10 we show in Part A the expected distribution of random sample *standard deviations* drawn from a *normal* universe. The universe standard deviation is 1.26% and all possible samples of 10 items have been presumed to be drawn. Note the positive skewness. The existence of positive skewness is as we would expect. A *below average* value for a sample standard deviation is restricted by a *floor at 0*. An *above average* value faces no such restriction. Hence the sample standard deviation has more room to wander in the plus direction than it does in the minus direction. The arithmetic mean of this distribution is 1.16%. Thus the mean of the sample standard deviations is *less than* the standard deviation of the universe. This is the same phenomenon

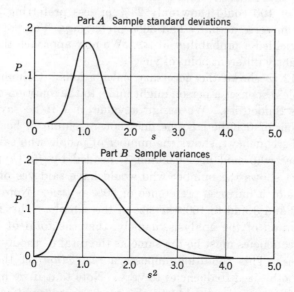

Fig. 12.10 Distribution of sample standard deviations and sample variances (see Table 12.13).

we have encountered previously.   If we multiply these sample standard

deviations by $\sqrt{\dfrac{2N}{2N-3}}$, or by $\sqrt{\dfrac{20}{17}} = 1.085$, we would get a mean

of 1.26%.

Part B of Fig. 12.10 shows the same distribution as Part A except for the use of the *variance*, or the *square* of the standard deviation, along the horizontal axis.   We find it much more convenient to work with this distribution than with that of the standard deviation.   In fact, in this case we first calculated the distribution of the variance and then derived the distribution of the standard deviation.   The greater convenience arises because the distribution of sample variances from a *normal* universe conforms to a well-known model distribution called the chi-square (χ^2) distribution.

The χ^2 Distribution

In Chapter 8 we discussed the problem the president of the Smoothies Co. had in making a decision about market share of Smoothies.   The available facts were a random sample of 100 consumer preferences for cereal which showed 28 preferring Smoothies. The president was concerned that the market share had fallen below 30%.   At that time we made some estimates of the probability that a sample of 100 could show only 28% or less preferring Smoothies when the universe actually had 30% preferring.   The normal curve estimate yielded a probability of .33.   We now approach the problem from a slightly different point of view.

Table 12.12 shows the necessary calculations.   Column 1 shows the possible responses a person might make to the question of whether he prefers Smoothies.   We assign a value of 1 if he says he does and a value of 0 if he says he does not.   Column 2, headed by f_0 (observed frequency), shows the number of people who said yes and the number who said no.   Column 3, headed by f_H (hypothesized frequency) shows the number who would have said yes or no if the hypothesis of a universe preference of 30% is true.   Note that both columns 2 and 3 add to 100, the size of the sample.   This is a necessary condition of the analysis, namely, that the total of the actual sample frequencies must be the same as the total of the hypothesized frequencies.   This condition imposes a *restriction* on the freedom of the hypothesized frequencies to vary.   Note that if we hypothesize that 30 of the people should say yes, we have *automatically and at the same time* said that 70 of the people should say no simply because we have imposed the condition that the total of yesses and

TABLE 12.12

Calculation of χ^2 for Hypothesis that Brand Share is 30% Given a Sample of 100 with a Share of 28%

(1)	(2)	(3)	(4)	(5)	(6)
X	f_0	f_H	$f_0 - f_H$	$(f_0 - f_H)^2$	$\dfrac{(f_0 - f_H)^2}{f_H}$
1	28	30	-2	4	.133
0	72	70	2	4	.057
	100	100	0	8	.190

Degrees of Freedom $(n) = 1$.
Probability of a χ^2 of *.190 or larger* is .66.
Probability of a sample proportion of *.28 or less* is .33
($\frac{1}{2}$ of .66).

nos must be 100. This condition is the basis of our saying that these data have only *one* degree of freedom even though we have *two* sets of frequencies to compare.

Column 4 shows the differences between the actual and hypothesized frequencies. The algebraic *sum* of these is necessarily 0 because of the condition of the equality of the total frequencies. Thus the algebraic sum of these differences cannot be used as an indication of the degree to which the actual frequencies differ from the hypothesized frequencies. If we ignored the signs of the differences, the resultant sum would reflect the over-all degree of difference. Unfortunately, to ignore the signs is to create some very awkward mathematical problems. Hence we prefer to solve the problem of signs by *squaring* the differences, thus making all the signs positive. (This is exactly how we solved the problem of signs when we talked about the problem of measuring the variation within a given series, a solution which led to the development of the *standard deviation* as a measure of variation.) The *sum* of the squared differences definitely does reflect the degree of difference between the actual and hypothesized frequencies. Here we have a total of squared differences of 8. If we had hypothesized frequencies of 32 and 68, we would have derived a total of 32.

If we wished, we could now analyze this total difference shown in column 5. We could calculate the probability that a difference of this magnitude or larger could have occurred by chance even though our hypothesis is true. This kind of analysis would be complicated, however, by the fact that *it would have to be particularized for this problem*. The resultant probability distribution would fit only the case in which we had an hypothesis of 30 and an N of 100. Various avenues could be selected to develop a *generalized* distribution that could be used to solve all problems, in the same way in which we are able to use the generalized normal distribution. The most convenient way currently available is that shown in column 6. Here the *squared* difference of column 5 is divided by the hypothesized frequency. This has the effect of making the result *independent* of the particular magnitude of the frequencies. The sum of these ratios in column 6 is what we *define as* χ^2.

The χ^2 distribution has the very important property that it is specified entirely in terms of n, the number of degrees of freedom in the analysis. For example, a given χ^2 distribution has a mean of n, a standard deviation of $\sqrt{2n}$, and a coefficient of skewness of $\sqrt{2/n}$. The fundamental assumption underlying the χ^2 distribution is that the *distribution of differences between actual and hypothesized frequencies is normal*. Thus it is assumed that the -2 shown in the first row of column 4 is only one of a *normally distributed set of such differences*. The same assumption applies to the $+2$, and, of course, correspondingly to any other differences if our problem had included more than two sets of differences. In our problem we know that this assumption is not *strictly* satisfied because these column 4 differences are actually *binomially distributed*. However, we also know that, with a sample as large as 100 and with p not too far from .5, we would find the normal curve to be a reasonably close approximation to the binomial. This assumption of normality is what causes us to suggest that one should use the χ^2 distribution with extreme caution unless (1) the generating universe is normal or (2) the frequencies in the various cells are moderately large, thus giving us some assurance that a normal approximation is reasonable.

The χ^2 distribution has very large positive skewness if n is small. This skewness declines as n increases, as can be seen from the fact that the coefficient of skewness $= \sqrt{2/n}$. In fact, the χ^2 distribution approaches the normal distribution as n increases indefinitely. Many analysts have adopted the dividing line of $n = 30$ as the point below which they use the specific χ^2 as an estimator and above which they use the normal curve. Figure 12.11 shows some χ^2 distributions for selected n.

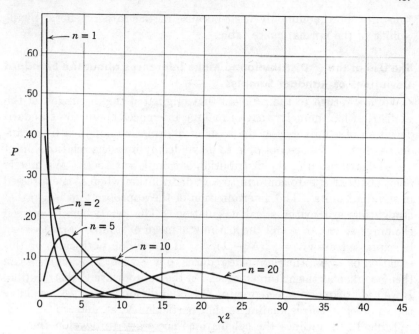

Fig. 12.11 The χ^2 distribution for selected degrees of freedom (n).

Let us now return to Table 12.12 and complete our analysis. The χ^2 in Appendix F tells us that with $n = 1$ a χ^2 of *.190 or more* could occur by chance about .66 of the time. But this includes not only the case where the sample f_0 is *less than* the hypothesized f_H but also the case where it is *more than* the hypothesized f_H. For example, we would also have had a χ^2 of .190 if f_0 had been .32. Thus, since in our problem we are concerned with the *fact* that f_0 is *less than* f_H, we must cut the probability of .66 in half, giving us a final probability of .33 that we could get a sample of 100 with a p of *.28 or less* if the universe had a proportion of .30. (This probability of .33 is exactly the same answer we got when we used the normal approximation in Chapter 8. It should be because the *fundamental* assumptions are precisely the same. In fact, the normal curve approach and the χ^2 approach are fundamentally the same, with the first working with *normally distributed* variations and the second working with the *squares of normally distributed variations.* In many problems, like this one of market share, we choose between them as a matter of taste and as a matter of availability of tables. Normal curve solutions are more commonly used because of the rather general availability of the normal curve table.)

The Use of the χ^2 Distribution to Make Inferences about the Standard Deviations of Random Samples

We now return to the problem that originated the discussion of the χ^2 distribution, namely, that of making inferences about the standard deviation of a universe on the basis of information supplied by a random sample. We are not able to delve deeply into the relationship of the χ^2 distribution to the distribution of sample variances. We merely point out that s^2's do conform to a χ^2 distribution when s^2 is expressed in standard units. The determination of the appropriate n is a rather straightforward arithmetical calculation. The relationship between the universe variance and the arithmetic mean of sample variances can be expressed as $\overline{X}_{s^2} = \sigma^2(N-1)/N$. If we divide both sides of this equation by σ^2/N, the right side reduces to $N-1$, or to n. This n can then be taken as the arithmetic mean of the appropriate χ^2 distribution. If we then take any selected value of s^2 and divide it by σ^2/N, we have the value of χ^2 corresponding to that particular N, s^2, and σ^2.

Table 12.13 outlines the calculations necessary to develop the distribution of sample standard deviations and sample variances from a normal universe.

Column 1 lists arbitrarily chosen values of sample standard deviations. These have been chosen with a constant interval of .12%.

Column 2 shows the squares of these standard deviations, or sample variances.

Column 3 multiplies each variance in column 2 by 6.29. The result is the χ^2 value corresponding to the given s^2. The calculation of the 6.29 is shown at the head of the table. It is simply the result of dividing N, or 10, by σ^2, or 1.59. (The χ^2 formula of Ns^2/σ^2 is the result of *dividing* s^2 by σ^2/N.)

Column 4 shows the probability of getting the column 3 χ^2 *or larger*. For example, there are .987 chances of getting a χ^2 of *2.26 or more* if the mean expectation is 9 (degrees of freedom); this mean expectation is the equivalent of the expected mean of the sample variances, or 1.43, or $(N-1)\sigma^2/N$.

Column 5 shows the intervals for s^2 that are the consequence of the arbitrarily chosen values of s given in column 1.

Column 6 shows the estimated probabilities that sample variances will fall in the intervals shown in column 5. These probabilities come from the cumulative probabilities of column 4. For example, column 4 shows that there is a probability of .953 that a χ^2 of at

TABLE 12.13

Inferences About Sample Variances From a Normal Universe

Given: $\sigma = 1.26\%$; $\sigma^2 = 1.59$; $N = 10$

$$\chi^2 = \frac{Ns^2}{\sigma^2} = \frac{10s^2}{1.59} = 6.29s^2$$

(1)	(2)	(3) $6.29s^2$	(4)	(5)	(6)	(7)	(8)
s	s^2	$= \chi_s^2$	$P(\chi^2 \geqq \chi_s^2)$	s^2	$P(s^2\,\vert\,\sigma^2, N)$	s_m^2	Ps_m^2
.36	.1296	0.82	1.000	.1296– .2304	.003	.1800	.00054
.48	.2304	1.45	.997	.2304– .3600	.010	.2952	.00295
.60	.3600	2.26	.987	.3600– .5184	.034	.4392	.01493
.72	.5184	3.26	.953	.5184– .7056	.073	.6120	.04468
.84	.7056	4.44	.880	.7056– .9216	.120	.8136	.09763
.96	.9216	5.80	.760	.9216–1.1664	.158	1.0440	.16495
1.08	1.1664	7.34	.602	1.1664–1.4400	.170	1.3032	.22154
1.20	1.4400	9.06	.432	1.4400–1.7424	.153	1.5912	.24345
1.32	1.7424	10.96	.279	1.7424–2.0736	.117	1.9080	.22324
1.44	2.0736	13.04	.162	2.0736–2.4336	.079	2.2536	.17803
1.56	2.4336	15.31	.083	2.4336–2.8224	.045	2.6280	.11826
1.68	2.8224	17.75	.038	2.8224–3.2400	.022	3.0312	.06669
1.80	3.2400	20.38	.016	3.2400–3.6864	.010	3.4632	.03463
1.92	3.6864	23.19	.006	3.6864–4.1616	.004	3.9240	.01570
2.04	4.1616	26.18	.002	4.1616–4.6656	.001	4.4136	.00441
2.16	4.6656	29.35	.001	4.6656–5.1984	.001	4.9320	.00493
					1.000		1.43656

least 3.26 will occur. There is also a probability of .880 that a χ^2 of at least 4.44 will occur. Therefore, there must be a probability of .953 − .880, or of .073, that a χ^2 between 3.26 and 4.44 will occur. A comparison of column 3 with column 2 shows that χ^2's between 3.26 and 4.44 are the equivalent of s^2's between .5184 and .7056.

Column 7 shows the midpoints of the intervals of column 5.

Column 8 is the result of multiplying the midpoints of column 7 by the probabilities of column 6. The total of column 8, or 1.437, is the arithmetic mean of the s^2's. This is slightly larger than the expected value of 1.430 because of the bias resulting from using midpoints to represent the intervals. Note that the intervals are skewed and that we have more intervals above the median interval than we have below it.

TABLE 12.14

Inferences About Sample Standard Deviations
(Basic Data Taken from Table 12.13)

(1) s	(2) s_m	(3) P	(4) Ps_m
.36– .48	.42	.003	.00126
.48– .60	.54	.010	.00540
.60– .72	.66	.034	.02244
.72– .84	.78	.073	.05694
.84– .96	.90	.120	.10800
.96–1.08	1.02	.158	.16116
1.08–1.20	1.14	.170	.19380
1.20–1.32	1.26	.153	.19278
1.32–1.44	1.38	.117	.16146
1.44–1.56	1.50	.079	.11850
1.56–1.68	1.62	.045	.07290
1.68–1.80	1.74	.022	.03828
1.80–1.92	1.86	.010	.01860
1.92–2.04	1.98	.004	.00792
2.04–2.16	2.10	.001	.00210
2.16–2.28	2.22	.001	.00222
		1.000	1.16376

The Bias in s² and in s.   The fact that the arithmetic mean of the s^2 is 1.43 [1] instead of 1.59 is a demonstration of the phenomenon that we first discovered in Chapter 7, namely that sample variances and sample standard deviations tend to be too small on the average. We also remind ourselves that the exact magnitude of this bias for the sample *variances* is related to N and $N-1$. Thus, if we multiply each s^2 by 10/9, we would find that the arithmetic mean of the s^2's would be 1.59, the variance of the universe. Also, if we had used χ^2 values of $(N-1)\hat{\sigma}^2/\sigma^2$ instead of Ns^2/σ^2 in our Table 12.13 calculations, we would have found that the $\hat{\sigma}^2$ would have averaged 1.59 (except for the minor upward bias due to use of midpoints).

Unfortunately, the exact adjustment that corrects s^2 for bias is not the same as the adjustment that corrects s for bias. Table 12.14 illustrates the source of the difficulty. Here we extend Table 12.13

---

[1] We will use the theoretically correct value of 1.43 instead of the calculated value of 1.437 in order to simplify the following discussion.

to make the implied inferences about s. The interval boundaries given in column 1 are the *square roots* of the interval boundaries given in column 5 of Table 12.13.

Column 2 gives the midpoints of the intervals. These midpoints are then multiplied by the probabilities of column 3 to derive column 4.

The sum of column 4, or 1.16%, is the arithmetic mean of the expected sample standard deviations. If we *square this mean* we get 1.35. Note that this is *not* the same as the *mean of the squares* given in column 8 of Table 12.13, which is 1.44. Nor would we expect it to be. The *square of the mean* of a set of numbers is not the same as the *mean of the squares* unless the numbers are all the same. In fact, one of the short-cut formulas for calculating the variance of a set of numbers is to subtract the square of the mean from the mean of the squares, namely, $s^2 = (\Sigma X^2)/N - \overline{X}^2$.

Thus we see that the $N - 1$ adjustment corrects the s^2 for bias but it does not completely correct the s. The arithmetic mean of the corrected s's, or the $\hat{s}$'s, would still be less than the σ of the universe. The amount by which it would be less is obviously related to the *variance* of the distribution of sample s's because this variance is equal to the difference between the mean of the squares of s and the square of the mean of s, or $\sigma_s^2 = \Sigma s^2/N - (\Sigma s/N)^2$, or $1.44 - 1.35 = .09$.

If we wish to make an unbiased estimate of σ, we can accomplish it approximately by the formula

$$\sigma_e^2 = s^2 \frac{2N}{2N - 3}. \qquad \text{(σ_e is taken to represent an unbiased estimate of σ.)}$$

If we apply this formula in this case, we get

$$\sigma_e^2 = 1.16^2 \frac{2 \times 10}{2 \times 10 - 3} = 1.59.$$

Thus $\sigma_e = 1.26\%$, the same as the standard deviation of the universe.

To summarize this section, we might point out that if we are satisfied to make the *best single estimate* we can of the universe *variance*, we can do this by the relation $\sigma^2 = s^2 N/(N - 1)$. The square root of this is not the best single estimate of the *standard deviation* of the universe. The best single estimate of the standard deviation of the universe can

be approximated from the relation $\sigma_e = s \sqrt{\dfrac{2N}{2N - 3}}$.

In the next section we consider the problem of making estimates of the *entire inference distribution* of σ^2 and of σ.

The Use of the χ^2 Distribution to Derive the Inference Distribution of the Variance and Standard Deviation of the Universe

It is a very formidable task to estimate the inference distribution of σ^2 and of σ. The difficulties are caused by the skewness in the distribution of χ^2 and by the fact that the various inference vectors will have different variances. This was the same kind of difficulty we had with the binomial. We can only approximate the inference ratios unless N is large enough to make the skewness negligible and the variances practically the same.

We can illustrate the procedure and the difficulties by referring to a specific example. Suppose we have a sample of 10 with a standard deviation of scrap percentages of .96%. Table 12.15 shows the calculations.

Column 1 shows the arbitrarily selected values of σ_I. We have again used an interval of .12% to facilitate reference to our preceding work.

Column 2 shows the squares of the column 1 standard deviations.

Column 3 shows the χ^2 values appropriate to the $\sigma_I{}^2$, the s^2, and the N. Note that the $\sigma_I{}^2$ is in the denominator of the ratio and that it varies as $\sigma_I{}^2$ varies. Thus we are using our now familiar technique of selecting *prior hypotheses* about σ^2. We then use such an hypothesis to calculate the χ^2 for the given s^2. We assign implicit *equal* weights to each of these prior hypotheses. Thus we are using the familiar Bayes's theorem. The final distribution of inference ratios shown in column 6 is the *posterior* distribution and is a revision of the *prior* distribution of equal probabilities.

Column 4 shows the probability that a χ^2 at least as large as that specified could have occurred by chance.

Column 5 lists the intervals for the possible values of $\sigma_I{}^2$.

Column 6 shows the inference ratio corresponding to each interval of $\sigma_I{}^2$.

The most interesting inference ratio is that for the interval 1.4400 to 1.7424. This is the interval which contains the $\sigma_I{}^2$ of 1.59 at its approximate center. If the universe variance really were 1.59, we would expect a sample variance between .81 and 1.04 to occur approximately .14 of the time. (See Table 12.13, columns 5 and 6.) Note, however, that we assign a probability of only .11 to a universe variance between 1.44 and 1.74 if we are given a sample variance of .92. Ideally these two probabilities should be about the same. The difference is caused by the skewness of χ^2 and by the variation of the variance from one inference vector to the next. If N were some-

TABLE 12.15

Inferences About the Variance of a Normal Universe

Given: $s = .96\%$, $N = 10$

$$s^2 = .9216$$

$$\chi^2 = \frac{Ns^2}{\sigma_I{}^2} = \frac{10 \times .9216}{\sigma_I{}^2}$$

(1)	(2)	(3)	(4)	(5)	(6)
σ_I	$\sigma_I{}^2$	$\dfrac{10 \times .9216}{\sigma_I{}^2} = \chi_I{}^2$	$P(\chi^2 \gtrless \chi_I{}^2)$	$\sigma_I{}^2$	$I(\sigma_I{}^2 \mid s^2, N)$
.48	.2304	40.00	.000	.2304– .3600	.002
.60	.3600	25.60	.002	.3600– .5184	.036
.72	.5184	17.78	.038	.5184– .7056	.122
.84	.7056	13.06	.160	.7056– .9216	.190
.96	.9216	10.00	.350	.9216–1.1664	.194
1.08	1.1664	7.90	.544	1.1664–1.4400	.155
1.20	1.4400	6.40	.699	1.4400–1.7424	.109
1.32	1.7424	5.29	.808	1.7424–2.0736	.072
1.44	2.0736	4.44	.880	2.0736–2.4336	.045
1.56	2.4336	3.79	.925	2.4336–2.8224	.027
1.68	2.8224	3.27	.952	2.8224–3.2400	.018
1.80	3.2400	2.84	.970	3.2400–3.6864	.011
1.92	3.6864	2.50	.981	3.6864–4.1616	.006
2.04	4.1616	2.21	.987	4.1616–4.6656	.005
2.16	4.6656	1.98	.992	4.6656–5.1984	.003
2.28	5.1984	1.77	.995	5.1984–5.7600	.001
2.40	5.7600	1.60	.996	5.7600–6.3504	.001
2.52	6.3504	1.45	.997	6.3504–6.9696	.001
2.64	6.9696	1.32	.998	6.9696–7.6176	.001
2.76	7.6176	1.21	.999	7.6176–8.2944	.001
					1.000

what larger, say, about 35, then this difference would be close to 0.

If we had a sample of 10 with a standard deviation of 1.56% and a variance of 2.43, we would find the inference distribution to be more dispersed than we just did for the case where $s = .96\%$. The contrast is made clear in Fig. 12.12. This illustrates the point that the variance of the inference vectors varies from one sample result to another. Ideally, we would like the variance of the sample

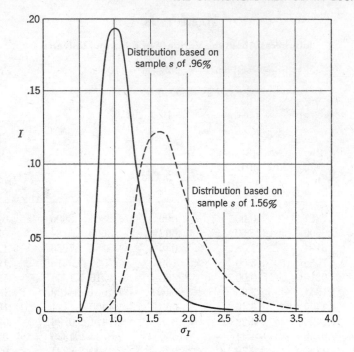

Fig. 12.12 Inference distributions of the standard deviation of a universe based on two different samples of 10 items.

variances to be independent of the variance. This, of course, would be quite a trick to achieve. Since we cannot achieve it, we must be satisfied with only crude approximations to our inference ratios.

If we wish to make our inferences for the standard deviation instead of for the variance, we could merely take the square roots of the various σ_I^2's. Or, if we felt the need to correct for the moderate bias, we could multiply each σ_I^2 by $(2N-2)/(2N-3)$ before taking the square root. Most people do not make this adjustment because they feel that the estimates are too crude to make such an adjustment practically meaningful.

Normal Curve Inferences About the Standard Deviation When *N* is Large

If we have a *normal* universe, and if the sample is large, say, 30 or more, the distribution of sample standard deviations is approximately normal with a standard deviation equal to approximately $\dfrac{\sigma}{\sqrt{2N}}$. If we must *estimate* the standard deviation of the universe, the usual case, we obtain $\hat{\sigma}_s = \dfrac{s}{\sqrt{2N-2}}$. For example, if we had a random sample of 50 yarn fibers with a standard deviation of breaking strength of 4.64 oz., we could make reasonably accurate inferences about the standard deviation of the universe of breaking strength by applying our usual procedure for normal curve estimates. The mean of such inferences would be approximated by $4.64 \sqrt{\dfrac{2N}{2N-3}}$, or 4.71 oz. in this case. The standard deviation of the assumed normal distribution would be approximately .47 oz. We do not carry out the rest of the calculations here. We merely note that there would be about .68 chances that the universe standard deviation falls between 4.24 and 5.18 oz.

Confidence Limits of σ and σ^2

If we are interested in specifying only parts of the distribution of inferences about σ and σ^2, we can proceed exactly as we did in setting confidence limits for the mean. We can pick out the proper limiting points from the whole inference distribution, or we can take advantage of special tables which provide the limiting points for the more conventionally used confidence coefficients. For example, suppose we wished the 90% confidence limits for σ^2 given a sample of 10 with a variance of .92 (our familiar scrap percentage problem). We wish to find the χ^2 values for $n = 9$ that cut off the lower 5% and upper 5% of the distribution. The lower 5% is the point *above* which *95%* of the cases fall. The χ^2 table in Appendix F shows a χ^2 value of 3.325 at the 95% point and a χ^2 of 16.919 at the 5% point. Our fundamental formula is $\chi^2 = Ns^2/\sigma_I^2$. Substituting values of χ^2, N, and s^2 and solving for the appropriate inference values of σ_I^2, we get 90% confidence limits of .54 and 2.77. These correspond quite closely to the values we would get if we interpolated in the inference distribution we worked out in Table 12.15.

Confidence limits for σ could be derived from the confidence limits of σ^2 by taking square roots of the σ^2. As before, we could first adjust the σ^2 in order to allow approximately for the bias in σ when it is calculated from σ^2.

PROBLEMS AND QUESTIONS

12.1 What do we mean when we say that the standard deviation of a random sample is a *biased* estimate of the standard deviation of the universe?

12.2 The actual or potential existence of skewness in a distribution is always a source of some concern to us because an attempt to allow for this skewness adds considerably to the difficulty of our work at the same time as such an allowance would improve our estimates.

What do we know about the behavior of skewness in samples that makes it possible for us to gracefully compromise our desire to avoid difficult work and our desire to make reasonably accurate estimates?

12.3 Our uncertainty about a future sample mean is a function of our uncertainty about the universe that is prevailing and our uncertainty about the particular sample that will occur from whatever universe is prevailing. Assume a case of a prior sample of 10 items. Then sketch a tree diagram to illustrate the sources of our uncertainty about the results in a second sample of 10 items.

Use your tree diagram as a reference and explain in nontechnical language why we would expect the variance of the expected sample results to be about *twice* the variance of our inferences about the universe. (Note: We can say twice only because our first and second samples have the same size. What would you say if the second sample were *three* times as large as the first sample?)

12.4 We find some very substantial analytical advantages if we work with distribution models that assume that the variable in question can take on *any value whatsoever* over an *infinite* range. We then use a frequency curve that shows a concentration of frequency near some central point of this infinite range and then tails off into lower frequencies on both sides of this concentration area, with the relative frequencies ultimately getting so small (e.g., .00000001) that we can afford to ignore them in a practical problem.

Analyze what you know about the following distributions from the point of view of determining whether it would be practical to assume that the distribution conformed to this model of a continuous distribution with an infinite range. (Note: Keep in mind that the difference between a probability of 0 and a probability of .00000001 is often of no consequence.)

(*a*) The distribution of heights of adult male human beings.

(*b*) The distribution of unit sales of a Woolworth store.

(*c*) The distribution of stock prices on the N.Y. Stock Exchange. (Note: You will have to face up to the problems of number of shares outstanding and number of shares traded at the particular prices.)

(*d*) The distribution of sample p's in samples of 500 from a universe with a π of .5.

(*e*) The distribution of sample p's in samples of 5 from a universe with a π of .05.

(*f*) The distribution of the dollar volume of sales that *might* occur next week in the neighborhood super market.

(*g*) The distribution of automobile tire sizes that have been manufactured in the United States during 1961.

12.5 Explain the logic of our saying that random samples from an infinite and continuous universe will yield pairs of sample means and sample standard deviations such that every possible standard deviation will appear paired with every possible mean. Furthermore, these pairs will occur in such relative frequencies that the *arithmetic mean* of all the standard deviations associated with a given sample mean will be the same as the arithmetic mean of the standard deviations associated with any other sample mean. Thus the inference matrix will show the same variance for each vector, both horizontally and vertically.

12.6 A study of the length of life of a particular brand of 75 watt light bulbs resulted in a sample of 50 bulbs showing an arithmetic mean life of 840 hours, a percentile equivalent of this mean of .64, and a standard deviation of 80 hours.

(a) Estimate an inference distribution for the universe mean life of these bulbs by the use of the binomial distribution and percentile equivalents.

(b) Estimate an inference distribution for the universe mean life of these bulbs by assuming a normal distribution of sample means.

(c) Compare your results in (a) and (b) and logically account for the directions of the observed differences.

12.7 Critically compare the distribution of Z (normal) with the distribution of t. Pay particular attention to the fact that the t distribution is derived from the normal.

12.8(a) Suppose 18-month-old Baby Boy A and 18-month-old Baby Boy B have both had perfect records of never having broken a flower vase equally exposed in both their homes. Which is the better behaved of these two boys if one considers that A has always been confined in a playpen when in the room in question while B has been allowed apparently unrestricted freedom in the room? Relate this problem to the concept of degrees of freedom.

(b) Attendance records show that during a given 10-week period the statistics course at the local college had daily patronage closer to capacity on the average than did the local movie theater. This is evidence that

1. The statistics instructor was putting on a better performance than the offerings of the local theater.

2. The students would have had to pay their own fee at the theater, an obvious deterrent to attendance, whereas the parents generally paid the fee for the statistics course as part of the tuition. Thus the students considered the statistics course was free of charge.

3. The statistics course was required for a degree and the instructor kept an attendance record. He also asked questions on examinations that were based on material available only in the lectures.

4. The students rarely had any alternatives that they preferred to the statistics course.

Discuss your choice of explanation(s) in the light of the freedom that the students had to exercise unrestricted choice.

(c) Young children have a strong urge to grow older in a hurry in order to have greater freedom to make their own choices. Have you found that you have really had greater freedom as you have grown older? In your answer consider such things as

1. Physical restrictions on your freedom of choice.

2. Psychological, sociological, moral, etc., restrictions.

3. The correlation between your freedom to make one decision and the effects of the decision (and its outcomes) on your freedom to make other decisions. For example, you initially have freedom to choose your intended career. However, once you decide to try for a medical degree,

you automatically impose all sorts of restrictions on your remaining available choices. At the same time, of course, your pursuit of your medical studies opens up a whole vista of choices that are denied to those who have not made the first choice.

(d) If you are trying to understand *why* you made a particular decision, would it be important to analyze the scope of the freedom you possessed in making the decision? Might you be unaware of some of the restrictions on your behavior because these restrictions are buried in your subconscious?

(e) Why is it often more accurate to predict a person's behavior on the basis of his past behavior rather than on the basis of what he says he is going to do?

(f) What would be your initial reaction to a company's financial budget that assumed a doubling of dollar sales in the next year compared with this year despite the fact that the past record of the company has never shown a year-to-year sales increase of more than 15%?

(g) A traffic light obviously restricts a person's freedom of choice as to when he may go through an intersection, particularly if there is a policeman on the corner. On the other hand, the existence of the light also creates some freedoms that might not have been available if the light were not there. What are some of these new-found freedoms? Do you feel better off on balance because the light is there?

(h) All laws and regulations are obviously restrictive of freedom. Otherwise there would be no point in the law or regulation. However, do laws and regulations also create freedom? Illustrate with respect to some of the more controversial laws and regulations existing or proposed in your environmental group.

(i) What sense, if any, would there be to an "index of the rate at which Americans have lost their freedom" which is based on the rate of increase in the number of laws and regulations "on the books" over the years?

12.9 Suppose you had a sample of only 10 light bulbs instead of the 50 referred to in Question 12.6. The mean life is still 840 hours and the standard deviation still 80 hours. We hesitate to calculate the percentile equivalent of the mean because of the serious interpolation problem presented when we have only 10 items. (If we overcome this hesitation, we estimate a percentile equivalent (P.E.$_{\bar{x}}$) of .58.)

(a) Estimate an infe.ence distribution for the mean life of these bulbs by the use of the t distribution.

(b) Make similar estimates by the use of the binomial distribution and percentile equivalents of the mean.

(c) Compare your estimates in (a) and (b). Explain the logic of the observed differences. (Note: You may have to be wary of reading errors which you made in switching from π_I to μ_I.)

12.10 Estimate the 80% confidence intervals of the universe mean based on the following sample information.

(a) Sample of 100 cigarette smokers shows a mean daily consumption rate of 14.7 cigarettes and a standard deviation of 3.9 cigarettes.

(b) Sample of 10 bolts shows a mean breaking strength of 1146 pounds and a standard deviation of 107 pounds.

(c) A sample of 100 people reveals that .75 of them claim to smoke fewer than 15 cigarettes per day. (Many of these people are nonsmokers.)

12.11 (a) A particular brand of fresh milk is claimed to have a mean butterfat content of 4.10%. A random sample of 20 quart bottles shows a mean of 4.00% and a standard deviation of .08%. What is your reaction to this hypothesis of a universe mean of 4.10%? Show the relevant probabilities.

(b) What is the probability that this milk is actually averaging as low as 4.00% butterfat?

12.12(a) An initial study of the life of light bulbs is performed with a sample of 15 bulbs. It resulted in a mean life of 790 hours and a standard deviation of 146 hours. The standard deviation impressed the researchers as too high to provide reliable information on the basis of such a small sample. Hence another study was made of 15 more bulbs. This sample yielded a mean of 820 hours and a standard deviation of 155 hours.

Pool the information of these two samples and make inferences about the mean life in the universe.

(b) Make inferences about the mean of the universe from the first sample and then pool these inferences with the information of the second sample in order to make final inferences about the mean of the universe.

(c) Does it make any difference whether you pool samples or inferences?

(d) Does your analysis indicate that it was reasonable to pool these two sets of evidence as though they came from the same universe? Justify your conclusion.

12.13(a) Construct the inference distribution of the *differences* that might exist between the means of the two universes from which the above two samples of light bulbs came.

(b) What is the probability that the second sample came from a universe with a *higher* mean life?

What would be your reaction if this probability turned out to be .50?

12.14(a) Given a sample of 20 light bulbs with a mean life of 800 hours and a standard deviation of 100 hours, construct the inference distribution for the expected mean life of a second sample of 30 bulbs from the same universe.

(b) Also construct the inference distribution for the mean of a second sample of 10,000 bulbs.

(c) Contrast your distributions in (a) and (b).

(d) Would you say that a sample of 10,000 is practically infinite in this case? Why or why not?

12.15 Explain the relationship of the χ^2 distribution to the normal distribution. Be very careful to note exactly what distribution it is that the χ^2 distribution assumes is normal.

12.16 It is believed that the student body at a given college is split 50–50 in their preferences for classes starting at 8 A.M. or at 8:30 A.M. A presumably random sample of 50 students is polled by the student newspaper. This sample shows 56% expressing a preference for the 8:30 start, with 44% expressing a preference for the 8:00 A.M. start.

(a) Why is it important to report this survey by referring to the sample as "presumably" random?

(b) Why is it important to state that the results reflect the "expressions" of preference rather than the preferences themselves?

(c) Test this .50 hypothesis against this sample result of .56 by the use of the following methods:

1. By use of the binomial distribution. (Note: Would it be a good idea to take only half of the frequency associated with a p of exactly .56? Explain.)

2. By use of the normal distribution. Use a mean of .5 and the appropriate associated standard deviation of sample p's.

3. By use of the χ^2 distribution.

4. Compare your answers in (a), (b), and (c). Should any of these answers be exactly the same except for rounding and/or arithmetical errors? Explain.

12.17 Suppose we have a universe with a standard deviation of $10. We then draw all possible random samples of 10 items each.

(a) Make up an inference distribution for *sample variances*. (See Table 12.13.)

(b) Make up an inference distribution for sample *standard deviations*.

(c) Calculate the arithmetic mean of the variances and of the standard deviations and compare them with the universe values and with each other.

(d) Chart each of your inference distributions and note any significant properties of these distributions.

12.18 An automobile battery manufacturer applies an accelerated life test to a sample of 20 batteries. His results show a mean life of 27.3 months and a standard deviation of 2.6 months.

Make up an inference distribution for the value of the universe standard deviation.

1. By the use of the χ^2 distribution. What assumption are you making about the distribution of the individual items in the universe? Do you think this is a reasonable assumption to make about the life of automobile batteries? Why or why not?

2. By the use of the normal curve.

3. Compare your distributions in (a) and (b) and account for the differences.

12.19 Use the information in Question 12.18 and estimate the proportion of batteries the manufacturer should expect to be returned for partial credit if the batteries are warranted to give a minimum of 24 months' service. (Note: There are at least two parts to this problem. One part is the problem of estimating the proportion of batteries that will last fewer than 24 months. The other part is to estimate the proportion of the owners of such defective batteries who will bother to claim a credit.)

12.20 A second sample of 20 batteries yielded a mean of 28.4 months and a standard deviation of 2.9 months. (See Question 12.18 for the results of the first sample.)

(a) Pool this sample with the first sample and estimate the inference distribution for the universe standard deviation from the pooled results.

(b) Estimate the probability that the second sample came from a universe with a higher standard deviation than the universe from which the first sample came.

12.21 Given the first sample with a mean of 27.3 months and a standard deviation of 2.6 months, estimate the probability of getting a second sample of 20 batteries from the *same universe* with a standard deviation of 2.9 months or more.

chapter 13

Reducing uncertainty by association: *the problem and the model for analysis*

13.1 The Fundamental Idea of Association

The process of learning by association is very familiar and the technique simple. It consists of noting that events occur simultaneously, or with a predictable lag. For example, freshening of the wind, distant thunder, and approaching dark clouds usually presage a rain shower. A prudent person can in this way be forewarned to make any appropriate preparations.

Association and Knowledge of "When"

In Chapter 2 we briefly discussed the various kinds of knowledge we might have about an event. Among the three kinds was knowledge of "When" an event would occur. This is exactly the same kind of knowledge as knowledge about association. Our remarks there apply equally well here, and it may be helpful to quickly review the relevant pages.

Association and Sorting, or Classifying

Television panel programs and many parlor games are really games of association. Success depends on our ability to associate the answers to questions with certain *classes* and *subclasses* of events. The trick is to progressively narrow the range of variation within a class until it is practically zero, leaving room for only one event, the one at issue.

We can best illustrate this process by a hypothetical example. Let us assume we have a set, or universe, of several hundred small blocks of wood. Each block has a number on it. The numbers run from 0 to 100, with a mean of 50 and a standard deviation of 10. The numbers are approximately normally distributed.

If we are told that one of the blocks has been drawn from the box that contained all of them and are asked to estimate the number on the block, what can we say? The best single guess we can make is "50." We could increase our confidence in guessing correctly by estimating a *range* of values, such as "between 40 and 60." We could now feel that we had about two chances out of three of being correct.

Let us next suppose that we are permitted to ask and have answered any question about the characteristics of the block except, of course, a question about the number itself. So we decide to ask about the *color* of the block because we have had some past experience that indicates that the numbers, to some extent, are *associated* with color. In fact, our past experience suggests the following subsets, or subuniverses, of blocks according to the color of the block:

Subset of red Range = 0–40 $\mu = 20$ $\sigma = 8$	Subset of green Range = 30–70 $\mu = 50$ $\sigma = 8$	Subset of yellow Range = 60–100 $\mu = 80$ $\sigma = 8$

We are told that the block is red. We can now estimate that the block has a number between 12 and 28 with about two out of three chances of being correct. Note that *knowledge of the color* has enabled us to reduce our uncertainty (as measured by σ) from ± 10 to ± 8, a reduction of .20 or 20%.

We then recall that the blocks have different shapes and that the shape is also associated with the number. In fact, our past experience suggests the following subsets of *red-square, red-triangle,* and *red-circle* blocks:

Red-square Range:0–20 $\mu:10$ $\sigma:5$	Red-triangle Range:10–30 $\mu:20$ $\sigma:5$	Red-circle Range:20–40 $\mu:30$ $\sigma:5$

We are told the block is circular, and we can now estimate that the block has a number between 25 and 35 with about two out of three chances of being correct. Note that *knowledge of shape* has enabled us to reduce our uncertainty from ± 8 to ± 5, or .375 below what it was when we knew only color. Also note that knowledge of both color and shape enable us to reduce our uncertainty from ± 10 to ± 5, or 50%.

Figure 13.1 shows all the subclasses of blocks we can presently distinguish. If we knew additional *associated characteristics* of the blocks, we might be able to reduce the uncertainty even further. For example, the blocks might have different weights, with the heavier blocks having the larger numbers. We would then subdivide each of the nine color-shape classes into the appropriate color-shape-weight classes. We have already carried the illustration far enough to illustrate the process, so we make no further effort to increase our knowledge about the numbers on the blocks.

Measuring the Extent of Association

Association exists between two events whenever we can make improved estimates of one of the events from knowledge about the other event. For example, we say that there is some association between the *color* of the blocks and the *numbers* on the blocks because knowledge of color enables us to make improved estimates of the numbers on the blocks. There is no association between events if knowledge of one tells us nothing about the other. For example, knowledge of the color, or of the suit, of an ordinary playing card tells us nothing about the number on the card. Hence there is no association between card color and card number. (Note, however, there is some association between card color and card suit.)

Perfect association exists between two events when knowledge about one of the events tells us all there is to know about the other event. For example, if all the red blocks had 6's on them, we would know the number whenever we knew the block was red.

Real-life examples of perfect association are practically nonexistent, as are real-life examples of no association. Most practical problems involve some intermediate degree of association between events. We can quantify the *degree of association* in many different ways. One of the simplest ways is by measuring the *reduction in error* that occurs when we take advantage of some associated knowledge. Let us use the standard deviation as a convenient measure of error. (Other measures could be used.) We discovered that the numbers on all the blocks have a standard deviation of 10. Thus, if all we know about a block is that it is a member of this set of blocks, we are subject to an error in the order of 10 as we estimate the number on the block. The red blocks have a standard deviation of

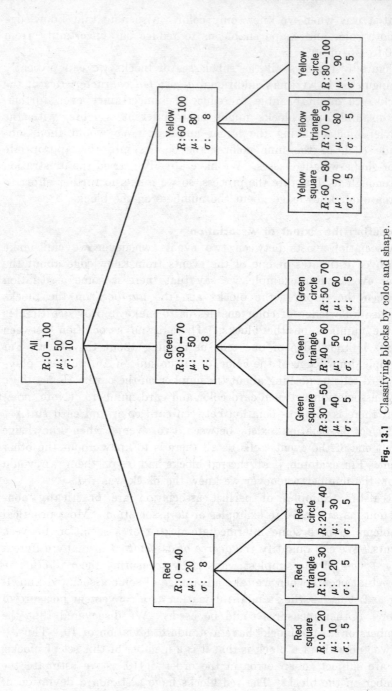

Fig. 13.1 Classifying blocks by color and shape.

only 8, as do the green blocks and the yellow blocks. Thus, if we know the color of the block, we are subject to an error in the order of 8. This is an *error reduction* of 2 on a base of 10, or a 20% reduction. Therefore, it would be proper to state that knowledge of color enables us to achieve a *relative reduction of error* of .20. We might call such a result a *coefficient of association,* which we can symbolize by the letter A.

Since most problems involve several associated variables, we have to use subscripts to clearly identify what it is we are associating. For example, we might label the coefficient of association between block *number* and block *color* as A_{nc}; that between *number* and *shape* (not shown in Fig. 13.1) as A_{ns}; and that between *number* and *shape, with color constant,* as $A_{ns \cdot c}$. The value of $A_{ns \cdot c}$ from Fig. 13.1 is $(8-5)/8$, or .375. The reason we say color is constant as we add knowledge about shape to color is that knowledge about color appears at both levels; thus any change in error from the second tier of cells to the third tier of cells is *independent* of color. We usually apply the term *partial association* to the degree of association between two variables when another, or other, variable(s) is (are) constant. We would say that .375 is the *degree of partial association between number and shape when color is constant.*

Association Works Both Ways

Since we were basically interested in the numbers on the blocks, we naturally tended to think of the association as helping to estimate the number. If there is an association between number and color, however, there is also an association between color and number, and if we know the number on a block, we also know something about the color of the block.

Similarly, we might have first sorted the blocks by shape and then by color, obviously ending up with the same cells in the third tier. For example, the second tier might then have looked as follows:

Subset of square Range: 0–80 μ: 40 σ: 9	Subset of triangle Range: 10–90 μ: 50 σ: 9	Subset of circular Range: 20–100 μ: 60 σ: 9

Note that there is less association between number and shape ($A_{ns} = .1$) than between number and color. The reverse might as well be true.

Association and Causation

No reasonable person would ever argue that the red blocks have small numbers *because* they are red, or that the small-numbered blocks are red *because* they are small numbered. The available evidence suggests only that red blocks tend to be small-numbered blocks. Why this association exists is not revealed by a simple examination of the association itself. If, on the other hand, we were to paint the red blocks green, and if the numbers on the blocks automatically changed to larger numbers, we would have some evidence that the numbers were caused by the color. But, if we were only able to *observe* that green blocks had larger numbers than red blocks, we would only be able to say that "green blocks have larger numbers than red blocks."

We all have an urge to infer a causal connection from observable evidence of association. This is perfectly respectable as long as we recognize that the particular inference is an expression of a personal opinion, and not a conclusion that logically follows from the observed facts. Such inferences are the same as unproved theories or hypotheses. If we plan to act on the basis of such inferences, we would be well-advised to act with caution until additional evidence appears to support our theory about the nature of the causal connection.

It is sometimes argued that we should pay no attention to an observed association unless we can "logically explain it," with "logically explain" meaning the same as "know the causes." For example, an often quoted "nonsense association" is that between ministers' salaries and liquor sales. It is a fact that ministers' annual salaries tend to be higher in those communities where per capita liquor consumption is high. We should not ignore this fact just because it has apparently illogical connotations *if we confuse association with causation.* This fact does not necessarily imply that ministers earn high salaries from the liquor trade, or that ministers encourage the consumption of liquor. It does not even necessarily imply what most people would consider the most logical explanation, namely, that people who can afford to pay high salaries to ministers also have enough money to buy liquor. The observable fact is just that, namely, an observable fact. Whether *we* know *why* this fact exists has nothing whatever to do with whether it is or is not a fact. It is never prudent to ignore a fact just because we do not understand it.

Statistical analysis is really a science for the *analysis of observations* and not capable of uncovering the *causes* of observed facts. The study of associations between variables may stimulate our imaginations as to underlying causes, but it cannot directly point to the causes. In effect, we can determine "what birds flock together" without being able to determine "why they flock together." We leave the latter task to the specialists in the particular area of knowledge involved, whether it be migratory habits of birds, reactions of employees to a change in the length of the coffee-break, or the effect of color on the reader response to an advertisement, etc.

Association: Conscious and Unconscious

Most of our associating is at the unconscious level. We develop habits of behavior and response which make it unnecessary to consciously think about each of the associated or coordinated events. There is much evidence to support the view that the conscious mind cannot consider more than two or three variables at a time. Since most of our problems require the consideration of many more than two or three variables, we find ourselves in a serious dilemma if we try to *think* about a problem. We solve the dilemma by a combination of *analysis* and *experimentation*. We analyze by breaking the problem into parts, each part presumably having few enough variables for us to mentally handle it; the other parts we temporarily ignore. We then shift our attention to the other parts. After having surveyed all the parts of the problem, we try to put the parts back together again, with more or less success. The process is not unlike what goes on when we put a complex puzzle together.

Experimentation is basically a cut-and-try technique. We systematically manipulate one variable while attempting to hold the others constant. The test of the effectiveness is the outcome. For example, if we increase the use of color in our advertisements, we would tentatively assume that variation in the results was attributable to the color. We say tentatively because we are never completely successful in holding other factors constant. If we are able to perform enough experiments, we can often gain additional confidence in our results because the disturbing effects of the other variables tend to average out. This cut-and-try technique is obviously very time-consuming. If each of us were restricted to the knowledge gained only from our own experiments, we would make very slow progress in trying to improve our estimates. Fortunately, however, considerable competitive activity is going on. As soon as we see one person getting good results, the rest of us quickly copy him, or at least as quickly as personal pride and the patent laws will allow.

It is possible to considerably extend the scope for conscious consideration of several variables by using mathematical tools. In subsequent pages we are not able to fully exploit these techniques, but we are able to explain some of the fundamentals and point the directions we might follow if we were to become more ambitious.

13.2 Some Practical Problems

The fundamental technique used in discovering and measuring associations is sorting or classifying as shown in Fig. 13.1. Unfortunately, we find it very difficult to use the technique in that form. The difficulty develops because of the need for a *large sample of experience* to make the technique effective. We need the large sample to get a reasonable number of items in each cell or subset. Our example had only three colors and three shapes, and even then we ended up with nine subsets. If we desired a minimum of 10 items in each subset to give us a fair idea of the mean and standard deviation of each subset, we would have to have a minimum of 90 items. (Actually we would probably need many more than 90 to give us a minimum of 10 per cell. Items would not occur with equal frequency in each of the cells unless we were able to control the frequency.) Imagine the problem that occurs if we needed, say, four variables and five divisions of each. This would lead to 5^4 ultimate subsets, or 625. With tremendous luck we could get two items in each cell with a sample of only 1350!

TABLE 13.1

Sample of Heights and Weights of Adult American Males

Height (inches)	Weight (pounds)	Height (inches)	Weight (pounds)
64	135	69	158
65	125	70	155
65	140	71	180
66	160	71	195
66	145	72	170
66	122	72	185
67	145	72	210
67	170	73	225
69	175	74	180
69	160	74	195

We solve the problem of sample size by using the simple idea that the various cells are *not completely independent of each other*. We really do not have to collect information on every cell to be able to say something intelligent about the items in that cell. A simple example makes the point. Consider the problem of the association between the height and weight of adult American males. Let us suppose we have selected a random sample of only 20 men and have measured their heights and weights. Table 13.1 shows the results. We then plot these 20 paired figures in Fig. 13.2*A*. (Such a plotting is called a *scatter diagram*, or scattergram for short.) It seems quite clear to the naked eye that tall men are *in general* heavier than short men. In fact, the eye almost irresistibly draws in a line to show how this relationship between height and weight progresses from left to right. Figure 13.2*B* shows one possible line.

What is the logic for drawing such a line? It is simply that experience and common sense suggest that a *smooth* line marks the progression from one weight to the next as we let height increase. There seems to be no logical reason why the progression should have any plateaus or any reversals. If we consider that each inch of height represents a separate subclass for determining the weight of those that fall in that class, we can use the smooth line as an estimate of the *mean* weight in each class. For example, we estimate that adult American males with a height between 67.5 and 68.5 inches

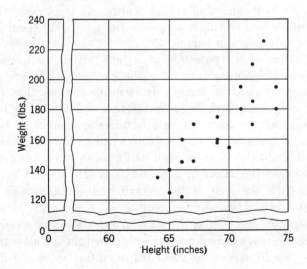

Fig. 13.2A Scatter diagram of heights and weights of adult American males.

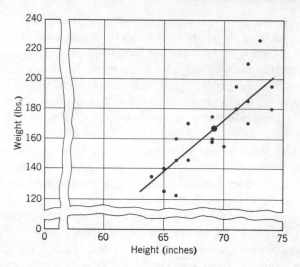

Fig. 13.2B Scatter diagram of heights and weights of adult American males with line of relationship fitted visually.

have an arithmetic mean weight of 160 pounds. Thus this line is really a basis for *interpolating* the various mean weight values for the given height values.

If we wished, we could treat the height factor as a *continuous* variable and divide the height groups into an *infinite* number of groups, each with an infinitesimal width. It is obvious that most of such cells would be empty of actual data. We fill them in by the use of the interpolation device.

The problem of the *variation* of weight within the height groups is not so comfortably solved as is the problem of determining the mean weight within the group. It is quite obvious that people of the same height can and do have different weights. The important issue is whether the degree of variation is the same in all the height classes. For example, suppose we happened to have substantial evidence that the males 66 inches tall had a mean weight of 140 pounds and a standard deviation of 7 pounds. Would it then make sense to assume that the men 74 inches tall had a mean weight of 195 pounds and *also a standard deviation of 7 pounds*. Most people would naturally expect that the standard deviation of weight within a class would increase as the mean weight within the class increased. Thus they would expect the standard deviation in the 74-inch class to be greater than 7 pounds. But how much greater? Would there be a *systematic* relationship between the mean and the standard deviation, say, something as convenient as a constant percentage relationship? For example, given a constant percentage relationship, and given a standard deviation of 7 on a mean of 140, we would expect a standard deviation of 9.75 pounds on a mean of 195.

Although there are ways to solve the problem of a variable standard deviation, the methods are outside the bounds of our treatment here. We use methods which *assume* that the *standard deviation of one variable is the same for all values of the other variable*. This assumption considerably simplifies the arithmetic and usually does not introduce gross errors. We do caution, however, to be alert to situations where this assumption would lead to gross errors.

13.3 A Model for Association (Correlation) Analysis

Any kind of mathematical analysis of data requires a model to provide the necessary steps of analysis and the basis of intelligent interpretation of the results. The *assumptions* underlying the model are the essence of the problem. We should always know exactly what they are and exactly in what way they may not be completely satisfied. Otherwise, we run the danger of applying our results in most inappropriate circumstances. We should have the same sort of reservations about applying an untested mathematical model as we would have about taking a trip in an untested airplane that conforms to the model that an engineer designed.

Associated Conditional Probability Distributions

Table 13.2 illustrates the first step in constructing our *correlation*[1] model. The left-hand scale, labeled X_1, shows values of the *dependent* variable, the variable we are primarily interested in estimating. We should not interpret the word *dependent* literally. This is a term that has been applied for years to any variable listed along the *vertical* axis. We do not mean to imply that the variable is really dependent on something. A more descriptive term would be the *estimated* variable.

The horizontal scale, labeled X_2, shows values of the *independent*

---

[1] Note the use of the term *correlation*. This is the conventional name applied to the statistical analysis of the association between variables. We tend to use the words association and correlation interchangeably most of the time. The word *relationship* is also used with essentially the same meaning.

variable. Again we caution against a literal interpretation. It is merely the conventional term for a variable listed along the horizontal axis. A more descriptive term for our purposes would be the *estimating* variable.

The vertical and horizontal vectors within the body of Table 13.2

TABLE 13.2

Correlation Model with Equally Likely Values of the Independent Variable

X_1	2	3	4	5	6	7	8	9	10	11	12	13	14	15	Total Frequency
25														1	"1000"
24													1	5	"1000"
23												1	5	17	"1000"
22											1	5	17	44	"1000"
21										1	5	17	44	92	"1000"
20									1	5	17	44	92	150	"1000"
19								1	5	17	44	92	150	191	"1000"
18							1	5	17	44	92	150	191	191	"1000"
17						1	5	17	44	92	150	191	191	150	"1000"
16					1	5	17	44	92	150	191	191	150	92	"1000"
15				1	5	17	44	92	150	191	191	150	92	44	"1000"
14			1	5	17	44	92	150	191	191	150	92	44	17	"1000"
13		1	5	17	44	92	150	191	191	150	92	44	17	5	"1000"
12	1	5	17	44	92	150	191	191	150	92	44	17	5	1	1000
11	5	17	44	92	150	191	191	150	92	44	17	5	1		"1000"
10	17	44	92	150	191	191	150	92	44	17	5	1			"1000"
9	44	92	150	191	191	150	92	44	17	5	1				"1000"
8	92	150	191	191	150	92	44	17	5	1					"1000"
7	150	191	191	150	92	44	17	5	1						"1000"
6	191	191	150	92	44	17	5	1							"1000"
5	191	150	92	44	17	5	1								"1000"
4	150	92	44	17	5	1									"1000"
3	92	44	17	5	1										"1000"
2	44	17	5	1											"1000"
1	17	5	1												"1000"
0	2	3	4	5	6	7	8	9	10	11	12	13	14	15	X_2
Total Frequency	1000	1000	1000	1000	1000	1000	1000	1000	1000	1000	1000	1000	1000	1000	

show *probability* distributions. All of these distributions are *normal* and *identical* except for the lateral displacement. Each value of X_2 is associated with a particular probability distribution for various values of X_1. For example, if we were given an X_2 value of 6, we would expect to find an associated value of X_1 to occur with the indicated frequency as shown in Table 13.3. This is taken from the column vector in Table 13.2 that corresponds to an X_2 of 6. This particular distribution has an arithmetic mean of X_1 of 9.5. If we look again at Table 13.2, we note that X_1 has a mean of 10.5 when X_2 equals 7, a mean of 11.5 when X_2 equals 8, etc. If we wished, we could generalize this relationship by using an equation. It would be $\bar{X}_1 = 3.5 + 1.0X_2$.

Note that this equation gives us the *mean* of the possible X_1 values that might be associated with a given X_2. If we wished to estimate *individual values* of X_1 that might be associated with a given X_2, we would have to allow for the variation within each vector. All of these vertical vectors have a standard deviation of 2. Thus, if we were given the information that X_2 had a value of 6, we would be 68% confident that the associated value of X_1 was between 7.5 and 11.5. (Recall that these probability distributions are normal.)

TABLE 13.3

Expected Value of X_1 when X_2 is Equal to 6

X_1	Probability, or Relative Frequency
17	.000
16	.001
15	.005
14	.017
13	.044
12	.092
11	.150
10	.191
9	.191
8	.150
7	.092
6	.044
5	.017
4	.005
3	.001
2	.000

Let us now return to Table 13.2, noting additional important features. The sum of each vertical vector is 1000. Here 1000 is really 1.000 in terms of probability, or relative frequency. Thus we are treating the X_2 values as *equally likely*, or as *given information*. Each of the associated probability distributions is called a *conditional* probability distribution because each distribution is applicable only on the *condition* that the given X_2 value prevails. We shortly look at *unconditional* probability distributions.

What we have just said about the vertical vectors applies equally well to the horizontal vectors. Note that these also all add to 1000, or at least they would if we extended the table to include more vertical vectors. We have enclosed 1000 in quotes in those cases that do not actually add up to 1000 in the table but which would if the table were extended. It so happens that the horizontal vectors also have a standard deviation of 2. It is, of course, not necessary for the vertical and horizontal vectors to have the same standard deviation. For example, if the unit of X_1 were halved, the standard deviation of the vertical vectors would become 4. What is important is that the horizontal vectors are also *normally distributed*. This is a direct consequence of having the vertical vectors normally distributed and also having the two variables related in the form of a *straight* line. (Note the diagonal straight line running through the means of the vertical, and also the horizontal, vectors.) If the relationship had been curved, and many relationships in practice are curved, no such simple relationship exists between the vertical and horizontal vectors and analysis becomes a bit more complex.

The Stereogram

Another useful way to picture the model shown in Table 13.2 is in the form of a *stereogram*, or a three-dimensional structure. Figure 13.3 shows how Table 13.2 looks if we show the probabilities as a third dimension.

Associated Unconditional Probability Distributions

Unless we have experimental control over our data, we do not find associated distributions appearing in the form shown in Table 13.2. The values of the independent variable (X_2) are generally not at all equally likely. For example, if we select a random group of men in order to correlate their height and weight, we would tend to find more men near the average height than we would men at the extremes of height. The same would be true of their weight, of course.

Fig. 13.3 Correlation model I. Conditional distribution of X_1. (Photograph by Herb Comess.)

So let us modify our model of Table 13.2 by assuming that the various values of X_2 would occur with the probabilities given by a *normal* distribution. We simply multiply each vertical vector in Table 13.2 by the probability that the given X_2 would occur. For example, let us assume that an X_2 of 8 has a probability of .0922 of occurring. We hence multiply each probability in the "$X_2 = 8$" vector of Table 13.2 by .0922. The result is as shown in the "$X_2 = 8$" vector of Table 13.4. The other vectors are similarly modified from those given in Table 13.2.

The probabilities are carried out to four decimal places to make it possible to see some of the detail near the tails of the distributions. It might be helpful to gain perspective for studying Table 13.4 if we look at Fig. 13.4. There we show the stereogram of Table 13.4.

All vectors are normally distributed, whether we consider the vertical vectors or the horizontal vectors. The truth of this statement follows directly from the fact that the vectors in Table 13.2 were normally distributed, and the only change we made from Table 13.2 to Table 13.4 was to multiply each vertical vector by a *constant,* an

TABLE 13.4

Correlation Model II—Unconditional Associated Probabilities

X_1	4	5	6	7	8	9	10	11	12	13	14	15	16	17	Total Frequency
24															
23												001	001	000	2
22										001	002	003	002	001	9
21									002	005	007	007	005	002	28
20								002	008	016	019	016	008	002	71
19							002	010	026	040	040	026	010	002	156
18						002	010	032	066	085	066	032	010	002	305
17					001	008	032	084	138	138	084	032	008	001	526
16					005	026	084	176	226	176	084	026	005		807
15				002	016	066	176	286	286	176	066	016	002		1092
14			001	007	040	138	286	364	286	138	040	007	001		1308
13			003	019	085	225	364	364	225	085	019	003			1392
12		001	007	040	138	286	364	286	138	040	007	001			1308
11		002	016	066	176	286	286	176	066	016	002				1092
10		005	026	084	176	226	176	084	026	005					807
9	001	008	032	084	138	138	084	032	008	001					526
8	002	010	032	066	085	066	032	010	002						305
7	002	010	026	040	040	026	010	002							156
6	002	008	016	019	016	008	002								71
5	002	005	007	007	005	002									28
4	001	002	003	002	001										9
3	000	001	001												2
2															
Total Frequency	0010	0052	0170	0436	0922	1502	1908	1908	1502	0922	0436	0170	0052	0010	(10000)

X_2

Diagonal Totals

	0010
	0052
	0170
	0436
	0922
	1502
	1910

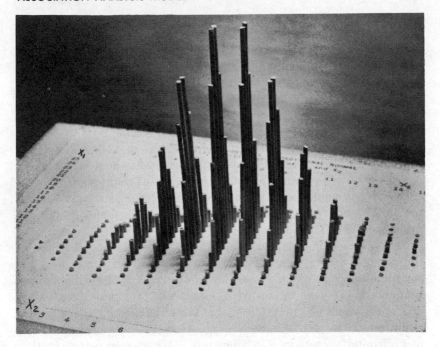

Fig. 13.4 Correlation Model II. Unconditional distributions of X_1 and X_2. (Photograph by Herb Comess.)

arithmetical operation which in no way alters the *shape* or *form* of the distribution.

The distribution of the *sums* of the *vertical* vectors is also normal. (These sums are shown along the horizontal axis just above the X_2 values.) This follows directly from the fact that we *assumed* that X_2 would occur with normally distributed probabilities.

The distribution of the *sums* of the *horizontal* vectors is also normal. (These sums are shown in the extreme right-hand column.) This is the distribution of X_1 we would expect *if we had no information about X_2.* We have more to say about this distribution later.

The distribution of the *diagonal sums* is also normal. (These sums are shown in the box in the lower left section of the table. They are the result of adding the probabilities along a line parallel to the line showing the mean values of X_1 for the various given values of X_2.) The probabilities below the main diagonal are not shown because of lack of space. They would be an exact mirrored image of the probabilities shown. The fact that these diagonal sums are identical with the vertical sums is a coincidence with this illustration. It is not generally true.

Note that the marginal probabilities and the diagonal sums add to 10,000. This is really 1.0000, with the decimal point ommitted for convenience. Thus we find that all of the probabilities together add to 1.0000, as any proper probability distribution should. Each cell in the figure gives the *unconditional* probability of finding a particular item occurring in the given cell. For example, we find that there is a probability of .0138 of finding an X_2 of 12 paired with an X_1 of 12 *provided* we have no prior information about either X_2 or X_1. Contrast this with a probability of .044 of finding an X_1 of 12 *if we already know that X_2 equals* 12. The latter is the *conditional* probability of X_1 *given* knowledge of X_2 and is found in the appropriate cell of Table 13.2.

(The dashed line diagonal on Table 13.4 is the line that passes through the means of all the *horizontal* vectors in contrast to the solid line diagonal which passes through the means of all the *vertical* vectors. If we were interested in estimating X_2 from given values of X_1, we would be interested in the dashed diagonal. Since we are not interested in such estimates, we ignore this line through the means of horizontal vectors in this discussion. We merely point out that these two diagonals would coincide if the association were perfect. They would be at right angles to each other and parallel to the respective axes if the association were 0. In an exercise at the end of the chapter, there is an opportunity to speculate on the logic of these statements.)

Comparing the Two Correlation Models

It is useful at this stage to review the properties of the correlation models and tie a few ends together.

1. Both models assume that the probabilities are *normally distributed* for all relevant distributions. This is the simplest model we know how to work with. If we do not use normal distributions, we have substantial difficulties in trying to estimate the probabilities in the various cells and vectors. If our actual distributions are not strictly normal, and they rarely are, we generally accept the resultant crudities in our estimates unless the departure from normal is so great that critical distortion occurs. If such distortion would occur, we have several avenues open to us. One is to try to *transform* the data by the use of logarithms, reciprocals, square roots, etc., into distributions that are more nearly normal than the original data. The use of transformations involves some mathematical and theoretical difficulties that are

beyond our present scope. Another way is to abandon the mean and the standard deviation as measuring devices and use medians and quartile deviations. A third avenue is not to bother with defining the nature of the association between two variables. This is not recommended unless the whole problem is so trivial that we can justify any work on it as only useful exercise to tone up our mental muscles.

2. Both models have vertical vectors so that the *standard deviations are all identical*. (The standard deviations of the horizontal vectors are also equal.) This is a very critical assumption, even more critical than the assumption of normality. It is this assumption that makes it possible to *combine* logically the separate bits of information we might have on the way the various X_1 values deviate around their mean for the given values of X_2. This is the assumption we referred to when we discussed the sample of only 20 pairs of heights and weights. If, for example, tall men show greater weight variation than short men, our problems are substantially magnified and we would find these models somewhat crude in their ability to approximate reality. We are not able to consider such additional complexities in this introductory discussion.

3. Both of these models assume that the relationship between the two variables is *linear*, that is, a straight line. Although it is likely true that there is no such thing as a linear relationship in real life, it is nevertheless true that a straight line does come tolerably close to most of the curvilinear relationships that we do find. Figure 13.5 illustrates a few of the types of curves that might occur. Parts A and B show two types that occur fairly often. In A the true relationship is rather steeply positive for low values of X_2 and tends to flatten out. B shows the same thing except that the relationship is negative (low values of X_2 associated with high values of X_1.) The important point about both of these is that the true relationship apparently never shifts from positive to negative, or vice versa, as does the relationship in Part C. In Part C, it is quite clear that a straight line misses the truth rather badly. In fact, it indicates no relationship whereas actually it is obvious that there is a clear relationship.

One of the real dangers in using straight lines to approximate curves is the temptation to *extrapolate* the line beyond the range of experience as shown by the dashed extension of the line in Part A. It is obvious that such an extension rather quickly leads to ridiculous answers. This is the kind of nonsense we can get into if we let our mathematics use us instead of our using our mathematics.

It is, of course, possible to use curved lines in our analysis. We, in later pages, indicate briefly how to do this. However, most of our attention is directed toward learning how to work with straight lines.

4. Practical correlation analysis involves working with observations that fall into a model like that shown as Model II, the model with *unconditional* probabilities, and then converting our results into a model like that shown as Model I, the model with the *conditional* probabilities. We then are able to make estimates of X_1 on the basis of any *given* values of X_2.

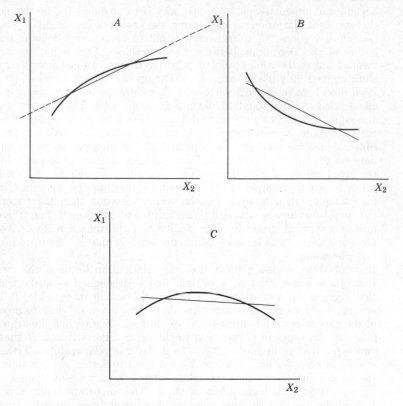

Fig. 13.5 Using a straight line to approximate a relationship.

13.4   The Statistical Tools

The Line of Relationship, or Line of Conditional Means

Our first task in a correlation analysis is to determine the line that passes through the means of the various vertical vectors. If we have information about the whole universe of X_1, X_2 pairs, and if these vector means fall in a straight line, our problem is quite simple. We would merely calculate the means for two widely spaced vectors and use these two means to determine the straight line that would pass through all of the means. We can write the general equation of such a line as

$$\mu_{12} = \alpha_{12} + \beta_{12}X_2 \qquad (13.1)$$

The symbol we use to represent the *universe mean* of X_1 is μ_{12}, *given* a particular value of X_2. For example, if the *mean* weight of all adult American males who are 69 inches tall is 160 pounds, we would say that μ_{12} has a value of 160 when X_2 equals 69. The α_{12} (alpha) defines the value of μ_{12} when X_2 equals 0. It is the point at which the line of relationship intercepts the vertical axis; α_{12} has a value of 3.5 in our model. Usually this is a nonsense value in a practical problem because it would be nonsense to talk about a 0 value for the X_2 variable. For example, to state that an adult American male 0 inches tall would tend to average a weight of *minus* 320 pounds is obviously nonsense. This kind of nonsense points up the necessity of remembering that the straight line is generally meaningful only within a middle range of the data. With a mathematical equation, however, we can make estimates anywhere we wish, of course. Thus it is very important that we exhibit the proper amount of common sense. The situation is not unlike the way an automobile steers wherever we wish. We should not blame the steering mechanism if we steer the car into a ditch. Similarly, we should not blame the line if we steer it into an area of nonsense answers.

The β_{12} (beta) refers to the change in μ_{12} per unit change in X_2. It is the *slope* of the line of relationship. In our model it has a value of 1.0. It has a value of about 7 pounds in our height-weight data shown in Table 13.1 and Fig. 13.2B. The word change implies that it is the variation in X_2 that *causes* the observed change in μ_{12}. This implication is unwarranted and is only a consequence of imperfections in our language. It would be more exact to define β_{12} as the *difference* we *observe* in μ_{12} for each unit *difference* we *observe* in X_2.

If we were dealing with a *curvilinear* relationship, the slope would be a variable rather than a constant as it is for a straight line. Our equation would then need some additional *parameters* beyond α_{12} and β_{12}. For example, we might have a second-degree parabola which would look somewhat similar to Part C of Fig. 13.5. This would have a general equation like

$$\mu_{12} = \alpha_{12} + \beta_{12}X_2 + \gamma_{12}X_2{}^2.$$

(We use parameter to refer to the mathematical constants in an equation that presumably describe the situation in the *universe*. We call the same constants *statistics* if we are dealing only with a *sample* of data. We would then replace the Greek α, β, and γ (gamma) with the English a, b, and c. Thus we carry forward our convention of using Greek letters for universe values and English letters for sample values. We also continue our convention of using the circumflex (ˆ) on top of a Greek letter to indicate an unbiased *estimate* of a universe value.)

(The subscripts attached to the various symbols are for the purpose of clearly specifying exactly what variables we are working with. We use the system of X_1, X_2, X_3, etc. to specify our various variables instead of the more familiar X, Y, and Z. We do this because most practical problems involve many more than three variables and a certain awkwardness develops after we pass Z. We must identify α and β by a subscript because in some problems we have more than one α and β. For example, we might have β_{13}. This would be the difference observed in X_1 for each unit difference observed in X_3. It is well worthwhile to take time to fix these various symbols in mind as we go along. If we do not understand our simple symbolic language, we will have considerable difficulty understanding the ideas being developed. We use the symbols in order to make it possible to express these ideas more clearly and more concisely. We add to our vocabulary as we go along.)

The Measure of Variation Around the Line of Conditional Means

We might measure the variation in the vertical vectors in many different ways; in fact, some of the early work in the development of correlation technique used quartile deviations. We, however, find the standard deviation the most convenient measure, particularly because of its simple relationship to normal curve probabilities, and we confine our work to the use of the standard deviation.

Since the vertical vectors all have the same standard deviation, we can measure the standard deviation of any one of them and use the result to apply to all the vertical vectors. In our model shown in Table 13.4 (or in the one shown in Table 13.2) the standard deviation of the vertical deviations around the line of relationship happens to be 2.0. This is calculated in the conventional way and is shown in Table 13.5 for the vertical vector at $X_2 = 10$ in Table 13.4.

Note the addition to our vocabulary of symbols. We label X_1 as $X_{1.2}$, the mean of X_1 as $\mu_{1.2}$, the standard deviation as $\sigma_{1.2}$. We do this to signify that we are talking about the X_1's for *some given value* of X_2, in this case an X_2 of 10. Thus we can say that X_2 is taken as a *constant* while we study this variation in X_1. We can also say that the observed variation in $X_{1.2}$ is *independent* of any variation in X_2. Or, we might alternatively say that this particular distribution of $X_{1.2}$ is *conditional* on X_2 being equal to 10. If X_2 had another value than 10, we would find a different conditional distribution of $X_{1.2}$. (We can see the various conditional distributions of $X_{1.2}$ if we look at the vertical vectors in Tables 13.2 and 13.4.)

If X_1 and X_2 were to be perfectly related, $X_{1.2}$ would always be *constant* for a given X_2 value. This follows logically from the fact

TABLE 13.5

Calculation of the Standard Deviation of Vertical Vectors Shown in Tables 13.2 and 13.4 (Illustrated with reference to vertical vector at $X_2 = 10$ in Table 13.4)

$X_{1.2}$	f	$fX_{1.2}$	$fX^2_{1.2}$
19	.0002	.0038	.0722
18	.0010	.0180	.3240
17	.0032	.0544	.9248
16	.0084	.1344	2.1504
15	.0176	.2640	3.9600
14	.0286	.4004	5.6056
13	.0364	.4732	6.1516
12	.0364	.4368	5.2416
11	.0286	.3146	3.4606
10	.0176	.1760	1.7600
9	.0084	.0756	.6804
8	.0032	.0256	.2048
7	.0010	.0070	.0490
6	.0002	.0012	.0072
	.1908	2.3850	30.5922

$$\mu_{1.2} = \frac{\Sigma fX_{1.2}}{N} = 12.5$$

$$\sigma_{1.2} = \sqrt{\frac{\Sigma fX^2_{1.2}}{N} - \left(\frac{\Sigma fX_{1.2}}{N}\right)^2} = \sqrt{\frac{30.5922}{.1908} - (12.5)^2}$$

$$= 2.0$$

that if X_1 and X_2 are perfectly related, and if we hold X_2 constant, $X_{1.2}$ must also be constant.

If X_1 and X_2 have no relationship whatever, all the $X_{1.2}$ distributions would be precisely the same regardless of the particular value of X_2. In such a case, the holding of X_2 constant makes no difference in the value of $X_{1.2}$.

The Measure of the Degree of Association

It is impractical to pay any attention to an associated variable if there is no association, or if the degree of association is negligible. To do so is a distractive waste of energy, and can sometimes be a serious error. For example, if we as an employer believed that intelligence were positively associated with head circumference and if we wished to hire only the most intelligent people, our personnel questionnaire would be quite simple. We would determine only a person's hat size and hire only the "big-headed." With average luck, we should end up with a pretty good cross section of all shades of intelligence, but certainly not with only the most intelligent people. Our trouble would develop as we asked these people to do tasks that require above average intelligence.

The simplest way to measure and to understand the *degree* of association is to compare the standard deviation of the *conditional* distribution of the $X_{1.2}$'s with that of the *unconditional* distribution of X_1. In our model we have already discovered that the standard deviation of the conditional distribution of $X_{1.2}$ is 2.0. Table 13.6

TABLE 13.6

Calculation of Standard Deviation of X_1 (Distribution taken from vertical margin of Table 13.4)

X_1	P	PX_1	PX_1^2
23	.0002	.0046	.1058
22	.0009	.0198	.4356
21	.0028	.0588	1.2348
20	.0071	.1420	2.8400
19	.0156	.2964	5.6316
18	.0305	.5490	9.8820
17	.0526	.8942	15.2014
16	.0807	1.2912	20.6592
15	.1092	1.6380	24.5700
14	.1308	1.8312	25.6368
13	.1392	1.8096	23.5248
12	.1308	1.5696	18.8352
11	.1092	1.2012	13.2132
10	.0807	.8070	8.0700
9	.0526	.4734	4.2606
8	.0305	.2440	1.9520
7	.0156	.1092	.7644
6	.0071	.0426	.2556
5	.0028	.0140	.0700
4	.0009	.0036	.0144
3	.0002	.0006	.0018
	1.0000	13.0000	177.1592

$$\mu_1 = 13.0 \qquad \sigma_1 = \sqrt{177.159 - (13.0)^2} = 2.9$$

shows the calculation of the standard deviation of the unconditional distribution of X_1. This distribution is taken from the vertical *margin* of Table 13.4. It is the *sum* of all the conditional distributions and gives us the expected values of X_1 if we have no prior knowledge of the value of X_2. The unconditional standard deviation happens to be 2.9. Thus we find that knowledge of the value of X_2 enables us to reduce our ignorance or uncertainty about X_1 from 2.9 to 2.0.

We can express this reduction in ignorance in *relative* terms by dividing the amount of error reduction, in this case .9, by the maximum possible reduction, in this case 2.9. We can call this result A_{12}, or the degree of association between X_1 and X_2. In formal terms we have

$$A_{12} = \frac{\sigma_1 - \sigma_{1.2}}{\sigma_1} = \frac{2.9 - 2.0}{2.9} = .31.$$

This *relative reduction in error* (or of uncertainty, or of ignorance) gives us a clearer idea of the *degree* of association than does the amount of error reduction alone. For example, if we had an unconditional standard deviation of 100 and a conditional standard deviation of 99.1, we would also have an error reduction of .9. But it is obvious that .9 on a base of 100 would indicate a trivial degree of error reduction. Similarly, if we could achieve a .9 reduction on a base of 1.0, we would have achieved a very substantial degree of error reduction.

Alternative Ways of Measuring the Degree of Association

Although the above method of measuring the degree of association is very simple and very logical, it is not customarily used. The accidents of historical development have given prominence to two other measures of association. It is probable that the method just given will eventually supersede the other two; however, it is necessary for us to clearly understand the other two as long as they are commonly used now.

Probably the most informative way to approach the other measures is to start at the historical beginnings of formal correlation analysis. Sir Francis Galton published an article in 1886 on "Regression towards mediocrity in hereditary stature."[1] His research interests were essentially in biology and anthropology, two areas wherein

[1] *Journal of Anthropological Institute,* Vol. 15, 1886, p. 246 as referred to by G. U. Yule and M. G. Kendall in *An Introduction to the Theory of Statistics,* 12th edition, J. B. Lippincott Company, 1940.

much of statistical method originated. In this article he was concerned with the degree of association between the heights of fathers and the heights of their male offspring. He approached his problem by collecting a sample of heights of fathers and sons and plotting the pairs on a scatter diagram. It can be likened to Fig. 13.6. The evidence of some kind of relationship was obvious to Galton. Tall fathers definitely tended to have tall sons and short fathers short sons. In those pioneering days Galton's problem was to figure out a way to place a line on this scatter diagram to express this relationship in the "best" way, that is, in such a way that nobody could draw a "better" line. Galton actually worked with notions of the median and of the quartile deviation in his development. We discuss his solution in terms of the mean and the standard deviation, the measures that were used by Karl Pearson, another English statistician, who picked up Galton's work and developed it in the directions that came to dominate statistics for over half a century.

The first step in discovering the path of the "best" line is to draw the lines on the chart corresponding to the mean height of fathers (the X variable) and the mean height of sons (the Y variable). The

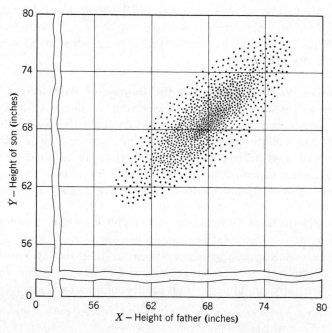

Fig. 13.6 Hypothetical relationship between height of a father and height of his son.

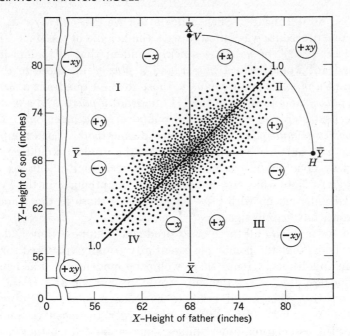

Fig. 13.7 Analysis of hypothetical relationship between height of a father and height of his son.

scatter diagram now looks as shown in Fig. 13.7. This divides the scatter into four quadrants. Note that there are more points in the IV and II quadrants than in the I and III quadrants. This imbalance is evidence of the positive association between heights of fathers and sons. If the points were more or less equally distributed through the four quadrants, the evidence would suggest no association. If they predominated in the I and III quadrants, negative association would be indicated, that is, tall fathers would tend to have short sons. If all of the points were located in the IV and II quadrants, we would have evidence of practically perfect association. In fact, it is possible to develop a crude measure of the degree of association by the relative *number* of points in the various quadrants.

The next step in analysis was to recognize that it was not enough to merely *count* the number of points in each quadrant. The *location* of the point within the quadrant was important. The further into a quadrant a point was, the more significant was it as a possible indicator of association. Hence each point was measured as a *deviation* from the mean. For example, if a father were 68 inches tall, and the mean height of fathers were 66 inches, the measurement would be recorded as $+2$ inches. Such a deviation we can call $X - \bar{X}$, or x. The same procedure was followed with the heights of the sons. These would be $Y - \bar{Y}$, or y. It is quickly evident that all points in the II quadrant would have a *plus* x and a *plus* y, all those in the IV quadrant a *minus* x and a *minus* y, those in the I quadrant a *minus* x and a *plus* y, and all those in the III quadrant a *plus* x and a *minus* y.

The next step was quite simple, but also quite ingenious. *The x in a pair was multiplied by the y in the same pair.* For example, if a given x, y pair had values of $+4$, $+3$, the product would be $+12$. This was done for all pairs. (We call such multiplications *cross products*.) Note what now happens. All the products in the IV and II quadrants end up with *plus* signs, and all those in the I and III quadrants have *minus* signs.

Now we may *add* all these cross products. Suppose they add to 0. This tells us that the points are essentially equally scattered through all four quadrants. Hence there would be evidence of 0 association and the best line of relationship would be horizontal. If the sum were positive, this would indicate a positive relative relationship between X and Y. In addition, the *larger* the positive sum the *greater* the association, other things being equal (which they are not as we see shortly). Similarly if the sum were *negative*.

But it is obvious that the magnitude of the sum of cross products depends on two factors other than the degree of association. They are the *units* of the two series and the *number* of cross products added. For example, if we measure height in inches, we obtain one sum of cross products; if we measure height in centimeters, we obtain a sum which would be somewhat larger. (It would be about 2.54^2 or 6.45 as large.) Since there is no way of selecting any one unit as more logical than any other unit, the trick is to *eliminate* all units. This can be done by dividing each x by the *standard deviation* of the x's and each y by the *standard deviation* of the y's. We would now have $\Sigma(x/\sigma_x)(y/\sigma_y)$. Since x and σ_x have the same unit, the unit cancels in the division. Similarly for the unit of y. We say the results of a division by the standard deviation are expressed in *standard units*.

The problem of the *number* of items added is very simple. We merely *divide* by the number of items, thus getting the familiar arithmetic mean.

If we put all these steps together, we get

$$\frac{\sum \dfrac{x}{\sigma_x}\dfrac{y}{\sigma_y}}{N}.$$

An exact description of this formula would be: the arithmetic mean of the cross products in standard units. If we followed the logic of its development, we also know that it must also be a measure of the degree of association. But, before we pursue that topic, let us return to Galton's problem of the "best" line. Common sense suggests that the best line would pass through the point where the mean of X and Y cross. In other words, no one is able to argue successfully against the notion that a father of *average* height should have a son of *average* height. The only issue remaining, then, is the *slope* of the line as it passes through that point. We already know that this line should have a slope of 0 if there is no association. We also know that

$$\frac{\sum \dfrac{x}{\sigma_x}\dfrac{y}{\sigma_y}}{N}$$

would have a value of 0 if there were no association. We also know that the slope would increase from 0 (assuming a positive relationship) as the degree of association increased. But how high might this slope logically become? Let us look at Fig. 13.7 and imagine our straight line rotating around the intersection of the two means. If we start at the horizontal and rotate counterclockwise, we infer that we are showing an *increase* in the degree of association until we reach the point marked 1.0, which corresponds to a line at a 45° angle. After that point, we infer that the degree of correlation is *decreasing* again until it reaches 0 when the line becomes vertical. Thus we can picture a 0 correlation as showing a *horizontal* line of relationship or a *vertical* line of relationship. Since we generally put our estimating variable on the horizontal axis and the estimated variable on the vertical axis, we normally do not think of drawing a vertical line of relationship. If, however, convention had started with the estimating variable on the vertical axis, we normally would not think of drawing a horizontal line of relationship. Actually both lines are equally logical in the abstract.

We thus see that any scatter diagram always has *two* logical lines of relationship, one for estimating Y from X and the other for estimating X from Y. If we now place the index finger of our hand on the point V on the vertical line in Fig. 13.7 and our thumb on point H, we can simulate what happens as the degree of correlation increases from 0. Draw the thumb and forefinger slowly together along the periphery of the circle, bringing them together at equal rates

At any stage of this operation the thumb and the forefinger would each indicate a line of *equal* degrees of association. If we continue this operation to the end, we discover that our thumb and forefinger come together at the point halfway between the horizontal and the vertical, the point of a 45° line. The two lines hence become one and the association is perfect. Thus we can say that the slope of either of these lines will measure the degree of association; or, conversely, the degree of association measures the slope of these lines.[1]

The final step in the logic of development we accept on faith. This step is the proof that

$$\frac{\sum \frac{x}{\sigma_x} \frac{y}{\sigma_y}}{N}$$

has a *maximum numerical value of 1.0.* (If we consider the *direction* of the association, we would say that the result might vary between $+1$ and -1. The logic of a negative relationship is precisely the same as that for a positive relationship. By using the lower right-hand quadrant of Fig. 13.7, we can duplicate all the steps we took in the upper right-hand quadrant.) We can now see that a value of 1 for

$$\frac{\sum \frac{x}{\sigma_x} \frac{y}{\sigma_y}}{N}$$

can be taken to correspond to a 45° line on the chart (if the variables are measured in standard units), a value of .5 to a 22.5° line, etc.

Thus we have the equivalent of Galton's solution to the problem of the "best" line, namely, a line that passes through the general mean with a slope equal to

$$\frac{\sum \frac{x}{\sigma_x} \frac{y}{\sigma_y}}{N}.$$

At the same time we have a measure of the *degree of association* that very conveniently varies between 0 and 1 (ignoring the sign). This is the measure that was finally developed by Pearson. He called it

---

[1] These statements assume that the slope is measured in standard units. They do not apply to a scatter diagram in natural units. Thus the statements do not really hold for Fig. 13.7. We use Fig. 13.7 merely for convenience of reference.

r (the coefficient of correlation), the first letter of the word regression (and coincidentally the first letter of the word relation). It has been known as the Pearsonian r ever since.

We cannot help be attracted to the logic and ingenuity of this line of development. Unfortunately, this method of measuring the degree of association, or of correlation, had an unsuspected tendency to lead to substantial misunderstanding. Many people naturally assumed that if an r of 0 indicated 0 correlation and an r of 1 indicated perfect correlation, an r of .50 would indicate 50% correlation. But this is not so in any practical interpretation of what we might mean by degree. It became the custom for teachers and textbook writers to caution the student against such a simple percentage scale interpretation of r. Rather the student was told that he would gradually learn by experience how much correlation was really represented by fractional values of r. He might also be told to be wary in the meantime of using the results of any correlation analysis unless r were at least as large as .80. Naturally this advice was largely ignored, and many people respected results that yielded r's as low as .15, etc.

Of course, many statisticians were unhappy with this situation. They felt they were dealing with a kind of magic that could be really understood only by a very few geniuses. Hence it was not surprising that a way would be found around such a vague method of measuring the degree of correlation. The measure that evolved, during the 1920's, was called the *coefficient of determination*. It can be calculated in many different ways, all of which are mathematical equivalents. One way is to simply *square* the value of r. For example, if $r = .5$, then $r^2 = .25$. Another way is to calculate the *relative reduction in square error*, or, to use our familar symbols, $(\sigma_1^2 - \sigma_{1.2}^2)/\sigma_1^2$. For example, if we go back to the illustration of our model, we would get $r^2 = (2.9^2 - 2.0^2)/2.9^2$, or $(8.41 - 4.00)/8.41$, or .52. (Note that we found a relative reduction of *error* of .31.)

There has been a rather strong tendency to foster an interpretation of r^2 that would permit a statement like, "an r^2 of .25 means that 25% of the variation in X_1 is explained by variation in X_2." We strongly oppose this because it simply replaces a misinterpreted r with a misinterpreted r^2, although with not quite so much misinterpretation.

The best way for us to unravel some of the mystery from the various ways of measuring the degree of association is to write out some of the alternative formulas for calculating them. We can then find the formulas that seem to provide the best links between these measures. We list some of these formulas below.

The Coefficient of Association—A

$$A_{12} = \frac{\sigma_1 - \sigma_{1.2}}{\sigma_1} \text{ (Relative reduction in error.)} \tag{13.2}$$

$$A_{12} = 1 - \underbrace{\sqrt{\underbrace{1 - \underbrace{r_{12}^2}_{\text{coefficient of determination}}}_{\text{coefficient of nondetermination}}}_{\text{coefficient of alienation}}}_{\text{coefficient of association}} \tag{13.3}$$

The Coefficient of Determination—r^2

$$r_{12}^2 = \frac{\sigma_1{}^2 - \sigma_{1.2}^2}{\sigma_1{}^2} \qquad \text{(Relative reduction in \textit{square} error.)} \tag{13.4}$$

$$r_{12}^2 = \frac{\sigma_{12}^2}{\sigma_1{}^2} \qquad \begin{array}{l}\text{(Proportion of total square variation that}\\ \text{has been explained.)}\end{array} \tag{13.5}$$

$$r_{12}^2 = 1 - \underbrace{\left(\underbrace{\left(1 - \underbrace{A}_{\text{coefficient of association}}\right)}_{\text{coefficient of nonassociation}}\right)^2}_{\text{square of coefficient of nonassociation}} \tag{13.6}$$

$$r_{12}^2 = (r_{12})^2 \qquad \begin{array}{l}\text{(Coefficient of determination is the}\\ \text{square of the coefficient of correlation.)}\end{array} \tag{13.7}$$

The Coefficient of Correlation—r

$$r_{12} = \sqrt{r_{12}^2} \qquad \text{(Square root of coefficient of determination.)} \tag{13.8}$$

$$r_{12} = \frac{\sum \frac{x_2}{\sigma_2} \cdot \frac{x_1}{\sigma_1}}{N} \qquad \begin{array}{l}\text{(Arithmetic mean of cross products in}\\ \text{standard units.)}\end{array} \tag{13.9}$$

$$r_{12} = b_{12} \frac{\sigma_1}{\sigma_2} \qquad \text{(Slope of line in standard units.)}$$

$$\tag{13.10}$$

$$= b_{21} \frac{\sigma_2}{\sigma_1} \qquad (\qquad\qquad `` \qquad\qquad)$$

(Remember that there are two lines, one for estimating X_1 from X_2 and the other for estimating X_2 from X_1. They both yield the same r.)

$$r_{12} = \frac{\sigma_{12}}{\sigma_1} \qquad \text{(13.11)}$$

(Ratio of standard deviation of conditional means to standard deviation of dependent variable.)

The formulas given are only a small sample of the various algebraic forms that can be used to calculate A, r^2, and r. They are enough to give us an idea of how fertile an area correlation analysis is for a person who likes to play with imaginative mathematics. We consider Eq. 13.2 the most logical and most natural way to measure the degree of association. Our argument is very simple and straightforward: Our fundamental purpose in studying association between variables is *to help us make estimates with smaller errors*. Hence we are naturally interested in the extent to which our knowledge about the association reduces our errors.

Equation 13.3 is very interesting; it is also very useful if we are presented with a study that uses r's and r^2's and we would like to convert them to A's. We should study this formula from the inside out by starting with the smallest circle. Here we have the *coefficient of determination*, which we know is a measure of the degree of association. If we subtract r^2 from 1, we have a measure of the degree of nonassociation. We call this measure the *coefficient of nondetermination*. If we then take the *square root* of $1 - r^2$, we still have a measure of the degree of nonassociation. We call this measure the *coefficient of alienation*. This is really the counterpart to the coefficient of correlation, which, as we know, is the *square root* of the coefficient of determination. Finally, if we subtract the coefficient of alienation (sometimes called k) from 1, we must have a measure of association; and, in fact, we do have A, the coefficient of association.

The Adding-up Problem. Many analysts have been bothered by the issue of whether a given measure of relationship (A, or r, or r^2) yielded a result of 1 when added to its counterpart measure of nonrelationship. For example, we know that the coefficient of determination plus the coefficient of nondetermination equals 1 because we have just noted that in the preceding paragraph. But consider the coefficient of correlation (r) and its counterpart, the coefficient of alienation (k). We have seen that $k = \sqrt{1 - r^2}$. Suppose $r = .8$. Then $r^2 = .64$; $1 - r^2 = .36$; and $\sqrt{1 - r^2} = .6$. Thus $r + k = .8 + .6 = 1.4$, substantially larger than 1. In general $r + k \geq 1$, with the sum 1 only when the correlation is 0 or perfect. This is obviously a very illogical situation. Two variables are either correlated or they are not, and the part that is not correlated must be correlated, and vice versa. Either r or k, or both, are too large.

If we accept the validity of A, and we do, and since $A = 1 - k$, we accept the validity of k. Thus we decide that r must be too large. It is relatively easy to demonstrate why r is too large. Consider Fig. 13.8. Here we show a stripped-down scatter diagram with only two points and two lines. Suppose we had to make an estimate of X_1 *without any knowledge at all of the value of X_2.* Our best procedure (assuming normality) would be to guess the mean of X_1 with some error allowance based on σ_1. Suppose the actual value turned out to be at A. Our mean estimate would have missed by the vertical distance shown as a. Now suppose we had *prior knowledge of X_2.* We would now use the line of conditional means (μ_{12}) as the basis of our estimate with an error allowance based on $\sigma_{1.2}$. Hence we would now miss by only the distance b. If we take the difference between a and b, we get c, which is the *distance between the line of unconditional means (μ_1) and the line of conditional means (μ_{12}).*

We are aware that we can take all such distances as a, the difference from an item to the mean, and calculate σ_1; and also that we can take

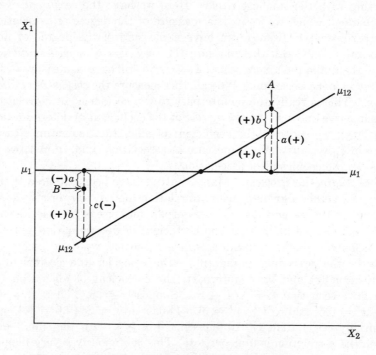

Fig. 13.8   Illustration of the bias in r.

the distances such as b, the difference between an item and the line of conditional means, and calculate $\sigma_{1.2}$. Similarly, we can take all such distances as c and calculate their standard deviation. We call this σ_{12}, or the *standard deviation of the conditional means*. This follows from the fact that the mean of all the conditional means is equal to the mean of the X_1's. (We place the line of relationship so that it passes through the general mean. Since this line is symmetrical in its extensions, the arithmetic mean of all the values along the line must equal the μ_1 part of the general mean.) If we now note that c is the deviation from μ_{12} to μ_1, and if we keep in mind that $\mu_{\mu_{12}} = \mu_1$, we can see that $\mu_{12} - \mu_1 = \mu_{12} - \mu_{\mu_{12}}$, and hence that σ_c must also be $\sigma_{\mu_{12}}$, which we usually abbreviate to σ_{12}.

If we put a, b, and c into words, we can see that the error we started with (a) *minus* the error we ended with (b) equals the error we eliminated (c); and all of this would have been accomplished by knowledge of the value of X_2 as we were estimating X_1. All of this makes very good practical sense.

But now let us look at a point like B. We again label the appropriate deviations as a, b, and c. If we add b and c *algebraically* (that is, with regard for the *sign* attached to the deviation), we would get a, just as we would for the point A. For example, a might be -2, b $+5$, and c -7. We, however, now notice a bit of nonsense. A value of c of 7 indicates that we have reduced our error 7 units by use of knowledge about X_2, and we accomplished this despite the fact that we had only an error of 2 to begin with! Actually, of course, knowledge of the value of X_2 causes us to make a *poorer* estimate here, and to claim an error reduction of 7 units is a serious misrepresentation.

We can picture what is happening by imagining that we start our analysis of the association of X_1 with X_2 with the horizontal line of unconditional means. We then mentally rotate this line counterclockwise around the point 0 until it reaches the line of conditional means. (See Fig. 13.9.) As we do this, we note that the line gets closer to *every point* for a while. But finally the line reaches some of the points. Any further rotation will definitely *increase* the errors of estimating these points. We continue to rotate, nevertheless, because we are trying to reduce our *average* error as much as possible. We find that the average error tends to decrease as long as we rotate *toward* more points than we rotate *away* from. Hence we stop the rotation when we have as many points above the line as we have below the line *at all points along the line*, or as near to this ideal as we can achieve. We must qualify by saying *all along the line* because

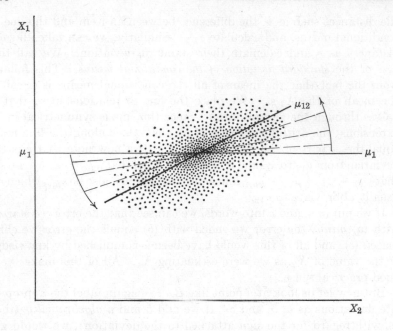

Fig. 13.9 Rotating the line of relationship to reduce average estimating error.

the line always has about the same number of points above as below.
The problem is that in some positions of the line all the points above
the line are at one end of the line and all the points below the line
are at the other end. Note that this is the situation with the line of
unconditional means.

If we have followed the argument to this point, we can now see
why σ_{12} is too big. It contains all the rotation for all the points.
Actually, however, we rotate too much for just about half of the
points because we must pass about half of the points in order to put
half of them on each side of the line and all along the line.

If we now recall that the coefficient of correlation is based on the
slope of this line that we have been mentally rotating, we can see
that r must have an *upward* bias. We can confirm this impression by
turning back to Eq. 13.11 on p. 513. There we see that r can also be
calculated by getting the ratio of the *standard deviation of conditional means* (with an upward bias in terms of error reduction) to
the *standard deviation of the dependent variable* (X_1).

We do not find the adding-up property of r^2 particularly compelling
because it requires us to think in terms of *square* errors. Square

crrors arc usually meaningless, and to know how much we have reduced them does not enlighten the situation.

A Simple Analogy. We can use a simple analogy to illustrate the relationship between A and r and the degree of association. Suppose we are the host (or hostess) at a dinner party and are asked by one of the guests to replenish the water in the water glass. More specifically, we are asked to half-fill the glass. This seems a simple instruction unless we have a thoughtful turn of mind and the glass is aesthetically shaped as shown in Fig. 13.10. Is the glass half-full as in Part A or as in Part B? If we think half-full means half-way up the vertical distance from the bottom to the top of the glass, Glass A is half-full. If we think half-full means half of the total *volume* in the glass, Glass B is half-full. If we think of the degree of association as being measured by the *volume* in the glass and the coefficient of correlation as measuring the *vertical distance* from top to bottom, we can see why the coefficient of correlation makes the glass look fuller than it really is. (We can see why commercial practice leads to glasses with narrow bottoms and wide tops to encourage the illusion of greater contents.) It is also interesting to note that the problem of different scales disappears at the extremes of full and

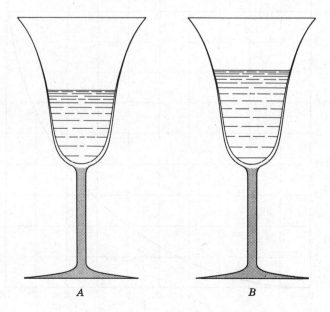

Fig. 13.10 Half a glass of water.

empty, just as it disappears at the extremes of complete and 0 association.

A Scale of Equivalence Between A and r.   Although the water glass analogy conveys the idea, it does not communicate the exact character of the relationship between A and r.   This is shown in Fig. 13.11.   Here r is shown on the horizontal scale and A on the vertical scale.   To convert a given r into A, or vice versa, we locate r on the horizontal scale and run a vertical line upward until it hits the curved line, as illustrated for a value of r of .80.   We then extend a horizontal from this point until it touches the A scale, in this case at .40.   It is interesting to note that the traditional intuitive idea that r should be at least .80 really means that there should be at least a 40% error reduction.   We think it best not to have any arbitrary boundaries for a minimum degree of useful correlation.   We deliberately selected an r of .80 as an illustration because it is that point at which r is exactly *twice* as large as A.   Values of r less than .8 are *more than twice* as large as the corresponding A (except at the limit of 0).   For example, an r of .20 corresponds to an A of only

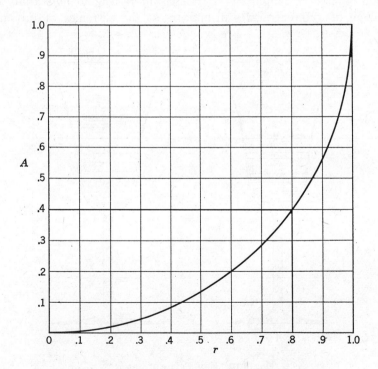

Fig. 13.11   Scale of equivalence between A and r.

.02, a 10 to 1 ratio. We can thus see why an r of .2 represents a trivially small degree of association. Values of r greater than .8 are *less than twice* as large as A. For example, an r of .95 corresponds to an A of .69, a 1.4 to 1 ratio.

13.5 The Next Step

The preceding pages have concentrated mainly on the essential ideas in the analysis of the association between two or more sets of events. In the next chapter we use these ideas and the associated techniques in a practical problem.

PROBLEMS AND QUESTIONS

13.1 Suppose you were faced with the task of selecting a sales manager for your company. To what extent would you be interested in each of the following characteristics of a prospect? Explain the basis of your answer in each case.

(*a*) Height.

(*b*) Sex.

(*c*) Age.

(*d*) Formal education.

(*e*) Years experience as a salesman of your line of products.

(*f*) Years experience as a sales manager, or assistant sales manager, for any line of products.

(*g*) Number of children.

(*h*) Weight of wife (or husband).

(*i*) Proportion of gray hairs on head.

13.2 We have learned to associate the temperature with the season of the year. For example, consider a 30-year experience in Chicago. The daily temperature has varied from an average low of 17.1 degrees F. to an average high of 85.3 if we ignore the season of the year; however, if we classify these temperatures by month, we find the range of the average low to average high temperature varying as follows:

Month	Range of the Daily Temperature Average Low	Average High	Month	Range of the Daily Temperature Average Low	Average High
January	17.1	32.7	July	63.9	85.3
February	19.8	35.0	August	62.3	83.0
March	29.0	45.0	September	55.2	75.9
April	38.6	57.6	October	43.9	64.3
May	48.7	69.7	November	31.3	47.6
June	58.8	80.0	December	20.6	35.3

(a) Determine the difference between the low and high figure for each month.

(b) Calculate the arithmetic mean of such differences.

(c) Compare your result in (b) with the difference between the low and high figure for the full year.

(d) What is the *degree* of association between the temperature and the month of the year?

13.3 (a) What *causes* the temperature in Chicago to be generally higher in July than in January?

(b) Are these the same causes that result in the reverse relationship in Buenos Aires?

13.4 The Crayle Co. has been considering the possibility of using the results of a finger dexterity test as an aid in the selection of employees for one of the assembly tasks in the production line. The Pixem Test has been given to 10 of its veteran employees with known production records. The scores and production records are as follows:

Worker	Average Daily Output X_1	Score on Pixem Dexterity Test X_2
A	220	11
B	270	14
C	230	17
D	270	19
E	320	21
F	340	27
G	320	30
H	390	31
I	370	39
J	420	43

(a) Construct a scatter diagram of these two series.

(b) Draw a smooth line on the graph to represent your best judgment of a line that measures the average output expected based on any given test score. Would you expect this line to be straight or curved? Is it possible that the line might actually turn negative for very high test scores? Explain.

(c) Extend your line to the left until it crosses the X_1 axis. Is there any common sense interpretation to this value of X_1 for a case in which X_2 equals 0? Is there any mathematical interpretation?

(d) Would you expect the variation in output among workers with the same test score to be the same for all test score groups? Explain.

(e) Suppose that these same workers were to be given this same test again. Would you expect each worker to get the same score as he did the first time? Why or why not?

(f) What are the implications of your answer in (e) to a proper interpretation of the specific test scores given above?

13.5 What type of relationship would you expect to find between the following pairs of variables? (For example, would you expect the relationship to be *straight* line or some kind of curve?) In each case, be very careful to note whether you are referring to the kind of relationship you would expect to *observe* if you collected data from the real world or to the kind of relationship you would *hypothesize* on the assumption that *other variables would be constant.*

(*a*) Relationship between height and weight of new-born babies.

(*b*) Relationship between price of a product and its volume of sales.

(*c*) Relationship between price of a product and its quality.

(*d*) Relationship between the size—in square inches of space—of a newspaper advertisement and the intensity of reader response as measured by purchase rate for product being advertised.

(*e*) Relationship between experience as measured by years on the job and the ability to do the job.

(*f*) Relationship between thickness of a coat of paint and its ability to survive the weather.

13.6 Distinguish between a dependent and an independent variable. Illustrate with reference to two variables that you have had some experience with.

13.7 Distinguish between a conditional probability distribution of a dependent variable and an unconditional probability distribution of that same variable.

13.8(*a*) What is the relevance to correlation analysis of the assumption that the vertical vectors be identical except for their averages?

(*b*) Suppose you had strong reason to believe that the *coefficients of variation* of the vertical vectors were practically the same in a given problem rather than the standard deviations being practically the same. What suggestions do you have for transforming the data so as to equalize the variations of the vertical vectors?

13.9 What are the theoretical and practical advantages of working with the assumption that the normal curve adequately describes the vector distributions in a correlation analysis?

13.10 Suppose we are given the information that the vertical vectors in a correlation problem are all normal and that they all have the same standard deviation. We are also told that the relationship is linear, at least within the relevant range of the data. What can we now say about:

(*a*) The horizontal vectors?

(*b*) The diagonals?

(*c*) The *sums* of the vertical vectors?

13.11 Why is it appropriate to call a line of relationship between two variables a line of *conditional averages?*

13.12 Use the test score—output data of Problem 13.4 and calculate as best you can the following:

(*a*) The standard deviation of the universe of worker outputs.

(*b*) The standard deviation of the universe of test scores.

(*c*) The conditional standard deviation of worker output, *given* the test score. Use the variations around your visually fitted line of Problem 13.4.

(*d*) Compare the relative sizes of your conditional and unconditional standard deviations of worker output.

13.13 Would you expect the universes referred to in Problem 13.12 to remain stable through time so that the results could be used as a guide for hiring future workers? Explain.

13.14 Use the standard deviations you calculated in Problem 13.12 to calculate the following. Interpret your results.

(a) The coefficient of correlation $-r$.

(b) The coefficient of determination $-r^2$.

(c) The coefficient of association $-A$.

(d) The coefficient of alienation $-k$.

(e) The coefficient of nondetermination $-k^2$.

chapter 14

Reducing uncertainty by association: *application of the model to practical problems*

So far our discussion of correlation, or association, has for the most part been confined to an ideal world. Except for our references to Galton's work, we have talked about correlations that might exist in a *universe*. Actually, of course, we never really know the content of any *real universes*. We come in contact only with *samples* that have happened to occur. Sometimes we may actually *select* a sample by random or other means. Usually these samples "just happen," the way the weather "just happens." Thus we come back to our familiar problem: How can we draw *inferences* from past sample data so we can make some *rational predictions* about the future samples which have yet to occur but which we will have to contend with? As before, we follow the path from past samples to future samples by detouring around through past and future universes. Also, as before, we do this by making the most judicious guesses we find practicable within the limits of time and costs.

14.1   Selecting Relevant Variables

Before we can formally correlate any variables, we must pick them out and obtain their measurements. Suppose we were a sales manager who was trying to gain some understanding of the variation in sales from one sales territory to the next. We would probably start our analysis by trying to think of the various factors which we consider to have something to do with sales. Suppose our product were electric blankets. Our list of factors might look something like the following:

1. The salesman—his ability, his energy, etc.
2. The size of the territory.
   a. The number of people.
   b. The number of people over 20 years of age.
   c. The square miles in territory, etc.
3. Average income in the territory.
4. Number of electric appliance and department stores.
5. Average temperature—by months—in the territory.
6. Cost of electricity.
7. Sociological factors that might affect the acceptability of electric blankets.
   a. Proportion of foreign born in population.
   b. Proportion of people over 45 years of age (habits set before introduction of electric blanket).
8. Competition in territory.
   a. Number of active competitive brands.
   b. Prices of competitive brands.
   c. Skill and energy of competitive salesmen.
   d. Volume of competitive promotional activity.
   e. Number of years competitors have been in market.
   f. Number of years we have been in market, etc.
9. How much do we help the salesman?
   a. Promotional activity.
   b. Salary and commission.
   c. Expense allowances.

We can undoubtedly think of many more possible factors that might help us understand the variation in sales from territory to territory. If we really knew something about the manufacture and merchandising of electric blankets, we could think of many more than that. Our list is long enough, however, to make a few practical points quite clear.

First, we note that if we select only *one* of these factors, say, population, to correlate with sales, we will be considering only a small part of the possibly relevant variables. No matter how fancy we get in this analysis, we should never lose sight of our limited scope.

Second, we note that if we try to correlate all these factors at once, we might confuse ourselves much as a golfer would if he tried to *consciously* think about the hundreds of muscles he must coordinate in order to hit a proper golf shot. Hence we should not forget that, as meritorious as a "scientific" analysis of our problem is, it is not a complete or necessarily a superior substitute for the kind of intuitive and unconscious coordination that can be performed by a person with several years of intelligently digested experience. The scientific analysis can help an intelligent person. It cannot create intelligence where none existed before.

Third, we have a definite problem of *choice* of which variable or variables we analyze in a formal way. Naturally we would like to analyze the most important ones, that is, the variables that will tell us the most about the variation in sales. But how can we do this in advance of analysis, particularly since one of the purposes of the analysis is to tell us which are the most important? This is a dilemma, so we do the only practical thing. We make an *advance guess* of which are the most important, and we use the results of the analysis to tell us how good our guesses were. In other words, we set up *hypotheses* about whether the variables are related and then we *test these hypotheses.* We use those hypotheses that survive the test and put aside those that do not. This approach works well over time if we do not acquire strong emotional attachments for some of our hypotheses and conveniently ignore the results of the tests when they are unfavorable. For example, it is not unusual for a sales manager to have a pet factor that he thinks is important as a measure of sales ability. He would never think of hiring a man who did not possess this attribute, and he would rarely fire a man who had a large amount of it, and all this despite the fact that available evidence suggests very strongly that this factor is at best neutral towards sales ability. He was probably victimized years ago by some very vivid experience where this factor happened to play a role, and it has colored his thinking ever since.

Our competitors will also be making guesses about which factors are most important. If they are luckier, or smarter, than we are, their guesses will be better, and they will gain an advantage because of this additional knowledge. If we do not have luck like this, or this kind of "smartness," we can still survive if we do not let our pride prevent us from imitating our successful competitor, at a respectful distance of course. Japanese businessmen, for example, have demonstrated an amazing ability to follow close behind the successful innovations of businessmen in England, Germany, and the United States. It is competitive imitation like this, of course, that leads to progress. If no one imitates our innovation, we can be assured that we will not make much money with it.

Most guesses about what factors seem worthwhile to analyze arise in a relatively haphazard way. Some of the best guesses come from the most unlikely sources. It is not uncommon to discover that some of the most foolish guesses turn out to be very fruitful. In fact, it is almost certain to be so because its very foolishness is what has prevented other people from investigating it sooner. We also have the problem of not being able to think of some factors until other factors are thought of first. It is as though the factors are piled up in interlocking layers and we have to unpeel them one by one. The situation is further complicated because many of the factors are *related to each other.* Thus things are not always what they seem. We sometimes find that we should do just the opposite of what common sense suggests. (Common sense is used here as a synonym for superficial observation.) For example, a beginning automobile driver tends to make turns with the brake partially on in order to make a slow turn for comfort and control. He eventually learns (or at least some do) that he should slow down before the turn and speed up while in the turn for much more comfort and control. Similarly, beginning golfers try to hit the ball into the air by lifting the ball. So they try to get the club under the ball. Because the earth is already in possession of the space under the ball, they do not have much success. They eventually learn (or some do) that the ball should be hit up into the air by hitting down on the ball, thus avoiding the attempt to move the earth out of the way first. It is quite a day when the golfer first discovers that it is not he but the lofted clubface that directs the ball into the air.

The only useful positive suggestion in helping to select factors is to get in the habit of making rough charts (called scatter diagrams) of potentially useful relations. If these sketches give the appearance of association, preferably of a high degree, we have a fairly good clue that further analysis will be fruitful. On the other hand, if our sketch shows evidence of little association, as indicated in Fig. 14.1, we might hesitate to plunge into an immediate investigation. But do not then assume that these variables are not related. Their relationship may be buried under some other variables that we have not noticed yet. We discuss this later after we acquire some technical knowledge on the analysis of more than two variables at the same time.

The Problem of Quantifying the Variables

So far we have carefully skirted the question of whether some of the variables are quantified, or even quantifiable. Some of these variables exist only in our mind, and frequently it is better to first think out an imaginary scatter diagram. In fact, even if we can measure these variables, we find that we can correlate the data mentally first. Most of us have never really seen a scatter diagram of measured heights and weights of men. Nevertheless we are quite capable of mentally picturing what such a scatter diagram would look like. We have been accumulating the points for such a mental

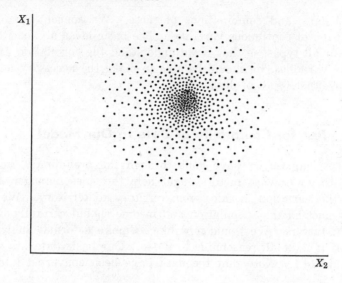

Fig. 14.1 An example of no apparent correlation.

scatter diagram over the years as we made mental notes of the heights and weights of men we have observed.

The problem of quantifying certain variables has prevented their being formally analyzed. Everyone who thinks of such a variable as a potential factor tends to dismiss it as unmeasurable or as too expensive to measure. One of the most interesting uses of correlation analysis, incidentally, is to quantify something *indirectly* by measuring something that is *related* to the variable we are trying to measure. For example, a thermometer does not measure *heat;* it measures the *relationship* between the size of some material and the variation in the heat, whether the material be liquid mercury or bimetallic bars. Another interesting application of correlation analysis to the problem of measurement is to make allowance for all the factors we can measure and then attribute any remaining variation to some remaining factor that we cannot otherwise measure. For example, suppose we wished to rate salesmen in their various territories. How do we measure sales performance? What we can do is allow for variation in population, income, etc., and then argue that any *remaining* vari ations in sales from territory to territory is a measure of the salesman's effectiveness. This sort of measuring goes on every day. We have occasion to examine it later.

Correlation techniques have been worked out to study data expressed in many forms, principal ones being data expressed as *continuous* variables, *discrete* variables, *attribute* data of all sorts, *ranked* data, and combinations of these. We concentrate on the correlation of continuous variables. The basic ideas are exactly the same for all types, so that if we understand the correlation of continuous variables, we should be able to make the necessary adaptations to other types of data.

14.2　Test for Conformity of Data to Our Model

Let us suppose we have gone through the preliminary work of trying to guess what factors might help the sales manager understand the variation in sales from territory to territory. We have finally guessed that population and income should certainly be important factors. We would now like to make a formal analysis of these if it is at all reasonable to do so. Our basic data are shown in Table 14.1. Note that the data have been converted into per-

TABLE 14.1

Sales, Population, and Income for the 15 Territories of The Tingle Company
(All data represent annual averages for the 3 years of 1957–60)

| Terri-tory | Sales 1000's | Popu-lation 1000's | Income $1 mil. | Territory Data as Percent of Company Total | | |
				Sales X_1	Popu-lation X_2	Income X_3
#1	6	5	16	4.0	2.4	8.9
2	4	6	12	2.7	2.9	6.7
3	10	8	17	6.7	3.8	9.4
4	8	9	15	5.3	4.3	8.3
5	6	11	11	4.0	5.2	6.1
6	9	11	15	6.0	5.2	8.4
7	12	12	15	8.0	5.7	8.4
8	9	14	9	6.0	6.7	5.0
9	12	15	13	8.0	7.1	7.2
10	11	17	11	7.2	8.1	6.1
11	10	17	8	6.7	8.1	4.4
12	13	20	12	8.7	9.5	6.7
13	12	21	8	8.0	10.0	4.4
14	15	22	12	10.0	10.5	6.7
15	13	22	6	8.7	10.5	3.3
	150	210	180	100.0	100.0	100.0

centages of the total for all territories. This has been done to simplify the application of the results in subsequent years. It would be very unlikely that there would be a stable relationship between the *actual quantities* over the years because of shifts in general acceptability of the product, shifts in prices, etc. However, if such shifts were to affect the various territories more or less equally, which they are likely to do, the relationships among the *percentages* of total should remain fairly stable. For example, if the company's total sales were to grow 10% faster than population, use of the actual quantities of population to estimate actual quantities of sales would result in general underestimation. However, if a territory retained the same percentage of population, it should retain its same percentage of sales.

Deciding on Shape of Line of Relationship

The first decision is that about the *shape* of the line of relationship, or the line of conditional averages. Our model requires that a straight line be a reasonable estimator of this shape. The obvious approach is to sketch a scatter diagram of the sample data. Figures 14.2, 14.3, and 14.4 show the scatter diagrams (scattergrams) for the sales–

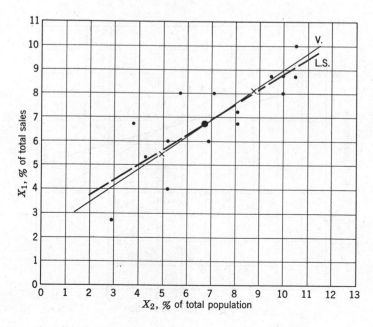

Fig. 14.2 Scattergram of relationship between sales and population. (Data from Table 14.1.)

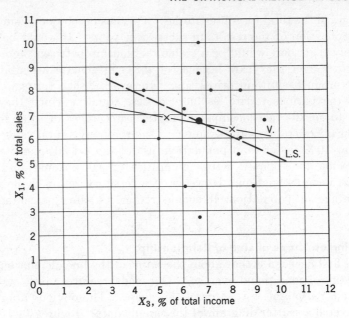

Fig. 14.3 Scattergram of relationship between sales and income. (Data from Table 14.1.)

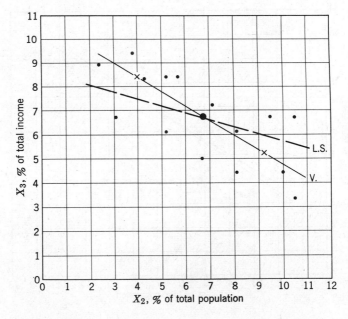

Fig. 14.4 Scattergram of relationship between population and income. (Data from Table 14.1.)

population, sales–income, and income–population relationships. In each case the large dot near the center of the graph shows the general mean of the data. This point was used as a pivot point for locating the visually fitted line shown on the graph as V. (The L.S. line is referred to shortly.) Each line was placed by pivoting around the center point until there were about as many points above the line as there were below the line on each side of the center point. A straight line seems to be a reasonable estimator in each case.

A useful trick in selecting the shape of the line is to divide the data into sections according to the size of the independent variable. For example, we divided the data into two sections, one for the values of the independent variable that were *below average* (to the left of the center point) and the other for the values *above average* (to the right of the center point). We fitted by eye an average for the dependent variable in each section. These are shown as X's on the graphs. We then drew the line as close to these averages, including the general average, as possible. If we had more items, we would have found it advantageous to divide the data into more than two sections. If the data tended to conform to a curved pattern, the section averages would very likely make this fairly clear. See Fig. 14.5 to illustrate such a case with a tentative curved line drawn in.

Always remember we are dealing with only a sample of data. We cannot expect exact conformity of any line to the various section

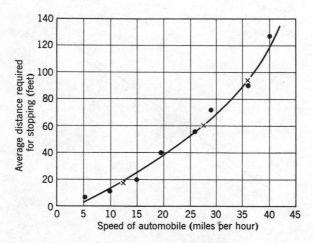

Fig. 14.5 Illustration of curvilinear relationship. (Data show the average distance required to stop an automobile for various speeds. Data taken from Ezekiel & Fox, *Methods of Correlation and Regression Analysis,* p. 100. By permission of the publisher, John Wiley and Sons.)

averages. On the other hand, do not use the excuse of a small sample to justify a straight line for almost any kind of data.

Deciding on Applicability of Arithmetic Mean as an Average

We are not really interested in using the arithmetic mean as such. The arithmetic mean is appropriate when we are interested in the *totals* of data. Here we are interested in making the closest possible estimate of the sales in a territory. The total of a set of such estimates is essentially irrelevant. The *median* of a set of values is *closest* to all the values. The arithmetic mean of a set of values will be the same as the median *if the distribution is symmetrical.* In addition, the arithmetic mean of a random sample is subject to smaller sampling errors than the median *if the universe is symmetrical.* Hence we prefer to use the mean rather than the median if the sample is sufficiently symmetrical to support the hypothesis of a symmetrical universe. There are additional mathematical conveniences if we use the mean. Thus we tend to use means as estimators unless there is reasonably strong evidence to the contrary.

An examination of Figs. 14.2 to 14.4 reveals no strong evidence contrary to the hypothesis of a symmetrical universe, and we are willing to use the arithmetic mean. If we had evidence of definite skewness, as illustrated in Fig. 14.6, we would then have the usual options available:

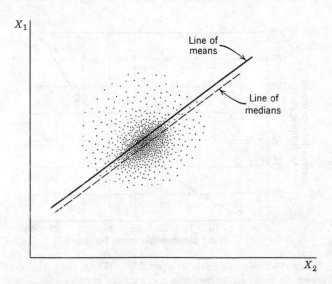

Fig. 14.6 Illustration of effects of skewness in X_1 on line of means.

1. We could ignore the skewness and continue to use the means with recognition that our results are somewhat crude.
2. We could try to transform the data, either one or both series, to see if such transformed data conformed reasonably well to a symmetrical distribution. For example, there is some evidence that the weights of adult males show definite positive skewness. If we correlate the *logarithms* of weight with the heights we might achieve a closer approximation to symmetry. (Incidentally, the most economical way to test a logarithmic transformation is to use paper with a logarithmic scale in either one or both axes, depending on our needs. Do not waste time looking up logarithms until such a relationship has been confirmed by a graphic analysis.)
3. We could judiciously omit any items that seemed to be out of line. This is a dangerous practice and should be done only when there is definite evidence that special and identifiable circumstances contributed to the departure of such items from a general symmetrical pattern.

Deciding on Applicability of Normal Curve Approximation

If we successfully jump the hurdles of linearity and symmetry, we are generally very ready to accept the applicability of a normal curve approximation. This is because experience suggests that practically all symmetrical distributions have a central tendency, or a tendency to bunch near the average. In such a case we find a normal curve approximation not only better than any competitive approximation, but also quite accurate in its own right.

The three graphs of the relationships among sales, population, and income represent such small samples that it is somewhat ludicrous to try to make any rational determination of whether a normal curve is a good approximation. This, unfortunately, is rather common in the analysis of business data. The trouble develops because the basic universes are shifting so rapidly that it is very difficult for us to collect large samples of homogeneous data, and consequently we tend to take the position of assuming the normal curve is appropriate *unless we find relatively strong contrary evidence*. This is, of course, a relatively weak position, but, again, we defend it because we have trouble finding a stronger position. Naturally, a prudent analyst keeps these limitations in mind as he draws any conclusions from his analysis.

Mathematical Tests of Conformity of Data to Model

The above tests were confined to what we could find out from graphic evidence. It is possible to apply mathematical tests to measure the conformity of the sample data to the conditions of this, or other, models. Such tests are outside the bounds of our limited discussion. Also, we point out that these mathematical tests can be applied only after we have fitted our model to the data. The tests then help us decide whether we should or should not use the results. Our discussion has been directed to the use of tests that help us decide whether we should fit the model or not. Thus it is a good idea to make the graphic tests even when we are planning to make the mathematical tests after our results are available. This is usually true even when we have access to an electronic computer to process the results. The computer is very quick, once we set it up, but it still costs money to operate, and very few businesses can afford to produce useless or misleading correlation analyses.

14.3   Estimating a Line of Relationship

Since we have only a sample of data, with many gaps in both the independent and the dependent variable, we cannot calculate a line of averages by calculating all the separate averages for each vertical vector. We must devise an interpolation technique. We have already seen how this can be done by hand and eye on a graph. We would now like to calculate such a line.

The Least Squares Property of the Arithmetic Mean

The arithmetic mean has two very useful and interesting mathematical properties:

1. The sum of the deviations from the mean equals 0.

$$\Sigma(X - \overline{X}) = \Sigma x = 0.$$

2. The sum of the *squares* of the deviations is a minimum.

$$\Sigma x^2 \text{ is a minimum.}$$

The *least-squares* property interests us the most at the moment. Suppose we did have all the universe data and that they conformed to the conditions of our model. We would then find that the conditional means would fall in a straight line and that the standard deviations around these means would all be the same. *Each* of these conditional means would be a *least-squares value* for the items in its vector. We could then label the line of means as a *least-squares line* in the sense that any other line would give a larger sum of squares of the deviations of the items from the line because, of course, any other line would not pass through all the conditional means.

Now let us turn to sample data. We argue that a least-squares line fitted to the sample data would be the best possible estimate of the least-squares line in the universe. This is the same principle we followed when we stated that the arithmetic mean of a sample is the best estimate of the arithmetic mean of the universe.

It is a good idea to keep in mind that a least-squares line is nothing more than a line of means and can be called an *arithmetic mean line.* It has all the characteristics, both good and bad, of the arithmetic mean.

The determination of how to calculate a least-squares (L.S.) line involves the mathematics of the calculus and hence is outside the scope of this book. It is useful, however, to sketch the line of reasoning used without getting into the mathematics. Thus we might dispel any notions that there is anything mystical about a L.S. line. The first step is to define the type of line we wish to fit. In our case this is a *straight line,* which can be represented in general form as

$$X_{12} = a_{12} + b_{12}X_2. \tag{14.1}$$

(It is not uncommon for students to get the idea that L.S. lines are *always straight lines,* primarily because that is the only kind they calculate in an introductory course. Actually a L.S. line can have any shape we desire. This follows obviously because the *means* of the vertical vectors do not necessarily have to form a linear pattern. In fact, it is more likely than not that such means will form a *nonlinear* pattern.)

The second step in reasoning is to subtract each actual X_1 value from the mean of its vector as estimated by X_{12}. Thus we have

$$X_1 - X_{12} = X_1 - (a_{12} + b_{12}X_2) \tag{14.2}$$

if we follow the conventional rule of treating both sides of an equation alike.

In the third step we *square* each of these deviations, with the result

$$(X_1 - X_{12})^2 = [X_1 - (a_{12} + b_{12}X_2)]^2. \tag{14.3}$$

The fourth step is very critical from the point of view of the assumptions of the model. Here we *add* all the *squared deviations* of Step 3. In other words we *pool* all the deviations, almost all of them from *different* vertical vectors, as though they all belonged to the *same distribution.* The logic behind this pooling is the assumption that all the vertical vectors have the same standard deviation. (We say a correlation matrix is *homoscedastic* when all its vertical vectors have the same standard deviation.) If this assumption is not true, we end up with a conditional standard deviation that is an *arithmetic mean* of the various vector standard deviations rather than a specific estimate for each vector. If we wished, we could measure the degree to which these vectors might have different standard deviations, or the degree of *heteroscedasticity*. Our sample is too small to do this successfully, however. We would need enough items in each vector to make it possible to estimate the standard deviations separately. We rarely have such large samples in practice, and we again use the backhanded rule that we adopt the hypothesis of homoscedastic vectors *unless we have fairly strong evidence to the contrary*.

Our equation now is

$$\Sigma(X_1 - X_{12})^2 = \Sigma[X_1 - (a_{12} + b_{12}X_2)]^2. \qquad (14.4)$$

The fifth and last step is to find a way of choosing values for a and b so that $\Sigma(X_1 - X_{12})^2$ is a minimum. (Those familiar with calculus can perform this step by taking partial derivatives with respect to a and b and then setting each of these equal to 0. Of course, it is better to simplify the equation first.) This step leads to two equations as follows:

$$(1) \qquad \Sigma X_1 = Na_{12} + b_{12}\Sigma X_2$$

$$(14.5)$$

$$(2) \quad \Sigma X_1 X_2 = a_{12}\Sigma X_2 + b_{12}\Sigma X_2{}^2.$$

If we fill in the appropriate sums and solve these two equations for a and b, we have values for a and b so that the *sums of the squares of the deviations of the sample items around our line will be a minimum*. There is no magic to these squares; we minimize their sum only because this gives us an *arithmetic mean line*.

Let us apply this technique to our problem of sales territories. Table 14.2 shows the detailed calculations for the relationship between sales and population. It also shows the results for the line of linear relationship between sales and income and that between income and population. These lines are plotted as the L.S. lines in Figs. 14.2 to 14.4. Note their close conformity to the V. lines. It is worthwhile to speculate on how much of the differences between and V. and L.S. lines is due to errors in the visual fitting and how much to the inapplicability of the L.S. model. Suffice it to say that we should not be too hasty in praising or condemning either line. (Remember also that if part of the test is to compare the standard

TABLE 14.2

Calculating a Least-squares Straight Line of Relationship between Sales and Population

X_1 = Sales as % of Total of All Territories
X_2 = Population " " "
X_3 = Income " " "

Territory	X_1	X_2	X_3	$X_1{}^2$	$X_2{}^2$	$X_3{}^2$	X_1X_2	X_1X_3	X_2X_3
1	4.0	2.4	8.9	16.00	5.76	79.21	9.60	35.60	21.36
2	2.7	2.9	6.7	7.29	8.41	44.89	7.83	18.09	19.43
3	6.7	3.8	9.4	44.89	14.44	88.36	25.46	62.98	35.72
4	5.3	4.3	8.3	28.09	18.49	68.89	22.79	43.99	35.69
5	4.0	5.2	6.1	16.00	27.04	37.21	20.80	24.40	31.72
6	6.0	5.2	8.4	36.00	27.04	70.56	31.20	50.40	43.68
7	8.0	5.7	8.4	64.00	32.49	70.56	45.60	67.20	47.88
8	6.0	6.7	5.0	36.00	44.89	25.00	40.20	30.00	33.50
9	8.0	7.1	7.2	64.00	50.41	51.84	56.80	57.60	51.12
10	7.2	8.1	6.1	51.84	65.61	37.21	58.32	43.92	49.41
11	6.7	8.1	4.4	44.89	65.61	19.36	54.27	29.48	35.64
12	8.7	9.5	6.7	75.69	90.25	44.89	82.65	58.29	63.65
13	8.0	10.0	4.4	64.00	100.00	19.36	80.00	35.20	44.00
14	10.0	10.5	6.7	100.00	110.25	44.89	105.00	67.00	70.35
15	8.7	10.5	3.3	75.69	110.25	10.89	91.35	28.71	34.65
	100.0	100.0	100.0	724.38	770.94	713.12	731.87	652.86	617.80

L. S. Equations

(1) $\Sigma X_1 = N a_{12} + b_{12} \Sigma X_2$ (1) $100.00 = 15 a_{12} + 100.00 b_{12}$

(2) $\Sigma X_1 X_2 = a_{12} \Sigma X_2 + b_{12} \Sigma X_2{}^2$ (2) $731.87 = 100 a_{12} + 770.94 b_{12}$

Solution:

Eq. (1) $\times$ 6.6667: (3) $666.67 = 100 a_{12} + 666.67 b_{12}$
Eq. (2) $-$ Eq. (3): $65.20 = 104.27 b_{12}$
                        $b_{12} = .625$
Substitute in Eq. (1): $100.00 = 15 a_{12} + 62.50$
                        $a_{12} = 2.50$

Hence L.S. equation equals:

$$\overline{X}_{12} = 2.50 + .625 X_2$$

Similarly:

$$\overline{X}_{13} = 8.65 - .297 X_3$$

and

$$\overline{X}_{32} = 9.79 - .469 X_2$$

---

deviations around these lines, we will *always* find the standard deviation around the L.S. line at least as small as that around the V. line. This is a direct consequence of the least-squares property of the L.S. line and has nothing to do with the applicability of the model itself.)

One of the most striking features of the calculation of a L.S. line is the rather large amount of arithmetic involved. The arithmetic would be greater if we had used curves for our lines. The routine used in Table 14.2 to solve the two equations is the one most commonly taught in high school algebra courses. There are other routines that some might find more comfortable. Since a curved line would involve the solution of at least three equations, the solution routine would then be somewhat more tedious. In fact, it would be so tedious that it is worthwhile to develop short-cut techniques. We encounter these short cuts later during our discussion of multiple correlation.

14.4   The L.S. Line as an Estimator of X_1

The acid test of the value of the L.S. line as an estimator of values of X_1, given values of X_2, would be a test which involved making estimates of *new data*, that is, data which were not available at the time of the calculation of the line. We would, however, like an *advance estimate* of how close the L.S. line will be to the future data. We make the advance estimate by using the only available data, namely, the *same data we used to calculate the line*. It should be obvious that the advance estimate tends to be on the optimistic side unless we are very stupid about the line we select to calculate. In effect, we are going to judge how accurate our *forecasting* system will be by seeing how well the same system would have worked with the past data, the same data we used to develop the system (the L.S. line). There is a bit of circular reasoning here unless the future shows the same patterns as the past, which it rarely does in any great detail. However, this is the best we know how to do. Thus it is important to be alert to the possible need to discount the apparent accuracy of a forecast system if its stated accuracy is based only on the data used to develop the system.

Table 14.3 outlines the routine for estimating X_1 and the standard deviation of the errors in such estimates. The estimates are shown in column 4. Since the arithmetic mean has been used as the basis of these estimates, the total should be exactly 100. The difference of .3 is due to rounding errors. Note that this rounding error disappears if we carry an additional decimal place as in column 3. This additional place is not mathematically significant, however, so it is better to tolerate the rounding error.

The sum of the errors (column 6) should add to 0 for the same reasons as above.

TABLE 14.3

Estimates of X_1, and Errors Thereof, Based on Given Values of X_2

X_2 (1)	$b_{12}X_2$ (2)	$a_{12} + b_{12}X_2$ (3)	$\overline{X}_{12}$ (4)	X_1 (5)	$X_1 - \overline{X}_{12}$ (6)	$x_{1.2}^2$ (7)
2.4	1.50	4.00	4.0	4.0	0.0	0.0
2.9	1.81	4.31	4.3	2.7	−1.6	2.56
3.8	2.38	4.88	4.9	6.7	1.8	3.24
4.3	2.69	5.19	5.2	5.3	.1	.01
5.2	3.25	5.75	5.8	4.0	−1.8	3.24
5.2	3.25	5.75	5.8	6.0	.2	.04
5.7	3.56	6.06	6.1	8.0	1.9	3.61
6.7	4.19	6.69	6.7	6.0	−.7	.49
7.1	4.44	6.94	6.9	8.0	1.1	1.21
8.1	5.06	7.56	7.6	7.2	−.4	.16
8.1	5.06	7.56	7.6	6.7	−.9	.81
9.5	5.94	8.44	8.4	8.7	.3	.09
10.0	6.25	8.75	8.8	8.0	−.8	.64
10.5	6.56	9.06	9.1	10.0	.9	.81
10.5	6.56	9.06	9.1	8.7	−.4	.16
100.0	62.50	100.00	100.3	100.0	−.3	17.07

$$s_{1.2} = \sqrt{\frac{\Sigma(X_1 - \overline{X}_{12})^2}{N}} = \sqrt{\frac{17.07}{15}} = 1.07\%$$

$$\hat{\sigma}_{1.2} = \sqrt{\frac{\Sigma(X_1 - \overline{X}_{12})^2}{N - k}} = s_{1.2}\sqrt{\frac{N}{N - k}} = 1.07\sqrt{\frac{15}{15 - 2}} = 1.07 \times 1.07$$
$$= 1.14\%$$

We have calculated both $s_{1.2}$ and $\hat{\sigma}_{1.2}$. $s_{1.2}$ is the standard deviation for this particular sample. If, however, we conceive of this particular sample as only one of the many different samples that might have occurred as far as we know, and if we are willing to assume that this sample generating process is *random* within the bounds of our present knowledge, we might recognize the standard deviation of random samples tends to be too small on the average. (We found this to be so for single variables. It is correspondingly true for variables that are varying jointly.) The adjustment for this downward bias was related to the *number of degrees of freedom* used up in the calculation. When we had a single variable and based the standard deviation on the *mean of that variable*, we used up 1 degree of freedom. The standard deviation around the line is based on the line and on all the constants used to define the line, in our case a_{12} and b_{12}. Hence the line uses up 2 d.f. (If our line were curved and had the constants a, b, c, and d, we would have used up 4 d.f.) Hence we make an *estimate of the universe conditional standard deviation*, or $\acute{\sigma}_{1.2}$, by allowing for the loss of 2 d.f., thus increasing the figure from 1.07 to 1.14.

Table 14.3 follows the straight definition of the procedure for calculating $s_{1.2}$ and $\acute{\sigma}_{1.2}$. This routine is relatively tedious, however. It is also subject to larger rounding errors. Hence we usually calculate $s_{1.2}$ by a short procedure that is analogous to that we used to calculate the standard deviation of a single variable. For a (L.S.) straight line this formula [1] is

$$s_{1.2} = \sqrt{\frac{\Sigma X_1{}^2 - a_{12}\Sigma X_1 - b_{12}\Sigma X_1 X_2}{N}}. \qquad (14.5)$$

For our present problem we get

$$s_{1.2} = \sqrt{\frac{724.38 - 2.50 \times 100.00 - .625 \times 731.87}{15}}$$

$$= 1.06\%. \qquad \acute{\sigma}_{1.2} = 1.13\%.$$

The difference between 1.07, the result of the direct calculation, and the 1.06, the result of the short-cut calculation, is due to rounding. The 1.06 is more accurate.

14.5 Random Sampling Errors in Estimating $\bar{X}_{12}$

It is very unlikely that our estimates of the line and standard deviations are strictly accurate. Hence we must make some allowance for the resultant uncertainty. The values of a_{12} and b_{12} are both subject to random sampling errors. Since both of them are really arithmetic means, their sampling errors are a function of the

---

[1] The above short-cut formula has some simple properties that make it relatively easy to remember. The first term $\Sigma X_1{}^2$ is always the sum of the squares of the *dependent* variable. We then subtract a stream of products that consist of the *first* constant of the equation times the left-hand member of the *first* L.S. equation; the *second* constant times the left-hand member of the *second* L.S. equation, etc. We have occasion to extend this principle to the case of multiple correlation.

relevant standard deviation and of the d.f. The appropriate formulas for estimating these sampling errors are

$$\hat{\sigma}_a = \frac{s_{1.2}}{\sqrt{N - k}} = \frac{\hat{\sigma}_{1.2}}{\sqrt{N}}. \tag{14.6}$$

$$\hat{\sigma}_b = \frac{s_{1.2}}{s_2\sqrt{N - k}} = \frac{\hat{\sigma}_{1.2}}{\hat{\sigma}_2\sqrt{N}}. \tag{14.7}$$

Note their close similarity to the formula for the standard error of the mean, which is

$$\hat{\sigma}_{\bar{x}} = \frac{s}{\sqrt{N - 1}} = \frac{\hat{\sigma}}{\sqrt{N}}.$$

The standard error of $\overline{X}_{12}$, the conditional mean, is a function of both the error in a and in b. We combine these errors in exactly the same way we learned to combine errors when we were pooling two sample means. There we discovered that the *variance of a sum equals the sum of the variances*. (We also discovered that the variance of a *difference* is also equal to the *sum* of the variances.) Hence we combine these two errors as follows:

$$\hat{\sigma}^2_{\bar{x}_{12}} = \frac{\hat{\sigma}^2_{1.2}}{N} + \frac{\hat{\sigma}^2_{1.2}}{N\hat{\sigma}^2_2}. \tag{11.8}$$

Equation 14.8 allows only for the error in b for each *unit* of X_2. Actually the error in b tends to accumulate as we move away from the mean of X_2. Figure 14.7 illustrates the phenomenon. The difference between the solid line and the dashed line is the error in $\overline{X}_{12}$ caused by the error in b. It is clear that this error is larger as we move away from the mean of X_2. Hence we must modify our formula as follows:

$$\hat{\sigma}^2_{\bar{x}_{12}} = \frac{\hat{\sigma}^2_{1.2}}{N} + \frac{\hat{\sigma}^2_{1.2}(X_2 - \overline{X}_2)^2}{N\hat{\sigma}^2_2}. \tag{14.9}$$

If we wish, we may factor out the $\hat{\sigma}^2_{1.2}$, leaving us with

$$\hat{\sigma}^2_{\bar{x}_{12}} = \hat{\sigma}^2_{1.2}\left[\frac{1}{N} + \frac{(X_2 - \overline{X}_2)^2}{N\hat{\sigma}^2_2}\right]. \tag{14.10}$$

Finally, again if we wish, we may take the square root of both sides and obtain

$$\hat{\sigma}_{\bar{x}_{12}} = \hat{\sigma}_{1.2}\sqrt{\frac{1}{N} + \frac{(X_2 - \overline{X}_2)^2}{N\hat{\sigma}^2_2}}. \tag{14.11}$$

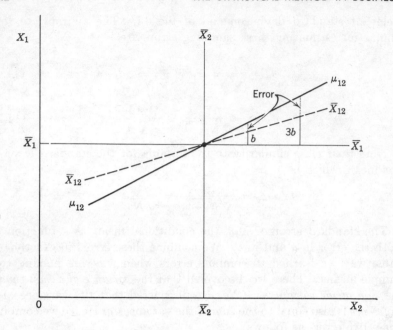

Fig. 14.7 Illustration of cumulating effect of an error in b_{12}.

Table 14.4 applies this formula to the problem of estimating the 75% confidence limits to the value of $\hat{\mu}_{12}$, the unknown universe value of the mean of X_1 for given values of X_2.[1] Since we are assuming that the universe is normally distributed, we can use the t distribution as the basis for estimation. A confidence coefficient of 75% corresponds to a t of 1.204 when we have 13 d.f.

Figure 14.8 shows the confidence band as it would appear on a graph. Note how it spreads as it moves away from the mean of X_2. Also note how we have terminated all the lines at the limits of the given values of X_2. Extrapolations beyond these limits should never be made without an explicit statement that the estimates are in an area beyond the bounds of past experience. Whenever circumstances force us to make estimates outside this experience range, we do so with some intuitively derived extra allowance for error. We become particularly concerned that the line may change its shape as its range extends.

[1] We show only the 75% confidence limits for $\hat{\mu}_{12}$. It is possible, of course, to show the whole inference distribution of $\hat{\mu}_{12}$ for any given value of X_2. We would use the same ideas and techniques described in Chapter 12.

TABLE 14.4

Estimating the 75% Confidence Limits to the Value of $\hat{\mu}_{12}$

$\bar{X}_{12}$	X_2	x_2	x_2^2	$\dfrac{x_2^2}{N\hat{\sigma}_2^2}$	$\dfrac{1}{N} + \dfrac{x_2^2}{N\hat{\sigma}_2^2}$	$\left(\dfrac{1}{N} + \dfrac{x_2^2}{N\hat{\sigma}_2^2}\right)^{1/2}$	$t\hat{\sigma}_{1.2}\left(\dfrac{1}{N} + \dfrac{x_2^2}{N\hat{\sigma}_2^2}\right)^{1/2}$	$\bar{X}_{12} + t\hat{\sigma}_{x_{12}}$	$\bar{X}_{12} - t\hat{\sigma}_{x_{12}}$
(1)	(2)	(3)	(4)	(5)	(6)	(7)	(8)	(9)	(10)
4.0	2.4	−4.3	18.49	.163	.230	.479	.651	4.65	3.35
4.3	2.9	−3.8	14.44	.127	.194	.440	.598	4.90	3.70
4.9	3.8	−2.9	8.41	.074	.141	.375	.510	5.41	4.39
5.2	4.3	−2.4	5.76	.051	.118	.343	.466	5.67	4.73
5.8	5.2	−1.5	2.25	.020	.087	.295	.401	6.20	5.40
6.1	5.7	−1.0	1.00	.009	.076	.276	.375	6.48	5.72
6.7	6.7	0.0	0.00	.000	.067	.259	.352	7.05	6.35
6.9	7.1	.4	.16	.001	.068	.261	.355	7.26	6.54
7.6	8.1	1.4	1.96	.017	.084	.290	.394	7.99	7.21
8.4	9.5	2.8	7.84	.069	.136	.369	.502	8.90	7.90
8.8	10.0	3.3	10.89	.096	.163	.404	.549	9.35	8.25
9.1	10.5	3.8	14.44	.127	.194	.440	.598	9.70	8.50
77.8	76.2	−4.2	85.64	.754	1.558	4.231	5.751	83.56	72.04

$N\hat{\sigma}_2^2 = 15 \times 2.75^2 = 113.4$

$\dfrac{1}{N} = \dfrac{1}{15} = .067$

$\hat{\sigma}_{1.2} = 1.13$

$t = 1.204$ (for 75% confidence limits and 13 d.f.)

$t\hat{\sigma}_{1.2} = 1.36$

Note: There are only 12 rows in the table because some of the 15 X_2 values are duplicates.

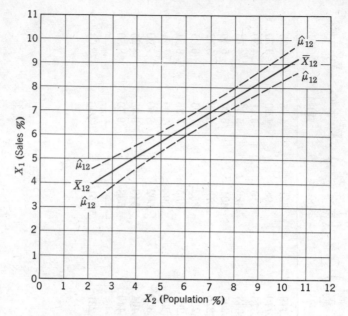

Fig. 14.8 75% confidence limits of $\hat{\mu}_{12}$ (see Table 14.4).

Allowing for the Sampling Error in the Standard Deviations

It is possible to estimate the distribution of the joint errors in both the line and the standard deviation around the line. We find, however, that the error in the standard deviation tends to be small enough to ignore as a practical matter, particularly since its estimation is fairly complex. Hence we ignore the problem here.

14.6   Random Sampling Errors in Estimating Individual Values of X_{12}

In the preceding section we were concerned only with the *mean* of the X_{12} values. More often than not we are more concerned with estimating *individual values of* X_{12}. The best single estimate we can make of these X_{12}'s is their *mean*, $\overline{X}_{12}$. (Recall we are assuming that X_{12} is a reasonably normal distribution.) However, we must make a larger error allowance than above because of the *dispersion of the items around their mean*. This involves only a simple modification in the error formula we used for the line of conditional means. The appropriate formula is

$$\hat{\sigma}^2_{x_{12}} = \hat{\sigma}^2_{1.2} + \frac{\hat{\sigma}^2_{1.2}}{N} + \frac{\hat{\sigma}^2_{1.2}(X_2 - \overline{X}_2)^2}{N\hat{\sigma}_2{}^2}. \qquad (14.12)$$

TABLE 14.5

Estimating the 75% Confidence Limits to Values of X_{12}. (Columns 1 to 5 would be exactly the same as in Table 14.4)

$1 + \frac{1}{N} + \frac{x_2^2}{N\hat{\sigma}_2^2}$	$\left(1 + \frac{1}{N} + \frac{x_2^2}{N\hat{\sigma}_2^2}\right)^{\frac{1}{2}}$	$t\hat{\sigma}_{1.2}\left(1 + \frac{1}{N} + \frac{x_2^2}{N\hat{\sigma}_2^2}\right)^{\frac{1}{2}}$	$X_{12} + t\hat{\sigma}_{\hat{x}_{12}}$	$X_{12} - t\hat{\sigma}_{\hat{x}_{12}}$
(6)	(7)	(8)	(9)	(10)
1.230	1.109	1.51	5.51	2.49
1.194	1.093	1.49	5.79	2.81
1.141	1.068	1.45	6.35	3.45
1.118	1.057	1.44	6.64	3.76
1.087	1.043	1.42	7.22	4.38
1.076	1.037	1.41	7.51	4.69
1.067	1.033	1.40	8.10	5.30
1.068	1.033	1.40	8.30	5.50
1.084	1.041	1.42	9.02	6.18
1.136	1.066	1.45	9.85	6.95
1.163	1.079	1.47	10.27	7.33
1.194	1.093	1.49	10.59	7.61
13.558	12.752	17.35	95.15	60.45

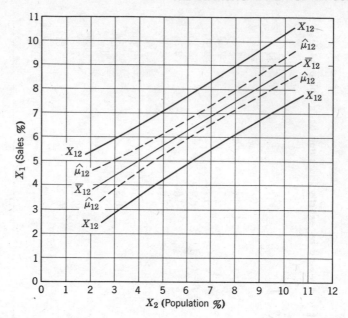

Fig. 14.9 75% confidence limits of X_{12} and of $\hat{\mu}_{12}$ (see Tables 14.4 and 14.5).

This is exactly the same as Eq. 14.9 except for the addition of the $\hat{\sigma}^2_{1.2}$. This is added to take care of the deviations of the X_{12} values from their mean. Figure 14.9 shows the 75% confidence limits for estimates of X_{12}. The 75% confidence limits to $\overline{X}_{12}$ are also shown for contrast. Note the very moderate rate of increase in the width of the confidence band for X_{12}, particularly when compared with that for $\overline{X}_{12}$. An examination of column 8 in Tables 14.4 and 14.5 conveys the same idea. Thus we discover that the variation in X_{12} is *dominated* by the difference between X_{12} and $\overline{X}_{12}$ and is only moderately affected by the sampling error in $\overline{X}_{12}$. Hence we usually do not bother with an attempt to allow for the widening confidence band when we are estimating *items*, particularly when the sample is moderately large.

Errors in Estimates When Sample is Large

If our sample is moderately large, $1/N$ and $x_2{}^2/(N\hat{\sigma}_2{}^2)$ become negligible, and we usually ignore them when we are estimating the values of individual items of the dependent variable. The only error we allow for is $\hat{\sigma}_{1.2}$. We still show the same concern, however, for the additional uncertainties as we extrapolate outside the range of past experience. Remember intuition and judgment are the only tools we have for handling the problem of extrapolation.

14.7 Estimating the Degree of Association

The results of our analysis of the association between sales and population, sales and income, and income and population can be summarized conveniently as shown in Table 14.6. Many analysts find this information sufficient for their purposes. However, it is often useful to rephrase this information by calculating the coefficients of association, such as A, r, and r^2. The coefficients for the sample data are:

$$A_{12} = \frac{s_1 - s_{1.2}}{s_1} = \frac{1.96 - 1.06}{1.96} = .46$$

$$r_{12}^2 = \frac{s_1^2 - s_{1.2}^2}{s_1^2} = \frac{3.84 - 1.12}{3.84} = .71$$

$$r_{12} = .84$$

$$A_{13} = -.15 \quad A_{32} = -.28$$

$$r_{13}^2 = .27 \quad r_{32}^2 = .49$$

$$r_{13} = -.52 \quad r_{32} = -.70$$

If we use the estimates of the standard deviations for the universe, these coefficients become:

$$\hat{A}_{12} = .45 \quad \hat{A}_{13} = -.12 \quad \hat{A}_{32} = -.27$$

$$\hat{r}_{12}^2 = .69 \quad \hat{r}_{13}^2 = .23 \quad \hat{r}_{32}^2 = .46$$

$$\hat{r}_{12} = .83 \quad \hat{r}_{13} = -.48 \quad \hat{r}_{32} = -.68$$

(Look again at Chapter 13, pp. 512–9, to review the interpretation of these coefficients.)

We can see that the universe estimates are not significantly smaller than those for the sample unless the degree of association is small, as it is in the case of sales and income. For this reason most practical analysts tend to use the sample coefficients, disregarding their slight upward bias. It is good practice, however, to not ignore this bias if we are working with small samples and if our results show relatively small associations.

Note that minus signs are placed before A_{13}, r_{13}, A_{32}, and r_{32}. They signify that the association is *negative*, that is, high values of one variable are associated with low values of the other. Negative

TABLE 14.6

Summary of Results of Analysis of Associations between Sales and Population, Sales and Income, and Income and Population

	Estimating Formula	Variation in Sample	d.f.	Estimated Variation in Universe	Estimated Item-forecast Error *
(1)	$\bar{X}_1 = 6.7\%$	$s_1 = 1.96\%$	14	$\hat{\sigma}_1 = 2.04\%$	$\hat{\sigma}_{x_1} = 2.11\%$
(2)	$\bar{X}_{12} = 2.50 + .625X_2$	$s_{1.2} = 1.06$	13	$\hat{\sigma}_{1.2} = 1.13$	$\hat{\sigma}_{x_{1.2}} = 1.17$
(3)	$\bar{X}_{13} = 8.65 - .297X_3$	$s_{1.3} = 1.67$	13	$\hat{\sigma}_{1.3} = 1.79$	$\hat{\sigma}_{x_{1.2}} = 1.85$
		Supplementary Data			
	$\bar{X}_3 = 6.7\%$	$s_3 = 1.76$	14	$\hat{\sigma}_3 = 1.83$	$\hat{\sigma}_{x_3} = 1.89$
	$\bar{X}_{32} = 9.79 - .469X_2$	$s_{3.2} = 1.26$	13	$\hat{\sigma}_{3.2} = 1.34$	$\hat{\sigma}_{x_{3.2}} = 1.38$

* The estimated item-forecast error is the result of adjusting the estimated variation in the universe for sampling error in the estimating formula. The general formula is

$$\hat{\sigma}_x = \hat{\sigma} \sqrt{1 + \frac{1}{N}}. \tag{14.13}$$

Since $N = 15$ in this problem, $\sqrt{1 + \dfrac{1}{N}} = 1.033$. Note that this ignores the sampling error in b.

association is, of course, as useful as positive association when it comes to reducing errors of estimate.

Sampling Errors in Measuring the Degree of Association

Coefficients of association based on sample data are subject to the usual problem of errors in random sampling. We are all familiar with *coincidence*, the simultaneous occurrence of two or more events that just happen to occur together. For example, the poorest golfer will occasionally correlate all his movements properly and make a good shot. Table 14.7 shows the results of random drawings from an ordinary card deck. Five cards were drawn with the right hand and five with the left. Very few people would conclude from this evidence that there is correlation between the hand used and the results we get despite the fact that the sample shows that the right hand drew larger cards on the average than the left hand. The problem is very easy with playing cards because everybody "knows" that the results of card drawing are "due to chance." The issue is

TABLE 14.7

Correlation between Value of Randomly Drawn Playing Cards and
Whether Cards Were Drawn with the Right or Left Hand

Values of Cards Drawn with

Right Hand	Left Hand
9	7
6	8
6	1
2	2
12	2
—	—
35	20

not as easily resolved with correlations in the world around us. We
believe the validity of correlations that make sense to us and discount those that do not.

Sampling Errors in r

We confine our discussion to sampling errors in the coefficient of
correlation r. Our remarks apply equally well to A and r^2 with the
obvious modifications. It is more convenient to work with r because
all the formulas and tables have been worked out in terms of r, which
is natural considering the long history of r.

Analysis of sampling errors in r (or r^2 or A) is considerably complicated because the sampling distribution of r is obviously skewed
except in the special case when there is no correlation in the universe, or when $\rho = 0$. (We use the Greek r, or ρ (rho), to refer to
universe.) We say obviously because common sense suggests that
if, say, $\rho = .80$, r cannot possibly be larger than 1.00, but it could
conceivably be as small as -1.00. Fortunately, we find as usual that
the central limit theorem applies, and that the distribution of r (r is
an arithmetic mean) approaches normal as N increases. This normal
curve approximation is better the closer ρ is to 0 because the skewness would then be less. (We except the special cases of ρ of $+1$ or
-1, when the sampling errors would be 0.)

The standard deviation, or standard error, of r depends only on ρ and on the sample size. The basic formula is

$$\sigma_r = \frac{1 - \rho^2}{\sqrt{N}}. \qquad (14.14)$$

If we note that $1 - \rho^2$ is the *coefficient of nondetermination*, and that the coefficient of nondetermination is based on the conditional variance, or $\sigma_{1.2}^2$, we can see that this is our usual sampling error formula. It has a measure of variation in the numerator and the size of the sample in the denominator.

In the special case when the universe correlation is 0, this formula reduces to

$$\frac{1}{\sqrt{N}}. \qquad (14.15)$$

The case when $\rho = 0$ has occupied a pre-eminent position in correlation analysis because many researchers have been most concerned with testing the null hypothesis, namely, the hypothesis that the universe contains *no* correlation. Our sample of 15 is rather small to use the *normal curve* as an approximator, but we test the null hypothesis anyway to illustrate the method. Namely

$$\sigma_r = \frac{1}{\sqrt{15}} = .258.$$

$$Z = \frac{r - \rho}{\sigma_r} = \frac{.84}{.258} = 3.26.$$

A Z of 3.26 leaves about .0006 in the tail of the normal curve. Hence we could say that there are about .0006 (6 out of 10,000) chances of getting a sample of 15 items with a coefficient of correlation of $+.84$ or more, even though the universe is uncorrelated. Miss David's Tables [1] of the exact distribution of r show a probability of about .0001 for this event.

The Use of Tables of the Sampling Distribution of r. Miss David hoped to solve the problem of a different distribution of r for every combination of ρ and N by constructing tables of enough exact distributions so that we could solve most practical problems with only moderate interpolation. Her tables are actually quite sparse in their

[1] F. N. David, *Tables of the Ordinates and Probability Integral of the Distribution of the Correlation Coefficient in Small Samples,* University College, London, 1938.

coverage, however, thus creating interpolation problems. She did make up some nomographs for selected confidence coefficients that some analysts have found quite useful. Figure 14.10 reproduces the nomograph for 90% limits. This nomograph yields 90% confidence limits for ρ_{12} of .64 and .93. Note the asymmetry in the limits around r_{12} of .84.

Fisher's z' Transformation of r. R. A. Fisher published a paper in 1921 which presented a method for transforming r into z', with z' having a distribution quite close to normal, even for samples as small as the neighborhood of 10. This discovery enabled us to largely dispense with tables like those Miss David eventually developed. The formula for the transformation is

$$z' = \tfrac{1}{2}[\log_e (1 + r) - \log_e (1 - r)], \qquad (14.16)$$

or
$$= 1.151 \log \frac{1 + r}{1 - r}. \qquad (14.17)$$

z' has a standard deviation of

$$\sigma_{z'} = \frac{1}{\sqrt{N - 3}} \quad \text{(approximately)}. \qquad (14.18)$$

Tables of z' are available to simplify the transformation. (See Appendix H.) Let us test the null hypothesis for our problem with the use of the z' transformation. An r of .84 is the equivalent of a z' of about 1.22. $\sigma_{z'} = 1/\sqrt{12}$, or .289. Hence, $Z = (z' - 0)/\sigma_{z'}$, or 1.22/.289, or 4.22. This leaves an area of about .00001 in the tail of the normal curve. If we compare this with the .0001 of the exact distribution and the .0006 of the normal curve, we see that for a sample of this size, the normal curve is a little too dispersed and the z' distribution is not dispersed quite enough. Actually, of course, the differences shown here would not cause most people any practical concern.

Confidence Limits of ρ. It is a relatively straightforward procedure to estimate confidence limits for ρ if we wish. We illustrate by setting 75% limits for ρ_{12}. r_{12} of .84 transforms into a z' of 1.22. 75% limits correspond to a Z of 1.15 in the normal curve. Hence our limits are at $1.22 + 1.15 \times .289$ and $1.22 - 1.15 \times .289$ in terms of z', or .89 and 1.55. Referring to Appendix H, we find that these correspond to $\hat{\rho}$'s of .71 and .91. Contrast these limits with those of .64 and .93 calculated from Miss David's nomograph for 90% limits.

14.8   When Is Correlation Significant?

The concept of significance has played a substantial role in the application of correlation results. The concept has been misinterpreted quite frequently and for this reason warrants a brief discussion. We have already referred to the null hypothesis, or the hypothesis that there is no correlation in the universe. In our problem we discovered that there was a probability of about .0001 of getting an $r_{12} \geq .84$ if there were no correlation in the universe. Thus we might conclude that there is definite evidence of *some* correlation because it is highly unlikely that there is *none*. Many analysts would now say that there is *significant* correlation between sales and population. What they mean, or at least what they should mean, is that the evidence casts considerable doubt on the hypothesis that there is *no* correlation. Unfortunately, many people have interpreted significant to mean much more. They have assumed it means that the correlation is sufficiently high to justify the use of the correlation results as a basis of practical prediction, if not as a basis for the presumption of some causal relationship. As we can imagine, the ultimate outcome often caused considerable disappointment and some disillusionment about the efficacy of correlation analysis in general. The fault was not of the correlation analysis but of the analysts and the interpreters.

We can illustrate by taking a case where a sample of 50 yields an r of .25. Since there are fewer than .05 chances of an $r \geq .50$ if ρ is 0, we would conclude that the "correlation is significant." We discover, however, that even if the true ρ is as high as .25, this amounts to only an error reduction of about 3%, actually very little. ($A = 1 - \sqrt{1 - r^2}$. This is how we translated .25 into 3%.)

14.9   Curvilinear Correlation

Most of the ideas and techniques of our linear normal curve model can be extended to cover the case of lines that are curved rather than straight. Some complications do arise, however, and there are some things we still do not understand about curvilinear correlation. We also have the problem of getting involved in the solution of more than two simultaneous equations when we introduce curvature. For these reasons, we do not pursue the study of curvilinear correlation in detail. We merely illustrate some of the routines by showing the calculations for fitting a second-degree parabola to our sales-population data. Our assumptions are essentially the same as for the linear model. We assume that the vertical vectors have equal standard deviations, but now these vectors have means that fall into a parabolic pattern instead of a linear pattern. Figure 14.11 shows the result we are going to get for our line of conditional means. We also assume that the vectors have at least symmetrical distributions, and preferably normal distributions. We desire the symmetry to make our *least-squares,* or arithmetic mean, line a reasonable approximation to a *least-error,* or median, line. We desire the normality to simplify the estimation of probabilities from the values of the standard deviations.

Our basic equation is

$$\bar{X}_{12} = a_{12} + b_{12}X_2 + c_{12}X_2{}^2. \qquad (14.19)$$

Note that there are three unknowns in this equation, and we need three equations to solve for these three unknowns. To get a *least-squares* solution, we must fill in and solve the following three equations:

(1) $\quad \Sigma X_1 \quad = Na_{12} + b_{12}\Sigma X_2 \quad + c_{12}\Sigma X_2{}^2$

(2) $\quad \Sigma X_1 X_2 = a_{12}\Sigma X_2 + b_{12}\Sigma X_2{}^2 \quad + c_{12}\Sigma X_2{}^3 \qquad (14.20)$

(3) $\quad \Sigma X_1 X_2{}^2 = a_{12}\Sigma X_2{}^2 + b_{12}\Sigma X_2{}^3 \quad + c_{12}\Sigma X_2{}^4.$

Note that the part of these equations enclosed in the rectangle is precisely what we used for our linear solution. We merely extend

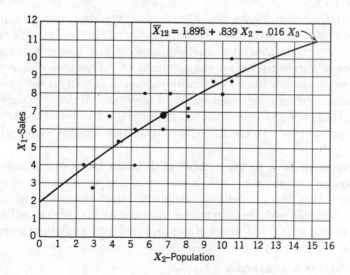

Fig. 14.11 A least-squares second-degree parabola fitted to the sales-population data.

these to the right and down by increasing the exponents of the X_2's by 1 in every case.

If we fill in these equations for the sales-population data, we get:

(1) $100.00 = 15.00a_{12} + 100.00b_{12} + 770.94c_{12}$

(2) $731.87 = 100.00a_{12} + 770.94b_{12} + 6533.18c_{12}$

(3) $6002.26 = 770.94a_{12} + 6533.18b_{12} + 58793.03c_{12}$

The resultant estimating equation is:

$$\overline{X}_{12} = 1.895 + .839X_2 - .016X_2{}^2.$$

The conditional standard deviation, $s_{1.2}$, is 1.06%, the same as that for the straight line. Actually it would be a little smaller for the curve than for the straight line if we were to carry more decimal places. These additional places would not represent significant digits, however, considering the accuracy of the original data. The practical identity of the $s_{1.2}$ for both these lines is clear evidence that the straight line is a very good fit to the data. Additional evidence is the very small value for c of $-.016$. Note that Fig. 14.11 shows the parabola is practically straight within the limits of the original data.

If we adjust $s_{1.2}$ for degrees of freedom to get an estimate of $\hat{\sigma}_{1.2}$, we find that the curved line is really a *poorer* estimator than the straight because we used up an additional degree of freedom in the calculation of c. Thus $\hat{\sigma}_{1.2} = s_{1.2}\sqrt{N/(N-k)}$, or $1.06\sqrt{15/12} = 1.06 \times 1.118 = 1.19\%$. When we used the straight line, we found a $\hat{\sigma}_{1.2}$ of 1.13.

This adjustment for degrees of freedom is very important for a proper interpretation of correlation results. A curved line will always *appear in the sample* to fit at least as well as a straight line, and the greater the number of curves the better the apparent fit. The price of curvature, however, is the additional constants needed in the equation, and each additional constant uses up a degree of freedom. Unless the curvature reduces $s_{1.2}$ enough to offset the loss of degrees of freedom, the curvature is a poor bargain. In the sales-population relationship we found such a poor bargain.

There is no limit to the number of different kinds of mathematical functions we might use to fit a line of means to a scatter diagram. We trust that the brief discussion given about the use of a second-degree parabola provides enough background so that we can safely try curve fitting within the limits of our knowledge of analytical geometry and, of course, our common sense.

PROBLEMS AND QUESTIONS

14.1 How would you go about selecting a location for a retail outlet? For example, suppose you were responsible for selecting appropriate locations for a gasoline station, or a supermarket, or a shoe store, etc. Select any one of these, or any other store type of interest.

(a) *List* the factors that you think might be relevant in estimating the future sales volume of such an outlet.

(b) *Rank* the five most important factors in their order of importance, that is, as you see their importance. Explain in a sentence or two for each factor *why* you think it has this degree of importance.

(c) Can you find quantitative data on each of these five principal factors? Where?

If the data are not yet available but nevertheless can be collected at reasonable (?) expense, outline briefly how you would proceed to collect such data.

(d) Suppose that you find that your most important factor is presently measurable only at exorbitant expense. How would you allow for this factor in selecting a location?

14.2 The personnel director of the Crayle Co. was so pleased with his first experience in using correlation analysis as an aid in selecting and rating personnel (see Problem 13.4) that he decided to make a more extensive correlation analysis of the factors that might be related to another job in the factory. After a few brainstorming sessions with the foremen, it was decided that the most promising factors among those on which they had measurements were:

X_2—Score on the Pixem Dexterity Test.
X_3—Number of months' experience on the job with the Crayle Co.
X_4—Score on a standard intelligence test.
X_5—Number of years of formal education.

Data on these variables were collected as of February 15, 1961. It was decided to use the arithmetic mean of the most recent 5 days' production records to measure the workers' performances. Thus the production data (X_1) refer to the mean output per 7½-hour day. Data were collected for a random sample of 50 workers out of the total of 247 who were working during that period. The data are given below.

	Production (Pieces) X_1	Dexterity Test Score X_2	Experience in Months X_3	Intelligence Test Score X_4	Formal Education Years X_5
1.	117	13	14	92	11
2.	112	14	9	76	10
3.	133	17	12	94	10
4.	119	18	5	87	9
5.	135	20	24	97	9
6.	120	20	15	90	10
7.	139	21	17	94	10
8.	130	21	20	84	9
9.	139	22	21	92	9
10.	144	23	23	93	10

	Production (Pieces) X_1	Dexterity Test Score X_2	Experience in Months X_3	Intelligence Test Score X_4	Formal Education Years X_5
11.	149	24	31	87	11
12.	148	24	18	102	9
13.	143	25	27	88	10
14.	167	26	40	100	9
15.	155	26	29	93	10
16.	157	27	21	91	12
17.	174	27	34	112	11
18.	161	27	26	94	12
19.	152	27	23	93	10
20.	154	28	24	91	10
21.	163	28	22	97	13
22.	173	28	36	99	10
23.	156	29	22	92	10
24.	161	29	25	97	9
25.	181	29	39	102	12
26.	174	30	37	95	11
27.	184	30	50	98	9
28.	179	30	43	100	10
29.	187	31	47	94	11
30.	176	31	40	99	10
31.	189	31	46	97	10
32.	201	31	83	96	9
33.	193	32	52	97	12
34.	195	32	65	99	11
35.	166	32	11	117	12
36.	152	33	3	108	13
37.	206	34	44	102	15
38.	205	34	55	101	12
39.	159	34	7	98	11
40.	201	35	59	104	10
41.	167	36	10	110	11
42.	155	37	4	100	10
43.	200	38	38	107	11
44.	225	38	74	113	12
45.	221	39	49	126	10
46.	208	39	53	108	10
47.	232	41	90	102	11
48.	234	42	79	107	11
49.	230	45	63	103	12
50.	229	48	57	101	10

(a) Use the data for the odd-numbered workers (or for the even-numbered) and analyze these factors by constructing the 10 scatter diagrams that are necessary to study each pair of factors. Consider the following in your analysis:

1. Is there any evidence of a meaningful correlation between the given pair of variables?

2. Do any of the independent variables show enough correlation with each other to justify eliminating one from further study because it is essentially duplicated by one of the other independent variables?

3. What seems to be an appropriate line to describe the average relationship in each case? Do any of the relationships appear to be curved?

4. Do the various relationships strike you as being logical in the sense that you more or less would expect such variables to be related in such a way? If some of the relationships do not appear logical, or if they had not appeared logical, what effect would such a finding have on any subsequent analysis?

5. Would you be willing to extrapolate any of these apparent relationships and make estimates based on such extrapolations? Explain.

6. Do the distributions around the lines of relationship appear to be reasonably symmetrical, or even normal? What is the significance of what you find on this matter?

7. Does the assumption of a constant variance in the vertical vectors appear to be a reasonable approximation in each case?

8. Rank the four independent variables in order of their apparent importance in explaining variations in output.

(b) The matrix below gives the various sums of cross products for these five variables.

	X_1	X_2	X_3	X_4	X_5
X_1	1,513,518	263,158	326,458	850,064	91,115
X_2		46,360	56,174	147,339	15,768
X_3			83,036	173,962	18,503
X_4				487,603	52,201
X_5					5,675

Calculate for each pair of variables:

1. The least-squares straight line of relationship.

2. The standard deviation of the dependent variable.

3. The conditional standard deviation of the dependent variable. (Also known as the standard error of estimate.)

4. 70% confidence interval for the expected *mean* of the dependent variable for selected values of the independent variable. (Select values throughout range of independent variable.)

5. 70% confidence interval for the expected *actual values* of the dependent variable for selected values of the independent variable.

6. Plot your least-squares lines and your 70% confidence ranges on your graphs of Problem 14.2(a). Evaluate the practical usefulness of these calculated results.

(c) Calculate the coefficients of association, determination, and correlation for each of your calculated relationships. Perform these calculations from the *sample* standard deviations and from the *estimated universe* standard deviations. Evaluate the practical significance of these coefficients.

(d) Estimate the 70% confidence limits for the coefficients of correlation you calculated in (c) above.

14.3 If you were the personnel director of the Crayle Co., to what extent would you pay attention to each of the four factors referred to in Problem 14.2? In answering this you might try to rank the factors in order of importance and assign relative weights to their importance.

14.4 Examine the results of your analysis and also the original data in order to assess the significance of "history" to this problem. For example, is there any evidence that the kind of men hired recently is different from those hired several years ago? If you find such a difference, how would such a finding affect your interpretation of your correlation results?

14.5 Suppose you have applicants who score as follows on the Pixem Dexterity Test: A—15; B—34; C—55. What estimate would you make of their output rate? *When* would you expect them to achieve this rate? Since you are given no information on the other independent variables, how do you allow for them, if at all?

14.6 Select from the above relationships (treated as straight lines above) that one that impresses you as the most likely to be reasonably well described by a second-degree parabola. Perform the necessary calculations to make a correlation study based on such a second-degree parabola. Are these results "significant"?

chapter 15

Reducing uncertainty by association: *multiple correlation analysis*

Up to this point we have analyzed the associations between sales and population and between sales and income, with each analysis *independent* of the other. We were in a position to make estimates of sales based on population alone, or to make estimates of sales based on income alone. There was no reason why these separate estimates should be particularly consistent with each other. For example, in Territory 2 we get an $\overline{X}_{12}$ of 4.3% and an $\overline{X}_{13}$ of 6.7%. (X_1 actually equalled 2.7%.) When we get different estimates like this, we should use the one that is based on the better estimator, in this case, X_2. Or, we might use an estimate based on a weighted combination of the separate estimates, with the weights proportional to the respective coefficients of association.

We now try to solve the problem of *simultaneously* analyzing the three variables of sales, population, and income. The method extends logically to cover any number of variables. The method is known as multiple correlation analysis.

15.1 The Underlying Idea of Multiple Correlation Analysis

Although the straightforward mathematical analysis we use may *look* as though we analyze the three variables *simultaneously*, we, in fact, analyze the variables *two at a time*, with the other variable *constant*. We then add the *net* correlations together to get estimates based on simultaneous variation of the independent variables.

It is easier to visualize the process of analyzing three variables if we draw graphs in three dimensions. It is possible to simulate three dimensions on two-dimensional paper by using projection techniques. Most people are not adept at this, so we do not attempt it here, but rather, we try to use the room in which *we are now sitting* so that we can see what three-variable analysis is.

First we specify the axes. Let us position ourselves so that we are near the center of the room and are facing one of the walls of the room. Imagine that we are measuring sales vertically, that is, from the floor to the ceiling. We will measure population from left to right, that is, along the wall that we are facing. We measure income from the back to the front, that is, along the wall to our left. Now let us check our bearings by "plotting" some of our data. Territory 1 has a sales of 4.0%, a population of 2.4%, and an income of 8.9%. We are going to place a golf ball in the space of the room to represent this combination of sales, population, and income. Starting at the origin, which is at the floor in the left corner facing us, mark off (mentally or actually) a distance of 2.4 units of population at floor level along the facing wall. (In selecting our units keep in mind that population runs from 2.4 to 10.5.)

Next mark off a distance from the 2.4 population point *parallel to the left wall* so that it covers 8.9 units of income. (Since 8.9 is more than the average of 6.7, this point should be to our left-front if we assume our original position in the center of the room.) The resultant coordinate point for population and income corresponds exactly to what we would have if we were planning to draw a scatter diagram of population and income *on the floor of our room*.

Finally, we measure a distance of 4.0 sales units straight up from this population-income coordinate point. We then hang the golf ball so that it occupies the resultant position.

The golf ball now has a position in the space of our room so that its distance from the floor measures the sales, its distance from the left wall measures population, and its distance from the rear wall measures income. (We are assuming we are in our original position in the center of the room.) Imagine we have placed golf balls to correspond to the sales-population-income of the other 14 territories. Thus there are now 15 golf balls hanging in the space of the room. If we were to take a photograph of the room from the rear, it would appear like Fig. 15.1. (We eliminate all irrelevancies from the room.)

What we would now like to do is place a flat piece of glass in the space of the room so that *there are about as many golf balls above the glass as there are below the glass all over the room*. (We assume

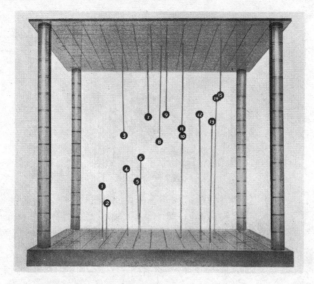

Fig. 15.1 Stereogram of relationship among X_1 (sales), X_2 (population), and X_3 (income). Sales measured from bottom to top, population from left to right, and income from back to front. (We assume we are sitting in middle of base and are facing the far "wall.") Numbers identify territories. See Table 14.1.

that we have no physical difficulty with the strings holding the golf balls. We have a special adhesive that enables us to place the balls in the air at any position!) Examination of Fig. 15.1 makes it rather apparent that the golf balls do follow a pattern in space. Figure 15.2 shows the glass in place.

We call this piece of glass a plane in three-dimensional space. It provides us with estimates of the *conditional mean* of sales, given some *combination* of population and income. If we measure the deviations of the golf balls from the plane, square them, divide by 15, and take the square root, we have the *conditional standard deviation*, or $s_{1.23}$. This is the variation in sales that is *independent* of variations in population and income, and hence the variation presumably associated with factors other than population and income.

The mathematical specifications of this plane are rather simple to determine. Suppose, for example, that we wished to give instructions to a carpenter so that he can build supports along the walls to hold this pane of glass. We might write something like this:

Nail a 2x2 in. strip of wood along the south wall so that the top edge of the strip is 5 in. above the floor at the southwest corner and so that the strip

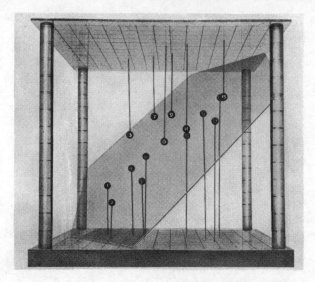

Fig. 15.2 Stereogram of relationship among sales, population, and income with fitted plane to describe average relationship. Note that Territories 1, 2, 4, 5, 6, 10, 12, 13, and 14 are below the plane and 3, 7, 8, 9, 11, and 15 above the plane. Also note that the territories further away, i.e., those that have higher incomes, tend to have higher sales for a given population.

rises .7 ft for every foot of distance along the south wall. Then nail a similar strip along the west wall, joining the south wall strip in the southwest corner, and rising .9 ft for every foot of distance along the west wall.

These two strips would be sufficient to hold the rigid pane of glass in place.

If our carpenter were a mathematician of moderate sorts, we could have economized on language by telling him to fit a plane with the following equation:

$$X_1 = .5 + .7X_2 + .9X_3,$$

where X_1 is the height of the plane for any given combination of X_2 (distance along the south wall) and X_3 (distance along the west wall). The .5 tells him the height of the plane in the southwest corner (where both X_2 and X_3 have values of 0); the .7 tells him the slope of the plane along the south wall (along which X_2 is measured); and the .9 tells him the slope of the plane along the west wall (along which X_3 is measured).

The general form of this equation would be

$$\overline{X}_{123} = a_{1(23)} + b_{12.3}X_2 + b_{13.2}X_3. \tag{15.1}$$

For our problem we would interpret this equation as:

$\overline{X}_{123}$ is an estimate of $\overline{X}_1$ (sales) based on given values of X_2 (population) and X_3 (income).

$a_{1(23)}$ is the estimated value of $\overline{X}_{123}$ when X_2 and X_3 have values of 0.

$b_{12.3}$ is the difference in $\overline{X}_{123}$ associated with a *unit* difference in X_2 *when X_3 is constant.*

$b_{13.2}$ is the difference in $\overline{X}_{123}$ associated with a *unit* difference in X_3 *when X_2 is constant.*

We can easily grasp the logic of referring to X_2 as *constant* if we mentally return to our room. Stand anywhere along the south wall (the original rear wall) with our back to the wall. Then we walk straight out along a line parallel to the west wall. As we walk along, we are walking from territories with small incomes to those with large incomes. But note that the *population is remaining constant* because we are along a line at right angles to some point on the population axis. The larger sales we encounter as we walk along this line are the differences in sales associated with differences in income when *population is constant.*

The Situation When We Have More Than Three Variables

The idea of three variables was relatively easy to express because we are all familiar with the three-dimensional world in which we live. If we add a fourth variable, we create the need for a fourth dimension; a fifth variable requires a fifth dimension; etc. One of the best ways to picture a fourth dimension is to imagine the skeleton of steel or concrete in the beginning stages of the construction of a multistory building. Assume we are concerned only with rooms to be built at the northwest corner of the building. Let us measure sales along the vertical axis as before. Let us measure population along the south wall and income along the west wall as before. What do we now do with number of retail outlets, our fourth variable? We measure the fourth variable along the same axis as we measure sales. The value of the fourth variable tells us what *floor of the building* to use in making our estimates. Each floor contains a room just like the one we used for our three-variable analysis. Each room, however, will have a *differently placed plane of glass,* the difference associated with variations in X_4. (We can immediately see that this is going to have to be a very tall building if X_4

is a continuous variable, and if we have a separate floor for each value of X_4.)

Suppose we have a fifth variable. We now need more than one room on each floor. Let us use the rooms along the north wall of the building to measure variations in the fifth variable. Each of these rooms has a typical three-dimensional set-up, each with its own plane. We now use X_4 to tell us what *floor* to use and X_5 to tell us what *room* to use *along the north wall*.

The rest of the rooms in this building are available to be used, so now we introduce a sixth variable. This variable indicates to us what room to use along the *west* axis of the building.

We have now completed this analogy and can review the whole picture. Imagine a very extensive multistory building. In *each* of the thousands of rooms we have a plane which measures the association among X_1, X_2, and X_3. Each room has a different plane, the differences depending on the particular values of X_4, X_5, and X_6 that prevail. We enter the building at the ground floor. We get on the elevator and get off at the floor indicated by the given value of X_4. We then consult the value of X_5 to find out how many rooms we must go along the north axis and the value of X_6 to find out how many rooms we must go along the west axis. We enter that room, consult the values of X_2 and X_3 and find our estimated value of X_{123456}, or more exactly, of $\overline{X}_{123456}$.

If we had a seventh, etc., variable, we could continue the analogy by stacking boxes in each room, with each box stacked with smaller boxes, etc.

An equation for a five-variable problem might look like

$$\overline{X}_{12345} = a_{1(2345)} + b_{12.345}X_2 + b_{13.245}X_3 + b_{14.235}X_4 + b_{15.234}X_5.$$

If some of our relationships were curvilinear rather than linear, our building would take on some very interesting futuristic shapes. We would also have some interesting engineering problems if the building is to stand.

15.2 Relationship of Multiple Correlation to Simple Correlation

While we have our three-dimensional model in mind, it is a good idea to compare our scatter diagrams for two variables with our stereogram for three variables. Figure 15.3 shows the scatter diagram of the relationship between X_1 and X_2 next to the stereogram

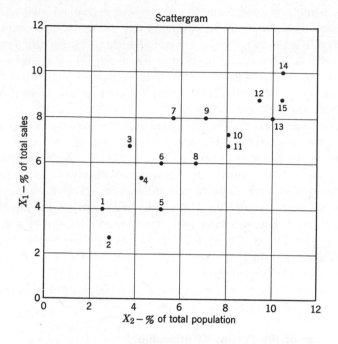

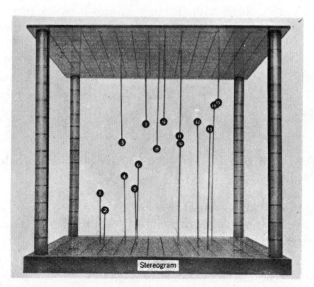

Fig. 15.3 Comparison of scattergram of relationship between sales and population and same relationship as it appears in the stereogram.

that is being observed from the same perspective. If we eliminate the factor of *depth* from the stereogram, we would get exactly the same result as shown in the scatter diagram. Since the factor of depth reflects *income,* elimination of the depth factor is the same as *ignoring* the income factor. This is, of course, exactly what we did when we drew the scattergram (a useful contraction of scatter diagram) for sales and population.

The contrast between a scattergram and a stereogram is even more vivid if we compare the scattergram of X_1 and X_3 with the stereogram from the same perspective. See Fig. 15.4. Note the *negative* slope of the relationship in the scattergram when we *ignore* population and the *positive* slope in the stereogram when we can observe X_1 and X_3 with X_2 *constant.* We can now see why our analysis of the relationship between sales and income showed a rather surprising *negative* association. Income and population are *negatively correlated* in our sample. Thus the depressant effects of a low population are sufficiently strong to offset the stimulating effects of a high income, with the result that income and sales appear negatively correlated when we ignore population.

The Concept of the Partial Relationship

When we are dealing with the relationship between two variables when one or more other variables are constant, it is a *partial* relationship. Thus we call $b_{12.3}$ the coefficient of *partial* regression, in contrast to b_{12}, which is the coefficient of regression. Similarly, we call $A_{12.3}$ the coefficient of *partial* association and $r_{12.3}$ the coefficient of *partial* correlation. We say more about these partial relations in later pages.

15.3   Assumptions Underlying Our Multiple Correlation Model

Our approach to the mathematical analysis of three variables parallels that we made of two variables. We make the same fundamental assumptions, namely:

1. The lines of conditional means are straight, or linear. This results in our plane being flat rather than contoured.
2. The conditional standard deviations are equal in all vertical vectors running above and below the plane. Imagine the plane being marked off in small squares or cells, with each square representing a particular combination of X_2 and X_3, and we can see the implication of this

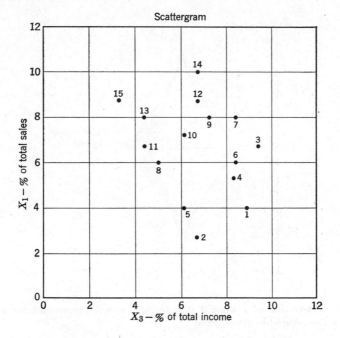

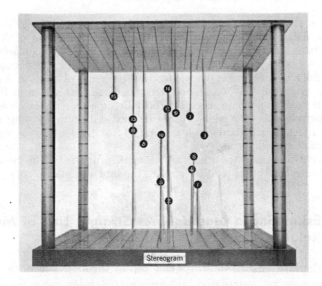

Fig. 15.4 Comparison of scattergram of relationship between sales and income and same relationship as it appears in the stereogram. The stereogram is viewed from the east side of Fig. 15.3.

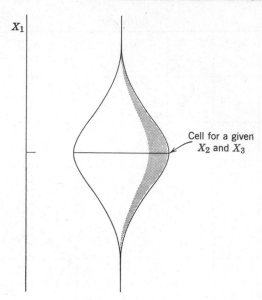

Fig. 15.5 Illustration of a normal distribution of cell frequencies for a single cell of a three-variable stereogram.

assumption. Assume that our sample is large enough so that each combination of X_2 and X_3 is paired with *several* values of X_1. Our golf balls for a given cell would tend to hang down like a stalactite from the roof of a cavern and also to project upward like a stalagmite from the floor of a cavern. We would thus get a distribution of X_1 values for a given cell that would look somewhat like that shown in Fig. 15.5. (Golf tees would be a more appropriate simulator of the distribution of the golf balls than would stalactites and stalagmites!) Our assumption of equal standard deviations refers to the equality of variations around these cell means.

3. The conditional distributions are essentially normal. This assumption facilitates the interpretation of our standard deviations.

15.4   Estimating a Least-squares Straight Line of Multiple Relationship

We calculate an *arithmetic mean plane* through the data for the same reasons we calculated an *arithmetic mean line* for a two-variable relationship. Again we accomplish this by taking advantage of the *least-squares* property of the arithmetic mean. We would like to obtain values of $a_{1(23)}$, $b_{12.3}$, and $b_{13.2}$ in the equation

$$\overline{X}_{123} = a_{1(23)} + b_{12.3}X_2 + b_{13.2}X_3 \qquad (15.1)$$

so that the sums of the squares of the deviations of the X_1 from the $\overline{X}_{123}$ is a minimum. The same mathematical routine that is used for a two-variable analysis indicates that we get such least-squares values if we solve the following three equations: (Equations for estimating least-squares lines are often called normal equations, the term originating with the idea that the least-squares line achieves its most reliable use when the underlying distributions are normal.)

(1) $\Sigma X_1 \quad = Na_{1(23)} + b_{12.3}\Sigma X_2 + b_{13.2}\Sigma X_3$

(2) $\Sigma X_1 X_2 = a_{1(23)}\Sigma X_2 + b_{12.3}\Sigma X_2{}^2 + b_{13.2}\Sigma X_2 X_3 \qquad (15.2)$

(3) $\Sigma X_1 X_3 = a_{1(23)}\Sigma X_3 + b_{12.3}\Sigma X_2 X_3 + b_{13.2}\Sigma X_3{}^2$

If we fill in all the required sums from the data in Table 14.2, we get

(1) $100.00 = \quad 15a_{1(23)} + 100.00b_{12.3} + 100.00b_{13.2}$

(2) $731.87 = 100a_{1(23)} + 770.94b_{12.3} + 617.80b_{13.2}$

(3) $652.86 = 100a_{1(23)} + 617.80b_{12.3} + 713.12b_{13.2}.$

These three equations can be solved simultaneously by any one of several different methods; however, we often find it more expeditious to take advantage of another property of the arithmetic mean and thereby reduce the three equations to two. This property is that the sum of the deviations from the mean is 0. Hence, if we measure all of our variables from their respective means instead of from the natural origin of 0, we find that our three normal equations reduce to:

(1) $\Sigma x_1 \quad = Na_{1(23)} + b_{12.3}\Sigma x_2 + b_{13.2}\Sigma x_3$

(2) $\Sigma x_1 x_2 = a_{1(23)}\Sigma x_2 + b_{12.3}\Sigma x_2{}^2 + b_{13.2}\Sigma x_2 x_3$

(3) $\Sigma x_1 x_3 = a_{1(23)}\Sigma x_3 + b_{12.3}\Sigma x_2 x_3 + b_{13.2}\Sigma x_3{}^2.$

All the circled sums are zero. Hence we find immediately that $a_{1(23)}$ is 0 when we measure all variables as deviations from their means. This is another way of saying that a territory with a mean population and a mean income should have mean sales. We are then left with the modified equations (2) and (3):

(2) $\Sigma x_1 x_2 = b_{12.3}\Sigma x_2{}^2 + b_{13.2}\Sigma x_2 x_3$

(3) $\Sigma x_1 x_3 = b_{12.3}\Sigma x_2 x_3 + b_{13.2}\Sigma x_3{}^2.$

(15.3)

(It is interesting to note the appearance of the *sums of the cross products of deviations* in these equations. These sums of cross products definitely do measure the degree of correlation, among other things.)

If we had to calculate directly these sums of cross products and sums of squares of deviations, the reduction to two equations would be no advantage. Fortunately, these sums are easily derived from data we already have in Table 14.2. The required formulas are:

$$\Sigma x_1 x_2 = \Sigma X_1 X_2 - \bar{X}_1 \Sigma X_2 = 731.87 - 6.67 \times 100 = 65.20$$

$$\Sigma x_1 x_3 = \Sigma X_1 X_3 - \bar{X}_1 \Sigma X_3 = 652.86 - 6.67 \times 100 = -13.81$$

$$\Sigma x_2 x_3 = \Sigma X_2 X_3 - \bar{X}_2 \Sigma X_3 = 617.80 - 6.67 \times 100 = -48.87$$

$$\Sigma x_2{}^2 = \Sigma X_2{}^2 - \bar{X}_2 \Sigma X_2 = 770.94 - 6.67 \times 100 = 104.27$$

$$\Sigma x_3{}^2 = \Sigma X_3{}^2 - \bar{X}_3 \Sigma X_3 = 713.12 - 6.67 \times 100 = 46.45$$

Note that all these formulas are fundamentally the same. The general formula is: the sums of products of deviations of two variables from their respective means is equal to the sums of products of the original variables *minus* the product of the mean of one variable and the sum of the other. If we recognize that the *square* of one variable is simply the *product* of two variables that happen to have the same value, we can see that this rule also extends to the sums of squares of deviations.

If we substitute these values in the two equations, we obtain

$$(2) \qquad 65.20 = 104.27 b_{12.3} - 48.87 b_{13.2}$$

$$(3) \quad -13.81 = -48.87 b_{12.3} + 46.45 b_{13.2}.$$

Solving these two equations simultaneously gives us

$$b_{12.3} = .959, \text{ or } .96,$$

and
$$b_{13.2} = .712, \text{ or } .71.$$

If we leave the origin at the general mean, $a_{1(23)} = 0$. It is, however, generally more convenient to have the origin at 0. The value of $a_{1(23)}$ at the natural origin is

$$a_{1(23)} = \bar{X}_1 - b_{12.3}\bar{X}_2 - b_{13.2}\bar{X}_3$$

$$= 6.667 - .959 \times 6.667 - .712 \times 6.667$$

$$= -4.47.$$

Thus the equation of our plane of conditional means is

$$\bar{X}_{123} = -4.47 + .96 X_2 + .71 X_3.$$

Our mathematically inclined carpenter could now build the supports for this plane in our room. We hope he would have the good sense to realize that we do not really wish him to cut a hole in the floor at the southwest corner so he could anchor his 2x2's 4.47 units *below* the floor level. We wish him to terminate at the floor level at a point so that *if* the 2x2 were extended, it would reach the corner 4.47 units below the floor.

The fact that $a_{1(23)}$ has a negative value points up the nonsense in extending our plane into the corner where a territory has 0 people and these 0 people have 0 income. (On the other hand, there is some logic to the presumption that if a sales manager shipped merchandise into an empty territory, there would probably be some loss before the merchandise could be rescued. It is unlikely, though, that -4.47 is a correct estimate of the probable loss!)

15.5 Estimating the Conditional Standard Deviation for a Three-variable Analysis

The standard deviation of the X_1 values around our plane can be calculated in the usual way. We measure the deviation of X_1 from $\overline{X}_{123}$ and square the result. We then add up all such squared deviations, divide by the number, or by the degrees of freedom, and take the square root. In symbols we get

$$s_{1.23} = \sqrt{\frac{\Sigma(X_1 - \overline{X}_{123})^2}{N}}, \tag{15.4}$$

or
$$\hat{\sigma}_{1.23} = \sqrt{\frac{\Sigma(X_1 - \overline{X}_{123})^2}{N - 3}}. \tag{15.5}$$

This is a tedious calculation, and so, unless we have other reasons to wish to calculate the $\overline{X}_{123}$ values, we prefer to use the short-cut version of the formula. (Remember that shortcuts almost always have more twists and turns than the long way.) The short-cut formula is

$$s_{1.23} = \sqrt{\frac{\Sigma X_1^2 - a_{1(23)}\Sigma X_1 - b_{12.3}\Sigma X_1 X_2 - b_{13.2}\Sigma X_1 X_3}{N}}. \tag{15.6}$$

(A shorter short-cut version would be

$$s_{1.23} = \sqrt{\frac{\Sigma x_1^2 - b_{12.3}\Sigma x_1 x_2 - b_{13.2}\Sigma x_1 x_3}{N}}.)$$

Substituting in this equation, we get

$$s_{1.23} = \sqrt{\frac{724.38 - (-4.47) \times 100 - .96 \times 731.87 - .71 \times 652.86}{15}}$$

$$= .59\%.$$

If we adjust, as we should, for degrees of freedom, we get

$$\hat{\sigma}_{1.23} = s_{1.23} \sqrt{\frac{N}{N-3}} = .59 \times 1.118 = .66\%.$$

15.6   A Summary of the Results of Our Analysis of Territory Sales

We can now extend Table 14.6 to include the results of our multiple analysis. Table 15.1 reproduces Table 14.6 except for the footnote and adds the results of our multiple analysis. It is quite evident that knowledge of *both* the population and income of a territory results in smaller estimating errors than if we knew only one or neither of these. If we were to introduce knowledge about other relevant variables, such as number of retail outlets, average annual temperature, etc., we probably could reduce $\hat{\sigma}_{1.23\ldots n}$ below the .66% which we achieved with knowledge of X_2 and X_3. We would probably have some trouble in making very large reductions, however, because of the few degrees of freedom we have to work with. If we enlarged our sample (assuming the company has some additional territories available) and introduced some additional variables, we would encounter a substantial increase in the amount of arithmetic involved. A four-variable analysis in-

TABLE 15.1

Summary of Results of Analysis of Sales in a Territory

Estimating Formula	Variation in Sample	Degrees of Freedom	Estimated Variation in Universe	Estimated Item-forecast Error
(1) $\bar{X}_1 = 6.7\%$	$s_1 = 1.96\%$	14	$\hat{\sigma}_1 = 2.04\%$	$\hat{\sigma}_{x_1} = 2.11\%$
(2) $\bar{X}_{12} = 2.50 + .625X_2$	$s_{1.2} = 1.06$	13	$\hat{\sigma}_{1.2} = 1.13$	$\hat{\sigma}_{x_{1.2}} = 1.17$
(3) $\bar{X}_{13} = 8.65 - .297X_3$	$s_{1.3} = 1.67$	13	$\hat{\sigma}_{1.3} = 1.79$	$\hat{\sigma}_{x_{1.3}} = 1.85$
(4) $\bar{X}_{123} = -4.47 + .959X_2 + .712X_3$	$s_{1.23} = .59$	12	$\hat{\sigma}_{1.23} = .66$	$\hat{\sigma}_{x_{1.23}} = .68$
Supplementary Data				
$\bar{X}_3 = 6.7\%$	$s_3 = 1.76$	14	$\hat{\sigma}_3 = 1.83$	$\hat{\sigma}_{x_3} = 1.89$
$\bar{X}_{32} = 9.79 - .469X_2$	$s_{3.2} = 1.26$	13	$\hat{\sigma}_{3.2} = 1.34$	$\hat{\sigma}_{x_{3.2}} = 1.38$

volves almost twice as much arithmetic as a three-variable analysis, for example. Such a formidable load of work has prevented any widespread use of multiple analysis of many variables. The development of the electronic computer promises to break this barrier, so that we should see a substantial increase in the use of multiple correlation techniques. Whether this upsurge will be accompanied by any significant amount of misuse is yet to be seen. There is a danger that some people forget that the computer follows instructions as given, with little facility for rejecting poor instructions.

Although we are not really interested in estimating income from population, we include the analysis as supplementary information to help us understand better the structure of our problem. Thus we can see that there is a reasonably high association between the two independent variables. This is the source of the rather dramatic shift of the slope of the sales-income line from negative to positive as we maintain population constant.

15.7 Sampling Errors in Multiple Correlation Analysis

Estimation of sampling errors in the estimation of the plane of conditional means parallels the reasoning we used for a line. The net error is a function of the error in $a_{1(23)}$, $b_{12.3}$, and $b_{13.2}$. The basic formula would be

$$\hat{\sigma}_{\bar{x}_{123}} = \sqrt{\frac{\hat{\sigma}_{1.23}^2}{N} + \frac{\hat{\sigma}_{1.23}^2 x_2^2}{N\hat{\sigma}_2^2} + \frac{\hat{\sigma}_{1.23}^2 x_3^2}{N\hat{\sigma}_3^2}}. \tag{15.7}$$

Note that this error increases as we depart from the general mean because of the cumulation of errors in $b_{12.3}$ and $b_{13.2}$.

If coefficients of *partial* association, or *partial* correlation have been calculated, they too are subject to sampling errors. For example, the coefficient of partial association between sales and population, with income constant is

$$A_{12.3} = \frac{s_{1.3} - s_{1.23}}{s_{1.3}} = \frac{1.67 - .59}{1.67} = .65,$$

and the coefficient of partial correlation of the same is

$$r_{12.3} = \sqrt{\frac{s_{1.3}^2 - s_{1.23}^2}{s_{1.3}^2}} = \sqrt{1 - (1 - A_{12.3})^2}$$

$$= .94.$$

Transformation of r into z' gives us 1.74. The standard deviation of z' (frequently called the standard *error*) is

$$\sigma_{z'} = \frac{1}{\sqrt{N - 3 - (k - 2)}} = \frac{1}{\sqrt{11}} = .30.$$

Note that the standard deviation of z' is slightly larger here than it was for the two-variable coefficient, the increase being due to the loss of one more degree of freedom. Seventy-five percent limits correspond to a Z of 1.15 in the normal curve. Hence the limits to $z'_{12.3}$ are $1.74 \pm 1.15 \times .30$, or 1.40 and 2.08. These correspond to limits for $\hat{\rho}_{12.3}$ of .89 and .97.

15.8   Note on the Coefficient of Multiple Correlation or Association

A coefficient of *simple* association measures the relative error reduction which takes place when we consider *one* independent variable in addition to the dependent variable. The coefficient of *partial* association measures the relative error reduction which takes place when we consider *one* independent variable while *holding one or more other independent variables constant*. Some people also like to measure the relative error reduction which takes place when we consider *two or more* independent variables. For example, if we calculate

$$A_{123} = \frac{s_1 - s_{1.23}}{s_1} = \frac{1.96 - .59}{1.96} = .70,$$

we have measured the relative error reduction which takes place when we consider both population and income. Such a calculation is the coefficient of *multiple* association, or the *multiple coefficient* of association.

Since multiple coefficients always involve at least *two* added variables, they tend to be rather large in numerical value. They are very difficult to interpret because of the addition of *two* or more variables. We have no basis of judging how much of the information was contributed by one of the variables and how much by the other or others. We can judge the latter only with reference to the *partial* associations, where we allow only *one* independent variable to vary at a time. Therefore we recommend avoiding the calculation of multiple coefficients because they contribute no precise and useful information and yield numbers so large that the uninitiated tend to be overimpressed.

15.9 The Relationship between Simple and Partial Correlations

When we found sales and income with a *negative* association and later found that the partial association was *positive* when we held population constant, we had empirical proof that the relationships between simple and partial associations are not as obvious as we might hope. We can get a more precise idea of the relationships between simple and partial coefficients if we show their exact mathematical function. For example, using r for convenience, we get

$$r_{12.3} = \frac{r_{12} - r_{13}r_{23}}{\sqrt{1 - r_{13}^2}\ \sqrt{1 - r_{23}^2}} \tag{15.8}$$

A few of the more obvious conclusions we can draw from this equation are:

1. Values of r_{13} and r_{23} are interchangeable. Each has the same and equal effect on the value of $r_{12.3}$.
2. If both r_{13} and r_{23} are 0, then $r_{12.3} = r_{12}$. We would infer this intuitively, because, if X_3 were uncorrelated with both X_1 and X_2, the holding of X_3 constant should have no bearing on the relationship between X_1 and X_2.
3. If r_{13} and r_{23} are both 1, then r_{12} *must* also be 1 and $r_{12.3}$ must be 0.
4. r_{12} is not completely independent of r_{13} and r_{23}. This is obviously true for the case mentioned in 3. It is also clear if we play with various combinations of values for r_{12}, r_{13}, and r_{23}. For example, suppose we know that $r_{13} = .8$ and $r_{23} = .5$. What can we say about the value of r_{12} and $r_{12.3}$? Substituting these given values we get

$$r_{12.3} = \frac{r_{12} - .40}{\sqrt{.36 \times .75}} = \frac{r_{12} - .40}{.52}.$$

If we give r_{12} a value greater than .92, then $r_{12.3}$ would have a value greater than 1, a logical impossibility. Similarly, if we give r_{12} a value less than $-.12$, then $r_{12.3}$ would have a value less than -1. Therefore we know that r_{12} must have a value between $-.12$ and .92, given that $r_{13} = .8$ and $r_{23} = .5$. If r_{13} is *minus* .8, with r_{23} remaining at .5, then r_{12} must be between $+.12$ and $-.92$, a complete reversal of signs from the case when r_{13} was positive.

These are enough to indicate the possibilities.[1] We can extend the list of logical deductions if necessary. This type of equation can

---

[1] Ruth W. Lees and Frederic M. Lord have prepared a nomograph for the calculation of partial correlation coefficients. It is published in the *Journal of the American Statistical Association,* Dec., 1961, p. 995. Errors have been discovered in this nomograph. A corrected nomograph will appear in a later issue.

be extended to cover higher order coefficients of correlation. (We frequently identify the order of a coefficient by the number of variables held constant. Thus r_{12} is a zero-order coefficient, $r_{12.3}$ a first-order coefficient, $r_{12.34}$ a second-order coefficient, etc.) The formula for $r_{12.34}$ is

$$r_{12.34} = \frac{r_{12.3} - r_{14.3}r_{24.3}}{\sqrt{1 - r_{14.3}^2}\sqrt{1 - r_{24.3}^2}}, \quad \text{or} \quad \frac{r_{12.4} - r_{13.4}r_{23.4}}{\sqrt{1 - r_{13.4}^2}\sqrt{1 - r_{23.4}^2}}.$$

$$(15.9)$$

The pattern of these formulas is fairly simple to discern, and we should be able to develop the appropriate formula for any coefficient we wish.

Although the coefficient of correlation is quite difficult to interpret by itself, analysis of the collection of them for a given problem will give us a good insight into the structure of the relationships among the variables. If we start with all the possible zero-order coefficients, we can derive all the first-order coefficients, and then all the second-order coefficients from the first-order ones, etc. It is also possible by a technique called *factor analysis* to discover the possible existence of an underlying factor that is apparently common to several variables.[1] For example, the relatively abstract factor of intelligence may be considered as an underlying factor that is common to several problem-solving abilities we might measure.

15.10   Spurious Correlation

One way to study the correlation between sales and income with population constant is with the multiple correlation type of analysis that we have done above. Another way is to correlate *per capita* sales with *per capita* income. The calculation of per capita data involves *dividing* a series such as sales by the population in each territory. Thus the resultant figures are *ratios* of one variable to another. When we divide each of two series by the same third series, and correlate the resultant ratios, we get a *spurious* correlation mixed with the so-called real correlation. We say that some spurious correlation develops when we calculate such ratios because the calculation of the ratios tends to *create* some correlation. The argument is based on the behavior of random series. Suppose we had

[1] See H. H. Harman, *Modern Factor Analysis,* University of Chicago, 1960.

two series of random numbers that were uncorrelated. Then suppose we had a third series of random numbers, uncorrelated with either of the first two, which we divide into the other two series. (We might as well *multiply* the first two series by the third to illustrate the principle.) When we divide by a *large* number, the resultant ratios tend to get very small *together*. When we divide by a *small* number, the resultant ratios tend to remain moderately large *together*. Thus the resultant ratios will tend to be *positively* correlated even though the original data were uncorrelated. If we refer back to our formula for the relationship between zero- and first-order coefficients, however, we note that if $r_{12} = 0$, $r_{13} = 0$, and $r_{23} = 0$, then $r_{12.3} = 0$. Nevertheless $r_{\frac{1}{3}, \frac{2}{3}}$ will tend to be positive.

There is nothing inherently wrong with the correlation of ratios like these or with spurious correlation. It is just as useful in prediction as nonspurious correlation. For example, if we were given information on the value of one of the ratios, say X_1/X_3, indicating that the ratio was low, we could make the valid inference that X_2/X_3 is also low. It is not surprising that the calculation of ratios alters the correlations between the primary series. In fact, we would not really think of calculating such ratios unless we believed that some alteration would take place. The difficult technical problem arises when it comes to estimating the number of degrees of freedom in the final estimates. We know that we lose 1 d.f. when we hold a third variable constant linearly, but we are not too confident that we know the restrictions that are imposed when we calculate the ratios. The issue is too complex for us to do any more than mention it here.

15.11   The Phenomenon of Joint Correlation

Our treatment of multiple correlation analysis assumed that the relevant relationships were all linear. More importantly, perhaps, the implication of this assumption is that *it makes no difference at which level we hold a third variable constant* when we study the correlation between two other variables. An analogy from the chemistry laboratory helps make the point. Suppose we are performing an experiment that involves water. Suppose further that we would like to hold the temperature of the room constant during the course of the experiment. The immediate question arises as to the *particular* temperature we would like to maintain constant. We would obviously get different results if we held the temperature constant at 20°F. than if we held it constant at 250°F. Thus the results of our experiment are valid *only within the limits* of temperature where it makes no difference where we hold it constant.

If we find that it does make a difference to a relationship depending on the level at which we hold a third variable constant, we are dealing with variables that have *joint* correlation. An everyday example of a joint correlation is found among life expectancy, weight, and age for human beings. We are aware that overweight people tend to have a shorter life expectancy than underweight people. What most people do not know, however, is that this statement applies *only* to *older* people, those about 50 years of age or more. To be underweight is not an asset for longevity at younger ages. In fact, at age 22, to be 20% underweight is more damaging to longevity than to be 20% overweight.[1]

The techniques for discovering and measuring joint correlation are outside our scope here. We merely mention its existence. Common sense will usually warn us at the proper time if we are at least aware of the possibility.

15.12 Nonlinear Multiple Correlation

We may wonder what we do if our linear model is not a reasonably accurate picture of reality. We merely use the so-called appropriate curves. We say so-called because it is not at all easy to decide on the proper curve in advance of any mathematics, and we cannot do any mathematics until we have selected a curve, proper or not. If time and money are plentiful, and if we have an electronic computer, we can always engage in a "fishing expedition." We fit all kinds of lines to the data and pick out the most appropriate at the end. But if time and money are restricted, we try to guess in advance the type of relationship that might be appropriate. Some people always guess "straight line," thus putting very little strain on their technical knowledge or their time and money. They never find out how much they might be missing by trying other possibilities.

Again it is possible to use the clues from scattergrams to facilitate accurate guessing. The problem here is more complicated because

---

[1] Mordecai Ezekial and Karl A. Fox, *Methods of Correlation and Regression Analysis,* John Wiley and Sons, New York, N.Y. This book is a very useful reference for the theoretical and practical aspects of correlation analysis, with no mathematics beyond elementary algebra required.

of its multidimensional character, really requiring complex stereo-grams. There are some graphic techniques available, however, that make it possible to achieve some multidimensional effects in two dimensions. An extensive discussion of these methods is in Ezekial and Fox. One useful point to know is that *if all simple correlation scattergrams indicate straight lines, the partial relationships will also be linear.* It is, therefore, always a good idea to draw at least rough scattergrams for all possible pairs of the relevant variables. We recall that we started our analysis of the sales-population-income problem by constructing the three possible scattergrams.

15.13 Using Correlation Analysis Results as a Measure of An Ignored Variable

Suppose our sales manager wanted to measure the effectiveness of his salesmen. The obvious thing is to look at the *sales performance* of the salesmen. If the sales manager desired, he might rate the salesmen according to their sales. For example, our data show that the salesman in territory 14 is the "best" because he has had the *highest* sales. (See Table 15.2.) Salesmen 12 and 15 are next best,

TABLE 15.2

Rating Salesmen According to Sales Performance
After Allowing for Population and Income

Territory or Salesman (1)	X_1 (2)	$\bar{X}_{12}$ (3)	$\bar{X}_{13}$ (4)	$\bar{X}_{123}$ (5)	x_1 (6)	R_1 (7)	$x_{1.2}$ (8)	$R_{1.2}$ (9)	$x_{1.3}$ (10)	$R_{1.3}$ (11)	$x_{1.23}$ (12)	$R_{1.23}$ (13)
1	4.0	4.0	6.0	4.2	−2.7	13.5	0	8	−2.0	13	−.2	7.5
2	2.7	4.3	6.7	3.1	−4.0	15	−1.6	14	−4.0	15	−.4	11
3	6.7	4.9	5.9	5.8	0	8.5	1.8	2	.8	6	.9	2
4	5.3	5.2	6.2	5.6	−1.4	12	.1	7	− .9	11	−.3	9
5	4.0	5.8	6.8	4.8	−2.7	13.5	−1.8	15	−2.8	14	−.8	15
6	6.0	5.8	6.2	6.5	− .7	10.5	.2	6	− .2	9	−.5	13
7	8.0	6.1	6.2	7.0	1.3	5	1.9	1	1.8	3	1.0	1
8	6.0	6.7	7.2	5.5	− .7	10.5	− .7	11	−1.2	12	.5	4.5
9	8.0	6.9	6.5	7.5	1.3	5	1.1	3	1.5	4	.5	4.5
10	7.2	7.6	6.8	7.6	.5	7	− .4	9.5	.4	8	−.4	11
11	6.7	7.6	7.3	6.4	0	8.5	− .9	13	− .6	10	.3	6
12	8.7	8.4	6.7	9.4	2.0	2.5	.3	5	2.0	2	−.7	14
13	8.0	8.8	7.3	8.2	1.3	5	− .8	12	.7	7	−.2	7.5
14	10.0	9.1	6.7	10.4	3.3	1	.9	4	3.3	1	−.4	11
15	8.7	9.1	7.7	8.0	2.0	2.5	− .4	9.5	1.0	5	.7	3
	100.0	100.3	100.2	100.0	− .5	120	− .3	120	− .2	120	0	120

and salesman 2 is the "poorest." Note that here we get the same ranking of salesmen whether we use the sales figure (X_1) or the deviation from the mean (x_1). In subsequent discussion we concentrate on deviations from the mean for obvious reasons.

Salesman 2 would probably be the first to complain about being rated solely according to sales performance. He would very likely claim that there are extenuating circumstances which make it comparatively difficult to sell in his territory, especially when we compare his territory with 14. An intelligent sales manager would want to investigate these extenuating circumstances. He might run a correlation analysis similar to what we have done, or possibly more comprehensive, and obtain results like those shown in Table 15.2.

We use Salesman 1 in Territory 1 as an example to explain the table. Salesman 1 actually sold 4.0% of the total (column 2). This performance put him 2.7% (column 6) below the average, a performance that tied him for the 13.5 rank (column 7). (A rank of 13.5 represents a tie for both the 13th and 14th rank. A proper way to handle ties for any ranks in a ranking operation is to give each tied rankee the arithmetic mean value of the ranks tied. For example, Salesmen 7, 9, and 13 all tied for ranks 4, 5, and 6. We assign each a rank of 5. This method of handling ties assures that the *sum* of all the ranks is the same whether or not there are any ties.)

However, Territory 1 had a relatively low population, which, when considered, gives us an arithmetic mean expectation of only 4.0% (column 3). This puts Salesman 1 right at the average (column 8) with a rank of 8 (column 9). Thus Salesman 1 rates much better if we consider population in the rating.

If we consider only income, we would expect mean sales of 6.0% in Territory 1, putting Salesman 1 2.0% below average (column 10) with a rank of 13 (column 11). Finally, considering both population and income, we would expect mean sales of 4.2% (column 5), putting Salesman 1 .2% below average (column 12) with a rank of 7.5 (column 13).

Thus we see that our rating of Salesman 1 varies from 7.5 to 13.5 depending upon whether we do or do not consider population and income factors. One of the most interesting outcomes is that for Salesman 14. He goes from a rank of 1 if we ignore population and income to a rank of 11 if we consider these factors. Presumably a good deal of his success is due to his territory rather than to his own efforts. Since such interesting things can happen if we consider population and income, it is only natural to ask what would happen if we considered even more factors. The answer is that it would depend on the degree of association between these additional factors and sales. If there were very little association, very little change would take place in the rankings. Note, for example, that knowledge of income makes very little difference in the rankings. (Compare columns 7 and 11.) On the other hand, knowledge of population makes a very definite difference. (Compare columns 7 and 9.) If we wished, we might measure the correlation between rankings, with a result of 0 corresponding to a correlation of 1 between sales and the factor.

If we are unsuccessful in finding additional factors that will significantly change the rankings, our sales manager might then assume that the ultimate rankings in terms of deviations measures the salesmen's performances with reasonable accuracy. Of course, there is always the problem of what to do with the unmeasurable factors. For example, the sales manager might visit a territory for a few days and call on a few customers with the salesman. The sales manager then claims to have developed a "feel" for the territory and its problems, and for the skill with which the salesman has been exploiting the territory. As a result he might substantially modify the results of a formal correlation analysis. There are no specific rules for making such modifications other than the appointment of a good sales manager. If we could really establish such rules, we could replace the sales manager with a statistician.

15.14 The Problem of Stability of Past Relationships

Correlation analysis is necessarily restricted to historical data. Any discovered relationships generally have practical value only when they can be applied to *future* events, and we again must concern ourselves with the problem of shifts in universes over time. For example, a change in consumer tastes may substantially alter the class of people who tend to buy a product. Such changes could easily alter the population-income relationships of the sort we measured. If a sales manager ignored such changes because he was not aware of them, his administration of the sales force would lag several years behind the facts, with possibly disastrous results unless the company had a sheltered monopoly.

The only way we can keep abreast of such changes over time is to stay alert to new data as they appear. This is best done by establishing some routine for recording new data and for assessing their consistency with measured past relationships. This is generally better than waiting until some disadvantaged people become sufficiently irritated to make complaints, or to resign, or to switch their business elsewhere, as the case may be.

15.15　The Problem of Cost

Again we must remind ourselves that knowledge is not without cost. There are always costs of some kind, whether in money, time, physical energy, pleasures given up, etc. Correlation analysis is nothing more than a formal method for acquiring knowledge, or for at least attempting to acquire knowledge. We must always be conscious of the need to make a *profit* by acquiring knowledge with the *promise* of a higher return than its cost. We emphasize promise because there is no way to be sure that any knowledge will have a return. The person who insists that he will not learn anything until he knows its value generally remains ignorant because he cannot find any honest person who will guarantee a return.

There is no formula for predetermining the value of knowledge. Each person must assess his own costs and the value of his rewards. Our only guide is past experience, our own and that of others. We can often catalogue some of the costs and potential rewards in some parts of a business but we can never do it completely.

We should also remember that knowledge is subject to depreciation and obsolescence, a type of cost we are likely to forget until we discover that a particular set of knowledge is worthless. We all know many things that are no longer true and many things that may still be true but that no one cares enough about to pay for. Some of this knowledge is useful for the personal pleasure it gives in its retelling, or for otherwise nourishing the ego.

PROBLEMS AND QUESTIONS

15.1 It was suggested in the text that weighting in proportion to coefficients of association (A's) might be appropriate if we wished to combine variables that have been treated independently of each other, the type of analysis we made in the preceding chapter. What is the logic, if any, to this use of weights?

What other possible weighting systems might be used?

15.2 Calculate a least-squares plane (linear) of relationship from the data of Problem 14.2 among:

(a) Production, dexterity test scores, and experience.
(b) Production, dexterity test scores, and intelligence test scores.
(c) Production, dexterity test scores, and formal education.

(d) Production, experience, and intelligence test scores.

(e) Production, experience, and formal education.

(f) Production, intelligence test scores, and formal education.

(g) Production, dexterity test scores, experience, and intelligence test scores.

(h) Production, dexterity test scores, experience, and education.

(i) Production, experience, intelligence test scores, and education.

(j) Production, dexterity, intelligence, and education.

(k) Production, dexterity, experience, intelligence, and education.

15.3 (a) For each estimating plane that you calculated in 15.2 make estimates of the expected production for the odd-numbered workers (or even-numbered).

(b) Construct a scattergram using your estimates in (a) as the independent variable and the actual production as the dependent variable.

1. Is there any evidence of a *systematic* variation around a straight line on this scattergram? (In other words, is there any evidence that the plane should probably be curved?) If so, what modifications do you suggest for your estimating equation in order to bend the plane in the appropriate directions? What clues for an appropriate modification do you find in the scattergrams you drew in Problem 14.2? What clues from the "logic" of the expected relationships?

15.4 Calculate the conditional standard deviation of production for each of the relationships you have calculated in Problem 15.2. (These should be unbiased universe estimates.)

15.5 Make 70% confidence estimates of the expected production for each of the following combinations of factors. Use only those factors included in your estimating equation. What is the practical significance of the ignored variables?

(a) $X_2 = 28$; $X_3 = 45$; $X_4 = 100$; $X_5 = 10$.

(b) $X_2 = 47$; $X_3 = 88$; $X_4 = 125$; $X_5 = 12$.

(c) $X_2 = 60$; $X_3 = 0$; $X_4 = 102$; $X_5 = 11$.

15.6 Construct a table like Table 15.1 which lists all the possible results of your correlation analysis of these Crayle Co. figures.

(a) Which formula has the least error?

(b) Might the apparent superiority of the formula with the least error be due to chance? Explain.

(c) What considerations would guide you in deciding which of these estimating formulas you would use:

1. In selecting new workers?

2. In evaluating the performance of a worker? For example, suppose you found a worker who was producing less than expected. (You *should* find about half the workers producing less than expected. Why? Suppose you find more than 60% producing less than expected. What would be your reaction?)

(d) Rank the four explanatory factors in order of importance. Also assign the most appropriate weights to each in order to signify their relative importance as you see them.

15.7 Your table in Problem 15.6 has several different estimates of the universe standard deviation, most of them being conditional on the availability of values of the independent variables. A coefficient of association (or of determination, or of correlation) involves comparing two such standard deviations with each other.

(a) Calculate the coefficients of association that give meaningful answers.

(b) Some of the coefficients calculated in (a) are known as coefficients of partial association. Explain what is meant by partial association.

(c) What have you learned from your calculation of these coefficients that you did not know before? (We are referring to what you have learned about this problem of personnel evaluation. You have undoubtedly learned about some other things too, such as the tedium of such calculations.)

15.8(a) Calculate all the zero-order coefficients of correlation for the Crayle Co. problem. (There are 10 of them. A cooperative effort is recommended.)

(b) Deduce from these the 28 coefficients of partial correlation.

(c) Deduce the 28 coefficients of partial *association* from your 28 coefficients of partial *correlation*. Do these results agree with those you calculated in 15.7a when you compared the standard deviations directly? Should they?

15.9(a) Below are given three random series. Verify that these series are practically uncorrelated by calculating r_{12}, r_{13}, and r_{23}. [A quick and convenient formula for calculating r_{12} is by calculating $\Sigma x_1 x_2 / N s_1 s_2$. r_{13} and r_{23} can be similarly calculated. The necessary sums of cross products (*not* yet in deviations from the mean) are given below.]

Item	X_1	X_2	X_3		
1.	5	3	9	$\Sigma X_1{}^2$	$= 299$
2.	7	3	8	$\Sigma X_1 X_2$	$= 205$
3.	7	6	6	$\Sigma X_1 X_3$	$= 265$
4.	1	2	3	$\Sigma X_2{}^2$	$= 282$
5.	2	7	7	$\Sigma X_2 X_3$	$= 273$
6.	2	3	3	$\Sigma X_3{}^2$	$= 369$
7.	7	0	0		
8.	1	9	6		
9.	6	7	2		
10.	9	6	9		
	47	46	53		

(b) Divide both X_1 and X_2 by the appropriate X_3 and calculate the coefficient of correlation between the resultant ratios. Explain why you did not get a result of 0.

(c) Is the ratio of X_2 to X_3 a valid base for estimating the *ratio* of X_1 to X_3? Explain.

(d) Is the ratio of X_2 to X_3 a valid base for estimating X_1? What is the relationship between X_1 and the ratio of X_2 to X_3?

15.10 Your multiple correlation analysis of the Crayle Co. problem assumed that the relationships between any pair of variables with one or more other variables constant are independent of the level at which the other variables were held constant. Does this seem a reasonable assumption in this problem? (In answering, keep in mind that the actual data will tend to stay within certain boundaries; hence what happens at hypothetical extremes may be irrelevant in practice.)

15.11 The attempt to use correlation analysis to eliminate the relationships of some variables to a dependent variable and thus leave a residual variation that might be attributed to some unmeasured variable sometimes creates a dilemma. (Refer in the text to the use of correlation analysis to rate the effectiveness of salesmen.) If we search assiduously for explanatory variables, we might end up leaving practically no residual to be attributed to the unmeasured variable. If we do not search assiduously, we take the risk of failing to find an explanatory variable that would explain a good part of the variation that we may end up attributing to the unmeasured variable.

(a) How would you proceed to cope with these opposite risks? Give particular attention to how you would utilize the concept of degrees of freedom in trying to reduce these risks. In order to lend some concreteness to your reply, use the example of rating salesmen and *devise a final ranking of salesmen in order of ability.* Defend the basis, or bases, of your rankings.

(b) Assign weights to your rankings so that we can tell *how much* superiority you think Salesman X has over Salesman Y.

chapter 16
The problem of changes over time

16.1 The Challenge of the Future

In the final analysis, the acid test of the efficacy of any knowledge is its usefulness in foretelling the future. Mere description of historical events is useless unless future events conform in some way to past patterns. So far we have merely mentioned the existence of the problem of whether past patterns have some stability through time. We now explicitly consider the problem of the relationship of the past to the future.

16.2 The Nature of Time

Time is best not defined; we assume that everybody knows what it is, and attempts to define it rigorously usually lead into an almost hopeless tangle of words. So let us turn directly to the problem of measuring time.

All kinds of physical phenomena could be used as reference points, but those currently used are based on the physical relationships of the earth, sun, and moon. The *year* is, of course, the time it takes the earth to complete one circuit around the sun. The *day* is the time it takes the earth to make one complete spin around its axis. The *month* is fundamentally rooted in the time it takes the moon to complete one circuit around the earth. Unfortunately, however, attempts at personal aggrandizement by ancient rulers have resulted in months with different numbers of days. Other units of time are subdivisions or multiples of these principal units.

It is useful to speculate briefly on why man has chosen to use the notions of the year, month, and day as units of time. Each of the physical phenomena referred to makes a significant difference to the amount of light and/or heat available to man, both of which are essential to man's survival and comfort, and man knows they are essential. There are very likely other physical phenomena equally essential to man's survival but which we so far have not been able to discern with sufficient precision to make their behavior meaningful measures of time. For example, the whole solar system is probably going somewhere in the same sense that the earth is going around the sun, but as yet we have not been able to clearly define any reference points or landmarks. It is also very possible that the earth, moon, and sun are all emitting and absorbing various kinds of energy, and very likely at systematic rates. If we could measure such energy transformations, we might better understand climatic changes on the earth, alternations of economic prosperity and depression, the long cycle of success of the New York Yankees, etc. In the meantime we struggle along with the relatively crude units of the year, etc.

The important point of this discussion of time is that there is no particular magic to time. It is simply a *dating* device that enables us to relate all other phenomena to *common reference points*. Its value to us is not unlike the value of a money system, whereby we are able to relate the value of all goods and services to a common reference point. Our time units are, of course, much more stable than our money units.

16.3 Time and Other Variables

We are not really interested in time as such. Rather we are interested in the other variables that we can understand better if we *date* these variables.

Problems in Meaningful Dating of Variables

Homogeneity of Data. An ideal *time series* (a series of *dated* measurements) is one in which the unit of measure remains constant over the full time period. This is not at all easy to accomplish in a dynamic society. For example, if we are dealing with the sales of a company, it is not unusual to find that the company has changed its line of products over time, or has purchased other businesses. Such sharp changes in the integral unit can easily lead to misinterpretation of the significance of time changes in the sales series. Similar things can happen to an industry sales series. Since very few companies deal in only one product or service, it is just about impossible to construct a homogeneous industry series by adding up the sales of individual companies. That is why we make strong attempts to collect *product* statistics, such as sales of washing machines, rather than sales of washing machine companies.

It is very important to familiarize ourselves with the definitions of the units of measure and the changes therein before we engage in any statistical analysis of a time series. It is very embarrassing to work up a very profound explanation of a variation and discover that a change in unit accounts for it, particularly if the change in unit is common knowledge within an industry. A careful worker must therefore pay attention to the footnotes and the appendices.

If we discover that there have been changes in units of a non-trivial type, we usually find that we should either confine our formal analysis to only the later sections of data, the period after the change in units, or we should modify the data by making some adjustment for the change in unit. Many analysts prefer to modify the data because they feel more comfortable with the larger sample of data that results than they would if they had to ignore the earlier data before a unit change. We usually prefer to modify data by adjusting the earlier data to conform to the new unit, rather than to adjust the later data to conform to the old unit. In this way we are able to add new data as they occur without any further adjustments, unless, of course, there are subsequent changes in units.

Exactly what we should do to modify data requires knowledge rather than technique. The important point is to know our data and then do what seems to make sense. The simplest *technique* of adjustment is to assume that the *relative changes* in the data would be about the same in both the new and old units. We adjust the *level* of the data only. Such an assumption is almost never correct, but it is frequently all that is available. Naturally we should not be too ambitious with our conclusions from the resultant series.

One of the advantages of analyzing data by the use of charts and experience-based intuition rather than formal mathematics is the flexibility for handling problems of heterogenous data. The corresponding disadvantage is, of course, that we might subconsciously bias the results toward desired conclusions. Thus an optimistic analyst is more likely to foresee a rosy future from a given set of data than is a pessimistic one.

Selection of Dates. An unlimited number of options is available for the selection of dates. We might check our cash balance every hour, or every day, or once a week, etc. We might cumulate sales daily, or hourly, or monthly, etc. Two analytical factors control the selection. The time period should be long enough to permit measurable and meaningful changes to occur. Otherwise we put ourselves in the position of trying to "see the corn grow." The other factor is the desirability of not having a time period so long that important changes are concealed within items rather than being shown as differences between items. For example, if we cumulate sales only annually, the data will conceal any seasonal variations. It is not necessarily wrong to conceal changes. In fact we often do it deliberately as an analytical device. What is wrong is to conceal changes that are significant to the conclusions we are drawing. A useful general rule to follow is that we should conceal only those movements that conform closely to a *linear interpolation* between the data that are recorded. Thus we could always make good estimates of the intermediate data if we had to.

Another factor important in selecting dates for recording data is *cost* vs. *benefits of additional knowledge.* A supermarket manager might find it useful to check cash register tapes every hour. Thus he can schedule check-out clerks, bundle boys, etc., for the most efficient use of their time without sacrificing customer convenience. An automobile dealer would probably find an hourly check of sales a particularly erratic and useless activity. Businessmen are continually concerned with collecting sufficiently detailed information without cluttering up the files with meaningless trivia.

Cumulative vs. Noncumulative Data

It is important to distinguish between two general classes of data that occur in business time series. *Cumulative* data are data that can be meaningfully *added* over time. Thus we can add daily sales to get weekly sales. Conversely, we can subdivide annual sales into monthly sales.

Noncumulative data are data that have different sizes at different dates but which make meaningless totals if we add the data for different dates. For example, if we add daily cash balances, we do not get a weekly or monthly cash balance. Similarly, if we add a person's height from year to year, we do not get his present height.

Data which appear on the income, or profit and loss, statement of a company are generally cumulative data. Data which appear on a balance sheet are generally noncumulative data.

General Classes of Variation in Time Series Data, Systematic vs. Nonsystematic Variations

The fundamental objective of the analysis of time series is to discover variations over time that *appear* to have some *pattern* or *system* to them. We then hope that a projection of this apparent system will produce useful estimates of future variation. We say *appear* because we can do no more than use what we ourselves can see. We do not really claim that the data themselves have the given system. Nor do we claim that data that have no apparent system actually do have no system. It may simply be that our perceptive abilities are inadequate. As a matter of fact, we prefer to believe that all variations are fundamentally systematic, just waiting for some man who is smart enough to discover the system.

Nonsystematic variations are simply those variations left over after we have extracted the presumed systems. In fact we often call them *residual* variations. They are of the nature of *random* variations and can sometimes be treated successfully with probability techniques.

Since different people bring different backgrounds of knowledge, experience, and analytical skills to a problem, it is not unusual to find different people classifying the variations differently. Neither person is technically wrong as long as he does the best possible job within the bounds of his own limitations. Nevertheless, one of the persons will produce better results. Unfortunately, it is not easy to decide which will be better. The one who sees the most system in the data may have only a very lively imagination coupled with a strong background in analytical geometry. The best we are able to do is develop the habit of rating people on the *results* they produce and to prefer the man with the better record of results. If we concentrate on elegance of method, we might be misled by the form and ignore the substance. Unorthodoxy of method seems to be almost a hallmark of outstanding achievement. Unfortunately, it is also a hallmark of poor achievement. Thus, if we aim for the best, we might achieve the worst. On the other hand, if we are willing to settle for good, but not outstanding, dependable performance, we would do well to concentrate on form. The situation is not unlike that in athletic achievement. Most golfers with bad form are bad golfers, just as most golfers with good form are good golfers. However, the outstandingly good golfers often have poor form, although we now call it unorthodox.

Types of Systematic Variation

Generally we do better in finding systematic behavior if we know what to look for. Man's experience in the physical sciences has given us most of the clues we look for in business data. The following broad classes of systematic variation have been found useful in studying business and economic data. Note that these systems are simply the result of *correlating* a series with *time* as an independent variable. Remember that there should be no connotation that time *causes* the systematic variation. The underlying causes would really be the other things that are *also happening as time passes*. We make no explicit attempt to identify these other things in a formal way. We do, however, make references to things that might be considered probable causes of the observed behavior.

Periodic, or Repetitive, Variation. Figure 16.1 shows a very simple periodic system, a familiar sine curve. This system shows a constant *amplitude* of movement and a constant *period* of movement. Thus each *cycle* is exactly like every other cycle. Forecasting the next wave is a very simple task of extrapolating the constant cycle.

If we measure the angle the sun's rays make every day at noon with some point on the earth's surface, we would find that this angle would pass through a repetitive cycle of sufficient stability to warrant

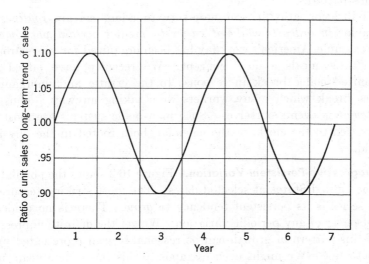

Fig. 16.1 A simple periodic system: the sine curve.

predicting the angle at any date many years into the future. This is the astronomical basis which, among a few other factors, causes a *seasonal variation* in temperature, rainfall, etc., at that point on the earth's surface. Unfortunately, the seasonal variations do not conform to as exact a pattern as the angle of the sun's rays. There is clear evidence that the *average* of many years of seasonal data will conform quite closely to a simple cycle. However, the specific year data will show departures, sometimes in a discernibly systematic way and other times in an apparently random way.

When we move from weather phenomena to such things as sales of bathing suits and of antifreeze, we find the departure from a simple cycle even more pronounced. Now we have to contend with events which are somewhat under the control of man and his institutions, and man is not always, or really ever, in precise control. Furthermore, man is not consistent in what he wishes to achieve with his controls. Hence we find seasonal variations in economic data exhibiting sometimes rather wide departures from the underlying cyclical phenomenon of the angle of the sun's rays.

Additional complications arise because of the institution of the *holiday*. As custom dictates certain kinds of traditional behavior at a holiday, definite patterns begin to appear in the relevant data. Customs change, however, and the resultant patterns also change, creating a real challenge for the analyst who is trying to *predict* future patterns.

Civilization also finds it necessary to adopt certain *routines* of behavior *in order to make it easier to predict certain phenomena*. For example, America's workday has been organized for years around the "three meals a day" concept. We recently have added the organized coffee break in response to the erratic and unorganized coffee break which many workers were taking anyway. Thus we *systematize* events ourselves. Such man-made systems are most always tied to the clock, or the calendar, both rooted in the physical world.

Progressive-Persistent Variation. Figure 16.2 shows the population of the United States at selected dates. The most striking feature of this series is its persistent tendency to *grow*. There is no evidence whatsoever of any periodic variation. We get the definite impression that this pattern of growth can be reasonably well represented by a smooth line. We might even extrapolate this line a few years into the future with some confidence that the actual population will not vary very much from such a line.

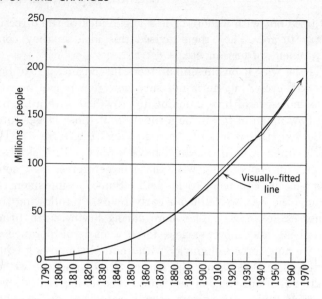

Fig. 16.2 Population of the United States, 1790–1960. (Source: United States Bureau of the Census, *Historical Statistics of the U.S., Colonial Times to 1957,* Washington, D.C., p. 7, and *Current Population Reports,* June 14, 1961.)

We call such a line a *secular trend,* or a trend over a long period of time. How long is long is not easy to determine. All we can say is long enough so that we have evidence of a *persistent* tendency to move in some general direction. This movement may not be *linear,* but we do require that it not have ups and downs. This does not mean that the actual series does not have ups and downs, but only that the *general persistent* movement has no ups and downs. The situation may be likened to the path of an ocean liner from New York to London. The *trend* of the liner is persistently toward London, although the disturbances of wind, current, and human error cause the liner to be almost always headed some other place, with corrections being made as soon as their need becomes apparent. The analogy is imperfect because we do not know the *destination* of United States population or of similar series. Estimating secular trend is more like plotting the general path of an ocean liner without ever knowing exactly where the liner is going. We steer for awhile in terms of where we think it *should* be going, then we revise this idea of destination as we come to realize it is not really going where we originally thought. Or perhaps a better analogy would be the problem of some of the early explorers of the American wilderness.

They started out with a more or less vague idea of the direction they should try to go. They then revised this idea as they confronted certain problems of terrain, etc.

This is the way a businessman steers his business. He hopes the business will grow, but he is not sure how fast it can or will grow. He is also not sure of how much of its growth is within his own control and how much of it will be a function of those larger forces that would be like the wind, the current, and the terrain. He must nevertheless plot a path; he must have a plan. With skill and luck he will end up cooperating with those larger forces and controlling the ones that he can bend to his will. Some businessmen still plot their course the way we built our early roads, by following the paths of the horses and cows. The more daring businessmen bring other forces to bear and more or less force a path of planned growth, the way we now force a highway with giant earthmoving equipment. One of the big issues facing the United States and the world is the rate of growth of our national economy. We do not really know what the practical limits are to our growth rate; nor do we know how much we should try to *force* the rate by use of governmental power. The problem is not made simpler by the fact that we do not know *what* it is that should grow. Gross national product is just a total of a vast number of specific goods and services. It is not enough to just make GNP grow, with no concern for the specific parts that make up the growth. The parts are of the essence, and one of our risks is that we may make the total grow temporarily by sacrificing some of the slow-growing parts, albeit crucial, in favor of some of the fast-growing parts.

The problem of the complexity of the growth process is a persistent concern of the business manager. We hear often of balanced growth and healthy growth. This must mean that thoughtful businessmen and economists can conceive of unbalanced growth and unhealthy growth, a kind of growth that somehow apparently alters the structure of the organism in unfavorable ways, thus ultimately precipitating retardation, or decline, or even death.

For example, the kind of growth that took place in the United States during the 1920's in real estate activities, automobile capacity, radio capacity, etc., turned out to be unsustainable. Much of this capacity remained unused until the advent of the inordinate demands of World War II. Some people still worry about what might have happened to the United States economy if the war had not seemingly solved what had begun to look like an almost unsolvable problem.

A person might be forgiven if he called the growth of the 1920's unhealthy. We might also mention that one of the prime tasks of the Federal Reserve Board is to encourage growth of the economy without letting the growth get unhealthy.

It should be obvious that we have to be very naive to assume that we can plot the path of future growth by simply extrapolating lines on charts, or by the equivalent use of mathematical equations. Plotting the growth of a business, or of any institution, or of any person's career, is more a matter of knowledge, faith, and courage than it is of statistical technique. Where our statistical technique can help us, however, is in pointing out the probable limits of what can possibly happen. For example, Fig. 16.2 indicates the unlikelihood that United States population will *double* over the next 10 years. Such an event would represent such a substantial break with past patterns of growth that we would necessarily have to have many other things change also, events which themselves would be very unlikely. Having said this, however, again we remind ourselves that past experience of this sort can also be a chain to our thinking. Statistical-minded people are notoriously conservative, with definite tendencies to plan for and to expect the *usual;* and they are right most of the time, because, of course, it is the usual that usually happens. The confident expectation of the improbable is not a characteristic of a statistician, but it is a characteristic of the pioneer. Until somebody figures out a rational way to decide when to bet on the improbable, society will just have to hope that its prevailing pioneers have good instinct, or whatever quality it is that makes a few pioneers geniuses while most of them turn out to be wastrels.

Momentum, or Runs, in Variation. Most of us are familiar with the behavior of a pendulum. If the pendulum is at rest and we push it, it will oscillate with steadily dampening movements until it eventually comes to rest again. Let us suppose that we had the problem of predicting the position of the pendulum. Let us suppose further that the force that activates the pendulum is essentially intermittent in its action, perhaps even essentially random as far as we know. Furthermore, the strength of the force varies, again intermittently. The best way to predict the position of the pendulum would be to study its past behavior. We soon notice this tendency of the swings to dampen unless the force were being applied so frequently that rarely would the pendulum complete two swings before it is impelled again. If the outside force appears frequently enough,

it may be that the pendulum never really shows this dampening effect to the naked eye. In fact, this is exactly what happens to the pendulum in a clock. (The clock is designed, of course, so that the outside force is as constant as possible in its strength and in its time interval, thus producing a pendulum with an essentially constant oscillation.)

Whenever we have a phenomenon that is being acted upon by two or more *opposite*, but not constantly equal, forces, we get a variation called a *run*, or *momentum*. This may be what goes on when we observe a business cycle. Economic activity has always been characterized by alternation of prosperity and depression. The ups and downs have not been too closely approximated by a periodic curve of constant amplitude and length. However, we definitely have not fluctuated from prosperity to depression on a day-to-day basis, although occasionally we have had panics that have caused rather sharp drops over very short time periods. Generally we find that it has taken *time* for activity to progress from peaks of prosperity to depths of depression. Since it does take time, it is possible to forecast tomorrow's activity by reference to today's. Furthermore, it is sometimes possible to predict a *continued rise* in activity (or a fall) because there has been a *run* of rises (or falls). What makes it tricky is that the run has to have a certain minimum length to assure us that it is unlikely to be a *random* rise; also the run cannot be too long because we then fear that it has exhausted itself and will give way to a reverse run.

Table 16.1 shows the lengths of runs in business activity in the United States as estimated by Geoffrey Moore of the National Bureau of Economic Research and extended by reference to the turning points of the Federal Reserve Board Index of Industrial Production. It is obvious that the lengths have varied over the years. Note that the runs of upswings have been generally longer than the runs of downswings, behavior consistent with the long-term growth of the economy. This differential in length is particularly pronounced during the last 15 to 25 years, with the lengths of downswings very short.

Some analysts would rather look upon the ups and downs in general business activity as disturbed cycles rather than runs. Their theory is that there are underlying cyclical forces similar to those affecting seasonal variation, but that these forces are being partially offset by disturbances which cause variations in the lengths and amplitudes of the cycles. These analysts try to discover the length and amplitude of this underlying cycle. For example, there has been

TABLE 16.1

Length of Cycle Phases in United States *

(As Indicated by National Bureau of Economic Research Reference Dates to
June, 1938 and by Federal Reserve Index of Industrial Production since)

Trough	Peak	Expansion (in Months)	Trough	Contraction (in Months)	Full Cycle (in Months)
Dec., 1854	June, 1857	30	Dec., 1858	18	48
Dec., 1858	Oct., 1860	22	June, 1861	8	30
June, 1861	Apr., 1865	46	Dec., 1867	32	78
Dec., 1867	June, 1869	18	Dec., 1870	18	36
Dec., 1870	Oct., 1873	34	Mar., 1879	65	99
Mar., 1879	Mar., 1882	36	May, 1885	38	74
May, 1885	Mar., 1887	22	Apr., 1888	13	35
Apr., 1888	July, 1890	27	May, 1891	10	37
May, 1891	Jan., 1893	20	June, 1894	17	37
June, 1894	Dec., 1895	18	June, 1897	18	36
June, 1897	June, 1899	24	Dec., 1900	18	42
Dec., 1900	Sept., 1902	21	Aug., 1904	23	44
Aug., 1904	May, 1907	33	June, 1908	13	46
June, 1908	Jan., 1910	19	Jan., 1912	24	43
Jan., 1912	Jan., 1913	12	Dec., 1914	23	35
Dec., 1914	Aug., 1918	44	Apr., 1919	8	52
Apr., 1919	Jan., 1920	9	July, 1921	18	27
July, 1921	May, 1923	22	July, 1924	14	36
July, 1924	Oct., 1926	27	Nov., 1927	13	40
Nov., 1927	June, 1929	19	Mar., 1933	45	64
Mar., 1933	May, 1937	50	June, 1938	13	63
June, 1938	Oct., 1943	64	Feb., 1946	28	92
Feb., 1946	Oct., 1948	32	July, 1949	9	41
July, 1949	July, 1953	48	Aug., 1954	13	61
Aug., 1954	Feb., 1957	30	Apr., 1958	14	44
Apr., 1958	May, 1960	25	Feb., 1961	9	34
Feb., 1961					
Average		28		21	49

* Adapted from Geoffrey H. Moore, *Statistical Indicators of Cyclical Revivals and
Recessions*, Occasional Paper 31 (New York: National Bureau of Economic Research, Inc., 1950), p. 6.

some evidence that there has been a building, or construction, cycle of about 18 years in length in the United States.

Another group of theorists looks upon the ups and downs of general business activity as analogous to the weaving path of a ship at sea or of an automobile on a highway. The economy tends to drift off course, or at least it tends to drift off what we think the course should be. But since we are never too sure of where we are or of where we are going, we usually recognize a drift only after we have apparently drifted quite far off course. We then tend to overcorrect, thus sending the economy into a drift in the opposite direction.

A theory related to the preceding theory emphasizes that the ups and downs are fundamentally a product of our remembered past experience. Since experience tells us that the economy has gone up and down, we assume that it will continue to go up and down. Hence we eventually take defensive actions after the economy has run up for awhile because "what goes up must come down." These defensive actions then precipitate the downswing, thus "confirming" the theory. Conversely, we assume that the economy can run down only so many months. Hence we start taking offensive action to take advantage of the expected upturn. These offensive actions then precipitate the upturn, again "confirming" the theory of the inevitability of the ups and downs.

It is not our task to pursue further the subtleties of *why* economic activity tends to run. We wish only to point to enough of the issues so we can recognize that *what we eventually do with our analysis of the evidence will depend to some extent on our theory of why the runs occur.* It is just about impossible to be completely objective in our analysis, and we are not at all confident that we should try to be completely objective. What we eventually accomplish with our personal career, or with our business, or with our national economy will depend at least in part on the faith we have in the goals we set. Although we wish to be realistic in setting our goals, we wish to avoid being so realistic that we never do more than reproduce past experience. Attempts to grow always involve a stepping out into the unknown, into areas where past experience is not a perfect guide to what might happen, and where failure is often more frequent than success.

Episodic Variations. When a modern nation gets involved in war, it finds that massive forces are released which rather completely alter the ordinary business of life. The nation tends to step up its efforts considerably, so much so that those remaining at home will frequently produce more than the nation produced before millions of people left the working force to become soldiers. War has a way of making clear what must be done, so we set about to do it, to the exclusion of many other things that normally distract and divide us. The resultant activity soon shows up in the economic figures and we have a "boom."

We call the economic consequences of such episodes as war, revolution, famine, etc., *episodic variations*. We assume that such events do not reoccur on any regular schedule. In fact, we hope that they never reoccur, although there is some evidence that such episodes may be necessary to toughen a society so that it will go on paths of future development that it could never have found without the stimulus of a crisis.

Some analysts believe that episodic variations are the principal sources of the disturbances referred to earlier and which set in motion the runs and oscillations in the economy. They believe that the economy would eventually become essentially stationary, similar to the kind of stagnation that prevailed during the so-called Middle Ages, unless it were to be occasionally shocked by episodic forces.

The essential point about episodic variations from an analytical viewpoint is that the episode and its economic consequences are so vivid that we have no trouble identifying the nature and source of the *initial* impact. The trouble develops as we try to trace through the ramifications of this initial impact. For example, the decade of the 1960's almost certainly will feel some of the effects of the forces set in motion by World War II, and perhaps even some of the effects of the forces set in motion by World War I. The same thing can be said about the ramifications of forces set in motion by major financial panics. Many of the men making the major decisions today in American corporations were brought up during the days of the 1929 crash. Their thinking is still colored by that traumatic experience. Although we feel confident that such secondary effects exist, we have had little success in working out methods for measuring them.

Residual Variations. After we have identified the periodic, the progressive-persistent, the runs, and the episodic variations in a given series, the remaining variation is the *residual* variation. This is the variation that presumably has no pattern or system beyond that which might easily have occurred by chance in a small sample. Thus it is in the nature of a *random* variation, a variation that we can predict only on a "how often" basis.

16.4 Relationship of Time Series Analysis to Correlation Analysis

We analyze time series in essentially the same way we analyzed a correlation problem. We take time as the independent variable and try to describe any relationship we think we see between variation in time and variation in the dependent series. The lines of relationship we look for are generally more complicated than the simple lines we generally use in ordinary correlation analysis. As we have already seen, we look for lines that describe a periodic relationship in addition to those that describe a progressive-persistent relationship. Progressive-persistent relationships are, of course, very analogous to a line of relationship in correlation analysis. In fact, some people calculate *least-squares* lines to estimate progressive-persistent movements.

There are some very important differences, however, between a time series problem and a correlation problem. The primary differences are: (1) the samples of data arise in different ways; (2) the relationship is much more complex in a time series; and (3) *extrapolation* is *required* in the practical application of the results of time series analysis. Let us look at these three sources of difference.

The Sample of Data in a Time Series

Suppose we take an ordinary deck of playing cards and draw out a random sample of *one* card at 12:01 P.M. of a given day. We then return this card to the deck, shuffle the deck, and draw out another random sample of *one* card at 12:02 P.M. Let us repeat this process until we have the results of 10 drawings, each a minute apart. Figure 16.3 shows the results of such a process. We now have a *time series* of card drawings.

Ordinarily we do not think of card drawings as constituting a time series because we *assume* that time makes no difference in the results. Therefore we do not even keep track of the time. Nevertheless, in a fundamental sense it is a time series. In fact, all events that can occur only *one at a time* are necessarily time series in the sense that time passes between the events. Whether or not time makes any difference is an *interpretation* we put on the data, and this interpretation should not be allowed to obscure the fact of whether the series is or is not a time series.

If we *date* each universe as of the time the sample came out, we

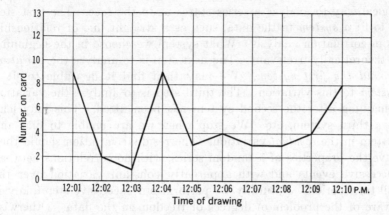

Fig. 16.3 Results of random drawing of 10 cards from an ordinary deck of playing cards. (Card replaced after each drawing.)

have the interesting case wherein it is impossible to ever draw *more than one item out of the exact-same universe.* For example, it is impossible for a company to get two *samples* of its monthly sales volume during the month of June, 1961. Only *one* sample can possibly occur. The next sample will occur in July. Any observed difference between the June and July sales may be associated with the passage of time or it may be associated with simply a random variation in monthly sales, in the same way that we might decide that the decline of 6 from 12:01 to 12:02 was simply a random variation and not associated with the passage of time. In either case, *we* have to decide what to call it. There is no law or fact that can determine it.

Since we can never get more than one sample item out of a given dated universe, we are obviously handicapped when it comes to drawing inferences about the universe from which this item came. We would have no information whatsoever about the *variation* that might have existed in that universe *as long as we confined our attention to that one item and that one universe.* We solve this problem the same way we solved the similar problem in correlation analysis. We *assume* that the *averages* of these universes differ *systematically* and that the *dispersions* within these universes are the *same,* or, if the dispersions are different, we assume that they differ *systematically.* Naturally, the systems we always refer to are those we think exist.

As soon as we adopt this model of the behavior of time series, the logical way to analyze a series stares us in the face. The first step is to fit a *system* to the data, such as a straight line of relationship as in correlation analysis. What system we choose in the beginning is theoretically irrelevant. The next step is to analyze the *variation around the first system*. We may then find it desirable to fit a *system* to this variation. The third step is to analyze the variation remaining after the second system has been fitted. This may lead to a third system, etc. We stop when we are unable to find any system in the *residual* variation. The residual variation should then have the properties of a random series, with no correlations between successive events and with apparently constant variation over the full time period. Naturally we perform our successive step analysis aware of the problem of degrees of freedom in the data. Otherwise we end up with systems that have been imposed on the data by the analyst rather than with systems that actually exist in the data; and it is probably worse to act as though we know, when we do not, than it is to act with a known degree of ignorance.

Time Series Relationships Are Complex

In view of the preceding discussion it is probably redundant to state that time series relationships are more complex than those we encounter in typical correlation analysis. They are so complex that we prefer to handle the problem by distilling several relatively simple systems rather than trying to discover some master system. This method of analysis creates some interesting problems of its own, but they are not serious deficiencies as long as we are aware of what we are doing.

The Need to Extrapolate

We emphasized the importance of distinguishing the *interpolation* range of the independent variable from the *extrapolation* range in the application of correlation analysis. The historical data always straddle the interpolation range. We, therefore, have reasonable confidence that future items that occur within this range will conform to the historical patterns. Although we find that the patterns within the interpolation range give us some *hints* of the probable patterns in the extrapolation range, we would never be so brash as to assume that we should have as much confidence with our extrapolations as we have with our interpolations.

Unfortunately, all future events in time series necessarily occur in the extrapolation range, with the possible exception of seasonal variations, which, of course, are only part of the total variation in the series. The year 1960 will never occur again, or at least not as far as we know. July will probably occur again, but it will be July of a later year.

The need to extrapolate makes time series analysis a "catch-as-catch-can" procedure. In fact, some analysts argue that *techniques of time series analysis* are meaningful to talk about only in the analysis of seasonal variations. Any other conversation is simply a way of padding a statistics course in a manner that would be tolerated only by a naive and/or captive audience. They would argue that intelligent analysis of time series is more a matter of becoming educated in the intricacies of the subject to be forecasted than a matter of technique. For example, the best place to get a weather forecast is from a meteorologist, not from a mathematical statistician. Similarly, a good source for a forecast of the sales of Chevrolet cars is the Chevrolet Division of General Motors.

While there is undoubtedly much merit in this discounting of technique, it is still stimulating to explore some of the technical aspects of time series analysis. A direct advantage may come from the stimulation and guidance it gives to our efforts to become educated in some particular area of application. Thus it might help in telling us what we should try to learn in a specific field of application. An indirect advantage may come from the fact that a minimum knowledge of technique often protects us from being mesmerized by the technical applications of others. We are no longer such a naive audience.

16.5 Correlating Two Or More Time Series

Since it is unlikely that time is really the underlying explanatory variable when we study a time series, it is not surprising that we frequently attempt to correlate various time series with each other rather than with time itself. For example, suppose our company sells a staple consumer product like sugar. We may reason that *population* growth would be the primary factor underlying the growth of our market. Hence we correlate the changes in population over the years with the changes in our sales and find a relatively high association. We could now forecast our sales by first *forecasting* population and then substituting the population forecast in the estimating equation. (Note that we would probably be working in the extrapolation range.)

This type of correlation analysis is very popular, whether done graphically or mathematically. It comes under severe censure by many people, however, if the analysis never gets more sophisticated than that described. One criticism is that this technique merely *transfers* the forecasting problem from one series to another, and we have no reason to believe that we can forecast the independent variable so accurately that the indirect forecast of the dependent variable would be any more accurate than if we had forecasted it directly as a time series. Another criticism is that this type of analysis merely correlates the *trends* of the two series. There might be other systematic movements in the two series that would also be correlated if we were to isolate them by standard types of time series analysis.

An interesting way to handle the first criticism is to search for other variables that *lead* movements in the dependent variable. This is obviously a very useful idea. If we found, for example, that movements in Series *A* preceded movements in Series *B* by 4 months on the average, we could forecast Series *B* by simply watching Series *A*. Thus we would have a *barometer* of movements in Series *B* the way air pressure is a barometer of precipitation in weather forecasting. Unfortunately, there are surprisingly few economic events that lead other economic events consistently enough and with enough lead to provide us with practical guides. One of our problems is that the lag in the reporting of information on the lead series is longer than the length of the average lead. The National Bureau of Economic Research has done considerable research into the existence of leads and lags in various economic series and has published lists of leading indicators of changes in business activity, coincident indicators, and lagging indicators.[1]

Another problem in trying to discover consistent leading indicators flows from the *reactions* of businessmen and consumers to any evidences of leading tendencies. Suppose, for example, that we were to discover that the price of General Motors common stock lagged 10 days on the average behind movements in the price of Standard Oil of New Jersey common stock. We would watch the price of Jersey Standard and then take the proper action with respect to General Motors. If Jersey went up, we would buy GM, and vice versa. If only *we* knew this, and if we had only a small capital fund, we could probably take advantage of this lead-lag phenomenon for many

[1] For current data on such indicators see *Business Cycle Developments,* published monthly by the United States Department of Commerce, Bureau of the Census.

weeks. What is more likely is that others would discover the same thing, or we would get greedy and try to increase our rate of purchases and sales. We would then discover that the length of the lead would begin to shorten as a result of the induced buying and selling action. If the knowledge of the lead became common, the lead would disappear entirely! The last entrants would probably find themselves actually victimized by a *lag* whereas there was a *lead* before because the induced market action, based on something that was no longer true, would push the price of General Motors higher or lower than could be sustained by the fundamental market forces.

In fact, we might generalize that no *discernible* lead in economic series will sustain itself if it is possible to make money by taking advantage of the knowledge of the lead. Thus, if we wish to make money by taking advantage of leads, we are going to have to do it before others know about it; and we are going to have to do it before indications of the lead are clear enough for others and us to be sure it exists; and we still have the risk that we are reading a system into the data that is not there.

16.6 The Use of Time as an Index of Other Variables

In an earlier chapter (Chapter 4) we pointed out we frequently measure one variable, such as ability to learn school subjects, by reference to another variable, such as age. We do this for many reasons, a few of which we mention here. One of the most commonly used measures is time, particularly as it reflects age. For example, seniority, the number of years on the job, is taken as a measure of the value of a worker. Automobile dealers have an association which publishes a book which tells the dealer how much a used car is worth with sole reference to the age of the car.

The assumption that underlies this practice of using time as an index of another variable is that the *correlation* between variations in time and variations in the other variable are sufficiently close so that the resultant errors are of little practical consequence. Most intelligent people use such a time index only as a *guide*. For example, the intelligent automobile dealer will start with the book price, and with the notion that this is a fair price for the *average* car of this vintage. He then modifies in the direction considered appropriate by the departure of the particular car from the average. The unimaginative dealer follows the book and offers too much for the poor cars, which he thereby acquires, and too little for the good cars, which therefore get sold to his competitors. Thus he systematically and objectively runs himself out of business.

The use of time as an index has two rather obvious advantages. One, it is very easy to measure and just about everybody understands it. (With the possible exception of people like Archie Moore and Satchel Paige.) Two, it has *objectivity*, a very desirable quality when we are dealing with people. For example, if we tell an executive he must retire because he is 65 years old and a company rule requires retirement at that age, we have none of the implications we would have if we tell the executive that he must retire because he is senile, or because he is forgetful, etc. Thus we find it very advantageous to work out book rules based on time. We make some mistakes when we apply these rules, but if we are intelligent about it, the cost of these mistakes will be less than the cost of trying to use other measures.

PROBLEMS AND QUESTIONS

16.1(*a*) Select a major United States corporation and collect its annual dollar sales figures for the most recent 15 years.

(*b*) Analyze the history of the corporation for existence of mergers, purchases of other companies, introduction of products in new fields, etc.

(*c*) *What* is measured by the variation in the company sales over the years? You should also consider the problem of price changes and the problem of changes in the "product and style mix."

(*d*) Chart your sales data on both arithmetic and logarithmic scales and then extrapolate the apparent average rate of change of sales. What assumptions are implied by your extrapolation with respect to the company's future rate of acquisition of other companies, expansion of the product line, price changes, general rate of growth of the American economy, etc.?

Do these assumptions strike you as reasonable?

What modifications would be necessary in your extrapolation to allow for any such assumption that you believe will *not* prevail?

16.2(*a*) As a business manager, what advantages do you see in having *daily* sales figures in contrast to only *monthly* sales figures?

(*b*) The electronics and computer people are already contemplating the day when an executive in a central office will be able to observe the minute-by-minute rate of sales of his products as fast as they take place all over the country. Such an elaborate set-up of computer equipment, leased telephone wires, and television projection and receiving facilities will obviously cost money. What advantages might such instantaneous reporting give a company that would justify its cost? Do you believe that such systems will eventually come to pass, or do you look upon this as "pipe dreams"?

16.3 Classify each of the following variables as being *cumulative* or *noncumulative*.

(*a*) Dollar sales of a company.

(*b*) Weekly wage of an employee.

(c) Your weight from year to year.

(d) Heights of school children.

(e) Unit cost of production from year to year, or from department to department, or from company to company.

(f) Accounts receivable from week to week.

16.4 Does it ever make sense to add up a *noncumulative* series? Explain. (Hint: Note that the calculation of the arithmetic mean involves adding up the set of quantities.)

16.5 What kinds of systematic behavior, or variation, are you aware of in the following phenomena? Note whether you are aware of any *changes* in these systems over the years.

(a) The number of leaves on an elm tree.

(b) The time at which you eat breakfast.

(c) Your weight since birth.

(d) The number of people lined up at the tellers' windows in the local bank.

(e) The Gross National Product of the United States.

(f) The Dow-Jones average of the daily closing price of 30 industrial common stocks sold on the New York Stock Exchange.

(g) The daily closing price of General Motors common stock on the New York Stock Exchange.

(h) The winner of the American League pennant? Of the National League pennant?

(i) Your personal sense of your own physical well being.

(j) Your blood pressure.

16.6(a) Use sales as a measure of size and collect data on the annual sales of some company that has experienced what appears to you as an exceedingly high rate of growth.

(b) Plot the sales on arithmetic and logarithmic scales and draw in a smooth line that describes your impression of the growth curve for this company.

(c) Has the company been growing too fast for its own future health? Explain. (In answering this you should refer to the "conditions of healthy growth" as you see them. You will probably find it fruitful to examine the balance sheets and income statements of your selected company.)

(d) Some economic theorists attribute a business decline to the "unhealthy excesses" that accompanied the preceding "boom." Do you agree that such a theory has some validity? What are some of the manifestations of "unhealthy excesses"?

16.7 Momentum and friction are forces commonly at work in the physical world, with momentum tending to keep a body in motion in its initial direction and friction tending to retard this motion. Similar forces are often thought to be at work in the political, economic, social, competitive athletics, etc., worlds. Analyze the following phenomena for evidence of the action of forces similar to momentum and friction. Make note of any impelling forces necessary to initiate the motion. Also note the path of variation followed by the given phenomenon as it responds to: 1. an impelling force, 2. momentum, and 3. friction.

(a) The speed of an automobile.

(b) The rate of sales of a new model of an automobile.

(*c*) The rate of production of pages per hour as you work on a term paper or on a report to your boss.

(*d*) The variation in the success ratio of a baseball, football, etc., team. (You might consider this variation as it takes place throughout a given game, or from game to game, or from season to season.)

(*e*) The rate of sales of the various salesmen in the weeks following the annual inspirational sales meeting. Contrast this with the variation in the rate of sales during the 8 weeks of a sales contest.

(*f*) The progress of the relations between the United States and Russia.

(*g*) The fluctuations in general business activity in the United States (as measured by variations in the Gross National Product).

16.8 The commonly quoted statement "you can't turn back the clock" contains considerable wisdom. In our terms, it is the equivalent of saying that we cannot go back and get another sample from the old universe because the old universe has since been replaced by a new one. (This is a hard lesson for us to learn, and one which we would prefer not to have to learn. For example, as children we frequently play games that permit "take-overs," a practice we find it harder and harder to get away with as we get older. We sometimes are successful in preserving this practice on the golf course by permitting "Mulligans" on the first tee.)

In each of the following cases indicate the degree to which you think the universe shifts as successive samples are drawn out. Or, in other words, in which of these cases is it possible to have take-overs?

(*a*) A coin is tossed 10 times in a row.

(*b*) Ten cards are dealt from an ordinary deck.

(*c*) You throw the same dart 10 times in a row at a given target and from the same distance.

(*d*) You throw 10 "different" darts at a target.

(*e*) You take 10 quizzes during a course and have a grade on each.

(*f*) You test a sales talk you have worked out by giving the "same" talk to 10 successive prospects. (Would an average of your results be a good measure of the future usefulness of this sales talk? Explain.)

(*g*) You select 10 successive annual figures for the United States Gross National Product.

16.9 Discuss the advantages and disadvantages we derive by using time to measure the following phenomena.

(*a*) It takes 4 years to earn a college degree.

(*b*) It takes 60 minutes to play a football game.

(*c*) It takes 40 hours to do a week's work.

(*d*) It costs $8 a day to rent a floor sander.

(*e*) It costs $100 a day to buy an attorney's time.

(*f*) A baby should be fed every 4 hours. (Some books say this.)

(*g*) Depreciation on a building should be charged at a rate of 2% per year.

(*h*) A soft-boiled egg should be boiled for 3 minutes.

16.10 Give three examples of events, or symptoms, which precede some other event on a reasonably consistent schedule as far as your experience goes. For example, does a sneeze presage a nose cold?

chapter 17
The anatomy of an economic time series

Several approaches are available for the analysis of an economic time series. We confine our attention to only two. In this chapter we examine the *anatomy of an historical time series* using a model that has a long history and a wide use, thus justifying its being called traditional. In the next chapter we examine an approach that is quite explicitly oriented toward *predicting* the future behavior of an economic time series. Before embarking on either approach it is important to remind ourselves that no mechanical approach is over very satisfactory. *Judgment* is, and should be, a very important part of the procedure, and preferably judgment born of knowledge and experience beyond that which is obvious from the numerical data.

17.1 The Traditional Model

A simple model of an economic time series is

$$A = T \times S \times C \times R.$$

A is the value of an item as it *actually* occurs; T is the value the actual item would have had if only the secular *trend* had been operating on it; S is the magnitude of the *seasonal* force on the actual item; and C is the magnitude of the force exerted by the ups and down in general business activity. Since this force used to be thought of as a *cyclical* force, it has become traditional to call it C. R is the *residual*, or, as some prefer, the *random* variation. Many analysts prefer to call it I for *irregular* because rarely are strong attempts made to purify the residual sufficiently to satisfy some people's conception of *random*. For example, it is not unusual to leave *episodic* factors in with the residual factors. In fact, it is not unusual to distill out only the trend and seasonal variations, leaving the cyclical and residual, etc., as an unrefined conglomeration.

Units in the Model

The actual item has some unit of measure, such as dollars, or tons. Since the four components of the model are *multiplied* together (for reasons described below), we cannot assign this unit to all four components and get a meaningful product. We assign this unit to only *one* of the components, traditionally the *trend* component. We treat the other components as *ratios;* for example, a typical result might be

$$A = T \times S \times C \times R$$

$$246 = 228 \times .91 \times 1.20 \times .99. \qquad \text{(Units in \$1 million)}$$

Thus the analysis would reveal that the sales would have been $228 million if trend had been the only force operating; however, during this particular season of the year, seasonal was a depressive factor of .09, or 9%. General business activity was .20 above average, thus raising the sales 20%. Finally, the residual forces resulted in a minor drop of .01.

The Logic Behind Multiplying the Components

Experience suggests that the forces acting on an economic time series are *relative* in impact. Sears Roebuck's total December sales are affected by the Christmas season in about the same *proportion* as is the small town department store's. Obviously, however, the increase in Sears' sales from November to December is in the hundreds of millions of dollars in contrast to the thousands of dollars of the department store.

The same kind of reasoning applies to the cyclical, secular, episodic, and residual forces. The big farm loses more corn to the grasshoppers than the small farm, but they both suffer about the same proportionately. (Assuming other conditions the same.)

The only other simple way to combine the components is by adding them together. Experience suggests, however, that this procedure would be inferior to multiplication. Attempts have been made to develop more complex and subtle ways of combining components, and they are still going on. No significant successes of general applicability have been recorded, so we mention such subtleties only in passing.

Estimating Components in the Model

$A = T \times S \times C \times R$ is only a general statement for any model for analyzing a time series. It merely tells how to combine the components *after* we get them. Each of the components must be estimated and we must have a model scheme for doing it. For example, the traditional model for estimating secular trend has been the correlation model with a least-squares estimating line. Seasonal variation has been estimated in many different ways, some naive and others sophisticated. Cyclical variation analysis has been more notable for the frustrations created than for any successful techniques. Analysis of the residual is customarily by-passed. Most of the techniques that have been used to analyze the residual are rooted in probability concepts, and traditional analysts have seriously questioned the applicability of probability concepts to any aspects of the analysis of economic time series. Their argument flows from a fundamental theory that economic events are *not independent*. This lack particularly applies to successive events of the same series, such as the monthly sales of Sears Roebuck. Nobody really questions this theory, but many analysts are inclined to worry only about *dependence that they can measure*. If they cannot measure it, they cannot take it into account, and they feel they must treat such variations *as though they were random*, and as though they were subject to probability considerations. In our discussion of randomness and probability we found this view as the most attractive. We might add that most of the traditionalists also treat such unrationalized variations as though they were random. The difference is more what they call them than what they do with them. This is because there is only one practical way to deal with variations we do not understand. Some people do it implicitly and reluctantly. Others do it explicitly and with enthusiasm, sometimes with too much of the latter.

17.2 Estimating Seasonal Variation

We start our analysis of the components with the seasonal variation because it is the one kind of variation that we know something about. We analyze the seasonal variation that has existed in United States gasoline demand from 1951 to 1961.

Homogeneity of Data

The first item we check is the definition of the data and any changes therein. We collected the data from various monthly issues of the *Survey of Current Business* and from the biennial issues of *Business Statistics,* both compiled by the United States Department of Commerce. The following information on the homogeneity of the data was obtained from the footnotes given in *Business Statistics.*

Data represent the apparent consumption in continental United States of refinery and natural gasoline (including aviation gasoline), naphtha used for industrial purposes, and, through 1952, the low-grade gasoline blend in jet fuels. Domestic demand is computed from production plus imports, minus exports, plus or minus the change in stocks. Figures beginning January, 1951 reflect adjustment to a new basis of reporting bulk-terminal stocks and, therefore, are not comparable with earlier data. The export figures used in computing domestic demand . . . include shipments to noncontiguous U.S. territories.

An idea of the magnitude of the effect of the change in definition of "bulk terminal" can be gained from the fact that monthly average domestic demand for gasoline was 91.0 mil. bbls. on the *old* basis for 1951 and 90.8 mil. bbls. on the *new* basis.

An idea of the effect of the exclusion of jet fuel after 1952 can be gleaned from the fact that 1.0 mil. bbls. of jet fuel is included in the monthly average figure for 1952.

The collected monthly data are shown in Table 17.1 for the years 1945 to 1961. Note that two sets of data are shown for 1951 and 1952. The revised figures have been lowered by 1.0 million per month to allow for the amount of jet fuel that had been included in the original data. We confine our formal analysis to the data from 1951 to 1961. We thereby avoid the problem of the change in definition of bulk terminals and also some of the problems of interpretation of the post-World War II adjustments to a civilian economy. We are, of course, still plagued with any problems associated with the Korean War.

Lest we make the error of attaching precise significance to small differences in the data, we should note that it is not unusual to find differences up to 1 million barrels between the preliminary and revised items of these estimates of gasoline consumption.

Variation in Number of Consumption Days in a Month. Interpretation of the monthly variations in gasoline consumption is partly confused by the monthly variations in numbers and types of consumption days. The more obvious source of this calendar variation is the differing *number* of days in the various months. February is a consistently low consumption month because of its fewer days, in addition, of course, to the fact that it is a poor month weather-wise in most of the country. February data are also affected by the

TABLE 17.1

Monthly Domestic Consumption of Gasoline in the United States
(including Armed Forces consumption)
Unit: 1,000,000 barrels.

	1945	1946	1947	1948	1949	1950	1951	1952	Revised 1951	Revised 1952
Jan	52.0	51.7	57.1	61.3	63.1	67.0	80.7	86.9	79.7	85.9
Feb	48.9	47.7	50.6	56.5	58.0	63.3	72.6	82.0	71.6	81.0
				(54.6)				(79.2)		(78.2)
Mar	55.4	56.7	60.0	68.2	73.3	78.8	86.7	87.1	85.7	86.1
Apr	59.0	62.1	63.3	72.2	75.3	80.4	87.3	98.7	86.3	97.7
May	60.7	66.8	70.9	77.2	81.7	89.0	99.4	101.1	98.4	100.1
Jun	60.6	63.2	71.2	78.0	83.4	90.2	96.3	99.3	95.3	98.3
Jul	66.2	69.1	73.4	81.4	82.1	91.7	100.5	105.3	99.5	104.3
Aug	70.1	66.7	72.1	80.3	84.7	94.5	101.1	103.0	100.1	102.0
Sep	64.5	62.3	71.4	76.2	80.8	86.7	91.3	100.1	90.3	99.1
Oct	55.7	66.6	73.3	75.2	79.3	89.1	100.5	103.7	99.5	102.7
Nov	53.5	61.3	64.1	72.6	76.3	82.7	88.0	91.3	87.0	90.3
Dec	49.7	61.1	67.5	72.2	75.6	81.0	85.2	95.8	84.2	94.8
Average	58.0	61.3	66.3	72.6	76.1	82.9	90.8	96.2	89.8	95.2
				(72.4)				(96.0)		(95.0)

	1953	1954	1955	1956	1957	1958	1959	1960	1961
Jan	88.1	89.2	97.2	100.5	109.3	107.3	114.7	111.3	114.5
Feb	84.6	85.7	89.5	98.0	96.7	95.5	99.8	108.9	105.6
				(94.6)				(105.1)	
Mar	96.7	100.8	106.6	112.4	113.2	108.9	119.0	120.5	126.6
Apr	100.1	103.4	112.2	113.0	115.8	118.5	124.9	129.1	
May	104.2	103.4	116.8	123.6	124.3	125.1	127.0	130.0	
Jun	112.6	112.9	121.4	126.8	121.6	125.4	133.7	138.9	
Jul	111.0	111.5	116.8	120.7	130.3	130.9	137.1	135.8	
Aug	106.8	109.6	122.8	125.8	128.8	129.9	132.9	138.4	
Sep	103.6	103.9	114.3	111.6	113.6	120.4	130.3	128.5	
Oct	103.4	105.0	113.9	119.2	119.4	125.1	120.9	126.2	
Nov	96.9	101.3	110.2	112.1	107.7	110.6	116.1	124.9	
Dec	97.7	103.8	112.2	108.1	112.8	120.3	123.6	124.9	
Average	100.5	102.5	111.2	114.3	116.1	118.2	123.3	126.4	
				(114.0)				(126.1)	

Note: See text for source and description of data.

occurrence of leap-year every 4 years. Revisions for leap-day in February, 1952, 1956, and 1960 are shown in parentheses under the actual figure in Table 17.1. (The adjustment was made by multiplying the actual figure by 28/29.) We have made no adjustment for the different days in the various months because it is customary practice to make estimates for *actual months,* which would include the factor of different numbers of days. Preliminary estimates for February of leap-year would have to be multiplied by 29/28 to correct to an actual month basis.

Another cause of calendar variations in the data would be the differences in number of Sundays, Mondays, etc., from month to month and from one month of one year to the same month of the next year. Insofar as gasoline consumption, or, more exactly, gasoline purchases, vary from day to day within the week, some of the monthly variations would be due to these calendar variations. We have no way of measuring these daily variations and their impact on monthly variations, and we leave them in the data to get left in the residual variations or to get absorbed into some other class of variation. We assume that these calendar variations are quite small and can be safely neglected.

One possible disadvantage in ignoring some of these calendar variations is the disturbance they create in what otherwise might be relatively smooth seasonal variations. Seasonal variation in gasoline consumption is fundamentally caused by variations in weather. If we average weather variations over many years, we find relatively smooth transitions from month to month, and even from day to day. Thus weather would tend to cause relatively smooth transitions from month to month in gasoline consumption, assuming the months have equal days and assuming that weather is the almost exclusive cause of the seasonal variation. If weather were almost the exclusive cause of seasonal variation in gasoline consumption, we would be very tempted to adjust all of our data to a daily average basis and thus be in a position to work with smooth transitions. However, such factors as holidays, week-ends, pay-days, etc., affect gasoline consumption. These tend to disturb any weather-induced smooth transitions from month to month.

Charts in the Analysis of Seasonal Variation

A visual examination of the relationships among the various monthly data serves several purposes. It gives us a preliminary impression of the *actual existence* of measurable seasonal variations.

The mathematical mechanics of seasonal analysis are quite tedious, and we do not like to plunge in without some reasonable assurance that we will discover useful results. Also there are occasions under which a *graphic analysis* will be sufficient to provide a reasonably accurate measure of seasonal for the purposes in mind.

A visual examination will also alert us to any idiosyncrasies of data that probably warrant further investigation before we plunge into any mathematical routines.

Figures 17.1 through 17.3 show three useful ways to chart data for the study of seasonal variations. Each chart has a *logarithmic* vertical scale to show the gasoline consumption variations. The logarithmic scale enables us to concentrate on the *relative* variations associated with seasonal forces.

Figure 17.1 shows all the monthly data chronologically. It is quite evident that the series has a general upward drift from year to year, a drift probably reflecting growth elements associated with population growth, development of improved highways, growing intensity of automobile use associated with growth in income, etc. The straight lines connecting February, 1951 with February, 1961 and August, 1951 with July, 1961 make it easier to compare this apparent growth with what it would have been if it had maintained a constant per-centage rate of increase over these 10 years. It appears that the relative rate of growth is slackening. We get a better perspective on this problem of growth when we examine more years of data in a later section.

There seems to be little evidence of any significant cyclical[1] or episodic variations in gasoline consumption, although we may decide later to associate some of the minor undulations with fluctuations in general business or with some factors more particular to gasoline consumption.

The most obvious variation in the data is that associated with the months of the year. There is clear evidence of a rather regular pattern of this within-year seasonal variation. Figures 17.2 and 17.3 make it even easier to judge the consistency of this pattern. Figure 17.2 is a year-over-year chart. It is the kind of chart many business analysts use to plot new data as they become available. Such a chart enables the analyst to get a rough idea of the operation of

---

[1] We will use the word cyclical as shorthand to refer to variations associated with fluctuations in general business activity. These fluctuations are not strictly cyclical, but do exhibit runs somewhat akin to a cyclical kind of movement.

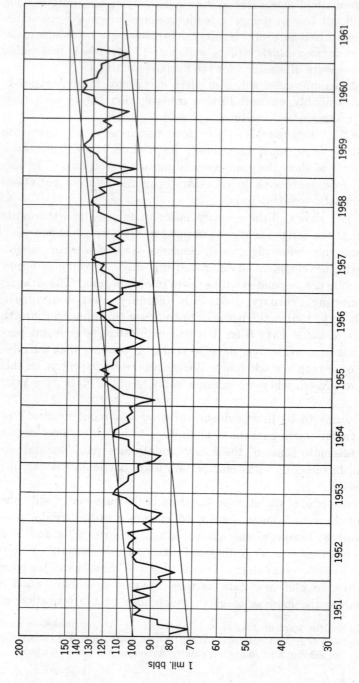

Fig. 17.1 Monthly domestic consumption of gasoline—United States, 1945-61. One million barrels. Vertical scale logarithmic. (See Table 17.1 for data.)

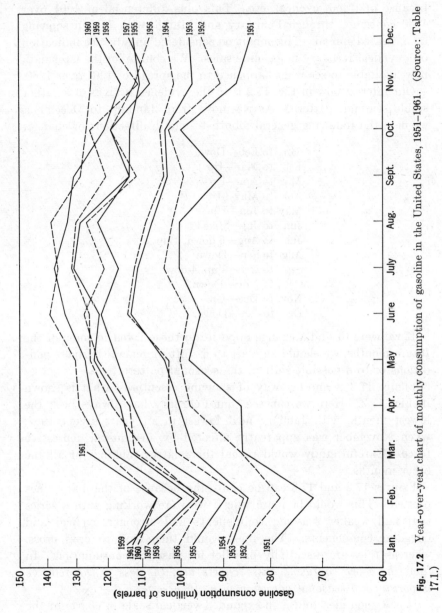

Fig. 17.2 Year-over-year chart of monthly consumption of gasoline in the United States, 1951–1961. (Source: Table 17.1.)

nonseasonal forces. For example, note that January, 1961 was slightly higher than January, 1960. This indicates a plus factor because of trend, cyclical, etc. This plus differential of 1961 over 1960 continued through February and March, with March showing an increased spread. This might be considered an advance indication of a cyclical recovery in gasoline sales. We could plot the later data now available to see what happened to the spread of 1961 over 1960.

Our interest now in Fig. 17.2 is in the evidence it gives of a rather stable seasonal pattern. As we move from January to December, we note the following general month-to-month directions of change:

> Jan to Feb—Down
> Feb to Mar—Up
> Mar to Apr—Up
> Apr to May—Up
> May to Jun—Up
> Jun to Jul—Mixed
> Jul to Aug—6 down, 4 up
> Aug to Sep—Down
> Sep to Oct—6 up, 4 down
> Oct to Nov—Down
> Nov to Dec—Up
> Dec to Jan—Down.

If we were to find a change opposite to those listed in some of the future months, we should be alert to a shift in general business conditions or to a possible shift in the seasonal pattern.

Figure 17.3 is another way of showing essentially what is shown in Fig. 17.2. Here we can see that February has always been the lowest month, with January next lowest in all years except 1957, when November was apparently affected by an unusual depressive force. Careful study would reveal the relative rankings of all the other months.

Figures 17.2 and 17.3 can be confusing because of the many lines plotted. This would be more true if we were working with a series that had weaker seasonal components and stronger cyclical and irregular components. The lines would then tend to criss cross, whereas they are essentially parallel for gasoline consumption. In fact, *the more confusing these charts are, the less is the relative importance of seasonal variation in a given series.*

It is a good idea to use an expanded vertical scale in charts of the 17.2 and 17.3 type in order to minimize the confusion in following the various lines.

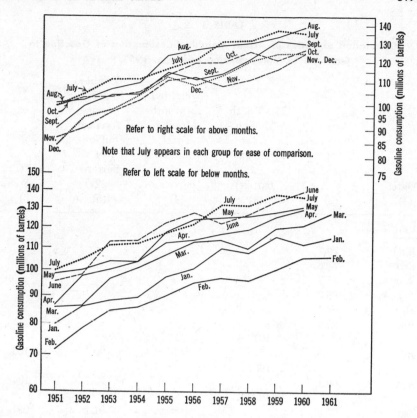

Fig. 17.3 Month-over-month chart of monthly consumption of gasoline in the United States, 1951–1961. (Source: Table 17.1.)

The One-year Moving Total and One-year Moving Arithmetic Mean

The theory behind our method of measuring seasonal variation is very simple. We start with an *actual* monthly item. We develop an item for the same month *from which the seasonal variation has been removed*. We then compare the two figures, with the *difference* being attributed basically to *seasonal* variation.

Since seasonal variation is a within-year movement, we would consider *annual* totals to be independent of seasonal. This independence would apply regardless of the particular calendar limits of the years. Although we ordinarily measure the year from January 1 to December 31, we might as well measure it from January 26 to January 25, etc. Column 3 of Table 17.2 lists the possible annual totals we can get from our gasoline data if we confine ourselves to terminal dates

TABLE 17.2

Calculation of Ratios of Actual Monthly Consumption of Gasoline to Centered 12-Month Moving Average, 1951 to 1961

Date (1)	Actual (millions of barrels) = A (2)	12-Month Moving Total (millions of barrels) (3)	Weighted 13-Month Moving Total (millions of barrels) (4)	Weighted 13-Month Moving Average (millions of barrels) = $TC'r$ (5)	$A/TC'r$ = Src' (6)
1951					
Jan	79.7				
Feb	71.6				
Mar	85.7				
Apr	86.3				
May	98.4				
Jun	95.3				
		1077.6			
Jul	99.5		2161.4	90.1	1.104
		1083.8			
Aug	100.1		2177.0	90.7	1.104
		1093.2			
Sep	90.3		2186.8	91.1	.991
		1093.6			
Oct	99.5		2198.6	91.6	1.086
		1105.0			
Nov	87.0		2211.7	92.2	.944
		1106.7			
Dec	84.2		2216.4	92.4	.911
		1109.7			
1952					
Jan	85.9		2224.2	92.7	.927
		1114.5			
Feb	78.2		2230.9	93.0	.841
		1116.4			
Mar	86.1		2241.6	93.4	.922
		1125.2			
Apr	97.7		2253.6	93.9	1.040
		1128.4			
May	100.1		2260.1	94.2	1.063
		1131.7			

TABLE 17.2 Continued

Date (1)	Actual (millions of barrels) = A (2)	12-Month Moving Total (millions of barrels) (3)	Weighted 13-Month Moving Total (millions of barrels) (4)	Weighted 13-Month Moving Average (millions of barrels) = $TC'r$ (5)	$A/TC'r$ = Src' (6)
1952					
Jun	98.3		2274.0	94.8	1.037
		1142.3			
Jul	104.3		2286.7	95.3	1.094
		1144.4			
Aug	102.0		2292.5	95.5	1.068
		1148.1			
Sep	99.1		2306.8	96.1	1.031
		1158.7			
Oct	102.7		2319.8	96.7	1.062
		1161.1			
Nov	90.3		2326.3	96.9	.932
		1165.2			
Dec	94.8		2344.7	97.7	.970
		1179.5			
1953					
Jan	88.1		2365.7	98.6	.894
		1186.2			
Feb	84.6		2377.2	99.0	.855
		1191.0			
Mar	96.7		2386.5	99.4	.973
		1195.5			
Apr	100.1		2391.7	99.6	1.005
		1196.2			
May	104.2		2399.0	100.0	1.042
		1202.8			
Jun	112.6		2408.5	100.4	1.122
		1205.7			
Jul	111.0		2412.5	100.5	1.104
		1206.8			
Aug	106.8		2414.7	100.6	1.062
		1207.9			
Sep	103.6		2419.9	100.8	1.028
		1212.0			

TABLE 17.2 Continued

Date (1)	Actual (millions of barrels) = A (2)	12-Month Moving Total (millions of barrels) (3)	Weighted 13-Month Moving Total (millions of barrels) (4)	Weighted 13-Month Moving Average (millions of barrels) = $TC'r$ (5)	$A/TC'r$ = Src' (6)
1953					
Oct	103.4		2427.3	101.1	1.023
		1215.3			
Nov	96.9		2429.8	101.2	.958
		1214.5			
Dec	97.7		2429.3	101.2	.965
		1214.8			
1954					
Jan	89.2		2430.1	101.3	.881
		1215.3			
Feb	85.7		2433.4	101.5	.844
		1218.1			
Mar	100.8		2436.5	101.5	.993
		1218.4			
Apr	103.4		2438.4	101.6	1.018
		1220.0			
May	103.4		2444.4	101.9	1.015
		1224.4			
Jun	112.9		2454.9	102.3	1.114
		1230.5			
Jul	111.5		2469.0	102.9	1.084
		1238.5			
Aug	109.6		2480.8	103.4	1.060
		1242.3			
Sep	103.9		2490.4	103.8	1.001
		1248.1			
Oct	105.0		2505.0	104.4	1.006
		1256.9			
Nov	101.3		2527.2	105.3	.962
		1270.3			
Dec	103.8		2549.1	106.2	.977
		1278.8			

TABLE 17.2 Continued

Date (1)	Actual (millions of barrels) = A (2)	12-Month Moving Total (millions of barrels) (3)	Weighted 13-Month Moving Total (millions of barrels) (4)	Weighted 13-Month Moving Average (millions of barrels) = TC'r (5)	A/TC'r = Src' (6)
1955					
Jan	97.2		2562.9	106.8	.910
		1284.1			
Feb	89.5		2581.4	107.6	.832
		1297.3			
Mar	106.6		2605.0	108.5	.982
		1307.7			
Apr	112.2		2624.3	109.3	1.027
		1316.6			
May	116.8		2642.1	110.1	1.061
		1325.5			
Jun	121.4		2659.4	110.8	1.096
		1333.9			
Jul	116.8		2671.1	111.3	1.049
		1337.2			
Aug	122.8		2679.5	111.6	1.100
		1342.3			
Sep	114.3		2690.4	112.1	1.020
		1348.1			
Oct	113.9		2697.0	112.4	1.013
		1348.9			
Nov	110.2		2704.6	112.7	.978
		1355.7			
Dec	112.2		2716.8	113.2	.991
		1361.1			
1956					
Jan	100.5		2726.1	113.6	.885
		1365.0			
Feb	94.6		2733.0	113.9	.831
		1368.0			
Mar	112.4		2733.3	113.9	.987
		1365.3			
Apr	113.0		2735.9	114.0	.991
		1370.6			

TABLE 17.2 **Continued**

Date (1)	Actual (millions of barrels) = A (2)	12-Month Moving Total (millions of barrels) (3)	Weighted 13-Month Moving Total (millions of barrels) (4)	Weighted 13-Month Moving Average (millions of barrels) = $TC'r$ (5)	$A/TC'r$ = Src' (6)
1956					
May	123.6		2743.1	114.3	1.081
		1372.5			
Jun	126.8		2740.9	114.2	1.110
		1368.4			
Jul	120.7		2745.6	114.4	1.055
		1377.2			
Aug	125.8		2756.5	114.9	1.095
		1379.3			
Sep	111.6		2759.4	115.0	.970
		1380.1			
Oct	119.2		2763.0	115.1	1.036
		1382.9			
Nov	112.1		2766.5	115.3	.972
		1383.6			
Dec	108.1		2762.0	115.1	.939
		1378.4			
1957					
Jan	109.3		2766.4	115.3	.948
		1388.0			
Feb	96.7		2779.0	115.8	.835
		1391.0			
Mar	113.2		2784.0	116.0	.976
		1393.0			
Apr	115.8		2786.2	116.1	.997
		1393.2			
May	124.3		2782.0	115.9	1.072
		1388.8			
Jun	121.6		2782.3	115.9	1.049
		1393.5			
Jul	130.3		2785.0	116.0	1.123
		1391.5			
Aug	128.8		2781.8	115.9	1.111
		1390.3			

TABLE 17.2 Continued

Date (1)	Actual (millions of barrels) = A (2)	12-Month Moving Total (millions of barrels) (3)	Weighted 13-Month Moving Total (millions of barrels) (4)	Weighted 13-Month Moving Average (millions of barrels) = $TC'r$ (5)	$A/TC'r$ = Src' (6)
1957					
Sep	113.6		2776.3	115.7	.982
		1386.0			
Oct	119.4		2774.7	115.6	1.033
		1388.7			
Nov	107.7		2778.2	115.8	.930
		1389.5			
Dec	112.8		2782.8	116.0	.972
		1393.3			
1958					
Jan	107.3		2787.2	116.1	.924
		1393.9			
Feb	95.5		2788.9	116.2	.822
		1395.0			
Mar	108.9		2796.8	116.5	.935
		1401.8			
Apr	118.5		2809.3	117.1	1.012
		1407.5			
May	125.1		2817.9	117.4	1.066
		1410.4			
Jun	125.4		2828.3	117.8	1.065
		1417.9			
Jul	130.9		2843.2	118.5	1.105
		1425.3			
Aug	129.9		2854.9	119.0	1.092
		1429.6			
Sep	120.4		2869.3	119.6	1.007
		1439.7			
Oct	125.1		2885.8	120.2	1.041
		1446.1			
Nov	110.6		2894.1	120.6	.917
		1448.0			
Dec	120.3		2904.3	121.0	.994
		1456.3			

TABLE 17.2   Continued

Date (1)	Actual (millions of barrels) = A (2)	12-Month Moving Total (millions of barrels) (3)	Weighted 13-Month Moving Total (millions of barrels) (4)	Weighted 13-Month Moving Average (millions of barrels) = TC'r (5)	A/TC'r = Src' (6)
1959					
Jan	114.7		2918.8	121.6	.943
		1462.5			
Feb	99.8		2928.0	122.0	.818
		1465.5			
Mar	119.0		2940.9	122.5	.971
		1475.4			
Apr	124.9		2946.6	122.8	1.017
		1471.2			
May	127.0		2947.9	122.8	1.034
		1476.7			
Jun	133.7		2956.7	123.2	1.085
		1480.0			
Jul	137.1		2956.6	123.2	1.113
		1476.6			
Aug	132.9		2958.5	123.3	1.078
		1481.9			
Sep	130.3		2965.3	123.6	1.054
		1483.4			
Oct	120.9		2971.0	123.8	.977
		1487.6			
Nov	116.1		2978.2	124.1	.936
		1490.6			
Dec	123.6		2986.4	124.4	.994
		1495.8			
1960					
Jan	111.3		2990.3	124.6	.893
		1494.5			
Feb	105.1		2994.5	124.8	.842
		1500.0			
Mar	120.5		2998.2	124.9	.965
		1498.2			
Apr	129.1		3001.7	125.1	1.032
		1503.5			

TABLE 17.2   Continued

Date (1)	Actual (millions of barrels) = A (2)	12-Month Moving Total (millions of barrels) (3)	Weighted 13-Month Moving Total (millions of barrels) (4)	Weighted 13-Month Moving Average (millions of barrels) = $TC'r$ (5)	$A/TC'r$ = Src' (6)
1960					
May	130.1		3015.8	125.7	1.035
		1512.3			
Jun	138.9		3025.9	126.1	1.102
		1513.6			
Jul	135.8		3030.4	126.3	1.075
		1516.8			
Aug	138.4		3034.1	126.4	1.095
		1517.3			
Sep	128.5		3040.7	126.7	1.014
		1523.4			
Oct	126.2				
Nov	124.9				
Dec	124.9				
1961					
Jan	114.5				
Feb	105.6				
Mar	126.6				

coinciding with the end of a month. For example, 1077.6 is the total of the 12 months of the year 1951; 1083.8 is the total of the last 11 months of 1951 and January of 1952; 1093.2 is total of last 10 months of 1951 and first 2 months of 1952, etc.

Since 1077.6, 1083.8, 1093.2, etc., are all annual totals, we argue that the differences among these figures must be independent of seasonal variation. If we could now compare such figures with data that include seasonal variation, we would be making progress toward measuring the seasonal component. We have two problems to solve first. First, we must *reduce the size* of these annual totals so they are of the same order of magnitude as the actual monthly data which contain seasonal factors. A simple and logical way to make such a reduction is to divide our annual totals by 12. Second, we must *re-date* these totals (or averages if we have already divided by 12) so that they correspond to the dates of the actual monthly data. Let us turn to the dating problem first.

The Problem of Dating Cumulative Time Series Data. The January, 1951 consumption was estimated to be 79.7 million barrels. It took the whole month of January to *accumulate* this total. Similarly it took the whole month of February to accumulate 71.6 million barrels in that month. Thus we can say that gasoline consumption has declined 8.1 million barrels between these two months. But, there is really nothing between January and February except the infinitesimal time interval between January 31 and February 1. Where, then, should we date these two figures in order to have a monthly time interval between them?

We must proceed by *assumption*. The conventional assumption is that the *middle* of the month is the best date to use to represent a month. If we take the 15th of the month as the middle, we can then say that, beginning with January 16th, we are starting to leave January and go into February. We continue to go into February until we reach February 15. After that we start leaving February and go into March, etc. Thus, we consider that the time between January and February is the time between January 15 and February 15, that between February and March is February 15 to March 15, etc. This assumption is also consistent with the equal distribution of ignorance rule which we find so commonly used. In essence we do not know which day of the month is the best to use to represent that month. As far as we know, each is equally good. The middle day, however, is the *closest* to all the days. (Remember the *least-error* property of the *median*.)

There are occasions in which we have definite reason to prefer one day within a month over another. For example, the date of Easter plays a definite role in the timing of sales in a department store, as does the date of Christmas, Independence Day, and other holidays. If such special dates are critical in a particular problem, we generally modify our analysis to allow for them. Generally, however, we find the effects practically negligible and use the more convenient 15th of month date.

To return now to our gasoline problem. If we date each monthly figure at the middle of the month, the average or total of the 12 months of a given calendar year would be dated at July 1, the middle of the year. Note that we placed the 1951 total of 1077.6 at a point midway between June and July, or at July 1. Similarly, the next total of 1083.8 is placed at August 1, etc. If we now add, or average, these two figures and two dates, we get a result that is dated at July 15. This latter date is the same as the date for the July actual figure of 99.5. Thus the 2161.4 in column 4 has a date corresponding to 99.5. Since 2161.4 is the result of adding 24 months of data (2 sets of 12-month data), we next divide the 2161.4 by 24 to get 90.1 shown in column 5. The figure 90.1 is a monthly figure for July which is *independent of seasonal* because it was based on *annual totals*.

We next divide the actual figure of 99.5 by the deseasonalized figure of 90.1 and get 1.104 shown in column 6. The departure of this ratio from 1 is presumably associated with seasonal to some extent. We analyze these column 6 figures shortly, but first we clear up a few points about column headings in Table 17.2.

Note that we headed column 4 with Weighted 13-Month Moving Total. This describes exactly what we did. The total of 1077.6 is the sum of the data from January, 1951 through December, 1951; 1083.8 is the sum from February, 1951 through January, 1952. Thus, if we add these totals together, we are really covering a span of *13 months* from January, 1951 through January, 1952. In covering this span, we really count the January, 1951 figure *once*, the February, 1951 through December, 1951 figures *twice*, and the January, 1952 figure *once*. We then have a *weighted 13-month moving total*, with 11 of the months given a weight of 2 and two of the months a weight of 1, and all the weights adding to 24. This is the 24 we divide by to get down to a monthly figure in column 5.

We label the monthly figure in column 5 as $TC'r$ to indicate that it has no seasonal. We put a prime on the C to alert us to the possibility that our averaging process has likely averaged out some of the cycle. We signify the residual by a lower case r to point up the strong likelihood that the averaging process has averaged out a significant part of the residual. Insofar as the residual behaves like a random series, it will tend to obey the same laws we have discussed in earlier chapters. Since we combined 24 monthly figures, with some double counting, we have the equivalent of a sample with 13 independent items. (The remaining 11 figures are not free because they depend on the other 13 in the sense that we can always deduce 11 from 13.) Hence we theoretically reduced the variation associated with residual by multiplying it by the factor $1/\sqrt{13}$,[1] or by approximately .28.

---

[1] This is based on our familiar formula: $\hat{\sigma}_{\bar{x}} = s/\sqrt{n-k}$

We label the ratios in column 6 as Src' to signify that we feel they contain practically all the seasonal, a significant part of the residual, and possibly vestiges of cyclical.

Our remaining task is to purify these column 6 ratios of Src' of the rc', thus leaving us with a measure of S.

Distilling the Vestiges of Residual and Cyclical Variation

The best way to see the nature of our remaining problem in the isolation of the seasonal variation is to chart the Src' ratios. Since the time sequence may be of some significance, we find it desirable to draw charts of the type shown in Fig. 17.4. Here we show the ratios separately for each month in chronological order. Our principal concern is whether the fluctuations from year to year in a given month's ratio show any evidence of systematic movements or of sharp shifts in level. We know, for example, that seasonal variation does not necessarily remain constant over the years. In fact, the gasoline consumption seasonal pattern has become a classic example of one that has shifted over the years. In the 1920's automobiles and highways were not conducive to winter travel. Hence the seasonal swing from July consumption to February consumption was quite wide. The gradual development of better antifreezes, the car heater, the immediate clearance of snow and ice, etc., tended to reduce this summer-winter differential substantially over the years. At the same time we were having regional shifts of population that resulted in a higher proportion of the population residing in the more temperate parts of the country. These changes are still going on to a degree, but they seem to be exerting a smaller net observable influence on the seasonal pattern of gasoline consumption. The development of the airplane industry, the mechanization of the farms, and the development of motor boats have combined to weaken the dominance of automobile consumption in the over-all seasonal pattern. If we look over the 12 charts in Fig. 17.4, we note no clear evidence of a shift of relative consumption from the summer to the winter months. Such shifts would have been quite noticeable during the decades preceding the one we are analyzing.

Analysis of charts like that of Fig. 17.4 is subject to considerable personal judgment. We are going to be seriously handicapped in exercising judgment because we know practically nothing about gasoline consumption beyond what shows up in the figures we have. We would be much better in our analysis if we had been working in the industry for years and had acquired specialized knowledge about the many factors that affect gasoline consumption. With these limitations in mind and with the strong possibility that we may legitimately differ in our interpretations, let us turn to these charts and make a few observations.

Although January shows a slight tendency toward higher ratios in the later years compared with those in the earlier years, we choose to practically ignore the possibility that January has shifted, or is continuing to shift, to higher levels. We have chosen to draw a horizontal line slightly above the median figure that happened to occur in 1955. The diamond at the right edge of the line is our forecast of the January ratio for the year 1962. We drew the line slightly above the median instead of at the median in order to make a slight concession to the possibility of this positive shift.

The February data make it very tempting to postulate the kind of downward drift shown by the curved line, although note that we have flattened the line to horizontal over the latest 3 years and into 1962. Note the circled dots in the February chart. These are the ratios we would have gotten for those leap years if we had not adjusted the data back to a 28-day basis. We can see that they are consistently out of line with the other items. A forecast for the next leap year in 1964 should, of course, allow for the extra day in February.

Incidentally, since February could not have become less important from 1952 to 1955 without another month or months becoming more important, we would not leave this declining line in February unless we could find where the increase apparently occurred. A quick glance through the other months shows that only in November was there any strong evidence of an increase from 1951 to 1955. Note how this increase in November not only stopped, but seems to have been replaced by a sharp shift back to the levels of the early fifties. The uncertainty about what we should now do with November points up the need to have some more information than available in these charts.

We make two more observations about these charts before concluding. Note that we have drawn a box around some of the ratios. These are ratios that seem to be sufficiently out of line to warrant a search for some episodic forces. We have not made such a search because it is best conducted by somebody who already knows considerably more about gasoline consumption than we do. We have generally ignored these boxed ratios in working out our lines and averages.

The other observation we wish to make is about our treatment of August. There seems to have been an abrupt upward shift from

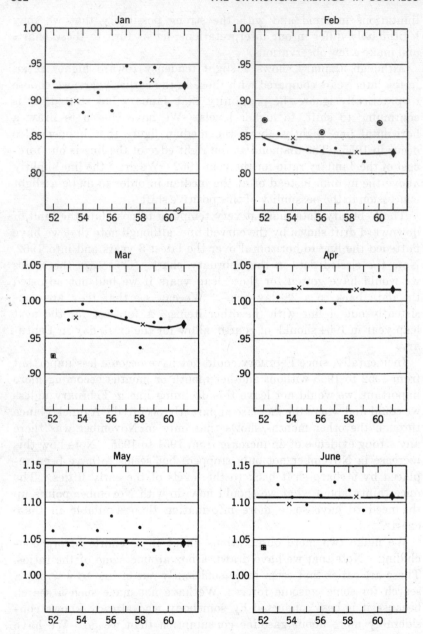

Fig. 17.4 Seasonal variation in United States gasoline consumption. (Data in Table 17.2.) Notes: 1. X's mark estimated averages of ratios for first half of years and second half of years. 2. Circled ratios in Feb highlight fact that these were "leap years." 3. Boxed ratios highlight very unusual ratios.

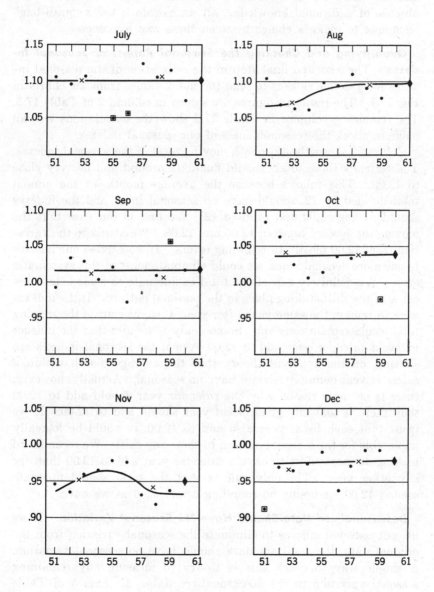

Fig. 17.4 Continued

1954 to 1955. On the other hand, it may have been that 1952, 1953, and 1954 just represented an unusual run of poor weather in August, and the series has now returned to its more typical level. In the absence of additional knowledge, all we can do is use a "grab-bag" technique to make a choice between these two hypotheses.

Quantifying and Checking the Seasonal Ratios, or Seasonal Indexes. The next and final step in the estimation of the seasonal indexes for gasoline sales is to read the index values from the charts in Fig. 17.4. The resultant figures are shown in column 2 of Table 17.3. The remaining columns in Table 17.3 show the calculations we can make to check the reasonableness of our seasonal indexes.

Column 3 shows the 12-month moving total of the seasonal indexes. Theoretically these totals should fluctuate around and be very close to 12.00. This follows because the average month, or the annual total divided by 12, should have no seasonal in it, and the indexes should average 1.00 and total to 12. We find in our case that the moving totals vary between 12.05 and 12.08. We attribute the variation from 12.00 mostly to rounding errors. If we carried our indexes to one more decimal place, we could eliminate most of this systematic error. We definitely expect the total to fluctuate to some extent because of the shifts taking place in the seasonal pattern. If the indexes were to remain the same year after year, then, of course, the moving total would remain constant. Some analysts require that the indexes *within a calendar year* add to 12.00 even if the seasonal indexes are shifting, on the apparent theory that the average month within a calendar year definitely should have no seasonal. Actually, however, there is no more reason why the *calendar* year should add to 12.00 than there is that any given *fiscal* year should add to 12.00. If we insist that each fiscal year also add to 12.00, it would be logically impossible for the seasonal pattern to show any shift. We recommend making no more effort to have a calendar year add to 12.00 than for any other year. The only rule is that the total should fluctuate around 12.00, assuming no rounding errors such as we have.

Deseasonalized Data Should Have No Seasonal Variation. If we use our seasonal indexes to eliminate the seasonal variation from the original data, the resultant data should have no seasonal variation. A simple way to check this is to try to measure any remaining seasonal variation in the deseasonalized data. Column 5 of Table 17.3 shows the deseasonalized gasoline consumption for the various months. It is calculated by *dividing* the actual data of column 4 by the seasonal indexes of column 2. The operation of *division* to elimi-

TABLE 17.3

Final Estimates of Seasonal Indexes of Gasoline Consumption, with Checks on Their Accuracy

Month (1)	Seasonal Index = S (2)	12-Month Moving Total of Seasonal Index (3)	Gasoline Consumption = A (4)	A/S (5)	Weighted 13-Month Moving Total of A/S (6)	Weighted 13-Month Moving Average of A/S (7)	Column 5 ÷ Column 7 (8)
1951							
Jan			79.7				
Feb			71.6				
Mar			85.7				
Apr			86.3				
May			98.4				
Jun			95.3				
Jul	1.10		99.5	90.5			
Aug	1.07		100.1	93.6			
Sep	1.01		90.3	89.4			
Oct	1.04		99.5	95.7			
Nov	.94		87.0	92.6			
Dec	.98		84.2	85.9			
		12.05					
1952							
Jan	.92		85.9	93.4	2209.5	92.1	1.014
		12.05					
Feb	.84		78.2	93.1	2215.5	92.3	1.009
		12.05					
Mar	.98		86.1	87.9	2225.9	92.7	.948
		12.05					
Apr	1.02		97.7	95.8	2237.7	93.2	1.028
		12.05					
May	1.05		100.1	95.3	2244.3	93.5	1.019
		12.05					
Jun	1.10		98.3	89.4	2258.6	94.1	.950
		12.05					
Jul	1.10		104.3	94.8	2271.8	94.7	1.001
		12.05					
Aug	1.07		102.0	95.3	2281.8	95.1	1.002
		12.05					
Sep	1.01		99.1	98.1	2300.2	95.8	1.024
		12.05					
Oct	1.04		102.7	98.8	2313.3	96.4	1.025
		12.05					
Nov	.94		90.3	96.1	2319.5	96.6	.995
		12.05					
Dec	.98		94.8	96.7	2336.4	97.4	.993
		12.05					
1953							
Jan	.92		88.1	95.8	2355.5	98.1	.977
		12.05					
Feb	.84		84.6	100.7	2366.1	98.6	1.021
		12.05					

TABLE 17.3 Continued

Month (1)	Seasonal Index = S (2)	12-Month Moving Total of Seasonal Index (3)	Gasoline Consumption = A (4)	A/S (5)	Weighted 13-Month Moving Total of A/S (6)	Weighted 13-Month Moving Average of A/S (7)	Column 5 + Column 7 (8)
1953							
Mar	.98		96.7	98.7	2375.1	99.0	.997
		12.05					
Apr	1.02		100.1	98.1	2380.2	99.2	.989
		12.05					
May	1.05		104.2	99.2	2386.7	99.4	.998
		12.06					
Jun	1.10		112.6	102.4	2395.6	99.8	1.026
		12.06					
Jul	1.10		111.0	100.9	2399.8	100.0	1.009
		12.06					
Aug	1.07		106.8	99.8	2403.6	100.2	.996
		12.05					
Sep	1.01		103.6	102.6	2410.4	100.4	1.022
		12.05					
Oct	1.04		103.4	99.4	2417.9	100.7	.987
		12.05					
Nov	.95		96.9	102.0	2420.5	100.9	1.011
		12.05					
Dec	.98		97.7	99.7	2420.0	100.8	.989
		12.05					
1954							
Jan	.92		89.2	97.0	2420.7	100.9	.961
		12.05					
Feb	.83		85.7	103.3	2422.9	101.0	1.023
		12.06					
Mar	.98		100.8	102.9	2424.9	101.0	1.019
		12.06					
Apr	1.02		103.4	101.4	2426.8	101.1	1.003
		12.06					
May	1.05		103.4	98.5	2431.9	101.3	.972
		12.07					
Jun	1.10		112.9	102.6	2441.6	101.7	1.009
		12.07					
Jul	1.10		111.5	101.4	2456.5	102.4	.990
		12.07					
Aug	1.08		109.6	101.5	2469.7	102.9	.986
		12.07					
Sep	1.01		103.9	102.9	2480.1	103.3	.996
		12.07					
Oct	1.04		105.0	101.0	2494.6	103.9	.972
		12.07					
Nov	.96		101.3	105.5	2515.9	104.8	1.007
		12.07					
Dec	.98		103.8	105.9	2536.4	105.7	1.002
		12.07					
1955							
Jan	.92		97.2	105.7	2549.0	106.2	.995
		12.07					
Feb	.83		89.5	107.8	2565.0	106.9	1.008
		12.08					

TABLE 17.3 Continued

Month (1)	Seasonal Index = S (2)	12-Month Moving Total of Seasonal Index (3)	Gasoline Consumption = A (4)	A/S (5)	Weighted 13-Month Moving Total of A/S (6)	Weighted 13-Month Moving Average of A/S (7)	Column 5 + Column 7 (8)
1955							
Mar	.98		106.6	108.8	2586.5	107.8	1.009
		12.08					
Apr	1.02		112.2	110.0	2605.3	108.6	1.013
		12.08					
May	1.05		116.8	111.2	2623.1	109.3	1.017
		12.08					
Jun	1.10		121.4	110.4	2641.0	110.0	1.004
		12.08					
Jul	1.10		116.8	106.2	2653.1	110.5	.961
		12.08					
Aug	1.09		122.8	112.7	2662.8	111.0	1.015
		12.08					
Sep	1.01		114.3	113.2	2674.9	111.5	1.015
		12.08					
Oct	1.04		113.9	109.5	2681.6	111.7	.980
		12.08					
Nov	.96		110.2	114.8	2688.9	112.0	1.025
		12.08					
Dec	.98		112.2	114.5	2700.3	112.5	1.018
		12.08					
1956							
Jan	.92		100.5	109.2	2708.7	112.9	.967
		12.08					
Feb	.83		94.6	114.0	2713.9	113.1	1.008
		12.09					
Mar	.98		112.4	114.7	2712.9	113.0	1.015
		12.09					
Apr	1.02		113.0	110.8	2715.3	113.1	.980
		12.09					
May	1.05		123.6	117.7	2722.4	113.4	1.038
		12.09					
Jun	1.10		126.8	115.3	2720.2	113.3	1.018
		12.09					
Jul	1.10		120.7	109.7	2725.6	113.6	.966
		12.09					
Aug	1.10		125.8	114.4	2737.7	114.1	1.003
		12.09					
Sep	1.01		111.6	110.5	2742.2	114.3	.967
		12.08					
Oct	1.04		119.2	114.6	2746.9	114.5	1.001
		12.08					
Nov	.96		112.1	116.8	2750.3	114.6	1.019
		12.08					
Dec	.98		108.1	110.3	2745.5	114.4	.964
		12.08					
1957							
Jan	.92		109.3	118.8	2750.2	114.6	1.037
		12.08					
Feb	.83		96.7	116.5	2761.7	115.1	1.012
		12.08					

TABLE 17.3 Continued

Month (1)	Seasonal Index = S (2)	12-Month Moving Total of Seasonal Index (3)	Gasoline Consumption = A (4)	A/S (5)	Weighted 13-Month Moving Total of A/S (6)	Weighted 13-Month Moving Average of A/S (7)	Column 5 ÷ Column 7 (8)
1957							
Mar	.97		113.2	116.7	2766.4	115.3	1.012
		12.08					
Apr	1.02		115.8	113.5	2768.6	115.4	.984
		12.08					
May	1.05		124.3	118.4	2766.6	115.3	1.027
		12.06					
Jun	1.10		121.6	110.5	2769.2	115.4	.958
		12.06					
Jul	1.10		130.3	118.5	2771.8	115.5	1.026
		12.06					
Aug	1.10		128.8	117.1	2768.2	115.3	1.016
		12.06					
Sep	1.01		113.6	112.5	2762.4	115.1	.977
		12.06					
Oct	1.04		119.4	114.8	2760.7	115.0	.998
		12.06					
Nov	.94		107.7	114.6	2764.1	115.2	.995
		12.06					
Dec	.98		112.8	115.1	2768.3	115.3	.998
		12.06					
1958							
Jan	.92		107.3	116.6	2772.3	115.5	1.010
		12.06					
Feb	.83		95.5	115.1	2773.8	115.6	.996
		12.06					
Mar	.97		108.9	112.3	2781.5	115.9	.969
		12.06					
Apr	1.02		118.5	116.2	2793.7	116.4	.998
		12.06					
May	1.05		125.1	119.1	2803.5	116.8	1.020
		12.05					
Jun	1.10		125.4	114.0	2815.5	117.3	.972
		12.05					
Jul	1.10		130.9	119.0	2831.3	118.0	1.008
		12.05					
Aug	1.10		129.9	118.1	2844.5	118.5	.997
		12.05					
Sep	1.01		120.4	119.2	2860.0	119.2	1.000
		12.05					
Oct	1.04		125.1	120.3	2876.7	119.9	1.003
		12.05					
Nov	.93		110.6	118.9	2884.9	120.2	.989
		12.05					
Dec	.98		120.3	122.8	2894.3	120.6	1.018
		12.05					
1959							
Jan	.92		114.7	124.7	2907.4	121.1	1.030
		12.05					
Feb	.83		99.8	120.2	2915.7	121.5	.989
		12.05					

TABLE 17.3 Continued

Month (1)	Seasonal Index = S (2)	12-Month Moving Total of Seasonal Index (3)	Gasoline Consumption = A (4)	A/S (5)	Weighted 13-Month Moving Total of A/S (6)	Weighted 13-Month Moving Average of A/S (7)	Column 5 ÷ Column 7 (8)
1959							
Mar	.97		119.0	122.7	2928.2	122.0	1.006
		12.05					
Apr	1.02		124.9	122.5	2933.9	122.2	1.002
		12.05					
May	1.05		127.0	121.0	2935.7	122.3	.989
		12.05					
Jun	1.10		133.7	121.5	2944.9	122.7	.990
		12.05					
Jul	1.10		137.1	124.6	2944.5	122.7	1.015
		12.05					
Aug	1.10		132.9	120.8	2947.2	122.8	.984
		12.05					
Sep	1.01		130.3	129.0	2955.1	123.1	1.048
		12.05					
Oct	1.04		120.9	116.2	2960.7	123.4	.942
		12.05					
Nov	.93		116.1	124.8	2967.7	123.7	1.009
		12.05					
Dec	.98		123.6	126.1	2975.4	124.0	1.017
		12.05					
1960							
Jan	.92		111.3	121.0	2979.1	124.1	.975
		12.05					
Feb	.83		105.1	126.6	2983.0	124.3	1.019
		12.05					
Mar	.97		120.5	124.2	2986.2	124.4	.998
		12.05					
Apr	1.02		129.1	126.6	2989.5	124.6	1.016
		12.05					
May	1.05		130.1	123.9	3004.1	125.2	.990
		12.05					
Jun	1.10		138.9	126.3	3014.9	125.6	1.006
		12.05					
Jul	1.10		135.8	123.5	3019.7	125.8	.982
		12.05					
Aug	1.10		138.4	125.8	3023.8	126.0	.998
		12.05					
Sep	1.01		128.5	127.2	3030.7	126.3	1.007
		12.05					
Oct	1.04		126.2	121.3			
		12.05					
Nov	.93		124.9	134.3			
		12.05					
Dec	.98		124.9	127.4			
		12.05					
1961							
Jan	.92		114.5	124.5			
		12.05					
Feb	.83		105.6	127.2			
		12.05					

TABLE 17.3   Continued

Month (1)	Seasonal Index = S (2)	12-Month Moving Total of Seasonal Index (3)	Gasoline Consumption = A (4)	A/S (5)	Weighted 13-Month Moving Total of A/S (6)	Weighted 13-Month Moving Average of A/S (7)	Column 5 ÷ Column 7 (8)
1961							
Mar	.97		126.6	130.5			
		12.05					
Apr	1.02						
		12.05					
May	1.05						
		12.05					
Jun	1.10						
		12.05					
Jul	1.10						
		12.05					
Aug	1.10						
		12.05					
Sep	1.01						
		12.05					
Oct	1.04						
Nov	.93						
Dec	.98						
1962							
Jan	.92						
Feb	.83						
Mar	.97						

nate seasonal variation is consistent with the model we started with. Our model stated that $A = TSCR$. If we divide both sides of this equation by S, we get $A/S = TCR$. The last three columns carry out the steps in the use of the 1-year moving average to isolate seasonal.

If we rearrange the column 8 data as shown in Table 17.4, we can better see whether there is any significant seasonal variation in these presumably deseasonalized data. We took the median ratio of each month as a simple check. Note that all medians hover around 1.00. If we wished, we could now adjust our original seasonal indexes to allow for the vestiges of seasonal variation still left in the data. Although we realize we may be just playing with rounding errors, we do go through the motions in Table 17.5 of making adjustments in order to illustrate the procedure. We show the adjustments only for the seasonal indexes as they appeared to stabilize in the last few years. Corresponding adjustments could be made in the earlier years when there seemed to be some evidence of shifting. Note that each

TABLE 17.4

Seasonal Analysis of Deseasonalized Gasoline Consumption
(Data are ratios of deseasonalized data to weighted 13-month moving averages of deseasonalized data)

	Jan	Feb	Mar	Apr	May	Jun	Jul	Aug	Sep	Oct	Nov	Dec
1952:	1.014	1.009	.948	1.028	1.019	.950	1.001	1.002	1.024	1.025	.995	.993
1953:	.977	1.021	.997	.989	.998	1.026	1.009	.996	1.022	.987	1.011	.989
1954:	.961	1.023	1.019	1.003	.972	1.009	.990	.986	.996	.972	1.007	1.002
1955:	.995	1.008	1.009	1.013	1.017	1.004	.961	1.015	1.015	.980	1.025	1.018
1956:	.967	1.008	1.015	.980	1.038	1.018	.966	1.003	.967	1.001	1.019	.964
1957:	1.037	1.012	1.012	.984	1.027	.958	1.026	1.016	.977	.998	.995	.998
1958:	1.010	.996	.969	.998	1.020	.972	1.008	.997	1.000	1.003	.989	1.018
1959:	1.030	.989	1.006	1.002	.989	.990	1.015	.984	1.048	.942	1.009	1.017
1960:	.975	1.019	.998	1.016	.990	1.006	.982	.998	1.007			
Median:	1.00	1.01	1.01	1.00	1.02	1.00	1.00	1.00	1.01	.99	1.01	1.00

TABLE 17.5

Adjusting Preliminary Seasonal Indexes for Vestiges of Seasonal Variation Discovered in Deseasonalized Data.
(Adjustments only to indexes that are applicable from 1959 on)

	Preliminary Indexes	Vestiges Indexes	Adjusted Indexes	Final Indexes
Jan	.92	1.00	.92	.91
Feb	.83	1.01	.84	.83
Mar	.97	1.01	.98	.97
Apr	1.02	1.00	1.02	1.01
May	1.05	1.02	1.07	1.06
Jun	1.10	1.00	1.10	1.09
Jul	1.10	1.00	1.10	1.09
Aug	1.10	1.00	1.10	1.09
Sep	1.01	1.01	1.02	1.01
Oct	1.04	.99	1.03	1.02
Nov	.93	1.01	.94	.93
Dec	.98	1.00	.98	.97
Total	12.05	12.05	12.10	11.98

of the adjusted indexes was reduced by .01 in order to make all 12 indexes add closer to 12.00.

The Notions of Average and of Specific Seasonal Variation

We all know that some summers are hotter than others. If a given series is affected by temperature, the magnitude of seasonal variation in a given *specific* year will depend on the temperatures *specific* to that year. If we analyze the seasonal variations, or the temperature variations over several years, we would expect most of these year-to-year variations to average out. If our seasonal indexes were based on such averages, we would have seasonal indexes that represented only *average expectation*, not the expectation specific to a given year. The seasonal indexes calculated in the preceding sections are *average indexes*. That is why we found the indexes practically the same in each year. Any differences which we showed in earlier years were not intended to represent *specific* seasonal variations. Rather they were to represent presumed *shifts in the average seasonal variation*. We were concerned with *patterns* of variation when we studied the 12 monthly charts. Thus our method of analysis automatically treats variations of specific seasonal from the average as *residual* variations.

If we wished to analyze specific seasonal variation, we would need more information than we have processed here. The only seasonal variation that we were able to analyze was that which was associated with *time*, in this case the months of the year. We paid no attention to any of the real variables that might actually be responsible for the seasonal variation in gasoline consumption. We make reference later to how we might use methods of multiple correlation analysis to solve the problem of specific seasonal variation.

17.3 Estimating Progressive-persistent Variations: The Secular Trend

In this section we confine ourselves to the estimation of the *historical* secular trend. In effect, we stand where we are now and look back to see the general path that we have apparently been traveling. We look forward only insofar as we must if we are going to judge where we have been going in the recent past.

Charts provide the best way to get perspective on where a given series has been going. They help us the same way the top of the mountain helps as a base if we would like to review the general path to the top. Figures 17.5 and 17.6 show the history of reported gasoline consumption in the United States from 1923 to 1960. Figure 17.5 has an equally-spaced vertical scale, or an *arithmetic* scale. Figure 17.6 has a *logarithmic* vertical scale. The logarithmic scale measures *relative* variations. If, for example, a straight line is drawn on a log scale, it would represent a *constant percentage* rate of change. The path of a savings account at 3% interest per year compounded would follow a straight line on a log scale.

Let us first examine Figure 17.5, the figure with an arithmetic scale. Let us ignore the smooth lines for the moment and concentrate on the actual data. First we note that we plot only *annual data,* in this case annual totals divided by 12 to put the series at the same order of magnitude as monthly data. By thus using annual data we avoid any concern with variations associated with seasonal variation. Beginning with 1923 the data show a very steady rate of increase until 1929. The increase continues to 1931 but at a slackening pace. If we recall our economic history, we remember that the fall of 1929 began the famous business collapse that ushered in the decade

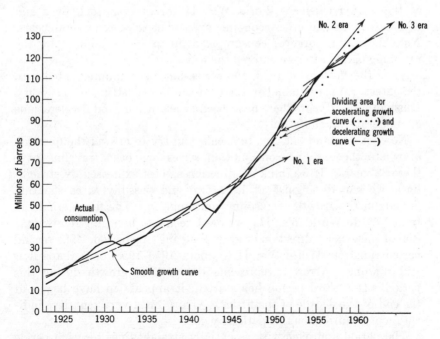

Fig. 17.5 Monthly average consumption of gasoline in the United States, 1923–1960, with visually fitted estimates of growth patterns. (Source: United States Department of Commerce, *Business Statistics,* various issues.)

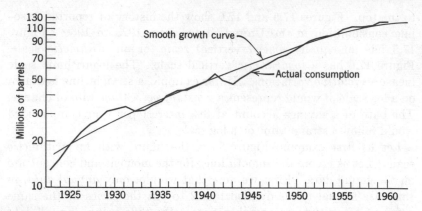

Fig. 17.6 Monthly average consumption of gasoline in the United States, 1923–1960, vertical scale logarithmic. (Source: United States Department of Commerce, *Business Statistics,* various issues.)

of the thirties. The data then turn up after the 1932 bottom and nearly parallel the rate of growth of the twenties except for hesitation at the 1938 recession. World War II forces then took over and dominated this and other economic events for the next several years. Note the initial surge of consumption up to 1941, followed by the rationing period after we entered the war.

Since the bottom of 1943, the series has risen uninterruptedly to the latest data available in 1960, an unbroken string of 17 years. During these 17 years there have been accelerations and decelerations of moderate amounts only.

Now let us stand back, so to speak, and try to answer the question of where the gasoline consumption series has been traveling over these 38 years. If we think of direction as best expressed by straight lines, we can distinguish at least two and possibly three separate periods in the growth of gasoline consumption. The first period ran from 1923 to World War II. Arrow 1 seems to be a fair representation of the general direction of growth during this period. The second period ran from World War II to about 1956–1958, or perhaps it is still running. Arrow 2 represents the path of growth during this period. If a third period has started, it appears to have begun at the end of the decade of the fifties. Arrow 3 is a very tentative indication of the direction this path may go.

The period approach with essentially straight lines for each period is attractive to those analysts who conceive of economic and political change as occurring in *waves,* or *eras,* with little logical continuity of movement from one era to the next. Such analysts might explain the period 1 era as the one dominated by the exploitation of the internal combustion engine in the automobile and truck, with the airplane making only moderate contributions. The second era witnessed the intensive application of the internal combustion gasoline engine to the airplane, boat motors, farm machinery, lawn mowers, etc. This was also the era of the trend toward big cars with high horsepower engines. The airplanes are now shifting to jet fuel (basically kerosene), the automobile public have become "economy-minded," the farms have been pretty much mechanized, and trucks now are usually run by diesel engines. Thus we may be entering a third era of growth of gasoline sales, with a rate slower than the decade of the fifties but faster than that of the twenties and thirties. What the fourth era will be like will depend on what happens to packaged atomic fuel, new developments in electricity storage techniques, etc. It may be that future generations will look back to the decade of the fifties as the golden era of the gasoline engine.

Other analysts are more inclined to try to make one era grow out of the preceding. The curved lines shown on Fig. 17.5 show the sort of growth paths they might draw. The theory is that growth is an essentially continuous phenomenon, with no real breaks between eras. Note that one of the curved lines shows only the one bend, with the line shooting upward at a pretty good clip at 1960. This line assumes that the last few years represent only a short-term departure from a continued strong upward growth. This departure would be identified as having been induced by the faddish concern with gasoline economy by otherwise profligate consumers, the moderate decline in general business, and a temporary plateau in the rate of technological advance in the gasoline engine. The surge of the fifties is presumably going to continue after these temporary depressants abate and after the development of the private airplane takes hold.

The other curved line has two bends in it and is really a smooth line connecting the three straight-line eras. A line of this shape, an elongated S, has had a very interesting history in man's attempts to discover the possible existence of *laws* of growth. The physical, chemical, and biological world we live in seems to have all sorts of rather inexorable laws of development and decline. It is not surprising, then, that man would look for similar laws in his social, political, and economic environment. One of the first phenomena studied scientifically on the basis of reasonably reliable data was population, both animal and human. It was hypothesized and then verified that population growth of certain insects would tend to follow the elongated S pattern provided the environmental conditions remained essentially the same. The insects had a natural tendency to reproduce themselves almost geometrically, just like the fabled rabbits. This tendency would produce the upward curving line like that shown in Fig. 17.5. This tendency, however, obviously could not continue indefinitely lest the particular type of insect were destined to inherit the earth. The general environment imposes certain restrictions on this tendency toward geometric growth. The restriction might be food supply, living space, natural enemies, etc. The effect of these restrictions is to impose a sort of moderately flexible ceiling on the maximum population. Starvation, disease, pestilence, warfare, etc. all combine to increase the death rate to levels consistent with the birthrate, the base population, and the restrictions. Thus the population curve turns from an accelerating, or geometric, rate of increase to a decelerating one, tracing a pattern very similar to that shown on Fig. 17.5 by the two-bend curve.

Such a theory of growth of population is very compelling. Its correctness has been rather well established in experiments with insects. The real problem is how to apply it intelligently to human populations and to economic and political institutions. The biggest stumbling block to making accurate predictions in human affairs is the same factor that gives man his greatest hope of preventing the inexorable playing out of such underlying physical laws. This is man's *adaptive* abilities. Although the history of man has been replete with starvation, disease, pestilence, warfare, etc., as population controls, the history has also been replete with examples of startling changes in the environmental restrictions. The gasoline engine, for example, may yet emancipate most of mankind from the threat of starvation as it finds even greater applications to the mechanization of farming. In fact, man has come to a stage in the Western World where incredible efforts are being expended to keep man alive under the most adverse conditions. Such efforts would never be made if we were already pressing the environmental limits for supporting our present population.

These adaptive movements that man makes suggest to some people that the notion of eras of growth and development as expressed by the separate lines on Fig. 17.5 is closer to the truth than any theory of continuous development. It is reasoned that man is not a *continuously adaptive* animal. Rather he tends to *shift*, and often rather abruptly, from one *routine* of behavior to another. A certain amount of pressure or discomfort has to develop before man is stimulated to make a change, and when he does make the change, he tends to leave a good many of the old habits behind. The reason that data on economic affairs do not show the changes as sharply as otherwise is that the data cover the behavior of thousands and millions of people. Each person may make an abrupt shift in a consumption pattern, but the timing of the shift differs from person to person. The spread of a fad throughout the United States and, even around much of the earth, illustrates the way a wave of adaptation takes place. The development of the communication arts in the modern world has made it possible for much of the earth to become aware of something at almost the same time. Thus we now find rather sharp shifts taking place in data that formerly were sluggish. For example, the cancer scare on cigarette smoking had an almost immediate and significant impact on total cigarette consumption. If it were communicated as in the 19th century, it would have been quite difficult to notice the impact of the scare on the data.

We have perhaps raised enough issues to make it clear that we do not feel at all competent to explain what *the* trend has been in gasoline consumption over the years. We suspect that there have been at least two eras of development, with the principal break between them occurring during and after World War II. What the future holds we would hesitate to guess without more knowledge than we have about the factors affecting the use of gasoline engines. Despite this hesitation, we nevertheless do make the guess that the decade of the sixties will show a growth pattern somewhere between those indicated by arrows 2 and 3. This is admittedly a fairly broad band, but any attempt to do better within the bounds of our present knowledge would run the risk of engaging in a bit of charlatanism.

Now let us look briefly at Fig. 17.6 where we have the gasoline data plotted on a logarithmic scale. A long sweeping curve has been drawn through the data to highlight the main feature of this chart, which is that the evidence is clear that there has been a *slackening* in the *percentage* rate of increase over the years. This impression is consistent with the notions we gained from studying the arithmetic scale chart. It is always a good idea to plot the data on both scales. Sometimes the patterns of development are clearer on arithmetic than on logarithmic and vice versa, and often the impressions reinforce each other. Occasionally we find that a straight line on logarithmic paper appears to be a very good description of the pattern of change. Then we would suspect that the series is undergoing a development that is still well within the environmental limits. The development of the electric power industry in the United States has shown a rather persistent percentage rate of increase over the years, for example. Various *particular* uses of electric power have run into saturation tendencies, but new uses have come forward fast enough to continually lift any apparent ceiling on industry development. It is possible that this development will continue until each consuming unit can have its own power cell, say in the form of an atomic-powered battery.

Estimating Specific Trend Values

If we wish to estimate specific trend values for various months or years, we can read them from our chart. The first question is, of course, to decide on the particular trend lines to use. We arbitrarily choose the three straight lines as our guides. We do this because we lean toward the theory of eras of growth, and also because we feel this procedure comes closest to what we would have done over the years if we had had to estimate trend at various times *during* the past, rather than having the advantage of the long look back. The natural human tendency is to plot a path of growth, say path 1, and then stick to it until events seem to call for a revision. The revision then usually leads to a definite departure from the previous path. Thus we might have revised to something like path 2, etc.

Column 3 in Table 17.6 shows the specific trend estimates which we have taken from the three straight lines on Fig. 17.5. Since the results are rounded to one decimal place, there is an occasional unevenness in the trend estimates that apparently belies the hypothesis of straight line changes. The monthly estimates are simple linear interpolations between the annual estimates taken from the chart.

The Use of Mathematical Methods in the Estimation of Secular Trend

It is possible to use mathematical methods rather than graphic methods in estimating a secular trend line. The mathematical method that has been most commonly used is the *least-squares* method, exactly the same technique we used in getting a line of relationship in correlation analysis. The theory of the use of a least-squares line as an estimate of secular trend is very simple. The path of the secular trend is essentially an *average* that runs through the data. If we use an *arithmetic mean* as the average, or a least-squares line, we are assuming that the *sum of the plus deviations around trend should equal the sum of the minus deviations*. (One of the properties of the arithmetic mean is that the sum of the deviations will equal zero.) This is another way of saying that there should

TABLE 17.6

Estimates of Trend, Seasonal, Cycle, and Residual Variations in U.S. Gasoline Consumption: 1951–60

	Actual (1)	Trend (2)	Seasonal (3)	Cycle Runs (4)	Residual (5)	Cycle and Residual (6)	7-Month Moving Average of CR (7)
1951							
Jan	79.7	83.7	.91			1.047	
Feb	71.6	84.1	.84			1.013	
Mar	85.7	84.5	.98			1.034	
Apr	86.3	84.8	1.01	1.040	.968	1.007	1.039
May	94.8	85.2	1.06	1.048	1.039	1.089	1.046
Jun	95.3	85.6	1.09	1.052	.971	1.021	1.048
Jul	99.5	86.0	1.09	1.061	1.001	1.062	1.060
Aug	100.1	86.4	1.06	1.068	1.023	1.093	1.068
Sep	90.3	86.7	1.01	1.062	.971	1.031	1.053
Oct	99.5	87.1	1.02	1.058	1.058	1.119	1.060
Nov	87.0	87.5	.94	1.054	1.004	1.058	1.058
Dec	84.2	87.9	.97	1.049	.941	.987	1.043
1952							
Jan	85.9	88.3	.91	1.044	1.024	1.069	1.051
Feb	81.0	88.6	.87	1.040	1.011	1.051*	1.041
Mar	86.1	89.0	.98	1.036	.954	.988	1.033
Apr	97.7	89.4	1.01	1.042	1.038	1.082	1.042
May	100.1	89.8	1.06	1.046	1.005	1.051	1.041
Jun	98.3	90.2	1.09	1.050	.952	1.000	1.044
Jul	104.3	90.6	1.09	1.053	1.003	1.056	1.060
Aug	102.0	91.0	1.06	1.056	1.001	1.057	1.054
Sep	99.1	91.3	1.01	1.058	1.015	1.074	1.055
Oct	102.7	91.7	1.02	1.060	1.036	1.098	1.061
Nov	90.3	92.1	.94	1.060	.984	1.043	1.064
Dec	94.8	92.5	.97	1.061	.995	1.056	1.064
1953							
Jan	88.1	92.9	.91	1.061	.982	1.042	1.061
Feb	84.6	93.2	.84	1.062	1.017	1.080	1.053
Mar	96.7	93.6	.98	1.062	.992	1.054	1.060
Apr	100.1	94.0	1.01	1.062	.992	1.054	1.061
May	104.2	94.4	1.06	1.062	.980	1.041	1.063
Jun	112.6	94.8	1.09	1.062	1.026	1.090	1.062
Jul	111.0	95.2	1.09	1.062	1.007	1.069	1.062
Aug	106.8	95.6	1.06	1.062	.992	1.054	1.062

TABLE 17.6   Continued

	Actual (1)	Trend (2)	Seasonal (3)	Cycle Runs (4)	Residual (5)	Cycle and Residual (6)	7-Month Moving Average of CR (7)
1953							
Sep	103.6	95.9	1.01	1.058	1.011	1.070	1.061
Oct	103.4	96.3	1.02	1.054	.999	1.053	1.049
Nov	96.9	96.7	.95	1.050	1.005	1.055	1.047
Dec	97.7	97.1	.97	1.046	.991	1.037	1.046
1954							
Jan	89.2	97.5	.91	1.042	.964	1.005	1.042
Feb	85.7	97.9	.83	1.037	1.017	1.055	1.032
Mar	100.8	98.2	.98	1.034	1.014	1.048	1.030
Apr	103.4	98.6	1.01	1.031	1.008	1.039	1.028
May	103.4	99.0	1.06	1.029	.957	.985	1.031
Jun	112.9	99.4	1.09	1.027	1.015	1.042	1.027
Jul	111.5	99.8	1.09	1.025	1.000	1.025	1.023
Aug	109.6	100.1	1.07	1.025	.998	1.023	1.023
Sep	103.9	100.5	1.01	1.033	.991	1.024	1.033
Oct	105.0	100.9	1.02	1.038	.983	1.020	1.033
Nov	101.3	101.3	.96	1.042	.999	1.041	1.037
Dec	103.8	101.7	.97	1.046	1.007	1.053	1.042
1955							
Jan	97.2	102.0	.91	1.050	.997	1.047	1.050
Feb	89.5	102.4	.83	1.054	.999	1.053	1.056
Mar	106.6	102.8	.98	1.056	1.002	1.058	1.060
Apr	112.2	103.2	1.01	1.059	1.017	1.077	1.057
May	116.8	103.6	1.06	1.062	1.002	1.064	1.062
Jun	121.4	104.0	1.09	1.064	1.007	1.071	1.066
Jul	116.8	104.4	1.09	1.066	.963	1.027	1.066
Aug	122.8	104.7	1.08	1.068	1.017	1.086	1.067
Sep	114.3	105.1	1.01	1.070	1.007	1.077	1.070
Oct	113.9	105.5	1.02	1.070	.990	1.059	1.070
Nov	110.2	105.9	.96	1.068	1.015	1.084	1.071
Dec	112.2	106.3	.97	1.066	1.021	1.088	1.068
1956							
Jan	100.5	106.6	.91	1.064	.974	1.036	1.063
Feb	98.0	107.0	.86	1.062	1.003	1.065	1.065
Mar	112.4	107.4	.98	1.060	1.008	1.068	1.063
Apr	113.0	107.8	1.01	1.058	.981	1.038	1.053
May	123.6	108.2	1.06	1.056	1.021	1.078	1.056

TABLE 17.6   Continued

	Actual (1)	Trend (2)	Seasonal (3)	Cycle Runs (4)	Residual (5)	Cycle and Residual (6)	7-Month Moving Average of CR (7)
1956							
Jun	126.8	108.6	1.09	1.054	1.016	1.071	1.047
Jul	120.7	109.0	1.09	1.052	.966	1.016	1.046
Aug	125.8	109.4	1.09	1.049	1.006	1.055	1.049
Sep	111.6	109.8	1.01	1.047	.961	1.006	1.038
Oct	119.2	110.2	1.02	1.045	1.015	1.061	1.039
Nov	112.1	110.6	.96	1.042	1.013	1.056	1.043
Dec	108.1	111.0	.97	1.039	.966	1.004	1.041
1957							
Jan	109.3	111.4	.91	1.037	1.040	1.078	1.043
Feb	96.7	111.8	.83	1.034	1.008	1.042	1.040
Mar	113.2	112.1	.97	1.031	1.010	1.041	1.030
Apr	115.8	112.5	1.01	1.028	.992	1.020	1.037
May	124.3	112.9	1.06	1.025	1.014	1.039	1.031
Jun	121.6	113.3	1.09	1.022	.964	.985	1.022
Jul	130.3	113.7	1.09	1.019	1.031	1.051	1.019
Aug	128.8	114.0	1.09	1.016	1.021	1.037	1.016
Sep	113.6	114.4	1.01	1.012	.971	.983	1.010
Oct	119.4	114.8	1.02	1.008	1.012	1.020	1.014
Nov	107.7	115.2	.94	1.005	.990	.995	1.005
Dec	112.8	115.6	.98	1.002	.994	.996	.995
1958							
Jan	107.3	115.9	.91	.998	1.019	1.017	.997
Feb	95.5	116.3	.83	.995	.995	.990	.995
Mar	108.9	116.7	.97	.995	.967	.962	.992
Apr	118.5	117.1	1.01	.995	1.007	1.002	.995
May	125.1	117.5	1.06	.995	1.009	1.004	.993
Jun	125.4	117.9	1.09	.998	.977	.975	.995
Jul	130.9	118.2	1.09	1.002	1.014	1.016	1.004
Aug	129.9	118.6	1.09	1.005	1.000	1.005	1.003
Sep	120.4	119.0	1.01	1.008	.994	1.002	1.006
Oct	125.1	119.4	1.02	1.011	1.016	1.027	1.016
Nov	110.6	119.8	.93	1.014	.978	.992	1.013
Dec	120.3	120.2	.98	1.016	1.006	1.022	1.014
1959							
Jan	114.7	120.5	.91	1.014	1.032	1.046	1.016
Feb	99.8	120.9	.83	1.012	.982	.994	1.009

TABLE 17.6   Continued

	Actual (1)	Trend (2)	Seasonal (3)	Cycle Runs (4)	Residual (5)	Cycle and Residual (6)	7-Month Moving Average of CR (7)
1959							
Mar	119.0	121.3	.97	1.010	1.002	1.012	1.010
Apr	124.9	121.7	1.01	1.009	1.007	1.016	1.011
May	127.0	122.1	1.06	1.008	.973	.981	1.003
Jun	133.7	122.4	1.09	1.006	.996	1.002	1.010
Jul	137.1	122.8	1.09	1.005	1.019	1.024	1.002
Aug	132.9	123.1	1.09	1.004	.986	.990	1.001
Sep	130.3	123.4	1.01	1.003	1.042	1.045	1.006
Oct	120.9	123.7	1.02	1.002	.956	.958	1.003
Nov	116.1	123.9	.93	1.001	1.006	1.007	1.002
Dec	123.6	124.2	.98	1.001	1.014	1.015	1.002
1960							
Jan	111.3	124.5	.91	1.000	.982	.982	.999
Feb	108.9	124.8	.86	1.000	1.014	1.014	1.001
Mar	120.5	125.0	.97	1.000	.994	.994	1.002
Apr	129.1	125.3	1.01	1.000	1.020	1.020	.998
May	130.1	125.6	1.06	1.001	.976	.977	1.002
Jun	138.9	125.8	1.09	1.001	1.012	1.013	1.000
Jul	135.8	126.1	1.09	1.001	.987	.988	.989
Aug	138.4	126.4	1.09	1.002	1.003	1.005	1.003
Sep	128.5	126.6	1.01	1.002	1.003	1.005	1.006
Oct	126.2	126.9	1.02	1.003	.972	.975	1.002
Nov	124.9	127.2	.93	1.003	1.053	1.056	1.003
Dec	124.9	127.4	.98	1.004	.996	1.000	1.005
1961							
Jan	114.5	127.7	.91			.985	
Feb	105.6	128.0	.83			.994	
Mar	126.6	128.2	.97		·	1.018	

be as much prosperity as depression over the course of the business cycle.

Before we can calculate a least-squares trend line, we must make two critical decisions, both based on personal judgment. The first is that of the *shape* of the trend line, whether a straight line, a compound interest or exponential type, or a parabola of some form, or an elongated S type, etc. The other concerns the *exact terminal years* on which to base the calculations. Different time periods will give different calculated lines. We have no objective standards on which to base a choice of time period. Bad choices in either decision will produce misleading trend lines, more so because the mathematics create an aura of authenticity in the mind of the uninitiated.

Since the proper use of mathematically-fitted trend lines requires a person highly skilled in both the mathematics and economics underlying his data, very few sophisticated analysts use mathematical trends. Their reasoning is that they might as well draw the trend freehand after they have made all the subjective analysis necessary for a mathematical line. As a matter of fact, a mathematical trend would not be considered a good trend unless it conformed to a line that "looked right" on a graph.

17.4 Estimating Cycle Runs and Residual

Now that we have estimated the seasonal and trend variations in gasoline consumption we can turn our attention to the cycle runs and residual in the data. The first step is to eliminate the seasonal and trend variations from the original data. Following our model, we do this by *dividing* the actual data by the seasonal and trend. In formula

$$\frac{A}{T \times S} = \frac{T \times S \times C \times R}{T \times S} = C \times R.$$

Column 6 of Table 17.6 shows the results of this elimination. (Column 6 is the result of dividing column 1 by the product of columns 2 and 3.)

We would now like to analyze these CR ratios for evidence of cycle runs. We could do this by plotting these ratios on a chart similar to Fig. 17.7. Actually, however, we prefer to try to average out some of the residual before trying to identify cycle runs. We have, for example, taken a 7-month moving average of the CR ratios and plotted these averages in Fig. 17.7. The averages themselves are shown in column 7 of Table 17.6. We then superimpose estimates of the cycle runs on these moving averages. We can undoubtedly find grounds for disagreement with the placing of some of these lines. Our timing of these runs would probably be considerably helped by any extra knowledge we might have about market factors affecting the sales of gasoline. In the absence of such knowledge, we merely draw lines that look good.

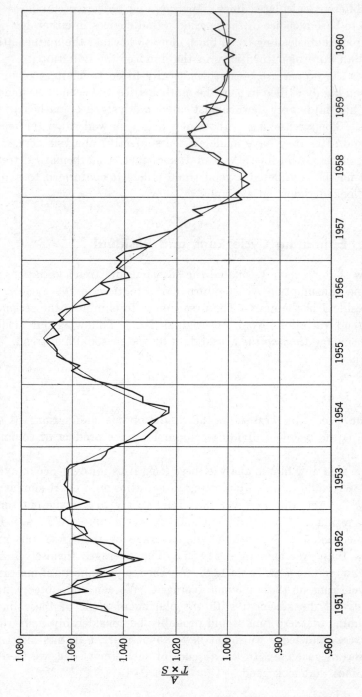

Fig. 17.7 Runs in cycles of gasoline consumption. (Data in Table 17.6.)

The *residual* variation is what is left. It is shown in column 5 of Table 17.6. This is calculated by dividing the estimates of cycle runs of column 4 into the CR ratios of column 6.

17.5 The Completed Model Anatomy of Gasoline Consumption

We set out to analyze gasoline consumption into the component variations of trend, seasonal, cycle runs, and residual. Columns 1 through 5 of Table 17.6 show the results of our analysis. The actual figure shown in column 1 should in each month be the product of the T, S, C, and R shown in the table. Since judgment played a major role in this analysis, it is fair to state that this anatomy is only one of several conceivable estimates that could have been made. It is likely, however, that other estimates would be fairly close to this because gasoline consumption tends to be dominated by reasonably strong and stable patterns, particularly in seasonal variation and trend. There would be much more room for disagreement in an industry like pig iron production where the patterns are neither strong nor stable. An idea of the relative strengths of the four components can be gained from the coefficients (V) of their respective variations. The coefficient of variation of the trend component is .123; that of the seasonal component is .073; that of the cycle runs is .023; and that of the residual is .022. Thus it can be seen that the series is fairly well dominated by trend and seasonal forces.

17.6 Auto-correlation in the Residual Variation

Theoretically, the residual variation should behave somewhat like a random series. That means that there should be no correlation between successive items, a condition that would make it impossible to predict the next residual variation from the preceding one. A simple way to test for the existence of correlation in the residual variations is to calculate the degree of *auto-correlation* in them. This is the degree of correlation between successive items in the residual variations. The independent, or predicting, variable is taken as the residual for the *preceding* month. Figure 17.8 illustrates this. On the horizontal axis are shown the values of the residual variations at time T. On the vertical axis are shown the values of the residual variations at time T plus one month. For example, the residual variation for April, 1951 was .968. What does this tell us about the residual variation for May, 1951, or, in general, what does the residual variation in one month tell us about the residual variation in the next month? We answer this question by pairing successive residual variations. .968 is the independent item associated with 1.039 of May, 1951; 1.039 then becomes the independent item associated with the .971 of June, 1951, etc. Figure 17.8 shows the scattergram of these 116 possible pairs. There is clear visual evidence of a negative association.

If we fit a least-squares straight line to this relationship, we get the equation

$$X_{t+1} = 1.421 - .421X_t.$$

The standard deviation around this line is .016 compared to a standard deviation in the residual variations of .022. Thus we get A of .27, or r of .78.

We find that there is a rather large amount of auto-correlation in these residual variations. It is quite evident that plus deviations

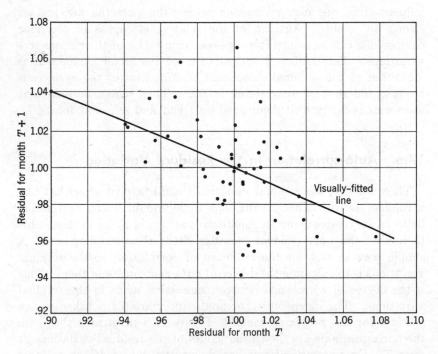

Fig. 17.8 Relationship between successive residuals in gasoline consumption. (Data in Table 17.7.)

tend to be followed by minus deviations, and minus deviations by plus deviations. If we wished, we could incorporate such an apparent systematic variation in our systematic elements as an oscillatory movement in the manner described by the least-squares equation. We hesitate to do this, however, for fear that we would be cutting our analysis rather thin. We suspect that we may have induced some of the auto-correlation by overrefined descriptions of the cycle runs. It is conceptually possible to always leave the residual variation with a high degree of negative correlation by simply running the cycle run lines through every little wave of the data. Successive residual variations would then almost always be on opposite sides of such a line. If we had confined our cycle runs to straight lines, we might have eliminated a good deal of the negative auto-correlation. The practical problem is to abstract as much system from the data as can be *relied on to persist into the future*. Unfortunately, the only way to test our skill in doing this is to wait until the future unfolds. The biggest criticism against most analyses of the type we have been describing is that the abstracted systems tend to disappear as the future unfolds. Most analysts have been far too generous in their allocations of variations to the trend, seasonal, and cycle categories with the result that they are unprepared for the large errors their forecasts tend to produce.

17.7 Criticisms of the Traditional Approach to Time Series Analysis

Traditional time series analysis based on $A = TSCR$ has enjoyed the popularity it has had more because there is a lack of reasonably simple competing analytical methods than because of any real successes in its application. The fundamental weakness in this approach is its lack of any operating rules to tell us how far we should go in superimposing systems of variation on the data. If we were to extrapolate the systems we discovered in gasoline consumption to make estimates, say, for the remaining months of 1961, it would be very hard to place any meaningful confidence limits on our estimates. Experience with this method suggests that the residual variation would be a poor standard for setting such limits because it tends to be too small, thus leading to overoptimistic forecasts (overoptimistic in the sense that we would imply a degree of error smaller than we should).

Two primary weaknesses are at the root of our difficulties with the traditional method. The first is that the formal method restricts itself to *only* the information supplied by the series itself, together with the *dates* of such information. Any attempt to allow for related variables such as temperature, population, etc., must be handled informally and intuitively. Since most analysts always know more than just the data, or at least they think they do, the final results will tend to reflect this undefined subjective knowledge in addition to the obvious data themselves. We have no practical way to judge the validity of such an analysis except by judging the analyst himself. If he has a reputation for skill and honesty, we accept his results at face value. Otherwise we apply appropriate discounts, themselves a matter of judgment.

The second weakness is that the method analyzes *all of the historical detail* as if all such information were really available in a practical problem. It is as though we were faced with the problem of making decisions about problems to which we already had the answers! It is not surprising that we derive answers that are consistent with the *known* outcomes. The problem in practice, however, is to make the decision *before* the fact, and to still come up with answers consistent with the outcome. Traditional time series analysis is really no more than a highly developed technique of second-guessing. A technique for first-guessing would be more appropriate.

In view of these criticisms, we should not now assume that the results of this type of analysis are totally useless. Much of value can be learned from such an analysis. We know, for example, that the seasonal variation will very likely continue with a pattern very similar to that which we found in the past data. We also know that gasoline consumption has had a clearly indicated *upward* trend over the years and that it will continue upward unless some very spectacular events occur. We are not at all confident of the *rate* of this upward trend, or of whether this rate may be starting to retard somewhat. Fluctuations in general business have had only very moderate influence on gasoline consumption, a characteristic common to many moderately-priced consumer necessities. We would expect this situation to continue. On the other hand, we are not as confident of our analysis of these cycle runs as the analysis implies. If we had had more confidence, we would have analyzed the runs for average length and average rate of change, thus hoping to gain some basis for anticipating future runs.

17.8 The Use of Multiple Correlation Techniques in the Analysis of Economic Time Series

An obvious way to improve the results of a time series analysis would be to bring in additional information about the various seasonal, trend, and cycle factors. For example, we might analyze gasoline consumption with some of the following associated factors, among others.

X_1—Actual monthly gasoline consumption.
X_2—Average temperature during month.
X_3—Rainfall during month.
X_4—Number of days in month.
X_5—Number of major holidays in month.
X_6—Number of Saturdays and Sundays in month.
X_7—Number of month (Jan = 1, Feb = 2, etc.).
X_8—Number of registered automobiles.
X_9—Number of airline passenger miles flown in piston engine aircraft.
X_{10}—Number of registered private airplanes.
X_{11}—Number of farm tractors in use.
X_{12}—Number of private motor boats in use.
X_{13}—Number of small gasoline engines in use on power mowers, go-carts, garden tools, motorcycles, etc.
X_{14}—Miles of improved highways in use.
X_{15}—Number of compact cars in use.
X_{16}—Rate of disposable personal income.
X_{17}—Federal Reserve Index of Industrial Production.
X_{18}—Average price of regular grade gasoline.
X_{19}—Military budget of Federal Government.
X_{20}—The number of the year.

In each case there is the possibility of using time lags.

If we were to analyze the above factors over a 15-year period, we would have 180 observations on each factor, or a total of 3600. If we confined our analysis to straight-line relationships, we would have to perform 34,200 multiplications to get the cross products. We would also have the squarings and additions to do and finally solve a considerable number of simultaneous equations. It is not surprising, then, that no one as yet has performed such an analysis to our knowledge. But somebody will over the next few years because of the possibility of doing the calculations on an electronic computer. It will be very interesting to see what the outcome of such studies will be. Although there are risks that we will again fall into the trap of overdrawing conclusions, such a multiple correlation analysis should certainly help to formalize interpretations of factors that are currently left to intuition and experience.

17.9   Attempts to Simulate Actual Forecasting Conditions

Even an elaborate multiple correlation analysis is simply a second-guessing technique in the sense that it utilizes the results it is trying to predict in working out methods of prediction. The methods are sure to look good within the bounds of the data used to develop the methods. The situation might be quite different, and usually is, when we apply the results to the future. In the next chapter we look briefly at a method of approach that attempts to confine itself to only the information that could possibly be available at the time a forecast had to be made. Such an approach tends to give very discouraging results because it leads to uncertainty about the future. Perhaps that is why it is almost never used. Most people would rather use methods which give deceptively accurate results and rationalize away their failures than use methods which give relatively inconclusive results, even though the inconclusive results are a direct consequence of our general state of ignorance about the future.

PROBLEMS AND QUESTIONS

17.1 Consider two of the various economic time series that you think you know something about and evaluate the applicability of the general model of the components of variation that reads

$$A = T \times S \times C \times R.$$

For example, do you see any reasons why it might be preferable to *add* some of these components together?

Also, are some of these components irrelevant in your series? Or, can you think of some additional components, perhaps some components that are *parts* of the major components referred to in the general model?

17.2(*a*) Use the monthly data on gasoline consumption given in Table 17.1 to construct a series of *quarterly* data on gasoline consumption. Use quarterly *totals*. Bring the data up to date.

(*b*) Plot your quarterly data on a year-over-year chart with a logarithmic vertical scale.

(*c*) Analyze the chart for clues of the various kinds of systematic movements that have apparently been occurring in gasoline consumption.

(d) Project the quarterly gasoline consumption for 6 quarters beyond the available data. Indicate your range of uncertainty by showing upper and lower limits such that you would feel 80% confident that the actual consumption will fall within your stated limits. (This 80% is the equivalent of betting at odds of 4 to 1 that your forecast is correct. You should choose limits that are narrow enough to tempt somebody to accept your odds at the same time that they are wide enough to give you a little more than 80% confidence. This can be done only by being a little less ignorant than the other fellow. Or at least you must think you are less ignorant.)

(e) Calculate a 4-quarter moving arithmetic mean for your data with the final results centered at the middle of a quarter for correct matching with the original data.

(f) Your 4-quarter moving arithmetic mean actually ends up as a 5-quarter *weighted* arithmetic mean because of the centering operation. Why is this true? What are the weights?

(g) Calculate the ratios of the original data to your moving averages. (Slide rule accuracy is sufficient.)

(h) Plot these ratios on a separate chart for each of the 4 quarters (in the manner of Fig. 17.4).

(i) What components of variation are presumably dominating the ratios? Explain.

(j) Draw in visually fitted lines that presumably measure the progress of the seasonal component for each quarter over these years. Extrapolate your lines to make a forecast of the seasonal component for the coming year.

(k) What plus-and-minus error allowance do you think you need for your historical lines? For your extrapolations? Does this error allowance vary from one quarter to another? (In other words, do you feel more confident about your estimates of seasonal in some quarters than you do in others?)

(l) Read off seasonal estimates from your graphs.

(m) Deseasonalize the historical data by dividing the actual data by your seasonal indexes.

(n) Measure any vestiges of seasonal in your deseasonalized data. Revise your original indexes.

17.3 A common method of reporting business information is to provide data for corresponding months of successive years. For example, a sampling of items on the financial pages of the Chicago Daily News of October 10, 1961 shows the following items:

1. "Income of International Business Machines Corp. for the first nine months soared to $152,887,977, Thomas J. Watson, Jr., chairman, announced Tuesday.

The earnings, equal to $5.55 a share, compare with net income of $119,088,057 or $4.34 a share in the nine-month period that ended Sept. 30, 1960.

Gross income from sales, service and rentals also was up—from $1,040,-572,434 a year ago to $1,244,491,206 in the latest nine-month period."

2. "Walgreen Co. sales set new records for September and the first nine months of 1961.

Sales in September totaled $27,662,444, up 5.4 per cent from September, 1960. For the nine months sales totaled $236,638,613, up 4.6 per cent from the corresponding period last year."

(*a*) What is the value of this kind of reporting?

(*b*) Contrast the method of reporting data for corresponding periods of consecutive years with that of reporting "seasonally-adjusted" data. For example, the U.S. News & World Report of October 9, 1961 reported on page 137 that

"The country's money supply rose sharply in early September. After seasonal adjustments, the total of currency outside banks and checking accounts averaged 143 billion dollars in the first half of September, up 1.2 billion from late August."

Does this latter method convey any different kind of message? Explain.

17.4(*a*) Collect annual data on passenger miles flown for commercial airlines in the United States and on passenger miles for United States railroads. Collect the best data you can back to 1920.

(*b*) Plot these data on charts and analyze the two series for evidence of growth patterns over the years. Draw freehand lines on your charts that reflect such growth patterns. Consider both the apparent patterns exhibited by the charts and any other general information or insights you might have. Make no effort to collect any additional information at this point of your analysis.

(*c*) Project your expected pattern of growth for each series for each of the next 10 years. Indicate the maximum and minimum levels you would expect on the assumption that you wish to be 80% confident that your projected range will include the truth. (You might keep in mind that it will never be possible to determine the exact truth even after the events have occurred.)

(*d*) You undoubtedly felt somewhat ignorant as you worked (*b*) and (*c*) above and recognize that there are several things you would like to investigate if you had the time and resources. Suppose you have been granted the free use of three research assistants for a period of 2 months. In what directions would you instruct them to collect information, etc., in order to help you derive a more expert opinion about the growth patterns—both past and future—of the airline and railroad passenger industries in the United States?

Consider the data you would try to collect, the charts you would have drawn, the correlations you would have run, the brainstorming sessions you would organize, the men you would have interviewed, etc.

(*e*) Do you see any evidence that the airline passenger business might follow the growth patterns that have been shown by the railroads, with the appropriate time lags of course?

(*f*) Do you see any evidence that either or both of these businesses have followed or will follow a pattern of growth that corresponds to any general law of growth like that exhibited by some animal and insect populations under certain environmental conditions? Explain.

(*g*) To what extent do you believe that the growth patterns in these businesses have and will be significantly under the control of the executives who have made and will make major decisions for the various companies in each of these industries? Or, in other words, if you were such an executive, to what extent do you feel that you could count on certain underlying forces of growth to propel your company and to what extent you would feel that you and your co-workers would have to create such forces?

(*h*) If it has not already occurred to you in your analysis of the above questions, you should now consider the likelihood that the railroad passenger business will experience a revival, say, somewhat like the revival of the phonograph record industry which was once apparently threatened by the radio industry but which has since enjoyed several decades of considerable growth. (You might also consider the early threat of television to the radio industry and the subsequent recovery of the radio industry both in broadcasting and receiving.)

(*i*) What recommendations do you have with respect to our national policy for the regulation of railroads and airlines in order to foster a healthy future growth in our passenger transportation facilities?

17.5 Select some corporation that you have an interest in (not necessarily financial—yet) and analyze the growth prospects for this company with an eye toward making a judgment about the investment value of this company's common stock. Assume you have $5000 to invest in this or other company. You need some sort of annual return from this investment in order to supplement your earnings. You also have resources sufficiently limited so that you could not easily laugh off the loss of a substantial proportion of your $5000. How much of this $5000 would you invest in this company's common stock at the current market price? Explain.

17.6(*a*) Use your final estimated trend lines in Problem 17.4 and read off numerical trend values for each year.

(*b*) Eliminate trend from the original data. What is measured by the resultant ratios? (Slide rule accuracy is sufficient.)

(*c*) Analyze your ratios of trend to actual data for evidence of runs or of cyclical variations. You should try to distill these runs from the ratios. What do you then have left? Can you detect any systems in these residuals?

(*d*) Which industry has been apparently more affected by cyclical fluctuations—airline passenger or railroad passenger? How much more? (Use your own ingenuity to summarize rate of the cyclical fluctuations in the two series.)

(*e*) Is there any evidence that the magnitude of cyclical fluctuations has changed over the years? If so, how do you explain such changes?

(*f*) Make an 80% confidence projection of the trend/actual ratios for the next two years for each of these industries.

(*g*) Do you note any significant evidence that the airline and railroad passenger miles have cyclical fluctuations with different *timing*, particularly at the turning points where the ratios shift from a positive run to a negative run, or vice versa? For example, is there any evidence that the airline business turns down before the railroads? Would you be able to make a sharper analysis of this matter of comparative timing if you had monthly data to work with? Explain.

17.7(*a*) Make a formal analysis of the degree of auto-correlation that exists in the residual variations you developed in Problem 17.6(*c*) above. Interpret your results.

(*b*) You very likely used one-year lags in measuring the auto-correlation in (*a*) immediately above. You might as well have used two-year lags, or three-year lags, etc. What would be the logical implications of such analyses? For example, might you find *negative* correlation with one-year lags and *positive* correlation with two-year lags? If so, what would this tell you about the behavior of the series?

17.8 Evaluate the following quotation.

"The current upturn in general business should run for at least 24 months because we have not had a shorter expansion period since the one that ended in 1929. However, we should be alert to signs of a downturn at the end of this 24 month period because 3 out of the last 4 expansions have terminated in 32 months or less." (See Table 16.1 for some historical evidence on the lengths of cyclical runs in general business in the United States)

17.9 Comment on the following.

"While it may very well be true that traditional methods of analyzing an economic time series give us a feeling of knowing more about the probable future than we really do, we should nevertheless not discount the psychological value we get from the results of such analyses. While overconfidence may not be a good state for action when we are dealing with events over which our actions have no control, there are times when the enthusiasm generated by a little overconfidence may help us to actually bring to pass events that would have been impossible if we had appraised the situation more 'realistically.' It is only when the analysis makes the situation look dark that we should guard against overconfidence in the correctness of our appraisal."

chapter 18

Forecasting an economic time series

In the preceding chapter we were concerned with the *past behavior* of an economic time series. In this chapter we are concerned with the problem of the *future behavior* of an economic time series. Our study of the past behavior consisted of trying to analyze a series into its component, or anatomical, parts. The knowledge gained from such a study is useful in predicting the future course of a time series, particularly the future course of the within-the-year variation. The method of approach, however, tends to overestimate what we know about a situation, and thus leads to forecasts that imply smaller errors than actually prevail.

As we switch our orientation from the past to the future, we are much more interested in the *whole* series than in any of the component parts, such as seasonal or secular trend. We find that it is the whole series that the businessman has to contend with, not with any hypothetical parts that we might distill by statistical methods. We try to avoid making *conditional forecasts,* that is, forecasts that assume certain things will be true. Naturally, it is always true that *some conditions* underlie any forecast. For example, we assume that there will be no nuclear war, or similar catastrophe during the range of the forecast. We also assume no miracles, such as the discovery of a perpetual motion machine or a simple way for human beings to subsist on air alone. We do not, however, make forecasts that assume a "steady rate of growth" or "no decline in general business," or "no particularly wet spring," etc. We consider our job either to predict such phenomena or to allow for their occurrence within the bounds of our expected error.

18.1   Naive Forecasting Methods

If we make a forecast of the future course of gasoline consumption in the United States based almost solely on the *past behavior of gasoline consumption,* we say that we are making a *naive forecast.* The simplest type of naive forecast assumes that the next period's figure will be the same as the last period's. For example, given a 1960 gasoline consumption of 126.1 million barrels per month, we might forecast that the 1961 consumption will also be 126.1 million barrels per month. We probably agree that such a forecast is very naive. What we may not be aware of, however, is that it is not at all easy to improve this forecast very much. We try in later pages, but the difficulties mount fairly rapidly.

A more complex naive system is to assume the latest rate of change will continue. For example, given a 1959 gasoline consumption of 123.3 million barrels per month and 126.1 for 1960, we might assume that 1961 will be 128.9 (up 2.8) or 129.0 (up 2.3%), depending on whether we wish to assume a constant *absolute* rate or a constant *percentage* rate. Again, although this is very naive, it is surprisingly difficult to surpass in general accuracy.

As we use more of the past history of the series in our forecasting system, the more complex the naive system becomes. For example, we might fit a secular trend line to the last 15 years of data and extrapolate this. This system would probably have a larger error in general than the assumption of no change. If we supported our trend system with a seasonal index and some estimate of the cycle run, we would have a very complex naive system, albeit still naive by our definition because the analysis paid *no explicit attention to any other information than that supplied by the history of gasoline consumption itself.* Actually, of course, unless the analyst is just as naive as his data, he cannot help giving some *implicit* consideration to such factors as the periods of major wars, etc.

In order to avoid the label of naive, a forecasting method must give some *explicit* attention to factors outside the series itself. For example, a study of seasonal variations in gasoline consumption might include temperature variations.

We should not get the idea that naive methods are somehow bad, or inefficient. They are perfectly proper and respectable, and often as effective as any other methods. But they are naive in the true meaning of the term. We consider naive methods sufficiently respectable to be worthy of discussion. The remainder of this chapter concentrates on such naive methods for forecasting an economic time series. The proper use of sophisticated methods which utilize multiple correlation techniques for analyzing related factors requires knowledge particular to the specific application and is better done by somebody with enough experience in the particular area to pick out meaningful factors. Such a specialized type of analysis is outside the scope of this book.

18.2 The Base and Range of a Forecast

Forecasting is using the knowledge we have at *one moment of time* to estimate what will happen at *another moment of time*. The forecasting problem is created by the *interval of time* between the two moments. The *base point* of a forecast is the knowledge point from which we jump across the time gap. The *range* of a forecast is the time interval between the base point and the forecast point. For example, suppose a company has a practice of forecasting the next month's sales as soon as the current month's figure is available. The base point for a February sales forecast would be January, with a range of 1 month. Similarly, the base point for a November forecast would be October. If there are lags in the reporting of data, a very common problem, we may find ourselves at the end of the month of February and just getting reports on December sales. Thus a March forecast would have to be based on December with a range of 3 months. It is often much more practical to spend money on speeding up data reporting than it is to spend money on forecasts over longer ranges. Some companies are in the very strong position of knowing what last month's sales were while their competitors are still guessing. Man has known for a long time that knowledge is more valuable than the best guess, or the best technique for guessing.

It is very important to know the base point and range of a forecast to develop a forecasting method *consistent with the base point and range*. To do otherwise would be the equivalent of a naval gunnery crew practicing from a fixed base at a 2-mile range to develop techniques for hitting targets 5 miles from a moving base.

We illustrate some of the techniques for making naive forecasts of gasoline consumption by using ranges of 1 month, 6 months, 1 year, and 5 years.

18.3   Month-to-month Forecasts of Gasoline Consumption

We are going to try to forecast gasoline consumption for a given month from the base of the preceding month. We start our analysis of the historical record by finding out *what kinds of changes have occurred in the past over a one-month range.* We can measure these changes in terms of *differences* between the successive months or in terms of the *ratios* of one month to its preceding month. We find it preferable to use the ratios because the ratios would be more comparable over the years than would be the actual differences. The actual differences are at least partly a function of the *size* of the series, and the series tends to have larger sizes at the later dates than at the earlier dates because of the growth in gasoline consumption over the years. The ratios are more or less independent of this size factor.

Table 18.1 shows the month-to-month ratios for gasoline consumption from 1951 to 1961. Such month-to-month ratios are often called *link relatives,* the analogy being to a chain that has many links tied together. Here we tie all the months together with ratios between successive months. This table gives us 122 observations on

TABLE 18.1

Monthly Link Relatives of Gasoline Consumption: 1951–1961.
(Original Data in Table 17.1) (Link relative is shown
for the date of the forecast month, not for the
date of the base month)

	1951	1952	1953	1954	1955	1956	1957	1958	1959	1960	1961
Jan	—	1.020	.929	.913	.936	.896	1.011	.951	.953	.900	.917
Feb	.898	.910	.960	.961	.921	.941	.885	.890	.870	.944	.922
Mar	1.197	1.101	1.143	1.176	1.191	1.188	1.171	1.140	1.192	1.147	1.199
Apr	1.007	1.135	1.035	1.026	1.053	1.005	1.023	1.088	1.050	1.071	
May	1.140	1.025	1.041	1.000	1.041	1.094	1.073	1.056	1.017	1.007	
Jun	.968	.982	1.081	1.092	1.039	1.026	.978	1.002	1.053	1.068	
Jul	1.044	1.061	.986	.988	.962	.952	1.072	1.044	1.025	.978	
Aug	1.006	.978	.962	.983	1.051	1.042	.988	.992	.969	1.019	
Sep	.902	.972	.970	.948	.931	.887	.882	.927	.980	.928	
Oct	1.102	1.036	.998	1.011	.997	1.068	1.051	1.039	.928	.982	
Nov	.874	.879	.937	.965	.968	.940	.902	.884	.960	.990	
Dec	.968	1.050	1.008	1.025	1.018	.964	1.047	1.088	1.065	1.000	

TABLE 18.2

Frequency Distribution of Monthly Link Relatives of Gasoline Consumption

Link Relative	f	d	fd	fd^2
.85–.90 *	10	−3	−30	90
.90–.95	19	−2	−38	76
.95–1.00	30	−1	−30	30
1.00–1.05	30	0	0	0
1.05–1.10	19	1	19	19
1.10–1.15	7	2	14	28
1.15–1.20	7	3	21	63
	122		−44	306

$$\text{Mean} = 1.025 + \frac{-44}{122} \times .05$$

$$= 1.007^-$$

$$\text{Median} = 1.0000 + \frac{61 - 59}{30} \times .05$$

$$= 1.0033$$

$$s = .05 \sqrt{\frac{306}{122} - 1.007^2}$$

$$= .061$$

$$D_1 = .90 + \frac{12.2 - 10.0}{19} \times .05 = .906$$

$$D_9 = 1.15 - \frac{12.2 - 7.0}{7} \times .05 = 1.113$$

P.E. (Percentile Equivalent) of Mean

$$= \frac{59}{122} + \frac{.007}{.05} \times \frac{30}{122} = .518.$$

* Lower Limit Inclusive.

the ratio of one month to the preceding. If we ignore the dates on the links and form a frequency series as shown in Table 18.2, we see what we face when we try to forecast a next month's figure. Note that the mean of the ratios is 1.007. This implies that the series has grown at about .7 of 1% per month over the 122 months.

We would, however, be very foolish to rely on this as a meaningful average rate of change from month to month. If we start with the January, 1951 consumption figure of 79.7 million barrels and let this grow at a compounded rate of .007 per month, we arrive at a figure for January, 1961 of 230.9 million barrels. The actual reported figure for January, 1961 was only 114.5 million barrels.

Thus we have a very practical illustration of the meaningless character of the arithmetic mean of ratios of this type. We discounted the arithmetic mean for such a purpose on theoretical grounds in Chapter 6. Although the arithmetic mean may have no *inherent* meaning unless we are actually interested in the total, it sometimes gains meaning *by coincidence* if it happens to be practically equal to the median. The median does have great inherent value as an estimator whenever we are interested in minimizing our errors of estimate, which we would certainly like to do in this problem of forecasting gasoline consumption. We find the median of these ratios to be approximately 1.0033. From the point of view of the *whole distribution of ratios,* the mean of 1.0070 does not differ very much from 1.0033. Note, for example, that the ratios range from .85 to 1.20. Also note that the percentile equivalent of the mean is .518, certainly not very far from .500. Thus the skewness of the distribution is quite moderate.

In this problem, however, the critical issue is the relationship of the average ratio to 1. From this point of view, we find that the rate of change represented by 1.0070 is *more than twice as great* as that represented by the median of 1.0033. In some problems we might find the mean and the median ratios even closer to each other than we have here and yet the practical significance of the difference may be quite substantial. For example, we might have a mean ratio of 1.0007 and a median ratio of .9996. The mean indicates a *growing* series, the median a *declining* series.

It is often argued that the proper average to use for averaging ratios of this type is the *geometric mean.* We discussed this in Chapter 6 in connection with the problem of the average value of an investment fund. Since one of our problems in that discussion was that we did not have any clear-cut idea of why we wished to know the average value of the investment fund, it might be worthwhile to raise again the issue of the geometric mean in our present context. We have a definite purpose for wishing to measure the average rate of change of gasoline consumption from month to month. This is to provide a basis for *forecasting* gasoline consumption *one* month in advance. Common sense suggests that we would like this forecast to be *as close as possible* to the actual consumption that will prevail. We have previously learned that the *median* is the average that will accomplish this. We have already found this median ratio to be 1.0033. What role might we now assign to the geometric mean?

The geometric mean is calculated by *multiplying* all the items together. The items in our present problem are the monthly link relatives. If we multiply all of them together, we find that *all* the consumption data for the months from February, 1951 to December, 1960 will *cancel,* leaving us only with the ratio of the January, 1961 consumption to the January, 1951 consumption. The reason for this is immediately apparent if we write out the detail of the multiplication of these links. For example, we would be multiplying products like the following: (See Table 17.1 for the source of the figures.)

$$\frac{71.6}{79.7} \times \frac{85.7}{71.6} \times \frac{86.3}{85.7} \times \frac{98.4}{86.3} \times \frac{95.3}{98.4} \cdots \frac{124.9}{124.9} \times \frac{114.5}{124.9} = \frac{114.5}{79.7}$$

We end up with the interesting result that the geometric mean is based on only the values of the *first* and the *last* items in this list of 121 items. It is just as though the other 119 items did not exist. In fact, we might arbitrarily assign any values we wish to the intermediate items. We still get the same geometric mean. This is why we say that the most efficient way to calculate the geometric mean of such ratios is to simply take the Nth root of the ratio of the last item to the first item. In this case we would have $\sqrt[120]{\dfrac{114.5}{79.7}}$. Solution of this by the use of logarithms gives us a geometric mean ratio of 1.0030, a result that *happens* to be quite close to the median ratio of 1.0033 in this problem. There is no particular inherent reason why the geometric mean and median should be this close.

The above analysis of the geometric mean should make it quite obvious that its value has no particular relationship to the *month-to-month* changes in gasoline consumption. Hence it would have no inherent relevance to our problem. It is a mere coincidence that it has a value so close to the median. The geometric mean definitely bears a *mathematical* relationship to the ratio of the last item (January, 1961) to the first item (January, 1951). The *practical* significance of this relationship is not at all apparent.

Our Present Uncertainty about Month-to-Month Changes in Gasoline Consumption. To be able to state a meaningful *average* rate of change from month to month is of some value, although a quite limited one. Practical work requires that we have some awareness of the *probable range* within which the actual rate might fall. The only basis we have for estimating such a probable range about *future* rates is the experience we have had with *past* rates. The distribution shown in Table 18.2 could be used as a crude base for estimating such a range. We hope to be able to improve this shortly; however, the best way to understand the degree to which we might be able to improve it is to have a rather specific idea of how ignorant we are at the moment. Let us arbitrarily decide that we would like the range that would give us about 80% confidence. We could, of course, select any confidence coefficient that seemed consistent with our own consequence matrix. We can estimate an 80% confidence belt by finding the two points in our distribution that exclude the lower and upper 10% of the past ratios. We would accomplish this by estimating the values of the 1st decile, or D_1, and of the 9th decile, or D_9. The calculation of these, shown in Table 18.2, yields results of .906 and 1.113.

If we feel inadequate because all we can say is: we estimate the ratio of next month's consumption to this month's consumption will be somewhere between .906 and 1.113, we can always give the *appearance* of more accuracy by using a narrower band. If we do this, however, we would have to accept a lower than 80% confidence. As long as our information is restricted to what is available in Table 18.2, there is no way that we can legitimately reduce our apparent uncertainty except by decreasing our confidence. Fortunately for our peace of mind, we are going to expand our knowledge of these ratios a little and see if we cannot *decrease the uncertainty band without at the same time decreasing our confidence.*

Before we acquire this greater knowledge, let us simply note that the difference between our upper and lower boundary to our 80% confidence belt is presently .207.

What Difference Do the Months Make in the Size of the Ratios?

We have probably wondered why we ignored the possibility that there may be a *pattern* to these link relatives or monthly ratios. Actually, we deliberately avoided such a possibility to set the scene so that we would be able to *measure* the significance of such a monthly pattern to the task of improving our forecasts. Hence we have tried to define our state of ignorance without any information about monthly patterns. We can then compare our state of ignorance with such information and our state without it and thus measure the value of the information.

The logical thing now is to separate the 122 classes into 12 subclasses, one class for each month of the year. For example, let us look at the historical behavior of just the February to January links, and then the March to February links, etc. The best way is with a chart like that shown in Fig. 18.1. This is the same kind of chart we drew when we analyzed the ratios of monthly data to the moving averages, and we have the same purposes in mind. The most prominent feature of the ratios that is made apparent by examination of Fig. 18.1 is that they have different sizes in the different months. For example, the March to February ratios are consistently around 1.14 to 1.19, whereas the September to August ratios are consistently around .90 to .97. (We should note parenthetically that no adjustment has been made for leap year. We assume we could make such an adjustment if necessary on the basis of our treatment of this problem in Chapter 17. We leave it out here in order to simplify our present discussion.)

What is not so clear from these charts in Fig. 18.1 is whether any of these ratios for a given month show any *shifting pattern* over the years. Most of the months show what could be runs for a few years, but no month seems to have shifted its level between the early years and the later years. There is some evidence of negative correlation between the ratios for successive months. Note, for example, the reverse patterns of variation in the May/April ratios and the June/May ratios. This is partly induced by the way the ratios themselves are calculated. For example, if a May figure is unusually *high*, it will lead to an unusually *high* May/April ratio. But this unusually high May becomes the denominator of the June/May ratio. Hence the June/May ratio would tend to be unusually *low*.

It is also possible that part of this negative correlation is caused by the actual behavior of gasoline consumption. We found quite a bit of auto-correlation in the residual variations in our analysis of gasoline consumption. At the time we thought that we might have induced some of this by an overambitious specification of cycle runs. Although we still do not discount the possibility of our having induced some of the auto-correlation, we must now recognize the possibility that auto-correlation of this oscillatory type may be an inherent part of the series. It might be due to a tendency for gasoline marketers to overcorrect their monthly errors in planning sales and inventories, in the same way a person might follow an oscillatory path in an automobile because of a tendency to overcorrect steering errors. Or, it might be due to a similar kind of error-correction technique followed by those who compile the gasoline consumption series. It is not unusual to find some variation induced in a series by the person or persons doing the measuring. We then have to decide whether we use as a target the data *as measured* or the data *as they would be if they were correctly measured*. Usually we are forced to tie into the data as measured for want of information about what they should be.

We are sufficiently confused about the source of this negative correlation to avoid any explicit attempt to take advantage of it. The correlation is available to be analyzed if we wish and if practical considerations make it seem worthwhile. We will assume that there is no reliable system in these year-to-year variations and treat them as essentially random.

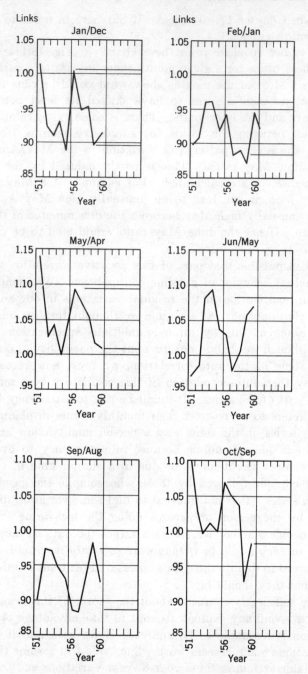

Fig. 18.1 Analysis of one-month link relatives of gasoline consumption. (Data in Table 18.1.)

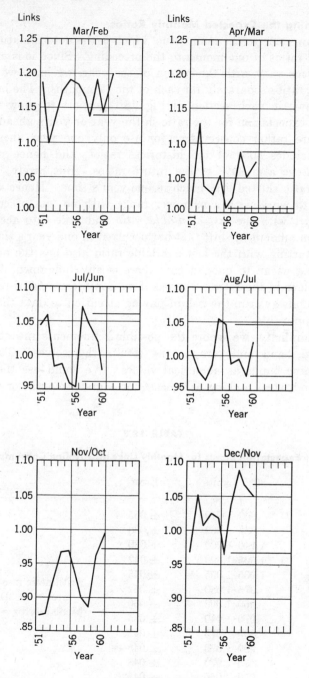

Fig. 18.1 Continued

Determining the Expected Monthly Ratios

We now come to the main issue, which is the determination of the *expected* ratios of one month to the preceding. Since it is clear that these ratios vary with the season of the year, we have worked out expected ratios separately for each of the 12 months. The horizontal lines drawn in each section of Fig. 18.1 purport to show the *80% range* of expectation for the ratio in the year or years ahead. These ranges are rather conservative for use only one year ahead. The range includes 80% of the historical ratios, and hence we hopefully believe also 80% of the future ratios. But rarely, however, has the ratio shifted that much in one year's time. Hence we might be able to work with a narrower range with no loss of confidence if we *start* with the *last available ratio* and take into account the maximum amount of shift that has occurred in one year's time in the past. Starting with the last available ratio also has the advantage of making us up to date in case there is any fundamental shifting taking place in the ratios, whereas if we consider some of the earlier ratios we always run the risk of paying attention to data that are no longer applicable.

For simplicity, we ignore the possible refinements in determining this 80% band and turn to the results themselves. Table 18.3 shows these bands as numerical values. We could use the specific error band when making a forecast for a given month, or we could

TABLE 18.3

80% Expectation Bands for Monthly Links of Gasoline Consumption

	80% Limits	Error	
Jan/Dec	.900–1.010	±.055	
Feb/Jan	.885– .960	±.038	
Mar/Feb	1.140–1.200	±.030	
Apr/Mar	1.005–1.090	±.042	
May/Apr	1.005–1.095	±.045	Arithmetic mean
Jun/May	.975–1.080	±.052	error = ±.044.
Jul/Jun	.960–1.060	±.050	Median error = ±.045.
Aug/Jul	.970–1.040	±.035	
Sep/Aug	.890– .975	±.042	
Oct/Sep	.980–1.070	±.045	
Nov/Oct	.875– .970	±.048	
Dec/Nov	.970–1.060	±.045	

use an *average* error band and apply it to all months equally. Using specific error bands reveals that March will likely be the easiest month to predict, with an error of $\pm.030$, and January will be the most difficult to predict with an error of $\pm.055$, almost twice as large as that for March. The average of all the error bands is about .045. We can now estimate the value of knowing these monthly patterns. If we do not know them, we have an 80% error band of approximately $\pm.104$. (This is 1/2 of .207. See p. 672.) Hence knowledge of these monthly patterns enables us to reduce our average expected error from .104 to .045, or about 57%.

When we are using charts like those in Fig. 18.1 as a basis of forecasts from month to month, we should keep the data up to date and modify the bands as the evidence warrants. We chose 80% bands in the illustration. Naturally, of course, we should use the confidence coefficient appropriate to the particular situation. The big advantage to this method of approach is the basis it provides for establishing some rationally determined confidence band for our expectations. And, finally, remember we can analyze these ratios for evidence of runs and of correlation between successive months and thus possibly narrow the confidence band.

18.4   Six-month Forecasts of Gasoline Consumption

As an additional illustration of the use of link relatives in forecasting we show the results for forecasting 6 months ahead in Tables 18.4 through 18.6 and in Fig. 18.2. These tables and the chart parallel the treatment we used on the 1-month links.

Let us first look at Table 18.5 where we show the frequency distribution of the 6-month links. Here we see a substantial increase in the variation in the links compared to the 1-month links, an increase in the standard deviation from .061 to .149. This is what we would expect. This illustrates the rather general finding that the further out we try to forecast the greater will the variation be in the variable being forecasted.

Where we are surprised, however, is in the charts of Fig. 18.2 and in the summary of monthly errors shown in Table 18.6. Here we discover that knowledge of the particular month enables us to substantially reduce our errors of estimate. The average expected error for 80% confidence is $\pm.037$ if we use information specific to each month. This represents an 83% reduction in error from the 80% confidence band of approximately $\pm.212$ if we ignore the monthly

TABLE 18.4

Six-month Link Relatives of United States Gasoline Consumption: 1951–1961
(Original data in Table 17.1)

	1951	1952	1953	1954	1955	1956	1957	1958	1959	1960	1961
Jan/Jul	—	.863	.845	.804	.872	.860	.906	.823	.876	.812	.843
Feb/Aug	—	.781	.829	.802	.817	.770	.769	.741	.768	.791	.763
Mar/Sep	—	.953	.976	.973	1.026	.983	1.014	.959	.988	.925	.985
Apr/Oct	—	.982	.975	1.000	1.069	.992	.971	.992	.998	1.068	
May/Nov	—	1.151	1.154	1.067	1.153	1.122	1.109	1.162	1.148	1.120	
Jun/Dec	—	1.167	1.188	1.156	1.170	1.130	1.125	1.112	1.111	1.124	
Jul/Jan	1.248	1.214	1.260	1.250	1.202	1.201	1.192	1.220	1.195	1.220	
Aug/Feb	1.398	1.304	1.262	1.279	1.372	1.330	1.332	1.360	1.332	1.317	
Sep/Mar	1.054	1.151	1.071	1.031	1.072	.993	1.004	1.106	1.095	1.066	
Oct/Apr	1.153	1.051	1.033	1.015	1.015	1.055	1.031	1.056	.968	.978	
Nov/May	.884	.902	.930	.980	.943	.907	.866	.884	.914	.961	
Dec/Jun	.884	.964	.868	.919	.924	.853	.928	.959	.924	.899	

TABLE 18.5

Frequency Distribution of 6-month Links of United States Gasoline
Consumption: 1951–1961

6-month Links	frequency f	d	fd	fd^2	
.70–.75 *	1	−6	−6	36	
.75–.80	6	−5	−30	150	
.80–.85	8	−4	−32	128	
.85–.90	11	−3	−33	99	
.90–.95	11	−2	−22	44	
.95–1.00	20	−1	−20	20	
1.00–1.05	9	0	0	0	$\text{Mean} = 1.025 + \dfrac{19}{117} \times .05$
1.05–1.10	11	1	11	11	
1.10–1.15	10	2	20	40	$= 1.0258$
1.15–1.20	12	3	36	108	
1.20–1.25	6	4	24	96	$s = .05 \sqrt{\dfrac{1159}{117} - 1.0258^2}$
1.25–1.30	4	5	20	100	
1.30–1.35	5	6	30	180	
1.35–1.40	3	7	21	147	$= .149$
	117		19	1159	

$$D_1 = .80 + \frac{11.7 - 7.0}{8} \times .05 = .829 \qquad \text{Median} = 1.0083$$

$$D_9 = 1.30 - \frac{11.7 - 8.0}{4} \times .05 = 1.254 \qquad \text{P.E.}\overline{X} = .527$$

* Lower Limit Inclusive.

TABLE 18.6

**80% Expectation Bands for 6-month Links of United States Gasoline
Consumption: 1951–1961 (Data from Fig. 18.2)**

	80% Limits	Error	
Jan/Jul	.815– .880	±.032	
Feb/Aug	.760– .820	±.030	
Mar/Sep	.950–1.020	±.035	
Apr/Oct	.970–1.070	±.050	
May/Nov	1.110–1.155	±.022	
Jun/Dec	1.110–1.175	±.032	
Jul/Jan	1.195–1.250	±.028	Mean = .037
Aug/Feb	1.280–1.370	±.045	Median = .036
Sep/Mar	1.005–1.105	±.050	
Oct/Apr	.980–1.060	±.040	
Nov/May	.885– .960	±.038	
Dec/Jun	.870– .960	±.045	
		.447	

information. Thus the seasonal factors are much more important
for the 6-month links than they are for the 1-month links. In fact,
we end up with smaller average errors for the 6-month forecasts
than we do for the 1-month forecasts (.037 vs. .045). This phenomenon of a smaller net error for a longer forecast than for a shorter
one is somewhat unusual, although it certainly does happen. In the
exercises there is a chance to check out the behavior of the links for
other time intervals and make reasonably specific comments on the
behavior of the residuals in gasoline consumption.

18.5   One-year Forecasts of Gasoline Consumption

Table 18.7 and Fig. 18.3 show the calculation and analysis of the
1-year link relatives of gasoline consumption. These are useful as
the basis of making a forecast one year ahead. We used data back
to 1923 even though there are questions about the strict homogeneity of the series for this period of time. We feel, however, that
the errors in the data are small compared to the basic variation in
gasoline consumption itself and that it is useful to observe the behavior of the links over this length of time.

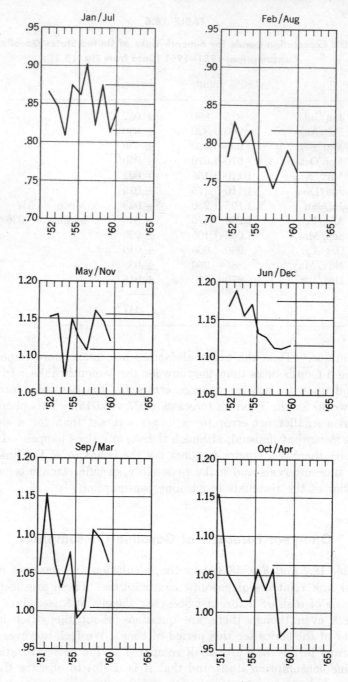

Fig. 18.2 Analysis of 6-month link relatives of gasoline consumption. (Data in Table 18.4.)

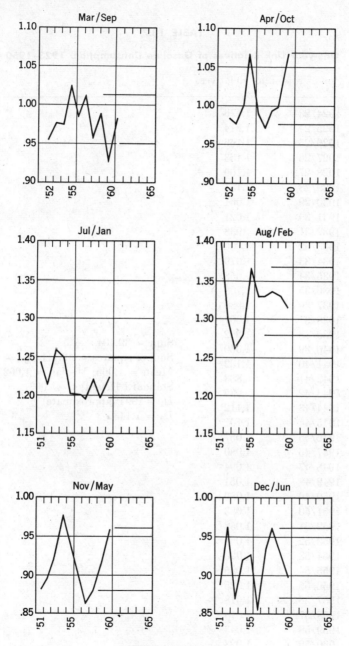

Fig. 18.2 Continued

TABLE 18.7

One-year Link Relatives of Gasoline Consumption: 1923–1960

Link Relatives

1924/23	1.176
1925/24	1.214
1926/25	1.166
1927/26	1.133
1928/27	1.109
1929/28	1.131
1930/29	1.061
1931/30	1.021
1932/31	.938
1933/32	1.006
1934/33	1.079
1935/34	1.058
1936/35	1.108
1937/36	1.080
1938/37	1.007
1939/38	1.062
1940/39	1.060
1941/40	1.132
1942/41	.883
1943/42	.965
1944/43	1.112
1945/44	1.101
1946/45	1.057
1947/46	1.080
1948/47	1.094
1949/48	1.051
1950/49	1.089
1951/50	1.083
1952/51	1.058
1953/52	1.058
1954/53	1.020
1955/54	1.085
1956/55	1.025
1957/56	1.018
1958/57	1.018
1959/58	1.043
1960/59	1.023

Sum = 39.404
Sum of squares = 42.111
Mean = 1.065; Median = 1.062
Standard Deviation = .063
D_1 = .994 (approximate)
D_9 = 1.143   "

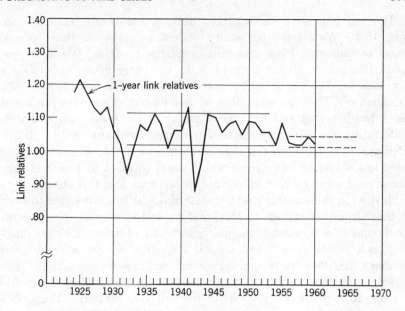

Fig. 18.3 1-year link relatives of gasoline consumption in the United States, 1923–1960. (Source: Table 18.7.) Note: The link relative is plotted against the terminal year of the linking period. See text for meaning of parallel lines.

If we take all the links and ignore their time sequence, we find that they average about 1.065 and have a standard deviation of .063. (The median ratio is about 1.062.)   Figure 18.3 makes it very clear, however, that the time sequence does make a difference.   The 1920's showed high annual rates that have not reappeared since, with the possible exception of the 1940 to 1941 rate which felt the effects of the beginning of World War II.   The two parallel solid lines running from the mid-thirties to the early-fifties show the boundaries of most of the ratios during this run of years.   (The World War II years have been ignored.)   It then appears that we might have moved into a new era in the early-fifties, an era which shows slightly lower annual rates than the previous two decades.   We detected the same tendencies in our study of the secular trend in gasoline consumption.

The problem is now to estimate the limits of annual change for the next year or so.   The parallel broken lines represent our judgment of a reasonable range of expectation for the annual rate of change from 1960 to 1961.   We would again venture an 80% confidence in this range.   In numbers, the range runs from a low of 1.0175 to a high of 1.0425, with an average expectation of 1.030.

It is obvious that we extracted quite a bit of information from Fig. 18.3. We started our study with a variation in these annual rates as indicated by a standard deviation of .063. We then proceeded to ignore all the data prior to the early fifties and made a forecast for 1961 with an expected error of only $\pm .0125$ for 80% confidence. Thus we were able to reduce our expected error about 84% (multiplying .063 by 1.28 to put it at the 80% level and then calculating the relative reduction from the resultant .080 to .0125). Perhaps we have been too ambitious in our use of Fig. 18.3. The acid test would be how people would react to the 4 to 1 odds if they knew only what we now know from these data and this chart.

Just as in the monthly and 6-month links, it is a good idea to keep a chart like that in Fig. 18.2 up to date and to modify the expectation band as new evidence might suggest. In addition, if we are making both monthly, say, and annual forecasts, we can correlate our findings and thus more quickly revise our expectation bands. For example, as the monthly data for 1961 become available, we should be able to improve our forecast of the full year of 1961. The first 3 months of 1961 suggest that the ratio of 1961 to 1960 is going to be above our minimum projection of 1.0175.

18.6 Five-year Forecasts of Gasoline Consumption

Table 18.8 and Fig. 18.4 show the analysis of the 5-year links in gasoline consumption. We find that the variation in these is substantially larger than in the 1-year links, a standard deviation of .235 vs. .063. Again we notice that the mean and the median are very close, thus indicating a reasonable amount of symmetry in the distribution of these ratios.

When we look at Fig. 18.4 we are not sure whether we should characterize what we see as very wild or very systematic. (Figure 18.4 has been drawn to the same scale as Fig. 18.3 to facilitate a visual comparison of the relative fluctuations in the 1-year and in the 5-year links.) We get a definite impression of rather wide swings in the ratios, at the same time we note that these swings are associated with rather well-known major events. The trough in the early thirties is the result of the Great Depression. The peak in the late thirties is the recovery from that depression. The height of this peak in the ratios is partly induced by the low swings 5 years earlier. We noticed some evidence of negative correlation between successive links in 1-month link relatives. Here we have 5-year link relatives

TABLE 18.8

Five-year Link Relatives of Gasoline Consumption: 1923–1960

Link Relatives

1928/23	2.092
1929/24	2.013
1930/25	1.759
1931/26	1.541
1932/27	1.275
1933/28	1.157
1934/29	1.103
1935/30	1.100
1936/31	1.193
1937/32	1.375
1938/33	1.375
1939/34	1.354
1940/35	1.356
1941/36	1.387
1942/37	1.134
1943/38	1.087
1944/39	1.138
1945/40	1.181
1946/41	1.103
1947/42	1.348
1948/43	1.527
1949/44	1.444
1950/45	1.429
1951/46	1.465
1952/47	1.435
1953/48	1.388
1954/49	1.347
1955/50	1.341
1956/51	1.269
1957/52	1.222
1958/53	1.176
1959/54	1.203
1960/55	1.134

Sum = 44.451
Sum of squares = 61.703
Mean = 1.347; Median = 1.347
Standard Deviation = .235
D_1 = 1.103
D_9 = 1.69 (approximate)

and again we note some evidence of a negative correlation between the links, but this time the correlation is between the links *5 years apart*. Note the lines running from 1932 to 1937, 1933 to 1938, etc. Since 1932 was an unusually low year, the link to that year was low. But when we get to 1937, we base the 1937 link on the year 1932.

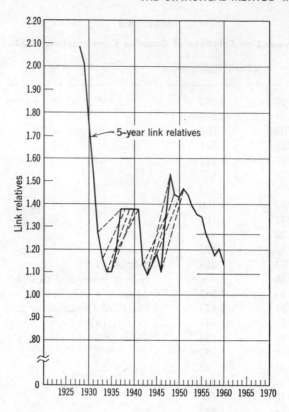

Fig. 18.4 5-year link relatives of gasoline consumption in the United States, 1923–1960. (Source: Table 18.8.)   Note: The link relative is plotted against the terminal year of the linking period. See text for meaning of parallel lines.

This gives 1937 a low base to jump from; hence it tends to have a high link.

We can see the same phenomenon at work if we compare the World War II low figures (due to rationing) with the postwar high figures.   Again we must keep in mind that part of the swing from low to high has been induced by our method of calculation.   Thus we might keep in mind the general rule that link relatives of time series tend to oscillate from high to low and vice versa over an interval equal to the range of the link.   Most of the time this induced oscillation is negligible and causes no trouble in analysis.   It becomes quite evident when we have a major outside force driving the data to one extreme or the other.   Interestingly enough, the oscillation tends to have only the single swing.   For example, the World War II artificial lows induced the postwar highs in the ratios; however, these postwar highs will not necessarily induce subsequent lows. They will do that *only if the postwar consumption is itself unusually high.* We do not believe that the postwar consumption was unusually high (except in comparison to the war-time artificial lows). Hence we do not expect the ratios in 1953, 1954, etc., to be low *because* of the preceding highs. If they are low, and they tend to be, we conclude that it is because the consumption rate in the fifties is itself tending to slacken its growth. We do not expect the links to bounce back from any "induced" lows in the late fifties the same way we would have expected the ratios to bounce back from the induced postwar highs.

We are now moderately ready to face the main issue of what we expect the consumption rate to be in 1965, 5 years beyond our base date of 1960. The two parallel lines indicate our 80% confidence range. This range runs from 1.09 to 1.26, or an average expectation of 1.175. This is more than five times our average expected 1-year rate because we are more inclined to anticipate a relatively large plus variation in consumption than a relatively large minus variation. This expected error of $\pm.085$ is approximately 72% less than we would have had if we had ignored the time sequence of these 5-year ratios. (As before, we multiplied the standard deviation of .235 by 1.28 to adjust to an 80% level. This adjustment raises the error to .301; .085 is about 72% less than .301.) Thus we apparently did not get as much from our charts with the 5-year links as we did with the 1-year links. In the latter case we were able to reduce our errors about 84%. Of course, in both instances we may be deluding ourselves, or we may be too conservative. The only way we could tell is to compare our judgments with those of a reasonable number of other people and perhaps make a few bets on our differences of opinion, with the bets possibly consisting of various decisions we might make with respect to investments in inventories, in refining facilities, in transportation facilities, in college graduate trainees, etc.

18.7   Long-term Forecasts

If we wished, we could analyze the 10-year link relatives, the 20-year link relatives, etc. If we did, we would find two things happening that would tend to discourage us. First, we would find very substantial variation in the links, with the variation increasing as we lengthened the range of the forecast. Second, we would have increasing difficulty in understanding our chart because we would

become most concerned that the links would be crossing from one era
to another in many instances, considerably increasing the possibility that we would be misled by what we see. As a result we would
end up with forecasts with such wide error bands that our forecasts
would have very little practical value. Very few businessmen find
it practical to plan on much of anything beyond a 5-year period.
Most investment decisions postulate a "payout" period of 3 to 5
years or the investment will not be made. This does not mean that
all investments turn out that way, but only that we do not *plan* on
less. Even then the average payout will be somewhat more than 5
years.

It also does not mean that businessmen are shortsighted and do
not look to the long-term future. Quite the contrary. It would be
very shortsighted to make plans for a 10-year period, say, *unless*
we were able to control events reasonably well over those 10 years.
Without such control, the plan probably will not be fulfilled. We
will begin to find ourselves in the essentially absurd position of acting according to a since out-dated plan in the face of developments
that make other action much more reasonable. It is not farsighted
to make plans for events that are beyond our range of vision. We
make plans for such out-of-range events by providing for *flexibility*
in plans. The greater the uncertainty, the greater is the necessity
to have *alternative* lines of action available. For example, a wise
military commander makes up battle plans with due consideration
for the expected weather, expected deployment of enemy troops,
expected depth of water at a river crossing, etc. But he had better
be ready with alternative plans if he finds the river too deep to wade.
Successful forecasting is as much the art of knowing what we *cannot
easily forecast* as it is the art of crystal ball gazing. That is why
it is so very important to have a reasonably clear idea of the *amount
of variation we have to contend with*.

18.8   Multiple Correlation Analysis of Link Relatives

We have so far confined ourselves to a naive type of analysis of
our link relatives. We confined our attention to information supplied by the gasoline consumption data themselves, with a few samples of subjective judgment added to intuitively reflect some phenomena such as major depressions and wars. If we wished, we
could still use our link relatives as our base and correlate such links
with additional information on temperature, number of registered

automobiles, etc. Such an analysis is outside our selected limits of coverage, however. We could pursue such a multiple correlation analysis on our own with a moderate amount of additional study of methodology and a considerable amount of knowledge of the particular area of application.

PROBLEMS AND QUESTIONS

18.1 It is sometimes recommended that a person, when driving an automobile, should not commit himself "further than he can see." Thus an intelligent driver presumably slows down at night and when approaching curves or the brow of a hill. An analogous line of reasoning is often applied to the problem of running a business. An intelligent businessman does not commit his company's resources "further than he can forecast."

If there is any merit in such a recommendation, it would seem that the job of the forecaster consists of more than trying to extend the range of vision into the future. In addition, the forecaster must be responsible for making quite clear *how far into the future his vision actually does extend*. Just as it is possible to drive a car at night without lights and at high rates of speed *on the assumption* that the road is straight and clear, it is possible to run a business by making substantial financial commitments *on the assumption* that "the road is straight and clear." We have a feeling, however, that we do not wish to be aboard in either case. There are times when prudence suggests that some provision be made for the uncertainties about the road ahead.

As a businessman, how would you protect yourself against sales fluctuations if you could not see these sales with 80% confidence any closer than:

(*a*) Plus or minus 2% 1 month ahead?

(*b*) Plus or minus 4% 6 months ahead?

(*c*) Plus or minus 20% 2 years ahead?

(*d*) Plus 100% and minus 50% 5 years ahead?

(*e*) Plus 300% and minus 80% 15 years ahead?

18.2 Suppose you are responsible for the company's policy in the hiring of college graduates as management trainees. What are the relative merits of a policy that advocates the hiring of several trainees who have exhibited erratic but occasionally brilliant performance in the hopes that one or two of the several will develop, with the others falling by the wayside?

Contrast this with a policy that advocates hiring a trainee only if it is considered "80%" probable that he will develop into a dependable and very useful executive, although possibly not given to flashes of genius.

18.3 Use your data on quarterly consumption of gasoline to develop naive forecasts of gasoline consumption for a range of:

(*a*) One quarter.

(*b*) Two quarters.

In each case, give explicit consideration to

1. The average expected rate of change. (Has it been changing?)

2. The 80% confidence limits for this rate. (Have these limits been changing?)

3. The relative reduction in ignorance that is achieved by paying attention to the particular quarter of the year that is used as a base.

18.4 Compare your ability to forecast gasoline consumption one quarter ahead with that to forecast two quarters ahead. Are you surprised at the direction and magnitude of the difference? Explain.

18.5 Use your annual data on airline passenger miles and railroad passenger miles and make naive forecasts for a range of:

(a) One year.

(b) Three years.

In each case, give explicit consideration to

1. The average expected rate of change. (Has it been changing?)

2. The 80% confidence limits for this rate. (Have these limits been changing?)

18.6 Compare your apparent ability to forecast airline passenger miles with that of forecasting railroad passenger miles.

Are these differences inherent in the nature of the two industries or are they a product of your greater ignorance about one industry than about the other? (Perhaps somebody else could have done better than you did in either or both of these two cases.) Explain.

18.7 Use your naive forecasts of Problem 18.5 as a base and analyze any additional related information that you anticipate will enable you to narrow your range of uncertainty.

State explicitly your 80% confidence limits *after* considering these other factors. Defend their validity.

Compare your naive limits with those after considering the additional information. Are they enough different to justify the extra time and effort you put into attempting to narrow the limits? Explain.

(Note: It is possible that your additional information may cause you to discount something that you thought was useful in developing your naive forecasts. Hence you may find that your 80% limits get wider rather than narrower with the additional information. In such a case would you now say that the additional information made your forecasts worse, or would you say something else?)

18.8 The attempt to combine some explicit statistical analysis of data (of the sort illustrated by your naive forecasts) with other information that may consist largely of the fruits of experience, etc., in order to arrive at a final forecast that uses all the available evidence, including that information embodied in the exercise of subjective judgment, can be likened to the use of prior probability distributions in combination with explicit new sample information to arrive at a final conclusion.

(a) Do you find the two procedures analogous? Explain.

(b) Do you see any way by which you might combine your feelings about the future of airline passenger miles with the historical data on such miles in order to develop explicitly an inference distribution of your expectations? Explain.

(c) Assume that you do see such a way, even though imperfectly. Would such an inference distribution have any family relationship to the inference distribution you might set up for the expected outcomes of the tossing of 10 coins? Explain.

(Hint: Do different people have to derive the same probability distribution for a problem in order for the distribution to be a proper probability distribution? Why or why not?)

18.9 Part I of *Business Cycle Indicators*, Vol. I. (Geoffrey H. Moore, Editor, a study by the National Bureau of Economic Research, Princeton University Press, Princeton, N.J., 1961) has 10 essays on the selection and interpretation of indicators. Select one essay and write a 5 to 10 page typewritten report on it. This report should:

(*a*) Tell the reader the main conclusions of the author of the essay;

(*b*) Outline the essential features of the evidence and/or the logical argument that supports such conclusions;

(*c*) Critically evaluate the practical usefulness of the indicators referred to or of the techniques of analysis referred to. This evaluation should proceed to the point of recommending exactly what an economic forecaster should now do about the substance of the essay in order to improve his own forecasting efforts.

chapter **19**

Index numbers: *the comparison of group characteristics*

19.1   The Group as a Standard of Comparison

We all frequently have occasion to rate a person, performance, institution, etc.; businessmen are no exception.   Although there are various ways of rating phenomena, one of the simplest and most common ways is to compare an individual item with the *group*, or *class*, to which it belongs.   For example, we conclude that the Houston Light and Power Company common stock has been a "fast grower" by comparing its rate of growth with the rate of growth of common stocks of similar public utilities, or with public utilities in general, or with common stocks in general, etc.   The problem that immediately arises, however, is that of characterizing the behavior of public utility common stocks.   Some of the stocks will have risen in price more than others.   Others might have fallen in price.   Some of the stocks have more shares outstanding than others and hence might be considered more important than others in the group.   Some of the stocks might be traded more than others, and not in proportion to shares outstanding.   These and other problems make it not so easy as first imagined to describe the behavior of the *group* of stocks.

It is obvious that an *average* behavior would be of interest.   We could then compare an individual stock with the average behavior and determine whether the individual stock price had risen more or less than average.

For example, suppose we have found that public utility common stock prices have risen 23.6% on the average over a given time interval.   Company A's stock rose 27.9% during the same interval.   Thus we can say that Company A's common has risen more than the

692

average. Exactly what we mean when we say that will depend on exactly how we calculated the average. We might have used an arithmetic mean of the prices of all the stocks, giving each stock a weight according to shares outstanding. Then we might find the average so dominated by the largest company that, say, as many as two thirds of the stocks actually rose in price more than the average of 23.6%. Thus Company A might be above average but still less than more than half the stocks. If we had used a median to average the group, we could then say unequivocally that Company A's stock did better than at least half of the companies'.

We sometimes are interested in how much above or below average a given item is. Given some average and the individual item, such as our average of 23.6% and the individual item of 27.9%, we can always calculate the relative difference between the two. Thus we might say that Company A's common stock rose 18% more than the average. (18% is the result of dividing the actual difference of 4.3% by the average of 23.6 and then multiplying by 100 to convert to percentages for ease of interpretation.) We might not be too clear about what we mean by 18% more than the average because we are not entirely clear about the meaning of the average of utility common stock prices having risen 23.6%. We might be much better informed if we could state such a comparison in terms of a *percentile ranking*. For example, if we knew that only 12% of all public utility common stocks rose more percentagewise than did Company A's, we would place Company A in a more exclusive position than if we could say only that 44% of all public utility common stocks rose more percentagewise than did Company A's. Either of these statements might be true given that the average was 23.6% and Company A's was 27.9%. Thus we find ourselves unable to clearly interpret a deviation from average unless we have some information about *all the deviations* from average, information supplied, say, by the standard deviation or the quartile deviation.

This is enough introduction to the kinds of problem we discuss in this chapter. We are concerned mainly with the problem of measuring *changes in groups of prices over time* and with *changes in physical outputs over time*. These are two of the most important problems in group comparisons over time for the general businessman, and also, for economists, government officials, and the general public. There are many other areas where similar problems arise, such as in psychological testing, grading of students, assessing the combined effects of the several elements making up soil fertility, etc. These areas have special problems of their own that require more specific knowledge of underlying factors than we presume to possess. In fact, we must confess a certain superficiality of treatment of the problems of price and output indexes because of lack of space to discuss properly the many difficult economic, social, and political issues that frequently cloud the practical work of constructing a price index. All we can do is point to the more general issues. Actual index number work is an extremely practical art. Compromise between theoretical niceties and budget considerations is very common. Errors in collecting data are often sufficiently large to make refinements of methodology somewhat like cutting firewood with scalpels. We probably tend in practice to pay far too much attention to variations in our indexes that are smaller than the basic errors in the data. A moderate amount of such self-delusion probably does no harm, particularly if it eases relations in the business family, but it would be well to avoid letting this become a way of life. The average citizen would be amazed to discover the many decisions that are being made, and the many more that are being recommended, on the basis of the movement of a few points in some of our major indexes, such as the Consumers' Price Index and the Dow-Jones Averages of Stock Prices.

19.2   An Inadequacy in Most Published Index Numbers

Most published index numbers provide only a single average figure at each date. Thus we cannot get any summary idea of the variation in the parts that make up the index. Most government indexes, however, are published with subindexes for various commodity classes and for various regions of the country. Thus we can get information on food prices as well as the behavior of Consumers' Prices in general. What we cannot get, however, is a summary evaluation, such as a standard deviation, of the degree to which, say, food prices differed in their price changes.

Thus it is necessary most of the time to try to get information on some of the more specialized index numbers if we wish to make evaluations of how much more a given price has varied than the average as shown by the general index. We should not try to draw more specific conclusions from an index number comparison than is really warranted by the available information.

19.3 The General Problems in Index Number Construction

It is convenient to discuss index numbers in terms of certain relatively distinct problem areas. We separate the problems into:

1. The specification of the *purpose* which underlies the principal uses of the indexes.
2. The specification of the exact *data* that are to be used in the index, the *sources* from which the data will be collected, and the specific *dates* at which the data will be collected.
3. The determination of the *base period* that will be used for any calculation of comparative relative changes.
4. The determination of the specific *weights* that will be attached to the various elements in the index.
5. The determination of the *type of average* that will be used to characterize the group behavior.
6. Determination of *revision* policy and procedures.

19.4 The Purpose that Underlies an Index Number Series

It has been semiseriously suggested that the primary use made of the Dow-Jones Averages of Common Stock Prices on the New York Stock Exchange is as a conversation ice-breaker on commuter trains. The conversation might start with something like "Wow, did you see that the Dow-Jones went off $6.74 today?" The conversation might then go almost anywhere from that beginning. If this were the only purpose for such an index, then we could build a good argument for an index formula that would insure enough volatility of movement to be a good conversation starter on almost any occasion. What the variation in the index really meant would be unimportant. The important thing would be for the index to *move*. In fact, it would be better for conversation purposes if we did not know what the variation meant. We could then have endless speculation on theories about why it did or did not move in certain ways.

The best way to find out what uses are really made of an index series is to be on hand when specific decisions are being made on the basis of turns in the index. Generally this is almost impossible to do. For example, with the Dow-Jones Averages, there are some people who make predictions about the Dow-Jones Averages based on theories about the past behavior of the Dow-Jones Averages. But this is a game that they play. What would be interesting to know is exactly what buy and sell orders are given for *specific* stocks based on the behavior of the Dow Averages. The indexes are supposed to represent the *whole list* of stocks in some way. But no one ever puts in an order to buy a cross section of the whole list of stocks. Specific stocks must be bought and sold, and it would be very interesting to know exactly what the behavior of a general index has to do with such specific transactions. We could then make proper decisions about the sample of stocks to include in the index, the frequency with which we should collect the prices, the weights we should assign to the various stocks in the index, the average we should use to summarize the individual stocks, etc.

Maybe it would be fruitful to turn the question around, and, instead of asking what our purposes are for an index, we find out how a given index is constructed and then ask what we can do with it as it is. For example, the Dow-Jones Average is essentially the *total* of the prices at the last transaction preceding the specification time, say at close of market, of a *selected list* of stocks, there being 30 issues included in the industrial stock section. Each price is given a weight of 1 in the index. The totals are compared at different times to find out what happened to stock prices. (Actually the totals are divided by factors that allow for stock splits, etc., over the years. For example, if a stock had been selling at $120 per share and it were split by issuing two new shares for each old share, the new price would immediately move to the neighborhood of $60. Actually, of course, there was no such spectacular decrease in the price of this company's stock. The Dow Average adjusts for this by using a smaller divisor than otherwise. In effect, the Dow Average is still on the old price level before the splits that have taken place. That is why we find the Dow Industrial Average in the neighborhood of $700 even though not a single issue in the list is priced as high as that. The point is that they theoretically would have been priced as high as that if the stocks had not been split over the years.) Table 19.1 shows a sample calculation of the industrials average for July 27, 1961.

What does movement in such an index mean? It obviously means what it is and what it does, namely, measures the changes in the total prices (or the arithmetic mean prices) of *the 30* issues, with one share of each being represented in the total. But this cannot be what interests most people because most people do not even know which 30 stocks are in the list. Presumably, then, the movement of the

TABLE 19.1

**Calculation of the Dow-Jones Average of 30 Industrial Stock Prices—
July 27, 1961 (Source of data: *The Wall Street Journal*, July 28, 1961)**

Company	Closing Price per Share	Company	Closing Price per Share
1. Allied Chemical	$ 63.625	16. Internat'l Nickel	$ 82.000
2. Aluminum Co.	74.250	17. Internat'l Paper	32.000
3. American Can	44.875	18. Johns-Manville	64.000
4. American Tel. & Tel.	124.250	19. Owens-Illinois Glass	86.250
5. American Tobacco	92.625	20. Proctor & Gamble	87.375
6. Anaconda	57.625	21. Sears Roebuck	68.375
7. Bethlehem Steel	42.875	22. Std. Oil of Cal.	52.250
8. Chrysler	46.000	23. Std. Oil of N.J.	45.875
9. DuPont	224.125	24. Swift & Co.	44.000
10. Eastman Kodak	104.000	25. Texaco	103.000
11. General Electric	65.625	26. Union Carbide	134.875
12. General Foods	83.000	27. United Aircraft	51.250
13. General Motors	47.375	28. U.S. Steel	86.500
14. Goodyear	43.875	29. Westinghouse Elect.	43.875
15. International Harvester	51.500	30. Woolworth	77.250
		Total:	$2224.50

Divisor: 3.165 (*Note*: This would be 30 except for the need to adjust for stock splits over the years.)

Average: $\dfrac{\$2224.50}{3.165} = \$702.80$

total of these 30 is hopefully supposed to represent the movement of something other than the total of these 30 issues.

What might this be? It might be the *total* of *all* the industrial issues, each with one share represented. It is entirely conceivable that the total of these 30 issues would go up, say, 10% if the total of all the industrials went up 10%. On the other hand, it is entirely conceivable that they would not parallel the relative movement of the total of the whole list. Suppose the movements were parallel. What would be the practical significance of the up and down movement in the total price of all the issues on the New York Stock Exchange? We could not even say that it represented the movement in the investment value of a cross section of American industry because of the equal weights given to each issue. A proper cross section certainly should make some allowance for the fact that different issues have more outstanding shares than others.

On the other hand, it is conceivable that the equally weighted total would move parallel to the variable weighted total. Suppose it did, what could we now say that would have practical significance? Given the validity of all these assumptions about the representativeness of our unweighted list of 30 issues as a counterpart to the weighted list of all issues, and given a little arithmetic, we could now make statements as sometimes appear in newspaper headlines such as "Market loses $4,500,000,000 of its value in a major sell-off!" This is certainly typical headline material, but what else is it? Would it mean that we as a citizen should support measures to reduce margin requirements, or to lower interest rates, or to eliminate taxation of dividends, or that we should sell our holdings, or sell short, or buy now to take advantage of the lower prices, etc.? It might be interesting to try to find out who lost this $4,500,000,000. Or, even better, who gained it from the losers, or was everybody a loser and the values just "disappeared" somewhere.

We ask questions like these not to embarrass us, or to be pedantically difficult, but only to emphasize that it is not easy to make a simple statement of purpose that will lead to simple rules for constructing an index number series. Most of the time we are not quite sure why we do want an index. We have a vague feeling that we will be better informed if we have some indexes of group behavior, even though we are not sure exactly what characteristic of the group is being summarized. More often than not we wistfully hope that we would get about the same answers to our index number calculations regardless of the various shadings of methodology we might adopt. For example, the hope that underlies almost all practical uses (conversation starters and headline material aside now) of the Dow and other stock price indexes is that the distribution of individual price movements is sufficiently symmetrical so that changes in the total or the arithmetic mean will parallel changes in the typical stock price. Thus, if a given stock increases in price more than the index, it would be fair to state that the given stock has performed better than the average, with the average now referring to typical behavior rather than an abstract total. Most people have a feeling they know what it means to compare an individual to a typical member of the group. They feel this even when they are not quite sure what is really typical. It is often as psychologically satisfying to say something is above average when we are mistaken as to what the average is as when we are correct in identifying the average.

Most published index numbers have not been constructed with any specific purpose in mind. Somebody thought it would be a good idea to measure changes in the behavior of some prices, say as an "additional service to subscribers." The first index was probably a simple arithmetic mean. Different people would have made many different uses of the index over the years, some reasonable and others quite farfetched. The advantages of familiarity and historical continuity would then work against most recommendations for improvements in the methods. Most indexes compiled and published by the Federal Government have started out as so-called general purpose indexes, thus providing the widest possible use. Most of the indexes are calculated by weighted totals or their equivalents. Frequent studies of the behavior of individual prices have revealed that most of the individual price changes form reasonably symmetrical distributions, particularly if the time interval is not more than a few years. Thus weighted totals, or aggregates, give about the same answers as would medians or the equivalent.

The problem of special purposes is handled not so much by different formulas as by the construction of subindexes to cover the changes in various component parts of the main index. If we are going to use any published index number series, we should investigate the conditions of selection of data, selection of weights, etc., to make sure we are using the best possible index for our purposes. It is particularly important to locate any specialized index, such as an index of wholesale steel prices if that is what we wish, rather than take a handy index of broader coverage, such as an index of ferrous metals prices.

If we are planning to construct our own indexes for a special purpose, such as DuPont does for the selling prices of its products, then, of course, we should make every effort to find out specifically how the indexes are going to be used throughout our company or by outsiders if we plan to publish our results. Then to protect the users and our reputation, we should clearly state sufficient detail on our data and methods so that if anyone misuses the index, it is done knowingly. There are no secrets in constructing index numbers, and people are just as suspicious of any secret methods we claim as we should be of any secret methods that others claim. It is the tedium of collecting data and calculating results that deters most people from making up their own indexes, not any lack of sufficient knowledge.

19.5   The Specification of the Basic Data to Be Used

We cannot collect data until we have specific knowledge of exactly what we want and of what can be made available within the current limits of custom in the trade. The American economic system is a veritable jungle of styles, sizes, colors, models, discounts, special deals, tie-in sales, etc. If we were to ask five people to find out what the price is of a 4-oz. jar of Maxwell House powdered coffee in Town X, we would very likely get five different answers. The five people would also return with a lot of questions they would now ask us so they could be more specific in satisfying our purpose. The situation would be even worse if we had asked them to find out the price of a man's white short-sleeved sport shirt, or the price of a 1958 Chevrolet 9-passenger station wagon "in good condition."

As bad as the situation may seem to be in the United States, it is considerably worse (from the point of view of easy collection of price data) in many other countries. Individual bargaining is the custom in many countries and our five people may find five different prices even though they all go to the same store and are waited on by the same clerk. Most American businesses have a price policy that stabilizes the price from customer to customer and day to day. In fact, the best way to collect price statistics in an A&P Super Market is to get the price lists from the regional office. Store prices will be the same except for laggardness on the part of the store manager and such specialized problems as deteriorating bakery goods.

Homogeneity of Data over Time

Suppose we were assigned the task of determining what happened to the price of a Ford sedan from 1959 to 1960. We would certainly have enough sense to realize that we should price the car at the same place each year and under the same sales conditions, say F.O.B. Detroit with full cash payment and no trade-in. We would also price the same basic model with respect to standard and optional equipment. But what do we do about the fact that the Ford Motor Company assures us in its advertisements that the 1960 car is supposed to be a better car dollar for dollar than the 1959 model despite the fact that the list price is $42 more in 1960? We now encounter a common phenomenon in American business, namely, that strictly comparable products from year to year do not exist. A 1960 car is not the same as a 1959 car, for both physical and psychological reasons. Nor is a brand new 1959 car available for sale in 1960 the same as a 1959 car available in 1959. How then do we determine what happened to the price of a particular model Ford sedan, or to the price of similarly so-called improved products? The answer is that we make arbitrary rules about such things and let the purists argue about it. A reincarnated Solomon could not separate that part of the price change that was due to a change in the product from that part that was due to a real price increase. The United States Bureau of Labor Statistics makes no claim to be Solomon, so it makes no effort to effect a separation. It treats the price change as entirely a price change. This distresses the auto manufacturers and bolsters the argument of some analysts that the Bureau's Consumer Price Index has an upward bias. The only time the U.S.B.L.S. finds it practical to allow for changes in the quality of the product is when the quality change has an obvious physical base which affects the product's durability or serviceability. Otherwise the U.S.B.L.S. finds it wiser to avoid the subtler changes in product quality.

The issue of what really gives a product economic value has long plagued economists and other social scientists. The issue has also been dealt with on a practical level by any practicing businessman who must try to sell a product at a price sufficiently high to cover all his costs. We all recognize the problem of trying to define an economic good or service so that we can measure the changes in its price without the confusion caused by changes in the product's qualities, both real and imagined. The disagreement arises when we try to rationalize the problem. One side, for example, would argue that the transportation aspect of the cost of living has gone up if the price of an automobile has gone up, quite irrespective of whether the car is a better car, or a more comfortable car, or a faster accelerating car, etc. The point is that we must buy what the rest of America is buying, and, of course, we can buy only those products that are available.

Another side argues that to classify a higher price for a better quality, and hence a higher standard of living, as an increase in the cost of living is to make the notion of measuring changes in the cost of living devoid of all practical meaning. The fact that it is difficult to define an unambiguous list of items that make up some meaningful standard of living over time is no excuse for abandoning the attempt entirely. Hence, this side would argue that a very serious effort should be made to estimate the prices of homogeneous units at different points in time, even if we have to imagine what the price might have been if the product had not changed. Thus, for example, if it is estimated that the 1959 Ford could have been profitably priced and sold in 1960 at $25 less than in 1959, then the price of the Ford car has gone down even though the only car available in 1960 is priced at $42 more than the car that was actually available in 1959. We can agree with this argument and still wonder who is going to decide what a car that is not going to be built or sold would cost to build and sell. Imagine the UAW and the Ford Motor Company arguing about this issue! They occasionally have difficulties with the facts about cars that are actually built and sold.

There is also the problem of classifying what happened to the elderly couple on a fixed income who tried to maintain a constant standard of living in the face of rising prices. Although it might conceivably have been true that they could have continued to buy some of their old items at the old prices if they were still available, the fact is that the old products are not available, and the elderly couple *must adopt a higher standard of living in some items whether they wish to or not!* Of course, if their resources are definitely limited, they will have to reduce their standard in, say, housing in order to increase their standard in food. Only a smooth talker could convince such a couple that their cost of living has not gone up as they move to poorer quarters.

We are in no position to rationalize the problems that get confused with economic, psychological, sociological, and political issues. We regret that they make a farce of any attempt to devise simple and unequivocal statistical procedures for measuring what happened to a few prices over time. We discover that the mechanical statistical procedures are indeed quite simple once we have the data in hand compared to the problems of getting good data in hand.

The Problem of When to Collect Price Data

If we were asked to find out what the price of United States Steel common stock was on the New York Stock Exchange on July 27, 1961, we would have an immediate problem of determining *when* on the 27th we wish to get the price. Hundreds of transactions occurred during the day, most at different prices. Do we wish the opening price, the closing price, the midday price, or an average price? The same problem exists if we wish to know the price of butter in the A&P during the month of July, 1961.

The ideal solution to the problem of what price to use to represent a day, or month, or year of prices would be a weighted arithmetic mean of the prices of all transactions. We would have to have a very unusual purpose to find another solution, such as a weighted geometric mean, preferable to the weighted arithmetic mean. Practical considerations make it virtually impossible to keep records on each transaction; hence compromises are usually made. The most common practice is to use the price prevailing near the *middle* of the time interval or to use the simple arithmetic mean of the prices at the beginning and end of the period. An exception to this rule has been the convention of using the end-of-day, or closing, price for stock exchange prices. These compromises likely do introduce errors for some applications, but they are justified by the saving in time and money.

There are occasions when simple solutions to the price-date problem are obviously seriously in error. The retail grocery trade has developed price policies that lead to a stream of week-end specials. The Thursday, Friday, and Saturday prices of many items are lower than the Monday, Tuesday, and Wednesday prices of the same items. A simple arithmetic mean would be a poor average because the week-end volume tends to be much higher than the beginning-week volume, so much so that many stores have begun to offer beginning-week specials to try to even out this imbalance that was partially caused by their week-end specials! The U.S.B.L.S. must be very judicious in its selection of the appropriate price for the week or the month.

The most important rule to follow in date selection is *consistency*. Since we are more interested in price *movement* than in price *level*, we often find that the comparison of two "too low" prices will give just about the same answer as two "too high" prices or two average prices. If bias is *consistent*, we can often ignore it in our final results provided we perform our calculations intelligently.

The Problem of Where to Collect Price Data

If we are constructing an index of prices of common stock on the New York Stock Exchange, we have no problem of deciding where we should get our prices. But, if we are constructing a Consumers' Price Index for the city of Chicago, we definitely have the problem of selecting the stores from which to get the prices. We certainly could not survey all the stores. Even if we did, we would still have the problem of properly weighting the various store prices in order to get an average for all stores. We solve this problem the same way we solve so many problems in economic data: We concentrate on the fact that we are interested in *movement* of prices over time and not the *level* of prices at any moment of time, and we assume that the intense competition in American business will force prices into line fairly quickly. For example, suppose the local independent grocery charges $.83 per pound for Land O' Lakes butter at the same time the A&P is charging $.79. If economic factors force the A&P to raise its price to, say, $.82, the same economic factors will probably affect the local independent grocer, and he will be forced to raise his price to, say, $.86. We would thus get about the same relative price change whether we measured the price change at the independent grocery or the A&P. (Note that there would be rounding errors because of the custom of quoting prices to the cent.)

We should not always rely on the force of competition to quickly adjust prices at all levels and thus solve our problem of where to collect our prices. For example, the postwar flowering of discount-house retail merchandising led to rather chaotic price conditions in the market for most household appliances. Old-style retailers did not react smoothly to these new competitive pressures, nor did the discount houses always know their costs well enough to maintain consistent price policies over time. As a result it became very difficult to find out what was happening to the price of a General Electric refrigerator, particularly since the manufacturer was also changing models every year. It took an experienced price collector to chart the course of such prices during those chaotic times, and even he would probably not have risked too much of his money or his reputation on the accuracy of his figures. We can see why monopolists, cartelists, and other strong believers in orderly markets might easily enlist the support of self-centered statisticians! In fact, nothing would make the price statistician's job easier than to have prices set by decree of some central authority; however, he would then have the problem of deciding to what extent he should take into account black market and gray market prices, a problem not at all foreign to the U.S.B.L.S. during World War II.

The Problem of the Sample of Data to Use

Suppose we were asked to make up a shopping list to cover the items purchased by a Philadelphia family during a month's time. We would then price this list in two separate months and calculate the difference in total cost, thus getting a measure of the changes in the total cost of a specified list of items that presumably represents the items of expenditure of a Philadelphia family. It is immediately apparent that we have the problem of deciding what family and what month of this family's purchases. The appropriate family would be a family typical for the group we are interested in. The Bureau of Labor Statistics uses the goods and services purchased by city wage-earner and clerical-worker families. They find a *typical list* rather than a *typical family*. Stratified random samples are taken of families, who then keep records of their expenditures. These various budget records are processed to develop a master typical expenditure list for families in that and similar cities. It is then assumed that this expenditure pattern will remain reasonably constant over several years, or until Congress can be persuaded to appropriate the money for another budget study. In the meantime, minor modifications are made in some of the items to allow for well-known and significant shifts in expenditures. For example, the rapid development of television necessitated some adjustments. Different lists are developed for each major city. The various resultant city indexes are then combined into a national index by the use of weights proportionate to the number of wage-earner and clerical-worker families in the various cities. Thus the national index is much more affected by price movements in New York City than in Augusta, Georgia.

Similar problems of sampling exist for most indexes. Ideally we try to get a cross section of the group that is purportedly represented by the index. This is best achieved by those who are familiar with the behavior patterns in the particular application. Most samples end up as a stratified-random sample, with the rules for stratification coming from the specialized knowledge that is available and the randomness coming from the ignorance that still remains. Usually we find the sample selection process so mixed up with judgmental and intuitive elements that we hesitate strongly to apply the routine probability formulas that we are familiar with to estimate the range of expected sampling errors. Most index numbers are calculated and published with no attempt to quantify the possible sampling errors in the final results. The user has to use his own judgment in deciding what significance he should attach to small movements in the indexes. That is one of the reasons why Congress and the U.S.B.L.S. have had frequent occasion to set up special commissions of interested and/or expert parties to evaluate the accuracy of the indexes. A formula just does not do an intelligent job.

19.6 The Determination of the Base Period

It is customary to express an index number as a percentage of some base. For example the U.S.B.L.S. Index of Consumers' Prices in May, 1961 was 127.4% of the 1947 to 1949 average. The index would be at a much higher figure if the base were 1933, or at a lower figure if the base were 1960. Theoretically, the particular base used should make no difference in the relative comparison of figures at different dates. For example, if we were to compare the figures given in column 2 of Table 19.2, we would get the same relative results regardless of which figure we used as a base. The other columns show a few of the possibilities. Figure 19.1 shows what happens to these various comparisons when they are plotted on a logarithmic scale, as they should be when we are interested in relative changes. Note that all the lines of comparison are parallel, including the line showing the actual data. This result is just what we would expect because all the change in base does is change the *unit of measure*.

The problem we have with the base is partly psychological and partly technical. The technical problem arises because it does make a difference what base we use if we *average* several individual series, which is of course what we often do in index number work. We consider this phenomenon in a later section. The psychological problems arise because people are impressionable and can be persuaded that, for example, prices are high because the index shows big numbers or low because it shows small numbers. This is what encourages advertising copy writers to talk about the giant 40-ounce size instead of the 2 1/2-pound size. There is some evidence that people are becoming more sophisticated in these matters and are perfectly capable of and willing to scrutinize the unit being used to generate such big or small numbers.

The base also becomes important when it comes to rationalizing

TABLE 19.2

Relative Differences in a Given Set of Figures with the Use of Different Bases

Time Period (1)	Data (2)	Period 1 as Base (3)	Period 2 as Base (4)	Period 5 as Base (5)
1	20	1.00	.67	.33
2	30	1.50	1.00	.50
3	40	2.00	1.33	.67
4	50	2.50	1.67	.83
5	60	3.00	2.00	1.00

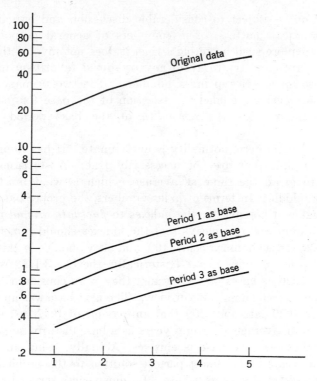

Fig. 19.1 Illustration of effects of a different base on the relative sizes of a series of numbers. (Source: Table 19.2.) Vertical scale is logarithmic.

some of the conflicts which arise in society. People have an understandable desire to argue for that base which bolsters their own argument. The farmer, for example, is most eager to point out how his relative price position has deteriorated since the 1910 to 1914 era. He naturally is not eager to discuss what a fine position he had during this era. The farmer is not alone in this attitude, however. Even college professors are not averse to pointing out how their relative income position in society has declined since the 1930's, with no reference to how it improved to that point.

The fact is that relative positions of prices, incomes, etc., have been shifting from year-to-year and decade-to-decade throughout the centuries. No group likes to see its relative position worsen, although it is perfectly willing to see it improved. The base used to compare such changes in relative positions is often of the

essence and is subject to considerable discussion and bargaining in
many practical matters.   The compilers of general purpose index
numbers deplore such bickering (when it does not involve their personal welfare) and try to avoid any presumed favoritism in selecting a base for a series of index numbers.   The two primary considerations which have guided the selection of the base for most government indexes are the *normality* of the base period and its
recency.

The use of the term normality is unfortunate.   It has implications
to some people that are not necessarily true.   A statistician uses
normal to mean the same as average, which is what most people
mean by middle.   In terms of index numbers, the proper base is that
which makes it possible for the indexes to *fluctuate around* the base
data.   In numbers, this means that the indexes should sometimes be
above 100 and sometimes below 100, and they should do this within
the experience of living men.   Historically, the U.S.B.L.S. used 1913
and then 1926 as bases partly because they were considered average
years from an economic point of view.   The next base was an *average*
of 1935 to 1939 data and after that an *average* of 1947 to 1949 data.
The use of an average of several years as a base disturbs some people
because they feel the base is elusive.   Actually, using an average
of several years is an almost perfect solution to the problem of selecting an average year as a base.   Its elusiveness serves to prevent
people from putting too much stock in the base as a source of argument.

A recent base is desirable for several reasons.   One reason is that
it tends to make the indexes fluctuate around 100 within recent experience, thus satisfying the desire for a base that is average.   Second, it provides a base that is within the memory span of many
people, thus simplifying judgments about the significance of the
measured changes.   To be told that consumers' prices today are six
times what they were during the Phoenician Wars provides most
people with very little information.   Third, it usually reduces the
heterogeneity in the data.   The 1960 Ford sedan is more like the
1959 or 1958 sedan than it is like the 1948 sedan.   Thus the price
comparison is more representative of a price difference instead of a
product difference if the base is reasonably recent.   Fourth, the
various prices in an index have less chance to wander off in different
directions over short periods of time than over long periods.   Hence
an average of short-period price changes tends to have less dispersion
around it than an average of long-period price changes.

19.7 Determination of the Specific Weights to Be Used

In most practical problems the particular weights to use for index numbers is fairly obvious. For example, it is difficult to argue against the use of the number of loaves of bread purchased during a month as the appropriate weight for the price of bread in a monthly index of consumers' prices. The monthly rate of purchase would be similarly logical for all other items in the list. A wholesale price index should be weighted according to the number of units sold at wholesale during the particular time period. A newspaper advertising lineage rate index should probably be weighted according to the number of circulation lines sold by a newspaper. Thus a newspaper with a circulation of 200,000 and with 50,000 lines of space sold would have its basic line rate assigned a weight proportional to the 200,000 × 50,000, or 10,000,000,000. Our most difficult problems occur with durable goods that are frequently sold and resold. The extreme example of such goods is a stock certificate. Another example would be a home. We now must choose between the number of *transactions* and the number of *units in existence* as weights. The issue is often debated of whether we should use "shares traded" as weights in a stock price index, or whether we should use "shares outstanding," or whether we should pay no attention to either as does the Dow-Jones Average. "Shares outstanding" as a weight is more attractive to financial people than "shares traded" for reasons that are best left to financial experts. On the other hand, "houses traded" has been used more often in indexes of real estate prices than "houses outstanding," for reasons that are most understood by real estate experts.

Incidentally, one of the apparent advantages of using shares outstanding in a stock price index is that the weights naturally stay quite constant over the years, thus avoiding the often very perplexing issue of the time period for the choice of proper weights. The number of shares traded fluctuates quite a bit, even from day to day, thus altering the relative importance, by this measure, of the various stock issues. The problem of when to select the weights and how often to revise them would be quite pressing under such circumstances.

The Problem of the Proper Time Period for the Determination of Weights

The relative frequency of purchase and sale of most commodities is in a constant state of flux. Most families do not maintain a fixed consumption pattern over any significant period of time. Various products gain and lose popularity over time. New products enter the market and often start to displace some of the old products. As soon as we try to give weights to commodity prices according to their relative importance, we immediately come to the question of *when*. The common sense solution to this problem is to use a time period that provides weights that are as applicable as possible to the points being compared. For example, if we were to measure changes in consumers' prices from 1955 to 1960, we would do well to use a list of items with weights that reflect the consumption patterns in both 1955 and 1960. The best way to do this is with an *average* of the patterns in the two years.

Although the use of weights based on the averages of the years being compared appeals to our sense of logic, it does not appeal to our pocketbook. We cannot average the weights unless we have information on them. The collection of such information is often a major task, or at least we have always thought of it as such, particularly when it pertains to family consumption patterns. Therefore we compromise our logical desires and usually use the weights that prevailed in a particular year as though they also prevailed in the other years being measured. We continue until our sense of propriety becomes sufficiently offended for us to spend the necessary funds to collect new information on consumption patterns. It is possible that some day a country as wealthy as the United States may set aside enough funds to make consumption pattern studies a continuing process.

We may wonder why the U.S.B.L.S. does not go back and revise all its indexes in the intervening years when new weight information becomes available. Thus, instead of an index for 1957 based on 1951–1952 weights, they might recalculate to get a 1957 index based on an average of, say, 1951–1952 and 1961–1962 weights. There is of course the clerical labor involved in such a task. More important, however, is the fact that the first published indexes were looked upon as *official* and became the basis of such decisions as the timing and magnitude of wage-rate changes. If revisions would make significant changes in such decisions, some people would be very upset. If they would make no significant differences in the original indexes, other people would wonder why so much money was spent on the revisions of the weights. Thus, it is perhaps as well that we do not know too much about what the force of the revisions might have been.

One factor we should always keep in mind when we are analyzing index number series over a period of years, however, is that we will be deluding ourselves if we pay much attention to every little change in the indexes. Many of these little changes are no more than statistical mirages whose form would have changed with another selection of weights.

19.8 The Determination of the Type of Average to Use in an Index Number Series

The subject of the proper type of *average* to use for the construction of index numbers has been quite thoroughly explored and discussed in the literature of the last 50 years or so. Economists have been the most concerned with the problem. Unfortunately, the discussion has not resulted in any really satisfactory resolution of the issues. The difficulty is caused by the existence of certain fundamental dilemmas. There are several very desirable properties that an index number series should have—if we look at each of these properties separately. But when we put all these desirable properties together, we find that some of them are self-contradictory. Hence the discussion rages on as each discussant pleads for the pre-eminent importance of one property rather than another. We merely indicate the bare outlines of the dilemmas involved and then go on to the types of solutions that are actually being used.

Purpose and the Choice of an Average

We emphasized the extreme importance of *purpose* in the choice of an average during our earlier discussion of the general problem of averages and their use. (See Chapter 6.) At that time we pointed out that there seemed to be only three general classes of purpose that would involve the use of an average. These were:

1. To select a figure that would have the property of being *as close as possible* to the various items in the group that the average was supposed to represent. If error in representation is important, such an average would have the advantage of *minimizing* such error. We discovered that the *median* had the inherent property of minimizing error, but we often used the *arithmetic mean* as a substitute when the distribution of items was *reasonably symmetrical*. We thus could take advantage of certain desirable properties of the mean without sacrificing our purpose.
2. To select a figure that would have the property of being the *most probable,* or the *most frequent.* This is a useful property when the size of an error makes no difference, or in situations of an "all or nothing" condition. We discovered that the *mode* had this inherent property. We asserted that there were very few such problem situa-

tions in real life outside the area of man-made games. Close does tend
to count in most other situations.

3. To select a figure that bears no inherent relationship to the *individual*
items in the group but which does have some inherent relationship to
some property of the group as a *mass*. The most commonly thought
of and most useful *mass property* of a group is the *total* of the group.
We discovered that this led us to the *arithmetic mean* as an average
that had inherent algebraic relationship to the *total* of a group. (The
harmonic mean does also, but we discovered that we could always
avoid the use of the harmonic mean by recasting the way of expressing
the data so that the arithmetic mean could be used instead.)

We also discovered that it is conceptually possible to calculate a
geometric mean that had the interesting property of being algebraically
related to the *product* of all the items in a series. We did have trouble,
however, in finding good reasons why a person would be interested in
the product of a series of numbers, particularly when the numbers had
units and the product would then have some most peculiar units attached to it. We now find the geometric mean again bothering us
because it has caused index number theorists much concern.

With this review we are now ready to face the problem of the
proper average in index number work. As we can imagine, since
indexes are concerned with the comparison of *groups*, averages are
at the very heart of all index number work.

The sine qua non of the proper average is that it satisfy a meaningful purpose. This rule is not changed when we consider index numbers. It is not accidental that practically all index numbers have
been calculated with the arithmetic mean. There are many reasons
for this, not the least of which has been its widespread familiarity.
But more importantly, it tends to satisfy one or the other, or both,
of the two purposes that dominate almost all uses of averages. It is
used because it represents the *total* and the total is often of great
practical significance. For example, the total of consumer expenditures on the items of family living is definitely a meaningful figure.
If the total increases because of price changes, this has significance
to the family and its budget.

The total of common stock prices, or of expenditures at wholesale,
has questionable practical significance. No one really tries to buy
a cross section of the available stock issues and thus build an investment portfolio that would have its total value move somewhat the
same as the movements in the total value of all the issues. (Perhaps
someone should. Most people try to select the best issues, but there
is some research that indicates that very few selected portfolios perform better than a random selection from the whole list. Perhaps
there is more logic to some of the methods used in the published
stock indexes than we suspect!) Similarly, no one really goes into

the retail business by trying to purchase a cross section of all goods offered at wholesale. The arithmetic mean might still be quite appropriate, however, if either of two conditions exists in the data. If the distributions of items are *symmetrical*, the mean and median will be the same. We then prefer the mean because of its familiarity and its ease of calculation. The other condition is the *stability of the shape of the distribution over time*. If the skewness remains essentially constant, the relative differences between the means and medians will remain essentially constant. The *ratio* between two means would then be approximately the same as the ratio of two medians; and it is these ratios that are of interest in index number work, not the actual levels of the averages. A simple example illustrates the point. Suppose our base distribution of prices has a median of $50 and a mean of $60, thus reflecting definite skewness. If prices then rise 50% on the average with no change in the general shape of the distribution, the new median would be $75 and the new mean $90. The ratio of $90 to $60 is the same as the ratio of $75 to $50. It is obvious, however, that the two means tend to overstate the level of prices in each period.

19.9   Some Technical Problems in Index Number Averages

Common sense suggests that index numbers should satisfy two very logical requirements. One, we should get consistent answers regardless of the *base* used in the calculation, and, second, a *price* index multiplied by a *quantity* index should give the same result as a *value* index from the same data. Let us consider them in turn.

The Base Reversal Test (Also Called the Time Reversal Test)

Let us consider a very simple problem with only two time periods and two commodities involved. Table 19.3 shows the basic data we use. We demonstrated earlier in Table 19.2 and Fig. 19.1 that the

TABLE 19.3

Basic Price Data for Illustrating the Base Reversal Test in the Calculation of Index Numbers

	Period 1	Period 2
Product *A*	$.10	$.20
Product *B*	.50	.25

base makes no difference if we are working with only *one* series of data. Now let us see what happens when we work with the *averages* of two or more series.

The Use of Simple Aggregates or Simple Arithmetic Means. Table 19.4 shows the possible results we obtain for our indexes if we use simple aggregates and simple arithmetic means as our summarization techniques. Note that we get the same answer with means as we do with totals. We should expect this because of the algebraic relationship of the mean to the total. Also note that the indexes in relative form are consistent regardless of whether we use Period 1 or Period 2 as a base; 100.0 to 75.0 is precisely the same as 133.3 is to 100.0. The last two numbers are each 1/3 larger than the first two. This phenomenon is always the result when we calculate index numbers by getting *relatives of means or of aggregates*. For example, if we had calculated the *geometric mean* price in each period and then taken relatives of the results, we would have obtained consistent results regardless of the base used. Table 19.5 shows such calculations. Note that the final answers are different from those when we used the mean, a difference we comment about later. At the moment

TABLE 19.4

Indexes Based on Simple Aggregates or Simple Arithmetic Means of Basic Data

	Period 1	Period 2
Product *A*	$ .10	$ .20
Product *B*	.50	.25
Totals:	$ .60	$ .45
Relatives of *Totals* with Period 1 as Base:	100.0 *	75.0
Relatives of *Totals* with Period 2 as Base:	133.3	100.0
Arith. Mean	$ .30	$ .225
Relatives of *Means*—1 Base:	100.0	75.0
Relatives of *Means*—2 Base:	133.3	100.0

* *Note*: In this and all subsequent tables we arbitrarily convert relatives to percentages without explicit calculations.

TABLE 19.5

Indexes Based on the Geometric Means of Actual Prices

	Period 1 Log of Price	Period 2 Log of Price
Product A	9.0000–10	9.3010–10
Product B	9.6990–10	9.3979–10
Sum of Logs:	18.6990–20	18.6989–20
Mean of Logs:	9.3495–10	9.3495–10
Geometric mean:	\$.2236	\$.2236
Relatives—1 Base:	100.0	100.0
Relatives—2 Base:	100.0	100.0

we are concerned only with the *internal consistency* of a given type of average, not with whether it gives the "right" answer.

The Use of Averages of Relatives.   When we compare two groups, we have the option of characterizing each group and then comparing these group characterizations, or of comparing the individual members and then characterizing these individual comparisons.   The same options are available for any kind of group comparisons.   Suppose, for example, we wished to compare the New York Yankee baseball team with the Los Angeles Dodgers.   We might evaluate the New York Yankees as a team and compare our evaluation with a similar evaluation of the Los Angeles Dodgers.   A comparison of team batting averages would be an example.   On the other hand, we might compare the New York catcher with the Los Angeles catcher, the New York first baseman with the Los Angeles first baseman, etc.; and then we would summarize all our comparisons.   Usually we would not get exactly the same answers.   That is why the sports writers usually make both kinds of comparisons.   Sometimes, as a matter of fact, we find a sports writer making a statement like, Team A is weaker at almost every position than Team B, but as a team they are still tougher to beat.   We find the same kind of apparent contradictions when we work with alternative ways of comparing groups of prices.

Table 19.6 shows the disconcerting results when we reverse the base in calculating the arithmetic mean of relatives.   Here we have an obvious contradiction, with prices apparently going up if we use

TABLE 19.6

Indexes Based on the Arithmetic Mean of Relatives

	Period 1 as Base		Period 2 as Base	
	Period 1 Relative	Period 2 Relative	Period 1 Relative	Period 2 Relative
Product *A*	100.0	200.0	50.0	100.0
Product *B*	100.0	50.0	200.0	100.0
Arithmetic Mean:	100.0	125.0	125.0	100.0

Period 1 as a base and going down if we use Period 2 as a base. Thus we can assert that the use of the arithmetic mean of relatives will not satisfy the *base reversal test*. We will get different results depending on the period we use as a base. Lest we get overly upset about such inconsistent results as just given, we should hasten to add that the above differences are very much larger than ever occur in practice. We have taken the very extreme case of one product doubling in price while the other one halved in order to draw the point very vividly.

If we now look at Table 19.7, we can see why the geometric mean

TABLE 19.7

Indexes Based on the Geometric Mean of Relatives

	Period 1 as Base		Period 2 as Base	
	Period 1 Relative	Period 2 Relative	Period 1 Relative	Period 2 Relative
Product *A*	100.0	200.0	50.0	100.0
Product *B*	100.0	50.0	200.0	100.0
Product of Relatives:	10000.0	10000.0	10000.0	10000.0
$\sqrt{}$ of Product:	100.0	100.0	100.0	100.0

Note: The geometric mean is here calculated strictly according to its definition, namely as the *n*th root of the product of all the items. Since we have only two items, this formula becomes: the square root of the product of the two items.

has attained such prominence in discussions of index number theory. Note that the geometric mean of relatives gives consistent answers regardless of the base. In fact, it gives exactly the same answers as we got when we took the relatives of the geometric means of the actual prices as in Table 19.5. Thus the geometric mean has the very interesting property of giving the same and consistent answers whether we compare the averages of groups or whether we average the individual comparisons. Before we try to evaluate the practical significance of this rather remarkable property of the geometric mean, we analyze the impact of *weights* on all of this and on related matters.

The Factor Reversal Test

Table 19.8 adds some quantity information to the price information given in Table 19.3. We are now in a position to calculate *weighted* price indexes, *quantity* indexes, and *value* indexes. Let us first calculate some weighted *price* indexes and check these for satisfaction of the *base reversal test* before going to the quantity and value indexes and the checking of the consistency of all three indexes with each other.

Table 19.9 shows the various results we get using the weighted aggregate formula with different combinations of weights. As expected, the base reversal test is satisfied in every instance. This is a direct consequence of not taking relatives until we have reduced the data of a given year to *one* figure. We did get different indexes, however, depending on whether we used first or second period weights, or an average of the two. This is as expected, also. If we did not get different results with different weights, then, of course, weights would not make any difference. We also found the indexes with the *average* weights falling between those with first or second period weights. This is a common sense expectation, and it confirms what we said earlier about the probable superiority of average weights.

TABLE 19.8

Prices and Quantities of Products A and B at Periods 1 and 2

	Period 1		Period 2	
	Price—p_1	Quantity—q_1	Price—p_2	Quantity—q_2
Product A	$.10	50 lbs.	$.20	80 lbs.
Product B	.50	15 gals.	.25	10 gals.

TABLE 19.9

The Use of Weighted Aggregates in the Construction of Price Indexes

A. Period 1 as Base; Period 1 Quantities as Weights

	$p_1 q_1$	$p_2 q_1$
Product A	$ 5.00	$10.00
Product B	7.50	3.75
	$12.50	$13.75

Indexes: $\dfrac{\Sigma p_1 q_1}{\Sigma p_1 q_1} = \dfrac{\$12.50}{\$12.50} = 100.0; \dfrac{\Sigma p_2 q_1}{\Sigma p_1 q_1} = \dfrac{\$13.75}{\$12.50} = 110.0$

B. Period 2 as Base; Period 1 Quantities as Weights

Indexes: $\dfrac{\Sigma p_1 q_1}{\Sigma p_2 q_1} = \dfrac{\$12.50}{\$13.75} = 90.9; \dfrac{\Sigma p_2 q_1}{\Sigma p_2 q_1} = \dfrac{\$13.75}{\$13.75} = 100.0$

Base Reversal Test: $110.0 \times 90.9 = 100.0$

C. Period 1 as Base; Period 2 Quantities as Weights

	$p_1 q_2$	$p_2 q_2$
Product A	$ 8.00	$16.00
Product B	5.00	2.50
	$13.00	$18.50

Indexes: $\dfrac{\Sigma p_1 q_2}{\Sigma p_1 q_2} = \dfrac{\$13.00}{\$13.00} = 100.0; \dfrac{\Sigma p_2 q_2}{\Sigma p_1 q_2} = \dfrac{\$18.50}{\$13.00} = 142.3$

D. Period 2 as Base; Period 2 Quantities as Weights

Indexes: $\dfrac{\Sigma p_1 q_2}{\Sigma p_2 q_2} = \dfrac{\$13.00}{\$18.50} = 70.3; \dfrac{\Sigma p_2 q_2}{\Sigma p_2 q_2} = \dfrac{\$18.50}{\$18.50} = 100.0$

Base Reversal Test: $142.3 \times 70.3 = 100.0$

E. Period 1 as Base; Average Quantities as Weights

	$p_1 \left(\dfrac{q_1 + q_2}{2} \right)$	$p_2 \left(\dfrac{q_1 + q_2}{2} \right)$
Product A	$ 6.50	$13.00
Product B	6.25	3.125
	$12.75	$16.125

Indexes: $\dfrac{\$12.75}{\$12.75} = 100.0 \quad \dfrac{\$16.125}{\$12.75} = 126.5$

F. Period 2 as Base; Average Quantities as Weights

Indexes: $\dfrac{\$12.75}{\$16.125} = 79.1 \quad \dfrac{\$16.125}{\$16.125} = 100.0$

Base Reversal Test: $126.5 \times 79.1 = 100.0$

Table 19.10 shows the use of the weighted aggregate formula in the construction of *quantity indexes*. The procedures are precisely the same as with price indexes except for the interchanging of all the p's and q's. Naturally, then, we would expect the quantity indexes on different bases to also satisfy the base reversal test. Table 19.10 does not show this test for all base and weight combinations because everything parallels Table 19.9. We show Parts C and D in Table 19.10 because we need these results in the calculations of Table 19.11.

We are now ready to check our price and quantity indexes to see if they are *consistent with each other*. For example, suppose we had information that the average prices of a group of agricultural commodities had gone up 12% as measured by an index of prices. We also had information that the average quantities sold had gone up 15%, again as measured by an index of quantities. We would then expect to be able to estimate what had happened to the *total value* of these agricultural commodities by *multiplying* the rates of change together, thus getting a joint rate of 1.12×1.15, or an increase of 28.8%.

Let us look at our already calculated price and quantity indexes and check their consistency. Table 19.11 shows the necessary calculations. There we see that the *total value* of our two products increased 48% from the first to the second period. If we multiply our price index with *period 1* weights by our quantity index with *period 1* weights, we get a product of only 114.4, considerably less than the true value. If we use the indexes based on *period 2* weights, we get a product of 191.4, considerably more than the true value.[1] If we use the indexes based on *average* weights, we get a product of 151.8, a value very close to the true value of 148.0. And finally, if we *cross* a price index with *period 1* weights with a quantity index with *period 2* weights, or vice versa, we obtain the true value exactly (except for rounding errors). The result of *crossing* weights is a direct consequence of the weighted aggregate formula. The proof is very simple. In symbols we have

$$\frac{\Sigma p_2 q_1}{\Sigma p_1 q_1} \times \frac{\Sigma q_2 p_2}{\Sigma q_1 p_2} = \frac{\Sigma q_2 p_2}{\Sigma p_1 q_1}$$

for the case of crossing a price index with period 1 weights with a quantity index with period 2 weights. Note that the left side of the

---

[1] It is of interest to note that the geometric mean of 114.4 and 191.4 is 148.0. This relation is always true and is easily proved algebraically.

TABLE 19.10

The Use of Weighted Aggregates in Constructing Quantity Indexes

A. Period 1 as Base; Period 1 Prices as Weights

	q_1p_1	q_2p_1
Product A	$ 5.00	$ 8.00
Product B	7.50	5.00
	$12.50	$13.00

Indexes: $\dfrac{\$12.50}{\$12.50} = 100.0$ $\dfrac{\$13.00}{\$12.50} = 104.0$

B. Period 2 as Base; Period 1 Prices as Weights

Indexes: $\dfrac{\$12.50}{\$13.00} = 96.2$ $\dfrac{\$13.00}{\$13.00} = 100.0$

Base Reversal Test: $104.0 \times 96.2 = 100.0$

C. Period 1 as Base; Period 2 Prices as Weights

	q_1p_2	q_2p_2
Product A	$10.00	$16.00
Product B	3.75	2.50
	$13.75	$18.50

Indexes: $\dfrac{\$13.75}{\$13.75} = 100.0$ $\dfrac{\$18.50}{\$13.75} = 134.5$

D. Period 1 as Base; Average Prices as Weights

	$q_1\left(\dfrac{p_1 + p_2}{2}\right)$	$q_2\left(\dfrac{p_1 + p_2}{2}\right)$
Product A	$ 7.50	$12.00
Product B	5.625	3.75
	$13.125	$15.75

Indexes: $\dfrac{\$13.125}{\$13.125} = 100.0$ $\dfrac{\$15.750}{\$13.125} = 120.0$

TABLE 19.11

Checking the Consistency of Price and Quantity Indexes against the Appropriate Value Index—Weighted Aggregate Formulas

A. Direct Construction of a Value Index

	p_1q_1	p_2q_2
Product A	$ 5.00	$16.00
Product B	7.50	2.50
	$12.50	$18.50

Value
Indexes: $\dfrac{\$12.50}{\$12.50} = 100.0;$ $\dfrac{\$18.50}{\$12.50} = 148.0$

B. Calculation of a Value Index by Multiplying a Price Index by a Quantity Index

1. Indexes using period 1 weights:

$$P_{21} \times Q_{21} {}^* = \frac{110.0 \times 104.0}{100} = 114.4.$$

2. Indexes using period 2 weights:

$$P_{21} \times Q_{21} = \frac{142.3 \times 134.5}{100} = 191.4.$$

3. Indexes using averages as weights:

$$P_{21} \times Q_{21} = \frac{126.5 \times 120.0}{100} = 151.8.$$

4. Price index with period 1 weights and quantity index with period 2 weights:

$$P_{21} \times Q_{21} = \frac{110.0 \times 134.5}{100} = 148.0.$$

5. Price index with period 2 weights and quantity index with period 1 weights:

$$P_{21} \times Q_{21} = \frac{142.3 \times 104.0}{100} = 148.0.$$

---

* Note: P is often used to indicate a price index, Q the quantity index, and V the value index. P_{21} means a price index for period 2 on period 1 as a base.

numerator cancels against the right side of the denominator, thus leaving us with a formula for a value index. The same result occurs if we cross the period 2 weighted price index with the period 1 weighted quantity index.

The last result is of great practical significance. We frequently have occasion to try to *deduce* a quantity index from given information on values and on a price index. If, say, the price index is a weighted aggregate with *base year* weights, a very common type of formula used, the division of the value series by the price series results in quantity indexes that have been weighted in the given year in each instance. For example, suppose we have a value index of 150.0 for 1960 on 1949 as a base. Suppose further that the corresponding price index is 128.6 for 1960 and also on a base of 1949. If we divide 150.0 by 128.6, getting a quotient of 116.6, we can now state that the quantities sold of these products have increased 16.6% on the average from 1949 to 1960 *if we use 1960 prices as weights*.

This testing of the logical consistency of price and quantity indexes is called the factor reversal test, with factor referring to the price or quantity elements in an index number formula.

Weighted Indexes Based on Relatives

Now let us review the effect of weights on indexes calculated by *averaging relatives* instead of by the *relatives of averages*. Table 19.12 shows the calculations of price indexes with the use of the weighted arithmetic mean of relatives and the weighted geometric mean of relatives. We show the results only for *period 1* weights. Period 2 weights would give the same kind of results with respect to the satisfaction of the base reversal test. First we note the weighted arithmetic mean of relatives gives quite inconsistent results as we change the base, with prices going up with period 1 as a base and going down with period 2 as a base. The geometric mean again gives consistent results, just as when the relatives were unweighted.

We should also note that the weighted arithmetic mean of relatives formula with base-year weights is the algebraic equivalent of the weighted aggregate with base-year weights. Hence the identical answer of 110.0 for the period 2 index on the period 1 base is not unexpected. The algebra of the equivalence is:

Weighted Arithmetic Mean with Base-Year Weights: $\dfrac{\Sigma p_1 q_1 \dfrac{p_2}{p_1}}{\Sigma p_1 q_1}$.

TABLE 19.12

The Use of Weighted Relatives in Price Indexes

Arithmetic Mean

A. Period 1 as Base; Period 1 Values as Weights

	$\dfrac{p_1}{p_1}$	p_1q_1	$p_1q_1\dfrac{p_1}{p_1}$	$\dfrac{p_2}{p_1}$	$p_1q_1\dfrac{p_2}{p_1}$
Product A	100.0	\$ 5.00	\$ 500	200.0	\$1000
Product B	100.0	7.50	750	50.0	375
		\$12.50	\$1250		\$1375

Indexes: $\dfrac{\$1250}{\$12.50} = 100.0$ $\qquad$ $\dfrac{\$1375}{\$12.50} = 110.0$

B. Period 2 as Base, Period 1 Values as Weights

	$\dfrac{p_1}{p_2}$	$p_1q_1\dfrac{p_1}{p_2}$	$\dfrac{p_2}{p_2}$	$p_1q_1\dfrac{p_2}{p_2}$
Product A	50.0	\$ 250	100.0	\$ 500
Product B	200.0	1500	100.0	750
		\$1750		\$1250

Indexes: $\dfrac{\$1750}{\$12.50} = 140.0$ $\qquad$ $\dfrac{\$1250}{\$12.50} = 100.0$

Base Reversal Test: $\dfrac{110.0 \times 140.0}{100} = 154.0$

Geometric Mean

C. Period 1 as Base; Period 1 Values as Weights

	$\log\dfrac{p_1}{p_1}$	$p_1q_1\log\dfrac{p_1}{p_1}$	$\log\dfrac{p_2}{p_1}$	$p_1q_1\log\dfrac{p_2}{p_1}$
Product A	2.0000	\$10.0000	2.3010	\$11.5050
Product B	2.0000	\$15.0000	1.6990	12.7425
		\$25.0000		\$24.2475
Mean of Logarithms:		2.0000		1.9398
Geometric Mean of Weighted Relatives:		100.0		87.1

D. Period 2 as Base; Period 1 Values as Weights

	$\log\dfrac{p_1}{p_2}$	$p_1q_1\log\dfrac{p_1}{p_2}$	$\log\dfrac{p_2}{p_2}$	$p_1q_1\log\dfrac{p_2}{p_2}$
Product A	1.6990	\$ 8.4950	2.0000	\$10.0000
Product B	2.3010	17.2575	2.0000	15.0000
		\$25.7525		\$25.0000
Means of Logarithms:		2.0602		2.0000
Geometric Mean of Weighted Relatives:		115.0		100.0

Base Reversal Test: $115.0 \times 87.1 = 100.2$ $\quad$ (Would be 100.0 except for rounding errors.)

TABLE 19.13

The Use of Weighted Relatives in Quantity Indexes

Arithmetic Means

A. Period 1 as Base; Period 1 Values as Weights

	$\dfrac{q_1}{q_1}$	$p_1q_1\dfrac{q_1}{q_1}$	$\dfrac{q_2}{q_1}$	$p_1q_1\dfrac{q_2}{q_1}$
Product A	100.0	\$ 500.0	160.0	\$ 800.0
Product B	100.0	750.0	66.7	500.0
		\$1250.0		\$1300.0

Indexes: $\dfrac{\$1250}{\$12.50} = 100.0 \qquad \dfrac{\$1300}{\$12.50} = 104.0$

B. Period 1 as Base; Period 2 Values as Weights

	$\dfrac{q_1}{q_1}$	$p_2q_2\dfrac{q_1}{q_1}$	$\dfrac{q_2}{q_1}$	$p_2q_2\dfrac{q_2}{q_1}$
Product A	100.0	\$1600.0	160.0	\$2560.0
Product B	100.0	250.0	66.7	166.7
		\$1850.0		\$2726.7

Indexes: $\dfrac{\$1850.0}{\$18.5} = 100.0 \qquad \dfrac{\$2726.7}{\$18.5} = 147.4$

Geometric Means

C. Period 1 as Base; Period 1 Values as Weights

	$\log\dfrac{q_1}{q_1}$	$p_1q_1\log\dfrac{q_1}{q_1}$	$\log\dfrac{q_2}{q_1}$	$p_1q_1\log\dfrac{q_2}{q_1}$
Product A	2.0000	\$10.0000	2.2041	\$11.0205
Product B	2.0000	15.0000	1.8239	13.6792
		\$25.0000		\$24.6997
Mean of Logarithms:		2.0000		1.9760
Geometric Mean of Weighted Relatives:		100.0		94.6

D. Period 1 as Base; Period 2 Values as Weights

	$\log\dfrac{q_1}{q_1}$	$p_2q_2\log\dfrac{q_1}{q_1}$	$\log\dfrac{q_2}{q_1}$	$p_2q_2\log\dfrac{q_2}{q_1}$
Product A	2.0000	\$32.0000	2.2041	\$35.2656
Product B	2.0000	5.0000	1.8239	4.5598
		\$37.0000		\$39.8254
Mean of Logarithms:		2.0000		2.1527
Geometric Mean of Weighted Relatives:		100.0		142.1

If we cancel p_1 in p_1q_1 of the numerator against p_1 in the denominator of the relative, we get the weighted aggregate formula of

$$\frac{\Sigma p_2 q_1}{\Sigma p_1 q_1}.$$

The calculation of quantity indexes with the weighted arithmetic mean and weighted geometric mean of relatives is shown in Table 19.13. We do not show the base reversal test here because we would get the same kind of results as for the price indexes, namely, the arithmetic mean will not satisfy the test and the geometric will. We are more interested in the consistency of these quantity indexes with the price indexes given in Table 19.12. The test for consistency of these indexes is shown in Table 19.14.

Thus we see that both the arithmetic mean and the geometric mean give inconsistent results if we try to derive a value index from the corresponding price and quantity indexes. We get the best results when we *crossed* the weights by using the arithmetic mean of price relatives with period 1 weights and the arithmetic mean of quantity relatives with period 2 weights. This result is consistent with what happened when we crossed weights in this way using the aggregate formula, with the cross of aggregates giving exact consistency.

TABLE 19.14

Checking the Consistency of Price and Quantity Indexes against the Appropriate Value Index—Weighted Average of Relatives Formulas

A. Weighted Arithmetic Mean of Price Relatives × Weighted Arithmetic Mean of Quantity Relatives—Period 1 Values as Weights in Each Case:

$$110.0 \times 104.0 = 114.4 \text{ vs. the true } 148.0.$$

B. Weighted Arithmetic Mean of Price Relatives with Period 1 Weights × Weighted Arithmetic Mean of Quantity Relatives with Period 2 Weights:

$$110.0 \times 147.4 = 162.1 \text{ vs. the true } 148.0$$

C. Weighted Geometric Mean of Price Relatives × Weighted Geometric Mean of Quantity Relatives—Period 1 Values as Weights in Each Case:

$$87.1 \times 94.6 = 82.4 \text{ vs. the true } 148.0$$

D. Weighted Geometric Mean of Price Relatives with Period 1 Weights × Weighted Geometric Mean of Quantity Relatives with Period 2 Weights:

$$87.1 \times 142.1 = 123.8 \text{ vs. the true } 148.0$$

19.10   Summary Remarks on the Problem of Choice of an Index Number Formula: the Average and the Weight Base

If we were to write down a set of rules for selecting an index number formula, the list might look like the following:

1. The *average* used should be consistent with the purpose. This means that users of the index should be able to understand exactly what is being averaged and how it is being averaged. Abstractions that presumably measure some undefinable properties of the series should be avoided.

    The two most understandable purposes are:
    a. To compare *totals* or *aggregates*, and
    b. To compare *typical* changes in the *individual* items.

    If the distribution of individual items being averaged is essentially symmetrical, or if the distributions being compared have essentially similar shapes, the *arithmetic mean* of relatives or its equivalent, the *aggregate* (properly weighted), can be used to satisfy both of these purposes.

2. The weights used should be as representative as possible of all periods being compared. Thus the use of *average* weights is strongly preferred. The only deterrent from the use of average weights should be practical considerations of the cost and time in collecting the necessary weight data. If we are forced to use only one set of weights, there seems to be no logical reason to prefer one year in the comparison over the other year. If we are comparing *several* years, the single year weights should be for an average year.

3. The index number formula should give *consistent* results for different base periods and also with its counterpart price or quantity index. No reasonably simple formula satisfies both of these consistency requirements. The geometric mean perfectly satisfies the base consistency requirement but fails badly on the factor reversal test.

    The best formula with which to approximate both results seems to be the *weighted aggregate with average weights*. We should never use any other formula unless we have strong and explicit reasons to the contrary. This formula is technically sound and satisfies most practical purposes.

4. The *base* used is largely a matter of arbitrary choice. The only recommendation is that "special pleading" bases should be avoided, or if unavoidable, they should always be matched with the figures from some other base that is equally logical.

19.11   The Concept of the Chain Index

Practical index number work is replete with many "tricks of the trade" to handle all the practical difficulties that arise because of lags in reporting data, sharp changes in weight patterns, the need to insert new commodities and drop old commodities, etc. We discuss only the *chain index*, perhaps the most useful "trick" of them all.

We found the *link relative* a useful tool in measuring the variation from one time period to another when we were analyzing time variations. We can illustrate the relationship of the *link* relative to the *chain* relative by reference to the following simple series of data:

	1950	1951	1952	1953	1954
Price:	$1	$2	$3	$4	$5

We get *link* relatives of these prices by *relating a price in one year to that in the immediately preceding year.* Such calculations are shown in Table 19.15. This is what we calculated when we were making year-to-year forecasts.

Suppose, now, that we wished to get the ratio of the 1954 price to the 1950 price. We could do this directly by obtaining a *fixed base* relative. Thus we would divide $5 by $1 and get a ratio, or relative, of 5.00. Or we could achieve the same result indirectly by working through the link relatives that we have calculated. For example, given that 1951/50 = 2.00 and that 1952/51 = 1.50, a simple multiplication of 1951/50 by 1952/51 and 2.00 by 1.50 gives us that 1952/50 = 3.00. This is, of course, exactly the same answer we would have obtained by dividing the 1952 figure by the 1950 figure directly. If we continue *to tie together* the links by multiplying them successively, we would get: 1951/50 × 1952/51 × 1953/52 × 1954/53 = 1954/50, and 2.00 × 1.50 × 1.33 × 1.25 = 5.00, again the same answer as if we had calculated the result directly.

Whenever we get the ratio of the data in one period to those of another period *by working through the links connecting the inter-*

TABLE 19.15

Link Relatives

Year	Price	Time Ratio	Link Relatives of Prices
1950	$1	—	
1951	2	1951/50	2.00
1952	3	1952/51	1.50
1953	4	1953/52	1.33
1954	5	1954/53	1.25

vening periods, we call the result a *chain* relative to distinguish it from the direct ratio which we call the *fixed base* relative. The terms are quite apt. Note that a whole *series of bases* are used in the calculation of a chain relative while only *one base* is used in the direct calculation.

We may wonder why anyone would go through the additional work required to obtain a chain relative when he could get the same result with one calculation. Our wonder is well founded. We do not very often calculate chain *relatives* outside statistics texts. Such calculation simply demonstrates the *logic* of a procedure that does have great practical application. Suppose, for example, we have calculated an index of consumers' prices from 1926 to 1936, using a set of weights that is reasonably representative of both of those periods. Suppose further that we had also calculated an index of consumers' prices from 1936 to 1946, using a set of weights that is reasonably representative of those two periods. Finally, suppose we now wanted an index of consumers' prices from 1926 to 1946. We could calculate this index directly, but the intervening span of years has led to such great shifts in the patterns of consumption that we are not at all happy with the representativeness of any set of weights we might use for both periods. So we now decide to compare 1946 with 1926 by *working through 1936*. Thus, if the 1936/26 ratio had been .768 and the 1946/36 ratio 1.497, we would estimate a *chain* index for 1946/26 of .768 $\times$ 1.497, or 1.150.

Note that we used the term chain *index* rather than chain *relative*. This is because we try to reserve the word *index* for comparisons of *groups* of items. Good sense recommends making *long-term* comparisons of *groups* of prices, or other elements, by working through a series of *short-term* comparisons. In this way we gain the advantages of reasonably homogeneous data over such short periods (the 1960 Ford is more nearly like the 1959 Ford than it is the 1926 Ford), and we are able to use weights that are reasonably representative of both periods. In this way we have found it possible to construct meaningful price indexes going back before the Civil War. A direct comparison would be a statistical farce. Practically no elements of consumption patterns are common to both periods, with the possible exception of such a minor consumption item as bourbon whiskey. But by working with chunks of this long span of time and chaining the chunks together, we feel that we have devised a meaningful, though imperfect, measure of changes over the full century.

Chain indexes are sometimes criticized because they do not give the same answers as a direct comparison would have. Such criticism misses the point of calculating a chain index. Of course chain indexes give different answers. If they did not, there would be no point in calculating the chain index. The chain index answer is considered better because it is based on *more homogeneous data* and *more representative weight patterns.*

19.12 Determination of Revision Policies and Procedures

It should be evident from the preceding discussion that practical index number work requires the resolution of dilemmas and several conflicting desires. It is almost impossible to construct a perfect index number series, and the more perfect the series is for some years the worse it is for other years. Thus an index number series should really be in a constant state of revision in data, sample, and weights. This is also impossible in practical affairs. Hence most compilers of index numbers may *research* the problem continuously but *revise* only periodically, either as the results of research dictate a revision or as necessary funds become available. The practical art of construction and use of index number series is still in the formative stages, having been practiced systematically only in this century. We are still trying to determine how much money it is worth spending on it. The United States Bureau of Labor Statistics is probably the most assiduous practitioner of the art and will probably enjoy larger budgets in the years ahead to make more frequent revisions possible. It is perhaps worth noting that most of the Bureau's indexes use the weighted aggregate, or its mathematical equivalent, the weighted arithmetic mean of relatives, with links and chains in order to facilitate weight changes in the years between major revisions.

19.13 Measuring the Dispersion within Groups

As of now very little effort has been made to publish index numbers that are supported by quantitative statements of the variation of the items within the group. Partial answers to the problem of variations within the group movements are provided by indexes for subclasses of items. There are also devices such as simple tallies of the number of items that have risen or fallen during a given period. This is done, for example, in the reporting of the behavior of stock prices.

But these devices are still inadequate, and there are opportunities for further development in measuring within-group variations.

PROBLEMS AND QUESTIONS

19.1   You have had many occasions in which you have made decisions based on an evaluation you have made of a *group* of events. Analyze each of the following group characterizations according to:

1. The particular *qualities* being measured. (For example, the relevant qualities in evaluating a meal at a restaurant may be the aroma of the coffee, the temperature of the soup, the politeness of the waiter, the toughness of the steak, etc.)

2. The method of *measuring* those qualities.

3. The method of *averaging* the measured qualities.

(Note: the *purpose* that underlies the desire to characterize the group is relevant in each of the above.)

(*a*) You would like to compare the meal you had at the "Ritz" Hotel with that you had at the dormitory.

(*b*) You would like to compare grammar school with high school.

(*c*) You would like to compare your house with that of your best friend.

(*d*) You would like to compare the new Chevrolet with the new Ford (or Plymouth, or Rambler, etc.).

(*e*) You would like to compare two different pairs of shoes in order to buy the better pair.

(One useful purpose served by having you struggle with problems like those given above is to get you to realize how simple a problem of price comparison really is!)

19.2   The following indexes are in rather common use in American life. What *specific* purposes do you think they can be used to satisfy? Give some sort of an evaluation of the accuracy they have in serving such purposes. Also indicate whether you feel that these indexes are sufficiently accurate for the purposes.

(*a*) Scores on intelligence tests.

(*b*) Dow-Jones Averages of Stock Prices.

(*c*) U.S.B.L.S. Index of Consumer Prices.

(*d*) Temperature-humidity index published by the weather bureau for a given city.

(*e*) Number of degree-days during a month.

(*f*) The won-lost percentages of baseball teams.

(*g*) The price of a quart of milk. (Or of any product.)

(*h*) The total weight of a human being (as possibly distinct from the weights of the various parts of the body).

(*i*) The cost per square foot of floor space in a new building.

19.3(*a*) What kind of an average is actually used in each case of Problem 19.2?

(*b*) What kind *should* be used to best satisfy the purpose? Explain.

(*c*) Is it possible that the actual average may work practically as well as the "correct" average? Explain.

19.4   How can you tell when each of the above indexes is high, or low, or about average, or very high? For example, suppose the following values occurred for the indexes referred to in Problem 19.2. State how large you think these values are. Explain the basis of your statement.

(a) 184.

(b) 306.

(c) 124%.

(d) 92.

(e) 300.

(f) .816.

(g) $.85.

(h) 275 pounds.

(i) $4.25.

19.5 Below are given some of the typical items that make up the consumption pattern of an American family. Analyze each item for homogeneity during the period 1945 to date. Consider the *physical* homogeneity, the *function* homogeneity (e.g., the ability of a washing machine to wash clothes), and the *psychological* homogeneity (the ability of the item to satisfy human wants). For example, the ownership of a horse and buggy may have provided more human satisfaction in 1900 than does the ownership of an automobile today.

Finally, indicate what it is that you think is measured by the changes in the *price* of the item. In order to make your answer more concrete, determine the 1945 price and the current price for each item and then account for the difference.

(a) A snowsuit for a 5-year-old male child.

(b) A television set.

(c) A pound of bacon.

(d) Mailing a letter from New York to California.

(e) A 4-year college curriculum at a selected college.

(f) A baseball game at Yankee Stadium.

(g) Police protection at the local, state, or national level.

(h) Religious instruction and inspiration at the church of your choice.

19.6 What *type* of average would you try to get in the following cases? Explain.

(a) The average price of a quart of home-delivered milk in the New York metropolitan area for purpose of including in a Consumers' Price Index. Also, for inclusion in an index to measure general changes in the value of the dollar to guide the Federal Reserve Board in its attempts to stabilize the value of the dollar. (Note: The variation we would be averaging is that from place to place within the area and from milk company to milk company.)

(b) The average price of a quart of home-delivered milk over the period of a year. (The variation we would be averaging is that from day to day, or month to month, etc.)

(Note on this question: The problem of which *average* to use in a problem is often essentially the same problem as that of determining the *kind of sample* to use when only one item is to be selected. Thus, the single *average* price of milk over the year is really a *sample* of the price of milk.)

19.7 Below are given the prices and quantities of two commodities at two different dates.

	Period 1		Period 2	
	Price p_1	Quantity q_1	Price p_2	Quantity q_2
Product A	$2.00	100	$2.50	150
Product B	$10.00	40	$12.00	30

(a) Calculate the following indexes

1. Simple aggregate of prices, Period 1 as base:
2. " " " " 2 " "
3. Simple arithmetic mean of price relatives, Period 1 as base.
4. " " " " " " 2 " "
5. " geometric " " " " 1 " "
6. " " " " " 2 " "
7. Weighted aggregate of prices, Period 1 weights, Period 1 base.
8. " " " " " " 2 "
9. " " " " " 2 " 1 "
10. " " " " " " 2 "
11. " " " " Average " 1 "
12. " " " " " " 2 "
13. Weighted Arithmetic Mean of Price Relatives, Period 1 Weights, Period 1 base.
14. " " " " " " 1 " 2 "
15. " " " " " " 2 " 1 "
16. " " " " " " 2 " 2 "
17. " " " " " Average " 1 "
18. " " " " " " " 2 "
19. " Geometric " " " " " 1 "
20. " " " " " " " 2 "
21. " " " " " Period 1 " 1 "
22. " " " " " " 1 " 2 "
23. " " " " " " 2 " 1 "
24. " " " " " " 2 " 2 "
25. Value index with Period 1 as base.
26. Value index with Period 2 as base.

(b) Analyze your results in Part (a) above for evidence of whether a given formula type (average and weights) satisfies the base reversal test.

(c) Repeat all the calculations of Part (a) above for the construction of *quantity* indexes rather than *price* indexes.

(d) Test your quantity indexes for ability to satisfy the base reversal test.

(e) Test your price and quantity indexes for ability to satisfy the factor reversal test.

(f) What practical significance do you find in the ability of an index number formula to satisfy the base reversal and factor reversal tests?

19.8(a) Collect data on the annual Gross National Product of the United States for the last 15 years. Compare the results for the data based on *current* dollars with the data based on *constant* dollars. Collect or calculate the ratios of the current dollar data to the constant dollar data. The resultant ratios are obviously a *price* index. What kind of formula (average and weights) underlies such an index number series? What kind of formula *should* it be? Explain.

(*b*) Collect annual dollar sales figures for some large multiproduct firm like General Motors, General Electric, Macy's, etc. Analyze the problem of finding a *price index* series that could be used to deflate the dollar sales series in order to estimate the changes in *physical volume* of sales over the years. (Deflation consists of *dividing* the dollar sales figures by appropriate price indexes.) Find the best price index you can and perform the calculations necessary to get the physical volume series.

Evaluate the results from the point of view of theoretical niceties and of practical usefulness.

19.9 Suppose you were constructing index numbers of physical volume of activity for a manufacturer of refrigerators. This company builds the refrigerator from such basic raw materials as sheet steel, insulation rolls, paint, etc. The company also handles a line of other household appliances such as electric and gas ranges, dishwashers, etc. These other items, however, are built almost entirely by subcontractors who do practically all the work on the products except for a few finishing touches, such as attachment of distinctive dials and of the name plates.

How would you give proper weight to the value of refrigerators vs. these other appliances in constructing your over-all index? (Hint: You would be concerned with the problem of estimating the value *added* by manufacture. You might relate your problem to that of the Federal Reserve Board in combining the output of sheet steel with the output of automobiles in its Index of Industrial Production. Note that some of the sheet steel would be embodied in the automobiles.)

19.10 Below are given data on three items of a Consumers' Price Index for 5 specific years spanning a period of 20 years.

	1940		1945		1950		1955		1960	
	Price	Quantity	Price	Quantity	Price	Quantity	Price	Quantity	Price	Quantity
Bread	$ .10	150 lbs.	$ .12	170	$ .19	160	$ .21	150	$ .24	140
Shoes	4.50	3.8 prs.	4.60	4.2	6.80	5.5	8.00	6.0	9.25	7.0
Gasoline	.14	600 gals.	.18	500	.29	650	.30	680	.34	750

(*a*) Construct the *best* possible index of changes in these prices considering the available information. Express the final indexes on 1940 as a base. (Hint: The use of links and chains, with the best weights used for each link, would be a useful approach.)

(*b*) Evaluate your final indexes from the point of view of

1. Their conforming to any theoretical and practical criteria of good indexes.

2. Their measuring something that has some practical meaning. For example, what difference might it make if the index went up 20% rather than going down 5%?

(*c*) What alternative method of construction would you recommend in the interests of saving some of the money needed to collect quantity data in each of these years? Do you think that such an alternative would result in changes in the indexes of any practical concern? Explain.

19.11 Suppose an index of common stock prices goes up 10%. What differences would it make if plus 10% were a result of:

(a) *All* stock prices increasing 10% each?

(b) 40% of the prices increasing by *more* than 10%?

(c) 30% of the prices increasing by more than 10% and 20% of them actually decreasing?

Appendix A

Squares, Square-Roots, and Reciprocals

n	n^2	$\sqrt{n}$	$\sqrt{10n}$	$1000/n$	n	n^2	$\sqrt{n}$	$\sqrt{10n}$	$1000/n$
					45	2 025	6.7082	21.213	22.222
1	1	1.0000	3.1623	1000.0	46	2 116	6.7823	21.448	21.739
2	4	1.4142	4.4721	500.00	47	2 209	6.8557	21.679	21.277
3	9	1.7321	5.4772	333.33	48	2 304	6.9282	21.909	20.833
4	16	2.0000	6.3246	250.00	49	2 401	7.0000	22.136	20.408
5	25	2.2361	7.0711	200.00	50	2 500	7.0711	22.361	20.000
6	36	2.4495	7.7460	166.67	51	2 601	7.1414	22.583	19.608
7	49	2.6458	8.3666	142.86	52	2 704	7.2111	22.804	19.231
8	64	2.8284	8.9443	125.00	53	2 809	7.2801	23.022	18.868
9	81	3.0000	9.4868	111.11	54	2 916	7.3485	23.238	18.519
10	100	3.1623	10.000	100.00	55	3 025	7.4162	23.452	18.182
11	121	3.3166	10.488	90.909	56	3 136	7.4833	23.664	17.857
12	144	3.4641	10.954	83.333	57	3 249	7.5498	23.875	17.544
13	169	3.6056	11.402	76.923	58	3 364	7.6158	24.083	17.241
14	196	3.7417	11.832	71.429	59	3 481	7.6811	24.290	16.949
15	225	3.8730	12.247	66.667	60	3 600	7.7460	24.495	16.667
16	256	4.0000	12.649	62.500	61	3 721	7.8103	24.698	16.393
17	289	4.1231	13.038	58.824	62	3 844	7.8740	24.900	16.129
18	324	4.2426	13.416	55.556	63	3 969	7.9373	25.100	15.873
19	361	4.3589	13.784	52.632	64	4 096	8.0000	25.298	15.625
20	400	4.4721	14.142	50.000	65	4 225	8.0623	25.495	15.385
21	441	4.5826	14.491	47.619	66	4 356	8.1240	25.690	15.152
22	484	4.6904	14.832	45.455	67	4 489	8.1854	25.884	14.925
23	529	4.7958	15.166	43.478	68	4 624	8.2462	26.077	14.706
24	576	4.8990	15.492	41.667	69	4 761	8.3066	26.268	14.493
25	625	5.0000	15.811	40.000	70	4 900	8.3666	26.458	14.286
26	676	5.0990	16.125	38.462	71	5 041	8.4262	26.646	14.085
27	729	5.1962	16.432	37.037	72	5 184	8.4853	26.833	13.889
28	784	5.2915	16.733	35.714	73	5 329	8.5440	27.019	13.699
29	841	5.3852	17.029	34.483	74	5 476	8.6023	27.203	13.514
30	900	5.4772	17.321	33.333	75	5 625	8.6603	27.386	13.333
31	961	5.5678	17.607	32.258	76	5 776	8.7178	27.568	13.158
32	1 024	5.6569	17.889	31.250	77	5 929	8.7750	27.749	12.987
33	1 089	5.7446	18.166	30.303	78	6 084	8.8318	27.928	12.821
34	1 156	5.8310	18.439	29.412	79	6 241	8.8882	28.107	12.658
35	1 225	5.9161	18.708	28.571	80	6 400	8.9443	28.284	12.500
36	1 296	6.0000	18.974	27.778	81	6 561	9.0000	28.461	12.346
37	1 369	6.0828	19.235	27.027	82	6 724	9.0554	28.636	12.195
38	1 444	6.1644	19.494	26.316	83	6 889	9.1104	28.810	12.048
39	1 521	6.2450	19.748	25.641	84	7 056	9.1652	28.983	11.905
40	1 600	6.3246	20.000	25.000	85	7 225	9.2195	29.155	11.765
41	1 681	6.4031	20.248	24.390	86	7 396	9.2736	29.326	11.628
42	1 764	6.4807	20.494	23.810	87	7 569	9.3274	29.496	11.494
43	1 849	6.5574	20.736	23.256	88	7 744	9.3808	29.665	11.364
44	1 936	6.6333	20.976	22.727	89	7 921	9.4340	29.833	11.236

Squares, Square-Roots, and Reciprocals

n	n^2	$\sqrt{n}$	$\sqrt{10n}$	$1000/n$	n	n^2	$\sqrt{n}$	$\sqrt{10n}$	$1000/n$
90	8 100	9.4868	30.000	11.111	145	21 025	12.042	38.079	6.8966
91	8 281	9.5394	30.166	10.989	146	21 316	12.083	38.210	6.8493
92	8 464	9.5917	30.332	10.870	147	21 609	12.124	38.341	6.8027
93	8 649	9.6437	30.496	10.753	148	21 904	12.166	38.471	6.7568
94	8 836	9.6954	30.659	10.638	149	22 201	12.207	38.601	6.7114
95	9 025	9.7468	30.822	10.526	150	22 500	12.247	38.730	6.6667
96	9 216	9.7980	30.984	10.417	151	22 801	12.288	38.859	6.6225
97	9 409	9.8489	31.145	10.309	152	23 104	12.329	38.987	6.5789
98	9 604	9.8995	31.305	10.204	153	23 409	12.369	39.115	6.5359
99	9 801	9.9499	31.464	10.101	154	23 716	12.410	39.243	6.4935
100	10 000	10.000	31.623	10.000	155	24 025	12.450	39.370	6.4516
101	10 201	10.050	31.781	9.9010	156	24 336	12.490	39.497	6.4103
102	10 404	10.100	31.937	9.8039	157	24 649	12.530	39.623	6.3694
103	10 609	10.149	32.094	9.7087	158	24 964	12.570	39.749	6.3291
104	10 816	10.198	32.249	9.6154	159	25 281	12.610	39.875	6.2893
105	11 025	10.247	32.404	9.5238	160	25 600	12.649	40.000	6.2500
106	11 236	10.296	32.558	9.4340	161	25 921	12.689	40.125	6.2112
107	11 449	10.344	32.711	9.3458	162	26 244	12.728	40.249	6.1728
108	11 664	10.392	32.863	9.2593	163	26 569	12.767	40.373	6.1350
109	11 881	10.440	33.015	9.1743	164	26 896	12.806	40.497	6.0976
110	12 100	10.488	33.166	9.0909	165	27 225	12.845	40.620	6.0606
111	12 321	10.536	33.317	9.0090	166	27 556	12.884	40.743	6.0241
112	12 544	10.583	33.466	8.9286	167	27 889	12.923	40.866	5.9880
113	12 769	10.630	33.615	8.8496	168	28 224	12.961	40.988	5.9524
114	12 996	10.677	33.764	8.7719	169	28 561	13.000	41.110	5.9172
115	13 225	10.724	33.912	8.6957	170	28 900	13.038	41.231	5.8824
116	13 456	10.770	34.059	8.6207	171	29 241	13.077	41.352	5.8480
117	13 689	10.817	34.205	8.5470	172	29 584	13.115	41.473	5.8140
118	13 924	10.863	34.351	8.4746	173	29 929	13.153	41.593	5.7803
119	14 161	10.909	34.496	8.4034	174	30 276	13.191	41.713	5.7471
120	14 400	10.954	34.641	8.3333	175	30 625	13.229	41.833	5.7143
121	14 641	11.000	34.785	8.2645	176	30 976	13.267	41.952	5.6818
122	14 884	11.045	34.929	8.1967	177	31 329	13.304	42.071	5.6497
123	15 129	11.091	35.071	8.1301	178	31 684	13.342	42.190	5.6180
124	15 376	11.136	35.214	8.0645	179	32 041	13.379	42.308	5.5866
125	15 625	11.180	35.355	8.0000	180	32 400	13.416	49.426	5.5556
126	15 876	11.225	35.496	7.9365	181	32 761	13.454	42.544	5.5249
127	16 129	11.269	35.637	7.8740	182	33 124	13.491	42.661	5.4945
128	16 384	11.314	35.777	7.8125	183	33 489	13.528	42.779	5.4645
129	16 641	11.358	35.917	7.7519	184	33 856	13.565	42.895	5.4348
130	16 900	11.402	36.056	7.6923	185	34 225	13.601	43.012	5.4054
131	17 161	11.446	36.194	7.6336	186	34 596	13.638	43.128	5.3763
132	17 424	11.489	36.332	7.5758	187	34 969	13.675	43.244	5.3476
133	17 689	11.533	36.469	7.5188	188	35 344	13.711	43.359	5.3191
134	17 956	11.576	36.606	7.4627	189	35 721	13.748	43.474	5.2910
135	18 225	11.619	36.742	7.4074	190	36 100	13.784	43.589	5.2632
136	18 496	11.662	36.878	7.3529	191	36 481	13.820	43.704	5.2356
137	18 769	11.705	37.014	7.2993	192	36 864	13.856	43.818	5.2083
138	19 044	11.747	37.148	7.2464	193	37 249	13.892	43.932	5.1813
139	19 321	11.790	37.283	7.1942	194	37 636	13.928	44.045	5.1546
140	19 600	11.832	37.417	7.1429	195	38 025	13.964	44.159	5.1282
141	19 881	11.874	37.550	7.0922	196	38 416	14.000	44.272	5.1020
142	20 164	11.916	37.683	7.0423	197	38 809	14.036	44.385	5.0761
143	20 449	11.958	37.815	6.9930	198	39 204	14.071	44.497	5.0505
144	20 736	12.000	37.947	6.9444	199	39 601	14.107	44.609	5.0251

Appendix B

Random Sampling Numbers *

97	58	55	23	12	87	39	84	32	23	26	91	01	11	26	01	24	06	58	20	33	46	38	86	23
84	95	87	34	95	31	23	12	64	75	89	28	38	15	91	81	89	08	86	08	88	20	02	11	67
11	52	38	09	94	32	47	35	42	67	39	33	89	97	16	28	94	86	93	86	96	13	43	85	99
38	69	94	97	10	44	42	85	46	88	56	56	63	58	22	89	19	26	82	25	94	15	54	65	62
23	99	36	33	41	99	76	22	29	19	92	53	92	15	71	47	57	74	69	03	65	57	90	53	17
09	15	95	74	87	09	63	82	63	29	84	57	45	80	07	13	57	40	58	34	21	93	90	39	21
55	75	91	36	57	38	30	89	64	42	01	84	83	12	79	32	09	56	03	81	90	88	00	71	02
84	62	29	92	42	03	92	37	46	19	90	75	68	84	49	53	80	62	19	20	31	14	42	11	17
79	25	70	07	80	85	32	53	87	11	33	79	14	20	04	12	40	31	74	39	80	21	37	65	20
40	10	91	52	27	21	18	64	61	04	85	55	16	90	71	31	95	15	86	74	87	80	75	71	27
93	18	86	63	72	22	53	44	23	89	38	06	46	04	79	67	77	33	21	75	40	51	74	60	53
63	71	69	30	23	12	85	90	05	07	67	33	56	52	60	21	50	72	26	28	48	67	31	87	61
05	29	95	78	06	10	41	62	18	37	42	91	98	43	33	20	58	62	80	65	19	90	07	84	49
30	04	29	90	89	64	25	66	36	41	99	59	15	43	86	34	10	05	99	83	08	02	18	01	22
75	50	83	42	46	80	76	77	34	16	04	05	06	28	86	60	70	04	13	28	98	76	78	43	69
68	82	44	11	33	11	20	42	00	22	40	03	06	12	45	06	32	34	44	18	01	26	36	78	42
51	38	78	69	65	25	98	73	40	31	12	04	99	51	09	49	04	32	68	68	54	64	15	25	68
98	41	81	63	70	58	43	39	93	18	54	46	98	33	01	47	85	39	81	11	48	84	07	64	76
08	44	37	01	53	59	67	11	11	53	16	98	16	52	52	39	32	22	18	22	04	03	06	77	17
17	30	92	82	09	42	37	88	43	35	11	54	89	05	61	10	46	27	43	33	88	92	72	62	01
74	87	89	10	02	19	45	29	65	70	77	81	98	78	67	05	62	57	08	79	30	32	62	91	87
61	81	52	99	80	11	55	21	98	02	08	26	01	20	16	07	42	88	56	51	31	96	14	85	49
55	08	43	08	22	50	28	03	18	00	80	79	60	18	33	92	36	13	50	41	43	59	82	16	65
44	38	47	15	16	96	03	51	42	15	35	96	40	87	91	56	91	13	58	85	40	06	36	04	30
12	45	97	68	57	62	36	61	03	29	46	60	79	85	99	91	13	99	95	58	75	14	74	88	12
19	95	23	05	45	01	87	81	18	92	36	94	07	14	08	90	32	51	29	61	50	60	34	92	25
71	55	86	72	94	77	08	55	65	50	33	53	94	81	52	36	31	53	12	74	88	59	99	35	95
07	32	94	03	20	66	29	98	75	65	70	30	56	59	08	24	51	75	48	73	11	29	77	08	36
10	35	58	59	25	89	62	60	77	71	24	13	38	20	83	02	48	11	67	95	38	97	15	58	18
62	99	34	08	06	81	46	09	16	82	95	17	13	46	36	51	36	87	56	10	80	79	40	48	82
19	44	35	31	20	16	05	25	26	38	98	94	18	38	88	10	90	29	01	12	48	85	52	97	22
77	76	94	64	49	45	39	58	07	88	32	11	43	09	51	32	69	31	63	02	33	47	08	94	85
97	43	81	59	46	59	26	04	63	86	87	31	55	50	66	11	37	04	68	14	57	17	08	82	48
09	77	93	46	95	36	98	08	77	39	71	44	48	10	19	54	80	24	83	47	06	79	01	78	43
71	09	43	23	16	33	93	21	87	89	16	53	05	53	16	98	96	30	89	49	83	32	23	13	32
25	19	47	70	48	16	91	39	59	80	66	77	96	02	08	59	58	48	91	81	04	31	64	65	15
43	23	23	81	42	61	42	37	17	76	75	40	18	81	33	51	68	04	41	00	72	82	28	68	03
50	57	81	53	79	98	04	75	77	30	49	18	17	01	70	06	01	53	04	76	49	93	39	68	00
81	04	78	50	20	33	21	64	10	00	49	43	08	86	53	25	50	24	70	63	01	08	52	66	67
19	62	59	60	23	26	11	30	12	63	26	60	61	15	83	27	41	02	61	80	72	19	91	56	53
32	52	48	94	61	60	43	08	29	67	86	20	90	03	18	48	22	42	82	59	84	31	00	92	15
79	73	88	64	27	89	92	95	64	78	40	06	16	28	66	54	93	14	19	00	39	11	13	27	55
05	12	93	24	38	18	25	64	65	51	81	15	80	43	36	94	49	89	58	80	80	76	25	65	69
59	72	45	18	64	49	67	78	83	66	72	92	63	42	78	21	14	35	00	16	05	92	74	20	31
22	75	30	52	34	00	43	50	50	91	10	64	18	60	30	48	99	84	23	37	20	03	50	50	05
86	21	48	23	45	01	80	49	33	99	57	92	46	06	55	60	98	81	40	20	72	45	67	83	67
47	02	27	40	96	41	44	06	54	76	83	52	32	56	15	09	45	22	54	07	49	70	54	48	84
36	76	21	72	44	85	55	63	87	29	62	84	18	48	29	23	75	29	90	68	02	56	04	32	34
43	84	04	45	20	18	42	25	25	95	70	15	92	80	82	47	10	21	18	57	83	54	02	09	53
88	82	00	84	16	82	67	66	77	89	78	31	98	11	56	27	07	76	59	71	87	56	99	27	28

* From Table XIX of A. Hald, *Statistical Tables and Formulas*, John Wiley and Sons, New York, 1952.

Random Sampling Numbers

```
90 78 82 54 47   20 83 80 10 41   35 22 23 03 98   79 74 41 35 05   78 73 95 47 83
78 58 68 87 41   11 08 81 29 89   71 23 10 01 79   25 06 00 45 80   64 70 95 34 29
51 42 21 03 88   20 05 35 93 00   68 12 09 55 09   36 54 95 22 82   48 30 09 56 87
93 15 07 60 86   67 37 94 24 35   82 44 19 92 96   21 84 29 04 29   83 32 05 10 48
27 12 31 66 62   09 54 17 31 23   27 30 37 36 79   75 50 39 57 12   67 23 22 09 33

79 44 83 55 47   96 50 93 56 82   58 16 35 18 87   64 08 22 47 93   86 43 43 30 17
89 73 43 91 03   57 91 35 40 64   13 61 94 37 16   09 93 96 25 87   30 23 42 54 31
29 30 90 00 58   15 99 93 33 67   80 08 59 21 66   13 54 56 85 25   05 32 03 52 52
97 33 17 26 25   04 73 18 10 05   34 40 32 65 07   28 68 29 31 97   89 57 95 55 16
07 15 44 92 47   28 50 93 03 53   37 70 19 68 59   95 39 87 90 46   98 64 46 24 71

82 50 35 50 80   23 67 81 25 02   83 08 12 70 00   25 31 33 80 06   19 86 14 59 27
59 21 86 16 30   27 85 16 26 34   50 15 87 22 69   71 36 95 90 76   90 99 79 63 21
04 19 60 33 05   29 02 33 74 56   38 84 21 07 35   93 54 70 18 47   14 62 75 45 02
96 91 44 09 94   06 89 50 88 83   82 50 11 82 51   30 68 91 06 28   86 65 17 45 20
31 71 03 53 38   94 02 52 72 15   44 49 53 42 43   00 36 97 67 64   12 27 46 00 18

03 70 22 67 59   98 10 64 68 08   79 06 89 48 41   85 72 10 87 24   96 04 20 68 00
08 45 79 46 89   74 73 67 60 15   70 37 61 44 07   67 89 81 54 26   57 17 63 27 74
37 80 05 75 64   48 51 68 68 27   71 75 45 32 27   76 35 26 58 88   67 74 48 90 94
90 63 56 69 37   19 74 48 63 31   52 36 84 40 66   72 66 03 41 87   65 29 12 36 64
22 69 38 02 88   89 71 43 01 87   41 79 42 99 29   41 08 47 32 19   45 29 59 69 90

05 79 69 67 64   36 14 82 65 26   40 51 63 42 48   85 48 34 12 04   33 26 52 26 52
48 91 53 03 82   64 24 06 31 03   97 44 82 24 89   88 48 66 54 10   41 27 09 11 61
94 64 97 27 25   62 23 94 40 54   56 32 97 78 90   58 86 41 75 19   42 90 85 36 68
15 85 82 52 08   52 96 26 92 88   93 11 03 23 52   78 23 57 85 43   53 90 42 22 22
09 81 37 66 56   99 08 59 19 48   29 69 21 64 95   12 08 15 24 45   59 25 22 76 96

43 83 99 02 76   12 16 45 52 66   35 70 93 09 52   75 40 34 35 62   65 42 27 20 59
31 98 09 80 62   75 26 64 57 26   46 41 47 90 97   99 46 10 51 42   73 28 98 89 91
81 35 42 62 84   37 02 59 78 16   17 96 05 71 39   88 05 34 05 92   22 43 89 66 89
97 95 56 39 75   65 47 61 86 33   14 88 55 33 69   70 87 79 94 46   17 61 72 27 01
37 63 35 93 23   17 30 14 51 51   17 28 21 74 67   12 11 57 19 27   38 70 73 82 92

39 22 96 00 48   52 49 62 09 40   08 30 27 54 70   96 06 52 12 80   36 12 38 68 05
61 29 84 34 51   60 19 77 82 16   64 45 02 27 04   65 55 90 95 04   20 39 29 96 28
38 84 18 10 29   19 09 66 06 78   37 09 60 50 21   52 72 01 52 70   29 65 05 37 16
64 29 48 04 08   55 72 25 25 77   54 26 27 24 39   66 67 06 40 00   99 35 70 69 58
64 02 32 99 63   62 42 89 32 20   81 14 08 40 45   22 15 37 49 38   96 51 19 08 27

13 83 39 51 30   31 49 94 83 66   02 50 95 18 98   58 84 90 58 81   00 40 91 12 46
83 30 90 09 35   41 12 87 93 66   85 96 20 65 34   23 13 05 41 01   91 48 95 59 45
46 63 53 97 63   18 86 37 56 20   35 62 66 11 37   30 91 89 97 51   64 78 06 95 65
54 43 40 02 41   55 70 52 96 87   02 82 61 21 88   60 65 98 42 09   03 61 20 83 01
27 18 65 62 01   97 45 79 51 37   74 47 20 11 48   97 93 73 86 50   46 61 95 01 24

45 42 16 13 20   34 51 08 71 52   39 17 71 39 84   97 27 72 49 42   81 62 32 87 22
35 92 97 02 34   93 32 95 81 13   92 05 40 70 95   71 66 61 24 08   77 32 73 66 79
60 55 35 57 24   52 95 84 90 64   38 39 72 70 17   98 42 85 96 67   41 11 83 17 78
43 17 21 09 60   58 86 12 31 11   66 61 43 96 00   93 97 00 15 20   37 96 73 56 63
07 85 74 58 28   38 74 68 32 61   87 14 71 83 47   90 11 96 70 08   67 04 34 46 08

33 00 29 08 87   42 59 40 24 97   44 99 13 56 87   95 02 47 97 89   23 51 45 37 83
97 14 00 42 23   72 03 19 02 41   11 23 36 98 32   19 91 42 03 58   62 23 74 45 06
68 58 32 80 82   40 49 71 83 37   93 49 99 60 72   88 14 26 88 95   48 69 35 40 63
39 87 38 16 06   82 92 62 32 75   67 64 50 49 39   29 55 53 92 97   04 48 60 53 90
37 73 01 84 87   42 88 30 93 75   01 18 34 73 30   28 44 28 18 01   00 38 26 38 57
```

Appendix C

Logarithms of n! *

n	log n!	n	log n!	n	log n!	n	log n!	n	log n!	n	log n!
I	0·0000	51	66·1906	101	159·9743	151	264·9359	201	377·2001
2	0·3010	52	67·9066	102	161·9829	152	267·1177	202	379·5054
3	0·7782	53	69·6309	103	163·9958	153	269·3024	203	381·8129
4	1·3802	54	71·3633	104	166·0128	154	271·4899	204	384·1226
5	2·0792	55	73·1037	105	168·0340	155	273·6803	205	386·4343
6	2·8573	56	74·8519	106	170·0593	156	275·8734	206	388·7482
7	3·7024	57	76·6077	107	172·0887	157	278·0693	207	391·0642
8	4·6055	58	78·3712	108	174·1221	158	280·2679	208	393·3822
9	5·5598	59	80·1420	109	176·1595	159	282·4693	209	395·7024
10	6·5598	60	81·9202	110	178·2009	160	284·6735	210	398·0246
11	7·6012	61	83·7055	111	180·2462	161	286·8803	211	400·3489
12	8·6803	62	85·4979	112	182·2955	162	289·0898	212	402·6752
13	9·7943	63	87·2972	113	184·3485	163	291·3020	213	405·0036
14	10·9404	64	89·1034	114	186·4054	164	293·5168	214	407·3340
15	12·1165	65	90·9163	115	188·4661	165	295·7343	215	409·6664
16	13·3206	66	92·7359	116	190·5306	166	297·9544	216	412·0009
17	14·5511	67	94·5619	117	192·5988	167	300·1771	217	414·3373
18	15·8063	68	96·3945	118	194·6707	168	302·4024	218	416·6758
19	17·0851	69	98·2333	119	196·7462	169	304·6303	219	419·0162
20	18·3861	70	100·0784	120	198·8254	170	306·8608	220	421·3587
21	19·7083	71	101·9297	121	200·9082	171	309·0938	221	423·7031
22	21·0508	72	103·7870	122	202·9945	172	311·3293	222	426·0494
23	22·4125	73	105·6503	123	205·0844	173	313·5674	223	428·3977
24	23·7927	74	107·5196	124	207·1779	174	315·8079	224	430·7480
25	25·1906	75	109·3946	125	209·2748	175	318·0509	225	433·1002
26	26·6056	76	111·2754	126	211·3751	176	320·2965	226	435·4543
27	28·0370	77	113·1619	127	213·4790	177	322·5444	227	437·8103
28	29·4841	78	115·0540	128	215·5862	178	324·7948	228	440·1682
29	30·9465	79	116·9516	129	217·6967	179	327·0477	229	442·5281
30	32·4237	80	118·8547	130	219·8107	180	329·3030	230	444·8898
31	33·9150	81	120·7632	131	221·9280	181	331·5606	231	447·2534
32	35·4202	82	122·6770	132	224·0485	182	333·8207	232	449·6189
33	36·9387	83	124·5961	133	226·1724	183	336·0832	233	451·9862
34	38·4702	84	126·5204	134	228·2995	184	338·3480	234	454·3555
35	40·0142	85	128·4498	135	230·4298	185	340·6152	235	456·7265
36	41·5705	86	130·3843	136	232·5634	186	342·8847	236	459·0994
37	43·1387	87	132·3238	137	234·7001	187	345·1565	237	461·4742
38	44·7185	88	134·2683	138	236·8400	188	347·4307	238	463·8508
39	46·3096	89	136·2177	139	238·9830	189	349·7071	239	466·2292
40	47·9116	90	138·1719	140	241·1291	190	351·9859	240	468·6094
41	49·5244	91	140·1310	141	243·2783	191	354·2669	241	470·9914
42	51·1477	92	142·0948	142	245·4306	192	356·5502	242	473·3752
43	52·7811	93	144·0632	143	247·5860	193	358·8358	243	475·7608
44	54·4246	94	146·0364	144	249·7443	194	361·1236	244	478·1482
45	56·0778	95	148·0141	145	251·9057	195	363·4136	245	480·5374
46	57·7406	96	149·9964	146	254·0700	196	365·7059	246	482·9283
47	59·4127	97	151·9831	147	256·2374	197	368·0003	247	485·3210
48	61·0939	98	153·9744	148	258·4076	198	370·2970	248	487·7154
49	62·7841	99	155·9700	149	260·5808	199	372·5959	249	490·1116
50	64·4831	100	157·9700	150	262·7569	200	374·8969	250	492·5096

* From Table XIII of A. Hald.

Appendix D[*]

Binomial Distribution

$$P = \binom{n}{x} \pi^x (1 - \pi)^{n-x}$$

Note: To find P when $\pi > .5$, find $P(n - x \,|\, 1 - \pi, n)$.

n	x	.05	.10	.15	.20	.25	.30	.35	.40	.45	.50
1	0	.9500	.9000	.8500	.8000	.7500	.7000	.6500	.6000	.5500	.5000
	1	.0500	.1000	.1500	.2000	.2500	.3000	.3500	.4000	.4500	.5000
2	0	.9025	.8100	.7225	.6400	.5625	.4900	.4225	.3600	.3025	.2500
	1	.0950	.1800	.2550	.3200	.3750	.4200	.4550	.4800	.4950	.5000
	2	.0025	.0100	.0225	.0400	.0625	.0900	.1225	.1600	.2025	.2500
3	0	.8574	.7290	.6141	.5120	.4219	.3430	.2746	.2160	.1664	.1250
	1	.1354	.2430	.3251	.3840	.4219	.4410	.4436	.4320	.4084	.3750
	2	.0071	.0270	.0574	.0960	.1406	.1890	.2389	.2880	.3341	.3750
	3	.0001	.0010	.0034	.0080	.0156	.0270	.0429	.0640	.0911	.1250
4	0	.8145	.6561	.5220	.4096	.3164	.2401	.1785	.1296	.0915	.0625
	1	.1715	.2916	.3685	.4096	.4219	.4116	.3845	.3456	.2995	.2500
	2	.0135	.0486	.0975	.1536	.2109	.2646	.3105	.3456	.3675	.3750
	3	.0005	.0036	.0115	.0256	.0469	.0756	.1115	.1536	.2005	.2500
	4	.0000	.0001	.0005	.0016	.0039	.0081	.0150	.0256	.0410	.0625
5	0	.7738	.5905	.4437	.3277	.2373	.1681	.1160	.0778	.0503	.0312
	1	.2036	.3280	.3915	.4096	.3955	.3602	.3124	.2592	.2059	.1562
	2	.0214	.0729	.1382	.2048	.2637	.3087	.3364	.3456	.3369	.3125
	3	.0011	.0081	.0244	.0512	.0879	.1323	.1811	.2304	.2757	.3125
	4	.0000	.0004	.0022	.0064	.0146	.0284	.0488	.0768	.1128	.1562
	5	.0000	.0000	.0001	.0003	.0010	.0024	.0053	.0102	.0185	.0312

[*] Adapted from *Tables of the Binomial Probability Distribution* (n from 2 to 49), National Bureau of Standards, Applied Mathematics Series, U.S. Govt. Printing Office, Wash., D.C., 1949, and from *50–100 Binomial Tables* by Harry G. Romig, John Wiley and Sons, 1953.

Binomial Distribution

n	x	.05	.10	.15	.20	.25	.30	.35	.40	.45	.50
6	0	.7351	.5314	.3771	.2621	.1780	.1176	.0754	.0467	.0277	.0156
	1	.2321	.3543	.3993	.3932	.3560	.3025	.2437	.1866	.1359	.0938
	2	.0305	.0984	.1762	.2458	.2966	.3241	.3280	.3110	.2780	.2344
	3	.0021	.0146	.0415	.0819	.1318	.1852	.2355	.2765	.3032	.3125
	4	.0001	.0012	.0055	.0154	.0330	.0595	.0951	.1382	.1861	.2344
	5	.0000	.0001	.0004	.0015	.0044	.0102	.0205	.0369	.0609	.0938
	6	.0000	.0000	.0000	.0001	.0002	.0007	.0018	.0041	.0083	.0156
7	0	.6983	.4783	.3206	.2097	.1335	.0824	.0490	.0280	.0152	.0078
	1	.2573	.3720	.3960	.3670	.3115	.2471	.1848	.1306	.0872	.0547
	2	.0406	.1240	.2097	.2753	.3115	.3177	.2985	.2613	.2140	.1641
	3	.0036	.0230	.0617	.1147	.1730	.2269	.2679	.2903	.2918	.2734
	4	.0002	.0026	.0109	.0287	.0577	.0972	.1442	.1935	.2388	.2734
	5	.0000	.0002	.0012	.0043	.0115	.0250	.0466	.0774	.1172	.1641
	6	.0000	.0000	.0001	.0004	.0013	.0036	.0084	.0172	.0320	.0547
	7	.0000	.0000	.0000	.0000	.0001	.0002	.0006	.0016	.0037	.0078
8	0	.6634	.4305	.2725	.1678	.1001	.0576	.0319	.0168	.0084	.0039
	1	.2793	.3826	.3847	.3355	.2670	.1977	.1373	.0896	.0548	.0312
	2	.0515	.1488	.2376	.2936	.3115	.2965	.2587	.2090	.1569	.1094
	3	.0054	.0331	.0839	.1468	.2076	.2541	.2786	.2787	.2568	.2188
	4	.0004	.0046	.0185	.0459	.0865	.1361	.1875	.2322	.2627	.2734
	5	.0000	.0004	.0026	.0092	.0231	.0467	.0808	.1239	.1719	.2188
	6	.0000	.0000	.0002	.0011	.0038	.0100	.0217	.0413	.0703	.1094
	7	.0000	.0000	.0000	.0001	.0004	.0012	.0033	.0079	.0164	.0312
	8	.0000	.0000	.0000	.0000	.0000	.0001	.0002	.0007	.0017	.0039
9	0	.6302	.3874	.2316	.1342	.0751	.0404	.0207	.0101	.0046	.0020
	1	.2985	.3874	.3679	.3020	.2253	.1556	.1004	.0605	.0339	.0176
	2	.0629	.1722	.2597	.3020	.3003	.2668	.2162	.1612	.1110	.0703
	3	.0077	.0446	.1069	.1762	.2336	.2668	.2716	.2508	.2119	.1641
	4	.0006	.0074	.0283	.0661	.1168	.1715	.2194	.2508	.2600	.2461
	5	.0000	.0008	.0050	.0165	.0389	.0735	.1181	.1672	.2128	.2461
	6	.0000	.0001	.0006	.0028	.0087	.0210	.0424	.0743	.1160	.1641
	7	.0000	.0000	.0000	.0003	.0012	.0039	.0098	.0212	.0407	.0703
	8	.0000	.0000	.0000	.0000	.0001	.0004	.0013	.0035	.0083	.0176
	9	.0000	.0000	.0000	.0000	.0000	.0000	.0001	.0003	.0008	.0020
10	0	.5987	.3487	.1969	.1074	.0563	.0282	.0135	.0060	.0025	.0010
	1	.3151	.3874	.3474	.2684	.1877	.1211	.0725	.0403	.0207	.0098
	2	.0746	.1937	.2759	.3020	.2816	.2335	.1757	.1209	.0763	.0439
	3	.0105	.0574	.1298	.2013	.2503	.2668	.2522	.2150	.1665	.1172
	4	.0010	.0112	.0401	.0881	.1460	.2001	.2377	.2508	.2384	.2051

Binomial Distribution

π

n	x	.05	.10	.15	.20	.25	.30	.35	.40	.45	.50
10	5	.0001	.0015	.0085	.0264	.0584	.1029	.1536	.2007	.2340	.2461
	6	.0000	.0001	.0012	.0055	.0162	.0368	.0689	.1115	.1596	.2051
	7	.0000	.0000	.0001	.0008	.0031	.0090	.0212	.0425	.0746	.1172
	8	.0000	.0000	.0000	.0001	.0004	.0014	.0043	.0106	.0229	.0439
	9	.0000	.0000	.0000	.0000	.0000	.0001	.0005	.0016	.0042	.0098
	10	.0000	.0000	.0000	.0000	.0000	.0000	.0000	.0001	.0003	.0010
11	0	.5688	.3138	.1673	.0859	.0422	.0198	.0088	.0036	.0014	.0005
	1	.3293	.3835	.3248	.2362	.1549	.0932	.0518	.0266	.0125	.0054
	2	.0867	.2131	.2866	.2953	.2581	.1998	.1395	.0887	.0513	.0269
	3	.0137	.0710	.1517	.2215	.2581	.2568	.2254	.1774	.1259	.0806
	4	.0014	.0158	.0536	.1107	.1721	.2201	.2428	.2365	.2060	.1611
	5	.0001	.0025	.0132	.0388	.0803	.1321	.1830	.2207	.2360	.2256
	6	.0000	.0003	.0023	.0097	.0268	.0566	.0985	.1471	.1931	.2256
	7	.0000	.0000	.0003	.0017	.0064	.0173	.0379	.0701	.1128	.1611
	8	.0000	.0000	.0000	.0002	.0011	.0037	.0102	.0234	.0462	.0806
	9	.0000	.0000	.0000	.0000	.0001	.0005	.0018	.0052	.0126	.0269
	10	.0000	.0000	.0000	.0000	.0000	.0000	.0002	.0007	.0021	.0054
	11	.0000	.0000	.0000	.0000	.0000	.0000	.0000	.0000	.0002	.0005
12	0	.5404	.2824	.1422	.0687	.0317	.0138	.0057	.0022	.0008	.0002
	1	.3413	.3766	.3012	.2062	.1267	.0712	.0368	.0174	.0075	.0029
	2	.0988	.2301	.2924	.2835	.2323	.1678	.1088	.0639	.0339	.0161
	3	.0173	.0852	.1720	.2362	.2581	.2397	.1954	.1419	.0923	.0537
	4	.0021	.0213	.0683	.1329	.1936	.2311	.2367	.2128	.1700	.1208
	5	.0002	.0038	.0193	.0532	.1032	.1585	.2039	.2270	.2225	.1934
	6	.0000	.0005	.0040	.0155	.0401	.0792	.1281	.1766	.2124	.2256
	7	.0000	.0000	.0006	.0033	.0115	.0291	.0591	.1009	.1489	.1934
	8	.0000	.0000	.0001	.0005	.0024	.0078	.0199	.0420	.0762	.1208
	9	.0000	.0000	.0000	.0001	.0004	.0015	.0048	.0125	.0277	.0537
	10	.0000	.0000	.0000	.0000	.0000	.0002	.0008	.0025	.0068	.0161
	11	.0000	.0000	.0000	.0000	.0000	.0000	.0001	.0003	.0010	.0029
	12	.0000	.0000	.0000	.0000	.0000	.0000	.0000	.0000	.0001	.0002
13	0	.5133	.2542	.1209	.0550	.0238	.0097	.0037	.0013	.0004	.0001
	1	.3512	.3672	.2774	.1787	.1029	.0540	.0259	.0113	.0045	.0016
	2	.1109	.2448	.2937	.2680	.2059	.1388	.0836	.0453	.0220	.0095
	3	.0214	.0997	.1900	.2457	.2517	.2181	.1651	.1107	.0660	.0349
	4	.0028	.0277	.0838	.1535	.2097	.2337	.2222	.1845	.1350	.0873
	5	.0003	.0055	.0266	.0691	.1258	.1803	.2154	.2214	.1989	.1571
	6	.0000	.0008	.0063	.0230	.0559	.1030	.1546	.1968	.2169	.2095
	7	.0000	.0001	.0011	.0058	.0186	.0442	.0833	.1312	.1775	.2095
	8	.0000	.0000	.0001	.0011	.0047	.0142	.0336	.0656	.1089	.1571
	9	.0000	.0000	.0000	.0001	.0009	.0034	.0101	.0243	.0495	.0873

Binomial Distribution

n	x	.05	.10	.15	.20	.25	.30	.35	.40	.45	.50
13	10	.0000	.0000	.0000	.0000	.0001	.0006	.0022	.0065	.0162	.0349
	11	.0000	.0000	.0000	.0000	.0000	.0001	.0003	.0012	.0036	.0095
	12	.0000	.0000	.0000	.0000	.0000	.0000	.0000	.0001	.0005	.0016
	13	.0000	.0000	.0000	.0000	.0000	.0000	.0000	.0000	.0000	.0001
14	0	.4877	.2288	.1028	.0440	.0178	.0068	.0024	.0008	.0002	.0001
	1	.3593	.3559	.2539	.1539	.0832	.0407	.0181	.0073	.0027	.0009
	2	.1229	.2570	.2912	.2501	.1802	.1134	.0634	.0317	.0141	.0056
	3	.0259	.1142	.2056	.2501	.2402	.1943	.1366	.0845	.0462	.0222
	4	.0037	.0349	.0998	.1720	.2202	.2290	.2022	.1549	.1040	.0611
	5	.0004	.0078	.0352	.0860	.1468	.1963	.2178	.2066	.1701	.1222
	6	.0000	.0013	.0093	.0322	.0734	.1262	.1759	.2066	.2088	.1833
	7	.0000	.0002	.0019	.0092	.0280	.0618	.1082	.1574	.1952	.2095
	8	.0000	.0000	.0003	.0020	.0082	.0232	.0510	.0918	.1398	.1833
	9	.0000	.0000	.0000	.0003	.0018	.0066	.0183	.0408	.0762	.1222
	10	.0000	.0000	.0000	.0000	.0003	.0014	.0049	.0136	.0312	.0611
	11	.0000	.0000	.0000	.0000	.0000	.0002	.0010	.0033	.0093	.0222
	12	.0000	.0000	.0000	.0000	.0000	.0000	.0001	.0005	.0019	.0056
	13	.0000	.0000	.0000	.0000	.0000	.0000	.0000	.0001	.0002	.0009
	14	.0000	.0000	.0000	.0000	.0000	.0000	.0000	.0000	.0000	.0001
15	0	.4633	.2059	.0874	.0352	.0134	.0047	.0016	.0005	.0001	.0000
	1	.3658	.3432	.2312	.1319	.0668	.0305	.0126	.0047	.0016	.0005
	2	.1348	.2669	.2856	.2309	.1559	.0916	.0476	.0219	.0090	.0032
	3	.0307	.1285	.2184	.2501	.2252	.1700	.1110	.0634	.0318	.0139
	4	.0049	.0428	.1156	.1876	.2252	.2186	.1792	.1268	.0780	.0417
	5	.0006	.0105	.0449	.1032	.1651	.2061	.2123	.1859	.1404	.0916
	6	.0000	.0019	.0132	.0430	.0917	.1472	.1906	.2066	.1914	.1527
	7	.0000	.0003	.0030	.0138	.0393	.0811	.1319	.1771	.2013	.1964
	8	.0000	.0000	.0005	.0035	.0131	.0348	.0710	.1181	.1647	.1964
	9	.0000	.0000	.0001	.0007	.0034	.0116	.0298	.0612	.1048	.1527
	10	.0000	.0000	.0000	.0001	.0007	.0030	.0096	.0245	.0515	.0916
	11	.0000	.0000	.0000	.0000	.0001	.0006	.0024	.0074	.0191	.0417
	12	.0000	.0000	.0000	.0000	.0000	.0001	.0004	.0016	.0052	.0139
	13	.0000	.0000	.0000	.0000	.0000	.0000	.0001	.0003	.0010	.0032
	14	.0000	.0000	.0000	.0000	.0000	.0000	.0000	.0000	.0001	.0005
	15	.0000	.0000	.0000	.0000	.0000	.0000	.0000	.0000	.0000	.0000
16	0	.4401	.1853	.0743	.0281	.0100	.0033	.0010	.0003	.0001	.0000
	1	.3706	.3294	.2097	.1126	.0535	.0228	.0087	.0030	.0009	.0002
	2	.1463	.2745	.2775	.2111	.1336	.0732	.0353	.0150	.0056	.0018
	3	.0359	.1423	.2285	.2463	.2079	.1465	.0888	.0468	.0215	.0085
	4	.0061	.0514	.1311	.2001	.2252	.2040	.1553	.1014	.0572	.0278

Binomial Distribution

n	x	.05	.10	.15	.20	.25	.30	.35	.40	.45	.50
16	5	.0008	.0137	.0555	.1201	.1802	.2099	.2008	.1623	.1123	.0667
	6	.0001	.0028	.0180	.0550	.1101	.1649	.1982	.1983	.1684	.1222
	7	.0000	.0004	.0045	.0197	.0524	.1010	.1524	.1889	.1969	.1746
	8	.0000	.0001	.0009	.0055	.0197	.0487	.0923	.1417	.1812	.1964
	9	.0000	.0000	.0001	.0012	.0058	.0185	.0442	.0840	.1318	.1746
	10	.0000	.0000	.0000	.0002	.0014	.0056	.0167	.0392	.0755	.1222
	11	.0000	.0000	.0000	.0000	.0002	.0013	.0049	.0142	.0337	.0667
	12	.0000	.0000	.0000	.0000	.0000	.0002	.0011	.0040	.0115	.0278
	13	.0000	.0000	.0000	.0000	.0000	.0000	.0002	.0008	.0029	.0085
	14	.0000	.0000	.0000	.0000	.0000	.0000	.0000	.0001	.0005	.0018
	15	.0000	.0000	.0000	.0000	.0000	.0000	.0000	.0000	.0001	.0002
	16	.0000	.0000	.0000	.0000	.0000	.0000	.0000	.0000	.0000	.0000
17	0	.4181	.1668	.0631	.0225	.0075	.0023	.0007	.0002	.0000	.0000
	1	.3741	.3150	.1893	.0957	.0426	.0169	.0060	.0019	.0005	.0001
	2	.1575	.2800	.2673	.1914	.1136	.0581	.0260	.0102	.0035	.0010
	3	.0415	.1556	.2359	.2393	.1893	.1245	.0701	.0341	.0144	.0052
	4	.0076	.0605	.1457	.2093	.2209	.1868	.1320	.0796	.0411	.0182
	5	.0010	.0175	.0668	.1361	.1914	.2081	.1849	.1379	.0875	.0472
	6	.0001	.0039	.0236	.0680	.1276	.1784	.1991	.1839	.1432	.0944
	7	.0000	.0007	.0065	.0267	.0668	.1201	.1685	.1927	.1841	.1484
	8	.0000	.0001	.0014	.0084	.0279	.0644	.1134	.1606	.1883	.1855
	9	.0000	.0000	.0003	.0021	.0093	.0276	.0611	.1070	.1540	.1855
	10	.0000	.0000	.0000	.0004	.0025	.0095	.0263	.0571	.1008	.1484
	11	.0000	.0000	.0000	.0001	.0005	.0026	.0090	.0242	.0525	.0944
	12	.0000	.0000	.0000	.0000	.0001	.0006	.0024	.0081	.0215	.0472
	13	.0000	.0000	.0000	.0000	.0000	.0001	.0005	.0021	.0068	.0182
	14	.0000	.0000	.0000	.0000	.0000	.0000	.0001	.0004	.0016	.0052
	15	.0000	.0000	.0000	.0000	.0000	.0000	.0000	.0001	.0003	.0010
	16	.0000	.0000	.0000	.0000	.0000	.0000	.0000	.0000	.0000	.0001
	17	.0000	.0000	.0000	.0000	.0000	.0000	.0000	.0000	.0000	.0000
18	0	.3972	.1501	.0536	.0180	.0056	.0016	.0004	.0001	.0000	.0000
	1	.3763	.3002	.1704	.0811	.0338	.0126	.0042	.0012	.0003	.0001
	2	.1683	.2835	.2556	.1723	.0958	.0458	.0190	.0069	.0022	.0006
	3	.0473	.1680	.2406	.2297	.1704	.1046	.0547	.0246	.0095	.0031
	4	.0093	.0700	.1592	.2153	.2130	.1681	.1104	.0614	.0291	.0117
	5	.0014	.0218	.0787	.1507	.1988	.2017	.1664	.1146	.0666	.0327
	6	.0002	.0052	.0301	.0816	.1436	.1873	.1941	.1655	.1181	.0708
	7	.0000	.0010	.0091	.0350	.0820	.1376	.1792	.1892	.1657	.1214
	8	.0000	.0002	.0022	.0120	.0376	.0811	.1327	.1734	.1864	.1669
	9	.0000	.0000	.0004	.0033	.0139	.0386	.0794	.1284	.1694	.1855

Binomial Distribution

n	x	.05	.10	.15	.20	.25	π .30	.35	.40	.45	.50
18	10	.0000	.0000	.0001	.0008	.0042	.0149	.0385	.0771	.1248	.1669
	11	.0000	.0000	.0000	.0001	.0010	.0046	.0151	.0374	.0742	.1214
	12	.0000	.0000	.0000	.0000	.0002	.0012	.0047	.0145	.0354	.0708
	13	.0000	.0000	.0000	.0000	.0000	.0002	.0012	.0045	.0134	.0327
	14	.0000	.0000	.0000	.0000	.0000	.0000	.0002	.0011	.0039	.0117
	15	.0000	.0000	.0000	.0000	.0000	.0000	.0000	.0002	.0009	.0031
	16	.0000	.0000	.0000	.0000	.0000	.0000	.0000	.0000	.0001	.0006
	17	.0000	.0000	.0000	.0000	.0000	.0000	.0000	.0000	.0000	.0001
	18	.0000	.0000	.0000	.0000	.0000	.0000	.0000	.0000	.0000	.0000
19	0	.3774	.1351	.0456	.0144	.0042	.0011	.0003	.0001	.0000	.0000
	1	.3774	.2852	.1529	.0685	.0268	.0093	.0029	.0008	.0002	.0000
	2	.1787	.2852	.2428	.1540	.0803	.0358	.0138	.0046	.0013	.0003
	3	.0533	.1796	.2428	.2182	.1517	.0869	.0422	.0175	.0062	.0018
	4	.0112	.0798	.1714	.2182	.2023	.1491	.0909	.0467	.0203	.0074
	5	.0018	.0266	.0907	.1636	.2023	.1916	.1468	.0933	.0497	.0222
	6	.0002	.0069	.0374	.0955	.1574	.1916	.1844	.1451	.0949	.0518
	7	.0000	.0014	.0122	.0443	.0974	.1525	.1844	.1797	.1443	.0961
	8	.0000	.0002	.0032	.0166	.0487	.0981	.1489	.1797	.1771	.1442
	9	.0000	.0000	.0007	.0051	.0198	.0514	.0980	.1464	.1771	.1762
	10	.0000	.0000	.0001	.0013	.0066	.0220	.0528	.0976	.1449	.1762
	11	.0000	.0000	.0000	.0003	.0018	.0077	.0233	.0532	.0970	.1442
	12	.0000	.0000	.0000	.0000	.0004	.0022	.0083	.0237	.0529	.0961
	13	.0000	.0000	.0000	.0000	.0001	.0005	.0024	.0085	.0233	.0518
	14	.0000	.0000	.0000	.0000	.0000	.0001	.0006	.0024	.0082	.0222
	15	.0000	.0000	.0000	.0000	.0000	.0000	.0001	.0005	.0022	.0074
	16	.0000	.0000	.0000	.0000	.0000	.0000	.0000	.0001	.0005	.0018
	17	.0000	.0000	.0000	.0000	.0000	.0000	.0000	.0000	.0001	.0003
	18	.0000	.0000	.0000	.0000	.0000	.0000	.0000	.0000	.0000	.0000
	19	.0000	.0000	.0000	.0000	.0000	.0000	.0000	.0000	.0000	.0000
20	0	.3585	.1216	.0388	.0115	.0032	.0008	.0002	.0000	.0000	.0000
	1	.3774	.2702	.1368	.0576	.0211	.0068	.0020	.0005	.0001	.0000
	2	.1887	.2852	.2293	.1369	.0669	.0278	.0100	.0031	.0008	.0002
	3	.0596	.1901	.2428	.2054	.1339	.0716	.0323	.0123	.0040	.0011
	4	.0133	.0898	.1821	.2182	.1897	.1304	.0738	.0350	.0139	.0046
	5	.0022	.0319	.1028	.1746	.2023	.1789	.1272	.0746	.0365	.0148
	6	.0003	.0089	.0454	.1091	.1686	.1916	.1712	.1244	.0746	.0370
	7	.0000	.0020	.0160	.0545	.1124	.1643	.1844	.1659	.1221	.0739
	8	.0000	.0004	.0046	.0222	.0609	.1144	.1614	.1797	.1623	.1201
	9	.0000	.0001	.0011	.0074	.0271	.0654	.1158	.1597	.1771	.1602

Binomial Distribution

π

n	x	.05	.10	.15	.20	.25	.30	.35	.40	.45	.50
20	10	.0000	.0000	.0002	.0020	.0099	.0308	.0686	.1171	.1593	.1762
	11	.0000	.0000	.0000	.0005	.0030	.0120	.0336	.0710	.1185	.1602
	12	.0000	.0000	.0000	.0001	.0008	.0039	.0136	.0355	.0727	.1201
	13	.0000	.0000	.0000	.0000	.0002	.0010	.0045	.0146	.0366	.0739
	14	.0000	.0000	.0000	.0000	.0000	.0002	.0012	.0049	.0150	.0370
	15	.0000	.0000	.0000	.0000	.0000	.0000	.0003	.0013	.0049	.0148
	16	.0000	.0000	.0000	.0000	.0000	.0000	.0000	.0003	.0013	.0046
	17	.0000	.0000	.0000	.0000	.0000	.0000	.0000	.0000	.0002	.0011
	18	.0000	.0000	.0000	.0000	.0000	.0000	.0000	.0000	.0000	.0002
	19	.0000	.0000	.0000	.0000	.0000	.0000	.0000	.0000	.0000	.0000
	20	.0000	.0000	.0000	.0000	.0000	.0000	.0000	.0000	.0000	.0000
40	0	.1285	.0148	.0015	.0001	—	—	—	—	—	—
	1	.2706	.0657	.0106	.0013	.0001	—	—	—	—	—
	2	.2777	.1423	.0365	.0065	.0009	.0001	—	—	—	—
	3	.1851	.2003	.0816	.0205	.0037	.0005	.0001	—	—	—
	4	.0901	.2059	.1332	.0475	.0113	.0020	.0003	—	—	—
	5	.0342	.1647	.1692	.0854	.0272	.0061	.0010	.0001	—	—
	6	.0105	.1068	.1742	.1246	.0530	.0151	.0031	.0005	—	—
	7	.0027	.0576	.1493	.1513	.0857	.0315	.0080	.0015	.0002	—
	8	.0006	.0264	.1087	.1560	.1179	.0557	.0179	.0040	.0006	.0001
	9	.0001	.0104	.0682	.1386	.1397	.0849	.0342	.0095	.0018	.0002
	10	—	.0036	.0373	.1075	.1444	.1128	.0571	.0196	.0047	.0008
	11	—	.0011	.0180	.0733	.1312	.1319	.0838	.0357	.0105	.0021
	12	—	.0003	.0077	.0443	.1057	.1366	.1090	.0576	.0207	.0051
	13	—	.0001	.0029	.0238	.0759	.1261	.1265	.0827	.0365	.0109
	14	—	—	.0010	.0115	.0488	.1042	.1313	.1063	.0575	.0211
	15	—	—	.0003	.0050	.0282	.0774	.1226	.1228	.0816	.0366
	16	—	—	.0001	.0019	.0147	.0518	.1031	.1279	.1043	.0572
	17	—	—	—	.0007	.0069	.0314	.0784	.1204	.1205	.0807
	18	—	—	—	.0002	.0029	.0172	.0539	.1026	.1260	.1031
	19	—	—	—	.0001	.0011	.0085	.0336	.0792	.1194	.1194
	20	—	—	—	—	.0004	.0038	.0190	.0554	.1025	.1254
	21	—	—	—	—	.0001	.0016	.0097	.0352	.0799	.1194
	22	—	—	—	—	—	.0006	.0045	.0203	.0565	.1031
	23	—	—	—	—	—	.0002	.0019	.0106	.0362	.0807
	24	—	—	—	—	—	.0001	.0007	.0050	.0210	.0572
	25	—	—	—	—	—	—	.0003	.0021	.0110	.0366
	26	—	—	—	—	—	—	.0001	.0008	.0052	.0211
	27	—	—	—	—	—	—	—	.0003	.0022	.0109
	28	—	—	—	—	—	—	—	.0001	.0008	.0051
	29	—	—	—	—	—	—	—	—	.0003	.0021

Binomial Distribution

π

n	x	.05	.10	.15	.20	.25	.30	.35	.40	.45	.50
40	30	—	—	—	—'	—	—	—	—	.0001	.0008
	31	—	—	—	—	—	—	—	—	—	.0002
	32	—	—	—	—	—	—	—	—	—	.0001
	33	—	—	—	—	—	—	—	—	—	—
50	0	.0769	.0052	.0003	—	—	—	—	—	—	—
	1	.2025	.0286	.0026	.0002	—	—	—	—	—	—
	2	.2611	.0779	.0113	.0011	.0001	—	—	—	—	—
	3	.2199	.1386	.0319	.0044	.0004	—	—	—	—	—
	4	.1360	.1809	.0661	.0128	.0016	.0001	—	—	—	—
	5	.0658	.1849	.1072	.0295	.0049	.0006	—	—	—	—
	6	.0260	.1541	.1419	.0554	.0123	.0018	.0002	—	—	—
	7	.0086	.1076	.1575	.0870	.0259	.0048	.0006	—	—	—
	8	.0024	.0643	.1493	.1169	.0463	.0110	.0017	.0002	—	—
	9	.0006	.0333	.1230	.1364	.0721	.0220	.0042	.0005	—	—
	10	.0001	.0152	.0890	.1398	.0985	.0386	.0093	.0014	.0001	—
	11	—	.0061	.0571	.1271	.1194	.0602	.0182	.0035	.0004	—
	12	—	.0022	.0328	.1033	.1294	.0838	.0319	.0076	.0011	.0001
	13	—	.0007	.0169	.0755	.1261	.1050	.0502	.0147	.0027	.0003
	14	—	.0002	.0079	.0499	.1110	.1189	.0714	.0260	.0059	.0008
	15	—	.0001	.0033	.0299	.0888	.1223	.0923	.0415	.0116	.0020
	16	—	—	.0013	.0164	.0648	.1147	.1088	.0606	.0207	.0044
	17	—	—	.0005	.0082	.0432	.0983	.1171	.0808	.0339	.0087
	18	—	—	.0001	.0038	.0264	.0772	.1156	.0987	.0508	.0160
	19	—	—	—	.0016	.0148	.0558	.1048	.1109	.0700	.0270
	20	—	—	—	.0006	.0077	.0370	.0875	.1146	.0888	.0419
	21	—	—	—	.0002	.0036	.0227	.0673	.1091	.1038	.0598
	22	—	—	—	.0001	.0016	.0128	.0478	.0959	.1119	.0788
	23	—	—	—	—	.0006	.0067	.0313	.0778	.1115	.0960
	24	—	—	—	—	.0002	.0032	.0190	.0584	.1026	.1080
	25	—	—	—	—	.0001	.0014	.0106	.0405	.0873	.1123
	26	—	—	—	—	—	.0006	.0055	.0259	.0687	.1080
	27	—	—	—	—	—	.0002	.0026	.0154	.0500	.0960
	28	—	—	—	—	—	.0001	.0012	.0084	.0336	.0788
	29	—	—	—	—	—	—	.0005	.0043	.0208	.0598
	30	—	—	—	—	—	—	.0002	.0020	.0119	.0419
	31	—	—	—	—	—	—	.0001	.0009	.0063	.0270
	32	—	—	—	—	—	—	—	.0003	.0031	.0160
	33	—	—	—	—	—	—	—	.0001	.0014	.0087
	34	—	—	—	—	—	—	—	—	.0006	.0044

Binomial Distribution

n	x	.05	.10	.15	.20	.25	.30	.35	.40	.45	.50
50	35	—	—	—	—	—	—	—	—	.0002	.0020
	36	—	—	—	—	—	—	—	—	.0001	.0008
	37	—	—	—	—	—	—	—	—	—	.0003
	38	—	—	—	—	—	—	—	—	—	.0001
	39	—	—	—	—	—	—	—	—	—	—
100	0	.0059	—	—	—	—	—	—	—	—	—
	1	.0312	.0003	—	—	—	—	—	—	—	—
	2	.0812	.0016	—	—	—	—	—	—	—	—
	3	.1396	.0059	.0001	—	—	—	—	—	—	—
	4	.1781	.0159	.0003	—	—	—	—	—	—	—
	5	.1800	.0339	.0011	—	—	—	—	—	—	—
	6	.1500	.0596	.0031	.0001	—	—	—	—	—	—
	7	.1060	.0889	.0075	.0002	—	—	—	—	—	—
	8	.0649	.1148	.0153	.0006	—	—	—	—	—	—
	9	.0349	.1304	.0276	.0015	—	—	—	—	—	—
	10	.0167	.1319	.0444	.0034	.0001	—	—	—	—	—
	11	.0072	.1199	.0640	.0069	.0003	—	—	—	—	—
	12	.0028	.0988	.0838	.0128	.0006	—	—	—	—	—
	13	.0010	.0743	.1001	.0216	.0014	—	—	—	—	—
	14	.0003	.0513	.1098	.0335	.0030	.0001	—	—	—	—
	15	.0001	.0327	.1111	.0481	.0057	.0002	—	—	—	—
	16	—	.0193	.1041	.0638	.0100	.0006	—	—	—	—
	17	—	.0106	.0908	.0789	.0165	.0012	—	—	—	—
	18	—	.0054	.0739	.0909	.0254	.0024	.0001	—	—	—
	19	—	.0026	.0563	.0981	.0365	.0044	.0002	—	—	—
	20	—	.0012	.0402	.0993	.0493	.0076	.0004	—	—	—
	21	—	.0005	.0270	.0946	.0626	.0124	.0009	—	—	—
	22	—	.0002	.0171	.0849	.0749	.0190	.0017	.0001	—	—
	23	—	.0001	.0103	.0720	.0847	.0277	.0032	.0001	—	—
	24	—	—	.0058	.0577	.0906	.0380	.0055	.0004	—	—
	25	—	—	.0031	.0439	.0918	.0496	.0090	.0006	—	—
	26	—	—	.0016	.0316	.0883	.0613	.0140	.0012	—	—
	27	—	—	.0008	.0217	.0806	.0720	.0207	.0022	.0001	—
	28	—	—	.0004	.0141	.0701	.0804	.0290	.0038	.0002	—
	29	—	—	.0002	.0088	.0580	.0856	.0388	.0063	.0004	—
	30	—	—	.0001	.0052	.0458	.0868	.0494	.0100	.0008	—
	31	—	—	—	.0029	.0344	.0840	.0601	.0151	.0014	.0001
	32	—	—	—	.0016	.0248	.0776	.0698	.0217	.0025	.0001
	33	—	—	—	.0008	.0170	.0685	.0774	.0298	.0043	.0002
	34	—	—	—	.0004	.0112	.0579	.0821	.0391	.0069	.0005

Binomial Distribution

n	x	.05	.10	.15	.20	.25	.30	.35	.40	.45	.50
100	35	—	—	—	.0002	.0070	.0468	.0834	.0491	.0106	.0009
	36	—	—	—	.0001	.0042	.0362	.0811	.0591	.0157	.0016
	37	—	—	—	—	.0024	.0268	.0755	.0682	.0222	.0027
	38	—	—	—	—	.0013	.0191	.0674	.0754	.0301	.0045
	39	—	—	—	—	.0007	.0130	.0577	.0799	.0391	.0071
	40	—	—	—	—	.0004	.0085	.0474	.0812	.0488	.0108
	41	—	—	—	—	.0002	.0053	.0373	.0792	.0584	.0159
	42	—	—	—	—	.0001	.0032	.0282	.0742	.0672	.0223
	43	—	—	—	—	—	.0019	.0205	.0667	.0741	.0301
	44	—	—	—	—	—	.0010	.0143	.0576	.0786	.0390
	45	—	—	—	—	—	.0005	.0096	.0478	.0800	.0485
	46	—	—	—	—	—	.0003	.0062	.0381	.0782	.0580
	47	—	—	—	—	—	.0001	.0038	.0292	.0736	.0666
	48	—	—	—	—	—	.0001	.0023	.0215	.0665	.0735
	49	—	—	—	—	—	—	.0013	.0152	.0577	.0780
	50	—	—	—	—	—	—	.0007	.0103	.0482	.0796
	51	—	—	—	—	—	—	.0004	.0068	.0380	.0780
	52	—	—	—	—	—	—	.0002	.0042	.0298	.0735
	53	—	—	—	—	—	—	.0001	.0026	.0221	.0665
	54	—	—	—	—	—	—	—	.0015	.0157	.0579
	55	—	—	—	—	—	—	—	.0008	.0108	.0484
	56	—	—	—	—	—	—	—	.0004	.0071	.0389
	57	—	—	—	—	—	—	—	.0002	.0045	.0300
	58	—	—	—	—	—	—	—	.0001	.0027	.0223
	59	—	—	—	—	—	—	—	.0001	.0016	.0159
	60	—	—	—	—	—	—	—	—	.0009	.0109
	61	—	—	—	—	—	—	—	—	.0005	.0071
	62	—	—	—	—	—	—	—	—	.0002	.0045
	63	—	—	—	—	—	—	—	—	.0001	.0027
	64	—	—	—	—	—	—	—	—	.0001	.0016
	65	—	—	—	—	—	—	—	—	—	.0009
	66	—	—	—	—	—	—	—	—	—	.0005
	67	—	—	—	—	—	—	—	—	—	.0002
	68	—	—	—	—	—	—	—	—	—	.0001
	69	—	—	—	—	—	—	—	—	—	.0001

Appendix E*

Cumulative Binomial

$$\sum_{s=x'}^{n} \binom{n}{s} \pi^s (1-\pi)^{n-s}$$

Note: To find P when $\pi > .5$, calculate $1 - P(n - x' + 1 \,|\, 1 - \pi, n)$. e.g. $P(x \geq 2 \,|\, \pi = .8, n = 6) = 1 - P(x \geq 5 \,|\, \pi = .2, n = 6) = 1 - .0016 = .9984$.

						π					
n	x'	.05	.10	.15	.20	.25	.30	.35	.40	.45	.50
2	1	.0975	.1900	.2775	.3600	.4375	.5100	.5775	.6400	.6975	.7500
	2	.0025	.0100	.0225	.0400	.0625	.0900	.1225	.1600	.2025	.2500
3	1	.1426	.2710	.3859	.4880	.5781	.6570	.7254	.7840	.8336	.8750
	2	.0072	.0280	.0608	.1040	.1562	.2160	.2818	.3520	.4252	.5000
	3	.0001	.0010	.0034	.0080	.0156	.0270	.0429	.0640	.0911	.1250
4	1	.1855	.3439	.4780	.5904	.6836	.7599	.8215	.8704	.9085	.9375
	2	.0140	.0523	.1095	.1808	.2617	.3483	.4370	.5248	.6090	.6875
	3	.0005	.0037	.0120	.0272	.0508	.0837	.1265	.1792	.2415	.3125
	4	.0000	.0001	.0005	.0016	.0039	.0081	.0150	.0256	.0410	.0625
5	1	.2262	.4095	.5563	.6723	.7627	.8319	.8840	.9222	.9497	.9688
	2	.0226	.0815	.1648	.2627	.3672	.4718	.5716	.6630	.7438	.8125
	3	.0012	.0086	.0266	.0579	.1035	.1631	.2352	.3174	.4069	.5000
	4	.0000	.0005	.0022	.0067	.0156	.0308	.0540	.0870	.1312	.1875
	5	.0000	.0000	.0001	.0003	.0010	.0024	.0053	.0102	.0185	.0312
6	1	.2649	.4686	.6229	.7379	.8220	.8824	.9246	.9533	.9723	.9844
	2	.0328	.1143	.2235	.3446	.4661	.5798	.6809	.7667	.8364	.8906
	3	.0022	.0158	.0473	.0989	.1694	.2557	.3529	.4557	.5585	.6562
	4	.0001	.0013	.0059	.0170	.0376	.0705	.1174	.1792	.2553	.3438
	5	.0000	.0001	.0004	.0016	.0046	.0109	.0223	.0410	.0692	.1094
	6	.0000	.0000	.0000	.0001	.0002	.0007	.0018	.0041	.0083	.0156

Cumulative Binomial

n	x'	.05	.10	.15	.20	.25	.30	.35	.40	.45	.50
7	1	.3017	.5217	.6794	.7903	.8665	.9176	.9510	.9720	.9848	.9922
	2	.0444	.1497	.2834	.4233	.5551	.6706	.7662	.8414	.8976	.9375
	3	.0038	.0257	.0738	.1480	.2436	.3529	.4677	.5801	.6836	.7734
	4	.0002	.0027	.0121	.0333	.0706	.1260	.1998	.2898	.3917	.5000
	5	.0000	.0002	.0012	.0047	.0129	.0288	.0556	.0963	.1529	.2266
	6	.0000	.0000	.0001	.0004	.0013	.0038	.0090	.0188	.0357	.0625
	7	.0000	.0000	.0000	.0000	.0001	.0002	.0006	.0016	.0037	.0078
8	1	.3366	.5695	.7275	.8322	.8999	.9424	.9681	.9832	.9916	.9961
	2	.0572	.1869	.3428	.4967	.6329	.7447	.8309	.8936	.9368	.9648
	3	.0058	.0381	.1052	.2031	.3215	.4482	.5722	.6846	.7799	.8555
	4	.0004	.0050	.0214	.0563	.1138	.1941	.2936	.4059	.5230	.6367
	5	.0000	.0004	.0029	.0104	.0273	.0580	.1061	.1737	.2604	.3633
	6	.0000	.0000	.0002	.0012	.0042	.0113	.0253	.0498	.0885	.1445
	7	.0000	.0000	.0000	.0001	.0004	.0013	.0036	.0085	.0181	.0352
	8	.0000	.0000	.0000	.0000	.0000	.0001	.0002	.0007	.0017	.0039
9	1	.3698	.6126	.7684	.8658	.9249	.9596	.9793	.9899	.9954	.9980
	2	.0712	.2252	.4005	.5638	.6997	.8040	.8789	.9295	.9615	.9805
	3	.0084	.0530	.1409	.2618	.3993	.5372	.6627	.7682	.8505	.9102
	4	.0006	.0083	.0339	.0856	.1657	.2703	.3911	.5174	.6386	.7461
	5	.0000	.0009	.0056	.0196	.0489	.0988	.1717	.2666	.3786	.5000
	6	.0000	.0001	.0006	.0031	.0100	.0253	.0536	.0994	.1658	.2539
	7	.0000	.0000	.0000	.0003	.0013	.0043	.0112	.0250	.0498	.0898
	8	.0000	.0000	.0000	.0000	.0001	.0004	.0014	.0038	.0091	.0195
	9	.0000	.0000	.0000	.0000	.0000	.0000	.0001	.0003	.0008	.0020
10	1	.4013	.6513	.8031	.8926	.9437	.9718	.9865	.9940	.9975	.9990
	2	.0861	.2639	.4557	.6242	.7560	.8507	.9140	.9536	.9767	.9893
	3	.0115	.0702	.1798	.3222	.4744	.6172	.7384	.8327	.9004	.9453
	4	.0010	.0128	.0500	.1209	.2241	.3504	.4862	.6177	.7340	.8281
	5	.0001	.0016	.0099	.0328	.0781	.1503	.2485	.3669	.4956	.6230
	6	.0000	.0001	.0014	.0064	.0197	.0473	.0949	.1662	.2616	.3770
	7	.0000	.0000	.0001	.0009	.0035	.0106	.0260	.0548	.1020	.1719
	8	.0000	.0000	.0000	.0001	.0004	.0016	.0048	.0123	.0274	.0547
	9	.0000	.0000	.0000	.0000	.0000	.0001	.0005	.0017	.0045	.0107
	10	.0000	.0000	.0000	.0000	.0000	.0000	.0000	.0001	.0003	.0010
11	1	.4312	.6862	.8327	.9141	.9578	.9802	.9912	.9964	.9986	.9995
	2	.1019	.3026	.5078	.6779	.8029	.8870	.9394	.9698	.9861	.9941
	3	.0152	.0896	.2212	.3826	.5448	.6873	.7999	.8811	.9348	.9673
	4	.0016	.0185	.0694	.1611	.2867	.4304	.5744	.7037	.8089	.8867
	5	.0001	.0028	.0159	.0504	.1146	.2103	.3317	.4672	.6029	.7256

Cumulative Binomial

n	x'	.05	.10	.15	.20	.25	.30	.35	.40	.45	.50
11	6	.0000	.0003	.0027	.0117	.0343	.0782	.1487	.2465	.3669	.5000
	7	.0000	.0000	.0003	.0020	.0076	.0216	.0501	.0994	.1738	.2744
	8	.0000	.0000	.0000	.0002	.0012	.0043	.0122	.0293	.0610	.1133
	9	.0000	.0000	.0000	.0000	.0001	.0006	.0020	.0059	.0148	.0327
	10	.0000	.0000	.0000	.0000	.0000	.0000	.0002	.0007	.0022	.0059
	11	.0000	.0000	.0000	.0000	.0000	.0000	.0000	.0000	.0002	.0005
12	1	.4596	.7176	.8578	.9313	.9683	.9862	.9943	.9978	.9992	.9998
	2	.1184	.3410	.5565	.7251	.8416	.9150	.9576	.9804	.9917	.9968
	3	.0196	.1109	.2642	.4417	.6093	.7472	.8487	.9166	.9579	.9807
	4	.0022	.0256	.0922	.2054	.3512	.5075	.6533	.7747	.8655	.9270
	5	.0002	.0043	.0239	.0726	.1576	.2763	.4167	.5618	.6956	.8062
	6	.0000	.0005	.0046	.0194	.0544	.1178	.2127	.3348	.4731	.6128
	7	.0000	.0001	.0007	.0039	.0143	.0386	.0846	.1582	.2607	.3872
	8	.0000	.0000	.0001	.0006	.0028	.0095	.0255	.0573	.1117	.1938
	9	.0000	.0000	.0000	.0001	.0004	.0017	.0056	.0153	.0356	.0730
	10	.0000	.0000	.0000	.0000	.0000	.0002	.0008	.0028	.0079	.0193
	11	.0000	.0000	.0000	.0000	.0000	.0000	.0001	.0003	.0011	.0032
	12	.0000	.0000	.0000	.0000	.0000	.0000	.0000	.0000	.0001	.0002
13	1	.4867	.7458	.8791	.9450	.9762	.9903	.9963	.9987	.9996	.9999
	2	.1354	.3787	.6017	.7664	.8733	.9363	.9704	.9874	.9951	.9983
	3	.0245	.1339	.2704	.4983	.6674	.7975	.8868	.9421	.9731	.9888
	4	.0031	.0342	.0967	.2527	.4157	.5794	.7217	.8314	.9071	.9539
	5	.0003	.0065	.0260	.0991	.2060	.3457	.4995	.6470	.7721	.8666
	6	.0000	.0009	.0053	.0300	.0802	.1654	.2841	.4256	.5732	.7095
	7	.0000	.0001	.0013	.0070	.0243	.0624	.1295	.2288	.3563	.5000
	8	.0000	.0000	.0002	.0012	.0056	.0182	.0462	.0977	.1788	.2905
	9	.0000	.0000	.0000	.0002	.0010	.0040	.0126	.0321	.0698	.1334
	10	.0000	.0000	.0000	.0000	.0001	.0007	.0025	.0078	.0203	.0461
	11	.0000	.0000	.0000	.0000	.0000	.0001	.0003	.0013	.0041	.0112
	12	.0000	.0000	.0000	.0000	.0000	.0000	.0000	.0001	.0005	.0017
	13	.0000	.0000	.0000	.0000	.0000	.0000	.0000	.0000	.0000	.0001
14	1	.5123	.7712	.8972	.9560	.9822	.9932	.9976	.9992	.9998	.9999
	2	.1530	.4154	.6433	.8021	.8990	.9525	.9795	.9919	.9971	.9991
	3	.0301	.1584	.3521	.5519	.7189	.8392	.9161	.9602	.9830	.9935
	4	.0042	.0441	.1465	.3018	.4787	.6448	.7795	.8757	.9368	.9713
	5	.0004	.0092	.0467	.1298	.2585	.4158	.5773	.7207	.8328	.9102

Cumulative Binomial

n	x'	.05	.10	.15	.20	.25	.30	.35	.40	.45	.50
14	6	.0000	.0015	.0115	.0439	.1117	.2195	.3595	.5141	.6627	.7880
	7	.0000	.0002	.0022	.0116	.0383	.0933	.1836	.3075	.4539	.6047
	8	.0000	.0000	.0003	.0024	.0103	.0315	.0753	.1501	.2586	.3953
	9	.0000	.0000	.0000	.0004	.0022	.0083	.0243	.0583	.1189	.2120
	10	.0000	.0000	.0000	.0000	.0003	.0017	.0060	.0175	.0426	.0898
	11	.0000	.0000	.0000	.0000	.0000	.0002	.0011	.0039	.0114	.0287
	12	.0000	.0000	.0000	.0000	.0000	.0000	.0001	.0006	.0022	.0065
	13	.0000	.0000	.0000	.0000	.0000	.0000	.0000	.0001	.0003	.0009
	14	.0000	.0000	.0000	.0000	.0000	.0000	.0000	.0000	.0000	.0001
15	1	.5367	.7941	.9126	.9648	.9866	.9953	.9984	.9995	.9999	1.0000
	2	.1710	.4510	.6814	.8329	.9198	.9647	.9858	.9948	.9983	.9995
	3	.0362	.1841	.3958	.6020	.7639	.8732	.9383	.9729	.9893	.9963
	4	.0055	.0556	.1773	.3518	.5387	.7031	.8273	.9095	.9576	.9824
	5	.0006	.0127	.0617	.1642	.3135	.4845	.6481	.7827	.8796	.9408
	6	.0001	.0022	.0168	.0611	.1484	.2784	.4357	.5968	.7392	.8491
	7	.0000	.0003	.0036	.0181	.0566	.1311	.2452	.3902	.5478	.6964
	8	.0000	.0000	.0006	.0042	.0173	.0500	.1132	.2131	.3465	.5000
	9	.0000	.0000	.0001	.0008	.0042	.0152	.0422	.0950	.1818	.3036
	10	.0000	.0000	.0000	.0001	.0008	.0037	.0124	.0338	.0769	.1509
	11	.0000	.0000	.0000	.0000	.0001	.0007	.0028	.0093	.0255	.0592
	12	.0000	.0000	.0000	.0000	.0000	.0001	.0005	.0019	.0063	.0176
	13	.0000	.0000	.0000	.0000	.0000	.0000	.0001	.0003	.0011	.0037
	14	.0000	.0000	.0000	.0000	.0000	.0000	.0000	.0000	.0001	.0005
	15	.0000	.0000	.0000	.0000	.0000	.0000	.0000	.0000	.0000	.0000
16	1	.5599	.8147	.9257	.9719	.9900	.9967	.9990	.9997	.9999	1.0000
	2	.1892	.4853	.7161	.8593	.9365	.9739	.9902	.9967	.9990	.9997
	3	.0429	.2108	.4386	.6482	.8029	.9006	.9549	.9817	.9934	.9979
	4	.0070	.0684	.2101	.4019	.5950	.7541	.8661	.9349	.9719	.9894
	5	.0009	.0170	.0791	.2018	.3698	.5501	.7108	.8334	.9147	.9616
	6	.0001	.0033	.0235	.0817	.1897	.3402	.5100	.6712	.8024	.8949
	7	.0000	.0005	.0056	.0267	.0796	.1753	.3119	.4728	.6340	.7228
	8	.0000	.0001	.0011	.0070	.0271	.0744	.1594	.2839	.4371	.5982
	9	.0000	.0000	.0002	.0015	.0075	.0257	.0671	.1423	.2559	.4018
	10	.0000	.0000	.0000	.0002	.0016	.0071	.0229	.0583	.1241	.2272
	11	.0000	.0000	.0000	.0000	.0003	.0016	.0062	.0191	.0486	.1051
	12	.0000	.0000	.0000	.0000	.0000	.0003	.0013	.0049	.0149	.0384
	13	.0000	.0000	.0000	.0000	.0000	.0000	.0002	.0009	.0035	.0106
	14	.0000	.0000	.0000	.0000	.0000	.0000	.0000	.0001	.0006	.0021
	15	.0000	.0000	.0000	.0000	.0000	.0000	.0000	.0000	.0001	.0003
	16	.0000	.0000	.0000	.0000	.0000	.0000	.0000	.0000	.0000	.0000

Cumulative Binomial

n	x'	.05	.10	.15	.20	.25	.30	.35	.40	.45	.50
17	1	.5819	.8332	.9369	.9775	.9925	.9977	.9993	.9998	1.0000	1.0000
	2	.2078	.5182	.7475	.8818	.9499	.9807	.9933	.9979	.9994	.9999
	3	.0503	.2382	.4802	.6904	.8363	.9226	.9673	.9877	.9959	.9988
	4	.0088	.0826	.2444	.4511	.6470	.7981	.8972	.9536	.9816	.9936
	5	.0012	.0221	.0987	.2418	.4261	.6113	.7652	.8740	.9404	.9755
	6	.0001	.0047	.0319	.1057	.2347	.4032	.5803	.7361	.8529	.9283
	7	.0000	.0008	.0083	.0377	.1071	.2248	.3812	.5522	.7098	.8338
	8	.0000	.0001	.0017	.0109	.0402	.1046	.2128	.3595	.5257	.6855
	9	.0000	.0000	.0003	.0026	.0124	.0403	.0994	.1989	.3374	.5000
	10	.0000	.0000	.0000	.0005	.0031	.0127	.0383	.0919	.1834	.3145
	11	.0000	.0000	.0000	.0001	.0006	.0032	.0120	.0348	.0826	.1662
	12	.0000	.0000	.0000	.0000	.0001	.0007	.0030	.0106	.0301	.0717
	13	.0000	.0000	.0000	.0000	.0000	.0001	.0006	.0025	.0086	.0245
	14	.0000	.0000	.0000	.0000	.0000	.0000	.0001	.0005	.0019	.0064
	15	.0000	.0000	.0000	.0000	.0000	.0000	.0000	.0001	.0003	.0012
	16	.0000	.0000	.0000	.0000	.0000	.0000	.0000	.0000	.0000	.0001
	17	.0000	.0000	.0000	.0000	.0000	.0000	.0000	.0000	.0000	.0000
18	1	.6028	.8499	.9464	.9820	.9944	.9984	.9996	.9999	1.0000	1.0000
	2	.2265	.5497	.7759	.9009	.9605	.9858	.9954	.9987	.9997	.9999
	3	.0581	.2662	.5203	.7287	.8647	.9400	.9764	.9918	.9975	.9993
	4	.0109	.0982	.2798	.4990	.6943	.8354	.9217	.9672	.9880	.9962
	5	.0015	.0282	.1206	.2836	.4813	.6673	.8114	.9058	.9589	.9846
	6	.0002	.0064	.0419	.1329	.2825	.4656	.6450	.7912	.8923	.9519
	7	.0000	.0012	.0118	.0513	.1390	.2783	.4509	.6257	.7742	.8811
	8	.0000	.0002	.0027	.0163	.0569	.1407	.2717	.4366	.6085	.7597
	9	.0000	.0000	.0005	.0043	.0193	.0596	.1391	.2632	.4222	.5927
	10	.0000	.0000	.0001	.0009	.0054	.0210	.0597	.1347	.2527	.4073
	11	.0000	.0000	.0000	.0002	.0012	.0061	.0212	.0576	.1280	.2403
	12	.0000	.0000	.0000	.0000	.0002	.0014	.0062	.0203	.0537	.1189
	13	.0000	.0000	.0000	.0000	.0000	.0003	.0014	.0058	.0183	.0481
	14	.0000	.0000	.0000	.0000	.0000	.0000	.0003	.0013	.0049	.0154
	15	.0000	.0000	.0000	.0000	.0000	.0000	.0000	.0002	.0010	.0038
	16	.0000	.0000	.0000	.0000	.0000	.0000	.0000	.0000	.0001	.0007
	17	.0000	.0000	.0000	.0000	.0000	.0000	.0000	.0000	.0000	.0001
	18	.0000	.0000	.0000	.0000	.0000	.0000	.0000	.0000	.0000	.0000
19	1	.6226	.8649	.9544	.9856	.9958	.9989	.9997	.9999	1.0000	1.0000
	2	.2453	.5797	.8015	.9171	.9690	.9896	.9969	.9992	.9998	1.0000
	3	.0665	.2946	.5587	.7631	.8887	.9538	.9830	.9945	.9985	.9996
	4	.0132	.1150	.3159	.5449	.7369	.8668	.9409	.9770	.9923	.9978
	5	.0020	.0352	.1444	.3267	.5346	.7178	.8500	.9304	.9720	.9904

Cumulative Binomial

n	x'	.05	.10	.15	.20	.25	.30	.35	.40	.45	.50
19	6	.0002	.0086	.0537	.1631	.3322	.5261	.7032	.8371	.9223	.9682
	7	.0000	.0017	.0163	.0676	.1749	.3345	.5188	.6919	.8273	.9165
	8	.0000	.0003	.0041	.0233	.0775	.1820	.3344	.5122	.6831	.8204
	9	.0000	.0000	.0008	.0067	.0287	.0839	.1855	.3325	.5060	.6762
	10	.0000	.0000	.0001	.0016	.0089	.0326	.0875	.1861	.3290	.5000
	11	.0000	.0000	.0000	.0003	.0023	.0105	.0347	.0885	.1841	.3238
	12	.0000	.0000	.0000	.0000	.0005	.0028	.0114	.0352	.0871	.1796
	13	.0000	.0000	.0000	.0000	.0001	.0006	.0031	.0116	.0342	.0835
	14	.0000	.0000	.0000	.0000	.0000	.0001	.0007	.0031	.0109	.0318
	15	.0000	.0000	.0000	.0000	.0000	.0000	.0001	.0006	.0028	.0096
	16	.0000	.0000	.0000	.0000	.0000	.0000	.0000	.0001	.0005	.0022
	17	.0000	.0000	.0000	.0000	.0000	.0000	.0000	.0000	.0001	.0004
	18	.0000	.0000	.0000	.0000	.0000	.0000	.0000	.0000	.0000	.0000
	19	.0000	.0000	.0000	.0000	.0000	.0000	.0000	.0000	.0000	.0000
20	1	.6415	.8784	.9612	.9885	.9968	.9992	.9998	1.0000	1.0000	1.0000
	2	.2642	.6083	.8244	.9308	.9757	.9924	.9979	.9995	.9999	1.0000
	3	.0755	.3231	.5951	.7939	.9087	.9645	.9879	.9964	.9991	.9998
	4	.0159	.1330	.3523	.5886	.7748	.8929	.9556	.9840	.9951	.9987
	5	.0026	.0432	.1702	.3704	.5852	.7625	.8818	.9490	.9811	.9941
	6	.0003	.0113	.0673	.1958	.3828	.5836	.7546	.8744	.9447	.9793
	7	.0000	.0024	.0219	.0867	.2142	.3920	.5834	.7500	.8701	.9423
	8	.0000	.0004	.0059	.0321	.1018	.2277	.3990	.5841	.7480	.8684
	9	.0000	.0001	.0013	.0100	.0409	.1133	.2376	.4044	.5857	.7483
	10	.0000	.0000	.0002	.0026	.0139	.0480	.1218	.2447	.4086	.5881
	11	.0000	.0000	.0000	.0006	.0039	.0171	.0532	.1275	.2493	.4119
	12	.0000	.0000	.0000	.0001	.0009	.0051	.0196	.0565	.1308	.2517
	13	.0000	.0000	.0000	.0000	.0002	.0013	.0060	.0210	.0580	.1316
	14	.0000	.0000	.0000	.0000	.0000	.0003	.0015	.0065	.0214	.0577
	15	.0000	.0000	.0000	.0000	.0000	.0000	.0003	.0016	.0064	.0207
	16	.0000	.0000	.0000	.0000	.0000	.0000	.0000	.0003	.0015	.0059
	17	.0000	.0000	.0000	.0000	.0000	.0000	.0000	.0000	.0003	.0013
	18	.0000	.0000	.0000	.0000	.0000	.0000	.0000	.0000	.0000	.0002
	19	.0000	.0000	.0000	.0000	.0000	.0000	.0000	.0000	.0000	.0000
	20	.0000	.0000	.0000	.0000	.0000	.0000	.0000	.0000	.0000	.0000
40	1	.8715	.9852	.9985	.9999	1.0000	1.0000	1.0000	1.0000	1.0000	1.0000
	2	.6009	.9195	.9879	.9985	.9999	1.0000	1.0000	1.0000	1.0000	1.0000
	3	.3233	.7772	.9514	.9921	.9990	.9999	1.0000	1.0000	1.0000	1.0000
	4	.1381	.5769	.8698	.9715	.9953	.9994	.9999	1.0000	1.0000	1.0000
	5	.0480	.3710	.7367	.9241	.9840	.9974	.9997	1.0000	1.0000	1.0000

Cumulative Binomial

						π					
n	x'	.05	.10	.15	.20	.25	.30	.35	.40	.45	.50
40	6	.0139	.2063	.5675	.8387	.9567	.9914	.9987	.9999	1.0000	1.0000
	7	.0034	.0995	.3933	.7141	.9038	.9762	.9956	.9994	.9999	1.0000
	8	.0007	.0419	.2441	.5629	.8180	.9447	.9876	.9979	.9998	1.0000
	9	.0001	.0155	.1354	.4069	.7002	.8890	.9697	.9939	.9991	.9999
	10	—	.0051	.0672	.2682	.5605	.8041	.9356	.9844	.9973	.9997
	11	—	.0015	.0299	.1608	.4161	.6913	.8785	.9648	.9926	.9989
	12	—	.0004	.0120	.0875	.2849	.5594	.7947	.9291	.9821	.9968
	13	—	.0001	.0043	.0432	.1791	.4228	.6857	.8715	.9614	.9917
	14	—	—	.0014	.0194	.1032	.2968	.5592	.7888	.9249	.9808
	15	—	—	.0004	.0079	.0544	.1926	.4279	.6826	.8674	.9597
	16	—	—	.0001	.0029	.0262	.1151	.3054	.5598	.7858	.9231
	17	—	—	—	.0010	.0116	.0633	.2022	.4319	.6815	.8659
	18	—	—	—	.0003	.0047	.0320	.1239	.3115	.5609	.7852
	19	—	—	—	.0001	.0017	.0148	.0699	.2089	.4349	.6821
	20	—	—	—	—	.0006	.0063	.0363	.1298	.3156	.5627
	21	—	—	—	—	.0002	.0024	.0173	.0744	.2130	.4373
	22	—	—	—	—	—	.0009	.0075	.0392	.1331	.3179
	23	—	—	—	—	—	.0003	.0030	.0189	.0767	.2148
	24	—	—	—	—	—	.0001	.0011	.0083	.0405	.1341
	25	—	—	—	—	—	—	.0004	.0034	.0196	.0769
	26	—	—	—	—	—	—	.0001	.0012	.0086	.0403
	27	—	—	—	—	—	—	—	.0004	.0034	.0192
	28	—	—	—	—	—	—	—	.0001	.0012	.0083
	29	—	—	—	—	—	—	—	—	.0004	.0032
	30	—	—	—	—	—	—	—	—	.0001	.0011
	31	—	—	—	—	—	—	—	—	—	.0003
	32	—	—	—	—	—	—	—	—	—	.0001
	33	—	—	—	—	—	—	—	—	—	—
	34	—	—	—	—	—	—	—	—	—	—
50	1	.9231	.9948	.9997	1.0000	1.0000	1.0000	1.0000	1.0000	1.0000	1.0000
	2	.7206	.9662	.9971	.9998	1.0000	1.0000	1.0000	1.0000	1.0000	1.0000
	3	.4595	.8883	.9858	.9987	.9999	1.0000	1.0000	1.0000	1.0000	1.0000
	4	.2396	.7497	.9540	.9943	.9995	1.0000	1.0000	1.0000	1.0000	1.0000
	5	.1036	.5688	.8879	.9815	.9979	.9998	1.0000	1.0000	1.0000	1.0000
	6	.0378	.3839	.7806	.9520	.9930	.9993	.9999	1.0000	1.0000	1.0000
	7	.0118	.2298	.6387	.8966	.9806	.9975	.9998	1.0000	1.0000	1.0000
	8	.0032	.1221	.4812	.8096	.9547	.9927	.9992	.9999	1.0000	1.0000
	9	.0008	.0579	.3319	.6927	.9084	.9817	.9975	.9998	1.0000	1.0000
	10	.0002	.0245	.2089	.5563	.8363	.9598	.9933	.9992	.9999	1.0000

Cumulative Binomial

π

n	x'	.05	.10	.15	.20	.25	.30	.35	.40	.45	.50
50	11	—	.0094	.1199	.4174	.7378	.9211	.9840	.9978	.9998	1.0000
	12	—	.0032	.0628	.2893	.6184	.8610	.9658	.9943	.9994	1.0000
	13	—	.0010	.0301	.1861	.4890	.7771	.9339	.9867	.9982	.9998
	14	—	.0003	.0132	.1106	.3630	.6721	.8837	.9720	.9955	.9995
	15	—	.0001	.0053	.0607	.2519	.5532	.8122	.9460	.9896	.9987
	16	—	—	.0020	.0308	.1631	.4308	.7199	.9045	.9780	.9967
	17	—	—	.0007	.0144	.0983	.3161	.6111	.8439	.9573	.9923
	18	—	—	.0002	.0063	.0551	.2178	.4940	.7631	.9235	.9836
	19	—	—	.0001	.0025	.0287	.1406	.3784	.6644	.8727	.9675
	20	—	—	—	.0009	.0139	.0848	.2736	.5535	.8026	.9405
	21	—	—	—	.0003	.0063	.0478	.1861	.4390	.7138	.8987
	22	—	—	—	.0001	.0026	.0251	.1187	.3299	.6100	.8389
	23	—	—	—	—	.0010	.0123	.0710	.2339	.4981	.7601
	24	—	—	—	—	.0004	.0056	.0396	.1562	.3866	.6641
	25	—	—	—	—	.0001	.0024	.0207	.0978	.2840	.5561
	26	—	—	—	—	—	.0008	.0100	.0573	.1966	.4439
	27	—	—	—	—	—	.0003	.0045	.0314	.1279	.3359
	28	—	—	—	—	—	.0001	.0019	.0160	.0780	.2399
	29	—	—	—	—	—	—	.0007	.0076	.0444	.1611
	30	—	—	—	—	—	—	.0003	.0034	.0235	.1013
	31	—	—	—	—	—	—	.0001	.0014	.0116	.0595
	32	—	—	—	—	—	—	—	.0005	.0053	.0325
	33	—	—	—	—	—	—	—	.0002	.0022	.0164
	34	—	—	—	—	—	—	—	.0001	.0009	.0077
	35	—	—	—	—	—	—	—	—	.0003	.0033
	36	—	—	—	—	—	—	—	—	.0001	.0013
	37	—	—	—	—	—	—	—	—	—	.0005
	38	—	—	—	—	—	—	—	—	—	.0002
	39	—	—	—	—	—	—	—	—	—	—
100	1	.9941	1.0000	1.0000	1.0000	1.0000	1.0000	1.0000	1.0000	1.0000	1.0000
	2	.9629	.9997	1.0000	1.0000	1.0000	1.0000	1.0000	1.0000	1.0000	1.0000
	3	.8817	.9981	1.0000	1.0000	1.0000	1.0000	1.0000	1.0000	1.0000	1.0000
	4	.7422	.9922	.9999	1.0000	1.0000	1.0000	1.0000	1.0000	1.0000	1.0000
	5	.5640	.9763	.9996	1.0000	1.0000	1.0000	1.0000	1.0000	1.0000	1.0000
	6	.3840	.9424	.9984	1.0000	1.0000	1.0000	1.0000	1.0000	1.0000	1.0000
	7	.2340	.8828	.9953	.9999	1.0000	1.0000	1.0000	1.0000	1.0000	1.0000
	8	.1280	.7939	.9878	.9997	1.0000	1.0000	1.0000	1.0000	1.0000	1.0000
	9	.0631	.6791	.9725	.9991	1.0000	1.0000	1.0000	1.0000	1.0000	1.0000
	10	.0282	.5487	.9449	.9977	1.0000	1.0000	1.0000	1.0000	1.0000	1.0000

Cumulative Binomial

n	x′	.05	.10	.15	.20	.25	.30	.35	.40	.45	.50
100	11	.0115	.4168	.9006	.9943	.9999	1.0000	1.0000	1.0000	1.0000	1.0000
	12	.0043	.2970	.8365	.9874	.9996	1.0000	1.0000	1.0000	1.0000	1.0000
	13	.0015	.1982	.7527	.9747	.9990	1.0000	1.0000	1.0000	1.0000	1.0000
	14	.0005	.1239	.6526	.9531	.9975	.9999	1.0000	1.0000	1.0000	1.0000
	15	.0001	.0726	.5428	.9196	.9946	.9998	1.0000	1.0000	1.0000	1.0000
	16	—	.0399	.4317	.8715	.9889	.9996	1.0000	1.0000	1.0000	1.0000
	17	—	.0206	.3275	.8077	.9789	.9990	1.0000	1.0000	1.0000	1.0000
	18	—	.0100	.2367	.7288	.9624	.9978	.9999	1.0000	1.0000	1.0000
	19	—	.0046	.1628	.6379	.9370	.9955	.9999	1.0000	1.0000	1.0000
	20	—	.0020	.1065	.5398	.9005	.9911	.9997	1.0000	1.0000	1.0000
	21	—	.0008	.0663	.4405	.8512	.9835	.9992	1.0000	1.0000	1.0000
	22	—	.0003	.0393	.3460	.7886	.9712	.9983	1.0000	1.0000	1.0000
	23	—	.0001	.0221	.2611	.7136	.9521	.9966	.9999	1.0000	1.0000
	24	—	—	.0119	.1891	.6289	.9245	.9934	.9997	1.0000	1.0000
	25	—	—	.0061	.1314	.5383	.8864	.9879	.9994	1.0000	1.0000
	26	—	—	.0030	.0875	.4465	.8369	.9789	.9988	1.0000	1.0000
	27	—	—	.0014	.0558	.3583	.7756	.9649	.9976	.9999	1.0000
	28	—	—	.0006	.0342	.2776	.7036	.9442	.9954	.9998	1.0000
	29	—	—	.0003	.0200	.2075	.6232	.9152	.9916	.9996	1.0000
	30	—	—	.0001	.0113	.1495	.5377	.8764	.9852	.9992	1.0000
	31	—	—	—	.0061	.1038	.4509	.8270	.9752	.9985	1.0000
	32	—	—	—	.0031	.0694	.3669	.7669	.9602	.9970	.9999
	33	—	—	—	.0016	.0446	.2893	.6971	.9385	.9945	.9998
	34	—	—	—	.0007	.0276	.2207	.6197	.9087	.9902	.9996
	35	—	—	—	.0003	.0164	.1629	.5376	.8697	.9834	.9991
	36	—	—	—	.0001	.0094	.1161	.4542	.8205	.9728	.9982
	37	—	—	—	.0001	.0052	.0799	.3731	.7614	.9571	.9967
	38	—	—	—	—	.0027	.0530	.2976	.6932	.9349	.9940
	39	—	—	—	—	.0014	.0340	.2301	.6178	.9049	.9895
	40	—	—	—	—	.0007	.0210	.1724	.5379	.8657	.9824
	41	—	—	—	—	.0003	.0125	.1250	.4567	.8169	.9716
	42	—	—	—	—	.0002	.0072	.0877	.3775	.7585	.9557
	43	—	—	—	—	.0001	.0040	.0594	.3033	.6913	.9334
	44	—	—	—	—	—	.0021	.0389	.2365	.6172	.9033
	45	—	—	—	—	—	.0011	.0246	.1789	.5387	.8644
	46	—	—	—	—	—	.0005	.0150	.1311	.4587	.8159
	47	—	—	—	—	—	.0003	.0088	.0930	.3804	.7579
	48	—	—	—	—	—	.0001	.0050	.0638	.3069	.6914
	49	—	—	—	—	—	.0001	.0028	.0423	.2404	.6178
	50	—	—	—	—	—	—	.0015	.0271	.1827	.5398

Cumulative Binomial

n	x'	.05	.10	.15	.20	.25	.30	.35	.40	.45	.50
100	51	—	—	—	—	—	—	.0007	.0168	.1346	.4602
	52	—	—	—	—	—	—	.0004	.0100	.0960	.3822
	53	—	—	—	—	—	—	.0002	.0058	.0662	.3086
	54	—	—	—	—	—	—	.0001	.0032	.0441	.2421
	55	—	—	—	—	—	—	—	.0017	.0284	.1841
	56	—	—	—	—	—	—	—	.0009	.0176	.1356
	57	—	—	—	—	—	—	—	.0004	.0106	.0967
	58	—	—	—	—	—	—	—	.0002	.0061	.0666
	59	—	—	—	—	—	—	—	.0001	.0034	.0443
	60	—	—	—	—	—	—	—	—	.0018	.0284
	61	—	—	—	—	—	—	—	—	.0009	.0176
	62	—	—	—	—	—	—	—	—	.0005	.0105
	63	—	—	—	—	—	—	—	—	.0002	.0060
	64	—	—	—	—	—	—	—	—	.0001	.0033
	65	—	—	—	—	—	—	—	—	—	.0018
	66	—	—	—	—	—	—	—	—	—	.0009
	67	—	—	—	—	—	—	—	—	—	.0004
	68	—	—	—	—	—	—	—	—	—	.0002
	69	—	—	—	—	—	—	—	—	—	.0001
	70	—	—	—	—	—	—	—	—	—	—

Appendix F

Poisson and χ² Distributions *

χ² (Chi-square) Distribution

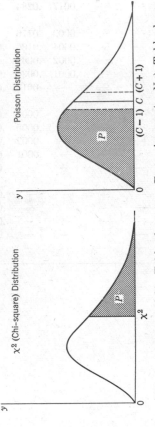

For a given n (d.f.), Table shows the probability of getting a χ^2 value equal to or greater than that given.

Poisson Distribution

$(C-1)\ C\ (C+1)$

For a given m (or Np), Table shows the probability of getting a c value less than that given.

n	$\chi^2=0.1$ $m=0.05$	0.2 0.10	0.3 0.15	0.4 0.20	0.5 0.25	0.6 0.30	0.7 0.35	0.8 0.40	0.9 0.45	1.0 0.50	c
1	0.75183	0.65472	0.58388	0.52709	0.47950	0.43858	0.40278	0.37109	0.34278	0.31731	1
2	.95123	.90484	.86071	.81873	.77880	.74082	.70469	.67032	.63763	.60653	
3	.99184	.97759	.96003	.94024	.91889	.89643	.87320	.84947	.82543	.80125	2
4	.99879	.99532	.98981	.98248	.97350	.96306	.95133	.93845	.92456	.90980	
5	.99984	.99911	.99764	.99533	.99212	.98800	.98297	.97703	.97022	.96257	3
6	.99998	.99985	.99950	.99885	.99784	.99640	.99449	.99207	.98912	.98561	
7		0.99997	0.99990	0.99974	0.99945	0.99899	0.99834	0.99744	0.99628	0.99483	4
8			.99998	.99994	.99987	.99973	.99953	.99922	.99880	.99825	
9				.99999	.99997	.99993	.99987	.99978	.99964	.99944	5
10					.99999	.99998	.99997	.99994	.99989	.99983	
11							.99999	.99998	.99997	.99995	6
12									.99999	.99999	

* Reproduced with permission from H. O. Hartley and E. S. Pearson, "Table of the χ^2 integral, and of the cumulative Poisson distribution," *Biometrika*, Vol. 37, June, 1950, pp. 313–325.

Poisson and χ² Distributions

n	$\chi^2=1{\cdot}1$ $m=0{\cdot}55$	$1{\cdot}2$ $0{\cdot}60$	$1{\cdot}3$ $0{\cdot}65$	$1{\cdot}4$ $0{\cdot}70$	$1{\cdot}5$ $0{\cdot}75$	$1{\cdot}6$ $0{\cdot}80$	$1{\cdot}7$ $0{\cdot}85$	$1{\cdot}8$ $0{\cdot}90$	$1{\cdot}9$ $0{\cdot}95$	$2{\cdot}0$ $1{\cdot}00$	c
1	0·29427	0·27332	0·25421	0·23672	0·22067	0·20590	0·19229	0·17971	0·16808	0·15730	
2	·57695	·54881	·52205	·49659	·47237	·44933	·42741	·40657	·38674	·36788	1
3	·77707	·75300	·72913	·70553	·68227	·65939	·63693	·61493	·59342	·57241	
4	·89427	·87810	·86138	·84420	·82664	·80879	·79072	·77248	·75414	·73576	2
5	·95410	·94488	·93493	·92431	·91307	·90125	·88890	·87607	·86280	·84915	
6	·98154	·97689	·97166	·96586	·95949	·95258	·94512	·93714	·92866	·91970	3
7	·99305	·99093	·98844	·98557	·98231	·97864	·97457	·97008	·96517	·95984	
8	·99753	·99664	·99555	·99425	·99271	·99092	·98887	·98654	·98393	·98101	4
9	·99917	·99882	·99838	·99782	·99715	·99633	·99537	·99425	·99295	·99147	
10	·99973	·99961	·99944	·99921	·99894	·99859	·99817	·99766	·99705	·99634	5
11	·99992	·99987	·99981	·99973	·99962	·99948	·99930	·99908	·99882	·99850	
12	·99998	·99996	·99994	·99991	·99987	·99982	·99975	·99966	·99954	·99941	6
13	0·99999	0·99999	·99998	0·99997	0·99996	0·99994	0·99991	0·99988	0·99983	0·99977	
14			·99999	·99999	·99999	·99998	·99997	·99996	·99994	·99992	7
15						·99999	·99999	·99999	·99998	·99997	
16									·99999	·99999	8

Poisson and χ² Distributions

n	$\chi^2=2.2$ $m=1.1$	2.4 / 1.2	2.6 / 1.3	2.8 / 1.4	3.0 / 1.5	3.2 / 1.6	3.4 / 1.7	3.6 / 1.8	3.8 / 1.9	4.0 / 2.0	c
1	0·13801	0·12134	0·10686	0·09426	0·08327	0·07364	0·06520	0·05778	0·05125	0·04550	1
2	·33287	·30119	·27253	·24660	·22313	·20190	·18268	·16530	·14957	·13534	2
3	·53195	·49363	·45749	·42350	·39163	·36181	·33397	·30802	·28389	·26146	3
4	·69903	·66263	·62682	·59183	·55783	·52493	·49325	·46284	·43375	·40601	4
5	·82084	·79147	·76137	·73079	·69999	·66918	·63857	·60831	·57856	·54942	5
6	·90042	·87949	·85711	·83350	·80885	·78336	·75722	·73062	·70372	·67668	6
7	0·94795	0·93444	0·91938	0·90287	0·88500	0·86590	0·84570	0·82452	0·80250	0·77978	7
8	·97426	·96623	·95691	·94628	·93436	·92119	·90681	·89129	·87470	·85712	8
9	·98790	·98345	·97807	·97170	·96430	·95583	·94631	·93572	·92408	·91141	9
10	·99457	·99225	·98934	·98575	·98142	·97632	·97039	·96359	·95592	·94735	10
11	·99766	·99652	·99503	·99311	·99073	·98781	·98431	·98019	·97541	·96992	11
12	·99903	·99850	·99777	·99680	·99554	·99396	·99200	·98962	·98678	·98344	
13	0·99961	0·99938	0·99903	0·99856	0·99793	0·99711	0·99606	0·99475	0·99314	0·99119	
14	·99985	·99975	·99960	·99938	·99907	·99866	·99813	·99743	·99655	·99547	
15	·99994	·99990	·99984	·99974	·99960	·99940	·99913	·99878	·99832	·99774	
16	·99998	·99996	·99994	·99989	·99983	·99974	·99961	·99944	·99921	·99890	
17	·99999	·99999	·99998	·99996	·99993	·99989	·99983	·99975	·99964	·99948	
18			·99999	·99998	·99997	·99995	·99993	·99989	·99984	·99976	
19				·99999	·99999	·99998	·99997	·99995	·99993	·99989	
20						·99999	·99999	·99998	·99997	·99995	
21								·99999	·99999	·99998	
22										·99999	

Poisson and χ^2 Distributions

c	6·0 3·0	5·8 2·9	5·6 2·8	5·4 2·7	5·2 2·6	5·0 2·5	4·8 2·4	4·6 2·3	4·4 2·2	$\chi^2=4·2$ m=2·1	n
	0·01431	0·01603	0·01796	0·02014	0·02259	0·02535	0·02846	0·03197	0·03594	0·04042	1
1	·04979	·05502	·06081	·06721	·07427	·08209	·09072	·10026	·11080	·12246	2
	·11161	·12176	·13278	·14474	·15772	·17180	·18704	·20354	·22139	·24066	3
2	·19915	·21459	·23108	·24866	·26739	·28730	·30844	·33085	·35457	·37962	4
	·30622	·32617	·34711	·36904	·39196	·41588	·44077	·46662	·49337	·52099	5
3	·42319	·44596	·46945	·49363	·51843	·54381	·56971	·59604	·62271	·64963	6
	·53975	·56329	·58715	·61127	·63557	·65996	·68435	·70864	·73272	·75647	7
4	·64723	·66962	·69194	·71409	·73600	·75758	·77872	·79935	·81935	·83864	8
	·73992	·75976	·77919	·79814	·81654	·83431	·85138	·86769	·88317	·89776	9
5	·81526	·83178	·84768	·86291	·87742	·89118	·90413	·91625	·92750	·93787	10
	·87337	·88637	·89868	·91026	·92109	·93117	·94046	·94898	·95672	·96370	11
6	·91608	·92583	·93489	·94327	·95096	·95798	·96433	·97002	·97509	·97955	12
	·94615	·95313	·95951	·96530	·97052	·97519	·97934	·98298	·98614	·98887	13
7	·96649	·97128	·97559	·97943	·98283	·98581	·98841	·99064	·99254	·99414	14
	·97975	·98291	·98571	·98816	·99029	·99213	·99369	·99501	·99610	·99701	15
8	·98810	·99012	·99187	·99338	·99467	·99575	·99666	·99741	·99802	·99851	16
	·99319	·99443	·99550	·99639	·99715	·99777	·99828	·99869	·99902	·99928	17
9	·99620	·99694	·99757	·99809	·99851	·99886	·99914	·99936	·99953	·99966	18
	·99793	·99836	·99872	·99901	·99924	·99943	·99958	·99969	·99978	·99985	19
10	·99890	·99914	·99934	·99950	·99962	·99972	·99980	·99986	·99990	·99993	20
	·99943	·99956	·99967	·99975	·99982	·99987	·99991	·99993	·99995	·99997	21
11	·99971	·99978	·99984	·99988	·99991	·99994	·99996	·99997	·99998	·99999	22
	·99986	·99989	·99992	·99994	·99996	·99997	·99998	·99999	·99999	·99999	23
12	·99993	·99995	·99996	·99997	·99998	·99999	·99999	·99999			24
	·99997	·99998	·99998	·99999	·99999	·99999					25
13	·99998	·99999	·99999								26
	·99999	·99999									27

Poisson and χ² Distributions

c	n	$\chi^2=6{\cdot}2$ $m=3{\cdot}1$	$6{\cdot}4$ $3{\cdot}2$	$6{\cdot}6$ $3{\cdot}3$	$6{\cdot}8$ $3{\cdot}4$	$7{\cdot}0$ $3{\cdot}5$	$7{\cdot}2$ $3{\cdot}6$	$7{\cdot}4$ $3{\cdot}7$	$7{\cdot}6$ $3{\cdot}8$	$7{\cdot}8$ $3{\cdot}9$	$8{\cdot}0$ $4{\cdot}0$
	1	0·01278	0·01141	0·01020	0·00912	0·00815	0·00729	0·00652	0·00584	0·00522	0·00468
1	2	·04505	·04076	·03688	·03337	·03020	·02732	·02472	·02237	·02024	·01832
	3	·10228	·09369	·08580	·07855	·07190	·06579	·06018	·05504	·05033	·04601
2	4	·18470	·17120	·15860	·14684	·13589	·12569	·11620	·10738	·09919	·09158
	5	·28724	·26922	·25213	·23595	·22064	·20619	·19255	·17970	·16761	·15624
3	6	·40116	·37990	·35943	·33974	·32085	·30275	·28543	·26890	·25313	·23810
	7	0·51660	0·49390	0·47168	0·45000	0·42888	0·40836	0·38845	0·36918	0·35056	0·33259
4	8	·62484	·60252	·58034	·55836	·53663	·51522	·49415	·47349	·45325	·43347
	9	·71975	·69931	·67869	·65793	·63712	·61631	·59555	·57490	·55442	·53415
5	10	·79819	·78061	·76259	·74418	·72544	·70644	·68722	·66784	·64837	·62884
	11	·85969	·84539	·83049	·81504	·79908	·78266	·76583	·74862	·73110	·71330
6	12	·90567	·89459	·88288	·87054	·85761	·84412	·83009	·81556	·80056	·78513
	13	0·93857	0·93038	0·92157	0·91216	0·90215	0·89155	0·88038	0·86865	0·85638	0·84360
7	14	·96120	·95538	·94903	·94215	·93471	·92673	·91819	·90911	·89948	·88933
	15	·97619	·97222	·96782	·96296	·95765	·95186	·94559	·93882	·93155	·92378
8	16	·98579	·98317	·98022	·97693	·97326	·96921	·96476	·95989	·95460	·94887
	17	·99174	·99007	·98816	·98599	·98355	·98081	·97775	·97437	·97064	·96655
9	18	·99532	·99429	·99309	·99171	·99013	·98833	·98630	·98402	·98147	·97864
	19	0·99741	0·99679	0·99606	0·99521	0·99421	0·99307	0·99176	0·99026	0·98857	0·98667
10	20	·99860	·99824	·99781	·99729	·99669	·99598	·99515	·99420	·99311	·99187
	21	·99926	·99905	·99880	·99850	·99814	·99771	·99721	·99662	·99594	·99514
11	22	·99962	·99950	·99936	·99919	·99898	·99873	·99843	·99807	·99765	·99716
	23	·99981	·99974	·99967	·99957	·99945	·99931	·99913	·99892	·99867	·99837
12	24	·99990	·99987	·99983	·99978	·99971	·99963	·99953	·99941	·99926	·99908
	25	0·99995	0·99994	0·99991	0·99989	0·99985	0·99981	0·99975	0·99968	0·99960	0·99949
13	26	·99998	·99997	·99996	·99994	·99992	·99990	·99987	·99983	·99978	·99973
	27	·99999	·99999	·99998	·99997	·99996	·99995	·99993	·99991	·99989	·99985
14	28		·99999	·99999	·99999	·99998	·99998	·99997	·99996	·99994	·99992
	29				·99999	·99999	·99999	·99998	·99998	·99997	·99996
15	30							0·99999	0·99999	0·99999	0·99998

Poisson and χ² Distributions

n	$\chi^2=8\cdot2$ / $m=4\cdot1$	$8\cdot4$ / $4\cdot2$	$8\cdot6$ / $4\cdot3$	$8\cdot8$ / $4\cdot4$	$9\cdot0$ / $4\cdot5$	$9\cdot2$ / $4\cdot6$	$9\cdot4$ / $4\cdot7$	$9\cdot6$ / $4\cdot8$	$9\cdot8$ / $4\cdot9$	$10\cdot0$ / $5\cdot0$	c
1	0·00419	0·00375	0·00336	0·00301	0·00270	0·00242	0·00217	0·00195	0·00175	0·00157	
2	·01657	·01500	·01357	·01228	·01111	·01005	·00910	·00823	·00745	·00674	1
3	·04205	·03843	·03511	·03207	·02929	·02675	·02442	·02229	·02034	·01857	
4	·08452	·07798	·07191	·06630	·06110	·05629	·05184	·04773	·04394	·04043	2
5	·14555	·13553	·12612	·11731	·10906	·10135	·09413	·08740	·08110	·07524	
6	·22381	·21024	·19736	·18514	·17358	·16264	·15230	·14254	·13333	·12465	3
7	0·31529	0·29865	0·28266	0·26734	0·25266	0·23861	0·22520	0·21240	0·20019	0·18857	
8	·41418	·39540	·37715	·35945	·34230	·32571	·30968	·29423	·27935	·26503	4
9	·51412	·49439	·47499	·45594	·43727	·41902	·40120	·38383	·36692	·35049	
10	·60931	·58983	·57044	·55118	·53210	·51323	·49461	·47626	·45821	·44049	5
11	·69528	·67709	·65876	·64035	·62189	·60344	·58502	·56669	·54846	·53039	
12	·76931	·75314	·73666	·71991	·70293	·68576	·66844	·65101	·63350	·61596	6
13	0·83033	0·81660	0·80244	0·78788	0·77294	0·75768	0·74211	0·72627	0·71020	0·69393	
14	·87865	·86746	·85579	·84365	·83105	·81803	·80461	·79081	·77666	·76218	7
15	·91551	·90675	·89749	·88774	·87752	·86683	·85569	·84412	·83213	·81974	
16	·94269	·93606	·92897	·92142	·91341	·90495	·89603	·88667	·87686	·86663	8
17	·96208	·95723	·95198	·94633	·94026	·93378	·92687	·91954	·91179	·90361	
18	·97551	·97207	·96830	·96420	·95974	·95493	·94974	·94418	·93824	·93191	9
19	0·98454	0·98217	0·97955	0·97666	0·97348	0·97001	0·96623	0·96213	0·95771	0·95295	
20	·99046	·98887	·98709	·98511	·98291	·98047	·97779	·97486	·97166	·96817	10
21	·99424	·99320	·99203	·99070	·98921	·98755	·98570	·98365	·98139	·97891	
22	·99659	·99593	·99518	·99431	·99333	·99222	·99098	·98958	·98803	·98630	11
23	·99802	·99761	·99714	·99659	·99596	·99524	·99442	·99349	·99245	·99128	
24	·99888	·99863	·99833	·99799	·99760	·99714	·99661	·99601	·99532	·99455	12
25	0·99937	0·99922	0·99905	0·99884	0·99860	0·99831	0·99798	0·99760	0·99716	0·99665	
26	·99966	·99957	·99947	·99934	·99919	·99902	·99882	·99858	·99830	·99798	13
27	·99981	·99977	·99971	·99963	·99955	·99944	·99932	·99917	·99900	·99880	
28	·99990	·99987	·99984	·99980	·99975	·99969	·99962	·99953	·99942	·99930	14
29	·99995	·99993	·99991	·99989	·99986	·99983	·99979	·99973	·99967	·99960	
30	0·99997	0·99997	0·99996	0·99994	0·99993	0·99991	0·99988	0·99985	0·99982	·99977	15
32	·99999	·99999	·99999	·99998	·99998	·99997	·99997	·99996	·99995	·99993	16
34						·99999	·99999	·99999	·99999	·99998	17

Poisson and χ^2 Distributions

n	$\chi^2=10\cdot5$ $m=5\cdot25$	$11\cdot0$ $5\cdot5$	$11\cdot5$ $5\cdot75$	$12\cdot0$ $6\cdot0$	$12\cdot5$ $6\cdot25$	$13\cdot0$ $6\cdot5$	$13\cdot5$ $6\cdot75$	$14\cdot0$ $7\cdot0$	$14\cdot5$ $7\cdot25$	$15\cdot0$ $7\cdot5$	c
1	0·00119	0·00091	0·00070	0·00053	0·00041	0·00031	0·00024	0·00018	0·00014	0·00011	1
2	·00525	·00409	·00318	·00248	·00193	·00150	·00117	·00091	·00071	·00055	2
3	·01476	·01173	·00931	·00738	·00585	·00464	·00367	·00291	·00230	·00182	3
4	·03280	·02656	·02148	·01735	·01400	·01128	·00907	·00730	·00586	·00470	
5	·06225	·05138	·04232	·03479	·02854	·02338	·01912	·01561	·01273	·01036	
6	·10511	·08838	·07410	·06197	·05170	·04304	·03575	·02964	·02452	·02026	
7	0·16196	0·13862	0·11825	0·10056	0·08527	0·07211	0·06082	0·05118	0·04297	0·03600	4
8	·23167	·20170	·17495	·15120	·13025	·11185	·09577	·08177	·06963	·05915	5
9	·31154	·27571	·24299	·21331	·18657	·16261	·14126	·12233	·10562	·09094	6
10	·39777	·35752	·31991	·28506	·25299	·22367	·19704	·17299	·15138	·13206	
11	·48605	·44326	·40237	·36364	·32726	·29333	·26190	·23299	·20655	·18250	
12	·57218	·52892	·48662	·44568	·40640	·36904	·33377	·30071	·26992	·24144	
13	0·65263	0·61082	0·56901	0·52764	0·48713	0·44781	0·40997	0·37384	0·33960	0·30735	7
14	·72479	·68604	·64639	·60630	·56622	·52652	·48759	·44971	·41316	·37815	8
15	·78717	·75259	·71641	·67903	·64086	·60230	·56374	·52553	·48800	·45142	9
16	·83925	·80949	·77762	·74398	·70890	·67276	·63591	·59871	·56152	·52464	
17	·88135	·85656	·82942	·80014	·76896	·73619	·70212	·66710	·63145	·59548	
18	·91436	·89436	·87195	·84724	·82038	·79157	·76106	·72909	·69596	·66197	

19	0·93952	0·92384	0·90587	0·88562	0·86[illegible]16	0·83857	0·81202	0·78369	0·75380	0·72260	
20	**·95817**	**·94622**	**·93221**	**·91608**	**·89[illegible]79**	**·87738**	**·85492**	**·83050**	**·80427**	**·77641**	**10**
21	·97166	·96279	·95214	·93962	·92513	·90862	·89010	·86960	·84718	·82295	
22	**·98118**	**·97475**	**·96686**	**·95738**	**·94618**	**·93316**	**·91827**	**·90148**	**·88279**	**·86224**	**11**
23	·98773	·98319	·97748	·97047	·96201	·95199	·94030	·92687	·91165	·89463	
24	**·99216**	**·98901**	**·98498**	**·97991**	**·973[illegible]7**	**·96612**	**·95715**	**·94665**	**·93454**	**·92076**	**12**
25	0·99507	0·99295	0·99015	0·98657	0·982[illegible]6	0·97650	0·96976	0·96173	0·95230	0·94138	
26	**·99696**	**·99555**	**·99366**	**·99117**	**·987[illegible]8**	**·98397**	**·97902**	**·97300**	**·96581**	**·95733**	**13**
27	·99815	·99724	·99598	·99429	·99208	·98925	·98567	·98125	·97588	·96943	
28	**·99890**	**·99831**	**·99749**	**·99637**	**·99487**	**·99290**	**·99037**	**·98719**	**·98324**	**·97844**	**14**
29	·99935	·99899	·99846	·99773	·99672	·99538	·99363	·99138	·98854	·98502	
30	**0·99963**	**0·99940**	**0·99907**	**0·99860**	**0·99794**	**0·99704**	**0·99585**	**0·99428**	**0·99227**	**0·98974**	**15**
32	**·99988**	**·99980**	**·99968**	**·99949**	**·9992[illegible]**	**·99884**	**·99831**	**·99759**	**·99664**	**·99539**	**16**
34	**·99996**	**·99994**	**·99989**	**·99983**	**·9997[illegible]**	**·99957**	**·99935**	**·99904**	**·99862**	**·99804**	**17**
36	**·99999**	**·99998**	**·99997**	**·99994**	**·9999[illegible]**	**·99985**	**·99976**	**·99964**	**·99946**	**·99921**	**18**
38			**·99999**	**·99998**	**·9999[illegible]**	**·99995**	**·99992**	**·99987**	**·99980**	**·99970**	**19**
40					**0·99999**	**0·99998**	**0·99997**	**0·99996**	**0·99993**	**0·99989**	**20**
42							**·99999**	**·99999**	**·99998**	**·99996**	**21**
44									**·99999**	**·99999**	**22**

Poisson and χ^2 Distributions

n	χ^2 = 15·5 m = 7·75	16·0 8·0	16·5 8·25	17·0 8·5	17·5 8·75	18·0 9·0	18·5 9·25	19·0 9·5	19·5 9·75	20·0 10·0	c
1	0·00008	0·00006	0·00005	0·00004	0·00003	0·00002	0·00002	0·00001	0·00001	0·00001	1
2	·00043	·00034	·00026	·00020	·00016	·00012	·00010	·00008	·00006	·00005	2
3	·00144	·00113	·00090	·00071	·00056	·00044	·00035	·00027	·00022	·00017	3
4	·00377	·00302	·00242	·00193	·00154	·00123	·00099	·00079	·00063	·00050	
5	·00843	·00684	·00555	·00450	·00364	·00295	·00238	·00192	·00155	·00125	
6	·01670	·01375	·01131	·00928	·00761	·00623	·00510	·00416	·00340	·00277	
7	0·03010	0·02512	0·02092	0·01740	0·01444	0·01197	0·00991	0·00819	0·00676	0·00557	4
8	·05012	·04238	·03576	·03011	·02530	·02123	·01777	·01486	·01240	·01034	5
9	·07809	·06688	·05715	·04872	·04144	·03517	·02980	·02519	·02126	·01791	6
10	·11487	·09963	·08619	·07436	·06401	·05496	·04709	·04026	·03435	·02925	
11	·16073	·14113	·12356	·10788	·09393	·08158	·07068	·06109	·05269	·04534	
12	·21522	·19124	·16939	·14960	·13174	·11569	·10133	·08853	·07716	·06709	
13	0·27719	0·24913	0·22318	0·19930	0·17744	0·15752	0·13944	0·12310	0·10840	0·09521	7
14	·34485	·31337	·28380	·25618	·23051	·20678	·18495	·16495	·14671	·13014	8
15	·41604	·38205	·34962	·31886	·28986	·26267	·23729	·21373	·19196	·17193	9
16	·48837	·45296	·41864	·38560	·35398	·32390	·29544	·26866	·24359	·22022	
17	·55951	·52383	·48871	·45437	·42102	·38884	·35797	·32853	·30060	·27423	
18	·62740	·59255	·55770	·52311	·48902	·45565	·42320	·39182	·36166	·33282	

	10	11	12	13	14	15	16	17	18	19
19	0·39458	0·42521	0·45684	0·48931	0·52244	0·55603	0·58987	0·62370	0·65728	0·69033
20	·45793	·48957	·52183	·55451	·58741	·62031	·65297	·68516	·71662	·74712
21	·52126	·55310	·58514	·61718	·64900	·68039	·71111	·74093	·76965	·79705
22	·58304	·61428	·64533	·67597	·70599	·73519	·76336	·79032	·81589	·83990
23	·64191	·67185	·70122	·72983	·75749	·78402	·80925	·83304	·85527	·87582
24	·69678	·72483	·75199	·77810	·80301	·82657	·84866	·86919	·88808	·90527
25	0·74683	0·77254	0·79712	0·82044	0·84239	0·86237	0·88179	0·89912	0·91483	0·92891
26	·79156	·81464	·83643	·85683	·87577	·89320	·90908	·92341	·93620	·94749
27	·83076	·85107	·87000	·88750	·90352	·91806	·93112	·94274	·95295	·96182
28	·86446	·88200	·89814	·91285	·92615	·93805	·94859	·95782	·96582	·97266
29	·89293	·90779	·92129	·93344	·94427	·95383	·96218	·96939	·97554	·98071
30	0·91654	0·92891	0·94001	0·94986	0·95853	0·96606	0·97258	0·97810	0·98274	0·98659
32	·95126	·95941	·96653	·97269	·97796	·98243	·98617	·98925	·99177	·99379
34	·97296	·97799	·98227	·98588	·98889	·99137	·99339	·99500	·99628	·99728
36	·98572	·98864	·99107	·99306	·99468	·99597	·99700	·99779	·99841	·99887
38	·99281	·99442	·99572	·99675	·99757	·99821	·99870	·99907	·99935	·99955
40	0·99655	0·99738	0·99804	0·99855	0·99894	0·99924	0·99947	0·99963	0·99975	0·99983
42	·99841	·99882	·99914	·99938	·99956	·99969	·99979	·99986	·99991	·99994
44	·99930	·99949	·99964	·99975	·99983	·99986	·99992	·99995	·99997	·99998
46	·99970	·99979	·99986	·99990	·99993	·99996	·99997	·99998	·99999	·99999
48	·99988	·99992	·99994	·99996	·99998	·99998	·99999	·99999		
50	0·99995	0·99997	0·99998	0·99999	0·99999	0·99999				
52	·99998	·99999	·99999							
54	·99999									

Poisson and χ² Distributions

n	χ²=21, m=10·5	22, 11·0	23, 11·5	24, 12·0	25, 12·5	26, 13·0	27, 13·5	28, 14·0	29, 14·5	30, 15·0	c
1	0·00001										1
2	·00003	0·00002	0·00001	0·00001							2
3	·00011	·00007	·00004	·00003	0·00002	0·00001	0·00001				3
4	·00032	·00020	·00013	·00008	·00005	·00003	·00002	0·00001	0·00001	0·00001	
5	·00081	·00052	·00034	·00022	·00014	·00009	·00006	·00004	·00002	·00002	
6	·00184	·00121	·00080	·00052	·00034	·00022	·00015	·00009	·00006	·00004	
7	·00377	·00254	·00171	0·00114	0·00076	0·00050	0·00033	0·00022	0·00015	0·00010	4
8	·00715	·00492	·00336	·00229	·00155	·00105	·00071	·00047	·00032	·00021	5
9	·01265	·00888	·00620	·00430	·00297	·00204	·00140	·00095	·00065	·00044	6
10	·02109	·01511	·01075	·00760	·00535	·00374	·00260	·00181	·00125	·00086	
11	·03337	·02437	·01768	·01273	·00912	·00649	·00460	·00324	·00227	·00159	
12	·05038	·03752	·02773	·02034	·01482	·01073	·00773	·00553	·00394	·00279	
13	·07293	·05536	·04168	0·03113	0·02308	0·01700	0·01244	0·00905	0·00655	0·00471	7
14	·10163	·07861	·06027	·04582	·03457	·02589	·01925	·01423	·01045	·00763	8
15	·13683	·10780	·08414	·06509	·04994	·03802	·02874	·02157	·01609	·01192	9
16	·17851	·14319	·11374	·08950	·06982	·05403	·04148	·03162	·02394	·01800	
17	·22629	·18472	·14925	·11944	·09471	·07446	·05807	·04494	·03453	·02635	
18	·27941	·23199	·19059	·15503	·12492	·09976	·07900	·06206	·04838	·03745	
19	0·33680	0·28426	0·23734	0·19615	0·16054	0·13019	0·10465	0·08343	0·06599	0·05180	10
20	·39713	·34051	·28880	·24239	·20143	·16581	·13526	·10940	·08776	·06985	11
21	·45894	·39951	·34398	·29306	·24716	·20645	·17085	·14015	·11400	·09199	12
22	·52074	·45989	·40173	·34723	·29707	·25168	·21123	·17568	·14486	·11846	
23	·58109	·52025	·46077	·40381	·35029	·30087	·25597	·21578	·18031	·14940	
24	·63873	·57927	·51980	·46160	·40576	·35317	·30445	·26004	·22013	·18475	

Note: the numbers printed vertically at the top of the table (13, 14, 15 … 35) form a secondary scale equal to half of the left-hand argument (they are shown against the even values: 13 ↔ 26, 14 ↔ 28, … 35 ↔ 70). The left-hand argument (25 … 70) indexes the rows.

arg	½										
25		0·22429	0·26392	0·30785	0·35588	0·40760	0·46237	0·51937	0·57756	0·63574	0·69261
26	13	·26761	·31108	·35846	·40933	·46311	·51898	·57597	·63295	·68870	·74196
27		·31415	·36090	·41097	·46379	·51860	·57446	·63032	·68501	·73738	·78629
28	14	·36322	·41253	·46445	·51825	·57305	·62784	·68154	·73304	·78129	·82535
29		·41400	·46507	·51791	·57171	·62549	·67825	·72893	·77654	·82019	·85915
30	15	0·46565	0·51760	0·57044	0·62327	0·67513	0·72503	0·77203	0·81526	0·85404	0·88789
32	16	·56809	·61916	·66936	·71779	·76361	·80603	·84442	·87830	·90740	·93167
34	17	·66412	·71121	·75592	·79755	·83549	·86931	·89871	·92360	·94408	·96039
36	18	·74886	·78972	·82720	·86088	·89047	·91584	·93703	·95425	·96781	·97814
38	19	·81947	·85296	·88264	·90838	·93017	·94815	·96258	·97383	·98231	·98849
40	20	0·87522	0·90122	0·92350	0·94213	0·95733	0·96941	0·97872	0·98568	0·99071	0·99421
42	21	·91703	·93622	·95209	·96491	·97499	·98269	·98840	·99250	·99533	·99721
44	22	·94689	·96038	·97116	·97955	·98592	·99060	·99394	·99623	·99775	·99871
46	23	·96726	·97630	·98329	·98854	·99238	·99509	·99695	·99818	·99896	·99943
48	24	·98054	·98634	·99067	·99382	·99603	·99754	·99853	·99916	·99954	·99976
50	25	0·98884	0·99241	0·99498	0·99678	0·99801	0·99881	0·99931	0·99962	0·99980	0·99990
52	26	·99382	·99592	·99739	·99839	·99903	·99944	·99969	·99984	·99992	·99996
54	27	·99669	·99789	·99869	·99922	·99955	·99975	·99987	·99993	·99997	·99999
56	28	·99828	·99894	·99937	·99963	·99980	·99989	·99994	·99997	·99999	
58	29	·99914	·99949	·99970	·99983	·99991	·99995	·99998	·99999		
60	30	0·99958	0·99976	0·99986	0·99993	0·99996	0·99998				
62	31	·99980	·99989	·99994	·99997	·99998	·99999				
64	32	·99991	·99995	·99997	·99999	·99999					
66	33	·99996	·99998	·99999							
68	34	·99998	·99999								
70	35	0·99999									

Poisson and χ² Distributions

n	c	χ²=31 / m=15·5	32 / 16·0	33 / 16·5	34 / 17·0	35 / 17·5	36 / 18·0	37 / 18·5	38 / 19·0	39 / 19·5	40 / 20·0
5	3	0·00001	0·00001								
6	4	·00003	·00002	0·00001	0·00001						
7	5	0·00006	0·00004	0·00003	0·00002	0·00001	0·00001				
8	6	·00014	·00009	·00006	·00004	·00003	·00002	0·00001	0·00001		
9	7	·00030	·00020	·00013	·00009	·00006	·00004	·00003	·00002	0·00001	0·00001
10	8	·00059	·00040	·00027	·00019	·00012	·00008	·00006	·00004	·00003	·00002
11	9	·00110	·00076	·00053	·00036	·00025	·00017	·00012	·00008	·00005	·00004
12	10	·00197	·00138	·00097	·00068	·00047	·00032	·00022	·00015	·00011	·00007
13	11	0·00337	0·00240	0·00170	0·00120	0·00085	0·00059	0·00041	0·00029	0·00020	0·00014
14	12	·00554	·00401	·00288	·00206	·00147	·00104	·00074	·00052	·00036	·00026
15	13	·00878	·00644	·00469	·00341	·00246	·00177	·00127	·00090	·00064	·00045
16	14	·01346	·01000	·00739	·00543	·00397	·00289	·00210	·00151	·00109	·00078
17		·01997	·01505	·01127	·00840	·00622	·00459	·00337	·00246	·00179	·00129
18		·02879	·02199	·01669	·01260	·00945	·00706	·00524	·00387	·00285	·00209
19		0·04037	0·03125	0·02404	0·01838	0·01397	0·01056	0·00793	0·00593	0·00442	0·00327
20		·05519	·04330	·03374	·02613	·02010	·01538	·01170	·00886	·00667	·00500
21		·07366	·05855	·04622	·03624	·02824	·02187	·01683	·01289	·00981	·00744
22		·09612	·07740	·06187	·04912	·03875	·03087	·02366	·01832	·01411	·01081
23		·12279	·10014	·08107	·06516	·05202	·04125	·03251	·02547	·01984	·01537
24		·15378	·12699	·10407	·08467	·06840	·05489	·04376	·03467	·02731	·02139
25		0·18902	0·15801	0·13107	0·10791	0·08820	0·07160	0·05774	0·04626	0·03684	0·02916
26		·22827	·19312	·16210	·13502	·11165	·09167	·07475	·06056	·04875	·03901
27		·27114	·23208	·19707	·16605	·13887	·11530	·09507	·07786	·06336	·05124
28		·31708	·27451	·23574	·20087	·16987	·14260	·11886	·09840	·08092	·06613
29		·36542	·31987	·27774	·23926	·20454	·17356	·14622	·12234	·10166	·08394

15	0.10486	0.12573	0.14975	0.17714	0.20808	0.24264	0.28083	0.32254	0.36753	0.41541	30
16	.15651	.18398	.21479	.24903	.28665	.32754	.37145	.41802	.46675	.51701	32
17	.22107	.25497	.29203	.33214	.37505	.42040	.46774	.51648	.56596	.61544	34
18	.29703	.33639	.37836	.42259	.46865	.51600	.56402	.61205	.65934	.70518	36
19	.38142	.42461	.46948	.51555	.56225	.60893	.65496	.69965	.74235	.78246	38
20	0.47026	0.51514	0.56061	0.60607	0.65092	0.69453	0.73632	0.77572	0.81225	0.84551	40
21	.55909	.60342	.64717	.68979	.73072	.76943	.80548	.83848	.86817	.89437	42
22	.64870	.68538	.72550	.76355	.79912	.83185	.86147	.88780	.91077	.93043	44
23	.72061	.75804	.79814	.82558	.85509	.88150	.90473	.92478	.94176	.95584	46
24	.78749	.81963	.84902	.87547	.89889	.91928	.93670	.95131	.96331	.97296	48
25	0.84323	0.86968	0.89325	0.91392	0.93174	0.94682	0.95935	0.96955	0.97769	0.98402	50
26	.88782	.90872	.92687	.94238	.95539	.96611	.97476	.98159	.98688	.99087	52
27	.92211	.93800	.95144	.96263	.97177	.97908	.98483	.98923	.99254	.99496	54
28	.94752	.95914	.96873	.97650	.98268	.98750	.99117	.99390	.99590	.99731	56
29	.96567	.97387	.98046	.98567	.98970	.99275	.99502	.99665	.99781	.99861	58
30	0.97818	0.98377	0.98815	0.99152	0.99406	0.99593	0.99727	0.99822	0.99887	0.99930	60
31	.98653	.99021	.99302	.99512	.99667	.99778	.99855	.99908	.99943	.99966	62
32	.99191	.99425	.99600	.99728	.99819	.99882	.99925	.99954	.99972	.99984	64
33	.99527	.99672	.99777	.99852	.99904	.99939	.99963	.99978	.99987	.99993	66
34	.99731	.99818	.99879	.99922	.99951	.99970	.99982	.99989	.99994	.99997	68
35	0.99851	0.99930	0.99936	0.99960	0.99975	0.99985	0.99991	0.99995	0.99997	0.99999	70

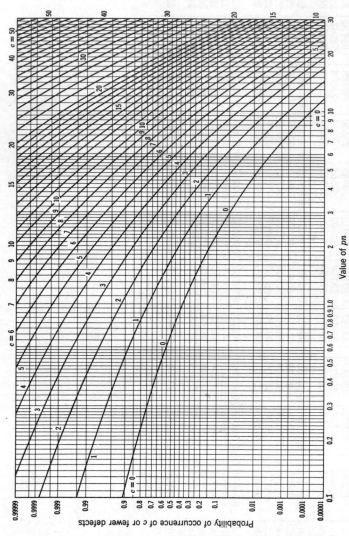

Cumulative probability curves of the Poisson exponential distribution (a modification of a chart given by Miss. F. Thorndike in *The Bell System Technical Journal*, October 1926). These curves may be used for determining the probability of *c* or less defects in a sample of *n* pieces selected from an infinite universe in which the fraction defective is *p*. They may also be used as an approximation under certain conditions for determining the probability of occurrence of *c* or less *defectives* for a given *p* and *n*. Further, they serve as a generalized set of OC curves for single sampling plans, when the Poisson distribution is applicable. (Used with permission from H. F. Dodge and H. G. Romig, *Sampling Inspection Tables*, John Wiley and Sons, Inc., New York, 1959, p. 35.)

Appendix G

Cumulative Distribution of t *

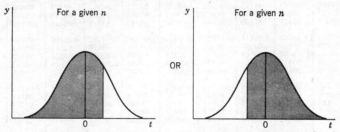

Table shows, for given n, probability of a t value equal to or less than the observed t when t is positive, or equal to or more than the observed t when t is negative.

* Reproduced with permission from H. O. Hartley and F. S. Pearson, "Table of the Probability Integral of the t-Distribution," *Biometrika*, Vol. 37, June 1950, pp. 168–172.

Cumulative Distribution of t

t \ n	1	2	3	4	5	6	7	8	9	10
0·0	0·50000	0·50000	0·50000	0·50000	0·50000	0·50000	0·50000	0·50000	0·50000	0·50000
0·1	·53173	·53527	·53667	·53742	·53788	·53820	·53843	·53860	·53873	·53884
0·2	·56283	·57002	·57286	·57438	·57532	·57596	·57642	·57676	·57704	·57726
0·3	·59277	·60376	·60812	·61044	·61188	·61285	·61356	·61409	·61450	·61484
0·4	·62112	·63608	·64203	64520	·64716	·64850	·64946	·65019	·65076	·65122
0·5	0·64758	0·66667	0·67428	0·67834	0·68085	0·68256	0·68380	0·68473	0·68546	0·68605
0·6	·67202	·69529	·70460	70958	·71267	·71477	·71629	·71745	·71835	·71907
0·7	·69440	·72181	·73284	·73875	·74243	·74493	·74674	·74811	·74919	·75006
0·8	·71478	·74618	·75890	·76574	·76999	·77289	·77500	·77659	·77784	·77885
0·9	·73326	·76845	·78277	·79050	·79531	·79860	·80099	·80280	·80422	·80536
1·0	0·75000	0·78868	0·80450	0·81305	0·81839	0·82204	0·82469	0·82670	0·82828	0·82955
1·1	·76515	·80698	·82416	·83346	·83927	·84325	·84614	·84834	·85006	·85145
1·2	·77886	·82349	·84187	·85182	·85805	·86232	·86541	·86777	·86961	·87110
1·3	·79129	·83838	·85777	·86827	·87485	·87935	·88262	·88510	·88705	·88862
1·4	·80257	·85177	·87200	·88295	·88980	·89448	·89788	·90046	·90249	·90412
1·5	0·81283	0·86380	0·88471	0·89600	0·90305	0·90786	0·91135	0·91400	0·91608	0·91775
1·6	·82219	·87464	·89605	·90758	·91475	·91964	·92318	·92587	·92797	·92966
1·7	·83075	·88439	·90615	·91782	·92506	·92998	·93354	·93622	·93833	·94002
1·8	·83859	·89317	·91516	·92688	·93412	·93902	·94256	·94522	·94731	·94897
1·9	·84579	·90109	·92318	·93488	·94207	·94691	·95040	·95302	·95506	·95669
2·0	0·85242	0·90825	0·93034	0·94194	0·94903	0·95379	0·95719	0·95974	0·96172	0·96331
2·1	·85854	·91473	·93672	·94817	·95512	·95976	·96306	·96553	·96744	·96896
2·2	·86420	·92060	·94241	·95367	·96045	·96495	·96813	·97050	·97233	·97378
2·3	·86945	·92593	·94751	·95853	·96511	·96945	·97250	·97476	·97650	·97787
2·4	·87433	·93077	·95206	·96282	·96919	·97335	·97627	·97841	·98005	·98134
2·5	0·87888	0·93519	0·95615	0·96662	0·97275	0·97674	0·97950	0·98153	0·98307	0·98428
2·6	·88313	·93923	·95981	·96998	·97587	·97967	·98229	·98419	·98563	·98675
2·7	·88709	·94292	·96311	·97295	·97861	·98221	·98468	·98646	·98780	·98884
2·8	·89081	·94630	·96607	·97559	·98100	·98442	·98674	·98840	·98964	·99060
2·9	·89430	·94941	·96875	·97794	·98310	·98633	·98851	·99005	·99120	·99208
3·0	0·89758	0·95227	0·97116	0·98003	0·98495	0·98800	0·99003	0·99146	0·99252	0·99333
3·1	·90067	·95490	·97335	·98189	·98657	·98944	·99134	·99267	·99364	·99437
3·2	·90359	·95733	·97533	·98355	·98800	·99070	·99247	·99369	·99459	·99525
3·3	·90634	·95958	·97713	·98503	·98926	·99180	·99344	·99457	·99539	·99599
3·4	·90895	·96166	·97877	·98636	·99037	·99275	·99428	·99532	·99606	·99661
3·5	0·91141	0·96358	0·98026	0·98755	0·99136	0·99359	0·99500	0·99596	0·99664	0·99714
3·6	·91376	·96538	·98162	·98862	·99223	·99432	·99563	·99651	·99713	·99758
3·7	·91598	·96705	·98286	·98958	·99300	·99496	·99617	·99698	·99754	·99795
3·8	·91809	·96860	·98400	·99045	·99369	·99552	·99664	·99738	·99789	·99826
3·9	·92010	·97005	·98504	·99123	·99430	·99601	·99705	·99773	·99819	·99852
4·0	0·92202	0·97141	0·98600	0·99193	0·99484	0·99644	0·99741	0·99803	0·99845	0·99874
4·2	·92560	·97386	·98768	·99315	·99575	·99716	·99798	·99850	·99885	·99909
4·4	·92887	·97602	·98912	·99415	·99649	·99772	·99842	·99886	·99914	·99933
4·6	·93186	·97792	·99034	·99498	·99708	·99815	·99876	·99912	·99936	·99951
4·8	·93462	·97962	·99140	·99568	·99756	·99850	·99902	·99932	·99951	·99964
5·0	0·93717	0·98113	0·99230	0·99625	0·99795	0·99877	0·99922	0·99947	0·99963	0·99973
5·2	·93952	·98248	·99309	·99674	·99827	·99899	·99937	·99959	·99972	·99980
5·4	·94171	·98369	·99378	·99715	·99853	·99917	·99950	·99968	·99978	·99985
5·6	·94375	·98478	·99437	·99750	·99875	·99931	·99959	·99975	·99983	·99989
5·8	·94565	·98577	·99490	·99780	·99893	·99942	·99967	·99980	·99987	·99991
6·0	0·94743	0·98666	0·99536	0·99806	0·99908	0·99952	0·99973	0·99984	0·99990	0·99993
6·2	·94910	·98748	·99577	·99828	·99920	·99959	·99978	·99987	·99992	·99995
6·4	·95066	·98822	·99614	·99847	·99931	·99966	·99982	·99990	·99994	·99996
6·6	·95214	·98890	·99646	·99863	·99940	·99971	·99985	·99992	·99995	·99997
6·8	·95352	·98953	·99675	·99878	·99948	·99975	·99987	·99993	·99996	·99998
7·0	0·95483	0·99010	0·99701	0·99890	0·99954	0·99979	0·99990	0·99994	0·99997	0·99998
7·2	·95607	·99063	·99724	·99901	·99960	·99982	·99991	·99995	·99997	·99999
7·4	·95724	·99111	·99745	·99911	·99964	·99984	·99993	·99996	·99998	·99999
7·6	·95836	·99156	·99764	·99920	·99969	·99986	·99994	·99997	·99998	·99999
7·8	·95941	·99198	·99781	·99927	·99972	·99988	·99995	·99997	·99999	·99999
8·0	0·96042	0·99237	0·99796	0·99934	0·99975	0·99990	0·99996	0·99998	0·99999	0·99999

n / t	11	12	13	14	15	16	17	18	19	20
0·0	0·50000	0·50000	0·50000	0·50000	0·50000	0·50000	0·50000	0·50000	0·50000	0·50000
0·1	·53893	·53900	·53907	·53912	·53917	·53921	·53924	·53928	·53930	·53933
0·2	·57744	·57759	·57771	·57782	·57792	·57800	·57807	·57814	·57820	·57825
0·3	·61511	·61534	·61554	·61571	·61585	·61598	·61609	·61619	·61628	·61636
0·4	·65159	·65191	·65217	·65240	·65260	·65278	·65293	·65307	·65319	·65330
0·5	0·68654	0·68694	0·68728	0·68758	0·68783	0·68806	0·68826	0·68843	0·68859	0·68873
0·6	·71967	·72017	·72059	·72095	·72127	·72155	·72179	·72201	·72220	·72238
0·7	·75077	·75136	·75187	·75230	·75268	·75301	·75330	·75356	·75380	·75400
0·8	·77968	·78037	·78096	·78146	·78190	·78229	·78263	·78293	·78320	·78344
0·9	·80630	·80709	·80776	·80833	·80883	·80927	·80965	·81000	·81031	·81058
1·0	0·83060	0·83148	0·83222	0·83286	0·83341	0·83390	0·83433	0·83472	0·83506	0·83537
1·1	·85259	·85355	·85436	·85506	·85566	·85620	·85667	·85709	·85746	·85780
1·2	·87233	·87335	·87422	·87497	·87562	·87620	·87670	·87715	·87756	·87792
1·3	·88991	·89099	·89191	·89270	·89339	·89399	·89452	·89500	·89542	·89581
1·4	·90546	·90658	·90754	·90836	·90907	·90970	·91025	·91074	·91118	·91158
1·5	0·91912	0·92027	0·92125	0·92209	0·92282	0·92346	0·92402	0·92452	0·92498	0·92538
1·6	·93105	·93221	·93320	·93404	·93478	·93542	·93599	·93650	·93695	·93736
1·7	·94140	·94256	·94354	·94439	·94512	·94576	·94632	·94683	·94728	·94768
1·8	·95034	·95148	·95245	·95328	·95400	·95463	·95518	·95568	·95612	·95652
1·9	·95802	·95914	·96008	·96089	·96158	·96220	·96273	·96321	·96364	·96403
2·0	0·96460	0·96567	0·96658	0·96736	0·96803	0·96861	0·96913	0·96959	0·97000	0·97037
2·1	·97020	·97123	·97209	·97283	·97347	·97403	·97452	·97495	·97534	·97569
2·2	·97496	·97593	·97675	·97745	·97805	·97858	·97904	·97945	·97981	·98014
2·3	·97898	·97990	·98067	·98132	·98189	·98238	·98281	·98319	·98352	·98383
2·4	·98238	·98324	·98396	·98457	·98509	·98554	·98594	·98629	·98660	·98688
2·5	0·98525	0·98604	0·98671	0·98727	0·98775	0·98816	0·98853	0·98885	0·98913	0·98938
2·6	·98765	·98839	·98900	·98951	·98995	·99033	·99066	·99095	·99121	·99144
2·7	·98967	·99035	·99090	·99137	·99177	·99211	·99241	·99267	·99290	·99311
2·8	·99136	·99198	·99249	·99291	·99327	·99358	·99385	·99408	·99429	·99447
2·9	·99278	·99334	·99380	·99418	·99450	·99478	·99502	·99523	·99541	·99557
3·0	0·99396	0·99447	0·99488	0·99522	0·99551	0·99576	0·99597	0·99616	0·99632	0·99646
3·1	·99495	·99541	·99578	·99608	·99634	·99656	·99675	·99691	·99705	·99718
3·2	·99577	·99618	·99652	·99679	·99702	·99721	·99738	·99752	·99764	·99775
3·3	·99646	·99683	·99713	·99737	·99757	·99774	·99789	·99801	·99812	·99821
3·4	·99703	·99737	·99763	·99784	·99802	·99817	·99830	·99840	·99850	·99858
3·5	0·99751	0·99781	0·99804	0·99823	0·99839	0·99852	0·99863	0·99872	0·99880	0·99887
3·6	·99791	·99818	·99838	·99855	·99869	·99880	·99890	·99898	·99905	·99911
3·7	·99825	·99848	·99867	·99881	·99893	·99903	·99911	·99918	·99924	·99929
3·8	·99853	·99874	·99890	·99902	·99913	·99921	·99928	·99934	·99939	·99944
3·9	·99876	·99895	·99909	·99920	·99929	·99936	·99942	·99948	·99952	·99956
4·0	0·99896	0·99912	0·99924	0·99934	0·99942	0·99948	0·99954	0·99958	0·99962	0·99965
4·2	·99926	·99938	·99948	·99955	·99961	·99966	·99970	·99973	·99976	·99978
4·4	·99947	·99957	·99964	·99970	·99974	·99978	·99980	·99983	·99985	·99986
4·6	·99962	·99969	·99975	·99979	·99983	·99985	·99987	·99989	·99990	·99991
4·8	·99972	·99978	·99983	·99986	·99988	·99990	·99992	·99993	·99994	·99995
5·0	0·99980	0·99985	0·99988	0·99990	0·99992	0·99993	0·99995	0·99995	0·99996	0·99997
5·2	·99985	·99989	·99992	·99993	·99995	·99996	·99996	·99997	·99997	·99998
5·4	·99989	·99992	·99994	·99995	·99996	·99997	·99998	·99998	·99998	·99999
5·6	·99992	·99994	·99996	·99997	·99997	·99998	·99998	·99999	·99999	·99999
5·8	·99994	·99996	·99997	·99998	·99998	·99999	·99999	·99999	·99999	·99999
6·0	0·99995	0·99997	0·99998	0·99998	0·99999	0·99999	0·99999	0·99999		
6·2	·99997	·99998	·99998	·99999	·99999	·99999				
6·4	·99997	·99998	·99999	·99999	·99999					
6·6	·99998	·99999	·99999	·99999						
6·8	·99998	·99999	·99999	·99999						
7·0	0·99999	0·99999								

Upper percentage points of t

$1-P$	$n = 1$	2	3	4	5	6	7	8	9	10
10^{-3}	318·3	22·33	10·21	7·17	5·89	5·21	4·79	4·50	4·30	4·14
10^{-4}	3183	70·7	22·20	13·03	9·68	8·02	7·06	6·44	6·01	5·69
10^{-5}	31831	224	47·91	23·33	15·54	12·03	10·11	8·90	8·10	7·53
5×10^{-6}	63652	316	60·40	27·82	17·89	13·55	11·22	9·79	8·83	8·15

t \ n	20	21	22	23	24	30	40	60	120	∞
0·00	0·50000	0·50000	0·50000	0·50000	0·50000	0·50000	0·50000	0·50000	0·50000	0·50000
0·05	·51969	·51970	·51971	·51972	·51973	·51977	·51981	·51986	·51990	·51994
0·10	·53933	·53935	·53938	·53939	·53941	·53950	·53958	·53966	·53974	·53983
0·15	·55887	·55890	·55893	·55896	·55899	·55912	·55924	·55937	·55949	·55962
0·20	·57825	·57830	·57834	·57838	·57842	·57858	·57875	·57892	·57909	·57926
0·25	0·59743	0·59749	0·59755	0·59760	0·59764	0·59785	0·59807	0·59828	0·59849	0·59871
0·30	·61636	·61644	·61650	·61656	·61662	·61688	·61713	·61739	·61765	·61791
0·35	·63500	·63509	·63517	·63524	·63530	·63561	·63591	·63622	·63652	·63683
0·40	·65330	·65340	·65349	·65358	·65365	·65400	·65436	·65471	·65507	·65542
0·45	·67122	·67134	·67144	·67154	·67163	·67203	·67243	·67283	·67324	·67364
0·50	0·68873	0·68886	0·68898	0·68909	0·68919	0·68964	0·69009	0·69055	0·69100	0·69146
0·55	·70579	·70594	·70607	·70619	·70630	·70680	·70731	·70782	·70833	·70884
0·60	·72238	·72254	·72268	·72281	·72294	·72349	·72405	·72462	·72518	·72575
0·65	·73846	·73863	·73879	·73893	·73907	·73968	·74030	·74091	·74153	·74215
0·70	·75400	·75419	·75437	·75453	·75467	·75534	·75601	·75668	·75736	·75804
0·75	0·76901	0·76921	0·76940	0·76957	0·76973	0·77045	0·77118	0·77191	0·77264	0·77337
0·80	·78344	·78367	·78387	·78405	·78422	·78500	·78578	·78657	·78735	·78814
0·85	·79731	·79754	·79776	·79796	·79814	·79897	·79981	·80065	·80149	·80234
0·90	·81058	·81084	·81107	·81128	·81147	·81236	·81325	·81414	·81504	·81594
0·95	·82327	·82354	·82378	·82401	·82421	·82515	·82609	·82704	·82799	·82894
1·00	0·83537	0·83565	0·83591	0·83614	0·83636	0·83735	0·83834	0·83934	0·84034	0·84134
1·05	·84688	·84717	·84744	·84769	·84791	·84895	·84999	·85104	·85209	·85314
1·10	·85780	·85811	·85839	·85864	·85888	·85996	·86105	·86214	·86323	·86433
1·15	·86814	·86846	·86875	·86902	·86926	·87039	·87151	·87265	·87378	·87493
1·20	·87792	·87825	·87855	·87882	·87907	·88023	·88140	·88257	·88375	·88493
1·25	0·88714	0·88747	0·88778	0·88807	0·88832	0·88952	0·89072	0·89192	0·89313	0·89435
1·30	·89581	·89616	·89647	·89676	·89703	·89825	·89948	·90071	·90195	·90320
1·35	·90395	·90431	·90463	·90492	·90519	·90644	·90770	·90896	·91022	·91149
1·40	·91158	·91194	·91227	·91257	·91285	·91411	·91539	·91667	·91795	·91924
1·45	·91872	·91908	·91942	·91972	·92000	·92128	·92257	·92387	·92517	·92647
1·50	0·92538	0·92575	0·92608	0·92639	0·92667	0·92797	0·92927	0·93057	0·93188	0·93319
1·55	·93159	·93196	·93230	·93260	·93289	·93419	·93549	·93680	·93811	·93943
1·60	·93736	·93773	·93807	·93838	·93866	·93996	·94127	·94257	·94389	·94520
1·65	·94272	·94309	·94342	·94373	·94401	·94531	·94661	·94792	·94922	·95053
1·70	·94768	·94805	·94839	·94869	·94897	·95026	·95155	·95284	·95414	·95543
1·75	0·95228	0·95264	0·95297	0·95327	0·95355	0·95483	0·95611	0·95738	0·95866	0·95994
1·80	·95652	·95688	·95720	·95750	·95778	·95904	·96030	·96156	·96281	·96407
1·85	·96043	·96078	·96110	·96140	·96167	·96291	·96414	·96538	·96661	·96784
1·90	·96403	·96437	·96469	·96498	·96524	·96646	·96767	·96888	·97008	·97128
1·95	·96733	·96767	·96798	·96827	·96852	·96971	·97089	·97207	·97325	·97441
2·0	0·97037	0·97070	0·97100	0·97128	0·97153	0·97269	0·97384	0·97498	0·97612	0·97725
2·1	·97569	·97601	·97629	·97655	·97679	·97788	·97896	·98003	·98109	·98214
2·2	·98014	·98043	·98070	·98094	·98116	·98218	·98318	·98416	·98514	·98610
2·3	·98383	·98410	·98435	·98457	·98478	·98571	·98663	·98753	·98841	·98928
2·4	·98688	·98712	·98735	·98756	·98774	·98860	·98943	·99024	·99103	·99180
2·5	0·98038	0·98961	0·98982	0·99000	0·99017	0·99094	0·99169	0·99241	0·99312	0·99379
2·6	·99144	·99164	·99183	·99200	·99215	·99284	·99350	·99414	·90475	·99534
2·7	·99311	·99329	·99346	·99361	·99375	·99436	·99494	·99550	·99603	·99653
2·8	·99447	·99463	·99478	·99492	·99504	·99557	·99608	·99657	·99702	·99744
2·9	·99557	·99572	·99585	·99596	·99607	·99654	·99698	·99740	·99778	·99813
3·0	0·99646	0·99659	0·99670	0·99681	0·99690	0·99730	0·99768	0·99804	0·99836	0·99865
3·1	·99718	·99729	·99739	·99748	·99756	·99791	·99823	·99853	·99879	·99903
3·2	·99775	·99785	·99793	·99801	·99808	·99838	·99865	·99890	·99912	·99931
3·3	·99821	·99829	·99837	·99844	·99849	·99875	·99898	·99918	·99936	·99952
3·4	·99858	·99865	·99871	·99877	·99882	·99904	·99923	·99940	·99954	·99966
3·5	0·99887	0·99893	0·99899	0·99904	0·99908	0·99926	0·99942	0·99956	0·99967	0·99977
3·6	·99911	·99916	·99920	·99925	·99928	·99943	·99957	·99968	·99977	·99984
3·7	·99929	·99933	·99937	·99941	·99944	·99957	·99967	·99976	·99984	·99989
3·8	·99944	·99948	·99951	·99954	·99956	·99967	·99976	·99983	·99989	·99993
3·9	·99956	·99959	·99961	·99964	·99966	·99975	·99982	·99988	·99992	·99995
4·0	0·99965	0·99967	0·99970	0·99972	0·99974	0·99981	0·99987	0·99991	0·99995	0·99997
5·0	0·99997	0·99997	0·99998	0·99998	0·99998	0·99999	0·99999			

Appendix H[*]

r Values for Given z' Values

z'	.00	.01	.02	.03	.04	.05	.06	.07	.08	.09
.0	.0000	.0100	.0200	.0300	.0400	.0500	.0599	.0699	.0798	.0898
.1	.0997	.1096	.1194	.1293	.1391	.1489	.1587	.1684	.1781	.1878
.2	.1974	.2070	.2165	.2260	.2355	.2449	.2543	.2636	.2729	.2821
.3	.2913	.3004	.3095	.3185	.3275	.3364	.3452	.3540	.3627	.3714
.4	.3800	.3885	.3969	.4053	.4136	.4219	.4301	.4382	.4462	.4542
.5	.4621	.4700	.4777	.4854	.4930	.5005	.5080	.5154	.5227	.5299
.6	.5370	.5441	.5511	.5581	.5649	.5717	.5784	.5850	.5915	.5980
.7	.6044	.6107	.6169	.6231	.6291	.6352	.6411	.6469	.6527	.6584
.8	.6640	.6696	.6751	.6805	.6858	.6911	.6963	.7014	.7064	.7114
.9	.7163	.7211	.7259	.7306	.7352	.7398	.7443	.7487	.7531	.7574
1.0	.7616	.7658	.7699	.7739	.7779	.7818	.7857	.7895	.7932	.7969
1.1	.8005	.8041	.8076	.8110	.8144	.8178	.8210	.8243	.8275	.8306
1.2	.8337	.8367	.8397	.8426	.8455	.8483	.8511	.8538	.8565	.8591
1.3	.8617	.8643	.8668	.8693	.8717	.8741	.8764	.8787	.8810	.8832
1.4	.8854	.8875	.8896	.8917	.8937	.8957	.8977	.8996	.9015	.9033
1.5	.9052	.9069	.9087	.9104	.9121	.9138	.9154	.9170	.9186	.9202
1.6	.9217	.9232	.9246	.9261	.9275	.9289	.9302	.9316	.9329	.9342
1.7	.9354	.9367	.9379	.9391	.9402	.9414	.9425	.9436	.9447	.9458
1.8	.9468	.9478	.9498	.9488	.9508	.9518	.9527	.9536	.9545	.9554
1.9	.9562	.9571	.9579	.9587	.9595	.9603	.9611	.9619	.9626	.9633
2.0	.9640	.9647	.9654	.9661	.9668	.9674	.9680	.9687	.9693	.9699
2.1	.9705	.9710	.9716	.9722	.9727	.9732	.9738	.9743	.9748	.9753
2.2	.9757	.9762	.9767	.9771	.9776	.9780	.9785	.9789	.9793	.9797
2.3	.9801	.9805	.9809	.9812	.9816	.9820	.9823	.9827	.9830	.9834
2.4	.9837	.9840	.9843	.9846	.9849	.9852	.9855	.9858	.9861	.9863
2.5	.9866	.9869	.9871	.9874	.9876	.9879	.9881	.9884	.9886	.9888
2.6	.9890	.9892	.9895	.9897	.9899	.9901	.9903	.9905	.9906	.9908
2.7	.9910	.9912	.9914	.9915	.9917	.9919	.9920	.9922	.9923	.9925
2.8	.9926	.9928	.9929	.9931	.9932	.9933	.9935	.9936	.9937	.9938
2.9	.9940	.9941	.9942	.9943	.9944	.9945	.9946	.9947	.9949	.9950
3.0	.9951									
4.0	.9993									
5.0	.9999									

[*] Reproduced with permission from Frederick C. Mills, *Statistical Methods*, Henry Holt and Company, New York, 1955.

Index

Ordinates of the Normal Curve *

$$\text{Values of } e^{-\frac{x^2}{2\sigma^2}}, \text{ or of } e^{-\frac{z^2}{2}}$$

z	.00	.01	.02	.03	.04	.05	.06	.07	.08	.09
0.0	1.00000	.99995	.99980	.99955	.99920	.99875	.99820	.99755	.99685	.99596
0.1	.99501	.99396	.99283	.99158	.99025	.98881	.98728	.98565	.98393	.98211
0.2	.98020	.97819	.97609	.97390	.97161	.96923	.96676	.96420	.96156	.95882
0.3	.95600	.95309	.95010	.94702	.94387	.94055	.93723	.93382	.93024	.92677
0.4	.92312	.91939	.91558	.91169	.90774	.90371	.89961	.89543	.89119	.88688
0.5	.88250	.87805	.87353	.86896	.86432	.85962	.85488	.85006	.84519	.84060
0.6	.83527	.83023	.82514	.82010	.81481	.80957	.80429	.79896	.79359	.78817
0.7	.78270	.77721	.77167	.76610	.76048	.75484	.74916	.74342	.73769	.73193
0.8	.72615	.72033	.71448	.70861	.70272	.69681	.69087	.68493	.67896	.67298
0.9	.66689	.66097	.65494	.64891	.64287	.63683	.63077	.62472	.61865	.61259
1.0	.60653	.60047	.59440	.58834	.58228	.57623	.57017	.56414	.55810	.55209
1.1	.54607	.54007	.53409	.52812	.52214	.51620	.51027	.50437	.49848	.49260
1.2	.48675	.48092	.47511	.46933	.46357	.45783	.45212	.44644	.44078	.43516
1.3	.42956	.42399	.41845	.41294	.40747	.40202	.39661	.39123	.38569	.38058
1.4	.37531	.37007	.36487	.35971	.35459	.34950	.34445	.33944	.33447	.32954
1.5	.32465	.31980	.31500	.31023	.30550	.30082	.29618	.29158	.28702	.28251
1.6	.27804	.27361	.26923	.26489	.26059	.25634	.25213	.24797	.24385	.23978
1.7	.23575	.23176	.22782	.22392	.22008	.21627	.21251	.20879	.20511	.20148
1.8	.19790	.19436	.19086	.18741	.18400	.18064	.17732	.17404	.17081	.16762
1.9	.16448	.16137	.15831	.15530	.15232	.14939	.14650	.14364	.14083	.13806
2.0	.13534	.13265	.13000	.12740	.12483	.12230	.11981	.11737	.11496	.11259
2.1	.11025	.10795	.10570	.10347	.10129	.09914	.09702	.09495	.09290	.09090
2.2	.08892	.08698	.08507	.08320	.08136	.07956	.07778	.07604	.07433	.07265
2.3	.07100	.06939	.06780	.06624	.06471	.06321	.06174	.06029	.05888	.05750
2.4	.05614	.05481	.05350	.05222	.05096	.04973	.04852	.04734	.04618	.04505
2.5	.04394	.04285	.04179	.04074	.03972	.03873	.03775	.03680	.03586	.03494
2.6	.03405	.03317	.03232	.03148	.03066	.02986	.02908	.02831	.02757	.02684
2.7	.02612	.02542	.02474	.02408	.02343	.02280	.02218	.02157	.02098	.02040
2.8	.01984	.01929	.01876	.01823	.01772	.01723	.01674	.01627	.01581	.01536
2.9	.01492	.01449	.01408	.01367	.01328	.01288	.01252	.01215	.01179	.01145
3.0	.01111	.01078	.01046	.01015	$.0^2$9846	$.0^2$9550	$.0^2$9262	$.0^2$8984	$.0^2$8665	$.0^2$8447
3.1	$.0^2$8189	$.0^2$7938	$.0^2$7695	$.0^2$7457	$.0^2$7229	$.0^2$7004	$.0^2$6785	$.0^2$6575	$.0^2$6369	$.0^2$6169
3.2	$.0^2$5976	$.0^2$5788	$.0^2$5605	$.0^2$5427	$.0^2$5254	$.0^2$5086	$.0^2$4923	$.0^2$4765	$.0^2$4612	$.0^2$4462
3.3	$.0^2$4319	$.0^2$4179	$.0^2$4041	$.0^2$3910	$.0^2$3780	$.0^2$3657	$.0^2$3537	$.0^2$3419	$.0^2$3306	$.0^2$3196
3.4	$.0^2$3088	$.0^2$2985	$.0^2$2885	$.0^2$2787	$.0^2$2695	$.0^2$2602	$.0^2$2514	$.0^2$2429	$.0^2$2346	$.0^2$2265
3.5	$.0^2$2188	$.0^2$2112	$.0^2$2039	$.0^2$1968	$.0^2$1900	$.0^2$1834	$.0^2$1770	$.0^2$1708	$.0^2$1648	$.0^2$1590
3.6	$.0^2$1534	$.0^2$1479	$.0^2$1427	$.0^2$1376	$.0^2$1327	$.0^2$1280	$.0^2$1234	$.0^2$1189	$.0^2$1146	$.0^2$1105
3.7	$.0^2$1065	$.0^2$1026	$.0^3$9886	$.0^3$9525	$.0^3$9177	$.0^3$8838	$.0^3$8513	$.0^3$8199	$.0^3$7893	$.0^3$7600
3.8	$.0^3$7317	$.0^3$7044	$.0^3$6780	$.0^3$6527	$.0^3$6282	$.0^3$6043	$.0^3$5815	$.0^3$5595	$.0^3$5382	$.0^3$5176
3.9	$.0^3$4981	$.0^3$4788	$.0^3$4605	$.0^3$4427	$.0^3$4256	$.0^3$4093	$.0^3$3933	$.0^3$3780	$.0^3$3632	$.0^3$3492
4.0	$.0^3$3354	$.0^3$3224	$.0^3$3096	$.0^3$2973	$.0^3$2858	$.0^3$2742	$.0^3$2634	$.0^3$2529	$.0^3$2428	$.0^3$2331
4.1	$.0^3$2237	$.0^3$2147	$.0^3$2061	$.0^3$1978	$.0^3$1898	$.0^3$1821	$.0^3$1746	$.0^3$1675	$.0^3$1607	$.0^3$1541
4.2	$.0^3$1477	$.0^3$1417	$.0^3$1358	$.0^3$1302	$.0^3$1248	$.0^3$1196	$.0^3$1146	$.0^3$1098	$.0^3$1053	$.0^3$1008
4.3	$.0^4$9661	$.0^4$9252	$.0^4$8861	$.0^4$8487	$.0^4$8126	$.0^4$7781	$.0^4$7450	$.0^4$7131	$.0^4$6826	$.0^4$6532
4.4	$.0^4$6252	$.0^4$5983	$.0^4$5725	$.0^4$5477	$.0^4$5239	$.0^4$5011	$.0^4$4793	$.0^4$4585	$.0^4$4384	$.0^4$4191
4.5	$.0^4$4006	$.0^4$3830	$.0^4$3662	$.0^4$3499	$.0^4$3344	$.0^4$3196	$.0^4$3053	$.0^4$2918	$.0^4$2787	$.0^4$2662
4.6	$.0^4$2542	$.0^4$2427	$.0^4$2318	$.0^4$2213	$.0^4$2113	$.0^4$2017	$.0^4$1925	$.0^4$1838	$.0^4$1754	$.0^4$1673
4.7	$.0^4$1597	$.0^4$1523	$.0^4$1453	$.0^4$1386	$.0^4$1322	$.0^4$1261	$.0^4$1202	$.0^4$1146	$.0^4$1093	$.0^4$1042
4.8	$.0^5$9929	$.0^5$9463	$.0^5$9019	$.0^5$8593	$.0^5$8189	$.0^5$7801	$.0^5$7432	$.0^5$7079	$.0^5$6743	$.0^5$6419
4.9	$.0^5$6114	$.0^5$5820	$.0^5$5542	$.0^5$5276	$.0^5$5021	$.0^5$4780	$.0^5$4547	$.0^5$4329	$.0^5$4118	$.0^5$3918

* Adapted from Table I in A. Hald, *Statistical Tables and Formulas*, John Wiley and Sons, New York, 1952. Above values are the result of multiplying Hald's values by $\sqrt{2\pi} = 2.50662827$.